# Tiberius

**Other titles by Lindsay Powell**

ALL THINGS UNDER THE SUN
How Modern Ideas Are Really Ancient

AUGUSTUS AT WAR
The Struggle for the *Pax Augusta*

BAR KOKHBA
The Jew Who Defied Hadrian and Challenged the Might of Rome

CAMPAIGN
The Bar Kokhba War AD 132–136:
The Last Jewish Revolt Against Imperial Rome

COMBAT
Roman Soldier versus Germanic Warrior, 1st Century AD

EAGER FOR GLORY
The Untold Story of Drusus the Elder, Conqueror of Germania

GERMANICUS
The Magnificent Life and Mysterious Death of
Rome's Most Popular General

MARCUS AGRIPPA
Right-Hand Man of Caesar Augustus

**Forewords, Introductions and Books edited by Lindsay Powell**

ANCIENT ROME ON THE SILVER SCREEN:
Myth versus Reality

GREEK ANCIENT ORIGINS

HANNIBAL OF CARTHAGE

JULIUS CAESAR

QUEEN CLEOPATRA

ROMAN ANCIENT ORIGINS

# Tiberius

## From Masterly Commander to Masterful Emperor of Rome

Lindsay Powell

Foreword by Penelope J. Goodman

Pen & Sword
MILITARY

First published in Great Britain in 2025 by
Pen & Sword Military
An imprint of Pen & Sword Books Limited
Yorkshire – Philadelphia



ISBN 978 1 47383 797 3



A CIP catalogue record for this book is available from the British Library.



Typeset by Mac Style
Printed in the UK by CPI Group (UK) Ltd, Croydon, CR0 4YY.

The Publisher's authorised representative in the EU for product safety is Authorised Rep Compliance Ltd., Ground Floor, 71 Lower Baggot Street, Dublin D02 P593, Ireland.
www.arccompliance.com

For a complete list of Pen & Sword titles please contact

PEN & SWORD BOOKS LIMITED
47 Church Street, Barnsley, South Yorkshire, S70 2AS, England
E-mail: enquiries@pen-and-sword.co.uk
Website: www.pen-and-sword.co.uk
or
PEN AND SWORD BOOKS
1950 Lawrence Road, Havertown, PA 19083, USA
E-mail: uspen-and-sword@casematepublishers.com
Website: www.penandswordbooks.com

**For Alan and Sue**

Ask for help from acquaintances, if you happen to be struggling;
No one is a better physician than a faithful friend.

*Auxilium a notis petito, si forte labores;*
*Nec quisquam melior medicus quam fidus amicus.*

M. Porcius Cato, *The Sayings of Cato* (*Disticha Catonis*) 4.13.

# Contents

# Foreword

by Penelope J. Goodman, University of Leeds

Though he may not have wished or willed it, Tiberius occupies a pivotal position in two major strands of Western History. Firstly, his accession to the Roman principate (rule by *princeps*, usually translated as 'emperor') in 14 CE clarified exactly what that system was. For as long as his predecessor Augustus had been *princeps*, the fiction that he was merely the best-qualified person to fulfil the role for the time being could be maintained. But when Tiberius, already equipped with the same political powers as Augustus, accepted the command of the armies and the Praetorian Guard after his death, the permanent and hereditary nature of the position became undeniable. Secondly, Tiberius was still *princeps* in 33 CE at the time of Jesus' crucifixion in the Roman province of Judaea. As such, he and the system of imperial rule which he represented are referenced in the Bible, and Tiberius plays an important if distant role in any narrative of Jesus' life and death.

What we know of Tiberius comes mainly from the accounts of ancient historians and biographers. These writers took a moralistic tone, sorting emperors into 'good' and 'bad' examples, partly because ancient history and biography had always offered its readers edifying moral content, but also because showing that 'good' emperors had prospered and 'bad' ones met sticky ends was one of the remaining means available to them to influence the rulers of their day. Their task was eased by the expectations of their readers. Though they knew they would lose credibility if they distorted matters of public record (laws passed, buildings built), they also knew that their audience prized literary style over precise factual detail. As such, they foregrounded whatever material supported their moral judgement of the subject (good or bad), described inner thoughts which they could not really have known, showcased their own speech-writing skills for occasions when no speech was documented or they considered the recorded one inadequate, and presented obviously scurrilous rumours with nothing but the thin disclaimer 'some said…'.

For most of our sources, Tiberius belongs firmly in the 'bad emperor' category. The Roman political elite took a dim view of behaviour which had reduced their influence, such as the prominence of Livia, treason trials held behind closed doors, and the power afforded to the Prefect of the Praetorian Guard. By comparison with some 'bad' emperors, though, he is lucky enough to benefit from a counter-narrative in the work of Velleius Paterculus, a contemporary writer who considered Tiberius a paradigm of good rule. Velleius has his own issues: he was personally close to Tiberius, wrote while the *princeps* was still alive and there were potential benefits to flattering him, and finished his account in 30 CE. This means that although he knew Tiberius had been living on Capri for four years, he may not have viewed the move as permanent and did not witness what Sejanus' downfall revealed about weaknesses of the set-up. Nonetheless, he provides a valuable alternative to the prevailing negative narratives.

From a modern perspective, of course, there is no such thing as a 'good' emperor. All were autocrats who suppressed political opposition, as well as imperialists who led the Roman state in conquering others, killing or enslaving many of them, and subjecting the rest to external rule and taxation. But we may still want to understand the system in which they operated, the choices they made, how their actions affected their contemporaries, and what their longer-term consequences were. This is what Lindsay Powell's biography of Tiberius offers.

In the pages which follow, Powell presents a clear and accessible account of Tiberius' life and career, scrupulously supported by a comprehensive knowledge of the ancient sources and modern scholarship. He carefully sets conflicting ancient accounts against each other and tests out the plausibility of the more lurid anecdotes, trying to ascertain what our sources could have known, what would have made sense from the point of view of the people involved and what might actually have happened. His account also sets itself apart from other modern treatments of Tiberius in two important ways. Firstly, Powell gives more space than his predecessors to Tiberius' life before becoming *princeps*: a full 54 years of his 77-year lifespan. This allows him to show how Tiberius' experiences during that period, particularly as a military commander and in diplomatic negotiations, may have shaped his later approach to ruling Rome and its empire. It also reveals much about how Tiberius the *princeps* was the product of his family background, the Roman political system and the wider society which he inhabited.

Secondly, Powell devotes two chapters to the reception and reassessment of Tiberius after his death in later Roman and Byzantine writers, Christian texts, portraits, drama, fiction, screenplays and modern academic accounts. These chapters are particularly welcome, as little attempt has so far been made to trace Tiberius' evolving posthumous reputation. Yet it undeniably shapes modern views of him even if we are not consciously aware of every step in the process. As Powell shows, the critical assessment of Tiberius which reached its definitive form with Tacitus circulated throughout antiquity and remains dominant in the modern era. The ancient tradition of presenting emperors as 'good' or 'bad' as a means of influencing absolute rulers continued in the medieval and early modern eras, and even after the advent of republics and constitutional monarchies it remained a powerful vehicle for political critique. As a result, Tacitus' portrayal of Tiberius as a gloomy, depraved, and distrustful persecutor of the Roman elite is absolutely present in popular culture today, right up to *Domina*.

Precisely because Tiberius the tyrant remains such a cultural touchpoint, modern readers may be surprised by Powell's account of the alternative sympathetic tradition developed by Christian writers, which has Tiberius acknowledging Jesus' divinity and protecting his followers. But we must remember that early Christians operated within the institutional structures of the Roman empire and the principate. Like their pagan counterparts, they too had an agenda, wishing to persuade later emperors that their predecessor in the time of Jesus had been receptive to him and benevolent to Christians, in the hope that they would behave similarly. Later, once the empire had fallen, the same narratives could be used in support of the primacy of Rome and the Papacy by suggesting that the embodiment of Roman political power had welcomed Christianity from the start.

In a speech to the Senate explaining his decision to decline a temple in Spain, Tacitus has Tiberius declare that after his death he wishes only for men to associate 'my deeds and the reputation of my name with praise and favourable recollection' (*The Annals* 4.38). Tacitus surely knew even as he wrote that his own history would help to ensure Tiberius enjoyed no such posthumous admiration. And if this was something Tiberius truly wished for, then some of his own decisions hardly helped his cause: particularly the move to Capri, which weakened his personal relationship with Rome and its political class and made him dependent on Sejanus. But Powell's book expertly guides the reader through the difficult and distorted source material for his life, allowing them to decide how they wish to remember Tiberius for themselves.

Leeds
August 2024

# Preface

The male members of the House of Augustus (*Domus Augusta*) have been my virtual companions for many years. I have had the good fortune to be able to research and then tell the extraordinary life stories of Caesar Augustus, Marcus Agrippa, Nero Claudius Drusus and Germanicus in a series of biographies published by Pen & Sword Books. One man has been a constant figure throughout: Tiberius (42 BCE–37 CE). Now it is *his* turn to receive the 'full treatment'. It seems fitting: my first biography for Pen & Sword was of Drusus the Elder, and I conclude this series with his devoted brother.

Tiberius' story is deeply woven into the dynastic fabric of the Julio-Claudian tapestry. He was stepson and later adopted son of Augustus, son-in-law to Agrippa, older brother of Drusus and uncle (later adoptive father) of Germanicus. He outlived them all, even living nearly two years longer than Augustus. Ultimately, he was picked by Augustus to succeed him as *princeps* ('First Man') and to continue the great project he began after the murder of his adopted father, C. Iulius Caesar, reigning for twenty-two years, six months and twenty-seven days. In fact, he was the seventh longest-serving *princeps* between 27 BCE and 476 CE (Augustus held the record at forty years, seven months and three days). He was related to future emperors too, as great-uncle of Caius Caligula, paternal uncle of Claudius and great-great uncle of Nero. If anyone does, Tiberius defines the term 'very important person' (VIP).

Tiberius himself lived an eventful life. His first fifty years were filled with adventure and derring-do, but it is his later life as *princeps* for which he is best known. Yet this position was not one he chose for himself. History has not been kind to the memory of Tiberius, second emperor of the Romans. Historians, ancient and modern, have often misunderstood him and, as a result, misrepresented him. They often mention his 'capable generalship' and 'sensible civic leadership', but describe his personality as 'dour' or 'boorish', then point to his 'self-imposed exile' and 'reclusive later life'. They recount his eagerness for 'treason trials' and his indulgence in 'sexual perversions', earning him the epithet 'tyrant' – or even 'monster'. Hearsay not refuted often becomes accepted fact. A publicist would have a tough time trying to explain such a man were he alive in today's world, but these characterizations of Tiberius go back centuries and have become his legend.

The challenge in writing about people of the ancient world is, of course, the paucity of accurate source material. Tiberius' own memoir is now entirely lost.[1] A biography of Tiberius is known to have been written by L. Mestrios Ploutarchos (Plutarch, *c.* 46–after 119 CE), composed a half-century or more after the emperor's death. It too is lost. Tiberius' speeches were available for Roman historians to study, and they sometimes included short excerpts in their published works, but even these may have been edited or rewritten by those authors. In this way, some of his sayings, which demonstrate his deep wisdom and dry sense of humour, have been preserved (see Appendix 1).

The only work of a primary source to come down to us by a writer who actually knew Tiberius personally, and can be properly called a witness, is the *Roman History* of M. (or C.) Velleius Paterculus (*c.* 19 BCE–31 CE), who served with Tiberius on military campaigns. Paterculus' account covers the years 14–30 CE – the first sixteen of Tiberius' twenty-seven-year reign. The other extant contemporary accounts are secondary sources. There are snippets in other works, such as the *Geography* of Strabon of Amasia (Strabo, 64/63 BCE–*c.* 24 CE) and *Memorable Deeds and Sayings* of Valerius Maximus (writing around 30 CE). Philon (Philo, *c.* 20 BCE–*c.* 40/50 CE), a Greek-speaking philosopher born into a prominent Jewish family in Alexandria, makes generally favourable remarks about Tiberius in his *Embassy to Caius*, an account of his diplomatic mission to the second emperor's successor, Caligula; it tells us how Tiberius was viewed in the years immediately after his death. Additionally, there are other books: the philosophical writings of L. Annaeus Seneca (Seneca the Younger, *c.* 4–65 CE); the *Natural History* of C. Plinius Secundus (Pliny the Elder, 23/24–79 CE), and his *German Wars*, which has long since been lost; the *Attic Nights* of A. Gellius (*c.* 125–after 180 CE); and the *Suda* (*Souda*), a tenth-century Byzantine encyclopaedia or lexicon of the ancient world.

Of the histories written in his day, which might have informed us of Tiberius' life and deeds, all are long gone. These include the writings of Verrius Flaccus; the *History* and *German War* of Aufidius Bassus, admired for his eloquence; the writings of M. Servilius Nonianus; the unnamed consul who wrote in his *Annals* about what he witnessed at one of Tiberius' dinner parties; the works of A. Cremutius Cordus (d. 25 CE), a historian lauded by Seneca the Younger in his letter of consolation *Ad Marciam*, who took his own life by starvation rather than face being tried for treason; and Fenestella, a writer of *Annals* and songs who died – of natural causes – in his 70s during Tiberius' reign.[2]

Yet even where ancient texts do survive, they are not without problems. Indeed, they are often the root cause of the problems for those who rely on them. Then as now, historians and writers tell *stories*. We have agendas and reasons for writing. The persona of each storyteller subtly *changes* the story. Some manipulate the narrative, while other narrators are completely unreliable. Some eighty years after Tiberius' demise, P. (or C.) Cornelius Tacitus (*c.* 56–*c.* 120 CE) published a history nowadays called *The Annals*. Tiberius appears in five out of the original six books (most of Book V and part of VI being lost), meaning his narrative on events of twenty-four years of his principate survive, missing the years 29–31 CE. Tacitus used Tiberius' speeches and other historians' works as sources of material.[3] Around the same time, C. Suetonius Tranquillus (*c.* 69–after 122 CE) wrote his *Life of Tiberius* as part of a much larger collection of portraits published as *Lives of the Caesars*. Another hundred years later, L. Cassius Dio (*c.* 155–*c.* 235 CE) wrote an epic *Roman History* in which Tiberius appears in Books 52–58. Paterculus, Tacitus, Suetonius, and Dio provide the most substantial documentation about Tiberius to survive from Antiquity.

Tiberius lived in the same period as Yeshua Ben Yosef (Jesus of Nazareth). In the four Gospels (Matthew, Mark, Luke and John), Tiberius is a remote, godfather-like figure. He is mentioned only once by name.[4] He was the Caesar in the saying, 'Render to Caesar the things that are Caesar's, and to God the things that are God's.'[5] He was also responsible for appointing Pontius Pilatus (Pontius Pilate), who sentenced Jesus to death by crucifixion. Later Christian writers bring him up in passing: Q. Septimius Florens Tertullianus (Tertullian, *c.* 155–*c.* 220 CE) refers to Tiberius as the emperor living at the beginning of the new faith throughout his *Apology*; Eusebius Pamphilius (265–339 CE), a bishop, writes about Tiberius' purported attitude to Jesus in Chapter 2 of *Church History* and lists key incidents in each year of Tiberius' reign in his *Chronicle*s, a *codex* written around 311 CE that presents chronology in an innovative tabular format; Eusebius Sophronius Hieronymus (Jerome, 342/347–420 CE) translated Eusebius' *Chronicle* into Latin and added new information in his own *Chronicles*; and Paulus Orosius (385–420 CE) outlines significant happenings in Tiberius' reign in Book 7 of his *History Against the Pagans*.

These are the sources for the story of Tiberius: 'some of them are true' (borrowing the famous tagline of my friend W. F. Strong of the University of Texas Rio Grande Valley), but which ones? During her Sather Classical Lecture for the University of California-Berkeley on 27 February 2021 entitled 'Imperial Transgressions', Dame Mary Beard, formerly classics professor at the University of Cambridge, discussed how Roman biographers and historians treated the life of the infamous young emperor Elagabalus (aka Heliogabalus, reigned 218–222 CE). She noted that they wrote of him according to opposing stereotypes of 'good emperors' and 'bad emperors'. They took aspects of his life and respectively created personas of a man behaving badly who pushed up against – or went further and transgressed – the conventions of what was deemed acceptable to the Roman elites. They depicted him inhabiting a topsy-turvy, dystopian world. For these writers, their subject's curious indulgences and repulsive excesses – in clothing, food, sex and religious cults – were the outward symptoms of the rotten system of autocracy. To serve their narrative purpose, they uncritically reported rumours and speculations as facts in their published accounts. For those outside the centre of imperial power on the Palatine Hill, who could tell what was real or what was fake? As a result, nothing about Elagabalus is quite what it seems. Indeed, my friend the novelist Steven Saylor writes that, even his death was not the end of the speculation:

> Elagabalus has accumulated a considerable *Nachleben*. That's a German word historians use to describe the cultural afterlife of a historical person and the transmutation of factuality into myth via poetry, opera, theater, painting, novels, etc.[6]

The same insights equally apply to the life of Tiberius.

Tiberius has been written about before, so why the need for another biography? Having closely studied the lives – personal, civilian and military – of Augustus, Agrippa, Nero Drusus, Germanicus and other members of the *Domus Augusta*, I believe I have a uniquely holistic, but nuanced, view of this man and his place in his family, society and times. In re-examining and reappraising the evidence afresh, some may anticipate that this new biography is a revisionist history. In some respects, it is, but as James M. Banner, Jr, visiting scholar in the history department of George Washington University, writes in *The Ever-Changing Past* (Yale University Press, 2021), 'History is not and has never been inert, certain, merely factual, and beyond interpretation.'[7] Thus, 'all historians are revisionists – at least in some respects. They are always trying to get a grasp on the past.'[8]

A major differentiator between this biography of Tiberius and the others is the space I devote to his life prior to becoming emperor. Many – indeed most – modern biographies cover the first fifty-six years of his life in just a few pages and devote the vast majority of their study to his principate of twenty-two years. In my opinion, this is a mistake. I believe that to fully understand the man who ruled the Roman Empire it is essential to examine in detail his life *before* he assumed the leadership position pioneered by Augustus *as well as after* because it helps to explain his approach to ruling as 'First Man'.

'The question for a biographer,' Walter Isaacson, author, journalist, and professor in history and American values at Tulane University, told *New York* magazine, 'is to show how the demons of a person are totally connected to the drive that gets their rockets to orbit. People who are driven by demons get shit done.'[9] This biography seeks to answer the following questions: Who was Tiberius? What kind of man was he? What did he do? What drove him? How did he get the reputation he has today?

It begins with an investigation of the known facts. The origin of the English word 'history' is *istoria*, the Greek for 'inquiry'. I begin by compiling an exhaustive chronology or timeline. To me, the job of a historian is to research, analyse and interpret events and the people who took part in them, in an attempt to 'to try to capture the past as it was', as James M. Banner, Jr, asserts.[10] In my case, there are of course no living survivors or witnesses to relate to me what they saw, but I do interview subject matter experts and record their insights. As an investigator, I conduct extensive research critically using ancient documentary sources, comparing them to epigraphy, numismatics (see Appendix 2), statuary and findings from archaeology, as well as insights from architecture, engineering, geography, military studies and medical science. I follow the leads wherever they take me. The 'abc' principles of the forensic scientist apply: 'assume nothing; believe nobody; check everything'. Throughout, I follow the dictum of investigative journalists, which is to 'work from the facts outwards: never a thesis inwards', letting the known facts speak for themselves. As Edward Gibbon did, I examine the evidence 'with impartiality', but not with 'indifference'.[11]

In chapters 1–9, I present what is known – or as best as can be deduced – from the sources of the life, deeds and times of Tiberius 'from womb to tomb', as the saying goes. Written in chronological order, the chapter breaks fall where I have determined the narrative takes a new direction, marking life turning points. These *Lebenswendepunkte*, as the Germans call them, may be linked to a career change or a significant historical event. If there are gaps in the story, it is because there are lacunae in the source material, as noted above. In other instances, the information in them is unclear, confused, conflated, contradictory, consciously omitted or outright contrived or concocted. I always try to point out these discrepancies in the text or endnotes.

In Chapter 10, I examine how Tiberius was remembered by his contemporaries and how those perceptions changed in the first few centuries after his death, becoming, in the process, his legend. In Chapter 11, I explore how Tiberius was essentially reinvented after 1453, with the fall of Constantinople, becoming the caricature of recent times.

Many modern biographers end their studies with a conclusion. As defined in a dictionary, a conclusion is a 'summing up' or 'a judgement or decision reached by reasoning'. As a biographer and historian, this seems to me to be too incontrovertible and categoric, as if there is some absolute truth in a human life. In this, as in my previous biographical works, I give, instead, an 'assessment' in Chapter 12. An assessment is 'the action of assessing someone or something': as anyone who has had a performance review during a career of employment knows, it focuses on measuring how well an individual has applied their knowledge, skills and abilities in carrying out their work.

Some explanation for my choices in respect of names of people, titles, places, dates and money are in order.

Names pose a particular challenge when writing about Tiberius' family. Tiberius grew up as Ti. Claudius Nero, becoming Ti. Iulius Caesar upon his adoption by Augustus in 4 CE. Augustus himself began as C. Octavius Thurinus, then became C. Iulius Caesar Octavianus upon his adoption by Iulius Caesar in 44 BCE, becoming Caesar *Divi filius* when Caesar was deified in 42 BC, then *Imperator* Caesar *Divi filius* around 38 BCE during the Civil Wars, only finally becoming *Imperator* Caesar *Divi filius* Augustus in 27 BCE. As with European royal families over the centuries, the same names were used by different generations. Rather than use *Maior* ('the Elder') or *Minor* ('the Younger'), or the numbers I or II, instead I follow Roman practice. Tiberius' father, Ti. Claudius Nero, appears as Ti. Nero. His brother, Nero Claudius Drusus, appears as Nero Drusus. His son, Drusus Iulius Caesar, is plain Drusus. His nephew, Ti. Claudius Nero (son of Nero Drusus), is plain Claudius (Rome's fourth emperor). As for his other nephews (sons of Germanicus), Drusus Iulius Caesar is Drusus Caesar, Nero Iulius Caesar is Nero Caesar and C. Iulius Caesar is Caius Caligula (Tiberius' successor). Augustus' adopted son, C. Iulius Caesar, is Caius, his brother, L. Iulius Caesar, is Lucius, while their brother, often referred to in modern history books as Agrippa Postumus, is Agrippa Caesar in this text to distinguish him from his natural father, M. Agrippa. I use Herod Agrippa rather than his Roman name, M. Iulius Agrippa. However, I do use *Maior* or *Minor* to differentiate between the women of the imperial family. For other Roman families, I use (I), (II) and (III) to distinguish between fathers, sons and grandsons who use the same name. Finally, I use Iulius and Seianus rather than the Anglicized forms Julius and Sejanus, as that is how the Romans spelled these names, there being no 'j' in Latin.

Modern historians refer to Tiberius as 'emperor', an Anglicizing of *imperator*. To translate the word this way is a mistake, however. To the Romans, it simply meant 'commander'. Originally it was a spontaneous commendation from the citizen soldiers – a Latin 'for he's a jolly good fellow' – as they, his countrymen, cheered their leader for bringing them victory on the battlefield. It was an honour to be proudly cited in the after-action report presented to the Senate, a title to be added after his name and carved on inscriptions for posterity. Hence '*TI[berivs] CAES[ar] DIVI F[ilivs] AVGVST[vs] IMP[erator]*', which appears on coins from 4–37 CE. It did not yet have the regal or despotic connotation of 'emperor' exhibited by Tiberius' later successors such as Elagabalus.

Where a city has a known, ancient name, I prefer to use it since the modern name creates a false impression of the scale and feel of the place in antiquity. However, I use modern Anglicized names for Athens and Rome. There is a list of ancient names of cities, towns, mountains and rivers and their modern equivalents at the end of the book.

For accuracy, the Latin version is also used for Roman military officer ranks, arms, equipment and battle formations throughout, since there is often no modern equivalent. Definitions of unfamiliar Roman (Latin or Greek) technical terms, which I have used in the text, are listed in the single Glossary at the end of the book.

The dating convention I use throughout is the 'Common (or Current) Era'. BCE – 'Before the Common Era' – equates to BC ('Before Christ') and ends with 1 BCE. CE – 'Common Era' – equates to AD ('*Anno Domini*') and begins with 1 CE (AD 1). No political correctness is intended; it is simply my choice as the author. There is, of course, no Year 0.

Sums of money are given in HS, the symbol for *sestertius* (pl. *sestertii*, Anglicized as sesterces) which was the principal denomination of coin used for prices and values under Augustus and Tiberius. It was an abbreviation of *semis tertius*, the Roman way to express '2½'. It was worth 2½ *asses* (the 'S' in HS referring to a *semis* or half *as*). The copper *as* (pl. *asses*) was the small change of the Early Empire. A regular soldier (*c.* 15 CE) earned about 10 *asses* per day, roughly 900 *sestertii* annually.[12] With it he could buy a cup of cheap wine at a bar for 1 *as*, a cup of fine quality Falernian wine for 4 *asses* and a loaf of bread for 2 *asses*, but there were deductions for the cost of food, clothing and armour, plus a contribution to a compulsory savings scheme, leaving the legionary around half of his pay to spend in hard cash.[13] Thus, 2½ *asses* = 1 *sestertius*, but 4 *sestertii* = 1 *denarius* (so 10 *asses* = 1 *denarius*). The *quinarius* was worth 5 *asses*, or half of a *denarius*. Under Augustus, a senator was required to own property equal to HS 1,000,000 (250,000 *denarii*), while an *eques* ('knight', literally 'horseman') had to possess a minimum of HS 400,000 (100,000 *denarii*).

My goal is to present as accurate and unbiased an account as possible of my findings 'without anger and passion', pointing out where any ambiguity or doubt lies.[14] My aim is to humanize the man, not to sanitize him. In explaining the material, my task as a writer is to make this story of the life of Tiberius compelling reading for you, the reader.

Long would be the tale of wrong,
long its winding course; but I will follow the high points of the story.

*Longa est iniuria,*
*longae ambages; sed summa sequar fastigia rerum.*
(Verg., *Aen.* 1.341–342).

Lindsay Powell
Anniversary of Tiberius' last day
March 2024
Austin, Texas

# Acknowledgments

There are several people who deserve my thanks for helping me with this special project.

To my commissioning editor, Philip Sidnell at Pen & Sword Books, who yet again responded enthusiastically to my proposal for this book and showed immense patience while waiting for the manuscript, I shall always be grateful. To the other hard-working members of the production team, Matt Jones and Dominic Allen at Pen & Sword, and Mat Blurton at Mac Style, I offer my sincere thanks for turning my virtual files into lovely, printed pages.

I feel deeply honoured that Penelope J. Goodman agreed to write the foreword. Penny is Senior Lecturer in Roman History, University of Leeds. She led the Commemorating Augustus project in 2014 which lay the ground for a twenty-first century re-evaluation of Rome's first emperor by exploring the wide range of responses to him expressed across the two millennia years since his death. Her work on the reception history of Augustus (published as *Afterlives of Augustus, AD 14–2014*, Cambridge University Press, 2018) is particularly germane for a study of the life of his successor, Tiberius. She has shown that Augustus has meant radically different things from one time and place to another; it is so with Tiberius.

One of the great joys of this project was conducting the field research. I am grateful to the many experts who kindly gave me their time. As I was editing the first draft of this volume, I learned that my friend and mentor Karl Galinsky, former Professor Emeritus, Floyd A. Cailloux Centennial Professor, University Distinguished Teaching Professor at The University of Texas at Austin, had passed away on 9 March 2024. He was 82. He had generously written the foreword to my *Augustus at War*. I had discussed this new project with him over coffee and cake in Austin. He shared my view that Tiberius has been misrepresented even into modern times and he encouraged me in my work. The Covid-19 pandemic and his five-year battle with cancer had restricted our ability to meet in person. It is my regret that he could not see this finished biography of the man who succeeded the individual about whom he was the undisputed international scholar. *Bene merenti fecit, Magister.*

This book tells the story of conflict in both words and pictures. For helping me to illustrate this volume, I offer my thanks to the many lovers of history on Wikimedia Commons who allow use of their photographs with attribution, especially: Apollo Numismatics; Carole Raddato of the 'Following Hadrian' blog in Frankfurt am Main, Germany; Classical Numismatics Group; The Coin Cabinet Ltd; The J. Paul Getty Center; Harlan J. Berk, Chicago; Münzkabinett Berlin, Onlinesammlung der Staatlichen Museen zu Berlin; Roma Numismatics Limited, London; and Victoria Numismatics. I should also like to thank the estate of Michael Leonard for allowing me to use the late artist's book jacket art, which appears as fig. 40.

War stories cannot be told without the aid of maps. I offer my thanks to Carlos de la Rocha of Sátrapa Ediciones for letting me use the map of Germanicus' campaigns in Germania, and to Erin Greb, who did a marvellous job of producing all the other maps in a similar style.

I have quoted extracts from several ancient authors' works whose voices lend authenticity to the narrative but have modified them to remove some of the archaic language. For the translations of classical texts, I used: Cassius Dio's *Romaike Historia* translated by Earnest Carey in *Roman History by Cassius Dio* (Loeb Classical Library, Harvard University Press, 1914–1927); Eusebius' *Historia Ecclesiastica* translated by Kirsopp Lake in *The Ecclesiastical History* (Loeb Classical Library, William Heinemann, 1926); Jerome's *Chronicon* translated and formatted by Roger Pearse and friends and graciously placed online with no restrictions at tertullian.org; Josephus' *Ioudaike Archaiologia* translated by William Whiston in *The Genuine Works of Flavius Josephus the Jewish Historian* (W. Bowyer, 1737); Julian's *Saturnalia* translated by W. C. Wright in *Julian. The Caesars* (Loeb Classical Library, Harvard University Press, 1913); Krinagoras' epigram in *The Greek Anthology* translated by W. R. Paton, William Heinemann (1927); Paulus Orosius' *Historiarum Adversum Paganos* translated by Irving Woodworth Raymond in *Seven Books of History Against the Pagans: The Apology of Paulus Orosius* (Columbia University Press, 1936); Pliny the Elder's *Naturalis Historia* translated by John Bostock and H. T. Riley in *The Natural History. Pliny the Elder* (Taylor and Francis, 1855); Seneca the Younger's *De Beneficiis* translated by Aubrey Stewart in *L. Annaeus Seneca. 'On Benefits'* (Bohn's Classical Library Edition, George Bell and Sons, 1887); Seneca the Younger's *De Clementia* translated by Aubrey Stewart in *L. Annaeus Seneca, Minor Dialogs Together with the Dialog 'On Clemency'* (Bohn's Classical Library Edition, George Bell and Sons, 1900); Strabo's *Geographika* translated by H. L. Jones in *Strabo: The Geography* (Loeb Classical Library, Harvard University Press, 1917–1932); Suetonius' *Vita Tiberi* translated by J. C. Rolfe in *Lives of the Twelve Caesars* (Loeb Classical Library, Harvard University Press, 1913–1914); Tacitus' *Annales* translated by Alfred John Church and William Jackson Brodribb in *The Annals of Tacitus* (Loeb Classical Library, Harvard University Press, 1931); Tertullian's *Apologeticus* translated by William Reeves in *The Apologies of Justin Martyr, Tertullian, and Minutius Felix, in Defence of the Christian Religion* (W. Churchill, 1716); and Velleius Paterculus'

*Historiae Romanae* translated by Frederick W. Shipley in *Compendium of Roman History* (Loeb Classical Library, Harvard University Press, 1924).

Finally, I thank Austin Public Library service in Austin, Texas, for providing access to the phenomenal JSTOR.org ('journal storage') website, the digital library of academic journals, books and primary sources, which greatly facilitated my research.

# List of Illustrations

# List of Maps

# List of Plates

# List of Tables

# Chronology

| BCE | Political and Social Events | Diplomatic and Military Events | Tiberius' Age |
|---|---|---|---|
| 42 | *16 November*: Birthday of Tiberius (Ti. Claudius Nero, son of Ti. Claudius Nero and Livia Drusilla). | *3 and 23 October*: Battle of Philippi, deaths of M. Iunius Brutus and C. Cassius Longinus, assassins of C. Iulius Caesar. | |
| 41 | M. Antonius meets Kleopatra VII at Tarsus. | Perusine War: L. Antonius and Fulvia occupy Perusia. | 1 |
| 40 | Tiberius flees with his parents to Sicily, seeking refuge with Sex. Pompeius.<br>Signing of Treaty of Brundisium. | Perusine War: *Imp*. Caesar (Octavian, heir of C. Iulius Caesar) defeats L. Antonius and Fulvia at Battle of Perusia. | 2 |
| 39 | Tiberius returns to Rome with his parents. | | 3 |
| 38 | *13 January*: Birth of Nero Claudius Drusus (Tiberius' brother).<br>Livia Drusilla marries *Imp*. Caesar. | | 4 |
| 37 | Second Pact of Tarentum.<br>Herod becomes King of Iudaea. | Romans seize Jerusalem from Parthia. | 5 |
| 36 | *31 January*: Birth of Antonia Minor (daughter of M. Antonius and Octavia Minor).<br>Lepidus appointed *Pontifex Maximus*. | M. Antonius campaigns in Parthia, suffers defeats, retreats to Egypt.<br>M. Agrippa defeats Sex. Pompeius at battles of Mylae and Naulochus; Sex. Pompeius flees to Asia. | 6 |
| 35 | | Illyrian War (*Bellum Illyricum*), Year 1: *Imp*. Caesar and M. Agrippa in Illyricum, campaign against Iapydes and Segestani.<br>Sex. Pompeius captured and executed at Miletus. | 7 |
| 34 | | Illyrian War, Year 2: *Imp*. Caesar and M. Agrippa pacify Illyricum.<br>M. Antonius in Armenia, captures Artavasdes II. | 8 |
| 33 | Death of Ti. Claudius Nero (Tiberius' father) in Rome: Tiberius gives the eulogy from the *Rostra Augusti*. | Illyrian War, Year 3:<br>M. Antonius annexes Media. | 9 |

| BCE | Political and Social Events | Diplomatic and Military Events | Tiberius' Age |
|---|---|---|---|
| 32 | *July*: Senate declares war upon Kleopatra VII.<br>Gallic and Hispanic provinces, Africa, Sicily and Sardinia swear oath of loyalty (*sacramentum*) to *Imp*. Caesar. | | 10 |
| 31 | *1 January*: *Imp*. Caesar consul (III). | Actian War (*Bellum Actiense*) – 2–3 *August*: Battle of Actium (*Bellum Actiacum*), *Imp*. Caesar with M. Agrippa defeats M. Antonius and Kleopatra in the Gulf of Ambracia.<br>*Imp*. Caesar acclaimed *imperator* (VI). | 11 |
| 30 | *1 January*: *Imp*. Caesar consul (IV).<br>*November/December*: *Lex Saenia*: adlects plebeians to the patrician class. | Alexandrian War (*Bellum Alexandreae*):<br>*1 August*: Alexandria falls to *Imp*. Caesar's troops; Egypt annexed as a province (Aegyptus).<br>*Imp*. Caesar acclaimed *imperator* (VII?) | 12 |
| 29 | *1 January*: *Imp*. Caesar consul (V).<br>*11 January*: Doors of Temple of Ianus closed.<br>Augustus purges the Senate. | Moesian War (*Bellum Moesum*), Year 1: M. Licinius Crassus campaigns against the Bastarnae, Moesi and 'other peoples'.<br>African War: unspecified conflict after which L. Autronius Paetus is acclaimed *imperator* and awarded a full triumph.<br>Dacian War (*Bellum Dacicum*): Cn. Cornelius Lentulus campaigns against the Getae under King Cotiso.<br>Sarmatian War (*Bellum Sarmaticum*): Cn. Cornelius Lentulus campaigns in Sarmatia.<br>Asturian and Cantabrian War (*Bellum Asturicum et Cantabricum*), Year 1: T. Statilius Taurus in command.<br>*13–15 August*: Caesar's 'Triple Triumph' for victories in Illyricum, Actium and Alexandria.<br>Revolts in Heroöpolis and Thebais, Egypt in protest at treatment by tax collectors. | 13 |

| BCE | Political and Social Events | Diplomatic and Military Events | Tiberius' Age |
|---|---|---|---|
| | *18 August*: Temple of Divus Iulius and *Curia Iulia* dedicated.<br>*28 August*: Altar of Victoria dedicated inside the *Curia Iulia*. | Cornelius Gallus sets Roman border between Egypt and Ethiopia at Meroē at the First Cataract; makes Ethiopia a Roman protectorate. | |
| 28 | *1 January*: *Imp.* Caesar consul (6) with Agrippa (2).<br>Restoration of *iura et leges populi Romani* ('the rights and laws of the Roman People'); *Imp.* Caesar named *princeps senatus* ('First Man of the Senate'); appointed *censor*: first purge of the Senate.<br>*9 October*: Temple of Apollo dedicated on Palatinus Hill. | Moesian War, Year 2: M. Licinius Crassus campaigns against the Bastarnae, Moesi and 'other peoples'; awarded a triumph by the Senate – claims the *spolia opima*; denied by Augustus, offered a triumph *in lieu*.<br>*26 May*: *C.* Calvisius Sabinus celebrates a triumph for victories in Hispania.<br>*14 July*: C. Carrinas celebrates a triumph for victories over the Galli.<br>Asturian and Cantabrian War, Year 2. | 14 |
| 27 | *1 January*: *Imp.* Caesar consul (7) with Agrippa (3).<br>*13 January*: *Imp.* Caesar granted control over a large number of provinces and permitted right to delegate their administration to *legati* (deputies); awarded *corona civica* (civic crown) for saving lives of citizens.<br>*16 January*: *Imp.* Caesar granted title *Augustus* and right to display the *clipeus virtutis* ('shield of virtue'); receives proconsular *imperium* for ten years.<br>Augustus goes to *Tres Galliae*, conducts census, holds assizes in Narbo.<br>Augustus falls seriously ill. | Asturian and Cantabrian War, Year 3.<br>Aquitanian War.<br>*July*: Triumph of M. Licinius Crassus for victories against the Bastarnae, Moesi and 'other peoples'.<br>*25 September*: Triumph of M. Valerius Messalla Corvinus for victories over the Aquitani. | 15 |
| 26 | *1 January*: Augustus consul (VIII).<br>Augustus in Hispania Tarraconensis. | Asturian and Cantabrian War, Year 4: P. Carisius, *Legatus Augusti Propraetore*; Tiberius in Hispania Tarraconensis as *tribunus militum*. | 16 |
| 25 | *1 January:* Augustus consul (IX).<br>Augustus in Hispania Tarraconensis.<br>Doors of Temple of Ianus closed for second time.<br>Marcellus marries Iulia.<br>Tiberius returns to Rome. | Asturian and Cantabrian War, Year 5.<br>Tiberius in Hispania Tarraconensis as *tribunus militum*.<br>Salassian War: Salassi defeated by M. Terentius Varro.<br>Watchtowers erected in Swiss Alps. | 17 |

| BCE | Political and Social Events | Diplomatic and Military Events | Tiberius' Age |
|---|---|---|---|
| | | German War: M. Vinicius invades Germania; Augustus acclaimed *imperator* (VIII).<br>Thracian War: M. Licinius Crassus campaigns against the Thraci and Moesi.<br>Aelius Gallus moves east into Arabia; encounters the Nabataeans; army struck down with sickness; returns to Egypt. | |
| 24 | *1 January*: Augustus consul (X).<br>Augustus falls seriously ill at Tarraco. | Asturian and Cantabrian War, Year 6. | 18 |
| 23 | *1 January:* Augustus consul (XI).<br>Tiberius *quaestor* with responsibilities for monitoring the *annona* and investigating *ergastulae* in Italy.<br>Marcellus *aedile*; death of Marcellus (aged 19).<br>Conspiracies of M. Primus (proconsul of Macedonia) and A. Terentius Varro Murena (consul).<br>*June*: Augustus resigns consulship, has consular *imperium* (*maius*?) renewed for five years; M. Agrippa granted consular *imperium* for five years.<br>Augustus falls seriously ill. | Asturian and Cantabrian War, Year 7.<br>Kandake of Kush invades southern Egypt; C. Petronius retaliates. | 19 |
| 22 | Augustus is offered, but refuses, powers of dictator and perpetual consulships, accepts *cura annonae.*<br>Tiberius prosecutes Fannius Caepio. | Asturian and Cantabrian War, Year 8.<br>Riots in Athens. | 20 |
| 21 | M. Agrippa marries Iulia. | Asturian and Cantabrian War, Year 9.<br>C. Petronius agrees peace treaty with Kandake of Kush. | 21 |
| 20 | Birth of C. Caesar (son of M. Agrippa).<br>Tiberius marries Vispania Agrippina (?).<br>Augustus agrees to settlement with Armenia and Parthia.<br>*3 June*: birth of L. Aelius Seianus. | Tiberius in Armenia; negotiates with the Parthian King Phraates IV: *aquilae* and *signa* lost at Cannae 53 BCE returned to Tiberius, brought back to Rome.<br>Asturian and Cantabrian War, Year 10.<br>M. Agrippa in *Tres Galliae*, crosses Rhine? | 22 |

| BCE | Political and Social Events | Diplomatic and Military Events | Tiberius' Age |
|---|---|---|---|
| | | *12 May*: Augustus acclaimed *imperator* (IX). Garamantian Campaign: L. Cornelius Balbus attacks Garamantes for raiding and captures fifteen of their settlements. | |
| 19 | Birth of M. Velleius Paterculus (?). <br> *12 October*: Augustus enters Rome, granted additional privileges, *summum imperium auspiciumque*. <br> *15 December*: Altar of Fortunae Redux dedicated. | *27 March*: Triumph of L. Cornelius Balbus (the last of the triumphs granted to a *privatus*). Asturian and Cantabrian War, Year 11: M. Agrippa restores morale to Roman Army and leads troops to victory; end of military campaigns in Iberian Peninsula after 200 years. Gallic Revolt: M. Agrippa squashes rebellion; refuses triumphal honours. | 23 |
| 18 | Augustus' and Agrippa's consular *imperium* renewed for five years. Augustus purges the Senate. *Lex Iulia de adulteriis coercendis* on adultery and criminal fornication. Agrippa granted *tribunicia potestas*. | | 24 |
| 17 | *May*–1–3 *June*: Celebration of the *Ludi Saeculares*. <br> *14 June–15 July*: Augustus adopts sons of M. Agrippa, renamed as C. Caesar and L. Caesar. | Lollian Disaster (*Clades Lolliana*): M. Lollius defeated by an alliance of Tencteri, Sugambri and Uspetes, led by warlord Maelo, which invades Belgica and takes the *aquila* of *Legio* V *Alaudae*. | 25 |
| 16 | Tiberius *praetor*, appointed *legatus Augusti pro praetore* of Gallia Comata and Belgica. <br> *24 May*: First possible year of birth of Nero Claudius Drusus (the future Germanicus Caesar), born in Rome. Tiberius and Drusus *Maior* stand in for Augustus at gladiatorial games. Augustus and Tiberius travel to Gallia Comata, stay in *Colonia* Copia-Lugdunum. M. Agrippa in Syria. | P. Silius Nerva campaigns against Camunni/Vennii/ Pannonii. | 26 |

| BCE | Political and Social Events | Diplomatic and Military Events | Tiberius' Age |
|---|---|---|---|
| 15 | Augustus reorganizes the provinces of the *Tres Galliae* (?).<br><br>*Procurator* Licinius affair (?).<br><br>*May 24:* Second possible year of birth of Nero Claudius Drusus (the future Germanicus Caesar) born in Rome.<br><br>*7 October*: First possible year of birth of Drusus (Tiberius' son). | Alpine War (*Bellum Alpinum*): Nero Drusus leads campaign against the Raeti via the Reschen Pass; Raeti continue attacks in *Tres Galliae*; joined by Tiberius with forces from Lugdunum, crush Vindelici.<br>*1 August*: Fall of *oppidum* of Genauni to Drusus.<br>Norican War (*Bellum Noricum*): Tiberius and Nero Drusus advance on the Kingdom of Noricum and annex it. Alpine nations provide auxiliary troops to Rome.<br>Augustus acclaimed *imperator* (X).<br>P. Sulpicius Quirinius campaigns against the Nasamones, Marmaridae and Garamantes in Cyrenaica. | 27 |
| 14 | Augustus in *Colonia* Munatia (Lugdunum).<br><br>Drusus appointed *legatus Augusti pro praetore* of *Tres Galliae*, relocates to *Colonia* Munatia.<br>Birth of Agrippina *Maior* (?).<br><br>*7 October*: Second possible year of birth of Drusus. | Nero Drusus (?) subdues the Comati, Alpes Maritimae subjugated, made a prefecture.<br>German War: Nero Drusus begins preparations for invasion of Germania, befriends the Batavi, establishes military camps along the Rhine. Work begins on excavating a canal (*fossa Drusiana*).<br>Revolt of Scribonius: M. Agrippa squashes usurper's rebellion in the Cimerian Bosporus; refuses triumphal honours.<br>Pannonian War (*Bellum Pannonicum*), Year 1: revolt of the Pannonii. M. Vinicius unable to contain the uprising. | 28 |
| 13 | *1 January*: Tiberius consul (1).<br>Augustus returns to Rome.<br>Augustus' and Agrippa's consular *imperium* renewed for five years.<br><br>Augustus purges the Senate.<br><br>*4 July*: Senate votes to erect *Ara Pacis Augustae* in Rome.<br>Theatre of Balbus inaugurated in Rome. | Augustus reforms pay, length of service and retirement benefits of the army.<br>Thracian War (*Bellum Thracicum*), Year 1: Raiskuporis I of Thrace slain in battle by Vologases, revolt of the Bessi.<br>Pannonian War, Year 2: M. Agrippa suppresses rebellion in Pannonia. | 29 |

| BCE | Political and Social Events | Diplomatic and Military Events | Tiberius' Age |
|---|---|---|---|
| | Census in *Tres Galliae* (?).<br>*7 October*: Third possible year birth of Drusus (Tiberius' son). | | |
| 12 | Roimetalkes succeeds Raiskuporis as King of Thrace.<br>Theatre of Marcellus inaugurated.<br>*6 March*: Lepidus dies: Augustus appointed *Pontifex Maximus*.<br>*March (?)*: M. Agrippa dies in Campania (aged 50/52).<br>Consecration of Altar of *Romae et Augustus* at Condate, *Colonia* Munatia.<br>Nero Drusus appointed *praetor urbanus*.<br>Fire in Rome. | Thracian War, Year 2: L. Calpurnius Piso engages the Bessi.<br>Pannonian War, Year 3: Tiberius goes to Illyricum; Tiberius and M. Vinicius campaign against the alliance of the Breuci.<br>Homonadensian War: P. Sulpicius Quirinus wages war against the Homonadenses in Cilicia and Galatia.<br>Nero Drusus foils a rebellion in *Tres Galliae*.<br>German War (*Bellum Germanicum*), Year 1: Nero Drusus launches an attack from Batavodurum against the Sugambri, Tencteri and Usipetes; takes fleet across Lacus Flevo; negotiates treaties with the Cananefates, Chauci and Frisii; navigates the Ems River and defeats the Bructeri in a river battle. On the return journey fleet is marooned on the Dutch coast but rescued by the Frisii.<br>Augustus acclaimed *imperator* (XI). | 30 |
| 11 | Tiberius and Nero Drusus receive *imperium proconsulare*.<br>Senate decrees doors of the Temple of Ianus to be closed but defers action.<br>Tiberius divorces Vipsania Agrippina, marries Iulia.<br>Death of Octavia Minor. | Pannonian War, Year 4: Tiberius campaigns against the alliances of Daesitiates and Breuci.<br>Nero Drusus' acclamation as *imperator* denied and claimed by Augustus (XII), but granted an *ovatio* with triumphal insignia.<br>Thracian War, Year 3: L. Calpurnius Piso defeats rebels.<br>German War, Year 2: Nero Drusus returns to *Tres Galliae*; launches campaign from Vetera along the Lippe River; engages the Cherusci, Marsi and Usipetes; reaches the Weser River; and narrowly avoids defeat at Battle of Arbalo at hands of Cherusci. | 31 |

| BCE | Political and Social Events | Diplomatic and Military Events | Tiberius' Age |
|---|---|---|---|
| 10 | Augustus and Tiberius return to *Colonia* Munatia.<br><br>*1 August*: Birth of Ti. Claudius Nero (future emperor Claudius) in Lugdunum; dedication of Altar of *Roma et Augustus* in *Colonia* Munatia before an assembly of the Gallic tribal leaders. Drusus *Maior* returns to Rome with Augustus and Tiberius. | Pannonian War, Year 3: final conquest by Tiberius.<br>German War, Year 3: Nero Drusus launches new phase of campaign from Mogontiacum; defeats the Chatti and Marcomanni; granted limited triumphal honours.<br>Dacian War (*Bellum Dacicum*)/ Sarmatian War (*Bellum Sarmaticum*): Cn. Cornelius Lentulus Augur engages the Daci and Sarmati.<br>Syllaeus/Nacebus challenge Herodes the Great. | 32 |
| 9 | *1 January*: Nero Drusus consul.<br>*30 January*: Dedication of *Ara Pacis Augustae* in Rome.<br><br>Tiberius in Illyricum.<br><br>Tiberius in Ticinum with Augustus.<br>*September (?)*: Tiberius rides 200 miles in twenty-four hours from Ticinum to join Nero Drusus; thirty days after his riding accident, Nero Drusus dies (aged 29); Tiberius accompanies body from Germania to Ticinum on foot, met by Augustus and Livia, and on to Rome for state funeral; Augustus gives funeral oration; ashes placed in Augustus' Mausoleum. | Augustus acclaimed *imperator* (XIII); Tiberius acclaimed *imperator* (I).<br>Tiberius' *ovatio*?<br>German War, Year 4: Nero Drusus launches second campaign from Mogontiacum, reaches the Elbe River; erects an altar on the banks of the Elbe River, turns back to the Rhine; fatally wounded in an accident. | 33 |
| 8 | Senate renews Augustus' consular *imperium* for ten years, and right to conduct a census.<br>Senate votes Nero Drusus and his male descendants the *agnomen* 'Germanicus', erects statues and a triumphal arch over the *Via Appia*; Rhine legions erect the *Tumulus* (Cenotaph – the *Eichelstein*) honouring him in Mogontiacum.<br>Reform of the calendar, with month *Sextilis* renamed *Augustus*.<br>Fire in Rome.<br>Doors of the Temple of Ianus closed (?). | German War, Year 5: Tiberius in Germania Magna, negotiates a peace settlement with all Germanic tribes; Maelo surrenders, Sugambri relocate to region around Vetera, renamed Cugerni, and thereafter supply auxiliary cavalry to Rome.<br>Augustus acclaimed *imperator* (XIV).<br>Tiberius acclaimed *imperator* (II).<br>Polemon of Pontus engages the Aspurgiani in Phanagoria, is defeated, taken prisoner and executed. | 34 |

| BCE | Political and Social Events | Diplomatic and Military Events | Tiberius' Age |
|---|---|---|---|
| 7 | *1 January*: Tiberius consul (II) with Cn. Calpurnius Piso. | *Tropaeum Alpium* (La Turbie) erected marking the complete subjugation of the Alps.<br>Tiberius celebrates *pompa triumphalis* in Rome for his victories in German War. | 35 |
| 6 | Senate renews Tiberius' consular *imperium*, grants him *tribunicia potestas* for five years.<br>Tiberius withdraws from public life unexpectedly and retires to Rhodes with Lucilius Longus. | | 36 |
| 5 | *1 January*: Augustus consul (XII).<br>Caius comes of age, designated *Princeps Iuventutis* ('Leader of the Youth'). | | 37 |
| 4 | Birth of Yeshua of Nazareth (?).<br>Birth of L. Annaeus Seneca (Seneca Minor) in Cordoba.<br>Death of Herodes (Herod the Great) in Jericho (?). | Revolts in Iudaea: Simon and Athronges *et al.* Varus intervenes from Syria. | 38 |
| 3 | Maroboduus of the Marcomanni forms a confederation of Germanic nations. | L. Domitius Ahenobarbus in Germania, crosses the Elbe River and builds *Pontes Longi* over marshland near Ems River. | 39 |
| 2 | *1 January*: Augustus consul (XIII) for last time.<br>*5 February*: Senate awards Augustus the accolade *Pater Patriae* ('Father of the Fatherland').<br>*12 May*: Dedication of the *Forum Augustum* and Temple of Mars Ultor.<br>Lucius comes of age, designated *princeps iuventutis*.<br>Iulia's scandalous private life exposed; arrested for adultery and *maiestas*, exiled to Pandateria; Tiberius divorces her.<br>*Autumn*: alternative date for birth of Yeshua of Nazareth. | | 40 |
| 1 | *29 January*: Caius departs Rome to begin his mission to the East with *imperium proconsulare*. | | 41 |

| CE | Political and Social Events | Diplomatic and Military Events | Tiberius' Age |
|---|---|---|---|
| 1 CE | *1 January*: Caius consul, in Syria.<br>Germanicus comes of age, assumes *toga virilis*.<br>Tiberius' consular *imperium* and *tribunicia potestas* expire. | Marmaridian (Marmaric) War, Year 1: campaign against the Marmaridae on the frontier of Cyrenaica.<br>German Revolt: L. Domitius Ahenobarbus *legatus Augusti pro praetore* of Germania, suppresses revolt, crosses the Elbe, engages Hermunduri and negotiates settlement with Maroboduus of the Marcommani; establishes an imperial cult altar and his headquarters at *Ara* Ubiorum.<br>Caius negotiates treaty with Phraatakes V of Parthia on an island in the Euphrates.<br>Augustus acclaimed *imperator* (XV). | 42 |
| 2 | Death of C. Marcius Censorinus<br>*20 August*: Death of Lucius at Massilia (aged 18); ashes placed in Mausoleum of Augustus.<br>Thrasyllus on Rhodes.<br>Tiberius returns to Rome from Rhodes. | Armenian War (*Bellum Armeniacum*), Year 1: Caius departs to lead expedition.<br><br>Marmaridian War, Year 1: P. Sulpicius Quirinius, proconsul of Africa, defeats the Marmaridae. | 43 |
| 3 | Augustus' *imperium* renewed for ten years. | Armenian War, Year 2:<br>*9 September*: Caius wounded at Artagira, Armenia.<br>Augustus acclaimed *imperator* (XVI). | 44 |
| 4 | Iulia permitted to relocate to Rhegium.<br>*21 February*: Death of Caius in Limyra (aged 23); ashes placed in Mausoleum of Augustus.<br>*26 June*: Tiberius adopts Germanicus.<br>*27 June*: Augustus adopts Tiberius and Agrippa Caesar.<br>Tiberius granted consular *imperium maius* and *tribunicia potestas* for five years.<br>*Lex Fufia Caninia* and *Lex Aelia Sentia* on manumission.<br>Walls of Saepinum completed (paid for by Tiberius and Drusus). | C. Sentius Saturninus *legatus Augusti pro praetore* of Germania.<br>German Revolt: Tiberius campaigns in Germania Magna, defeats the Bructeri and recalls Cherusci to loyalty. | 45 |

| CE | Political and Social Events | Diplomatic and Military Events | Tiberius' Age |
|---|---|---|---|
| 5 | Germanicus marries Agrippina *Maior*.<br>Earthquake strikes Rome.<br>Tiber River floods.<br>Famine in Rome.<br>*Lex Valeria Cornelia* regulating the procedure for elections of consuls and praetors. | German Revolt: Tiberius in Germania; reaches the Elbe River.<br>Augustus acclaimed *imperator* (XVII).<br>Tiberius acclaimed *imperator* (III).<br>C. Sentius Saturninus awarded triumphal honours. | 46 |
| 6 | *27 January*: Tiberius rededicates the restored Temple of Castor and Pollux in his and Nero Drusus' names.<br>Famine continues in Rome.<br>Fire destroys parts of the city.<br>Germanicus appointed *augur*.<br>Germanicus and his brother Claudius sponsor games in honour of their father.<br>Birth of Nero Caesar (first son of Germanicus). | Augustus establishes the *aerarium militare* to fund army retirements.<br>*Cohortes Vigilum* founded.<br>Numerous (unidentified) cities in revolt.<br>Brigandage rife in Sardinia.<br>Judaean Revolt: led by Iudas (of Gamala) the Galilean against the census, crushed by Quirinius. Qurinius against the Homanadenses.<br>Coponius appointed *Praefectus Iudaeae*.<br>Isaurian Revolt: in Asia Minor Cornelius Cossus (M. Plautius Silvanus?, *legatus* of Galatia-Pamphylia) squashes revolt of Isauri.<br>Gaetulican War (*Bellum Gaetulicum*): in Africa, proconsul Cossus Cornelius Lentulus defeats Gaetulici and Musulami: awarded triumphal ornaments and *agnomen* Gaetulicus.<br>Marcomannic War: Tiberius and C. Sentius Saturninus launch invasion of Bohaemium but abort it when forces have to be redeployed to suppress a major revolt in Illyricum (Dalmatia and Pannonia).<br>Batonian War (*Bellum Batonianum* or Greater Dalmatian War or Great Illyrian Revolt), Year 1: Bato of the Breuci, Bato of the Daesidiates agree to work together.<br>In Rome, Germanicus raises an army of freedmen, marches to Illyricum. | 47 |
| 7 | Germanicus *quaestor*.<br>Birth of Livia Iulia (daughter of Drusus and Livilla).<br>Agrippa Caesar banished to Planasia. | Batonian War, Year 2: Tiberius and Germanicus with reserves in Illyricum. Battle at *Mons* Claudius, Volcaean Marshes.<br>Tiberius holed up at Siscia. | 48 |

| CE | Political and Social Events | Diplomatic and Military Events | Tiberius' Age |
|---|---|---|---|
| 8 | Iulia Minor banished to Tremirus.<br>Ovid banished to Tomis.<br>Birth of Drusus Caesar (son of Germanicus). | Batonian War, Year 3: Tiberius and Germanicus in Illyricum.<br>*3 August*: Pannonii submit after defeat at Bathinus River.<br>Bato of the Breuci murdered by Bato of the Daesitates.<br>Augustus acclaimed *imperator* (XVIII); Tiberius acclaimed *imperator* (IV). | 49 |
| 9 | Tiberius' consular *imperium* and *tribunicia potestas* renewed for five years.<br><br>Germanicus *praetor*. | Batonian War (*Bellum Delmaticum*), Year 4: Tiberius and Germanicus campaign in Illyricum. Bato of the Daesidiates surrenders, revolt squashed. Augustus acclaimed *imperator* (XIX); Tiberius acclaimed *imperator* (V); Germanicus acclaimed *imperator* (II). Tiberius granted triumphal ornaments.<br>*September* (?): Varian War (*Bellum Varianum*) or Varian Disaster (*Clades Variana*): P. Quinctilius Varus and *Legiones* XVII, XIIX and XIX annihilated at Teutoburg Pass by Germanic alliance forces led by Arminius of the Cherusci.<br>Tiberius takes conscripts from Rome to Rhine forts.<br>M. Ambilibus appointed *Praefectus Iudaeae*. | 50 |
| 10 | *16 January*: Consecration of Temple of Concordia rebuilt by Tiberius.<br>Senate passes *Senatus Consultum Silanianum* on the interrogation and execution of household slaves. | German War: Tiberius campaigns in Germania Magna (?) | 51 |
| 11 | Artabanus II becomes King of Parthia. | German War: Tiberius campaigns in Germania Magna with Germanicus on military exercises; celebrates Augustus' birthday (23 September) on German soil: Augustus acclaimed *imperator* (XX); Tiberius acclaimed *imperator* (VI). | 52 |
| 12 | *1 January*: Germanicus consul (I).<br>Decree on restrictions for exiles.<br>*31 August* (?): Birth of Caius, nicknamed 'Caligula' (son of Germanicus), in Antium. | Annius Rufus appointed *Praefectus Iudaeae*.<br>*23 October*: Tiberius celebrates full triumph in Rome for victories in Illyricum ('Greater Dalmatian War'). | 53 |

| CE | Political and Social Events | Diplomatic and Military Events | Tiberius' Age |
|---|---|---|---|
| 13 | Augustus' consular *imperium* renewed.<br>Tiberius' consular *imperium* made equal with Augustus' (*imperium maius quam*); *tribunicia potestas* renewed for five years.<br>Germanicus made *legatus Augusti pro praetore* in *Tres Galliae* and Germania. | Gallic Revolt: Germanicus puts down insurrection in *Tres Galliae* (?), acclaimed *imperator* (I).<br>Augustus acclaimed *imperator* (XXI).<br>Tiberius acclaimed *imperator* (VII). | 54 |
| 14 | Census of Rome: 4,190,117 recorded citizens.<br>Tiberius travels to Capreae with Augustus.<br>*1 August*: Augustus at Neapolis for the Sebasta Games.<br>Tiberius departs via Beneventum to Illyricum; recalled to Nola.<br>*19 August*: Death of Augustus at Nola (aged 75). Soldiers in Italy swear oath of allegiance to Tiberius.<br>Death of Agrippa Caesar (aged 25).<br>*3 September*: Tiberius returns with body of Augustus to Rome.<br>*4 September:* Senate meets; Drusus reads Augustus' will.<br>*6 or 8 September*: Augustus' state funeral; Tiberius and Drusus give eulogies in the *Forum Romanum*; cremation.<br>*11 September*: Ashes placed in Mausoleum of Augustus.<br>*17 September*: Senate meets: agrees to deification of Augustus (*Divus Augustus*); Tiberius formally assumes role of *Princeps Senatus*.<br>Germanicus granted *imperium proconsulare maius*.<br>Tiberius institutes *Sodales Augustales*.<br>Death of Iulia (aged 52/53). | Seianus appointed *Praefectus Praetorio*.<br>*30 or 31 August*: Mutiny of legions stationed in Pannonia.<br>*31 August* or *1 September*: Blaesus sends envoys to Tiberius.<br>*c. 7/9–18 September:* Drusus travels to Pannonia.<br>*26 September*: Drusus negotiates with mutinying legions in Pannonia; lunar eclipse; mutiny ends.<br>*Late October*: Mutiny of legions stationed in Germania Inferior: Germanicus negotiates a settlement with legions; mutiny ends; punitive expedition against the Marsi.<br>*Late November?*: Germanicus returns to Rome. | 55 |
| 15 | *1 January*: Drusus consul (I).<br>*10 March*: Tiberius *pontifex maximus*.<br>Following riots in a theatre, Tiberius rejects calls for actors to be flogged, agrees to restrict their pay.<br>Following flooding of the Tiber, Tiberius creates a commission; Senate votes against its proposals.<br>Dismissal of case against Falanius for selling a statue of Augustus and Rubrius, violating Augustus' divinity by perjury.<br>Trial and acquittal for *maiestas* of Granius Marcellus. | German War, Year 1: Germanicus leads Roman troops to *saltus Teutoburgiensis*, buries bones; returning fleet shipwrecked off Frisian coast.<br>Valerius Gratus appointed *Praefectus Iudaeae*. | 56 |

| CE | Political and Social Events | Diplomatic and Military Events | Tiberius' Age |
|---|---|---|---|
| 16 | *13–14 September*: Trial and death of M. Livius Drusus Libo Drusus for *maiestas*.<br>*Senatus Consultum* expelling 'Chaldeans' and 'Magians' from Italy.<br>Arrest and execution of conspirator Clemens. | German War, Year 2:<br>*Spring*: Germanicus leads troops at Battle of Weser River; Battle of Idistaviso; and final Battle of the Angrivarian Wall; Tiberius acclaimed *imperator* (VIII); fleet destroyed by storms on return journey.<br>Triumphal honours for German War granted to Germanicus.<br>King of Parthia deposed. | 57 |
| 17 | Earthquakes destroy cities in Asia; Tiberius provides financial assistance to blighted communities.<br>Trial and acquittal for *maiestas* of Appuleia Varilla. | Germanicus leaves Germania.<br>Drusus in Illyricum.<br>*26 May*: Triumph of Germanicus in Rome.<br>Exile of Rheskuporis.<br>Unrest in Armenia, Iudaea, Syria; Tacfarinas leads revolt in Africa Proconsularis.<br>Triumphal honours for Tacfarinas War granted to M. Furius Camillus.<br>Germanicus appointed *Praepositus Orienti*, granted *imperium proconsulare maius* and travels to the East. | 58 |
| 18 | *1 January*: Tiberius consul (III), Germanicus consul (II); Tiberius resigns after a few days.<br>Birth of Iulia Livilla on Lesbos.<br>Piso insults Germanicus; arrives in Syria.<br>Death of Ovid in Tomis (aged 59–61). | Fall of Maroboduus.<br>Germanicus in the East, installs Q. Veranius in Cappadocia and Q. Servaeus in Commagene, crowns Zenon-Artaxias III in Armenia. | 59 |
| 19 | Germanicus in Egypt, returns to Syria, falls ill at Antiocheia on the Orontes.<br>*Senatus Consultum* banning *equites*, senators and women from performing on the stage and in the arena.<br>*10 October*: Death of Germanicus (aged 34).<br>*16 December*: *Senatus Consultum de Honoribus Germanici Decernendis*.<br>*?19 or 20*: Birth of Drusus' twin sons, Germanicus Gemellus and Ti. Gemellus.<br>Expulsion of Egyptian cults and Jewish converts and from Rome. | Revolt of Clemens (slave and Agrippa Caesar imposter); Clemens captured and secretly executed.<br>Rebel army of Cn. Calpurnius Piso defeated by Cn. Sentius Saneus (interim governor of Syria) at Celendris, Cilicia. | 60 |

| CE | Political and Social Events | Diplomatic and Military Events | Tiberius' Age |
|---|---|---|---|
| 20 | Agrippina Maior returns to Rome with Germanicus' ashes.<br>*March*: Funeral of Germanicus.<br>*Lex Papia Poppaea* amended.<br>*December*: Trial of Cn. Calpurnius Piso for *maiestas*; death of Piso, apparently by suicide.<br>*16 December*: Senate gives verdicts in trial of Piso; decree of the *Senatus Consultum de Cn. Pisone Patre*.<br>Death of Vipsania Agrippina (aged 55/56). | Tacfarinas continues revolt in Africa Proconsularis; defeated by Apronius Caesianus.<br>Death of Arminius (?). | 61 |
| 21 | *1 January*: Tiberius consul (IV), Drusus consul (II); Tiberius resigns after three months.<br>Tiberius in Campania.<br>Fire destroys the Theatre of Pompeius Magnus; Seianus intervenes to stop it spreading in Rome.<br>Trial of Clutorius Priscus the poet for *maiestas* in Tiberius' absence; executed.<br>Senate issues decree to require an interval of ten days between sentencing to death and its execution. | Revolt in Africa Proconsularis: Q. Iunius Blaesus selected to lead the counter-insurgency.<br>Revolt in Thracia: Raiskuporis II rescued by P. Vellaeus.<br>Revolt of Iulius Florus in Gallia Belgica and Iulius Sacrovir in Gallia Lugdunensis; defeated by C. Silius. | 62 |
| 22 | Drusus granted *tribunicia potestas*.<br>Trial of C. Iunius Silanus for extortion and *maiestas* (banished).<br>Tiberius rebuilds the Theatre of Pompeius destroyed by fire; statue of Seianus erected in theatre.<br>Death of Asinius Saloninus, Ateius Capito and Iunia. | Tacfarinas defeated by Q. Iunius Blaesus.<br>*Castra Praetoria* constructed at Rome. | 63 |
| 23 | Death of Lucilius Longus.<br>Seianus divorces Apicata.<br>Tiberius bans actors from performing in Rome.<br>*14 September*: Death of Drusus (aged 36).<br>Death of Drusus Caesar (aged 24/25).<br>Death of Germanicus Gemellus (aged 4).<br>Birth of C. Plinius Secundus (?).<br>Trial and banishment of Lucilius Capito for unauthorized use of troops in Asia.<br>Temple voted to Tiberius and Livia in Asia. | Triumphal honours for Tacfarinas War granted to Q. Iunius Blaesus. | 64 |

| CE | Political and Social Events | Diplomatic and Military Events | Tiberius' Age |
|---|---|---|---|
| | Trial and acquittal of two men on charges of supplying grain to Tacfarinas.<br>Trial of Aelius Saturninus (executed) for having recited some improper verses about Tiberius. | | |
| 24 | Trials for *maiestas* of L. Calpurnius Piso (suspended), C. Silius (commits suicide) and T. Cassius Severus (exiled).<br>Trial of M. Plautius Silvanus for defenestrating his wife (Silvanus commits suicide).<br>Trial of Cn. Cornelius Lentulus (dismissed), L. Seius Tubero (dismissed), Vibius Serenus (banished) and Caecilius Cornutus on charges of inciting rebellion (Cornutus commits suicide).<br>Trial of Catus Firmius (expelled from Senate) for falsely accusing his sister of *maiestas*.<br>Trial of P. Suillius Rufus (exiled) for bribery.<br>*17 September*: Tenth anniversary of Tiberius' principate; renewal of Tiberius' *imperium proconsulare maius*; *Decennalia* festival. | Death of Tacfarinas in Africa; Numidia and Mauretania annexed.<br>Triumphal honours for Tacfarinas War refused to P. Cornelius Dolabella.<br>Slave revolt in Italy led by T. Curtisius squashed by Curtius Lupus. | 65 |
| 25 | Cremutius Cordus and Fonteius Capito accused of defamatory remarks about Augustus (Cordus commits suicide).<br>*April*: Trial of Calpurnius Salvianus (banished).<br>Fonteius Capito acquitted of all charges.<br>Tiberius refuses a request by a delegation from Hispania to erect a temple to himself and Ausgusta.<br>Tiberius settles a dispute between Messenia and Sparta over the *Ager Dentheliales*.<br>Trial of Votienus Montanus (banished) for slandering Tiberius.<br>Apidius Merula struck off the senatorial rolls.<br>Seianus refuses Livilla (Livia Iulia). | Revolt in Thracia. | 66 |

| CE | Political and Social Events | Diplomatic and Military Events | Tiberius' Age |
|---|---|---|---|
| 26 | Trial of Claudia Pulchra for immorality and *maiestas* (convicted).<br>Tiberius leaves Rome for Campania; dedicates temples at Capua and Nola.<br>Seianus saves the life of Tiberius at a dinner party at Spelunca.<br>Seianus put in charge of affairs in Rome.<br>Pontius Pilatus posted to Iudaea.<br>Q. Haterius dies (aged 88). | Pontius Pilatus appointed *Praefectus Iudaeae.*<br><br>Revolt in Thracia; C. Poppaeus Sabinus granted triumphal ornaments. | 67 |
| 27 | Tiberius in Campania; abandons Spelunca and relocates to Capreae.<br>Fire in Rome destroys buildings on the *Caelius*; Tiberius covers losses of property owners.<br>Collapse of amphitheatre of Atilius at Fidenae; Tiberius compensates the 20,000 injured.<br>Death in exile of Votienus Montanus. | | 68 |
| 28 | Entrapment of Titius Sabinus. | Revolt of the Frisii; defeated by L. Apronius. | 69 |
| 29 | Trial and death of Sabinus.<br>Marriage of Agrippina Minor to C. Domitius Ahenobarbus.<br>Death in exile of Iulia Minor.<br>Altar to *Clementia* and *Amicitia* with Tiberius and Seianus.<br>Tiberius and Seianus in Campania, returns to Capreae.<br><br>*28 September*: Death of Livia Drusilla/ Iulia Augusta (aged 86).<br>Agrippina Maior exiled to Pandataria.<br>Nero Caesar exiled to Pontia. | | 70 |
| 30 | Drusus Caesar charged with misconduct; confined to the *Palatium*.<br>C. Asinius Gallus imprisoned.<br>Death of Fufius Geminus and wife Mutilia Prisca.<br>Seianus betrothed to Livia Iulia.<br>Velleius Paterculus publishes his *Roman History*.<br>Death of Shammai. | | 71 |
| 31 | *1 January*: Tiberius consul (V), Seianus consul (I); Tiberius resigns on Ides of May.<br>Death of M. Velleius Paterculus (?). | | 72 |

| CE | Political and Social Events | Diplomatic and Military Events | Tiberius' Age |
|---|---|---|---|
| | Death of Livia Iulia.<br>Death of Nero Caesar (aged 24/25).<br>Tiberius makes Caius Caligula his heir.<br>Disloyalty of Seianus exposed and brought to Tiberius' attention (by Antonia Minor?).<br>Naevius Sutorius Macro *Praefectus Praetorio.*<br>*18 October*: Seianus denounced, executed (aged 50).<br>Execution of Q. Iunius Blaesus.<br>Trials and deaths of Seianus' supporters. | | |
| 32 | *April*: Crucifixion of Jesus of Nazareth (according to Jerome).<br>*April Passover Day*: Lunar eclipse.<br>Earthquake destroys buildings in Bithynia and Nikeia.<br>Saul of Tarsus (Paul) becomes an evangelist of *Christos* (?). | Honours awarded to *Cohortes Pretoriae*.<br>Dispute of Iunius Gallio over privileges of veteran *Praetoriani*. | 73 |
| 33 | Tiberius on mainland Italy but does not visit Rome.<br>Sex. Marius charged with incest or *maiestas* (?) (executed).<br>Death of Asinius Gallus.<br>Financial crisis: Tiberius provides loans from the *fiscus* and sets up a commission to enforce laws on usuary.<br>Caius Caligula *quaestor*; marries Iunia Claudia.<br>*September* (?): Death of Drusus Caesar (aged 24/25).<br>*18 October*: Death of Agrippina Maior (aged 46).<br>Facing a renewed murder charge, Munatia Plancina commits suicide.<br>Suicide of M. Cocceius Nerva, despite Tiberius' pleas.<br>*December*: natural deaths of L. Aemilius Lamia and L. Pomponius Flaccus. | Hiberus temporarily *Praefectus Aegypti*.<br>A. Avillius Flaccus *Praefectus Aegypti*.<br>Tiberius complains to the Senate about the lack of talent for military leadership positions. | 74 |
| 34 | Tiberius on mainland Italy at Tusculum but does not visit Rome.<br>Trials of prominent Romans for *maiestas*.<br>Suicide of Mamercus Aemilius Scaurus and his wife.<br>Death of M. Aemilius Lepidus.<br>*17 September*: Twentieth anniversary of Tiberius' principate. | Attempt to indict Cn. Cornelius Lentulus Gaetulicus, *legatus Augusti propraetore* Germania Superior, as an associate of Seianus fails. | 75 |

| CE | Political and Social Events | Diplomatic and Military Events | Tiberius' Age |
|---|---|---|---|
| 35 | Trials of prominent Romans for *maiestas*.<br>Suicide of L. Fulcinius Trio.<br>Tiberius writes his will. | L. Vitellius in Syria; war in Armenia and Parthia against Artabanus II. | 76 |
| 36 | Trials of prominent Romans for *maiestas*.<br>Attempted suicide of Vibullius Agrippa.<br>Suicide of C. Sulpicius Galba after being turned down for a governorship.<br>Suicide of Aemilia Lepida.<br>Pontius Pilatus recalled to Rome (?).<br>Tiberius advocates for consecration of Christ, but Senate rejects the motion (?); Tiberius issues decree setting severe penalties against all who accuse the worshippers of Christ (?).<br>*1 November:* Fire in Rome damages *Circus Maximus* and buildings on the *Aventinus*; Tiberius (encamped near Rome) gives HS 1 million, managed by a special commission, to rebuild destroyed property.<br>Death of Thrasyllus. | L. Vitellius defeats Artabanus II, crowns Tiridates III in Parthia; Artabanus II returns.<br>Revolt of the Clitae in Cappadocia: defeated by M. Trebellius.<br>Marcellus appointed *Praefectus Iudaeae*. | 77 |
| 37 | Trials of prominent Romans for *maiestas*.<br>Suicide of L. Arruntius.<br>Death of Maroboduus of the Marcomanni at Ravenna.<br>Tiberius departs Latium and returns to Campania.<br>*16 March*: Death of Tiberius at Misenum (aged 77½).<br>*18 March*: Senate annuls Tiberius' will, which appointed Caius Caligula and Ti. Gemellus as joint heirs; accession of Caius Caligula as *princeps* (aged 25).<br>*29 March*: Tiberius' body arrives in Rome.<br>*3 April*: Funeral of Tiberius in Rome; Caius Caligula gives the oration; his ashes placed in Mausoleum of Augustus.<br>*9 April*: Earthquake damages Antioch on the Orontes.<br>*1 May*: Death of Antonia Minor (aged 72).<br>Death of M. Iunius Silanus.<br>Murder of Ti. Gemellus (aged 18).<br>*15 December*: Birth of L. Domitius Ahenobarbus (future *princeps* Nero). | | |

# List of Consuls

| Year | First Consul | Second Consul |
|---|---|---|
| 42 BCE | M. Aemilius Lepidus II | L. Munatius Plancus |
| 41 | L. Antonius Pietas | P. Servilius Isauricus II |
| 40 | Cn. Domitius Calvinus II | C. Asinius Pollio |
| *suff.* | L. Cornelius Balbus | P. Canidius Crassus |
| 39 | L. Marcius Censorinus | C. Calvisius Sabinus |
| *suff.* | C. Cocceius Balbus (after 2 October) | P. Alfenus Varus (after 2 October) |
| 38 | Ap. Claudius Pulcher | C. Norbanus Flaccus |
| *suff.* | L. Cornelius Lentulus (from 1 July) | L. Marcius Philippus (from 1 September) |
| 37 | M. Agrippa | L. Caninius Gallus |
| *suff.* | | T. Statilius Taurus |
| 36 | L. Gellius Poplicola | M. Cocceius Nerva |
| *suff.* | L. Nonius Asprenas (from 1 September) | Q. Marcius Rufus (from 1 July) |
| 35 | L. Cornificius | Sex. Pompeius |
| *suff.* | P. Cornelius Dolabella (from 1 September) | T. Peducaeus (from 1 July) |
| 34 | M. Antonius II (1 January only) | L. Scribonius Libo |
| *suff.* | L. Sempronius Atratinus | |
| *suff.* | Paullus Aemilius Lepidus (from 1 July) | C. Memmius (from 1 July) |
| *suff.* | | M. Herennius Picens (from September or November) |
| 33 | Imp. Caesar II (1 January only) | L. Volcacius Tullus |
| *suff.* | L. Autronius Paetus | |
| *suff.* | L. Flavius (1 May – before October) | C. Fonteius Capito (1 May – before October) |
| *suff.* | M. Acilius Glabrio (1 July – before October) | |
| *suff.* | L. Vinicius (from 1 September) | |
| *suff.* | Q. Laronius (from 1 October) | |
| 32 | Cn. Domitius Ahenobarbus | C. Sosius |
| *suff.* | L. Cornelius (Balbus? Cinna?) | M. Valerius Messalla |
| 31 | M. Antonius III (in the East) | Imp. Caesar III |
| *suff.* | M. Valerius Messalla Corvinus (from 1 January) | |
| *suff.* | M. Titius (from 1 May) | |
| *suff.* | Cn. Pompeius (from 1 October) | |
| 30 | Imp. Caesar IV | M. Licinius Crassus |
| *suff.* | | C. Antistius Vetus (from 1 July) |
| *suff.* | | M. Tullius Cicero (from 1 September) |
| *suff.* | | L. Saenius |
| 29 | Imp. Caesar V | Sex. Appuleius |

| Year | First Consul | Second Consul |
|---|---|---|
| *suff.* | | Potitus Valerius Messalla |
| 28 | Imp. Caesar VI | M. Agrippa II |
| 27 | Imp. Caesar Augustus VII | M. Agrippa III |
| 26 | Imp. Caesar Augustus VIII | T. Statilius Taurus II |
| 25 | Imp. Caesar Augustus IX | M. Iunius Silanus |
| 24 | Imp. Caesar Augustus X | C. Norbanus Flaccus |
| 23 | Imp. Caesar Augustus XI | A. Terentius Varro Murena (abdicated) |
| *suff.* | L. Sestius Albanianus Quirinalis (from 1 July) | Cn. Calpurnius Piso |
| 22 | M. Claudius Marcellus Aeserninus | L. Arruntius |
| 21 | M. Lollius | Q. Aemilius Lepidus |
| 20 | M. Appuleius | P. Silius Nerva |
| 19 | C. Sentius Saturninus | Q. Lucretius Vespillo (after 1 August) |
| *suff.* | M. Vinicius (after 1 August) | |
| 18 | P. Cornelius Lentulus Marcellinus | Cn. Cornelius Lentulus |
| 17 | C. Furnius | C. Iunius Silanus |
| 16 | L. Domitius Ahenobarbus | P. Cornelius Scipio |
| *suff.* | | L. Tarius Rufus |
| 15 | M. Livius Drusus Libo | L. Calpurnius Piso |
| 14 | M. Licinius Crassus Frugi | Cn. Cornelius Lentulus (Augur) |
| 13 | Ti. Claudius Nero | P. Quinctilius Varus |
| 12 | M. Valerius Messalla Appianus | P. Sulpicius Quirinius |
| *suff.* | C. Valgius Rufus (by 6 March) | |
| *suff.* | C. Caninius Rebilus (after 29 August) | L. Volusius Saturninus (after 29 August) |
| 11 | Q. Aelius Tubero | Paullus Fabius Maximus |
| 10 | Africanus Fabius Maximus | Iullus Antonius |
| 9 | Nero Claudius Drusus | T. Quinctius Crispinus Sulpicianus |
| 8 | C. Marcius Censorinus | C. Asinius Gallus |
| 7 | Ti. Claudius Nero II | Cn. Calpurnius Piso |
| 6 | D. Laelius Balbus | C. Antistius Vetus |
| 5 | Imp. Caesar Augustus XII | L. Cornelius Sulla |
| *suff.* | Q. Haterius (after 11 April) | L. Vinicius (after 11 April) |
| *suff.* | | C. Sulpicius Galba (by 13 August) |
| 4 | C. Calvisius Sabinus | L. Passienus Rufus |
| *suff.* | C. Caelius | Galus Sulpicius (after 1 July) |
| 3 | L. Cornelius Lentulus | M. Valerius Messalla Messallinus |
| 2 | Imp. Caesar Augustus XIII | M. Plautius Silvanus |
| *suff.* | C. Fufius Geminus (by 18 September) | L. Caninius Gallus (by 1 August) |
| *suff.* | Q. Fabricius (by 1 December) | |
| 1 BCE | Cossus Cornelius Lentulus (Gaetulicus) | L. Calpurnius Piso (Augur) |
| *suff.* | A. Plautius | A. Caecina Severus |
| | | |
| 1 CE | C. Caesar | L. Aemilius Paullus |
| Jul. | | M. Herennius Picens |
| 2 | P. Vinicius | P. Alfenus Varus |
| Jul. | P. Cornelius Lentulus Scipio | T. Quinctius Crispinus Valerianus |
| 3 | L. Aelius Lamia | M. Servilius |

| Year | First Consul | Second Consul |
|---|---|---|
| Jul. | P. Silius | L. Volusius Saturninus |
| 4 | Sex. Aelius Catus | C. Sentius Saturninus |
| Jul. | Cn. Sentius Saturninus | C. Clodius Licinus |
| 5 | L. Valerius Messalla Volesus | Cn. Cornelius Cinna Magnus |
| Jul. | C. Vibius Postumus | C. Ateius Capito |
| 6 | M. Aemilius Lepidus | L. Arruntius |
| Jul. | | L. Nonius Asprenas |
| 7 | Q. Caecilius Metellus Creticus Silanus | A. Licinius Nerva Silianus |
| Jul. | | Lucilius Longus |
| 8 | M. Furius Camillus | Sex. Nonius Quinctilianus |
| Jul. | L. Apronius | A. Vibius Habitus |
| 9 | C. Poppaeus Sabinus | Q. Sulpicius Camerinus |
| Jul. | M. Papius Mutilus | Q. Poppaeus Secundus |
| 10 | P. Cornelius Dolabella | C. Iunius Silanus |
| Jul. | Ser. Cornelius Lentulus Maluginensis | Q. Iunius Blaesus |
| 11 | M'. Aemilius Lepidus | T. Statilius Taurus |
| Jul. | L. Cassius Longinus | |
| 12 | Germanicus Iulius Caesar | C. Fonteius Capito |
| Jul. | | C. Visellius Varro |
| 13 | C. Silius | L. Munatius Plancus |
| *suff.* | C. Caecina Largus | |
| 14 | Sex. Pompeius | Sex. Appuleius |
| 15 | Drusus Iulius Caesar | C. Norbanus Flaccus |
| Jul. | | M. Junius Silanus |
| 16 | Sisenna Statilius Taurus | L. Scribonius Libo |
| Jul. | C. Vibius Rufus | C. Pomponius Graecinus |
| 17 | L. Pomponius Flaccus | C. Caelius Rufus |
| *suff.* | C. Vibius Marsus | L. Voluseius Proculus |
| 18 | Ti. Caesar Augustus III (January) | Germanicus Iulius Caesar II (January–April) |
| *suff.* | L. Seius Tubero (February–July) | Livineius Regulus (May–July) |
| *suff.* | C. Rubellius Blandus (August–December) | M. Vipstanus Gallus |
| 19 | M. Iunius Silanus Torquatus | L. Norbanus Balbus |
| Jul. | | P. Petronius |
| 20 | M. Valerius Messalla Barbatus | M. Aurelius Cotta Maximus Messalinus |
| 21 | Ti. Caesar Augustus IV | Drusus Iulius Caesar II |
| *suff.* | Mam. Aemilius Scaurus | Cn. Tremellius |
| 22 | D. Haterius Agrippa | C. Sulpicius Galba |
| 23 | C. Asinius Pollio | C. Antistius Vetus |
| *suff.* | | C. Stertinius Maximus |
| 24 | Ser. Cornelius Cethegus | L. Visellius Varro |
| Jul. | C. Calpurnius Aviola | P. Cornelius Lentulus Scipio |
| 25 | Cossus Cornelius Lentulus | M. Asinius Agrippa |
| Sep. | C. Petronius | |
| 26 | Cn. Cornelius Lentulus Gaetulicus | C. Calvisius Sabinus |
| *suff.* | Q. Iunius Blaesus | L. Antistius Vetus |

| Year | First Consul | Second Consul |
|---|---|---|
| 27 | L. Calpurnius Piso | M. Licinius Crassus Frugi |
| *suff.* | P. Cornelius Lentulus | C. Sallustius Passienus Crispus |
| 28 | Ap. Iunius Silanus | P. Silius Nerva |
| *suff.* | L. Iunius Silanus | C. Vellaeus Tutor |
| 29 | C. Fufius Geminus | L. Rubellius Geminus |
| Jul. | A. Plautius | L. Nonius Asprenas |
| 30 | L. Cassius Longinus | M. Vinicius |
| Jul. | L. Naevius Surdinus | C. Cassius Longinus |
| 31 | Ti. Caesar Augustus V | L. Aelius Seianus |
| 9 May | Faustus Cornelius Sulla | Sex. Tedius Valerius Catullus |
| Jul. | | L. Fulcinius Trio |
| Oct. | P. Memmius Regulus | |
| 32 | Cn. Domitius Ahenobarbus | L. Arruntius Camillus Scribonianus |
| Jul. | | A. Vitellius |
| 33 | L. Livius Ocella Sulpicius Galba | L. Cornelius Sulla Felix |
| Jul. | L. Salvius Otho | C. Octavius Laenas |
| 34 | Paullus Fabius Persicus | L. Vitellius |
| Jul. | Q. Marcius Barea Soranus | T. Rustius Nummius Gallus |
| 35 | C. Cestius Gallus | M. Servilius Nonianus |
| Jul. | D. Valerius Asiaticus | A. Gabinius Secundus |
| 36 | Sex. Papinius Allenius | Q. Plautius |
| Jul. | C. Vettius Rufus | M. Porcius Cato |
| 37 | Cn. Acerronius Proculus | C. Petronius Pontius Nigrinus |
| 1 Jul. | C. Caesar Augustus Germanicus | Ti. Claudius Nero Germanicus |
| 1 Sep. | A. Caecina Paetus | C. Caninius Rebilus |

*Suff.* = *Suffectus* (suffect consul).

# Roman Names

### M. Caelius T. *f.* Lemonia Bononia

This is the official name of a centurion of *Legio* XIIX preserved on an inscription now in the Rheinisches Landesmuseum in Bonn, Germany (*CIL*, XIII, 8648 = *AE* 1952). His name embodies the elements of Roman naming practice. It translates as:

**Marcus Caelius, son of Titus, of the voting tribe of Lemonia, from Bononia**

Marcus is his forename (*praenomen*) by which his family and close friends called him. In inscriptions, public records and narrative texts, it was abbreviated. The standard abbreviations for common *praenomina* were:

| | | | |
|---|---|---|---|
| A. | Aulus | M'. | Manius |
| Ap. | Appius | P. | Publius |
| C. *or* G. | Caius or Gaius | Q. | Quintus |
| Cn. *or* Gn. | Cnaeus or Gnaeus | Ser. | Servius |
| D. | Decimus | Sex. | Sextus |
| L. | Lucius | Sp. | Spurius |
| M. | Marcus | T. | Titus |
| Mam. | Mamius | Ti. | Tiberius |

Caelius is his clan or family name (*nomen gentilicium* or *nomen*). His clan is *gens Caelia*. Many of these clans, such as the *Claudii* and *Cornelii*, were famous old families of Rome with proud traditions. Then follows the filiation or patrymonic of the father's *praenomen*, whose full name would have been Titus Caelius. As a Roman citizen, his family was associated with one of thirty-five voting tribes: in elections, Caelius voted with the Lemonian tribe. The final element is the place of his birth (*origo*) or domicile (*domus*), which is in this case Bononia, modern Bologna in Italy. Together, these distinguished this particular Marcus Caelius from another bearing the same name. To clearly tell men apart with the same name, with their warped sense of humour, Romans often adopted a third nickname (*cognomen*) such as Rufus 'red haired', Paulus 'shorty' or Brutus 'stupid'. Men who had achieved great victories in war might be granted use of a honorific title commemorating where they were won, such as *Africanus* meaning 'the African' (or 'of Africa') or *Germanicus*, 'the German' (or 'of Germania').

Footnote: M. Caelius died in 9 CE during the *Clades Variana* or Battle at the Teutoburg Pass.

Something greater and loftier is expected of a *princeps*, and while everybody takes to himself the credit of right policy, one alone has to bear the odium of every person's failures …

Such, Conscript Fathers, are the anxieties which the *princep*s has to sustain, and the neglect of them will be utter ruin to the *Res Publica.*

*Maius aliquid et excelsius a principe postulatur; et cum recte factorum sibi quisque gratiam trahant, unius invidia ab omnibus peccatur …*

*Patres Conscripti, curam sustinet princeps; haec omissa funditus Rem Publicam trahet.*

Tiberius' letter to the Senate in 22 CE, quoted in Tacitus, *Annals* 3.53–54.

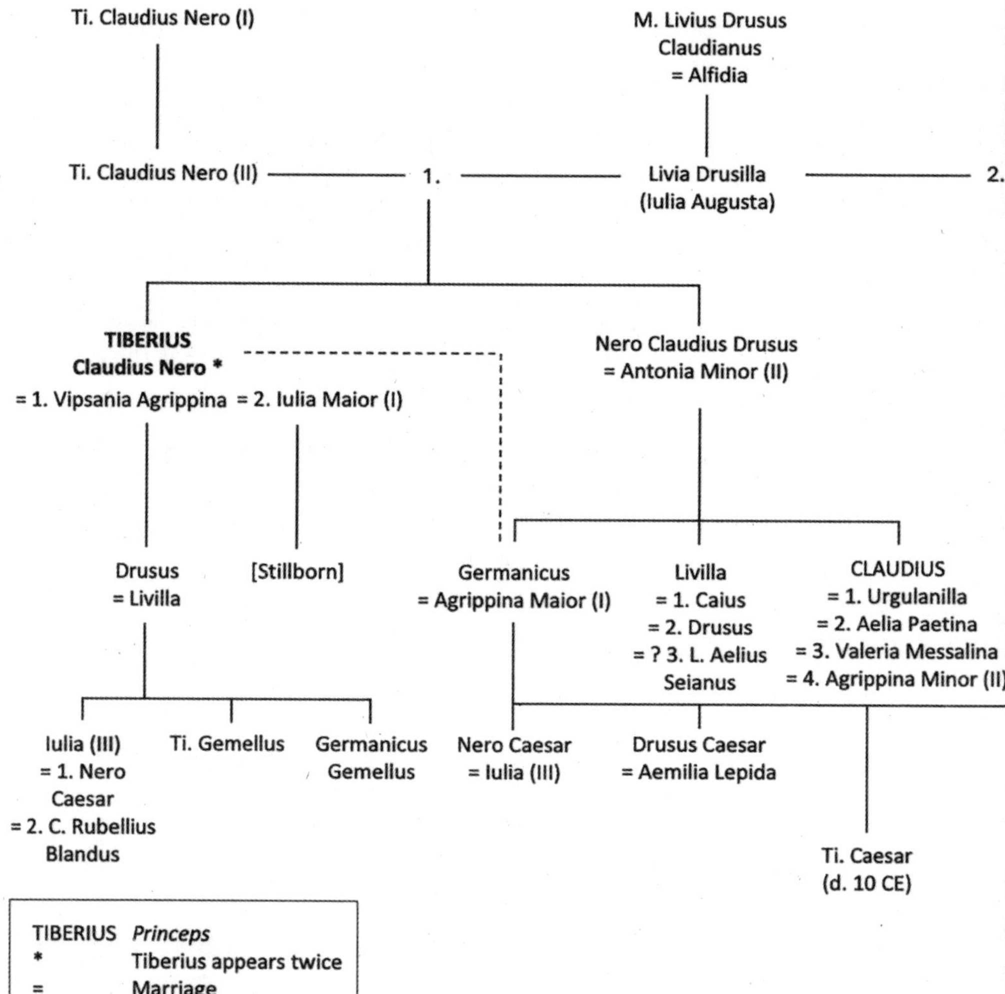
Ti. Claudius Nero (I)
M. Livius Drusus Claudianus = Alfidia
Ti. Claudius Nero (II)
1.
Livia Drusilla (Iulia Augusta)
2.
TIBERIUS Claudius Nero *
= 1. Vipsania Agrippina
= 2. Iulia Maior (I)
Nero Claudius Drusus = Antonia Minor (II)
Drusus = Livilla
[Stillborn]
Germanicus = Agrippina Maior (I)
Livilla = 1. Caius = 2. Drusus = ? 3. L. Aelius Seianus
CLAUDIUS = 1. Urgulanilla = 2. Aelia Paetina = 3. Valeria Messalina = 4. Agrippina Minor (II)
Iulia (III) = 1. Nero Caesar = 2. C. Rubellius Blandus
Ti. Gemellus
Germanicus Gemellus
Nero Caesar = Iulia (III)
Drusus Caesar = Aemilia Lepida
Ti. Caesar (d. 10 CE)
TIBERIUS Princeps
* Tiberius appears twice
= Marriage
-- Adoption

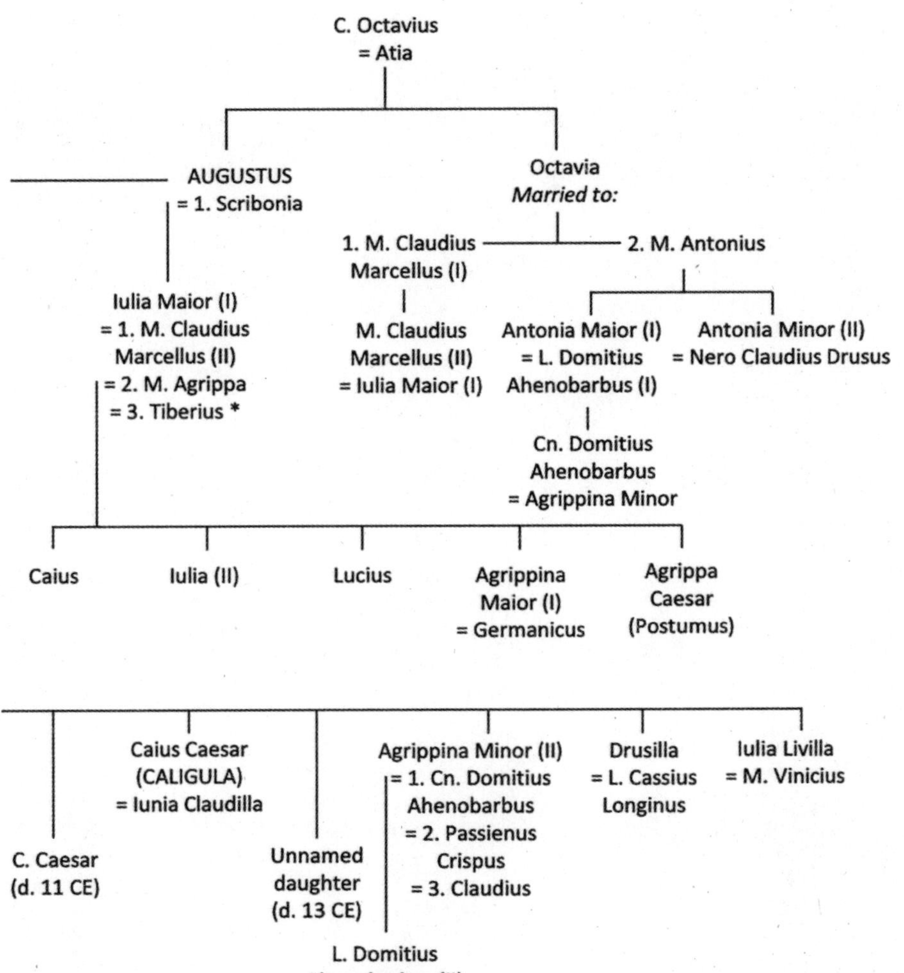

C. Octavius
= Atia
AUGUSTUS
= 1. Scribonia
Octavia
Married to:
1. M. Claudius Marcellus (I)
2. M. Antonius
Iulia Maior (I)
= 1. M. Claudius Marcellus (II)
= 2. M. Agrippa
= 3. Tiberius *
M. Claudius Marcellus (II)
= Iulia Maior (I)
Antonia Maior (I)
= L. Domitius Ahenobarbus (I)
Antonia Minor (II)
= Nero Claudius Drusus
Cn. Domitius Ahenobarbus
= Agrippina Minor
Caius
Iulia (II)
Lucius
Agrippina Maior (I)
= Germanicus
Agrippa Caesar (Postumus)
C. Caesar
(d. 11 CE)
Caius Caesar (CALIGULA)
= Iunia Claudilla
Unnamed daughter
(d. 13 CE)
Agrippina Minor (II)
= 1. Cn. Domitius Ahenobarbus
= 2. Passienus Crispus
= 3. Claudius
Drusilla
= L. Cassius Longinus
Iulia Livilla
= M. Vinicius
L. Domitius Ahenobarbus (II)
(NERO)

# Chapter 1

# Growing Up in Turbulent Times: 42–19 BCE

In the summer of 4 CE, a military convoy left Rome.[1] At a brisk pace, it moved northwards through Italy, over the Alps and across the Gallic provinces. The soldiers of the Praetorian Cohorts marched in disciplined lines as befitted the elite of the Roman Army.[2] Riding with the troops, to take up his new posting as *praefectus equitum* ('prefect of cavalry') on the Rhine was a young man in his mid-20s named M. Velleius Paterculus.[3] He was attached to the staff of the new imperial legate who was leading the column.[4] As they passed through cities along the journey, curious onlookers turned out to watch. Paterculus witnessed first-hand how they reacted.

Some of the older men in the crowds, Paterculus later wrote in his *Roman History*, became emotional when they recognized the *imperator* ('commander') on his horse.[5] They were retired veterans of the legions who had served with him. Tears of joy welled up in their eyes at the sight of the senior officer. Some felt the familiar urge to salute him and longed to shake his hand as they might a close friend. Others called out to their old comrade.

'Is it really you that we see, *imperator*?' asked one in amazement.

'Have we received you safely back among us?' shouted another.

'I served with you, *imperator*, in Armenia!'

'And I in Raetia!'

'I received my decoration from you in Vindelicia!' said one, beaming with pride.

'I got mine in Pannonia!'

'I received mine in Germania!'[6]

Between them, these veterans had served with the legate in camps and combat theatres along the Euphrates, Danube, Rhine and Sava rivers. Even in retirement, all still felt a close bond with the man who now rode past them.

At the times these men were on active service, the legate had been just one of two of the *princeps*' stepsons. A few weeks before the convoy left Rome on this latest tour, the now 45-year-old commander had been formally adopted by the ageing Caesar Augustus.[7] The new son had become the second most important man in all the empire. Perhaps to his regret, his life would never be the same.

History remembers him by his *praenomen*, Tiberius. This is his extraordinary story.

* * *

The life of Tiberius begins with a mystery. When and where he was born is not entirely certain. Suetonius, the Roman collector of biographical facts and fictions about the Caesars, writes in the first decades of the early second century CE:

> Some have supposed that Tiberius was born at Fundi, on no better evidence than that his maternal grandmother was a native of that place, and that later a statue of Good Fortune was set up there by decree of the Senate. But according to the most numerous and trustworthy authorities, he was born at Rome, on the Palatinus, on the 16th day before the Kalends of December, in the consulship of M. Aemilius Lepidus (I) and L. Munatius Plancus (the former for the second time) [42 BCE] while the war of Philippi was going on. In fact, it is so recorded both in the calendar and in the public gazette. Yet, in spite of this, some write that he was born in the preceding year, that of Hirtius and Pansa [43 BCE], and others in the following year, in the consulate of Servilius Isauricus and L. Antonius [41 BCE].[8]

These details might even have been deliberately suppressed so that astrologers could not produce his horoscope and learn about his life and death.[9]

Assuming 16 November of the year 42 BCE to be correct, his birthday was barely a month after the official end of a brutal civil war.[10] That grave conflict, which had pitted Roman against Roman, followed the murder of C. Iulius Caesar, *dictator perpetuo*, on the Ides of March 44 BCE.[11] Tiberius' own parents were swept up in the ensuing maelstrom, a fact which may also explain why the date of his birth is confused. Indeed, turmoil was to mark the earliest years of his life.

His father was Ti. Claudius Nero, 'a man of noble character and high intellectual training'.[12] He had done rather well by associating himself with the old military commander. During the Alexandrian War (48–47 BCE), fought between the Ptolemy brother and sister for control of Egypt, Iulius Caesar had appointed Ti. Nero as *quaestor* and he had acquitted himself well in combat.[13] To qualify for one of the forty available positions, the candidate had to be at least 30 years of age. Meaning 'investigator' or 'judge', in peacetime the *quaestor classicus* was responsible for administering the public treasury (*Fiscus*); but this was wartime, and he was also charged with distributing the spoils.[14] He proved his worth when he commanded a fleet, and his leadership contributed materially to the victorious outcome for Caesar.[15] Caesar rewarded him with the position of *pontifex*, a member of a college of priests (*collegium*), replacing P. Scipio. Now a trusted and favoured deputy, in 46 BCE Caesar dispatched Ti. Nero to Gallia Narbonnensis, Rome's oldest province, with the important commission of establishing new *coloniae* for the honourably discharged veterans of the legions he had himself raised and now disbanded.[16] His personal fortunes changed, however, in the aftermath of Caesar's assassination.

The *praenomen* Tiberius was an antique Latin name, perhaps derived from *Tiberis*, and meant 'one who lives by the Tiber River'.[17] Tiberius was a frequent choice of first name for male members of *gens Claudia*. Indeed, Ti. Nero was descended from a patrician branch of the Claudian clan with roots among the Sabines of central Italy in the sixth century BCE. It produced a long line of high-profile, high-performance individuals. Suetonius counted 'twenty-eight consulships, five dictatorships, seven censorships, six triumphs, and two ovations' among its members' distinctions.[18] 'It is notorious besides,' writes the biographer, 'that all the *Claudii* were aristocrats and staunch upholders of the prestige and influence of the patricians.'[19] Love of freedom (*libertas*) and a certain bloody-mindedness were character traits of the family. Through his maternal grandfather's adoption into it, Ti. Nero was also connected to the family of the plebeian *gens Livia*. It too was 'of great prominence and had been honoured with eight consulships, two censorships, and three triumphs, as well as with the offices of *Dictator* and *Magister Equitum* ['Master of the Horse'].'[20] The *Drusi* were a branch of this clan too, noted for their derring-do on the battlefield and daring deeds in the service of the *Res Publica* ('Commonwealth'). Ti. Nero was a personable individual who got along with people of influence.[21]

In 50 BCE, Ti. Nero had planned to marry Tullia, the daughter of M. Tullius Cicero, the consul for 63 BCE and a self-promoting orator and writer.[22] Political loyalties made that an impossible choice. After his campaigns in Gallia Comata, Iulius Caesar had been instructed to surrender his legions, return to Rome and face an inquiry into his activities by his peers in the Senate. Famously, he crossed the Rubico River with a legion and, in so doing, provoked a civil war.[23] The Senate and the statesman stood with Cn. Pompeius Magnus as their champion and evacuated Rome, intending to join him and his army in Macedonia and Thrace.[24] Ti. Nero, however, aligned with Iulius Caesar and stayed in the city.[25] The marriage with Tullia never took place.

Ti. Nero's judgment was tested again in the weeks after the conspirators' twenty-three dagger blows struck down Iulius Caesar. Strangely, he now turned against his old patron. There was a debate on 17 March 44 BCE in which M. Antonius (Caesar's former *Magister Equitium* and the current consul) called for moderation. As *praetor*, Ti. Nero surprised many that day. 'When all the others voted for an amnesty through fear of mob violence,' writes Suetonius, 'he even favoured a proposal for *rewarding* the tyrannicides.'[26] The amnesty, which was agreed, meant the conspirators got away with murder. A month after the assassination, they slipped out of Rome unscathed. C. Cassius Longinus moved to Syria, while M. Iunius Brutus went to Macedonia, and his cousin, Dec. Iunius Brutus Albinus, settled in Mutina (Modena) as the new governor (*proconsulis*) of Gallia Cisalpina.[27] Following the end of his consulship in December 44 BCE, Antonius was himself given the governorship of Macedonia.[28] Piqued that Dec.

Brutus had landed the better provincial appointment, since it would offer him easier access to Rome in the event of trouble, Antonius marched his troops from Macedonia to the north of Italy to seize Mutina.[29]

Caesar's legal heir was an unexpected choice, namely his great-nephew C. Octavius Thurinus.[30] After seeing brief military service in Hispania, in the spring of 44 BCE he had been in Apollonia in Illyricum training with troops in readiness for an expedition to be led by Caesar himself against the Getae nation and the Parthian Empire.[31] Learning of the murder by letter, Octavius and his close friends – among them M. Agrippa (b. 64/63 BCE) – secretly returned to Italy.[32] Encouraged by Cicero, initially Octavius sided with the majority in the Senate. Then just 19 years old, he had inherited the deceased dictator's name and fortune, and with them the loyalty of the veterans who had served with him on countless battlefields. His heir now 'recalled' (*evocati*) these men to new legions.[33] In its struggle against Antonius, the Senate urgently needed an army.[34] In the spring of 43 BCE, on the promise of receiving a consulship for services to be rendered, Octavius lent his legions to the consuls A. Hirtius and C. Vibius Pansa for the purpose of relieving Dec. Brutus and defeating Antonius.[35] The Senate had no intention of honouring its promise to the young upstart, however.[36] Realizing he had been duped, after the battle Octavius turned around and marched on Rome,[37] where he secured his consulship – the first of many.[38]

Dec. Brutus was captured, and then executed as he tried to escape and join the other conspirators.[39] The reckoning with them would come soon after. Driving Octavius was an obsession to avenge his adoptive father's murder and seize the power imbued in his rich political legacy.[40] Reconciling with Antonius, the former adversaries joined with M. Aemilius Lepidus (I) to form a commission of 'Three Men to Reform the Commonwealth' (*Tresviri Rei Publicae Constituendae*) with legal powers lasting five years.[41] Under this arrangement, Octavius assumed responsibility for the two provinces in Africa, Sardinia and Sicily, Lepidus took the provinces in Hispania and Gallia Narbonensis, and to Antonius went Gallia Comata and Belgica, as well as the region south and north of the Alps.[42] In 42 BCE, Antonius and Caesar – now proudly using the inherited name instead of Octavius – set off to Macedonia to take down the ringleaders of the conspiracy.[43] On 3 and 23 October that year, their forces engaged the armies of Brutus and Cassius and defeated them.[44]

In these tempestuous times, around 43 or 42 BCE, the Claudian bachelor married 14-year-old Livia Drusilla (fig. 1).[45] Velleius Paterculus described her as 'the most eminent of Roman women in birth, in sincerity, and in beauty'.[46] Tacitus writes of her:

> In the purity of her home life, she was of the ancient type, but was more gracious than was thought fitting in ladies of former days. An imperious

> mother and an amiable wife, she was a match for the diplomacy of her husband and the dissimulation of her son.[47]

Figure 1. Portrait bust identified as Livia Drusilla. Smart and strong-willed, she was 17 years old when she gave birth to Tiberius.

Her father, M. Claudius Drusus Claudianus, may have been a personal friend of Ti. Nero; she may have been orphaned when her father died in the civil war, perhaps at Philippi fighting with Brutus and Cassius.[48] Newly married, Nero wasted no time in producing an heir.[49] His first child by Livia was born in November.[50] Nine days later, on the *dies lustricus* 'day of purification', he officially accepted the boy as his own by taking him in his arms (*tollere*), naming him after himself, as was Roman custom.[51] He remained active in the administration of the *Res Publica*. By the end of 42 BCE, Ti. Nero was due to serve out his praetorship. Yet, when the time came, he refused to stand down and insisted on retaining his bodyguard of *lictores* with their ceremonial bundles of axes and rods (*fasces*).[52]

The conspirators having been eliminated, and with it the reason for their political association, enmity grew between the *triumviri*. Ti. Nero left Rome for Perusia (Perugia) to join consul L. Antonius, the brother of M. Antonius, and his wife, Fulvia, who were occupying the city in an act of rebellion against Caesar's growing power.[53] L. Antonius' luck proved fleeting. In 40 BCE, the young Caesar and his friend M. Agrippa besieged the city.[54] They took no prisoners, but when Perusia fell, Ti. Nero, his young wife and baby managed to escape.[55] They fled south to Praeneste (Palestrina), but, finding no sanctuary there, moved on to Neapolis (Naples).[56] Paterculus blames Ti. Nero for starting a war in Campania, where he 'now came forward as the protector of those who had lost their lands.'[57] Caesar's arrival in the region quickly squashed the rebellion. Failing to acquire a party of slaves to assist them, even with the promise of manumission granting them their freedom, the hapless couple took to the sea. Eventually they reached Sicily, where Pompeius Magnus' youngest son, Sex. Pompeius (I), offered them refuge.[58] Maintaining the resistance established by his deceased father, Sextus was successfully using the tactics of a pirate to interrupt shipments of grain from the big island to Rome and to harass the cities on the Italian coast, all with the purpose of undermining support for Caesar's heir.[59] The face-to-face meeting Ti. Nero had hoped to have with Sextus in Sicily did not take place; indeed, the rebel leader denied him the right to continue receiving the protection of the *fasces*.

Insulted by the slight, Ti. Nero sailed to Achaea in Greece, where he threw in his lot with M. Antonius instead.[60] Suetonius offers a poignant description of the seemingly unending travails endured by little Tiberius Claudius Nero:

> He passed his infancy and his youth amid hardship and tribulation, since he was everywhere the companion of his parents in their flight; at Neapolis indeed he all but betrayed them twice by his crying, as they were secretly on their way to a ship just as the enemy burst into town, being suddenly torn from his nurse's breast and again from his mother's arms by those who tried to relieve the poor women of their burden because of the imminent danger. After being taken all over Sicilia also and Achaea, and consigned to the public care of the Lacedaemonians, because they were dependents of the *Claudii*, he almost lost his life as he was leaving there by night, when the woods suddenly caught fire all around them, and the flames so encircled the whole company that part of Livia's robe and her hair were scorched.[61]

This was a tough upbringing for a boy who had not yet reached the age of 3. Yet the youngster charmed the renegade's family: 'The gifts, which were given him in Sicilia by Pompeia (sister of Sex. Pompeius (I)) – a cloak and clasp, as well as amulets [*bullae*] of gold – are still kept and exhibited at Baiae.'[62]

The *triumviri* settled their differences with a new accord signed at Brundisium (Brindisi) in October 40 BCE.[63] The following spring, they agreed a non-aggression pact with Sex. Pompeius (I) at Misenum (Miseno); to show his support for it, Caesar divorced his wife, Claudia, and married Scribonia, who was the niece or sister of Sextus' wife.[64] One of the pact's stipulations was an amnesty for refugees; among the beneficiaries were Ti. Nero, his wife and son, who returned to Italy and, finally, to Rome.[65]

In mid-39 BCE, Livia was pregnant again. In the meantime, she had caught the eye of Caesar, now a 24-year-old statesman with considerable political and military clout. He insisted that Ti. Nero divorce his 19-year-old wife.[66] Not in a position to refuse, Nero consented. Caesar divorced Scribonia on the very day she gave birth to his only daughter, Iulia.[67] In his autobiography, he gave as his reason that he was 'unable to put up with her shrewish disposition'.[68] Remarkably, Ti. Nero himself presided over the wedding of his former wife to her new partner on 17 January 38 BCE.[69] Just days before, Livia had given birth to a second boy.[70] The timing of the delivery caused some to speculate that the boy had been fathered by Caesar, blessed by some miracle of speed, though it was never proved.[71] Ti. Nero accepted the boy as his own son and named him Dec. Claudius Drusus.[72] The two boys lived with their natural father, while their mother moved in with her new husband.

Ti. Nero *pater* died unexpectedly in 33 BCE. Tiberius *filius*, now 9 years old, gave the oration at the funeral from the *Rostra* in the *Forum Romanum*.[73] It was his first public appearance. What Tiberius' feelings were towards his father are unknown, but they would seem to have been respectful, if not affectionate. In later years, he and his brother celebrated the memory of Ti. Nero with games (*munera*) held in the *Forum*.[74] He clearly cherished his lineage as a descendant of the *Claudii Nerones*. He also commemorated his grandfather's life with games: they were notable for being held in the new theatre built by T. Statilius Taurus, the first structure of its kind built in stone, inaugurated in 29 BCE; among those fighting were retired gladiators (*rudiarii*) who had been induced 'to appear with the rest by the payment of HS 100,000 to each.'[75] He sponsored theatre-plays too, though he did not attend them in person; all were lavish productions paid for by his mother and stepfather.[76]

Ti. Nero's sons moved to be with their mother in Caesar's house on the *Mons* Palatinus (Palatine Hill). Their new home – the *Palatium*, which had previously belonged to M. Antonius – was of modest size, decorated plainly but comfortably furnished, reflecting the tastes of its new owner.[77] It was, however, a place filled with people. The boys now shared their upbringing with the extended First Family from various marriages. Caesar's daughter, Iulia, had her home here. Caesar's elder sister, Octavia, lived in the house with her five children, among them four daughters, including Antonia Minor, and her only son, M. Claudius Marcellus, who was some six months older than Tiberius.[78] Sometimes, sons of kings and potentates stayed, either as guests or hostages. Caesar and his wife encouraged the children to read literature and appreciate culture.[79] The girls were taught the traditional domestic skills of spinning and weaving.[80] The boys' education encompassed a much broader curriculum, with its emphasis on command of language and public speaking. Tiberius enjoyed his studies of Latin and Greek texts, most of them moral and poetic works, and developed fluency in this second language.[81] He took an impish delight in challenging his teachers' command of their subjects – and of their patience. Suetonius records:

> Yet his special aim was a knowledge of mythology, which he carried to a silly and laughable extreme; for he used to test even the *grammatici*, a class of men in whom, as I have said, he was especially interested, by questions something like this: 'Who was Hecuba's mother?' 'What was the name of Achilles among the maidens?' 'What were the Sirens in the habit of singing?'[82]

Beyond the front doors of the *Palatium*, the world remained a dangerous place. Since signing the pact in Brundisium, the triumvirs had fallen out. Antonius had departed for his designated territory in the East, based at Antiocheia (Antioch on the Orontes), while Caesar stayed in the West, based at Rome; Lepidus (I) had since been removed, assuming the sacred position of *pontifex maximus* as a consolation.[83] To bind them closer, Caesar offered his highly respected sister,

Octavia, to be Antonius' wife; he accepted.[84] From 41 BCE, Antonius aligned with Queen Kleopatra VII Thea Philopator of Egypt, who financed his wars against Parthia (36 BCE), and to whose family members he later illegally distributed Roman territories (32 BCE).[85] Meantime, Caesar, with M. Agrippa's help, had defeated Sex. Pompeius (I) (36 BCE) and then successfully put down revolts in Illyricum (36–35 BCE).[86] Antonius called for support to bolster his failing expedition. Octavia brought him troops and, after accepting them, he sent her away; Antonius was emotionally entangled with, and also now married to, Kleopatra.[87] Caesar and Antonius traded personal insults.[88] By decree of the Senate in 32 BCE, Caesar, using the form *Imperator* Caesar *Divi filius* ('Commander Caesar Son of God'), declared war on the Egyptian queen.[89] After a months-long war of attrition, M. Agrippa overwhelmed the fleet of Antonius and his royal patron at Actium by early morning of 3 September 31 BCE, while the army led by *Imp.* Caesar finally took Egypt and all its wealth with the fall of Alexandria on 1 August 30 BCE.[90] Fourteen years after the murder of Iulius Caesar, his adopted son who now bore his name was the undisputed military leader (*dux*) of the Roman world.

Safely back in Italy, the great wars in which *Imp.* Caesar had scored major victories were celebrated in a magnificent 'Triple Triumph' held over three days in 29 BCE in Rome.[91] Tiberius himself, now 12, took part in the military parade on 14 April marking the victory in the Actian War.[92] He rode the left trace-horse of the triumphal chariot (*currus triumphalis*) driven by Caesar, while M. Claudius Marcellus (b. 42 BCE), son of Octavia and the same age as Tiberius, rode the one on the right.[93] This carefully choreographed arrangement communicated to the Roman world that Marcellus was preeminent and that *Imp.* Caesar regarded him as superior to Tiberius.[94] Starring in one of the greatest spectacles of Roman history, with its carnival atmosphere as it wound through the city's streets, along the *Via Sacra* and up to the *Capitolium*, would have left a deep impression on the teenagers. There would never again be a triumph on anything like this scale.

On 13 January 27 BCE, with his powers of *triumvir* expiring, *Imp.* Caesar negotiated a political agreement with the Senate (fig. 2).[95] This shared the administration of Rome's sprawling dominions between them (map 1). The 'Provinces of the Senate and People', which were generally free of war and conflict, would be administered by civilian proconsuls chosen by lot each year, while the rest, dubbed 'Provinces of Caesar', would be administered for ten years by military propraetorian legates (*legati Augusti pro praetore*), each handpicked every three years by Caesar, who was granted special legal power to command (*imperium proconsulare*) for a period of ten years.[96] Significantly, he had control of twenty-two legions (out of a total of twenty-eight) and as many or more auxiliary units stationed in these territories, 'alleging that they were insecure and precarious and either had enemies on their borders or were able on their own account to begin a serious revolt'.[97] Recognizing the reasonable way in which

Figure 2. Imp. Caesar *Divi Filius* opened the rebuilt the Senate House in 29 BCE, an achievement he proudly noted in his Res Gestae (19).

he had negotiated the terms and conditions of the settlement, the Senate hailed Caesar as 'Augustus' (plate 2), 'signifying that he was more than human – for all the most precious and sacred objects are termed *augusta*'.[98] From this time on, he would be known as *Imperator* Caesar *Divi filius* Augustus.

On 24 April 27 BCE, Tiberius went through the all-important rite of passage marking a freeborn Roman boy's graduation to manhood (plate 3).[99] In a traditional ceremony – attended by his stepfather, mother, close family and friends – he removed the *bulla* and chain from his neck and donned the pure white *toga virilis* ('manly gown') over his white tunic.[100] He was then escorted to the *Tabularium*, the records office which overlooked the *Forum Romanum*, where his name was officially entered into the rolls of Roman citizens. He was now a full citizen (*civis Romanus*), with all its rights, privileges, protections and obligations before the law.

Tiberius was once again at the centre of attention when, later that same year, as leader of the squadron of older patrician boys (*ductor turmae puerorum maiorum*), he took part in the Game of Troy (*Ludus Troiae*).[101] His cousin, Marcellus, may have led the other squadron of younger boys. Held every four years, these 'Trojan Games' were a display of mock combat routines performed by freeborn Roman boys of different ages.[102] It was a precision equestrian tournament calling for expert horsemanship, close co-ordination between the participants and tight discipline to correctly perform the required exercises, all while under the critical gaze of their family and the public in the *Circus Maximus*. They were *Imp.* Caesar's favourite spectacle, 'thinking that it was a practice both excellent in itself, and sanctioned by ancient usage, that the spirit of the young nobles should be displayed in such exercises'.[103] They instilled in a young man the warrior's

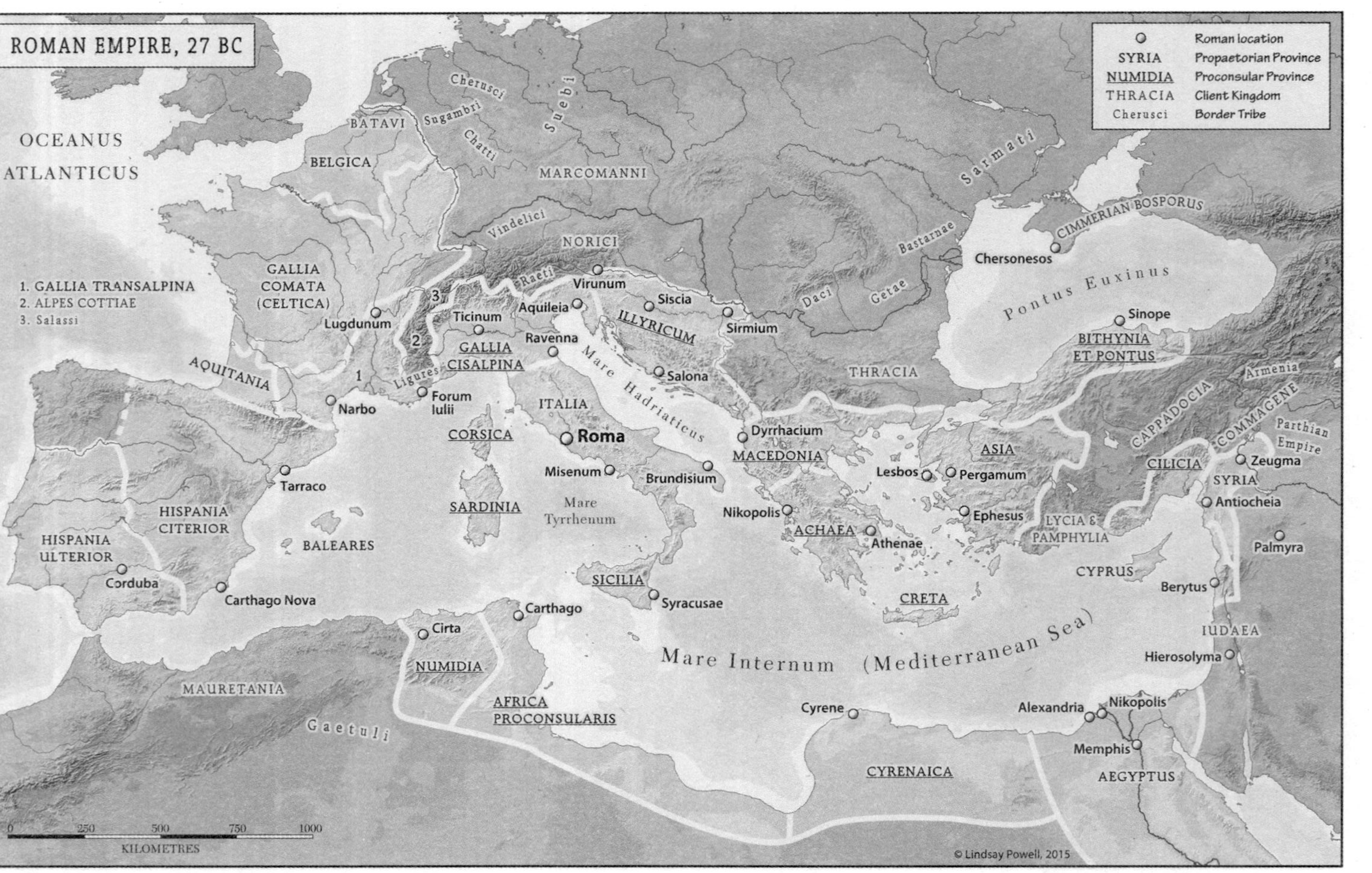


Map 1. The Roman Empire, 27 BCE.

ethos of courage, honour, competition and brotherhood, and the importance of persistence. The *Ludus* entailed some risk of bodily harm: Nonius Asprenas was made lame when he fell from his horse during a performance.[104]

Tiberius was a good student who thrived on learning.[105] He was passionate about the liberal arts (*artes liberales*), about which he could read and debate in both Latin and Greek.[106] He and Marcellus both studied under Greek teacher Nestor, perhaps also Athenaeus, who was an expert in history and law, and Theodoros of Gadara, a Sophist whose servile birth is noted by the source although it was not unusual for high-status Roman families to employ them.[107] Expertise in public speaking was a vital skill for a man, whether used for addressing a jury in a courtroom, the Conscript Fathers in the Senate House or his fellow soldiers before battle.[108] In his rhetoric, Tiberius followed M. Valerius Messalla Corvinus (I), an accomplished military commander, author and patron of poets.[109] He had a house close by the *Palatium*, which also once belonged to M. Antonius.[110] Corvinus had followed Cicero and was known for his affected, artificial style, yet it was one that later came to be regarded as superior to the famous stateman's.[111] Oratory was a learned skill and, in the process of acquiring it, a speaker would form his own *elocutio* or 'style'.[112] Tiberius' eloquence is noted by Philo.[113] A speaker was expected to teach, entertain and move his listener. A Roman orator *performed* a speech with a practiced manner of delivery and a repertoire of formal hand gestures.[114] For all the training, speaking publicly still felt awkward for Tiberius; he was uncomfortable being an actor who recited a script. Suetonius remarks that Tiberius 'so obscured his style by excessive mannerisms and pedantry, that he was thought to speak much better extempore than in a prepared address'.[115] He was 'a master of the art of weighing words – powerful, moreover, in the expression of his views, or, if ambiguous', observes Tacitus, 'ambiguous by design'.[116] Indeed, Augustus would pillory Tiberius, 'who sometimes hunted up obsolete and pedantic expressions'.[117] However, Dio reports that, even in informal conversation, Tiberius appeared to some to dissemble. In turn, people's confused reactions seemed to anger him:

> He never let what he desired appear in his conversation, and what he said he wanted he usually did not desire at all. On the contrary, his words indicated the exact opposite of his real purpose; he denied all interest in what he longed for and urged the claims of whatever he hated. He would exhibit anger over matters that were very far from arousing his wrath and make a show of affability where he was most vexed.[118]

Yet Tacitus also observes that in his speech, Tiberius 'usually combined jesting and seriousness'.[119]

In the spring of 27 BCE, Augustus (fig. 3) left Rome. In his absence, his trusted friend Agrippa would manage affairs in the city.[120] The time was right. Iulius

Caesar had been avenged. The civil wars were over, and law and order had been restored. Augustus' own legal position was secure for the next decade. He could turn his attention to pacifying the regions now in his care. High among his priorities was addressing the unfinished business in the West. Iulius Caesar had campaigned in Gallia Comata and Belgica (58–50 BCE), but 'the affairs of the Gauls were still unsettled', writes Dio, 'as the civil wars had begun immediately after their subjugation'.[121] Augustus' *imperium proconsulare* gave him control over a huge swath of Roman territory. To justify having that power, he needed to show the Senate that he was making progress in pacifying his *provincia*. Hoping for a quick victory, he also planned to subjugate the Astures and Cantabri once and for all.[122] They stood in the way of complete conquest of the Iberian Peninsula, which had begun with the outbreak of the Second Punic War nearly two centuries before.

Figure 3. Shown in a portrait bust wearing the *corona civica* awarded in 27 BCE, Augustus projected an image of himself as youthful, sensible and patriotic.

The trip would certainly not be a holiday, but it would be a family affair. Accompanying Augustus were Livia, Marcellus and Tiberius, and possibly Nero Drusus (who had dropped the *praenomen* Decimus and replaced it with Nero) too. For the older boys, this would be an opportunity to take their first career step with a plum assignment in the army on active campaign. 'It is the Roman nature to act bravely,' C. Mucius was reported to have told the Senate of the then newly founded *Res Publica*, 'and to suffer bravely.'[123] An aspiring Roman citizen eager to play his part in society competed in the 'race for honour' (*cursus honorum*). A formal career ladder, it combined military as well as civilian postings of increasing responsibility and geographic scope. Positions were elected or chosen by lot. Laws and customs stipulated the sequence and age requirements for each posting. The entry-level posting in the army for an eligible man of the senatorial class in his late teens, like Tiberius, was that of a senior military tribune with 'the broad stripe' (*tribunus laticlavius*), named after the width of the decorative purple stripes on his tunic. Each legion of nominally 6,000 men had one such tribune in charge of five junior tribunes of 'the narrow stripe' (*tribuni angusticlavius*) recruited from the *Order Equester*.[124] Many a junior tribune had previous experience, usually as a *praefectus* commanding an auxiliary infantry cohort; despite being the senior officer, Tiberius arrived with no prior military training.[125] As *tribunus laticlavius*, he reported to the legate of the legion (*legatus legionis*), the commander personally appointed by Augustus from the senatorial class. The lower-ranked *tribunus angusticlavius* mostly undertook staff work in the legate's headquarters (*principia*) but on campaign, he could also lead two cohorts of 480 men each.[126] There were ten cohorts per legion; a cohort comprised six centuries (*centuriae*) of eighty men, each led by a *centurio*, all well-equipped and highly trained professionals.[127] Being a *tribunus laticlavius* was a very responsible and high-profile position in which Tiberius would need to learn to work with men from different social classes and age groups in executing assigned orders. As Iulius Caesar had done, Augustus personally chose the military tribunes each year and decided their postings.[128] Tiberius and Marcellus were each assigned to a legion preparing to campaign against the Cantabri, starting in 26 BCE.[129]

Three years before, T. Statilius Taurus had scored major victories over the Cantabri and the neighbouring Astures in the north and north-west of the Iberian Peninsula.[130] Yet these nations refused to accept defeat and continued to resist full annexation.[131] Together, they represented a real threat to peoples already subjugated by Romans, with their constant harassments.[132] Brigandage (*latrocinium*) was also an abiding problem.[133] Here was an opportunity for Augustus to solve it. Taking a direct and personal interest in the matter, Augustus decided to lead the military campaign himself (map 2).[134] He assembled a massive taskforce (*expeditio*), comprising eight legions and as many auxiliary units, representing some 52,000 troops.[135] Assisting him in the campaign were two experienced *legati*.[136] C. Antistius Vetus, suffect consul in 30 BCE, was the former proconsul of Gallia Narbonnensis who brought experience of mountain warfare.[137] P. Carisius had served in the war against Sex. Pompeius (I) in Sicily on Caesar's side and was now eager for a senior command role.[138] As a legionary tribune, Tiberius would have been a member of the legate's leadership team, able to listen first-hand to battle-hardened prefects and centurions discussing campaign strategy and battle tactics. There were no military academies in Ancient Rome. Learning on the job from experienced practitioners, and taking active part in combat operations, was how a novice officer such as Tiberius became familiar with, and skilled in, the arts of war.

Over many decades, the lightly armed cavalry and infantry warriors of the two native Iberian peoples had proved able to resist Roman attempts to subjugate them. From their strongholds dotted among the hills and valleys of the Cantabrian Mountains, they forced their enemy, which had trained to fight set-piece battles on open plains, to engage them in a guerrilla-style war.[139] In a three-pronged attack, Augustus led one of the army groups from his base at Segisama in the south through the mountainous country, with Vetus and Carisius leading the other two.[140] The first recorded battle of the campaign against the Cantabri was fought under the walls of Attica or Vellica (Helechia).[141] Initial victory was swift. The Cantabri withdrew to *Mons* Vindius (or Vinnius, possibly Peña Santa).[142]

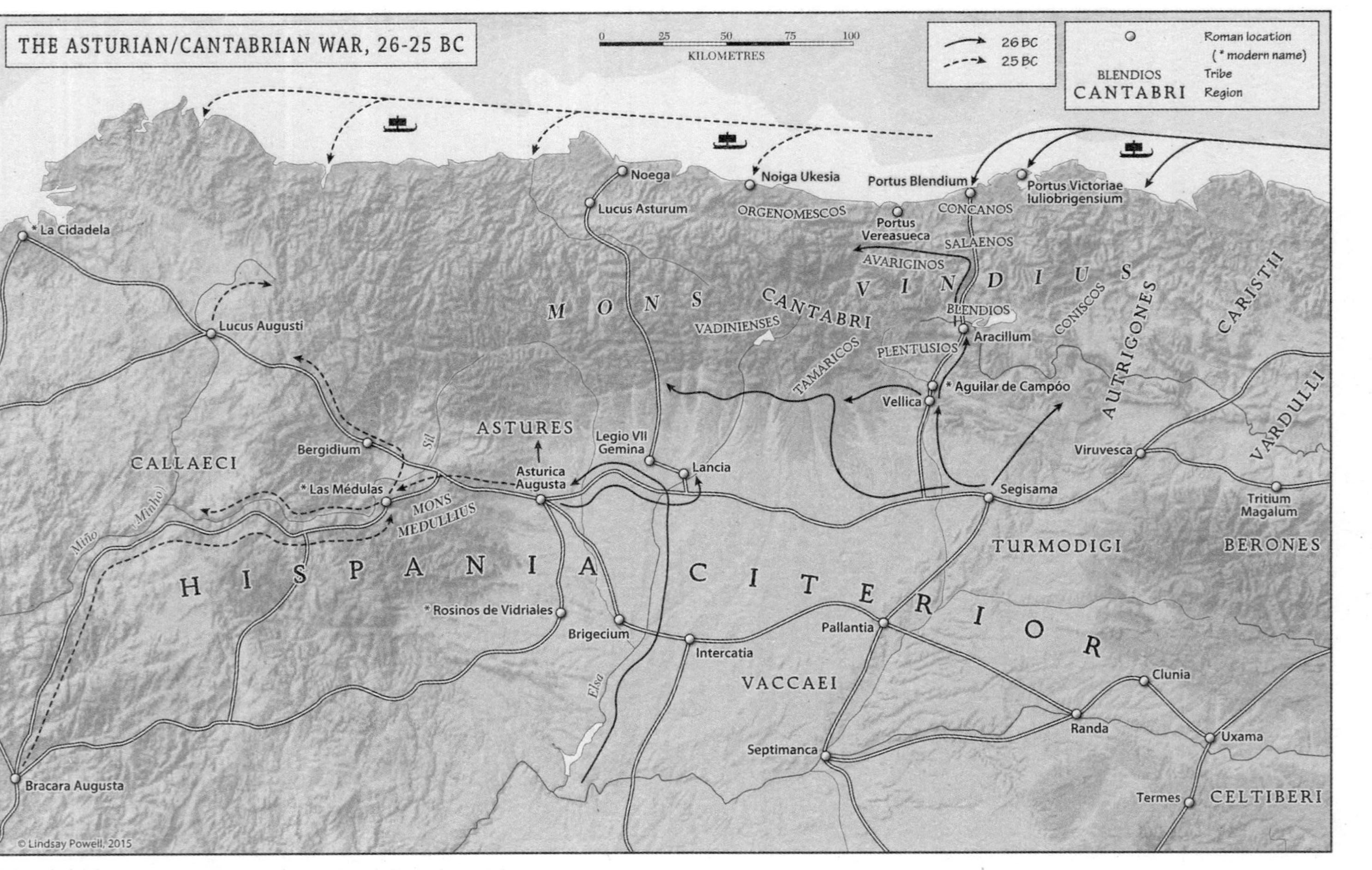


Map 2. Military Operations in Asturia and Cantabria, 25–23 BCE

Vindius fell when the people trapped inside began to starve and surrendered.[143] Other local strongholds (*oppida*) were also assaulted. Excavations at Monte Bernorio (plate 14) and the adjacent Roman Army camp at El Castillejo have produced finds of trilobate projectiles, the point of a javelin (*pilum*), hobnails from soldiers' boots and work tools of this period that strongly suggest a siege.[144] With Roman forces now advancing upon the rebels on several sides, they gradually 'enclosed its fierce people like wild beasts in a net'.[145] At the end of the first season, the Roman combat units suspended hostilities and withdrew to their winter camps.

Marcellus returned to Rome by the year's end. There, he married Augustus' daughter, Iulia, with Agrippa overseeing the ceremony since her father was still preoccupied with the war.[146] It is likely that Tiberius remained with Augustus. In the spring of 25 BCE, the campaign against the Cantabri started anew, but there was a major setback when Augustus fell ill. Dio suggests overexertion and anxiety, while Suetonius says, 'he was in such a desperate plight from abscesses of the liver', though it is quite possible his sickness was typhoid.[147] He withdrew from the war zone and retired to Tarraco (modern Tarragona) on the Mediterranean coast, where he remained in the care of his wife, Livia, and personal physician, Antonius Musa.[148] Augustus sent his signet ring, with which he authorized correspondence, to Agrippa, and his personal briefing papers about the army deployments and state finances to his co-consul, Cn. Calpurnius Piso (I).[149] Augustus would never again lead a military campaign in person: from this time on, he would rely completely on his *legati* to fight his wars for him.

The last recorded battle in the *Bellum Cantabricum et Asturicum* is the siege of *Mons* Medullus (possibly Peña Sagra) above the Minius (Miño) River.[150] The Roman Army surrounded it with a continuous earthwork and began a direct assault.[151] Whether Tiberius was there is not recorded in the extant sources. Supplies were no longer able to get into the stronghold, and all routes of escape from it were blocked. Trapped inside, the defenders were eventually forced to surrender. Carisius declared victory and erected the traditional *tropaeum* on the site.[152] The war was over.

However, Augustus was still sick. Musa attended him and tried various treatments, some increasingly risky.[153] The usual hot treatments he administered gave his patient no relief, and with concern growing about his welfare, Augustus was advised to try cold ones. These worked.[154] In 24 BCE, Augustus had sufficiently recovered to be able to leave Tarraco and return to Rome.[155] When he reached the city, the Romans expressed their joy for his recovery and safe return, granting him various privileges. Having acquitted themselves well on the warfront, there were honours for the two teenage boys as well:

> Marcellus was given the right to be a senator among the ex-praetors and to stand for the consulship ten years earlier than was customary, while Tiberius

> was permitted to stand for each office five years before the regular age; and he was at once elected *quaestor* and Marcellus' *aedile*.[156]

Doctor Musa was also handsomely rewarded.[157]

In Rome, Tiberius took up the post of *quaestor* in 23 BCE, as his father had done before him, giving him the opportunity to demonstrate the skills of persuasion and jurisprudence he had learned under his tutors.[158] Steeped in debating culture and resplendent in a purple-bordered *toga*, he prosecuted his first case, a defence of King Archelaus of Cappadocia.[159] Cases followed involving the people of Tralles and of Thessaly, 'the charge in each being different'.[160] In each trial, Augustus was the presiding magistrate. Tiberius also made a plea before the Senate on behalf of the citizens of Laodicea, Thyatira and Chios, who had suffered losses from an earthquake and had begged for assistance.

More consequential was a prosecution for treason. Tiberius arraigned Fannius Caepio, who had allegedly conspired with A. Terrentius Varro Murena to kill Augustus.[161] The *quaestio maiestatis* exclusively heard cases for the crime of *maiestas minuta populi Romani*, 'the diminution of the majesty of the Roman People'.[162] The bar to secure a guilty verdict in a treason trial was high. Tiberius failed to secure the jury's unanimous guilty verdict, though there were enough votes for Caepio's and Murena's condemnation and execution.[163] The philosopher Athenaeus of Seleucia in Cilicia – who had been in Rome at the time and was found while fleeing with Murena – was pardoned by Augustus on the basis that there was insufficient evidence for a conviction.[164] Augustus' close friend and advisor, C. Cilnius Maceanas, the husband of Murena's sister, had made representations on his behalf, but to no avail. Indeed, the damage to their friendship was so great it never recovered.[165] Augustus made a law that, in trials at which the defendant was not present, the jury's vote should not be taken in secret and that the defendant should be only convicted by a unanimous vote.[166] The experience of working on the case of *maiestas* would inform Tiberius' decisions on these matters in later life.

Augustus' relations with the Senate had become strained. To ameliorate the situation, he resigned the consulship mid-year, yet he secured his right to rule by other means. In 23 BCE, he took the powers, but not the office, of the tribune (*tribunicia potestas*), the ancient right of the plebeian tribune to veto decisions of the Senate and the legal inviolability it granted its holder.[167] Counting the number of times he held the power was how he measured the years of his rule from this point on. Moreover, after trading some of his provinces with the Senate, he retained his territory, while his *imperium proconsulare* to operate there, was enhanced to become *maius*, which meant his power of command was made greater than all other proconsuls.[168] These developments were pivotal. Augustus' assumption of the *tribunicia potestas* combined with the *imperium maius* established beyond dispute the legal basis of his rule. Agrippa's *imperium* was similarly extended for five years.[169] By making these incremental manoeuvres, Augustus gradually made his political position virtually unassailable. Augustus 'subjected it [the *Res Publica*] to power under the title of *princeps*', but he did not hold a *principatus* (an office of 'head of state').[170]

Augustus was a complex man and is an enigma today. What is known about his appearance and personality mostly comes from Suetonius, who writes:

> He had clear, bright eyes, in which he liked to have it thought that there was a kind of divine power, and it greatly pleased him, whenever he looked keenly at anyone, if he let his face fall as if before the radiance of the sun; but in his old age he could not see very well with his left eye. His teeth were wide apart, small, and ill-kept; his hair was slightly curly and inclining to golden; his eyebrows met. His ears were of moderate size, and his nose projected a little at the top and then bent slightly inward. His complexion was between dark and fair. He was short of stature (although Iulius Marathus, his freedman and keeper of his records, says that he was 5 feet 9 inches in height), but this was concealed by the fine proportion and symmetry of his figure, and was noticeable only by comparison with some taller person standing beside him.[171]

He had a weakness in his left hip, thigh and leg, and even limped slightly at times.[172] Indeed, he was often sick.[173] Nevertheless, he was unadventurous in his tastes for life at home and ate simple foods in moderate quantity.[173] Augustus had a versatile intellect, employing his talents to great effect as a political strategist and leader of war.[174] He was a workaholic, attentively dealing with state business and travelling extensively for that purpose.[175] While he could be generous, he was fiscally conservative.[176] When he spoke in public, he read from prepared notes in order not to forget points he wished to cover.[177] Yet he had a quick temper and could seethe with rage if upset.[178] He was a traditionalist in matters of religion, re-establishing several rites which had fallen out of favour, and believed in the value of dreams, omens, divinations and horoscopes to predict the future.[179] He was unsettled by thunder and lightning and carried a seal skin as protection.[180] He found making friends difficult, valuing moderation and loyalty, detesting excess and treachery.[181] Such was Tiberius' stepfather.

Still a *quaestor*, Tiberius undertook two additional public charges. One related to the corn supply (*annona*).[182] Despite having dealt with the interruptions caused by Sex. Pompeius (I), supply was deficient. The appetite of the citizens eligible for the daily corn dole was insatiable. Ensuring security of supply was crucial to Augustus maintaining the popular support for his precarious regime. Ships sailed from Sicily and Egypt on long circuitous routes to Ostia only while the shipping lanes were open from April to September. As *quaestor Ostiensis*, he had to ensure adequate inventory of corn was warehoused in the port at the mouth of the Tiber to serve demand the whole year round.[183] He accomplished his task well and successfully dealt with the scarcity of supply, ensuring that there were no problems for Augustus.[184] In his relationship with his stepfather, Tiberius had sufficient self-confidence to raise an objection, as revealed in an episode recorded by Suetonius:

> When Tiberius complained to him of the same thing in a letter, but in more forcible language, he [Augustus] replied as follows:
>
> 'My dear Tiberius, do not be carried away by the ardour of youth in this matter, or take it too much to heart that anyone speak evil of me; we must be content if we can stop anyone from *doing* evil to us.'[185]

Tiberius' second charge was to investigate the large slave-prisons (*ergastula*), which operated throughout Italy.[186] The owners of these dreadful institutions had gained a bad reputation. There were allegations that, in addition to slaves, lawful travellers – the victims of banditry and kidnapping – as well as men trying to avoid military service were chained up in them at night after being forced to labour hard during the day.[187] His mission was to ensure that these prisons operated within the law.

That year, Marcellus fell gravely ill. Antonius Musa tried his hot and cold treatments again, but this time to no avail.[188] In the height of summer 23 BCE, the young man died. He was just 19 years old. The *Palatium*, usually alive with chatter and gossip, was plunged into mourning.[189] The funeral was held in public. Augustus gave the oration before the body was cremated and placed the ashes in the recently finished family mausoleum.[190] To memorialize him, Augustus named the new entertainment complex – the ground of which he had already broken – the Theatre of Marcellus (*Theatrum Marcelli*).[191] He further ordered that a golden image of his nephew and son-in-law, as well as a golden crown and a curule chair, should be carried aloft into the theatre at the Roman Games (*Ludi Romani*) and then placed in the middle of the presiding officials.[192]

Family matters would preoccupy Augustus for years to come. Even when facing his own mortality in Tarraco, however, he did not designate a successor.[193] Perhaps he was confident of recovery or realized it looked too much like the act of a dynast or, worse, a king. Now in his 40s, and recognizing the variability of his health, Augustus was increasingly concerned about his legacy. Fast-tracked through the *cursus honorum*, Marcellus had been widely seen as the man most likely to succeed him. His premature death suddenly created uncertainty. Producing children – potential heirs – was what mattered now.[194] Augustus' 18-year-old widowed daughter Iulia, was available. Close in age to Marcellus, Tiberius was a potential candidate to be his new son-in-law, but Augustus did not pick him. He turned instead to his lifelong friend, M. Agrippa, who was now 42 or 43 and immensely popular in his own right. After two years had passed, in

21 BCE, Agrippa divorced Marcella and married Iulia.[195]

The circumstances leading up to the decision caused great public speculation. While Augustus had been campaigning in the Cantabrian Mountains, Agrippa had left Rome early in 23 BCE (fig. 4), ostensibly for Syria. Some thought Marcellus was upset by Augustus' decision to hand his signet ring to his friend and not to him, then his son-in-law.[196] The rumour reported by later Roman authors was that, learning of Marcellus' distress, Augustus had requested Agrippa to go to the East as a way for the older man with his great reputation to step aside and let the younger develop his credentials and profile in Rome.[197] Agrippa did not reach Syria, however; at the start of summer, he remained on Lesbos. Rather than Antiocheia on the Orontes, from where Roman commanders normally operated when on assignment in the Orient, he chose Mytilene.[198] This only added to the speculation that there had been a squabble between the two best friends.

Figure 4. In every respect, M. Agrippa was Augustus' right-hand man, a loyal and reliable deputy in political and military matters, and a close and trusted friend who gave no-nonsense counsel.

Yet there was a very good reason for Agrippa to be in the East: Rome's nemesis, Parthia. Relations between the Ancient World's two superpowers remained tense. Antonius' expeditions beyond the Euphrates River from 40–33 BCE had failed spectacularly. Egyptian treasure may have paid for them, but Roman lives and honour had been lost. Ten years later, the Parthians still retained Roman prisoners of war and the eagle standards (*aquilae*) and unit ensigns (*signa*) of their legions. In his final year of life, Iulius Caesar had been planning for a war of vengeance. Augustus was planning something very different: détente. He would not, however, meet the Parthian King of Kings in person. In his place, he would use his experienced deputy to negotiate the terms of a peace accord. Already in place, Agrippa was headquartered at his island residence beside its deep harbour with its excellent access by sea to the legates and military staff in Syria as his agents. This may have been the real reason Augustus' most trusted friend and deputy was in the region.[199]

An almost equal partner in power, and now imbued with *imperium proconsulare*, Agrippa had a full-time role in the management of Augustus' *provincia*.[200]

Augustus must have realized that he needed to train a close member of his family to take on more responsibilities of the day-to-day operations. His best and only candidate now was Tiberius. In 22 BCE, Augustus left Rome and headed south to Sicily.[201] Tiberius accompanied him on this new tour. On the island, Augustus founded a new *colonia* for retired soldiers at Syracusae (modern Siracusa).[202] Keeping army veterans happy with the retirement benefits he had promised them was a necessary part of the defence policy which he had begun soon after Actium. He demobbed vast numbers of citizen soldiers who had served with him or Antonius in the Actian and Alexandrian Wars, reducing the total number of legions by half.[203] He had given the sensitive task of resettling them in Italy to Agrippa.[204] It was one of the many thankless duties Agrippa did for him, which Tiberius would be expected to undertake.

In 22 BCE, the Roman People offered Augustus the post of *dictator* which came with twenty-four lictors, but he declined. The cause for the emergency powers was an acute shortage of grain for the free dole. Augustus is reported to have knelt before the People, imploring them to desist when they were pressing him to accept this terrible power, even stripping off his *toga praetexta* in a dramatic protest.[205] Normally, Augustus could rely on the quaestors to manage the grain distribution in Rome, Tiberius having been one the previous year. Instead, Augustus now created a commission in charge of the grain supply chain, with two magistrates appointed annually from among the ex-praetors and assumed one of the positions for himself.[206] He declined, however, to stand as consul for 21 BCE. M. Lollius, fresh from his assignment in Macedonia, was duly sworn in as one of the two senior magistrates. Riots broke out in Rome when the public was disappointed to learn that Augustus was not to be the other consul and that the position was still up for election.[207] Two men – Q. Aemilius Lepidus, a son of *triumvir* M. Aemilius Lepidus (I), and L. Iunius Silvanus – bitterly contested the vacancy. Lollius appealed to Augustus to return to settle the matter, but he refused and summoned the rival candidates to meet him in Sicily.[208] Chastened by a stern lecture from him, the senators returned to Rome, but when they arrived, riots more violent than the first broke out. Only when Lepidus was finally elected did peace return to the city's streets. Also lending his authority was Agrippa, who arrived back in Rome by the autumn, which is when he married Iulia.

Continuing the tour, the away team sailed from Sicily to Achaea in Greece. In the convoy of adjutants (*adiutores*), Praetorian Cohorts (*Cohortes Praetoriae*), freedmen (ex-slaves, *liberti*) and slaves (*servi*) was a young Roman from Cremona. P. Quinctilius Varus was due to take up his appointment as *quaestor* in the province.[209] In the years after Iulius Caesar's assassination, the Greeks had been poorly treated by Romans, who saw them as a bank to rob to fund their military campaigns. Rather than a warm welcome, the reception Augustus received in

Athens was hostile.[210] Smarting from the episode, he decided to spend the winter layover of 21/20 BCE offshore, dividing his time between the islands of Aigina and Samos.[211]

In the spring of 20 BCE, Augustus continued eastwards, travelling through Bithynia and Asia Minor.[212] Augustus reassigned lands among certain potentates, creating new dependent territories in the process.[213] Arriving in Syria, he received emissaries from Armenia. The delegation asked for his urgent assistance to replace the incumbent king, Artaxes, with his brother, Tigranes.[214] Knowing Tigranes, who had been a refugee in Rome for almost a decade, Augustus agreed to the request. He decided that he would not himself go to Armenia. Assigned the special, and potentially risky, mission of leading an army to help in the ousting of the King of Armenia was Tiberius.[215] Assured that Roman troops were coming to their aid, the Armenians themselves assassinated their unpopular king.[216] Riding at the head of his expeditionary force, Tiberius reached the capital city of Artaxata, where he personally crowned Tigranes (fig. 5).[217]

The act of installing a pro-Roman king in Armenia decisively tipped the scales of power in the region. Phraates IV, the 'King of Kings' (fig. 6), had lost his leverage. Tiberius was informed that the king – apparently 'awed by the reputation of so great a name' – was finally prepared to accept the terms of the settlement that had been proposed three years earlier.[218] Tiberius was Augustus' personal representative responsible for concluding the diplomatic process. It required a deft but firm touch from the 22-year-old. The formal ceremony took place on the banks of the Euphrates River (plate 15), which marked the natural boundary between the Roman and Parthian empires.[219] The handover of the legionary eagle standards (fig. 7) and the Roman war captives, and the official

Figure 5. Bringing Armenia into the Roman sphere of influence helped Rome establish a durable peace in the region with rival Parthia.

Figure 6. In 20 BCE, Phraates IV of Parthia, 'king of kings', negotiated the release of his son, kidnapped by the usurper Tiridates II, who had since fled to Rome. Tiberius played a prominent role in the final settlement.

signing of the accord, proceeded without a hitch. To show their commitment to the pact, 'Phraates entrusted to Augustus Caesar his children and also his children's children, thus obsequiously making sure of Caesar's friendship by giving hostages.'[220] It was a historic moment. When the news reached the *princeps*, Tiberius' stepfather was delighted:

> Augustus received them as if he had conquered the Parthian in a war; for he took great pride in the achievement, declaring that he had recovered without a struggle what had formerly been lost in battle.[221]

Figure 7. Augustus considered the return of the *aquilae* and *signa* lost at Carrhae in 53 BCE and M. Antonius' failed expeditions of 40 and 36 BCE against Parthia one of his singular achievements, which he recorded in his *Res Gestae* (29).

This affirmed for Augustus that diplomacy *was* a viable alternative to war. It was an important insight too for Tiberius, one that would inform his judgement in the future.

The mission in the East having been accomplished, it was time to return to Italy. Arriving on Samos, Augustus decided to spend the winter there. While resting on the island in the Aegean, he received several potentates and even a guest from India.[222] By chance, when the entourage finally reached Athens, it met P. Vergilius Maro (Vergil). Despite having plans of his own, the poet was persuaded to accompany Augustus' party to Italy. At Megara he fell sick. As the ship carrying the passengers arrived at Brundisium, on 21 September 19 BCE, Vergil died.[222] He had expressly requested that his incomplete poem about Rome's foundation should be destroyed. Augustus could not consent to it, however, and the *Aeneid* was saved for posterity.

Augustus, who had been absent for nearly three years, arrived almost undetected in Rome on the night of 12 October 19 BCE – despite the plans of the city's magistrates to lay on an official welcome.[224] He was never one for undue fuss. With him were the *aquilae* and *signa* recovered from the Parthian king.[225] The following day, he granted Tiberius the rank of ex-*praetor* (*propraetor*), which permitted him to be considered for governorship of a province. He also allowed his brother Nero Drusus to stand for various political offices fully five years earlier than was the custom.[226] While Augustus was away, the Senate had granted him several honours, which he mostly refused upon his return. However, he did accept the *summum imperium auspiciumque*, enlarging his powers over all officials governing provinces of the empire. He also accepted the position of supervisor of morals (*Curator Legum et Morum*) for five years, and assumed the authority of *censor* for the same period as well as the powers of consul for life. In consequence, this gave Augustus the right to be attended by twelve lictors with *fasces* at all times and everywhere he went, and the privilege of sitting on the curule chair between the two men who were the serving consuls at the time.[227]

On 15 December 19 BCE, the Altar of *Fortuna* Redux was dedicated in gratitude for his safe return from his long journey abroad.[228] The anniversary of his safe arrival in Rome was henceforth numbered among the public holidays and called the *Augustalia*.[229] The altar dedicated to the goddess who oversaw safe returns from dangerous journeys was erected beside the *Porta* Capena.[230] Dio reports that Augustus 'rode into the city on horseback and was honoured with a triumphal arch'.[231] Tiberius likely was in the procession riding behind him. Coins struck at the time express the *princeps*' great pride in the accomplishment – one achieved entirely without bloodshed.[232] The sacred battle standards were carried up to the *Capitolium* and placed in the temporary Temple of Mars Avenger (*Templum Marti Ultori*) for safekeeping.[233]

That year, or the following one, Tiberius married Vipsania Agrippina.[234] In a society in which arranged marriages were the norm, they had been betrothed since 33 BCE, when he was 9 and she only a year old.[235] Vipsania was daughter of M. Agrippa by his marriage to Pomponia Caecilia Attica. She was, thus, granddaughter of T. Pomponius Atticus, the great friend and confidant of Cicero, to whom he wrote many letters.[236] The arrangement spliced together the disparate branches of the hybrid family tree of Augustus, forming stronger dynastic ties between him and his loyal associates. The arrangement was good for Tiberius too. He was truly in love with his new wife, finding stability and fulfilment in this relationship.[237]

The previous ten years would prove to be among the happiest of Tiberius' life. The next decade would be very different.

# Chapter 2

# Counting Loves and Losses: 18–9 BCE

Back in Rome, Tiberius (plate 4) settled into civilian life. He turned his talents to poetry, composing verses in Greek in imitation of Euphorion of Chalcis, Rhianos of Crete and Parthenios of Nikaeia – three poets of whom, we are told, he was particularly fond.[1] Their sophisticated works, which exist today only as fragments, were variously epic and epigrammatic, dealing with mythological, romantic and erotic themes.[2] None of Tiberius' own poetry survives by which to judge the quality of his work, with the possible exception of one. The translation into Latin of Aratos of Soli's Greek *Phaenomena* – a reworking of the prose treatise by Eudoxos of Knidos, which taught the reader to identify constellations and to forecast the weather – may have been the work of Tiberius.[3] Its style is poetic verse, though it often departs far from the original text. The list of constellations of the zodiac described in just five unadorned lines in the Greek is reinterpreted and amplified in the Latin version as thirty-three lines, which include the myths explaining how the stars came to be configured.[4]

Meanwhile, Augustus reasserted his place in the political system. The overwhelmingly positive feeling towards the *princeps* continued with the renewal of both his and Agrippa's *imperium* for an additional five years. Among Augustus' first acts of 18 BCE, he purged the Senate of men who did not meet the wealth qualifications or for their lack of support of his agenda.[5] Exercising his powers to enforce traditional moral standards, Augustus introduced the *Lex Iulia de adulteriis coercendis* on adultery and criminal fornication (*stuprum*),[6] which would have an impact neither Augustus nor Tiberius could have anticipated.

The following year would mark the end of the first decade (*decennium*) since Augustus had accepted his unique, but honorific, position as the preeminent citizen in Roman society. He contrived to align his own anniversary with that of Rome in new *Ludi Saeculares* ('Century Games').[7] Normally held every 110 years, he envisioned a festival celebrating both the city's and its citizens' achievements. Whether Tiberius had a role in organizing the celebration is not known, though with his experience and skills he could surely have contributed to the project. Preparations began in May, with heralds announcing the Games. On 1 June 17 BCE, the great and good of the Roman elite assembled and for three days witnessed a once-in-a-lifetime production of songs, sacrifices and spectacles.

Augustus had commissioned his favourite poet Q. Horatius Flaccus (Horace) to write a poem for the occasion, the *Carmen Saeculares* ('Century Poem'), which formed the climax of the celebrations. A choir of twenty-seven boys and twenty-seven girls sang in unison its penultimate verse:

> Lov'st thou thine own Palatial Hill,
> Prolong the glorious life of Rome
> To other cycles, brightening still
> Through time to come![8]

These were words to inspire a nation.

Securing his legacy into this glorious future was becoming a matter of concern for Augustus. Having no male heir of his own, his strategy was to expand his immediate family. On a day between 14 June and 15 July, he formally adopted Caius and Lucius, the sons of Agrippa and his daughter Iulia.[9] They took the names C. Iulius Caesar and L. Iulius Caesar. It was an extraordinary act by one friend to another. Caius was nearly 3 years old, while his brother was barely 1. Augustus' intention was likely that one of these boys would succeed him at the appropriate time. It was plain for all to see that this decision not only pushed their natural father, Agrippa, further back in the line of succession, but also effectively eliminated Tiberius as a candidate. His brother, Nero Drusus, however, had the affection of Augustus, who 'always named him joint heir along with his sons, as he once declared in the Senate'.[10]

The celebratory mood of the city was interrupted late in the summer of 17 BCE when reports reached Rome that there had been a military disaster in Belgica. The governor of the province – the most northerly of the Gallic territories – was M. Lollius. Germanic tribes living on the right bank of the Rhine (Rhenus) had crossed the river and raided deep into Roman territory. 'The Cherusci, Suebi, and Sugambri,' explains the historian L. Annaeus Florus (*c.* 74–130 CE),

> had begun hostilities after crucifying twenty of our centurions, an act which served as an oath binding them together, and with such confidence of victory that they made an agreement in anticipation of dividing up the spoils.[11]

The geographer Strabo (64/63 BCE–*c.* 24 CE) writes in his contemporary account of the episode that 'it was the Sugambri, who live near the Rhenus, that began the war'.[12] Their leader was Melo (or Maelo).[13] The Sugambri made a pact with their neighbours, the Tencteri and Usipetes.[14] During their incursion, an *ala* of Roman cavalry was ambushed.[15] Fleeing, it crashed headlong into *Legio* V *Alaudae* ('The Larks'), which was on the march under Lollius' command, and it too was then attacked. In the struggle, its *aquila* standard was seized by the invaders.[16] The loss of a legionary eagle was considered shameful (*infamia*) by the Romans. Assigning blame to the Roman commander, the event soon acquired the moniker *Clades*

*Lolliana* ('Lollian Disaster').[17] It was humiliating to Augustus that one of his own handpicked legates had lost the *aquila*, especially when he and Tiberius had recovered the eagles from the Parthians just three years before.[18] Augustus had to act. When news reached the Germanic war band leaders that Augustus was preparing to travel to the Gallic provinces, they retreated across the Rhine. Suing for peace, they even handed over hostages (*obses*) as proof of their good faith.[19]

Before setting off to take command of the situation in person, Augustus first dedicated his restored Temple of Quirinus (the god who had significance to *gens Iulia*), which stood prominently on the Quirinalis (Quirinal Hill) in Rome.[20] While he made his travel arrangements, the Senate approved his request to permit Tiberius and his brother to sit in for him as sponsors (*editores*) of gladiatorial games held to mark the special occasion.[21] That year, Drusus married Antonia Minor (Antonia the Younger), M. Antonius' daughter by marriage to Octavia, the sister of Augustus.[22] She was regarded as a young woman of great moral virtue and charm, like her mother.[23] Tiberius would form an enduring friendship with his sister-in-law. On 24 May 16 BCE, Nero Drusus and Antonia Minor had a son, who was named after his father.[24]

In 16 BCE, Tiberius accompanied Augustus on the long trip by road.[25] When they arrived at Narbo Martius (Narbonne) in Gallia Narbonnensis, they found that order had been restored.[26] While Augustus was holding assizes at Narbo, he conducted an official census.[27] He learned of the abuses of Licinius, the procurator responsible for collecting taxes, which the Gauls deemed as much a threat to their wellbeing as any invasion by the Germans from the other bank of the Rhine.[28] Despite their earnest complaints, the wily Licinius was allowed to remain in post. Augustus was still infuriated by his deputy's ineptitude, however, and relieved Lollius of his duties. In his place he appointed Tiberius to govern. Lollius did not take his dismissal well.

Only a generation separated Iulius Caesar's departure as conqueror and Tiberius' arrival as governor. In his *Commentarii de Bello Gallico* ('Commentaries of the Gallic War'), Caesar had observed that 'all Gallia is divided into three parts.'[29] As *legatus Augusti propraetore*, Tiberius was responsible for administering Aquitania, Belgica and Gallia Comata ('Long Haired Gaul').[30] The three territories of this province of Caesar were slowly undergoing transformation – economic, political, social and military – into Roman dominions. The process of assimilating the sixty native tribal communities (*nationes*) through urbanization, observance of Roman law and religious practice, taxation of its income and wealth – what modern historians call 'Romanization' – had begun tentatively after Caesar's campaigns of 58–50 BCE.[31] It had since been delayed by civil wars among the Romans. The native Gallic peoples, who had suffered such large numbers of deaths at the hands of Caesar's troops during the conquest that it has been called a genocide in modern times, had been left to largely remain in, or live close to, their traditional *oppida*. Augustus recognized the economic potential of the region. While governor in 39–37 or 19 BCE, Agrippa had constructed a road network connecting the principal tribal settlements with *Colonia* Copia Felix Munatia (Lugdunum, modern Lyon), the city founded in 43 BCE by L. Munatius Plancus, one of Iulius Caesar's legates.[32] Agrippa established his residence at the palatial *praetorium* on the highest point of the acropolis of Fourvière, formed by the confluence of the rivers Rhône (Rhodanus) and Saône (Arar).[33] It was likely here, in his father-in-law's former villa, that Tiberius established his office and a home for his wife, Vipsania, and their slaves.

This was a major career step for the 25-year-old Tiberius. Under the terms Augustus agreed with the Senate in 27 BCE, his deputies were treated differently to the men who administered provinces of the People.[34] Unlike the *toga*-wearing civilian proconsuls and quaestors who were chosen annually by lot, Augustus' hand-picked legates were propraetorian – military appointments – serving three-year assignments and reported directly to him. Tiberius was now imbued with the *princeps*' personal legal power (*imperium*) to make decisions semi-autonomously and to carry them out in his name within the law – to even execute soldiers.[35] On duty, he was required to wear the panoply and sword (*parazonium*) of a commander, and he was accompanied by five (not six) lictors with *fasces*. His mission was to keep his province 'pacified and quiet'.[36] He had explicit legal duties to perform in his provinces.[37] He directly commanded the 'Army of *Tres Galliae*', comprising several legions as well as units of auxiliary cavalry and infantry at winter camps (*in hiberna*) scattered across the territory.[38] He was to promote and protect the interests of resident Roman citizens in his provinces, and was to encourage the local Gallic aristocracies to build self-sustaining urban communities in the Roman model.[39] He had to ensure that the local population enjoying Roman protection paid their taxes or tribute.[40] Located at *Colonia* Munatia from 15 BCE was the mint striking the silver *denarii*, guarded by a single unit of the *Cohortes Urbanae*.[41] Like his civilian counterparts, he assumed the decorations of his position of authority when he entered his appointed province and would lay them aside immediately upon completing his term of office.[42]

The plundering of towns and farms in Gallia Belgica was a reminder that, with an unprotected border along the Rhine, all of Gaul – and Italy too – was constantly exposed to Germanic incursions.[43] A raid could be a precursor to an invasion. It was a nightmare scenario, recalling the invasions of the Cimbri and Teutones who had destroyed Roman legions at Arausio in 105 BCE (near Orange in south-east France), in what was Rome's greatest military disaster; C. Marius had finally halted their southward march at the Battle of Vercellae four years later.[44] How Augustus and Tiberius conducted the biggest review of northern frontier policy since Caesar had fought there can now only be surmised by interpreting the ensuing operations on the ground. Around 16 BCE, Augustus

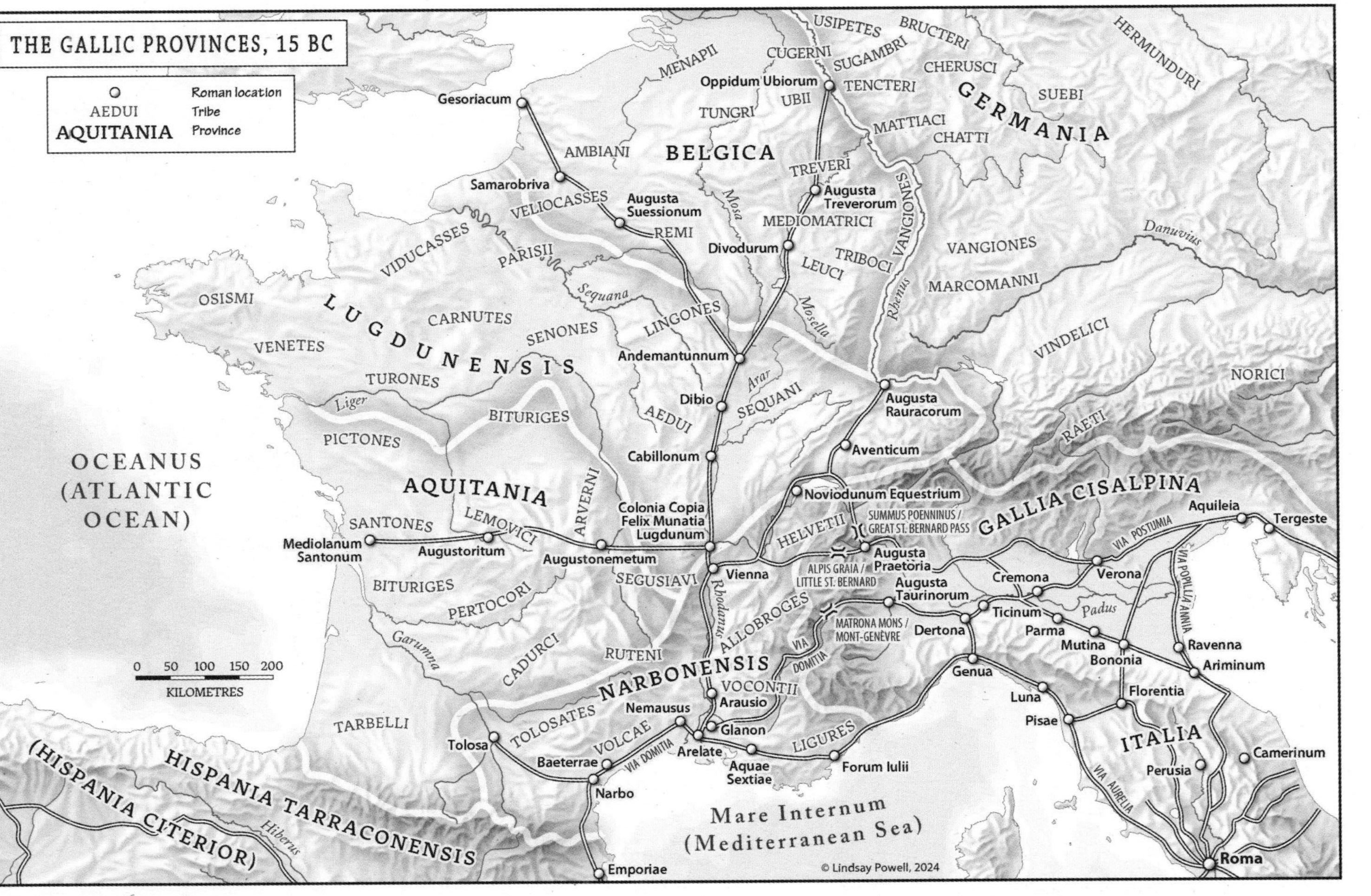

Map 3. *Tres Galliae*, 15 BCE.

reorganized the internal boundaries of Aquitania, Belgica and Gallia Comata into Gallia Aquitania, Gallia Belgica and Gallia Lugdunensis respectively, known collectively as the *Tres Provinciae Galliae* (map 3).[45] There was just a single military installation on the left bank of the Rhine.[46] Upriver was *Oppidum* Ubiorum, the urban community (*civitas*) of the Ubii – people resettled from the right bank by Agrippa – who were obligated to defend the area if invaded.[47] Directly south by south-west of it, Agrippa had also established *Augusta* Treverorum, the new *civitas* of the Treveri, on the Moselle River.[48] The border of the three Gallic provinces could be relatively easily secured by redeploying the army units to new positions, which would be a matter for Tiberius to execute as the *legatus Augusti*.

The security of Italy, however, also depended on capturing the remaining region north of the Po River and parts of the central Alps called Gallia Cisalpina ('This Side Gaul'). In these areas, native Iron Age peoples were not yet under direct Roman control. They considered Roman travellers traipsing through their lands as an interference and legitimate targets for attack.[49] A confederation of tribes known as the Raeti lived on the southern slopes of the Alps.[50] On its northern slopes, in the Voralpenland, lived the Vindelici, and to the east of them the Norici, who were Roman allies.[51] To execute this part of the campaign plan, Augustus turned to his two stepsons. It was a bold decision by the *princeps*. Just 23 years old (plate 10), this would be Nero Drusus' first duty as a military commander in any capacity or rank.[52] Paterculus describes him as:

> [A] young man endowed with as many great qualities as men's nature is capable of receiving or application developing. It would be hard to say whether his talents were the better adapted to a military career or the duties of life; at any rate, the charm and the sweetness of his character are said to have been inimitable, and also his modest attitude of equality towards his friends. As for his personal beauty, it was second only to that of his brother.[53]

In 15 BCE, the Claudian brothers embarked on a joint military campaign to subjugate Gallia Cisalpina, Raetia and Vindelicia (map 4).[54] The Roman accounts imply a prearranged, co-ordinated strategy between the two commanders. Velleius Paterculus describes them attacking the Raeti and Vindelici 'from different directions'.[55] Dio states that 'both leaders then invaded Raetia at many points simultaneously, either in person or through their deputies'.[56] This maximum effort mission would test the abilities of the two men as they worked together to achieve a common military objective. The *Bellum Alpinum* (Alpine War) began when Drusus' army group from Gallia Cisalpina – perhaps one or more of the available legions, VIIII *Hispana*, XIII *Gemina*, XIIII *Gemina*, XVI *Gallica* or XXI *Rapax* and auxiliaries – swept down upon the Veneti. The surviving milestones of the *Via Claudia Augusta* (the route of which connected Altinum, near present-day Venice, to the River Danube) specifically acknowledge the debt to Nero Drusus,

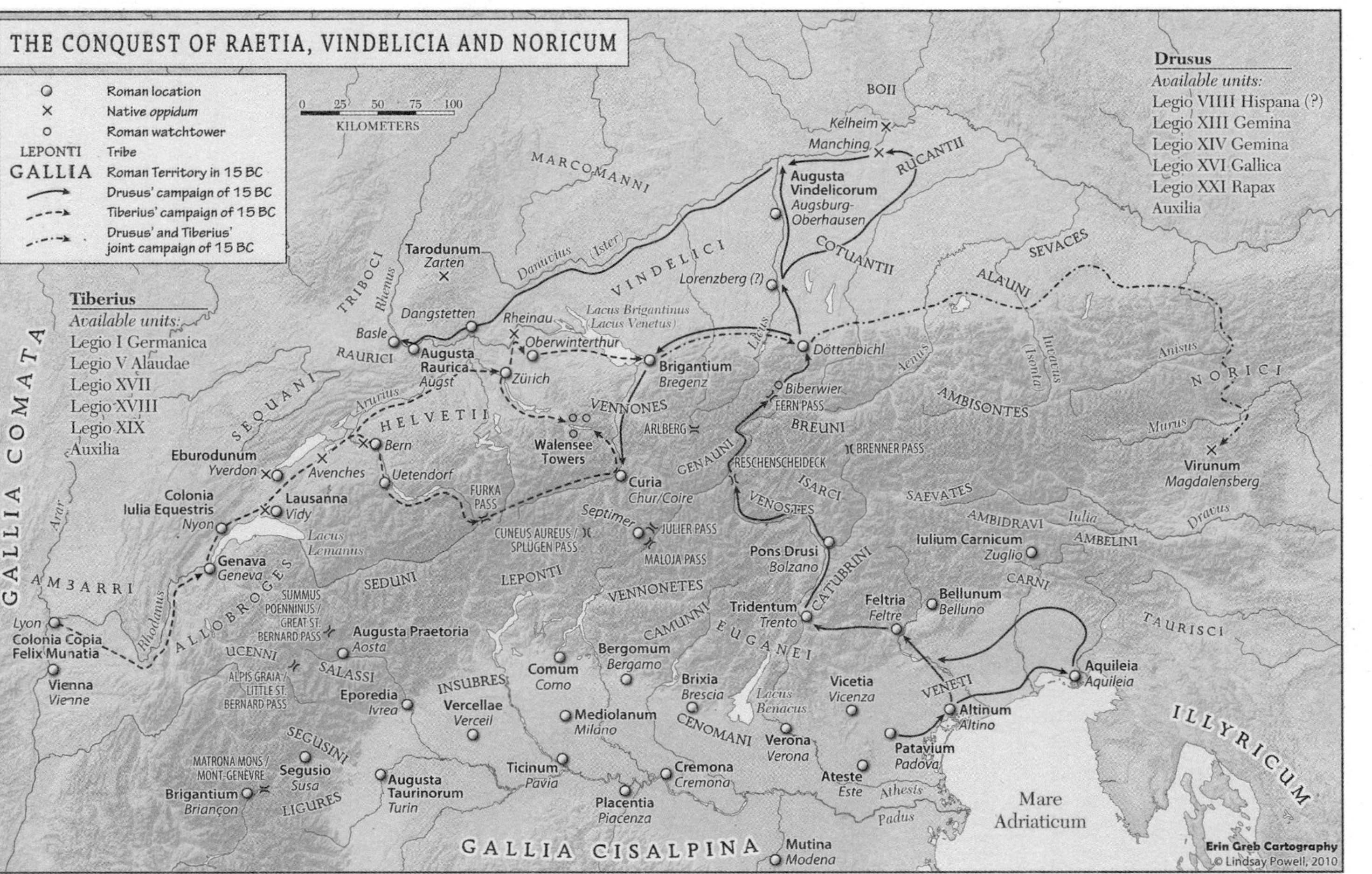


Map 4. The Conquest of Raetia, Vindelicia and Noricum, 15 BCE.

who 'had made [the way] passable after the opening up of the Alps by war'.[57] With his rear sector secured, he turned north-west to Tridentum (modern Trento). Establishing a crossing at *Pons Drusi* ('Drusus' Bridge', present-day Bolzano), he moved north through the Tridentine Mountains, likely over the Reschenpass, picking off individual tribes of the Raetian confederation as he encountered them. As each one fell, Nero Drusus moved ever northwards, eventually reaching the slopes of the Voralpenland. For his swift victories, Augustus made him *praetor*.[58]

Meanwhile, Tiberius mobilized his army group to attack the Raeti from the west. It would have comprised some or all of the units under his command in the *Tres Galliae*. From *Colonia* Munatia, he likely followed the course of the River Rhône (Rhodanus) or the Jura Mountains. In so doing, he would have marched through the *Alpes Poeninae*. The route between the Jura and Rhône was particularly hazardous in places. Caesar writes in his *Commentaries* of mountain passages narrowing to such an extent that wagons could move only in single file or a few men at a time.[59] Part of Tiberius' army group may have gone via the Furka Pass Oberwinterthur, and part via the Julier Pass (where *Legiones* III, X and XII are attested) to reach Curia; at the same time, Nero Drusus' army now marched from its position in the Voralpenland along the River Lech to the source of the Rhine, or followed the Danube River (Danuvius, Ister) to its source.[60] Advancing through the valleys of the Alps, the Claudian brothers executed a pincer movement. They fought in pitched battles that resulted in light Roman casualties but imposed heavy losses on their opponents.[61] Displaying boldness in his tactical thinking, when Tiberius reached a major lake, rather than go around it, he went *over* it. He ordered his men to board boats, with which they launched an audacious amphibious operation to deliver troops to the other side.[62] A unit of Tiberius' men established a camp temporarily in the Vindelician territory of the Brigantes near their native *oppidum* of Brigantia (Bregenz) at the eastern end of Lake Constance (Bodensee, plate 16).[63] Meanwhile, Nero Drusus' men stormed 'many towns and strongholds' with ruthless efficiency; defeated men who were old enough to fight were removed from their homeland or joined the Roman Army as auxiliary troops.[64]

Having defeated the Raeti, Nero Drusus – probably without Tiberius' assistance – continued eastwards into the territory of the Norici. This new phase, called the *Bellum Noricum* ('Norican War'), aimed to annex land which had rich reserves of iron (*ferrum Noricum*). Nero Drusus laid siege to the principal city of Virunum, a strongly fortified *oppidum* atop the Magdalensberg.[65] With its fall, resistance ceased. To prevent trouble in future, many of their able-bodied men were deported from the region to serve the Romans under their tribal leaders in cavalry and infantry auxiliary units, leaving just enough to work the land.[66]

Augustus was delighted by the victorious outcome of the war. In a single summer campaign, his stepsons had collaborated to vanquish several belligerent nations and brought an end to their destabilizing incursions.[67] Roman armies now controlled the passes of the Alps, connecting the Mediterranean world under Rome's influence through the Voralpenland of southern Germany by road to the banks of the Danube. Later, in his *Res Gestae*, Augustus would boast: 'The Alps, from the region which lies nearest to the Adriatic as far as the Tuscan Sea, I pacified.'[68] In Tiberius and Nero Drusus, Augustus had two young, all-Roman heroes whom he could hold up as champions of the new age.[69] Gold and silver coins were struck at the mint in *Colonia* Munatia, showing the figure of Augustus in a *toga*, seated on curule chair set upon a raised tribunal, with his right arm outstretched, reaching down to receive branches from two armed figures wearing cloaks (plate 21), interpreted to be Tiberius and Nero Drusus. Below *in exergue* is the legend *IMP X*, recording Augustus' tenth acclamation as *imperator* by the men of the legions. On the obverse, a fine portrait of an ever-youthful Augustus is surrounded by the legend *AVGVSTVS DIVI F.*[70] Perhaps at Augustus' own urging, in 13 BCE, Horace crafted the fourth in his series of poems.[71] He sang of how the brothers seemed invincible in the face of even the most savage of barbarian foes:

> What will not Claudian hands achieve?
> Jove's favour is their guiding star,
> And watchful potencies unweave
> For them the tangled paths of war.[72]

In September or October 15 BCE, buoyed by their victory, Tiberius and Nero Drusus returned to *Colonia* Munatia. There to welcome them was their mother, Livia, and stepfather, Augustus. The *princeps* had important news: Nero Drusus would be taking over from his brother as *legatus Augusti propraetore* of the *Tres Galliae*.[73] Tiberius would be returning to Rome.

How Tiberius spent his time in 14 CE is not recorded. His brother, meanwhile, embarked on a massive building of military infrastructure. In addition to his duties as *legatus Augusti propraetore* for *Tres Galliae*, he was to put an end to Germanic incursions once and for all by leading a campaign to annex the land across the Rhine. Seven legions were redeployed from *Tres Galliae* or drawn down from Hispania Tarraconensis to five new legionary camps established along the river at key points to control access to it and its tributaries at Batavodurum (Nijmegen-Hunerberg), Vetera (Xanten), Novaesium (Neuss), *Oppidum* Ubiorum (Cologne) and Mogontiacum (Mainz).[74] A military road connected the bases with the provincial command centre at *Colonia* Munatia. Forts for auxiliary units and supply dumps were constructed along this road at Andernach, Argentorate (Strasbourg), Asciburgium (Asberg), Bingen, Bonna, *apud* Confluentes (Koblenz), Speyer and Urmitz. A fort dating to this period, garrisoned by Treveri, has been identified at Trier.[75] A canal, the *Fossa Drusiana*, was dug to connect the Rhine with *Lacus*

Flevo (the Ijsselmeer) for a fleet (*Classis Germanica*) being constructed from scratch.[76] Nearly a quarter of Augustus' legions were now stationed along this riparian border.[77]

Late in 14 BCE, the Senate voted to elect Tiberius as consul for the following year, with P. Quinctilius Varus as his colleague.[78] Aged 28, Tiberius was significantly younger than the normal age for the consulship, but this was the direct result of Augustus' award to him recognizing his service. This position, the highest political office – one of two – in the *Res Publica*, entitled him to a bodyguard of twelve *lictores*, each carrying *fasces*. On 1 January 13 BCE, he sat upon a curule chair (*sella curulis*) in the *Curia Iulia* beside Varus in front of the assembly of Conscript Fathers. In the Senate House, as co-consul, Tiberius would oversee discussions and votes on matters of singular importance to Augustus. For Tiberius, the year would be a masterclass in government.

With Augustus' return from his tour of the western provinces in 13 BCE, the Senate approved the motion of renewing the *imperium* of both the *princeps* and Agrippa for another five years.[79] Tiberius put the vote first to L. Cornelius Balbus (a non-Roman by birth) to honour him for building the theatre, which had been funded by proceeds from the war in Africa.[80] The Conscript Fathers agreed to Augustus' proposal to reform the pay and conditions of the army: the years of service of the *Cohortes Praetoriae* were reduced from sixteen to twelve, while for the legions and auxiliaries the term was set at sixteen.[81] Men retired honourably from the legions would now receive a cash lump sum rather than a tract of land – a fairer way to prepare men on their return to civilian life. Commemorating the pact between Augustus and Rome, on 4 July that year the Senate approved funds for an altar, the *Ara Pacis Augustae*, to be constructed on the *Via Flaminia* beside his mausoleum on the *Campus Martius*.[82] The same year, the qualification for men to enter the Senate was raised to HS 1,000,000, a measure which effectively purged the assembly of its impoverished families.[83] After personally vetting candidates, Augustus assisted several of the most talented so that they could continue to serve as Conscript Fathers. Tiberius was also given a lesson in the need to strictly follow protocol. Augustus publicly rebuked him, because at a festival given under Tiberius' management, in fulfilment of a vow for the *princeps'* return, he had seated Caius Caesar beside Augustus; the people were similarly chastised for honouring Caius with applause and eulogies.[84]

On 7 October 13 BCE (though 15 and 14 BCE are possible alternatives), Tiberius and Vipsania had their first child together. He was named after Tiberius' younger brother.[85] Nero, a Sabine word meaning 'strong' or 'valiant', was a popular choice for sons of *gens Claudia*.[86] Tiberius and Vipsania are recorded as having had only two children together.

While most of the empire was tranquil, the Balkans were again mired in conflict and bloodshed. On the eastern side, L. Calpurnius Piso (I) was trying to suppress the Bessi in Thrace, where King Raiskuporis I had fallen in battle fighting the rebel Vologases. In the west, M. Vincius had been struggling to contain an uprising of the Breuci nation, which was now into its second year. No stranger to the region, Agrippa left Rome in late 13 BCE to deal with the situation. News of his imminent arrival was apparently enough by itself to quell the Pannonii.[87] On the return trip to Italy in early 12 BCE, Agrippa became sick. He retired to his summer house in Campania to rest and recuperate. His adjutants grew concerned at his deteriorating condition. They wrote to Augustus, who was away at the Panhellenic Festival, urging him to come soon.[88] Startled by the news, he raced to be with Agrippa, but he arrived too late. In his fifty-second year, Agrippa was already dead.[89] Bereft, Augustus arranged a state funeral for his best friend. After the required rituals, Agrippa's body was ceremoniously carried to Rome. There, in the *Forum Romanum*, it was laid in state.[90] The order of the funeral procession would be the model for Augustus' own.[91] In his funeral oration, Augustus recalled his friend's selfless service to Rome. As his sons in law, Tiberius (plate 9) and Varus each delivered a eulogy.[92] In a final snub to a man they had always perceived as undeserving of his high position in society, many senators did not attend the funeral.[93] Augustus placed his friend's ashes in his own mausoleum, which now contained the remains of two men he had marked out to be potential successors.[94] From here, directly visible from the tomb across the open expanse of the *Campus Martius*, Agrippa's elegant Pantheon stood as his monument.[95]

Agrippa's loss was a terrible personal blow to Augustus. Since his teens, Augustus had relied on his best friend for honest advice before making important decisions.[96] He would not – could not – now change the habit of a lifetime. Urgently needing a new right-hand man, he found a potential candidate in his oldest stepson. Fully twenty years younger than Agrippa, Tiberius had great potential. Circumstances had demanded that he grow up quickly, and he had risen to each of the challenges Augustus had put before him. Velleius Paterculus, who knew Tiberius personally, was effusive in his assessment of the man and his achievements:

> Nurtured by the teaching of eminent tutors, a youth equipped in the highest degree with the advantages of birth, personal beauty, commanding presence, an excellent education combined with native talents, Tiberius gave early promise of becoming the great man he now is.[97]

Tiberius' Jewish contemporary, Philo, recognized his intelligence and acuteness, writing that even while he was still a young man, many called Tiberius 'The Old Man' as a mark of respect because of his great wisdom.[98] His ethic for working hard (*industria*) and his self-restraint (*moderatio*) were traits of character that particularly appealed to Augustus,[99] who also greatly appreciated his stepson's devotion to him.

Tiberius was now a mature man at the start of his third decade of life. Drawing on the official records and images then available to him, Suetonius describes Tiberius' physical appearance:

> He was large and strong of frame, and of a stature above the average; broad of shoulders and chest; well-proportioned and symmetrical from head to foot. His left hand was the more nimble and stronger, and its joints were so powerful that he could bore through a fresh, sound apple with his finger, and break the head of a boy, or even a young man, with a fillip. He was of fair complexion and wore his hair rather long at the back, so much so as even to cover the nape of his neck; which was apparently a family trait. His face was handsome but would break out suddenly with many pimples. His eyes were unusually large and, strange to say, had the power of seeing even at night and in the dark, but only for a short time when first opened after sleep; presently they grew dim-sighted again.[100]

Portraits of Tiberius on busts (fig. 8) and coins do, indeed, emphasize the large eyes and particular styling of the hair (plate 6a, 6b and 7, also worn by other members of the extended family). These inanimate relics of the past do not, however, convey the peculiar mannerisms of the living Tiberius. Suetonius preserves these observations:

> He strode along with his neck stiff and bent forward, usually with a stern countenance and for the most part in silence, never or very rarely conversing with his companions, and then speaking with great deliberation and with a kind of supple movement of his fingers. All of these mannerisms of his, which were disagreeable and signs of arrogance, were remarked by Augustus, who often tried to excuse them to the Senate and People by declaring that they were natural failings, and not intentional.[101]

Figure 8. Portrait bust of Ti. Claudius Nero as a young man. It was originally part of a statue.

Tiberius was fastidious about his diet and physical fitness, and as a result, his strong constitution served him well. 'He enjoyed excellent health, which was all but perfect during nearly the whole of his reign,' remarks Suetonius, 'although from the thirtieth year of his age he took care of it according to his own ideas, without the aid or advice of physicians.'[102] His self-discipline about eating prevented him from becoming corpulent, even into old age.[103] Drinking was quite another matter. Suetonius reports: 'Even at the outset of his military career his excessive love of wine gave him the name of "Biberius", instead of Tiberius, "Caldius" for Claudius, and "Mero" for Nero.'[104] The punning nickname created by his fellow soldiers played on the Latin words for 'drink-loving' or 'thirsty' (*bibulus*) and 'hot wine' (*calidus mero*). Augustus could cope with these foibles, provided the man proved a loyal and wise counsellor.

Augustus' first order for Tiberius sent him on a mission to Illyricum to jointly command operations with M. Vinicius. What Romans considered pacification in practice meant its subjects submitting unconditionally to *their* way. The Breuci's refusal to kowtow meant Tiberius and Vinicius having to break their resistance by force. Such counterinsurgency campaigns, however, brought less glory for its principal protagonists than wars of conquest. However, they were essential to establishing the *Pax Augusta*, 'peace achieved through victories', as Augustus himself defined it.[105] His recent experience of fighting in the Alps would prepare him well for combat in the Balkans. 'The Old Man' would spend many seasons in this region, becoming deeply familiar with its tribes, turmoils and terrains – and with them learn the true cost of achieving the Roman peace.[106]

The conflict continued into 11 BCE, during which Tiberius campaigned against the alliances of the Daesitiates and Breuci, both formidable opponents practiced in guerilla warfare on the fertile plains and vales astride the Sava River (in what is now Bosnia). Taking advantage of his absence, the Delmatae and then the Pannonii rebelled against Roman rule. 'He made war upon both of them at once, shifting now to one front and now to the other,' writes Dio.[107] Slow but steady gains were made in this, the fourth year of the counterinsurgency. The native warriors preferred ambuscading and raiding to confronting the Romans in set-piece battles, asymmetrical encounters advantaging the former over the latter. One consequence of this kind of war was that the Senate added Illyricum to the province of Augustus, 'because of the feeling that it would always require armed forces both on its own account and because of the neighbouring Pannonii'.[108]

Agrippa's death had left Iulia a widow. Augustus decided that his daughter needed a new husband: it was to be Tiberius. The marriage was a clear statement of his growing appreciation of his stepson's importance in his family. However, there was a problem as Tiberius was already married to Vipsania Agrippina. Back in Rome, Tiberius resisted; Augustus insisted. Vipsania was even expecting their second child.[109] Swapping Agrippa's daughter for Agrippa's widow was a political marriage – love did not come into it. The divorce proceeded regardless. Tiberius took it very hard:

> This caused him no little distress of mind, for he was living happily with Agrippina, and disapproved of Iulia's character, having perceived that she had a passion for him even during the lifetime of her former husband, as was in fact the general opinion.[110]

Hardly a year after Agrippa's death, Iulia and Tiberius were hurriedly married.[111] He deeply resented the new arrangement:

> But even after the divorce he regretted his separation from Agrippina, and the only time that he chanced to see her, he followed her with such an intent and tearful gaze that care was taken that she should never again come before his eyes.[112]

Now Augustus' son-in law, Tiberius tried to make the marriage work. For a while the couple seemed to be genuinely in love.[113] They even tried for a child together in the first weeks. What joy Augustus may have felt at the time was turned to grief with the death of his sister, Octavia.[114] After her body was laid in state at the shrine of Iulius Caesar, Nero Drusus gave a funeral oration from the *Rostra*.[115] Her ashes were taken to the Mausoleum of Augustus.

The following year, 10 BCE, Tiberius returned to Illyricum, Nero Drusus to Germania. While the older brother faced the grinding chore of battling the familiar Balkan nations, the younger one was garnering glory conquering the ferocious German tribes. Starting his campaign to annex the lands across the Rhine River in 12 BCE, he had made good progress, reaching along the North Sea coast down the Ems and up the Lippe rivers.[116] The great Elbe River seemed within reach.[117] Meanwhile, in the *Tres Galliae*, work on the ritual complex proceeded at Condate. Named in honour of Roma and Augustus (plate 22), it was intended to be a meeting place for the leaders of the Gallic nations. In the summer of that year, the construction work was complete. Nero Drusus could withdraw from the German front for a while to supervise the dedication ceremony. Already in *Colonia* Munatia was Augustus, who was residing there awaiting news from him of the war in Germania.[118] He was later joined by Tiberius.[119] By happy coincidence, on 1 August 10 BCE, Antonia gave birth to a son; he was named Ti. Claudius Nero, the name of his paternal grandfather and of his uncle.[120] On the surface at least, the reunion was a time for a family celebration too.

Suetonius reports an allegation that Tiberius secretly harboured feelings of hatred (*odium*) towards his brother. As evidence, he records an occasion – time and place undisclosed – when Tiberius produced 'a letter of his, in which Drusus discussed with him the question of compelling Augustus to restore liberty'.[121] Nero Drusus' desire to see a return to the old style of government and a move away from the principate pioneered by Augustus was apparently well known, and he made no secret of it.[122] The story of the letter is the only example in the extant literature alleging Tiberius' fraternal hatred. Nevertheless, his brother's star was rising fast, almost eclipsing his own achievements. Furthermore, Nero Drusus' successful, love-filled marriage to Antonia contrasted starkly with Tiberius' own to Iulia. His had failed. His feelings towards Iulia had steadily grown cold. The rift reached its sad conclusion when their only child died in infancy at Aquileia, where Iulia stayed while her husband was in action in Illyricum.[123] Tiberius chose to sleep, and ultimately to live, completely separately from her.

The Senate voted to close the doors of the Temple of Ianus Geminus as recognition that Roman forces were no longer fighting. They had to remain open, however, when the Daci crossed the Danube and invaded the territory of the Pannonii, raiding it for booty, and the Delmatae refused to pay the Romans tribute, taking up arms against them.[124] Almost as soon as the inauguration ceremony in Condate had concluded, Tiberius swiftly returned to Illyricum to retake command of combat operations.[125] Army life provided him with both a family in which he felt at home and a refuge from domestic demands. Sleeping under a goatskin *papilio* suited him better than under the tiled roof of the *Palatium*.

At the end of the campaign season of 10 BCE, the two Claudian brothers met with Augustus again in Rome, where decrees recognizing their victories awaited them.[126] One of these was the vote in favour of Nero Drusus being consul for 9 BCE.[127] Yet the start to the New Year was inauspicious. In Rome, lightning storms severely damaged the temples of Jupiter Capitolinus (*Aedes Iovis Optimi Maximi Capitolini*) and Concordia (*Aedes Concordiae*). Tiberius vowed to one day rebuild the building sacred to the goddess of harmony.

The bad weather cleared. On 30 January, the day of Livia's birthday, the extended family of Augustus assembled on the west side of the *Via Flaminia* in the north-eastern corner of the *Campus Martius*. From there, they processed with priests and members of the religious colleges to the site of the new *Ara Pacis Augustae*. Voted for by the Senate five years earlier, it was now ready for its official dedication. It was an impressive edifice, erected to acknowledge the glory of Augustus' aspirations. The altar to the *Pax Augusta* was set upon a pedestal reached by steps, surrounded by an ornately decorated wall.[128] On the outside, flanking the front and rear openings, were depictions of gods and heroes.[129] Along the sides of the perimeter wall was a frieze depicting a line of dignitaries (*familiares*) led by priests (*flamines*) and sacrificial animals – perhaps a record of the foundation ceremony that had taken place on 4 July 13 BCE when Tiberius was consul.[130] Tiberius was among the *familiares* carved into the white Carrara marble (fig. 9); he is shown wearing a *toga* and facing the viewer, with a laurel crown upon his head.[131] Unique among the figures, Nero Drusus was presented wearing the *paludamentum* of an active commander. Establishing and enforcing the *Pax Augusta* required a willingness to engage in war. Once the ceremony

Figure 9. Scene from the *Ara Pacis Augustae* in Rome, consecrated on Livia's birthday in 9 BCE. The full male figure on the far right is believed to be Tiberius. The man with his *toga* over his head is identified as M. Agrippa.

concluded, Nero Drusus set off for the Rhine, while Tiberius headed to the Danube. Both men, for different reasons, were eager to join their troops.

The counterinsurgency went well for Tiberius. It might have been in this year that he showed his genius as a field commander, which earned him a place in Sex. Iulius Frontinus' compendium of successful military stratagems. In an undated battle, he records,

> when the barbarians in warlike mood had formed for battle at the very break of day, Ti. Nero held back his own troops and allowed the enemy to be hampered by the fog and to be drenched with the showers, which happened to be frequent that day. Then, when he noticed that they were weary with standing, and faint not only from exposure but also from exhaustion, he gave the signal, attacked and defeated them.[132]

In this campaign, Tiberius received his first acclamation as *imperator*; Augustus counted it among his own, now totalling thirteen.[133] It was an ancient honour in the gift of the soldiers to their field commander for bringing them victory, over the Delmatae and Pannonii in his case. For his victories in Illyricum, Augustus and the Senate granted Tiberius an ovation (*ovatio*) – 'a new kind of distinction never before conferred upon anyone', according the victor the right to ride along the *Via Sacra* upon a horse in triumph – which he celebrated upon his return to Rome, even as his brother was in Germania.[134] A recognition of military achievement, it was also a religious occasion, one in which the victor provided a feast for the people; some were gathered on the Capitolinus Hill, with the rest assembling in many other places around the city.[135] At the same time, his mother, Livia, with his wife, Iulia, hosted a celebratory dinner exclusively for the women. Anticipating a successful conclusion to his campaign, the same festivities granted to Tiberius were being planned for Nero Drusus, including holidays (*Feriae*) and a triumph when they were to be formally announced.[136]

Expectations were high for Nero Drusus as he entered the fourth year of the war across the Rhine. Augustus continued to take an active interest in the campaign. Rather than sojourn in *Colonia* Munatia or Narbo, this year he relocated to Ticinum (Pavia) in northern Italy (map 3), located between Rome and Drusus' forward base of operations.[137] Nero Drusus was pushing hard towards the Elbe River.[138] By the time he finally reached its banks, however, the campaign season was already coming to an end, and it was too late to cross to the other side. He ordered his men to erect a trophy, assembled from spoils collected at battles won along the way; the *Tropaeum Drusi* ('Trophy of Drusus') was the most northerly structure ever built by Romans on mainland Europe.[139] Then he told his officers to withdraw to the winter camps on the Rhine. Somewhere between the Weser and Saal rivers, he fell from – or was struck off – his horse.[140] The animal fell back on him, its bulk shattering his leg.[141] The troops struck camp while his medic urgently attended to their commander's nasty wound. Nero Drusus soon became very sick.[142] A message was dispatched to Augustus with the grave news. Receiving it, he told Tiberius, who was now himself in Ticinum, to go at once to his brother.[143]

In a state of panic, Tiberius rode in a carriage (*vehiculis*), accompanied only by Antabagius, 'a conquered barbarian', as his guide.[144] Their route took them over the Alps, and to keep up the frantic pace, they changed horses at intervals.[145] Tiberius reached the camp 'in three stages, travelling day and night on the road; the distance of each stage being 200 miles'. Indeed, they covered the ground so fast it was the land speed record of the Ancient World, worthy to be cited by Pliny the Elder in his *Natural History*.[146] Tiberius arrived to find the army consumed by gloom. The soldiers had taken to calling it the *Castra Scelerata* ('Accursed Camp'), after some reported seeing ghoulish sights.[147] Nevertheless, even in his deteriorating state, Nero Drusus gave orders that his men must turn out with their unit standards to greet the visiting commander, that the tent to the right of his own be made available to him and that he wished to be addressed as consul and *imperator*.[148] Tiberius was able to exchange a few final words with him. Thirty days after his accident, Nero Claudius Drusus was dead.[149] He was 29 years old.[150]

Tiberius, bereft, decided that his deceased brother would be taken back to Rome.[151] The complicated logistics would mean travelling through newly conquered country, putting the returning party at great risk. Regarding Nero Drusus as a worthy opponent, however, the Germanic nations agreed to suspend hostilities.[152] Tiberius attended his brother's body on the long journey, 'going before it on foot all the way'.[153] The centurions and military tribunes of the legions of his expeditionary army carried it over the first stage as far as their winter camps on the Rhine.[154] Thereafter, the leading men of each town and *colonia* along the road took turns to bear it.[155] Reaching Rome, the body was taken into the care of the quaestors' assistants.[156] It was laid in state, as had Marcellus' and Agrippa's before.[157] On the day of the funeral, Tiberius gave the first eulogy, addressing the crowd in the *Forum* from the *Rostra*.[158] The body was removed to the *Circus Flaminius*, where Augustus gave the second eulogy, in which spoke warmly of his stepson and called upon the gods to give his sons as glorious a death, when their time came, as they had accorded Nero Drusus.[159] Then members of the *Ordo Equester* carried the body one last time and laid it upon the pyre (*ustrinum*) in the *Campus Martius*, where it was set alight. The ashes were collected in an urn, which was placed in the mausoleum with an inscription composed by Augustus himself that lauded his praises.[160]

Nero Drusus 'had been the favour of the crowd'.[161] In recognition of his achievements, posthumous public honours were awarded.[162] Among them, the Senate voted Nero Drusus a triumphal arch of marble adorned with trophies on the *Via Appia*, and the *cognomen* '*Germanicus*' – meaning 'The German' or 'Of Germania' – for him and, significantly, his male descendants.[163] His troops raised a monumental tower in his honour at the fortress of Mogontiacum on the Rhine, around which they would run in ceremonial games held each year on an agreed holiday, which the cities of the *Tres Galliae* were mandated to observe with prayers and sacrifices.[164] The inconsolable grief of his mother, Livia, was acknowledged when statues of Nero Drusus were erected to honour his memory.[165]

Tiberius had to bear his own sorrows privately. He had suffered an accumulation of deeply personal losses – of the woman he loved, the father-in-law he respected and now the brother he adored. It was the speed with which these emotional blows fell – just three years. Grieving and unable to find solace in his marriage, Tiberius must have felt quite alone in the long, dark nights of the winter of 9 BCE.

## Chapter 3

# Paying the Price for Disloyalty: 8 BCE–5 CE

The Senate renewed Augustus' *imperium* for another ten years. Despite the loss of Nero Drusus, he was still committed to the project of pacifying the Germanic peoples.[1] To lead it, he turned to Tiberius.[2] On the campaign, he was to be joined by Caius, Augustus' 12-year-old adopted son, undertaking his first military commission.[3] As soon as Tiberius arrived in the Rhineland, the Germans sought terms: Tiberius removed 40,000 Sugambri to land on the Left Bank of the Rhine located between the Ubii and Batavi.[4] They had been the principal instigators behind the humiliation of 17 BCE and Augustus sought to punish them for it. When their envoys appeared, they were summarily arrested.[5] Separated from each other, they were taken to different cities in the *Tres Galliae*, where some committed suicide rather than face captivity far from their own people. The Sugambri would never again pose a threat to Roman interests. Meanwhile, Tiberius led his troops into action across the river. According to Velleius Paterculus, who was himself on the campaign:

> He [Tiberius] carried it on with his customary valour and good fortune, and after traversing every part of Germania in a victorious campaign, without any loss of the army entrusted to him – for he made this one of his chief concerns – he so subdued the country as to reduce it almost to the status of a tributary province.[6]

Complete pacification of Germania was still elusive. Archaeological evidence suggests a new policy of consolidation of Roman conquests under Tiberius. The massive, but unfinished, installation at Oberaden established by Nero Drusus on the Lippe (Lupia) River, was abandoned and a new fort, large enough for a single legion, was erected in timber further downstream at Haltern (plate 20).[7] Nevertheless, pleased by Tiberius' performance, Augustus permitted his son-in-law to use the acclamatory title *imperator* for the second time.[8] The soldiers were rewarded too. For ensuring Caius' safety, Augustus issued a special bonus in cash to the troops who had served with him.[9] Tiberius was recognized with a full triumph, the highest military honour for a Roman commander.[10]

At the end of the year, notices appeared in Rome announcing that Tiberius was standing for the consulship (plate 8).[11] The appointment was approved by the Senate. On 1 January 7 BCE, Tiberius took a curule chair for the second time in his political career. As Tiberius still held the *imperium* of a wartime commander, however, the first meeting of the Conscript Fathers was held in the *Curia Octaviae*, which stood outside the *pomerium*.[12] His colleague for the year was Cn. Calpurnius Piso (II), a man known to be irascible and difficult. Tiberius and Piso were not strangers; they had likely served together in the Cantabrian and Asturian War (26–25 BCE), and perhaps during the Alpine War (15 BCE) or the counterinsurgencies in Illyricum (11–9 BCE).[13] Piso came from an old plebeian family with a formidable reputation. He is described by Tacitus as 'a man of violent temper, without an idea of obedience, with indeed a natural arrogance inherited from his father'.[14] He asserts that Piso 'would hardly be the inferior of Tiberius, and as for Tiberius' children, he looked down on them as far beneath him'.[15] Remarkably, the two men were able to form a workable relationship, even a friendship (*amicitia*). Trust between them was essential for a successful political partnership, especially as Tiberius was to be absent for part of the year. Among his promised acts, Tiberius committed to rebuild the Temple of Concordia (*Aedes Concordiae*) that was damaged during the storm of early 9 BCE.[16]

Now permitted to enter Rome, Tiberius celebrated the triumph awarded to him the previous year.[17] Significantly, his was the first full-scale triumph (*pompa triumphalis*) granted to anyone since 19 BCE.[18] In awarding it to Tiberius, Augustus was acknowledging publicly that his son-in-law was acting on his *own* auspices and not under the *princeps*' as supreme commander. The exact date of the triumphal procession is lost, but a depiction of it survives on an extraordinary, embossed silver *skyphos* cup from Boscoreale, which has been dated on stylistic grounds to the Augustan era.[19] It is believed to have belonged to someone of high status who may have had a personal connection to the events. One side of the 'Tiberius Cup'

Figure 10. Tiberius riding his chariot in his full curule triumph of 7 BCE, depicted on one of the so-called Boscoreale Cups. He is accompanied by soldiers and preceded by sacrificial animals.

(fig. 10) depicts the triumphal procession in high relief in exquisite detail.[20] A man stands in a chariot drawn by four horses (*quadriga*). From the profile of the head and the facial features, this man is very likely Tiberius. He wears a gown (*toga picta*) over a tunic (*tunica palmata*), which together were the official garb of the victorious commander celebrating his triumph (*triumphator*). In his right hand he holds a laurel branch, in his left a sceptre topped with an eagle. Directly behind him stands the public slave (*servus publicus*), his right hand raised over Tiberius' head. His official role was to assist the *triumphator* by holding the crown made of bay or laurel leaves (*corona triumphalis*) or gold (*corona Etrusca*) over his head.[21] The right side of the cockpit of the triumphal chariot (*currus triumphalis*) is decorated with an image of Victoria, the personification of winged victory; the front above the draft pole is decorated with the *insignis corona triumphalis*. Behind the chariot walk four men in tunics with high ankle boots, suggesting that they are officers; all wear laurel crowns and one bears a torc (a gold or silver neck decoration typical of Iron Age Gallic warriors) around his neck while holding a laurel branch in his right hand. Among the horses is a man in a tunic and a *paludamentum* wearing military-issue *caligae*, his laureate head turned back towards Tiberius; this was a place of honour in the order of a triumphal ceremony. In front of the chariot walks a man stripped to the waist, straining to hold the reins of the four horses. A group of four men with poles, probably *lictores* with *fasces* (rods but missing the axes) consistent with his consular rank, walk beside the horses. In front of the procession is a group of men walking with the sacrificial victim (fig. 11). One carries a heavy axe on his shoulder, another holds the jaw of the garlanded head of the huge bull

Figure 11. The sacrifice of a bull before the *Capitolium* during Tiberius' full curule triumph of 7 BCE is depicted on one of the so-called Boscoreale Cups.

and leads it forward to meet its destiny at the *Capitolium*. The exquisite detail recorded in the scene can only have been taken from life – the artwork in precious metal memorializing a real event.

The shared joy of victories won in fields of glory far away was short lived. Later in the same year, reports arrived in Rome of trouble in Germania. Like Nero Drusus and other Claudians before him, Tiberius chose to lead the military operation in person.[22] The campaign may have largely amounted to a series of skirmishes, as Dio writes, somewhat dismissively, that 'nothing worthy of mention happened in Germania'.[23] It was enough that enemy blood was spilled to assert Rome's claim to the barbarian lands. Tiberius then returned to Rome to continue his consular duties for the remainder of the year.

Through his actions, Tiberius had demonstrated not only his capability as a highly successful military leader, but his unswerving loyalty to Augustus as Rome's 'first citizen'. He had steadily accumulated prestige from his successive political offices.[24] The one legal capacity he did not yet exercise was the *tribunicia potestas*, the power of a plebeian tribune. In 6 BCE, at the age of 36, Tiberius finally received it.[25] This was a public statement of Augustus' confidence in him as it accorded Tiberius the same powers as Augustus himself possessed.[26] Notably, Tiberius was significantly younger than Agrippa, who was 45 when it was given to him.[27] For the next five years, his person would be inviolate; anyone attacking him could face prosecution.[28] Tiberius could now convene and preside over meetings of the Senate, and he could pass legislation in the People's Assembly (*Comitia*). Through the right of *intercessio*, he could also block legislation and public actions simply by stating '*veto!*' ('I forbid!').[29] This, and the powers of arrest and prosecution (*coercitio*), established him in the historically important role going back to 493 BCE as protector of the People's interests and as their defender from injustices.

Augustus had a new task for Tiberius. In the East, the death of Tigranes III in exile in 8 BCE had left his kingdom, a client of Rome, at risk of slipping from the orbit of Roman influence and into the sphere of the Parthians. Augustus assigned Tiberius to re-establish good diplomatic relations with his son and successor, Tigranes IV, who was unpopular among his own people.[30] Tiberius received *imperium maius* empowering him to command the legions and govern the provinces in the East.[31] Years before, in 23 BCE, Augustus had sent M. Agrippa on a similar mission to Mytilene on Lesbos, from where he helped to negotiate a long peace treaty with Rome's oriental neighbour, sealed when Tiberius went in person to take back the ensigns and prisoners three years later.[32]

Yet just at the moment Tiberius reached the highest position and influence in the *Res Publica*, Augustus was advancing his adopted sons up the public service career ladder. By popular demand, Caius was 'elected' consul, but Augustus firmly rejected the vote, insisting that he was far too young to take on the responsibilities of the great office.[33] To Augustus' great disappointment, both seemed rather immature for their age, especially

> when he saw that Caius and Lucius were by no means inclined of their own choice to emulate his own conduct, as became young men who were being reared as members of the imperial house – they not only indulged in too great luxury in their lives but were also inclined to insolence.[34]

The root of the problem was their popularity and sense of entitlement. From the time when they were small boys, people fêted and flattered them everywhere they went.[35] Augustus himself was culpable to some extent, having been overindulgent with them as they grew up. Belatedly, to improve their attitudes and behaviours, he realized that tough love was now needed. Augustus decided the best approach was to expose them to life in the army, far away from the fawning crowd at Rome, as soon as practicable. In the meantime, he offered Caius a priesthood and the opportunity to attend meetings of the Senate.[36] However, Caius felt offended by this.[37]

Tiberius then did something that has perplexed historians ever since: he suddenly asked Augustus for permission to take a break from his obligations.[38] The noun both Velleius Paterculus and Suetonius use in their account of the event – *commeatus* – can refer to a soldier requesting leave of absence from his unit.[39] However, it appears he was not asking for a short interval but to withdraw or retire *completely* (Suetonius also uses the word *secedere*) from public life.[40] The officer-turned-historian explains that he needed 'to rest from the unbroken succession of his labours'.[41] Similarly, the biographer states that Tiberius initially gave as his reason 'weariness of office and a desire to rest'.[42] As reported by both the historian and the biographer, he subsequently changed his justification to argue that he did not want to overshadow the glory of Augustus' sons.[43] According to Dio, he feared that Caius and Lucius would be angry at him, and he was concerned that his own achievements should not detract from theirs; in fact, by leaving he was following Agrippa's example by not appearing to be a rival.[44] Either way, he intended to leave Rome on *his* terms.

Augustus, taken aback by the request, talked with Tiberius in an attempt to change his mind.[45] Frustrated when that did not work, he complained to the Senate that he felt 'he was being forsaken' by his son-in-law.[46] Tiberius was resolute. His mother also spoke with him with urgent entreaties, but that did not work either. Both parents applied pressure to force him to stay. Refusing to yield, Tiberius began 'a four-day hunger strike' in protest.[47] Augustus finally relented. Tiberius, he conceded, could go to the place of his choice without a specified return date. The narrative put out by the *Palatium* was that he was going to Rhodes because 'he needed incidentally a bit of instruction'.[48]

Tiberius, intending to avoid attracting attention from the public, planned a discrete, low-key departure from Rome. Allowed, at last, to leave, 'he left his wife and son in Rome and went down to Ostia in haste, without saying a single word to any of those who saw him off, and kissing only a very few when he left'.[49] Tiberius' behaviour had the opposite effect. People began to speculate about the real reasons behind the sudden departure of Augustus' son-in-law – especially as he was the man now widely seen as his successor. Dio writes:

> He made the journey as a private citizen … and when he reached Rhodes, he refrained from haughty conduct in both word and deed. This is the truest explanation of his journey abroad, though there is also a story that he took this course on account of his wife Iulia, because he could no longer endure her; at any rate, she was left behind in Rome. Others said that he was angry at not having been designated as Caesar, and yet others that he was expelled by Augustus himself, on the ground that he was plotting against Augustus' sons. But that his departure was *not* for the sake of instruction *nor* because he was displeased at the decrees passed, became plain from many of his subsequent actions, and particularly by his opening his will immediately at that time and reading it to his mother and Augustus. But all possible conjectures were made.[50]

Exile (*exilium*) was seen by Romans as a voluntary way of circumventing the death penalty.[51] While their political leaders had in the past frequently left the city of their own free will for rest and recuperation, they normally returned to the great city.[52] Tiberius' decision to quit of his own accord was viewed as very odd indeed.

The outbound sailing was briefly interrupted:

> From Ostia he coasted along the shore of Campania, and learning of an indisposition of Augustus, he stopped for a while. But since gossip was rife that he was lingering on the chance of realising his highest hopes, although the wind was all but dead ahead, he sailed directly to Rhodes.[53]

Tiberius could never entirely escape rumour and gossip. He was now just too public a figure.

His retreat from the public gaze was the ninth largest of the islands in the Mediterranean, located off the south coast of Asia Minor (now Turkey). Rhodes was a lucky find for Tiberius, 'for he had been attracted by the charm and healthfulness of that island ever since the time when he put in there on his return from Armenia' in 20 BCE.[54] He took a modest house inland and a villa that was not much bigger in the suburbs of the city of Rhodes.[55] His entourage was small, comprising his support staff of adjutants, messengers, bodyguard of lictors and *familia* of personal slaves. Staying with him were three companions: Licilius Longus, a senator of humble background, who Tiberius considered an intimate friend; and Vescularius Flaccus and Iulius Marinus, who were two of his oldest friends from the equestrian order.[56] Some imagined that Tiberius preferred to shun society on this island paradise to hide the fact that he enjoyed a voluptuous lifestyle. 'In the seclusion of Rhodes', it was said that 'he had acquired the habit of avoiding company and taking his pleasures by stealth'.[57] In practice, Tiberius lived a simpler life at a slower pace. While on the island, he adopted a kinder, more considerate approach in his interactions.[58] He went on walkabouts, often without a lictor or a messenger, and happily exchanged pleasantries with the local people as though they were his equals.[59] He preserved his personal physical fitness by working out at the gymnasium and practicing his swordsmanship and horsemanship.[60]

He maintained his intellectual agility by reading and conversing. He regularly attended the schools and lecture-rooms of teachers of philosophy. On one recorded occasion, a heated dispute arose among rival sophists in class.[61] When Tiberius participated in the discussion and appeared to favour one side, a fellow student subjected Tiberius to a tirade of abuse. Maintaining his calm, Tiberius withdrew and went to his house. Quickly returning with his lictors and attendants, and instructing his crier to summon the foul-mouthed offender before his tribunal, Tiberius had him hauled off to prison. Though now a private citizen, he still had the rights and privileges of a tribune.[62] This ambiguous status could create problems for his staff. Suetonius preserves an example.[63] One morning, while arranging his programme for the day, Tiberius announced that he wanted to visit people who were sick in the city.[64] This wish was misunderstood by his staff as an instruction. They issued orders that all the unwell people should be taken to a public portico and arranged according to the nature of their ailments. When escorted there, Tiberius was shocked at this unexpected sight. Embarrassed, for a while he was not sure what to do. Gathering his composure, he approached each one, apologizing for what had happened, 'even to the humblest and most obscure of them'.[65]

Tiberius' presence on the island drew visitors who were very important in their own right. Velleius Paterculus writes:

> I ought to say that all who departed for the provinces across the sea, whether proconsuls or legates appointed by the emperor, went out of their way to see him at Rhodes, and on meeting him they lowered their *fasces* to him though he was but a private citizen – if such majesty could ever belong to a private citizen – thereby confessing that his retirement was more worthy of honour than their official position.[66]

Among them was P. Sulpicius Quirinus, an advisor to Caius in Armenia, who treated Tiberius with courtesy and respect.[67] Notable by his absence was King Archelaus of Cappadocia, to whom Tiberius took a long-term dislike.[68] The longer Tiberius was away from Rome, however, the greater the risk that Augustus could manage without him. In 4 BCE, P. Quinctilius Varus – Tiberius' partner in the consulship of 13 BCE – quashed riots in Iudaea which followed the death of Herodes (Herod the Great) using detachments of legions stationed in Syria under his command.[69] Like many Roman governors, he had exploited his appointment for personal gain. Paterculus remarked that 'he entered the rich province a poor man but left it a rich man and the province poor'.[70] In 3 BCE, L. Domitius Ahenobarbus (I) took an army across the Elbe River, achieving what Nero Drusus had not. Although known to be 'haughty, extravagant and cruel', he was politically astute enough to erect an altar to Augustus on one of its banks.[71] Augustus was also preparing his sons to take on greater responsibilities – the same ones he had relied on Tiberius to carry out. Caius came of age in 5 BCE and was designated *Princeps Iuventutis* ('Leader of the Youth').[72] Similarly recognized was his brother, Lucius (fig. 12), when he came of age three years later.[73]

Unbeknownst to the boys, their mother, Iulia, was leading a secret life of debauchery. The extent of it finally became known in 2 BCE. There were reports that she had indulged in drunken revelries and orgiastic parties, at least one even taking place in public in the *Forum*.[74] Augustus suspected that she was involved in some sort of mischief, but had chosen not to believe it.[75] Tiberius too was aware of something wrong, feeling 'disgust at his wife, whom he dared neither accuse nor put away, though he could no longer endure her'.[76] Humiliated by his one and only daughter, Augustus had to make a deeply consequential decision. Under the *Lex Iulia de adulteriis coercendis* on adultery and criminal fornication that he had himself authorized in 18 BCE, he now banished her to Pandateria (the island of Ventotene, west of Naples).[77] She was joined, voluntarily, by her mother, Scribonia. Her lover, Iullus Antonius – a surviving son of M. Antonius who had been raised in Augustus' household – was arrested on the charge that

Figure 12. Augustus' adoption of the two sons of M. Agrippa was well received by the Roman People. Caius and Lucius are presented as *principes iuventutis* on this *denarius*, each togate, holding a spear and resting a hand on a shield.

he was conspiring against the *princeps* and executed.[78] Others implicated in the crime met a similar end.

When Tiberius learned of her banishment and that a bill of divorce had been sent to her in his name by the authority of Augustus, he initially welcomed the news.[79] Nevertheless, Tiberius considered it his duty, as the former husband, to make every possible effort to reconcile the father to his daughter, and he wrote numerous letters to Augustus in support of her. Regardless of her crimes, Tiberius allowed her to keep any gifts he had given her. The former son-in-law now re-evaluated his reasons for being on Rhodes. The point of his retirement, he had told Augustus, was to avoid the suspicion of rivalry with Caius and Lucius.[80] As they were now grown men and had an undisputed claim to succeed Augustus, Tiberius wanted to be allowed to visit his relatives in Rome, whom he sorely missed. Augustus' reply was clear and harsh: he denied his request and, moreover, admonished him for having given up any consideration for his family, which he had so eagerly abandoned in 6 BCE. Tiberius had seriously misjudged his position. Then in 1 CE, his *tribunicia potestas* expired. He was now an ordinary citizen without any legal authority, and one living far away from Rome – in effect he was in self-imposed exile.[81]

Tiberius' mood changed from confidence and contentment to concern and contrition. He wrote to his mother to intercede on his behalf. With her help, he received permission that, while away from Rome, he could use the title of *Legatus Augusti* ('Deputy of Augustus') as a way, in the view of Suetonius, to conceal his disgrace.[82] Visitors still stopped at Rhodes to meet with him, no matter how hard he tried to avoid them and despite moving into the house inland from the coast.[83] There was one relationship he realized that he needed to mend; that was with Caius. Augustus had since appointed him to lead the diplomatic mission to Armenia and given him proconsular powers to carry it out.[84] Learning that he was on Samos, Tiberius urgently sailed to meet with him.[85] Caius was surrounded by men of dubious character. On his staff was Cnaeus, son of L. Domitius Ahenobarbus (I), 'a man hateful in every walk of life'.[86] Caius' chief of staff and guardian (*comes et rector*) was M. Lollius, the former propraetorian legate of *Tres Galliae* dismissed by Augustus.[87] A deep odium had existed between the two men ever since. Lollius sought to undermine Tiberius at every opportunity. He slandered Tiberius before the meeting with Caius and now he was spreading word of rebellion to certain unnamed shady characters via centurions he had appointed who were returning from leave to their army bases.[88] The reception Tiberius received from Caius was frosty. It was made abundantly clear that he was not welcome there.

For the next two years, Tiberius lived in fear of his safety.[89] To thwart any suggestion that he represented a threat to Augustus or his sons, he even took the precaution of giving up his training with arms and horses. He tried to blend in with the local people by swapping his Roman *paludamentum* and *calcei* for a Greek *himation* and a pair of *embantes*.[90] Inadvertently, he had now become a hate figure. It is reported that in Gallia Narbonnensis, a mob in Nemausus (modern Nîmes) pulled down statues and busts of him, while someone at a dinner party threatened to sail to Rhodes and cut off the head of the man now disdainfully called *Exulis* ('The Exile') – he just needed Caius to give him the word.[91] This level of personal antagonism shook Tiberius. He wrote to his mother, pleading with her to lobby Augustus on his behalf to allow him to return to Rome. The *princeps* replied that he would consent so long as Caius (fig. 13) – who was elected consul for 1 CE – agreed to the request.[92] As it happened, Caius *was* now willing to consider it. His relationship with Lollius had since changed for the worse.[93] During a meeting with Phraatakes (Frahâtak) V of Parthia, he had learned that his 'companion and guide' had accepted bribes from kings of the East.[94] Exposed and shamed, Lollius took his own life; his death was received with joy.[95] Separately, Caius had dismissed Cn. Domitius Ahenobarbus for his outrageous behaviour.[96] Now independent of his reprobate advisors, the young man could finally think for himself. Caius acceded to Augustus' wishes.

Keeping a low profile and having so much free time, Tiberius took to studying astrology (*mathematicae*), or 'divination by means of the stars'.[97] This ancient 'science' (*scientia*) had fascinated him for years and had even become something of an obsession; indeed, he was 'firmly convinced that everything was in the hands of Fate'.[98] In astrological terms, Tiberius was born under Libra in the original zodiac of thirteen signs, or a Scorpio in that of twelve signs which was becoming the accepted model in the first century CE.[99] As characterized by the astrologers M. Manlius (a contemporary of Tiberius), Vettius Valens and Claudius Ptolemaeus, Libra men could be masculine, airy, noble and just, but also malicious and envious.[100] Valens specifically mentions that men born under the sign of the weighing scales were best suited to be placed in charge of measures, posts and the grain supply, whereas those born under the sign of the scorpion were commonly

Figure 13. While Tiberius was at Rhodes, Augustus expedited the political advancement of his adopted son, Caius, through the *cursus honorum*.

accomplices in murder, poisonings and other crimes, and haters of their own family.[101] Tiberius would have been fully aware of the traits of his natal sign. 'It was just at this time,' writes Suetonius, 'that he was convinced of the powers of the astrologer [*mathematicus*] Thrasyllus, whom he had attached to his household as a learned man.'[102] Thrasyllus came from a distinguished family in Alexandria or Mendes. A scholar on the works of Plato, Tiberius needed his expertise as a teacher (*magister*) in making calculations for the casting of horoscopes.[103] Yet he had nagging doubts about the man. Many of the predictions Thrasyllus had made turned out to be adverse or the opposite. Whenever Tiberius sought advice on astrological matters, he would use the top floor of his house and the services of one freedman who, though illiterate, had great physical strength.[104] This impressive man always walked in front of the person whose knowledge of divination (*scientia Chaldaeorum artis*) Tiberius was testing. They would all walk along an unfrequented and precipitous path near the house, which was built on a rocky location. If there was any suspicion of fakery or trickery, the man would hurl the astrologer, as he returned, into the sea beneath to ensure that no one would betray the secret. Thrasyllus was now led up the same path. Indeed, Tiberius had already made up his mind to push the man off it.[105] Then, at that moment, Thrasyllus spotted a ship on the horizon and declared that it brought good news. His conjecture proved right: it was a letter from his mother, Livia.[106] Taking what he had said to be a prediction, thereafter Tiberius counted him among his most intimate friends, granting him the name Ti. Claudius Thrasyllus.[107]

Throughout his life, omens and prophecies had seemed to point to his destiny.[108] Suetonius records a few instances:

> When Livia was with child with him [Tiberius] and was trying to divine by various omens whether she would bring forth a male, she took an egg from under a setting-hen, and when she had warmed it in her own hand and those of her attendants in turn, a cock with a fine crest was hatched. In his infancy the astrologer Scribonius promised him an illustrious career and even that he would one day be king, but without the crown of royalty; for at that time of course the rule of the Caesars was as yet unheard of. Again, on his first campaign, when he was leading an army through Macedonia into Syria, it chanced that at Philippi the altars consecrated in bygone days by the victorious legions gleamed of their own accord with sudden fires. When later, on his way to Illyricum, he visited the oracle of Geryon near Patavium, and drew a lot which advised him to seek an answer to his inquiries by throwing golden dice into the fount of Aponus, it came to pass that the dice which he threw showed the highest possible number; and those dice may be seen today under the water.[109]

One day in 2 CE, an eagle – a bird never seen before in Rhodes – perched itself upon the roof of Tiberius' house.[110] The previous day, when Tiberius received official notification that he could return Rome, it was seen that his tunic seemed to blaze as he was changing his clothes.[111]

Augustus expected – even demanded – unswerving loyalty from his family, friends and hand-picked deputies. He could be forgiving of mistakes too, but he would extract a price for Tiberius' 'error of judgement'. The condition for his return to Rome was that he should have no role in the political life of the *Res Publica*.[112] Thus, it was as a private citizen that Tiberius returned home in 2 CE. It was a humiliation for a man proudly descended from the Claudian line. He took up residence at the gardens of C. Cilinius Maecenas on the *Esquilinus* Hill – the former owner having died in 8 BCE, by which time the old friend had lost the trust of Augustus.[113] Effectively neither seen nor heard, Tiberius attended to his personal affairs, only raising his profile to introduce his son, Drusus, now 16 years old, to public life.[114] Drusus was a close friend of Herod Agrippa, the grandson of the late King Herodes.[115] Herod had emigrated to Rome in 5 BC, when 6 years old, after his father, Aristobulus IV, was executed – possibly with the complicity of his mother, Berenike (daughter of Salome). The Roman capital was actually safer for a member of the Hasmonean dynasty than Caesarea in Iudaea. He found refuge with Antonia Minor and became a thoroughly Romanized young man, taking the name M. Iulius Agrippa.

That year, Lucius, who was en route to his first military assignment with the legions in Hispania Tarraconensis, died unexpectedly at Massilia (Marseilles) from unknown causes.[115] He was just 18. His body was returned to Rome and his ashes were placed in the Mausoleum of Augustus.[117] In his stepson's honour, Tiberius composed a lyric poem entitled *Conquestio de Morte L. Caesaris* ('A Lament for the Death of Lucius Caesar').[118] Meanwhile, in the East, his older brother continued campaigning. When Ariobarzanes, a Mede who joined the Romans, was installed as King of Armenia, outright war with Parthia was averted.[119] In 3 CE, Caius' mission stalled at Artagira, a stronghold occupied by a force led by a man named Addon.[120] Caius eventually captured his adversary, and was acclaimed *imperator* for it, but during the siege he was seriously wounded.[121] His health failing, he now wrote to Augustus asking him to be allowed to resign his commission and withdraw to Syria to live there as a private citizen.[121] Distraught, Augustus agreed to his wishes, but the young man's injuries proved fatal. Reaching Limyra on the southern coast of Asia Minor aboard a merchant ship on 21 February 4 CE, Caius died.[123] He was 23 years old. His body was returned to Rome with the pomp and ceremony due his status, and his ashes were also placed in the Mausoleum of Augustus.[124] Iulia was not permitted to attend the funerals of either of her two boys. She was, however, allowed to move to Rhegium on the Italian mainland.[125]

With the deaths of his two adopted sons, the line of succession that Augustus had so carefully laid over many years was broken. To carry on his work and reduce the risk of a challenger emerging or of civil war resulting, he needed to ensure that his dynasty would prevail. Pragmatism was always the hallmark of his problem-solving, and the answer to his problem was Tiberius; he was to be rehabilitated and his status elevated once again.[126] At Augustus' request, and as a condition of his own adoption, Tiberius was compelled (*coactus*) to first adopt his nephew, Germanicus (plate 12), now 19 years old, as *his* son and heir.[127] Augustus had briefly considered adopting Germanicus directly, but he was apparently persuaded otherwise by his wife.[128] On 27 June 4 CE, Augustus formally adopted Tiberius, and with it his name changed to Ti. Iulius Caesar thereby severing forever his family ties to the Claudian line.[129] The ceremony for this act of *adrogatio* took place in public in the *Comitia Curiata* ('Centuriate Assembly') of the Roman People in the *Saepta Iulia*, presided over by the *Pontifices*.[130] Augustus declared, under oath, '*hoc Rei Publicae causa facio*' ('This I do for reasons of state').[131] It meant that,

> from that time on he [Tiberius] ceased to act as the head of a family, or to retain in any particular the privileges which he had given up. For he neither made gifts nor freed slaves, and he did not even accept an inheritance or any legacies, except to enter them as an addition to his personal property.[132]

Tiberius' adopted son assumed the new name Germanicus Iulius Caesar, making him Augustus' grandson. Tiberius' own son similarly changed his name to Drusus Iulius Caesar.[133] Additionally, Augustus adopted M. Agrippa's surviving son of the same name, who had been born after his friend's death; he took the name Agrippa Iulius Caesar.[134] The arrangement positioned Tiberius as the preferred successor, with Germanicus and his sons next in line; it placed Drusus and Agrippa Caesar as 'spares'.

Augustus made a speech to the Senate requesting that Tiberius be given *tribunicia potestas* for five years.[135] There may have been resistance from some senators. He was complimentary about his son, but felt compelled to explain 'his manners, style, and habits of life, which he meant as reproaches, yet he seemed to excuse'.[136] The motion was approved. Tiberius' *imperium proconsulare maius* was restored too. He was once again the second most powerful man in the Roman Empire. Now aged 66, Augustus was becoming noticeably frailer. He needed his right-hand man more than ever. 'On him all centred,' writes Tacitus, '[as] son, colleague in power.'[137] When an embassy from Parthia arrived in Rome to meet the *princeps*, it was asked to present its credentials (*mandata*) to Tiberius.[138] Augustus also needed to trust him like never before. A test of his faith in him arose when he sent Tiberius once again to deal with the unruly nations of Germania. Thought to be subjugated, they had been in general revolt (*immensum bellum*) for the last three years under its military governor, M. Vinicius.[139] Donning his military panoply for the first time in well over a decade, Tiberius went to the *Forum Augustum*, from where, since its opening in 2 BCE, commanders officially received their insignia and blessings from Augustus in front of the Temple of Mars Ultor.[140] Tiberius' orders were 'to pacify the Germans' in a new war – the *Bellum Germanicum*.[141]

On the road from Rome, riding through Italy and the *Tres Galliae*, Tiberius was greeted spontaneously by veterans with whom he had served.[142] He was a soldier's soldier, and he was still popular with them many years later. It was his no-nonsense manner that appealed to them:

> Let me also add the following trait, which, like the others I have described, will be immediately recognized as true by anyone who participated in that campaign. [Tiberius] Caesar alone of commanders was in the habit of also travelling in the saddle, and, throughout the greater portion of the summer campaign, of sitting at the table when dining with invited guests. Of those who did not imitate his own stern discipline he took no notice, in so far as no harmful precedent was thereby created. He often admonished, sometimes gave verbal reproof, but rarely punishment, and pursued the moderate course of pretending in most cases not to see things, and of administering only occasionally a reprimand.[143]

Soldiers and officials appreciated his fairness, pragmatism and principled stance on matters. When he stopped at Bagacum (Bavay, north-east France), a local official named Cn. Licinius Navos celebrated Tiberius' visit by setting up an inscription.[144] Finally, upon reaching the frontier with several legions under his direct command, Tiberius could have easily challenged his adoptive father, but he did not.[145] He and his legionaries' *gladii* were pointed towards the Germans.

What lay across the Rhine was territory and an enemy Tiberius knew well. It was already mid-summer when he jointly launched the campaign of 4 CE with C. Sentius Saturninus, *legatus Augusti propraetore* of Germania. According to Paterculus, who was himself involved in the offensive, '[Tiberius] Caesar claimed for himself every part of the war that was difficult or dangerous', leaving Saturninus 'in charge of expeditions of a less dangerous character'.[146] The five legions supported by auxiliary infantry and cavalry units thrust through the central region, engaging with the Cherusci and Bructeri as they advanced.[147] Temporary marching camps have been identified near the Weser River at Minden and Hameln, and at Barkhausen, Porta Westfalica in northern Germany.[148]

Suetonius records that, while Tiberius spent time meticulously preparing for combat operations, his belief in his good luck also played a role in his success:

> Although he left very little to fortune and chance, he entered battles with considerably greater confidence whenever it happened that, as he was working at night, his lamp suddenly and without human agency died down

> and went out; trusting, as he used to say, to an omen in which he had great confidence, since both he and his ancestors had found it trustworthy in all of their campaigns.[149]

Paterculus relates the story of a surprise encounter between Tiberius and a Germanic warrior:

> Even in the midst of these great events I cannot refrain from inserting this little incident. We were encamped on the nearer bank of the aforesaid river, while on the farther bank glittered the arms of the enemies' troops, who showed an inclination to flee at every movement and manoeuvre of our vessels, when one of the barbarians, advanced in years, tall of stature, of high rank, to judge by his dress, embarked in a canoe, made as is usual with them of a hollowed log, and guiding this strange craft he advanced alone to the middle of the stream and asked permission to land without harm to himself on the bank occupied by our troops, and to see [Tiberius] Caesar. Permission was granted. Then he beached his canoe, and, after gazing upon Caesar for a long time in silence, exclaimed: 'Our young men are insane, for though they worship you as divine when absent, when you are present they fear your armies instead of trusting to your protection. But I, by your kind permission, Caesar, have today seen the gods of whom I merely used to hear; and in my life have never hoped for or experienced a happier day.' After asking for and receiving permission to touch Caesar's hand, he again entered his canoe, and continued to gaze back upon him until he landed upon his own bank.[150]

Turning north-west, the Romans marched against the Attuarii and Canninefates on the North Sea coast.[151] Unusually for the Roman Army in combat, Tiberius extended the campaign season into December. He established a base on the Lippe River, where his troops billeted for the winter. The archaeological record shows that on the Lippe, a new fort, large enough for a single legion, was erected in timber at Anreppen some 100 kilometres (65 miles) upstream from Haltern.[152] Then Tiberius left for Rome. Dio reads a motive into his constant return trips to the city in between fighting. 'This was partly, to be sure,' he writes, 'on account of various business, but chiefly because he was afraid that Augustus might take advantage of his absence to show preference to somebody else.'[153] This remark likely refers to Germanicus or Agrippa Caesar, who had become eligible for military service.[154]

Invigorated by his winter sojourn, Tiberius returned to the theatre of war in the spring of 5 CE. With the central and north-west regions of Germania secured, the focus of the new campaign was the east and north-east. The army advanced – perhaps Tiberius moving from Vetera (Xanten) and Saturninus from Mogotiacum (Mainz) – to the Weser River.[155] Thereafter, reaching the Elbe River (Albis) was a strategic imperative, both as a way to outflank the German resistance and to facilitate the logistics supporting the taskforce:

> And with this wonderful combination of careful planning and good fortune on the part of the leader, and a close watch upon the seasons, the fleet which had skirted the windings of the seacoast sailed up the Albis from a sea hitherto unheard of and unknown, and after proving victorious over many tribes effected a junction with [Tiberius] Caesar and the army, bringing with it a great abundance of supplies of all kinds.[156]

The Roman expeditionary force engaged and defeated the Langobardi, 'a tribe', writes Paterculus, 'surpassing even the Germans in savagery'.[157] The climax of the season was reached when 'finally – and this is something which had never before been entertained even as a hope, much less actually attempted – a Roman Army with its standards was led 400 miles beyond the Rhenus as far as the Albis River, which flows past the territories of the Semnones and the Hermunduri'.[158]

As a participant in, and veteran of, the German War, Paterculus gives an effusive testimonial of a surrender ceremony (*deditio*):

> Good Gods, how large a volume could be filled with the tale of our achievements in the following summer under the generalship of Tiberius Caesar! All Germania was traversed by our armies, races were conquered hitherto almost unknown, even by name; and the tribes of the Cauchi were again subjugated. All the flower of their youth, infinite in number though they were, huge of stature and protected by the ground they held, surrendered their arms and, flanked by a gleaming line of our soldiers, fell with their warlords upon their knees before the tribunal of the commander.[159]

For the Romans, this was the very act of pacification. In contrast, writing two centuries later, Cassius Dio – ever the critic – dismissed the entire year's campaigning with the comment that 'nothing noteworthy was accomplished at this time'.[160] Yet he had to acknowledge that Tiberius earned an imperial acclamation for himself and for Augustus, while Saturninus received triumphal honours, for negotiating a truce with the Germanic nations.[161]

Contemporary poet Krinagoras of Mytilene wrote in celebration of Tiberius' achievements:

> East and West are the limits of the world,
> and through both ends passed the exploits of Nero.
> The Sun as he rose saw Armenia subdued by his hands
> and Germania as he went down the sky.
> Let us sing of his double victory in war!
> Araxes knows it and Rhine, drunk now by the enslaved.[162]

The verse writer's choice of the Rhine was prescient. The Roman Army would never reach the Elbe again.[163]

## Chapter 4

# Fighting for the *Pax Augusta*: 6 CE–13 CE

A severe famine afflicted the people in Rome in 6 CE.[1] In the scramble to obtain supplies, the price of grain spiked such that five *modii* sold for HS 110.[2] To reduce demand, gladiators and slaves offered for sale were sent at least 100 miles away from the city, and the leading families did all they could to reduce the size of their retinues and so cut the number of mouths to feed.[3] Emergency measures were introduced to apply strict oversight on the distribution of the available stock of wheat, prioritizing those qualifying for the *annona*.[4] Augustus even postponed the feast to celebrate his birthday. Rumour spread that a certain P. Rufus was behind the scarcity and that he was plotting a revolution.[5] Rewards were offered for information leading to Rufus' apprehension.[6] Making the situation worse, a fire broke out, destroying parts of the city. To deal with such calamities in future, Augustus founded seven cohorts of *Vigiles* comprised of freedmen equipped with firefighting equipment.[7] Stationed across the fourteen regions (*vici*) of Rome, the 6,000 men of the *Cohortes Vigilum* proved very popular with the citizenry.[8] The unit was funded by a tax on the sale of slaves.

Tiberius returned to a tense Rome. Perhaps with his help, the famine crisis was eventually solved. Gladiatorial games were given in honour of Nero Drusus by his sons, Germanicus and Claudius.[9] This opportunity to memorialize Nero Drusus provided great comfort to the people.[10] Tiberius himself was finally able to fulfil a vow he had made several years before when serving as consul.[11] With the proceeds from the disposal of war spoils (*ex manubiis*) from his campaigns, Tiberius paid for the restoration of the Temple of Castor and Pollux (*Templum Castoris*).[12] His generosity complied with Augustus' regulation of 17 BCE requiring his *legati* to invest some of their booty in monuments to beautify the city or improve its infrastructure.[13] Located in the south-east corner of the *Forum Romanum*, the temple butted right up against the triple victory Arch of Augustus (*Arcus Augusti*).[14] The temple had been damaged by fire in 14 BCE or 9 BCE.[15] Now fully rebuilt, he rededicated it on 27 January 6 CE.[16] Tiberius was not particularly devout, being 'somewhat neglectful of the gods and of religious matters'.[17] In the historian Livy's view, 'The neglect of the gods' was the historical cause of civil war because it unsettled the *Pax Deorum* ('Peace of the Gods'), a situation he believed still prevailed in his age.[18] However, Tiberius well understood the role of

Figure 14. Tiberius rebuilt the Temple of Castor and Pollux by investing a portion of the proceeds from his war spoils. Its unusual ground plan is shown in this fragment of the *Forma Urbs Romae* created under the emperor Septimius Severus between 203 and 211 CE.

religious observance in Roman life and of publicly fulfilling his vow by keeping his promise to the gods.

The temple was an imposing structure designed to impress. The front elevation (fig. 14) featured twin staircases on the sides of the podium, with a speaker's platform in between. Built upon a high podium, the octastyle temple was reconstructed in white marble and tufa, and surrounded by graceful Corinthian columns (fig. 15), all surmounted by an entablature with a plain frieze and modillion cornice.[19] On the entablature above the entrance was an inscription stating that Tiberius had dedicated the building 'in his own name and that of his brother'.[20] Dio records:

> For this mark of honour to the memory of Drusus comforted the people, and also the dedication by Tiberius of the Temple of the Dioscuri [Castor and Pollux], upon which he inserted not only his own name – calling himself 'Claudianus' instead of 'Claudius', because of his adoption into the family of Augustus – but also that of [Nero] Drusus.[21]

The Dioscuri twins had particular significance for him and his brother: devoted to each other, they were associated in people's minds with the divine twins.[22] Tiberius' decision to renovate the building was shrewd. The temple was high visibility, a focal point of daily life in Rome, since the Dioscuri appealed to a wide cross-section of Roman society.[23] Whenever they gathered there to do business, high above their heads were the names of Rome's famous Claudian brothers. The opening of the temple provided some good news in an otherwise bleak time.

Figure 15. Only three columns of the Temple of Castor and Pollux rebuilt by Tiberius still stand in the *Forum Romanum*.

While in Rome, Tiberius worked with Augustus to address one of the pressing matters of the day, ensuring the long-term financing of the standing army. They created a new fund which they called the *Aerarium* ('Military Treasury'), one kept separate from the *Fiscus*.[24] In his own name and that of Tiberius, Augustus made the initial deposit. He directed that three ex-*praetors* should be chosen by lot to administer it for three years, each having the protection of two lictors and any further assistance they requested.[25] He tasked the Senate to find other sources of revenue for the *Aerarium*, finally settling on a 5 per cent tax on inheritances and bequests.[26] The three ex-consuls successfully reduced some costs and cut others altogether.[27]

Around the Roman world – in Africa, Asia Minor, Iudaea, and Sardinia – Roman armies were engaged in conflicts.[28] Several of the Germanic nations with whom Rome had agreed truces just the previous year now reneged on their commitments. The Romans knew not to trust them to keep their word, and preparations for a major offensive were already in hand.[29] For this third phase of the war in Germania, Tiberius assembled a massive force consistent with Augustus' own military doctrine. Augustus was known to follow the dictum, 'Better a steadfast commander than a bold one'.[30] He would not risk the lives of his soldiers unless the calculus was overwhelmingly in their favour:

> He used to say that a war or a battle should not be begun under any circumstances, unless the hope of gain was clearly greater than the fear of loss; for he likened such as grasped at slight gains with no slight risk to those who fished with a golden hook, the loss of which, if it were carried off, could not be made good by any catch.[31]

With risk mitigation in mind, Tiberius brought overwhelming force to his latest venture. A new fort, large enough for a single legion, had been erected on a meander in the Main River at a place now called Marktbreit in Bavaria.[32] A camp able to accommodate two or three legions plus auxiliaries was constructed on an escarpment overlooking the Danube at Carnuntum (near modern Vienna); with a road connection to Aquileia, this was Tiberius' base of operations.[33] Scale was crucial, as the army would be facing a formidable opponent this coming season.

The enemy to be defeated was Maroboduus, leader of the Marcomanni. Through Roman eyes, Maroboduus was a friend-turned-foe. Considered intelligent and resourceful, he had lived in Rome as an ally, earning Augustus' patronage and friendship.[34] In 10 BCE, after sixteen years, he returned to his people across the Danube. The Marcomanni were located in the south-western region of Germania. In 3 BCE, L. Domitius Ahenobarbus (I) had settled the Hermunduri in lands belonging to the Marcomanni.[35] A charismatic leader, he convinced his people to migrate to new land 'in the plains surrounded by the Hercynian Forest', which the Romans called Bohaemium (now Bohemia and Moravia in Czechia) (plate 17).[36] By relocating, he hoped not only to avoid conflict with Rome, but to make his own position unassailable with his own people.[37] Through diplomacy and war, he built up the Marcomanni as a confederation, which became a rallying point of resistance for nations refusing to bow to Rome or yield to other Germanic aggressors.[38] 'His policy toward Rome,' writes Paterculus, 'was to avoid provoking us by war, but at the same time to let us understand that, if he were provoked by us, he had in reserve the power *and* the will to resist.'[39] By 6 CE, he could muster a force of some 70,000 infantry and 4,000 cavalry.[40] While among the Romans, perhaps as an auxiliary unit commander, he had learned their military doctrine. Replicating their training and by constant drilling, he had brought his own troops almost to the Roman standard of discipline.[41] Through war with his neighbours, those same troops had become battle-hardened. From a strategic viewpoint, Augustus deemed this large and diverse force on his northern border to be a significant threat to Rome's interests, even to Italy.[42] 'Nothing remained to be conquered in Germania except the people of the Marcomanni,' writes Paterculus – and it was now Tiberius' mission to eliminate that threat.[43]

Tiberius planned a two-pronged attack, co-ordinated with Saturninus. The strategy is known from Paterculus, who as a *praefectus equitum* was an active participant in this campaign.[44] Saturninus had instructions to lead his Rhine legions from his base eastwards through the country of the Chatti, cutting a passage through the densely wooded Hercynia *Silva*. Meanwhile, Tiberius would lead the Danube legions, supported by auxiliary troops from Illyricum, northwards from his base at Carnuntum. They would all rendezvous in Bohaemium, where the combined armies would mount a full-scale assault against the Marcomanni.

Archaeology may have revealed tantalizing evidence of the actual invasion route taken by Tiberius' army group. On the left bank of the Danube, where it meets the Morava (March) River some 10 kilometres (6 miles) west of Carnuntum, the

Figure 16. View of the confluence of the Morava River and the Danube River. Archaeological evidence suggests that it was here that Tiberius crossed with his taskforce from Carnuntum to engage Maroboduus of the Marcomanni in 6 CE.

stone foundations of a watchtower and barracks have been found. The Castle Hill (fig. 16) site in Bratislava-Devín has produced finds of military equipment, brooches and Arretine *terra sigillata* fragments, strongly suggesting a military presence in the Augustan period.[45] It may indicate that Tiberius' column marched northwards along the course of the Morava, its provisions being carried on boats rowed up the river, which was normal Roman logistical practice in wartime.[46]

Behind each legion's *aquila*, long lines of legionaries, marching four or eight abreast, organized in their assigned cohorts, followed their centurial *signa* on their way to intercept the target. The two army groups closed in:

> [Tiberius] Caesar had already arranged his winter quarters on the Danuvius and had brought up his army to within five days' march of the advanced posts of the enemy; and the legions which he had ordered Saturninus to bring up, separated from the enemy by an almost equal distance, were on the point of effecting a junction with Caesar at a predetermined rendezvous within a few days.[47]

Tiberius was now 'deep in enemy territory'.[48]

The *legatus Augusti* of Illyricum, M. Valerius Messalla Messallinus (II), had joined the expeditionary force with auxiliary units drawn from the Danube region of his province, later known as Pannonia.[49] Messallinus was a man 'who was even more noble in heart than in birth'.[50] Conspicuous by their absence were the auxiliaries from the coastal region of the province known as Dalmatia – after the Delmatae who lived there – that he had ordered to mobilize.[51] Unbeknownst to him, when the auxiliary units from Dalmatia had assembled, they had realized – perhaps for the first time – their immense numbers.[52] Their leaders began to question why they were risking their lives in wars of conquest *for* Rome when they could be defending their own country *from* Rome. They also shared a common grievance about punitive levels of taxation and tribute.[53] One Bato, leader of the Daesidiates nation, openly revolted.[54] The uprising quickly spread throughout the province. Some proceeded to invade the neighbouring province of Macedonia, which resulted in significant civilian casualties and extensive damage to property.[55] A third group had designs on Italy.[56] Paterculus puts the number in Illyricum who rebelled in excess of 800,000, of whom some 200,000 were trained infantry and 9,000 were cavalry, who, moreover, were 'under the orders of energetic and capable leaders'.[57] His estimates may be greatly overstated. However, if the Romans believed them to be true, they would have determined that they faced a very grave challenge.

A messenger brought Tiberius news that Illyricum was in open revolt.[58] For Tiberius, who had spent so many campaign seasons there, this must have been a deeply personal blow, not least because some of the rebels had their sights on Italy.[59] 'Fortune sometimes breaks off completely, sometimes merely delays, the execution of men's plans', in Paterculus' words.[60] Tiberius faced a terrible dilemma: whether to continue with the campaign now well under way in Bohaemium or to suspend hostilities and withdraw to deal with the rebellion in Illyricum. Far from Rome, he could not consult with Augustus, and time was of the essence. Tiberius' instinct was to protect Rome's hard-won gains in the Balkans, and so save the Italian homeland.[61] 'Glory was sacrificed to necessity,' writes the cavalry prefect-cum-historian of his commander's decision.[62] An emissary was dispatched to urgently seek a truce with Maroboduus. The king accepted, for it suited him to do so. A war with Rome was not in his interests; his geographical location afforded him profitable trade as a middleman between the peoples in Germania and the Baltic region to the north and the Romans to the south.[63] Under the terms of the treaty, Maroboduus agreed to be an ally (*socius*) of the Romans.[64] It meant the Marcomanni would have to stay out of conflicts with Rome initiated by German nations and come to the Romans' assistance by providing men and matériel when called upon.

Tiberius gave the general order to march south, sending Messallinus ahead of the main army (map 5). His small advance force tried to suppress the rebels, but in that initial encounter the men failed.[65] When Messallinus arrived in person, the two sides fought again. He found himself surrounded by the army of the enemy and 'supported by only *Legio* XX, and that at but half its normal strength, but he routed and put to flight more than 20,000', a victory which earned him

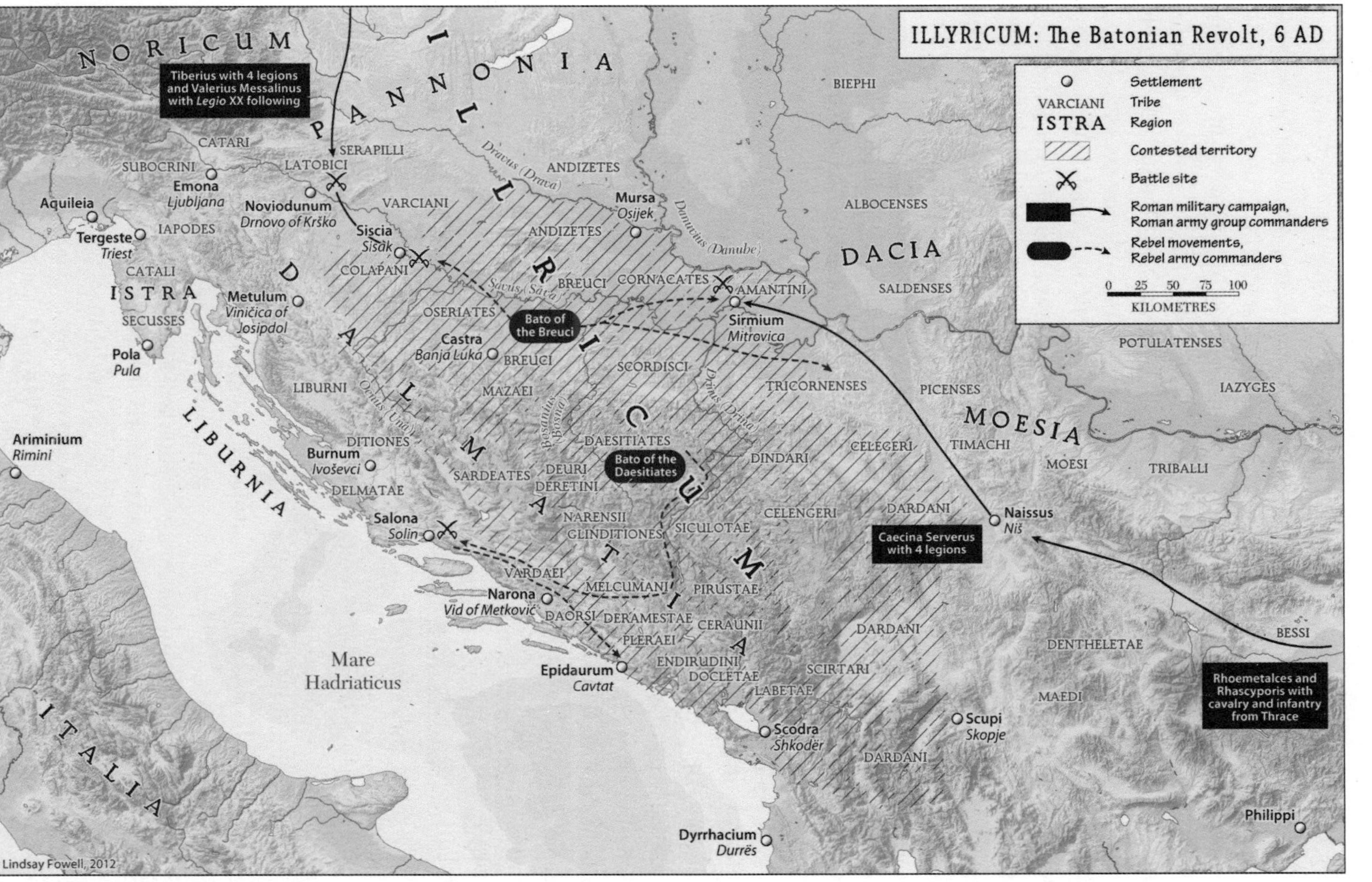

Map 5. Military Operations in Illyricum, 6 CE.

the honour of triumphal ornaments.[66] Bato of the Daesidiates seemed to have the stronger force in an open battle, but he was defeated in an ambush, where the rebels usually had the advantage.[67] Bato then marched on *Colonia* Martia Iulia Salonnae (Salona, modern Solin, Croatia), the administrative capital of the province.[68] The city was situated on the Dalmatian coast (plate 18) and surrounded by strong walls and towers. Without artillery and siege equipment, Bato could not assault it by force.[69] He was wounded when struck by a stone fired from a Roman *ballista* or a bullet (*glandes*) from a sling, but not fatally. Withdrawing his men, he dispatched some of his warband to ravage the countryside and its settlements. They reassembled at Apollonia further up the coast, where they scored a victory over the Romans.[70] Meanwhile, in the north of the province, two war leaders of the Breuci nation in Pannonia – Bato and Pinnes – moved on the city of Sirmium (Mitrovica).[71] Arriving from neighbouring Moesia, *legatus Augusti* A. Caecina Severus (b. *c.* 50 BCE) engaged them at the Drava River, and while taking casualties themselves, the Romans defeated the Breuci, who then retreated.[72] Nevertheless, their uprising emboldened others to join them. The leader of the Breuci asked to meet the leader of the Daesidiates, and they agreed to combine their forces against a common enemy and to encamp together in the Dinaric Alps on a mountain called Alma.[73]

Tiberius now arrived in Illyricum with the main expeditionary force. He and Messallinus moved into Siscia (Šišák), securing the route from Illyricum to Italy and using it as their base to direct the counterinsurgency.[74] Seeking a quick end to the uprising, Tiberius tried to tempt the rebels into a fight, but

> they would engage in no pitched battle with him, but kept moving from one place to another, causing great devastation; for, owing to their knowledge of the country and the lightness of their equipment, they could easily proceed wherever they pleased.[75]

Instead, they roamed the country to forage and pillage. During the winter months, they raided into Macedonia, wreaking havoc there too.[76] Jointly leading their armies, Roimetalkes (Rhoemetalces) I and his brother, Raiskuporis (Rhesuporis) II, succeeded in halting the rebels as they attempted to enter their kingdom of Thrace.

The realization that Italy was at risk of invasion sent Augustus into a panic.[77] By design, there were no longer any legions stationed in Italy, only the *Cohortes Praetoriae*.[78] At the start of 7 CE, the rebels held the land between the Danube, Sava and Drina rivers, right across the Dinaric Alps to the shore of the Adriatic Sea – everything except for a narrow arc of territory between the cities of Siscia and Salonnae (map 6). 'Men heard the *Princeps* say in the Senate, that, unless precautions were taken, the enemy might appear in sight of the city of Rome within ten days,' writes Paterculus.[79] The war was now perceived as 'the most

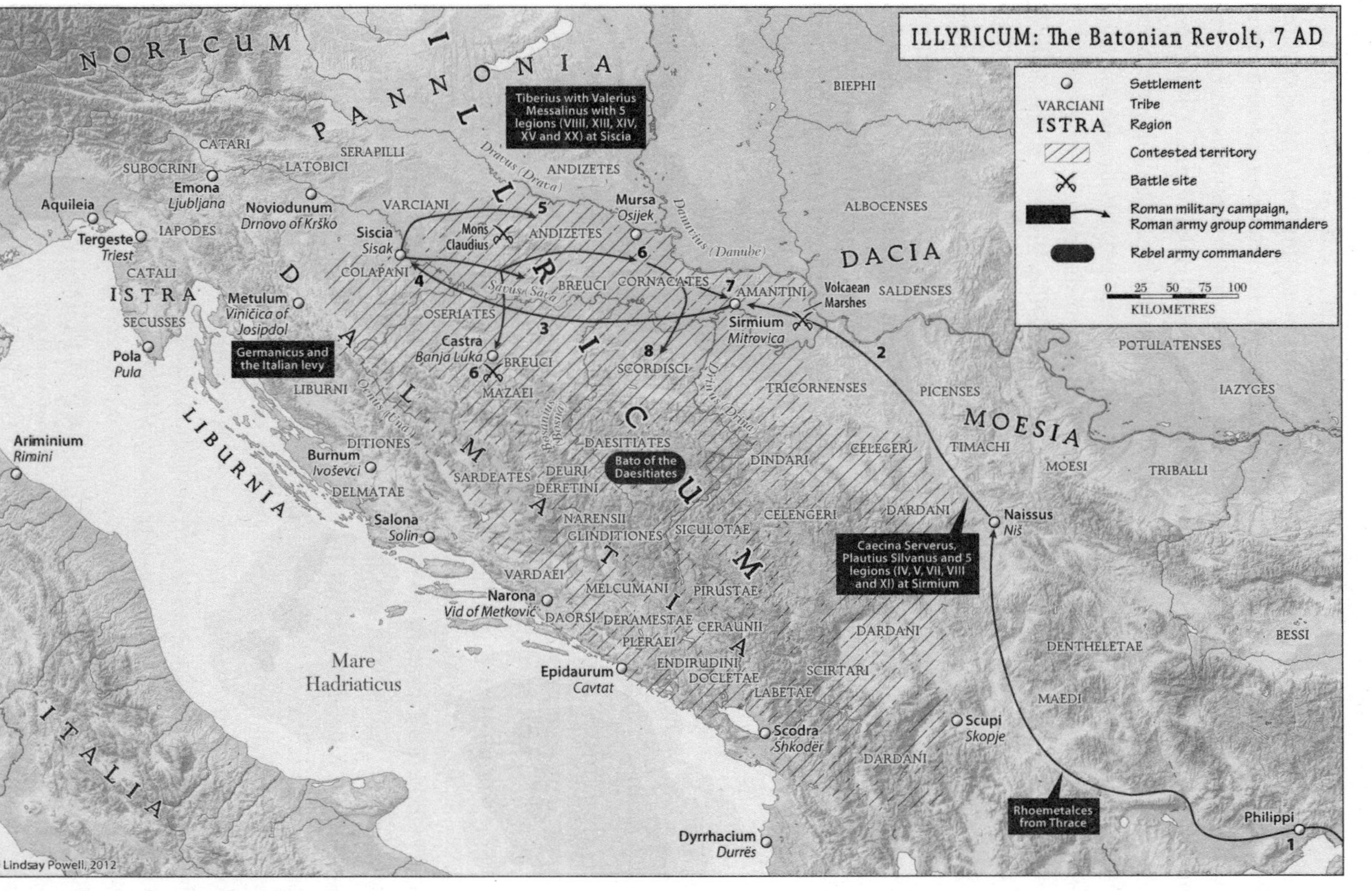


Map 6. Military Operations in Illyricum, 7 CE.

serious of all foreign wars since those with Carthage'.[80] The Conscript Fathers looked to their best commander to prevent this Doomsday scenario occurring. 'As a final measure of protection,' Paterculus writes, 'the *Res Publica* demanded from Augustus that Tiberius should be leader of the war.'[81] Augustus acceded to their wishes. Tiberius' primary objective was to wrench back control of Illyricum from the rebels as soon as practicable. His strategy was to co-ordinate his army group's manoeuvres with those of the governors of the neighbouring provinces, using the combined forces to encircle and crush the insurgents.[82]

Every man trained to use a sword counted in the defence of the *Res Publica*. Veterans of the legions (*evocati*) were recalled, and there was a general levy (*delictus ingenuorum*) conscripting able-bodied citizens to bolster the manpower available to prosecute the war.[83] In early 7 CE, Tiberius was joined by his adopted son, Germanicus, then a *quaestor*.[84] Now 21-years old, this was his first military deployment. He too was expected to play his part. Germanicus had been tasked by Augustus late in the previous year to form and train new units of the *Cohortes Voluntariorum* from scratch.[85] Each unit comprised some 480 citizens – both volunteer (*volones*) and conscripted – or freedmen; Augustus even bought slaves from their owners and manumitted them specifically to enlist in these cohorts.[86] That such units were only raised in times of emergency is an indication of just how gravely Augustus perceived the threat from the Balkans.[87]

The one man who would not contribute was young Agrippa Caesar, however. He was considered by his family to be a wastrel, spending his time fishing, on account of which he called himself by the nickname Neptunus.[88] Remarkably, unlike his brothers, Caius and Lucius, he had received neither honours nor assurances of advancement through the political system. He rowed with Augustus about being denied access to his father M. Agrippa's legacy and insulted Livia.[89] When his rage over the matter went too far, Augustus abdicated him, stripping him of his Julian name and banishing him to Planasia (modern Pionosa).[90] Through a decree of the Senate, his exile on the tiny island near Corsica was made permanent and enforced with a guard of soldiers.[91] There was now no possibility for him to ever succeed Augustus.[92]

In this the second year of the 'War of the Batos' (*Bellum Batonianum*), perhaps 80,000 men in total were deployed across Illyricum; it was a larger gathering of troops than the Cantabrian and Asturian War of 26 BCE, in which Tiberius had participated as an inexperienced 16-year-old military tribune.[93] According to Paterculus,

> there were now gathered together in one camp 10 legions, more than 70 *cohortes*, 14 *alae* of cavalry and more than 10,000 veterans, and in addition a large number of volunteers and the numerous cavalry of the king.[94]

Tiberius let the men remain for a few days to recover from their long marches; it was good for morale. Assembled in one place, the troops, seeing their great numbers and sensing the prospect of victory, were highly motivated.[95] However, considering it was too large a group to manage effectively for longer, not least logistically, he gave the commanders their new orders. Some units would be returning to their own provinces to ensure internal security, escorted part way by men of his own army to ensure their protection from rebel attacks.[96] Those remaining in Illyricum marched to their zones of operation. Tiberius returned with his troops to Siscia (plate 19).

Even with the advantage of this great professional army, the Romans struggled to take ground from the enemy. Based in the north of the province, Tiberius and Messallinus were only able to skirmish with the rebels. When they formed their men up in battle lines before the Dalmatian stronghold on *Mons* Claudius, the enemy stayed behind their ramparts and fended off the Roman attacks.[97] Tiberius besieged Seretium, but could not take it.[98] At one low point, Tiberius found himself trapped with his army in a dangerous place; Bato let the Romans escape. Rather than allowing his men to be idle, Tiberius had them use their time to construct a great canal between the Kulpa (Kolops) River, which flowed past the walls of Siscia, and the Sava, providing both a means to deliver supplies and a protective moat around the city.[100] In the south-east, Caecina Severus returned from Moesia to the war theatre, bringing with him Plautius Silvanus (b. *c.* 45 BCE) and five legions, joined by Roimetalkes and his Thracian cavalry and other allies. They were attacked with nearly disastrous consequences.[101] The senior officers had failed to debrief the scouts (*exploratores*) sent ahead to gather field intelligence, and were completely unaware of the enemy waiting for them. The rebels sprang their ambush, routing the Thracian riders. Seeing this, the infantry cohorts panicked and turned, causing the legions to waver momentarily. Several military tribunes were killed in the confusion, along with a *praefectus castrorum*, many *praefecti equitum* and a few centurions – including some ranked *primus pilus*. It was the unbending discipline and dogged determination of the common legionaries (*milites gregarii*), men like L. Caesius Bassus, that 'wrested a victory from a desperate plight' and saved the day for the Romans.[102] Later in the same season, Caecina was attacked at his camp in the Volcaean Marshes.[103] Again, the regular Roman soldiers stood their ground, fought gallantly and defeated the rebels. Germanicus' novice *Cohortes Voluntariorum* also performed well in their first engagements against the Mazaei in Dalmatia (Banja Luka in Bosnia-Herzegovina), which reflected well on him.[104]

Reviewing his strategy, Tiberius decided to break the legions into smaller detachments (*vexillationes*) of a few cohorts each, marching under their own *vexillum* standards so that they could cover more territory.[105] 'Whatever is done well enough is done quickly enough' was a maxim favoured by Augustus.[106] Yet, sitting in Rome, Augustus was impatient for news from his commander in the field. He is reported to have been disappointed by the results achieved thus far. According to Dio:

> When Augustus learned of these things, he began to be suspicious of Tiberius, who, as he thought, might speedily have overcome [the rebels], but was delaying purposely, in order that he might be under arms as long as possible, with the war as his excuse.[107]

The insinuation is more likely Dio's than that of Augustus, who knew well the difficulties of the terrain and people that Tiberius faced. He had personally led campaigns in the region with M. Agrippa – besieging Siscia, which he occupied in the war of 36–35 BCE – and sustained injuries himself.[108] Indeed, in several letters that probably date to this time, Augustus alluded to Tiberius as 'the most able expert in military matters and the sole defence of the Roman People'.[109] Suetonius records extracts from some of his personal correspondence:

> Farewell, most charming Tiberius, and success go with you, *as you war for me and for the Muses*. Most charming and valiant of men and most *legitimate* of leaders, or may I never know happiness, farewell.[110]
>
> I have only praise for the conduct of your summer campaigns, dear Tiberius, and I am sure that no one could have acted with better judgment than you did amid so many difficulties and such apathy of your army. All who were with you agree that the well-known line could be applied to you:
>
> *One man alone by his foresight has saved our dear country from ruin.*[111]
>
> If anything comes up that calls for careful thought, or if I am vexed at anything, I long mightily – so help me Heaven – for my dear Tiberius, and the lines of Homer come to my mind:
>
> *Let him but follow and we too, though flames round about us be raging,*
> *Both may return to our homes, since great are his wisdom and knowledge.*[112]

When Tiberius wrote that he was fatigued and had fallen sick, Augustus was deeply concerned:

> When I hear and read that you are worn out by constant hardships, may the Gods confound me if my own body does not wince in sympathy; and I beseech you to spare yourself, that the news of your illness may not kill me and your mother, and endanger the Roman People in the person of their future ruler.[113]
>
> It matters not whether I am well or not, if *you* are not well.[114]
>
> I pray the Gods to preserve you to us and to grant you good health now and forever, if they do not utterly hate the Roman People.[115]

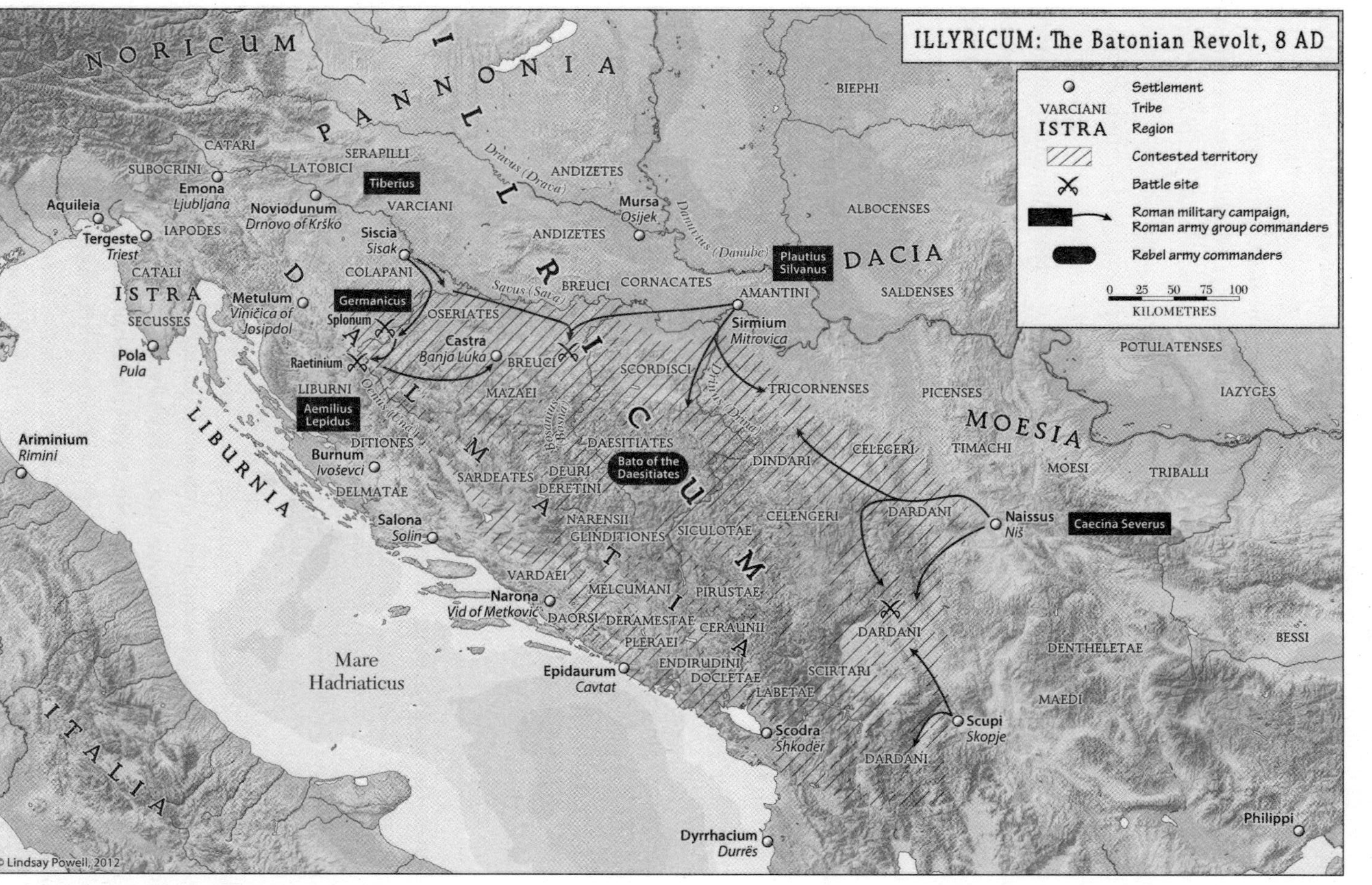


Map 7. Military Operations in Illyricum, 8 CE.

By the end of the year, it is recorded that Tiberius had driven back the Delmatae and Sarmatae.[116]

Another winter came and went, and the counterinsurgency dragged on into 8 CE (map 7). To receive reports from the warzone quicker, Augustus moved from Rome to Ariminum (Rimini) with his escort of *Praetoriani*.[117] This third season went badly for the rebels. Having spent the previous summer and autumn in combat, the crops they had grown had not been harvested and stored, and the rebel army of Illyricum now faced famine.[118] Disease then spread among the combatants. Many wanted to negotiate terms with the Romans, but they were outnumbered by others who did not – having mutinied from the army, they faced severe punishments if captured – so the resistance continued. A certain Scenobardus, pretending that he was going to switch sides, expressed this real fear of retribution to M'. Ennius, the commander of the garrison in Siscia.[119]

In the version of the events of 8 CE recorded by Dio, Bato had since betrayed Pinnes and secured the exclusive right to rule over the Breuci. It was a shortlived reign, however; he was captured in a skirmish with the other Bato and summarily executed by him in the presence of the army when he learned that the man, suspicious of his own commanders, had been demanding hostages from each garrison.[120] Bato of the Daesidiates was now in charge of the disunited army of discontented rebels. Many of the men of his own nation then rose in revolt.[121] Exploiting the divisions among the insurgents, Silvanus led an offensive against them. He succeeded in defeating the Breuci, finally getting the surrender of the other tribes in Pannonia without a fight.[122] In Paterculus' version, it was in the summer that

> those fierce warriors, many thousand in number, who had but a short time before threatened Italia with slavery, now brought the arms they had used in rebellion and laid them down, at a river called the Bathinus, prostrating themselves one and all before the knees of the commander; and how of their two supreme commanders, Bato and Pinnes, the one was made a prisoner and the other gave himself up.[123]

There were some holdouts in Pannonia, but to all intents and purposes the fire of revolt had been extinguished. Bato retreated to the south-west of the country to the homeland of his Daesidiates. From there he led a guerrilla war, striking out at the Romans as opportunities arose.[124] In the autumn of 8 CE, Tiberius led his soldiers back to Siscia to recuperate and repair their equipment. They remained there over the winter.

In the spring of 9 CE, Tiberius and Germanicus left for Rome to meet Augustus. When Tiberius arrived in the city, 'clad in the purple-bordered *toga* and crowned with laurel', he received a hero's welcome.[125] Augustus came out to greet him in person in the *Suburra* located in the notoriously stinking and noisy valley of the

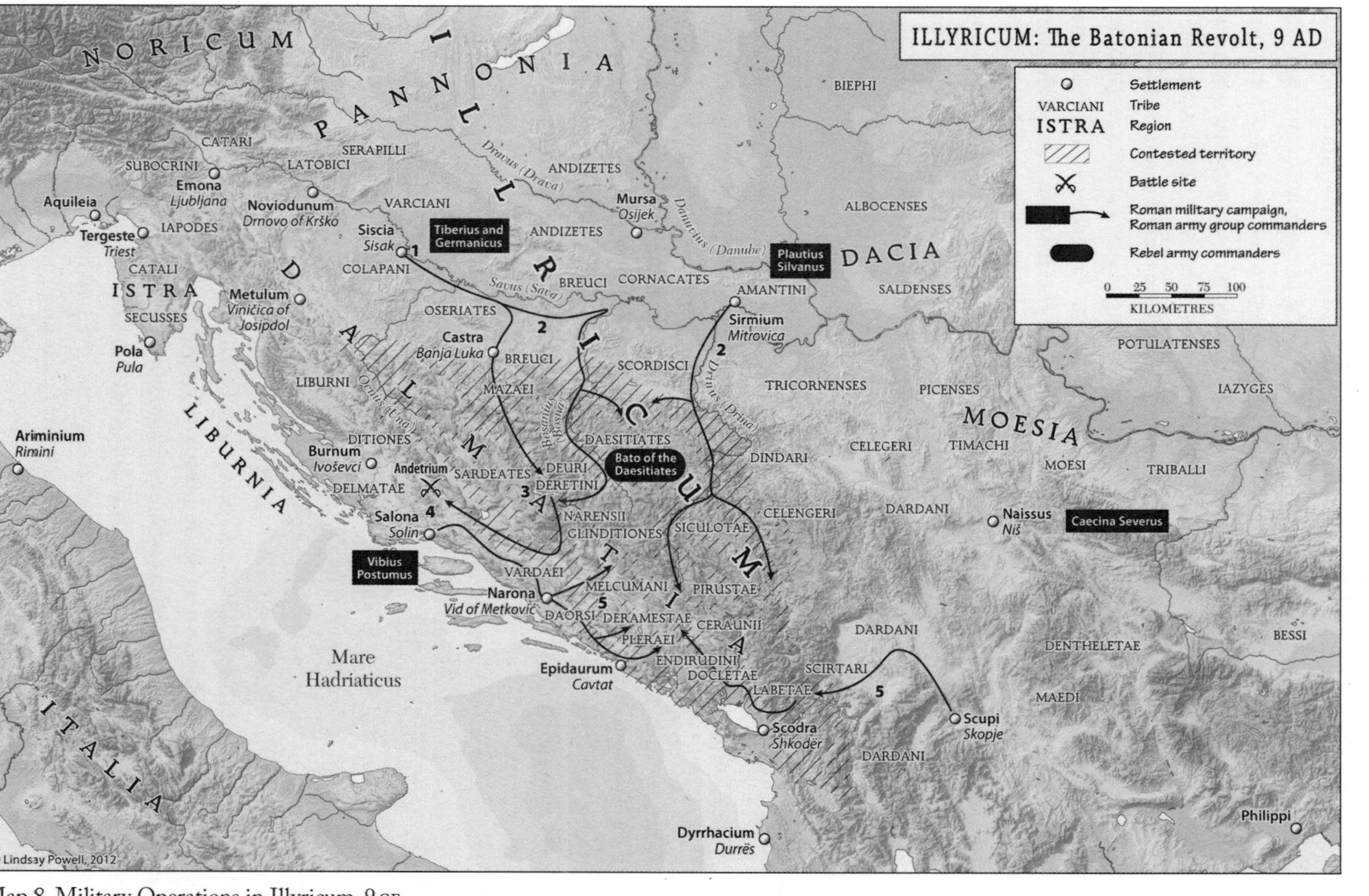


Map 8. Military Operations in Illyricum, 9 CE.

Viminalis and Esquilinus hills – its eclectic mix of business owners, labourers and merchants briefly stopping their work to watch.[126] The *princeps* accompanied him to the *Saepta*, recently built by the late M. Agrippa in the *Campus Martius*. From a tribunal erected in the great open colonnaded square with its painted walls and marble tablets, Tiberius took a curule chair. He sat beside Augustus between the two consuls, Q. Sulpicius Camerinus and C. Poppaeus Sabinus, and from there greeted the crowd of people.[127] After performing all the solemn ceremonies required for the return of a victorious commander (*adventus*), Tiberius was escorted around the temples to pay his respects and the new consuls of the year opened the triumphal games.[128]

The fourth year of the war in Illyricum would yet prove to be one of the most difficult of the entire counterinsurgency (map 8). Before leaving for Rome, Tiberius had appointed M. Aemilius Lepidus (II) – a son of *triumvir* M. Aemilius Lepidus (I) – to direct the campaign. Highly regarded by Paterculus, Tiberius saw in him a courageous, no-nonsense and loyal deputy.[129] Additionally, having shown talent for command and the responsibilities that came with it, Tiberius promoted Germanicus to oversee his army group of legions and auxiliaries at Siscia. Remaining himself in Rome a while longer, Tiberius ordered Germanicus back to Illyricum ahead of him.[130] Once in theatre, Germanicus launched a new offensive in what is now Bosnia and the Dinaric Alps. The terrain was a challenge. Roman combat doctrine – where the highly trained legionary could fight the enemy in formation alongside his fellow soldiers, throwing his *pilum* before moving in for close-quarters stabbing and thrusting with the double-edged *gladius* – was most effective in set-piece battles on the open plain. Yet even in valleys and mountain passes, Romans could still win, as his father, Nero Drusus, and then uncle, Tiberius, had demonstrated in the Alpine War of 15 BCE. In that conflict, they had also besieged and captured hilltop *oppida*. In the Dalmatian War (*Bellum Delmaticum*), Germanicus captured the fortified stronghold at Splonum, in part through the courage and initiative of a Germanic auxiliary cavalryman named Pusio.[131] Germanicus' assault on Raetinum, however, was made difficult without the necessary siege equipment, particularly heavy stone-throwing artillery (*ballistae*, *onagri*) used to demolish walls and battering rams (*aries*) to break down gates. An error of judgement was made when many of the Roman troops, ordered to advance, eagerly rushed in through the gates and found themselves surrounded by buildings set on fire by the rebels, resulting in heavy casualties and fatalities from severe burns.[132] Elsewhere, Seretium, attacked two years before by Tiberius, was finally stormed and razed to the ground, and other rebel installations were seized.[133]

Returning to Illyricum on Augustus' orders, Tiberius, as war leader (*dux*), went in pursuit of Bato.[134] He knew that while Bato was free, there would be no prospect of an end to the conflict. Tiberius divided the expeditionary army into three groups, one commanded by himself and Germanicus, one by Silvanus and one by Lepidus (II). Silvanus and Lepidus scored early victories. Silvanus moved south. Simultaneously striking south-east, Lepidus employed a policy of *vastatio*, inflicting great loss on those who barred his way by devastating fields, burning houses and slaying the inhabitants.[135] Meanwhile, Tiberius and Germanicus explored the country looking for the leader of the Daesidiates.[136] They hunted for him among the Perustae, Daesiadates and Delmatae, 'who were almost unconquerable on account of the position of their strongholds in the mountains, their warlike temper, their wonderful knowledge of fighting, and, above all, the narrow passes in which they lived'.[137]

At last, the Romans tracked Bato down to Andetrium near Salonnae, where he staged what would be his last stand.[138] Tiberius and his men prepared for a prolonged siege, a form of warfare that usually suited Roman strategy. Sieges employed their talent for military engineering in constructing siegeworks to seal off the defenders, and exploited the element of time, which Tiberius must have considered to be on his side since he could be provisioned with new supplies and relieved with new troops. However, he underestimated the challenge facing him. Andetrium was a well-fortified stronghold built upon a rocky hill encircled by deep ravines, through which torrents poured when it rained, presenting a besieging army with difficult access to its walls and gateways.[139] Bato had also prepared well in advance: the rebels had stockpiled food and were still able to add to their supplies by carrying them over the mountain passes which they still controlled. Indeed, they were able to harry the Roman logistics chain, with the result that 'Tiberius, though supposed to be besieging them, was himself placed in the position of a besieged force'.[140] Uncharacteristically, Tiberius was stuck.[141] With the ringleader of the revolt safely in the well-defended fort, Tiberius could neither advance nor retreat.

Making no obvious progress, yet ever exposed to danger, the morale of the Roman soldiers began to seep away. Some of the men became restless. At one point, a rowdy contingent created such a ruckus that the rebels encamped below Andetrium thought the Romans were attacking and ran for their lives.[142] Angered by his men's indiscipline, but delighted by the enemy's retreat, Tiberius called his troops together in a *contio*. He spoke to them, selectively giving out rebukes and admonitions, but he told them that they would remain until the rebels surrendered.[143] The prospect that Bato could win a victory was increasingly remote. Realizing his fate was sealed, he sent a herald to the Roman lines to ask Tiberius for a truce. The other men in Andetrium, however, would not follow him and remained behind its stout stonewalls.

This was Tiberius' opportunity. Determining that he could defeat the rebel holdouts without serious losses on his side, he gave the order for his men to advance against the stronghold.[144] In his account of the siege, Dio describes how

Tiberius had a platform erected on the hillside, from where he could view the unfolding events; he knew not only that his men would fight harder because their commander watched, but he could pick the right moment to send in the relief troops.[145] In a detail recorded by Dio, Tiberius held several units in reserve in a dense defensive square (*acies quadratum*) formation. When the order to advance came, some of his units could move faster over the smoother terrain while others had to navigate gullies, which slowed them down. The Delmatae warriors rushed out of the compound, assembling outside the walls on a steep ledge. From their high vantage point, they unleashed a barrage of missiles: some threw rocks, spears or slingshot; some rolled wheels or whole waggons loaded with rocks; others pushed circular chests or barrels packed full of stones down the hill.[146] Moving up the steep slope, the Romans took the full force of the incoming munitions, their lines breaking in places as the men moved aside to let the objects pass through or as men fell because of injury.[147]

Tiberius was acutely aware of his responsibility when he sent his men into harm's way, making their welfare his top priority.[148] Paterculus praised his commander:

> There was a horsed vehicle ready for those who needed it, his own litter was at the disposal of all, and I, among others, have enjoyed its use. Now his medic, now his kitchen, and now his bathing equipment, brought for this one purpose for himself alone, ministered to the comfort of all who were sick. All they lacked was their home and domestics [slaves], but nothing else that friends at home could furnish or desire for them.[149]

On the steep mountainside, the opponents edged closer together. In the ensuing mêlée, men shouted encouragement to each other, urging themselves to greater feats, others screaming as they gave or took blows.[150] Gradually, the Romans in the front ranks, relieved by those behind, were supplemented by men from the reserves.[151] To stop the Delmatae from fleeing, Tiberius sent a detachment to one side of the battlefield where escape was still possible, preventing them from retreating into their stronghold. The enemy who had managed to flee cast off their body armour and dropped their shields to move faster.[152] The Romans pursued them relentlessly and found them hiding in the forests around Andetrium, where they were slaughtered 'like so many wild animals'.[153] With all hope lost, only then did the men in the stronghold surrender. The mopping up operations completed, Tiberius turned to deal with the prisoners of war.

Separately, Germanicus was away fighting the remaining pockets of resistance at Arduba. Even though his army was larger than the defenders', he still struggled to secure the target.[154] The women in the stronghold urged their men to continue with the war, some even killing their own children in protest, but many still deserted. Arduba finally fell.[155] The forts and towns nearby surrendered soon after. Leaving Vibius Postumius as 'Overseer of the Delmatae' (*Praepositus Delmatiae*) with L. Apronius, Germanicus rejoined Tiberius.[156]

Tiberius was now ready for Bato to lay down his arms in a formal act of submission. Establishing the *Pax Augusta* demanded it – it was an act depicted on coins, cups and reliefs.[157] The rebel leader took the precaution of sending his son, Sceuas, to negotiate the terms of his capitulation. He offered to surrender himself and his followers if Tiberius would pardon them. The Roman commander accepted.[158] With that assurance, Bato arrived at the Roman camp by night. The following day, he was presented to Tiberius, who was seated upon a tribunal. The rebel war leader spoke the most important words of his life, as reported by Dio:

> He [Bato] asked nothing for himself, even holding his head forward to await the stroke, but on behalf of the others he made a long defence. Finally, upon being asked by Tiberius why his people had taken it into their heads to revolt and to [wage] war against the Romans so long, he replied: 'You Romans are to blame for this; for you send as guardians of your flocks, not dogs or shepherds, but wolves!'[159]

Romans recognized courage (*virtus*) in an honourable enemy. Tiberius, remembering that Bato had been generous to him when he could have easily dealt him a decisive blow during the war, showed Bato clemency (*clementia*), staying his execution and presenting him with rich gifts in gratitude. He was freed and permitted to retire peacefully to Ravenna.[160] Germanicus declared victory was theirs, and it was likely at this heady moment that the troops acclaimed Tiberius and Germanicus each as *Imperator* (Tiberius for a fifth and Germanicus a first time), adding a nineteenth to Augustus' running total.[161]

Paterculus asserts that the enemy were 'then at last pacified, not now under the mere generalship, but by the armed prowess of [Tiberius] Caesar himself, and then only when they were almost entirely exterminated'.[162] Augustus claimed the victory, later including it amongst his noteworthy achievements.[163] Suetonius observes that the war had tied up 'fifteen legions and a corresponding force of auxiliaries' – over half of the empire's professional military manpower – for three years.[164] Dio remarks that the re-subjugation of Illyricum came at great cost in blood and treasure, 'for ever so many legions were maintained for this campaign and but very little booty was taken'.[165] Casualty figures for the war are not recorded in any of the sources, but they were likely to have numbered in the tens of thousands.

For the living, there were big rewards. Augustus consented to grant Tiberius a full triumph, and to Germanicus, while to Vibius Postumus, Apronius and the other senior commanders he awarded the *ornamenta triumphalia*; he also agreed that two victory arches be erected in Pannonian Illyricum.[166] Commemorating this celebration may have been the reason the so-called *Gemma Augustea* was created. This magnificent cameo cut from double-layered Arabian onyx by Dioskourides (plate 28) depicts Augustus receiving Tiberius as he steps down from his triumphal chariot as Germanicus stands watching, while below is a scene of a *tropaeum* being erected as war captives observe dejectedly. There were calls for Tiberius to be given the honorary surname (*agnomen*) of *Pannonicus* ('The Pannonian'), *Invictus* ('Invincible') or *Pius* ('Dutiful'). Augustus, however, vetoed them all, 'reiterating the promise that Tiberius would be satisfied with one which he would receive at his father's death'.[167] In addition, Germanicus was elevated to the rank of *praetor*, being given the privilege of voting immediately after the ex-consuls and of holding the consulship earlier than custom allowed. Included in the honours, Tiberius' natural son, Drusus, was also granted the privilege of attending the meetings of the Senate before officially becoming a member of it, and of voting ahead of the ex-praetors as soon as he became *quaestor*.[168]

The Romans seemed finally to have ended conflicts within their sprawling dominions (map 9), but the celebrations would have to wait, however. Just five days after the end of operations in Illyricum, a report was delivered to Augustus in Rome about a revolt in Germania.[169] Initial details were probably sketchy, and likely to have come from L. Asprenas, the deputy serving under the *legatus Augusti Propraetore* in Germania.[170] His uncle, P. Quinctilius Varus, had completed successful governorships in Africa and Syria and been handpicked by Augustus in 6 CE to pacify the territory across the Rhine.[171] Varus had interpreted his mission as one of Romanizing its peoples by application of the law rather than the sword. With that mindset, 'he entered the heart of Germania as though he were going among a people enjoying the blessings of peace, and sitting on his tribunal he wasted the time of a summer campaign in holding court and observing the proper details of legal procedure'.[172] Varus had seriously underestimated his adversaries. Paterculus saw him as 'somewhat slow in mind as he was in body, and more accustomed to the leisure of the camp than to actual service in war'.[173] Those among the natives he had considered trusted allies had taken advantage of his 'mild character and quiet disposition'.[174] He paid for this misjudgement with his life.[175] Varus, along with three legions – XVII, XIIX and XIX – had been slaughtered by Germanic warriors; all eagles were lost and perhaps 14,000 souls.[176] It was deeply embarrassing for Augustus.[177] From the high of a victory over one set of rebels, he was suddenly plunged to a new low by a defeat from another. He grieved for the loss of his soldiers' lives.[178] Suetonius writes:

> In fact, they say that he was so greatly affected that for several months in succession he cut neither his beard nor his hair, and sometimes he would dash his head against a door, crying: 'Quintilius Varus, give me back my legions!' And he observed the day of the disaster each year as one of sorrow and mourning.[179]

The incident soon acquired the moniker *Clades Variana* ('Varian Disaster').[180]

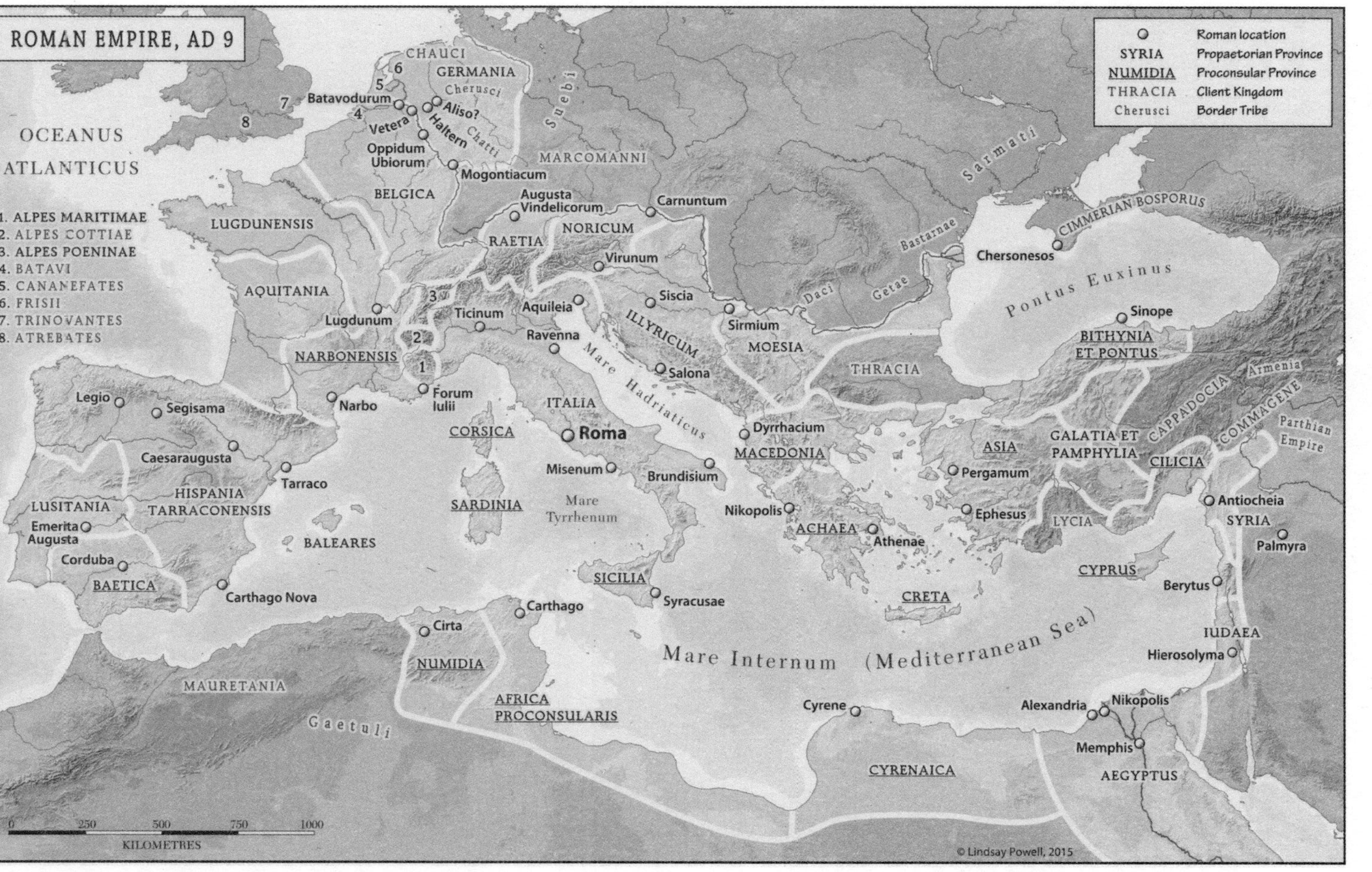


Map 9. The Roman Empire, 9 CE.

Similar reports reached Tiberius at around the same time. He needed to move fast to contain the situation. Asprenas had, in the meantime, secured the bridge over the Rhine and was providing what assistance he could to troops fleeing from the rebels; he was ready with his two legions to defend against incursions and had contacted the Germanic allies to ensure their loyalty.[181] From Illyricum, Tiberius sent Germanicus ahead to take charge while he raced to Rome.[182] Tactfully, with the city in shock over the disaster in Germania, Tiberius himself postponed his triumph – though, if Suetonius' account is to be believed, he entered Rome in the garb of a victorious commander.[183] Augustus was worried for the security of the provinces and he acutely feared that the enemy would march against Italy and Rome itself – just as he had done in 6 CE.[184] Compared to that fateful year, Rome's capacity to respond in 9 CE was now much reduced, not only from the destruction of three legions and their support troops, but also the number of men available for a new *dilectus*.[185] As Germanicus had done years earlier, Tiberius now raised as many *Cohortes Voluntariorum* from scratch as he could. In these desperate times,

> when no men of military age showed a willingness to be enrolled, he made them draw lots, depriving of his property and disfranchising every fifth man of those still under 35 and every tenth man among those who had passed that age. Finally, as a great many paid no heed to him even then, he put some to death. He chose by lot as many as he could of those who had already completed their term of service and of the freedmen.[186]

A story is reported of Augustus selling a Roman *eques* and his property at public auction, because he had cut off the thumbs of his two young sons to render them unfit for military service; without a thumb, they could not hold a sword.[187] The forced recruitment led many of the press-ganged individuals to be deeply resentful. As a precaution, Tiberius relocated the men of Augustus' own bodyguard (the *Germani Corporis Custodes*), comprising Gauls and Germans, and any of those nations serving in the Praetorian Cohorts whom he feared might foment rebellion, to certain unnamed islands, ordering those who were unarmed to leave the city.[188] Native Romans and Italians would now protect the person of the *princeps*.

Later that autumn, a box was delivered to Augustus that had been sent by Maroboduus. It contained the severed head of Varus.[189] Evading capture, the Roman commander had committed suicide and his adjutants had attempted to burn his body. Nevertheless, the Germans decapitated his charred corpse. Arminius had sent the head to the king to convince him to join his coalition against Rome. Horrifying as the object was, it proved that the king of the Marcomanni had kept his word as Roman ally. It also allowed the members of *gens Quinctilia* to bury their relative with some dignity and, moreover, Varus was not condemned to the dismal fate of *damnatio memoriae*.[190]

In the middle of the ensuing winter, there was one occasion for much-needed celebration in the gloomy city. The Temple of August Concordia (*Aedes Concordiae Augustae*) that Tiberius had vowed to rebuild in 7 CE was now finished, and he was in Rome on 16 January 10 CE to consecrate it.[191] The temple was originally vowed by Camillus during patrician–plebeian struggles in 367 BCE. If Concordia stood for the harmony between the social orders, there was no better time than this for national unity. Like the Temple of Castor, Tiberius dedicated it in his and his dead brother's name.[192] The new hexastyle building was deemed so impressive that it was featured on a *sestertius* (plate 23) struck around the same time.[193] It shows that statues stood upon the walls flanking the steps rising up the podium, and more statues and decorations adorned the roofline. Its cornices were exquisitely detailed, suggesting that Tiberius spared no expense on the project.[194] The money to pay for it came from war spoils from Germania and Illyricum.[195] The plan of Tiberius' temple greatly enlarged the footprint of the earlier building. The front porch now featured a wide transverse cell at the rear.[196] The interior space was used as a gallery to display paintings and statuary acquired by Tiberius himself, perhaps while on Rhodes. Some items were later catalogued by Pliny the Elder in his encyclopaedic *Natural History*, revealing that Tiberius had a collector's eye for famous masterpieces.[197] They were now available for the public to enjoy.

Once the roads cleared of ice and snow, Tiberius marched his new *Cohortes Voluntariorum* from Italy to Germania. He was never one for rash moves. Rather than launch a hasty campaign to punish the Germanic rebels, he consulted his commanders in council to critically assess intelligence about the situation across the Rhine.[198] He would have learned about the enemy's leader, Arminius, son of Segimerus of the Cherusci.[199] Tiberius might have known – or at least known of – him. He was a former hostage taken in 7 BCE, then raised in Rome as an *eques* who went on to lead an auxiliary unit, possibly seeing service in Illyricum.[200] Perhaps disillusioned by what he saw of the reality of Roman rule over newly conquered peoples, he formed a coalition of the Cherusci, Angrivarii, Bructeri and Marsi to win back their lands. He had been clever. Gaining Varus' complete trust and confidence, he had lured the Roman commander and his troops into a trap deep in the heart of what he considered a province undergoing pacification. He sprang it when the Roman Army returned from summer deployment to its winter camps. The coalition forced them to march through a place called *Saltus Teutoburgiensis* (the 'Pass' or 'Ravine' of Teutoburg) and ambushed them over several days.[201] As well as three legions, six *cohortes* of auxiliary infantry and several *alae* of cavalry were massacred.[202]

There *were* survivors; some escaped back to the Rhine, others were still being held as hostages by the Germans who offered them to their relatives for ransom, and a few were even liberated from their slavery decades later.[203] The three lost legions, however, would never be reconstituted; whether this was decided by Augustus or Tiberius is not clear. Tiberius' first priority was to ensure the Rhine was adequately guarded, which meant redeploying the remaining legions, some from Hispania Tarraconensis.[204] The land in Belgica adjacent to the left bank of the Rhine down to the North Sea was reconstituted as two smaller jurisdictions, reducing the Gallic province in size.[205] Germania Superior enclosed the territory from the source of the river in the Alps, south to the territories of the Helvetii and Rauraci and west to Confluentes (modern Koblenz), with Mogontiacum appointed as its administrative centre. Four legions were stationed in this new Upper Germania: *Legiones* XIV *Gemina* and XVI *Gallica* now shared the base at Mogontiacum, *Legio* II *Augusta* occupied Argentorate (Strasbourg) and the XIII *Gemina* was at Vindonissa (Windisch). Neighbouring Germania Inferior defined the lower section of river, with *Ara* Ubiorum as its principal city. Four legions were stationed in this new Lower Germania: *Legio* V *Alaudae* billeted with XXI *Rapax* at the base located outside the civilian settlement at *Ara* Ubiorum, along with the conscripted men of the *Cohortes Voluntariarum*; I *Germanica* and XX *Valeria Victrix* were co-located at Vetera with marines of the *Classis Germanica*.[206]

Tiberius' second priority was to firmly establish Rome's intention of retaking Germania north of the Rhine. Doing so would be a major undertaking, but he was particularly well briefed for the task. Suetonius notes that, in contrast to Varus' 'rashness and lack of care', Tiberius 'observed more scrupulous care than usual'.[207] Tiberius knew from first-hand experience the terrain and trouble that he and his army would face. On the forthcoming expedition, his men would travel light to move fast:

> When on the point of crossing the Rhenus, he reduced all the baggage to a prescribed limit, and would not start without standing on the bank and inspecting the loads of the waggons, to make sure that nothing was taken except what was allowed or necessary.[208]

Moving into hostile country meant that the men would need to be alert at all times. He instituted procedures to ensure that his instructions were understood and strictly followed:

> Once on the other side, he adopted the following manner of life: he took his meals sitting on the bare turf, often passed the night without a tent, and gave all his orders for the following day, as well as notice of any sudden emergency, in writing; adding the injunction that if anyone was in doubt about any matter, he was to consult him personally at any hour whatsoever, even of the night.[209]

He would not tolerate sloppiness among his men, regardless of rank:

> He required the strictest discipline, reviving bygone methods of punishment and ignominy, and even degrading the *legatus legionis* for sending a few soldiers across the river to accompany one of his freedmen on a hunting expedition.[210]

When he was satisfied that the preparations were finally complete, Tiberius launched the offensive. It is not clear if the campaign lasted two years (starting in 10 CE), or if it was of only a single year's duration (occurring in 11 CE).[211] Assuming that there were two offensives, as he had done before, Tiberius' army moved through Germania over land and along its rivers.[212] The sources do not disclose the exact routes taken and the enemies encountered, but *Legiones* I *Germanica* and XX *Valeria Victrix* are known to have participated.[213] Despite all of the precautions in place, danger lurked – even for Tiberius, who was attended by guards of the Praetorian Cohorts.[214] It was a necessary precaution. 'He narrowly escaped assassination,' writes Suetonius, 'by one of the Bructeri, who got access to him among his attendants, but was detected through his nervousness; whereupon a confession of his intended crime was wrung from him by torture.'[215] In the Caesia *Silva* ('Caesian Forest'), located somewhere between the *Lacus* Flevo (IJsselmeer) and the Lippe River, he ordered a ditch and rampart constructed, forming a *limes* to demarcate German from Roman territory; Tacitus does not disclose if a unit was left to man it.[216] When Tiberius was sure that the mission objectives had been accomplished, he withdrew to the Rhine. On his return to Italy, using restraint rather than punishment, he settled heated disputes which had broken out among the Viennenses in Gallia Narbonensis.[217]

In the spring of 11 CE, Tiberius returned with Germanicus (now imbued with *imperium proconsulare* if Dio is correct) to lead joint operations across the Rhine.[218] The sources have little to say about the new offensive. Dio writes only that they 'overran portions of it [Germania]', adding:

> They did not win any battle, however, since no one came to close quarters with them, nor did they reduce any tribe; for in their fear of falling victims to a fresh disaster they did not advance very far beyond the Rhenus.[219]

On 23 September, the 74th birthday of Caesar Augustus was celebrated with a horserace held on German soil under the direction of the legionary centurions. The troops acclaimed Augustus *imperator* for the twentieth time and Tiberius for his sixth.[220] Then they all returned to the comforts of their winter camps. This was the last time that Tiberius would take the field in person.

At the start of the following year, 12 CE, Germanicus began his term as consul.[221] Augustus was pleased by his grandson's progress. He wrote a letter commending Germanicus to the Senate and the latter to Tiberius. Unable to make himself heard in the Senate House, Augustus passed the letter to Germanicus to read aloud.[222] Now frail, he asked senators not to meet him at his home and informed them not to be offended if he failed to attend public banquets – an indication of the constant attention he still received in the *Curia* and *Forum*.[223] Nevertheless, he maintained his heavy workload. One significant law he passed related to exiles. While there were men who had committed crimes for which the punishment was to be banished from Rome, they still expected the comforts of home. The strictures were extensive:

> As there were many exiles who were either living outside of the districts to which they had been banished or living too luxuriously in the proper places, he ordered that no one who had been debarred from fire and water should live either on the mainland or on any of the islands within 50 miles of it, except Cos, Rhodes, Samos, and Lesbos; for he made an exception in the case of these alone for some reason or other. Besides this, he enjoined upon the exiles that they should not cross the sea to any other point, and should not possess more than one ship of burden having a capacity of 1,000 *amphorae* and two ships driven by oars; that they should not employ more than twenty slaves or freedmen, and should not possess property to the value of more than 125,000 [*drachamai*]; and he threatened to punish not only the exiles themselves but all others as well who should in any way assist them in violating these commands.[224]

The exclusions were significant: Tiberius had lived on Rhodes and M. Agrippa on Lesbos as 'voluntary exiles'. His daughter, Iulia, would have been included had she still been living on Pandataria. Her son, Agrippa Caesar, living on Planasia, and P. Ovidius Naso (Ovid), at Tomis in Thrace on the Black Sea – who was exiled by personal order of Augustus in 8 CE – *were* covered by the regulation.[225]

There were two high points of the year for Tiberius. The first was his new grandson, born to Germanicus and Agrippina on 31 August; they named him Caius.[226] The second was the celebration of his triumph. Delayed since the winter of 9 CE, his recent successes in Germania revived memory of his great victories in Illyricum. On 23 October, Tiberius rode in the *triumphator*'s chariot along the same processional route through Rome he had travelled in 7 BCE. This time, the *legati* who had helped him win the war, including consul Germanicus, rode on horseback behind him along the *Via Sacra* consistent with the triumphal ornaments accorded them.[227] Paterculus writes with evident pride of

> the most eminent leaders of the enemy [who] were not slain in battle, ... but were taken captive, so that he exhibited them in chains in his triumph. It was my lot and that of my brother to participate in this triumph among the men of distinguished rank and those who were decorated with distinguished honours.[228]

Among the captives displayed was Bato of the Daesidiates. Treated with respect, he returned to Ravenna afterwards.[229] Before turning the corner of the *Forum* and up the Capitolinus Hill, Tiberius 'dismounted from his chariot and fell at the knees of his father, who was presiding over the ceremonies'.[230] It was acknowledgement that everything Tiberius had achieved was done under the aegis of Augustus. After the ritual sacrifices at the *Capitolium*, Tiberius gave a banquet for the people laid on a thousand tables, and distributed largesse of HS 300 to every man.[231] A gold *aureus* (plate 25) and a silver *denarius* was later struck showing Tiberius in his triumphal regalia on the observe.[232]

For the first time since 6 CE, Tiberius spent an entire year in Rome. Augustus requested of the Senate that Tiberius 'should have in all the provinces and armies a power equal to his own', since 'he who was foremost in bearing aid should not be considered an equal in the honour to be won'.[233] The Conscript Fathers and the Roman People decreed Tiberius' proconsular *imperium maius quam* – the same as that of Augustus, his own having been renewed for another ten years at the start of 12 CE.[234] They also agreed to Augustus' motion that deliberations resolved with Tiberius and a body (*consilium*) of twenty counsellors – the consuls, consuls designate, his grandsons and certain others – should be taken as though approved by the entire Senate, including the annual election of consuls.[235] Tiberius' *tribunicia potestas* was also renewed for five years. Lest there be any doubt among Romans, Tiberius was now as powerful as the *princeps*, missing only the prestige and influence that came with the honorific titles of Augustus and *Pater Patriae*. He was, in effect, *princeps* designate. Augustus needed the relief from constantly working. While reading one of the volumes of his *Rescripta Bruto de Catone* ('Reply to Brutus on Cato') to a group of his intimate friends, he became tired and handed it to Tiberius to finish.[236]

Upon completion of his year as consul, Germanicus was assigned to the *Tres Galliae* as *Legatus Augusti Propraetore*.[237] He too was rising in the race for honours in the *Res Publica*. On his way to the provinces, he dealt with a disturbance in the Alps or Pyrennes, or perhaps a raid by Germans across the Rhine – the sources are obscure.[238] The victory over the opponent earned him his second acclamation as *imperator* – one more added to Augustus' tally, now twenty-one, and Tiberius' at seven.[239] Like his father, Nero Drusus, in 14 BCE, his primary duty was to ensure order in his province of sixty Gallic nations. There was one other mission that he would have in common with him: dealing with the Germans. Augustus wanted to stop the threat of hostilities from across the Rhine, ordering him 'to put an end to such traces of the war as still remained'.[240]

# Chapter 5

# Following in Augustus' Wake: 14–16 CE

Augustus had a new mission for Tiberius: he was to return to Illyricum 'to strengthen by pacifying the regions he had subjugated in war'.[1] To ensure that the Western Balkans would never again descend into conflict, around this time Illyricum was divided into two smaller provinces, and the army units there were redeployed – almost certainly with recommendations from Tiberius.[2] The region along the coast and all of the Dinaric Alps became Dalmatia, administered from Salonnae by P. Cornelius Dolabella.[3] Two legions, VII *Macedonica* and *Legio* XI, were co-located at Tilurium (Gardun, near Trilj), though the VII may have shared the fortress at Burnum (Kistanje) with *Legio* XI – the evidence is not clear.[4] The region from its border with Dalmatia up to the Danube River was designated Pannonia and administered from Carnuntum or Sirmium. Three legions were stationed in the province: VIII *Augusta* encamped near Poetovio (Ptuj), VIIII *Hispana* at Siscia and XV *Apollinaris* at Carnuntum.[5] Tiberius planned to visit and inspect the legions in person.

First, however, there would be time to relax. Tiberius left Rome with Augustus and travelled to Astura, a seaside resort in Campania, and from there the party took a ship to Capreae, where Augustus had a villa.[6] Over four days, he enjoyed watching exercises performed by *epheboi* on the island, awarding them prizes of fine clothes and a banquet.[7] Tiberius and Thrasyllus joined the *princeps* for an evening meal and shared jokes with him.[8] During the return by sea to Neapolis, Augustus began to feel sick.[9] Nevertheless, he was scheduled to attend an athletics competition in Neapolis and, not wishing to disappoint the participants, he went.[10] Father and son parted company at Beneventum.[11] Tiberius rode upon the ancient *Via Appia* in the direction of Brundisium, from where he would go by ship to Illyricum. Augustus went to the house of his natural father, C. Octavius, in Nola.[12] By now, his health had been deteriorating for several days.[13] Growing steadily weaker, he dispatched a rider to find Tiberius and urgently bring him to Nola.[14] Having just reached Illyricum, Tiberius raced back to Campania.[15]

Upon arriving at Nola, the two men discussed affairs of state in private, Augustus 'commending to him the continuation of their joint work'.[16] Suetonius remarks: 'I know that it is commonly believed, that when Tiberius left the room after this confidential talk, Augustus was overheard by his chamberlains to say:

"Alas for the Roman People, to be ground by jaws that crunch so slowly!'"[17] Friends and associates wanted to pay their last respects, and he talked with them.[18] It is reported that at this time, he told them all of his wishes, finally adding: 'I found Rome of clay; I leave it to you of marble.'[19]

On what would be his final day, he asked from time to time whether he was the cause of any disturbance outside. Calling for a mirror, he had his hair combed and his lazy jaw set straight. Augustus asked whether, in their view, he had played well his part in the comedy of life, quoting the line:

> Since well I've played my part, all clap your hands
> And from the stage dismiss me with applause.[20]

The story reported by Suetonius – perhaps repeating the official version – is that Augustus then dismissed everyone so he could be alone with his wife. Slipping into a coma, he suddenly called out in terror that forty men were dragging him away.[21] He settled again. As he was kissing his wife, he uttered his last words to her: 'Livia, live mindful of our wedlock, and farewell.'[22] Augustus died on 19 August 14 CE at the ninth hour, aged 75 years, 10 months and 26 days – just thirty-five days short of his 76th birthday.[23] He had led the *Res Publica* after his victory at Actium for almost forty-four years.[24]

The sequence of events and their timings immediately after are confusing, but it can be partially reconstructed.[25] News of Augustus' death was deliberately withheld for a few days.[26] In Dio's version, Tiberius was still on his way from Dalmatia and Livia was waiting for him to arrive, fearing the possibility of civil unrest – or worse. Livia and Tiberius needed time together to make arrangements. He gave the watchword to the *praefecti* of the Praetorian Cohorts – L. Seius Strabo and Valerius Ligur – who would likely have been at Nola with their commander-in-chief, and then sent a letter from there with the news to all the commanders of the legions and auxiliary units, and governors of the provinces, without claiming to be *princeps*.[27] On or around 19 August, the soldiers in Italy were required to swear an oath of allegiance (*sacramentum*) to Tiberius, copying what Augustus had done in 31 BCE on the eve of the Actian War.[28] Everywhere the news was received, there was dismay that Augustus was dead.[29] A rumour spread that he had insisted on only eating pears from his own tree and that Livia had smeared poison on the fruit, thereby implicating her in Augustus' death.[30] Another story circulated that Augustus 'met his death through the wiles of Tiberius, aided and abetted by Cn. [Calpurnius] Piso (II)'.[31] Neither claim was ever proved.

There was the unavoidable issue of what to do about Agrippa Caesar, the posthumous son of M. Agrippa and Iulia. It was alleged that Augustus had secretly visited him imprisoned on his island and had made provision for him to be his successor, not Tiberius.[32] According to Tacitus, C. Sallustius Crispus, grandson of the famous historian who shared the secret, sent the written order to the tribune, and Agrippa was then killed by a centurion.[33] In the version related by Suetonius, Agrippa Caesar was murdered by a tribune in charge of his security detail on Planasia.[34] Who issued the execution order became an embarrassment when the public found out. The tribune stated that he had received a letter in which he was ordered to do the deed. However, it was not at all clear whether Augustus had left this letter when he died – allegedly intending to remove a potential problem in the succession – or whether Livia wrote it herself in the name of her late husband; and if she had, whether it was with or without the knowledge of Tiberius. When the tribune reported that he had carried out the instructions in the letter, Tiberius replied that *he* had given no such order, and that the man must submit an official account to the Senate.[35] Suetonius blamed Tiberius entirely for what he frames as a political assassination. Tiberius was seen as trying to avoid the bad feelings towards him that the whole affair would cause among the Roman People. Whatever the case, people forgot about the matter with time. In contrast, Velleius Paterculus makes no mention of the episode at all. Of the uncertainty generally felt in the days following the death of Augustus, he writes:

> Suffice it for me to voice the common utterance: 'The world whose ruin we had feared we found not even disturbed, and such was the majesty of one man that there was no need of arms either to defend the good or to restrain the bad.'[36]

In the heat of summer, there was now some urgency in taking Augustus' body from Nola to Rome and performing the traditional funeral rites. Accompanying the body were Livia, Tiberius and men of the Praetorian Cohorts. As city magistrates had done for Nero Claudius Drusus decades before, *decuriones* of the colonial and municipal cities along the route carried the body upon their shoulders as far as Bovillae.[37] On the final leg to Rome, men of the *Ordo Equester* bore the body, moving by night and entering the city after dark, as Augustus himself had preferred to do in life.[38] The journey had taken some fifteen days.[39] The body was then taken to the *Palatium* and laid in state.[40]

The following day, attended by a squad of soldiers, Tiberius (fig. 17) proceeded to the *Curia Iulia* for a meeting with the Senate, which he had convened by invoking his power as a tribune.[41] The proclamation was brief and modest: 'He would provide for the honours due to his father, and not leave the lifeless body, and this was the only public duty he now claimed.'[42] To preside over the proceedings on 4 September, Tiberius was ritually purified and granted absolution to cleanse himself for having escorted and touched the corpse – such intimacy with the dead was normally forbidden because it polluted the living.[43] Tiberius would not allow normal business to be transacted on this day.[44] The agenda was restricted to a reading of Augustus' will, discussion of arrangements for the funeral and the awarding of posthumous honours.[45] Tiberius began to speak but was suddenly overcome with emotion and could not continue.[46] In his place, his son Drusus (plate 11), dressed in dark clothing, produced the will, which he had retrieved from the Vestal Virgins, and checked the seals as authentic.[47] Augustus' freedman, Polybius, then read aloud the text written in two books, each comprised of multiple blackened wax-covered tablets.[48] 'Since a cruel fate has bereft me of my sons Caius and Lucius,' the first line read, 'be Tiberius Caesar heir to two-thirds of my estate.'[49] The words only added to the suspicion of those who believed that Augustus had named Tiberius his successor out of necessity rather than from personal choice. The legacy made Tiberius immensely wealthy, Augustus leaving him with ~~HS~~ 100 million.[50] Livia was his other heir, receiving the remaining one-third of his estate.[51] Personal effects and sums of cash were given to relatives and various other persons.[52] To the Roman People he bequeathed ~~HS~~ 40 million (or 10 million *denarii*), likely the recipients of the free corn dole who each received ~~HS~~ 260. He provided for the soldiers too, giving ~~HS~~ 1,000 each to the men of the Praetorian Cohorts, ~~HS~~ 500 each to the Urban Cohorts and ~~HS~~ 300 each to the legionaries, equivalent to one-third of a year's pay.[53]

Figure 17. Statue of Tiberius wearing a *tunica* and *toga* along with the *calcei* of a senator. It would likely have been painted to appear life-like in Roman times.

Books of scrolls were given to Drusus, who read them to the men sitting attentively in the *Curia Iulia*:

> In one of the three rolls he included directions for his funeral; in the second, an account of what he had accomplished, which he desired to have cut upon bronze tablets and set up at the entrance to the Mausoleum; in the third, a summary of the condition of the whole empire (how many soldiers there were in active service in all parts of it, how much money there was in the Public Treasury and in the privy-purse, and what revenues were in arrears).[54]

Senators proposed various honours, but the assembly decreed that any suggestions should first be submitted in writing to Tiberius, and that he should select the ones he deemed appropriate, though his mother would also have a say in the matter.[55] When some senators moved to vote that Tiberius become *princeps* and take the title *Augustus*, Tiberius refused, insisting that the present discussion should focus on plans for the funeral (*mandata de funere*).[56] He did ask, however, for the Senate to provide him a bodyguard as a protection from any rioters who might cause trouble on the day of the funeral, as they had done on the occasion of Iulius Caesar's.[57] Seeing his armed men, one member called out that he already had soldiers, to which Tiberius replied: 'The soldiers do not belong to me, but to the *Res Publica*.'[58] Just in case, an edict prohibiting disturbances on the day of Augustus' funeral was also issued.[59] A period of mourning following the funeral was decreed.[60]

After Augustus' body had lain in state, on 6 or 8 September, the funeral took place.[61] The magnificence of the event even outdid the funerals of Cornelius Sulla and Iulius Caesar.[62] It combined the traditional aspects of the last rites with the pomp of a military triumph.[63] A wax effigy of Augustus dressed in the clothes of a *triumphator* reclined on a couch mounted on the funeral bier above the casket which contained the body.[64] From the *Palatium*, it was carried down the hill and placed on the *Rostra* in front of the Temple of *Divus* Iulius.[65] At the other end of the *Forum Romanum*, Drusus read a prepared eulogy to the assembled crowd from the old *Rostra Augusti* next to the Senate House.[66] Then, standing beside the body, as decreed by the Senate, Tiberius spoke.[67] In his *laudatio*, he praised Augustus' virtues, described how in his many public offices he had served the *Res Publica* and talked of the great victories which had brought glory to the Roman People.[68] Preceded by the statue of Victoria, which normally stood in the *Curia Iulia*, the bier was lifted up and carried in a great procession.[69] Wax images of Augustus' ancestors worn by actors, the family mourners, priests, state officials and a golden statue of Augustus mounted on a triumphal chariot (fig. 18) all moved slowly towards the *Campus Martius*.[70]

Reaching the crematory (*ustrinum*) in the Mausoleum precinct, the bier was placed on the prepared pyre.[71] The priests of the several colleges surrounded it. Men of the Praetorian Cohorts performed a final parade for their former commander-in-chief.[72] With flaming torches in hand, a group of centurions lit the combustible material and the body was soon engulfed by flames.[73] In an act of devotion, Livia remained at the site for five days with the leading men of the equestrian order; then, on 11 September, they gathered up the ashes, poured them into a casket and, joined by Tiberius, placed it inside the sepulchre Augustus had built, where members of his family were already entombed.[74]

On 17 September, the Senate met again. When an ex-*praetor* came forward who claimed he had witnessed the shades of the departed ascend to the sky, the late *princeps* was declared immortal and deified as *Divus* Augustus (plate 24).[75] With Tiberius' consent, decrees for honours, shrines, the *Ludi Augustales* games and authorization for the tribunes to be given charge of the *Augustalia* were passed in his memory.[76] Livia was appointed the first priestess of the new cult

Figure 18. Coins showing a representation of the cart carrying the wax effigy of Augustus pulled by four elephants during his funeral on 6 or 8 September 14 CE.

devoted to *Divus* Augustus, being assigned one *lictor*.[77] She was ennobled as the *Augusta* (plate 1) – Tiberius rejecting other proposed honours to her as excessive.[78] Tiberius himself already possessed all of the political and military powers imbued in Augustus when alive. The contentious issue now was defining his official role in the *Res Publica*. Of this pivotal decision, Paterculus writes that 'the Senate and the Roman People wrestled with [Tiberius] Caesar to induce him to succeed to the position of his father, while he on his side strove for permission to play the part of a citizen on a parity with the rest rather than that of a *princeps* over all'.[79] The ensuing discussion can be partially reconstructed from the accounts of Tacitus and Dio.

Understanding the thankless burden Augustus had undertaken as 'First Man', Tiberius was disinclined to bear it alone. In Tacitus' account, Tiberius expressed the view that, in a state which had so many eminent men as did Rome, the Conscript Fathers ought not foist the responsibilities on any one individual. Indeed, he said, 'the business of the *Res Publica* would be more easily carried out by the joint efforts of a number'.[80] Yet rather than discuss how a pluralistic solution might be achieved, several members of the Senate implored him alone to lead. Tiberius requested a second reading of Augustus' book – the *Breviarum Totius Imperii* – containing a detailed account of the deployments of the army and the empire's revenues and expenditures (map 10).[81] In it, Augustus urged that military strategy should remain fundamentally unchanged:

> He advised them to be satisfied with their present possessions and under no conditions to wish to increase the empire to any greater dimensions. It would be hard to guard, he said, and this would lead to danger of their losing what was already theirs. This principle he had really always followed

Map 10. The Roman Empire, 14 CE.

> himself not only in speech but also in action; at any rate he might have made great acquisitions from the barbarian world, but he had not wished to do so. These, then, were his injunctions.[82]

Augustus had provided the financial support for the army, establishing the *Aerarium Miliare* in 6 CE, with a senatorial commission to supervise its administration.[83]

Tiberius suggested he might assume a duty the Senate decided for him.[84] He proposed a tripartite approach, modelled on the settlement agreed between Augustus and the Senate in 27 BCE:

> [H]e asked for some associates and colleagues, though not with the intention that they should jointly rule the whole empire, as in an oligarchy, but rather dividing it into three parts, one of which he would retain himself, while giving up the remaining two to others. One of these portions consisted of Rome and the rest of Italy, the second of the legions, and the third of the subject peoples outside.[85]

More senators implored him. Then Asinius Gallus spoke: 'I ask you, Caesar, what department do you wish to be assigned you?'[86] Not anticipating the question, Tiberius thought for a while and answered that it would not at all become his modest nature to select or shun any part of a burden from which he would prefer to be wholly excused. 'Choose whichever portion you wish,' replied Gallus. Tiberius retorted: 'How can the same man both make the division *and* choose?'[87] Gallus replied that he had asked the question, not in the hope that he would divide the inseparable, but to elicit from Tiberius his acknowledgement that the empire ought to be governed by *one* man. He praised Augustus and urged Tiberius to remember his own victories and the brilliant work which he had done year after year in the pursuit of making peace. Tiberius, however, was now quite irritated with Gallus, having despised the man ever since his marriage to Vipsania.[88]

L. Arruntius now spoke, recounting conversations he had with Augustus about suitable candidates to lead the *Res Publica* after his death.[89] Among them were M. Aemilius Lepidus (II) and C. Asinius Gallus, with Cn. Calpurnius Piso (II) or Arruntius (suggesting himself) as alternatives. Each candidate was eliminated after discussion, at Tiberius' urging. C. Haterius then asked: 'How long, Caesar, will you permit the *Res Publica* to lack a head?'[90] Tiberius sternly rebuked him. Mamercus Aemilius Scaurus remarked that, since he had not used his power as tribune to veto the consuls' motion, there was still hope that Tiberius would accede to the wishes of the Senate. Tiberius did not respond. Other senators clamoured for him to accept. Worn down by the theatrics, Tiberius finally, but reluctantly, agreed 'up to the point, *not* of acknowledging that he assumed the power, but of ceasing to refuse and to be entreated'.[91] The consuls Sex. Pompeius (II) and Sex. Apuleius were the first to swear allegiance to him; in their presence, the oath was taken by Seius Strabo and C. Turranius, respectively *praefectus praetorio* and *praefectus annonae* (who supervised the corn dole).[92] The Senate, the soldiers and the Roman People followed thereafter. 'Tiberius would inaugurate everything with the consuls as though the *Res Publica* remained,' notes Tacitus, 'and he hesitated about being in command.'[93] He later disregarded a vote of the Senate, refusing to allow an oath to obey his enactments.[94]

Tiberius was very sensitive to forms of address. He would not allow himself to be called *dominus* ('master') by freedmen or *imperator* except by soldiers.[95] He refused the title of *Pater Patriae* – the one cherished by Augustus.[96] He did not formally adopt the appellation *Augustus* – according to Dio, he never even permitted a vote in the Senate on the matter – although he did not object to hearing it spoken or to reading it when written, and whenever he sent messages to kings and potentates, he would regularly include this title in his letters.[97] On coins struck at the mints in Rome and *Colonia* Munatia, the formula '*TI. CAESAR AVGVSTVS*' or '*TI. CAESAR DIVI AVG[vstvs] F[ilivs] AVGVSTVS*' was used on the obverse around a profile of his head, and the number of years he held the '*TR[ibvnicia P[otestas]*' on the reverse (Appendix 2(a)).[98] In general, he preferred the form Caesar, sometimes Germanicus (from the exploits of his son), and also *Princeps Senatus*.[99]

His first act as *princeps* was to request proconsular power for Germanicus (fig. 19), which was granted, and envoys were dispatched to the *Tres Galliae* to officially confer it on him.[100] The same request was not made for his brother, Drusus, however, because he was consul designate for 15 CE and already in Rome. Twelve candidates were named for the praetorship – as stipulated by Augustus – and when the Senate urged Tiberius to increase the number, he swore on oath never to exceed it.

Figure 19. Portrait bust identified as Germanicus. Son of Nero Claudius Drusus, he was adopted by Tiberius on 26 June 4 CE.

Outside the Senate, there were challengers. L. Scribonius Libo Drusus was secretly plotting a revolution.[101] He was a distant relation of Tiberius, being a son or grandson of Livia's adopted brother.[102] Tiberius became aware of this intrigue when he was approached by his old friend Vescularius Atticus, who had been given information by Firmius Catus, a senator and close friend of Libo's.[103] As

Libo had been elected to the praetorship for 15 CE, Tiberius decided not to reveal what he knew – at least yet.[104] The greatest threat came, unexpectedly, from the legions.[105] Without their support, a *princeps* could not hold on to power for long. On or around 30 or 31 August, some of the legionaries stationed in Pannonia mutinied. The following day, Q. Iunius Blaesus urgently sent an envoy – his son, who was a tribune in the legion – to Tiberius bearing the mutineers' demands.[106] On either 1 or 2 September, some of the legionaries stationed in Germania Inferior also mutinied.[107] In both cases, the revolts seem to have been triggered by news of Augustus' death and the uncertainty – or opportunity – it created for them. Several days after leaving Pannonia, the messenger arrived in Rome. Tiberius charged Drusus to deal with the matter and he left Rome with an escort of two Praetorian Cohorts led by L. Aelius Seianus some time between 7 or 9 and 18 September.[108] Meanwhile, on his own initiative, Germanicus made haste to confront the mutineers on the Rhine.[109] He arrived in the camp of *Legiones* I and XX a few days later.[110] In the two provinces, events moved quickly. The delay of several days in sending reports and receiving rescripts back meant that Tiberius' deputies had to act in his name with the powers he had delegated them. He had to trust them to make sensible decisions on the spot; they would be held accountable for them upon their return to Rome.

Drusus arrived at the summer base of three legions encamped together under the command of Iunius on 26 September.[111] Drusus found the men in disarray and disrespectful of his rank. He learned that a legionary named Percennius, aggrieved by his low compensation and poor conditions, had convinced his fellow soldiers to strike.[112] They compared their low pay for serving in harm's way on the frontier with the high pay of the *Praetoriani*, who served in relative security in Rome.[113] They were also angry at the brutal treatment of *Praefectus Castrorum* Aufidienus Rufus when constructing a bridge, which led them to beat and ridicule him.[114] Upon their return to camp, the soldiers were arrested, flogged and imprisoned, but they succeeded in inciting the other men to mutiny.[115] The mutineers freed the soldiers and rampaged through the camp, ejecting the tribunes and camp prefect and plundering the fugitives' belongings. Lucilius, a centurion, was killed; he was nicknamed *Cedo Alteram* ('Gimme Another') because he would demand a replacement for his vinestaff (*vitis*) when it snapped on a recalcitrant soldier's back.[116] Men of two legions came to blows over a centurion named Sirpicus ('Serpentine'), with *Legio* VIII demanding his death and *Legio* XV coming to his defence; order and discipline were only restored when soldiers of *Legio* VIIII intervened.[117] In Paterculus' words, 'Drusus employed the severity of the Romans of old.'[118] He began to read out a letter from Tiberius.[119] He tried to hear their grievances voiced through their chosen spokesman, the centurion Clemens.[120] But the soldiers were in a violent mood, particularly against the 67-year-old ex-consul, Cn. Cornelius Lentulus (II), thinking him to be hardening Drusus' resolve and at whom they throw stones. The battered and bleeding victor of campaigns against the Daci had to be rescued by Drusus' guard detail.[121] That night, when a lunar eclipse occurred, the superstitious soldiers interpreted the celestial event as a bad omen, and they finally backed down.[122] They accepted the terms Drusus offered and suspended the mutiny.[123] Men from the *Cohortes Praetoriae* seized the instigators and summarily executed them.[124]

In Germania Inferior, Germanicus encountered a similar situation, but one with added complications.[125] The legions under Caecina Severus were in their temporary summer camps (*in aestivis*) too.[126] The men had turned on several centurions and thrown some of them into the Rhine. Their grievance was the corruption rife among the senior officers, who demanded bribes from their men in return for less arduous duties or time off, with punishments for those who did not comply.[127] Caecina, afraid for his own life, let the mutineers execute a centurion named Septimius who had appealed to the legate to save him. A *praefectus castrorum* was restrained and confined. The men talked of sacking the civilian city at *Ara* Ubiorum and then marching on Gallia Belgica.[128]

Arriving at the camp of *Legiones* I and XX, Germanicus was met with men in disarray.[129] Addressing the men from a tribunal, he demanded that they assemble with their *signa*. Slowly, they complied, but only after first having shown their scars and bruises from the harsh treatment of their officers and telling their stories of service extended beyond the agreed twenty-year term.[130] Germanicus agreed to reduce service to sixteen years with conditions, granted honourable discharges for anyone with twenty years and offered cash settlements for outstanding pay and bonuses for all.[131] The soldiers of *Legiones* I and XX accepted, but those of V and XXI rejected the deal, egged on by the disaffected conscripts from the 'rabble of city slaves' in the ranks of the *Cohortes Voluntariorum*.[132] Germanicus offered them more generous terms, which they accepted.[133] When one soldier urged Germanicus to seize power for himself, saying the men would stand with him, he adamantly refused and swore his unswerving loyalty to Tiberius.[134]

During the night, a band of soldiers arrived at Germanicus' house (*praetorium*) in *Ara* Ubiorum. Surrounding the building, they demanded to have the legionary *aquila*, even seizing as hostage Germanicus' wife, Agrippina, and youngest son, Caius, then just 2 years old.[135] They let his wife go but held the boy. The legionaries referred to him affectionately by the nickname Caligula ('Little Boot'), on account of the child-size armour and boots (*caligae*) he wore around the camp.[136] When a deputation of senators led by Munatius Plancus arrived in *Ara* Ubiorum, they were threatened by the unruly gang, who thought they had come to revoke the newly agreed terms and conditions.[137] Plancus fled to the camp of *Legio* I and hid in the strongroom of the *principia* where the men's pay and legion's ensigns were kept.[138]

The following day, Germanicus berated the soldiers, especially the men of *Legio* XX.[139] The deputation left *Ara* Ubiorum with an armed escort provided by an auxiliary *ala* – the legionary cavalry having sided with the mutineers. When Germanicus said he would send his wife and son to *Augusta* Treverorum for their safety, and hugged them farewell, the mutineers began to question exactly what they were trying to achieve.[140] Germanicus finally persuaded the men to hand over the ringleaders and, when they complied, the mutiny finally ended. Hastily convened military tribunals meted out summary justice to those found guilty by their fellow soldiers.[141] A plan agreed between Germanicus and Caecina to arrest the men responsible for the revolt in *Legiones* V and XXI ended in disaster, however, when the tribunes carried out the order without the legate present; many innocent men were killed as a result.[142] To restore discipline and unit cohesion, in late October Germanicus agreed to lead the men in a raid across the Rhine.[143] A vexillation of soldiers picked from *Legiones* I, V, XX and XXI, plus twenty-six *cohortes* and eight *cohortes equitata* – approximately 12,000 men – marched into Germania.[144] They reached the entrenchments laid by Tiberius four years before in the Caesia *Silva*.[145] On their return they attacked the Marsi, butchering men, women and children alike.[146] Throughout the crisis, the legions of Germania Superior under C. Silius had remained true to their military oaths.[147] Some in Rome criticized Germanicus for not calling on Silius to assist in suppressing the renegade legions.[148] Nevertheless, Germanicus returned home to Rome to a hero's welcome. Though ordered to remain in their urban lodgings, the *Praetoriani* joined the crowds who came out to greet Tiberius' adopted son.[149]

When debriefed, the reports Drusus and Germanicus shared must have outraged their father and commander-in-chief. The legions and their legates were all known to Tiberius personally from his time in the field in both regions. Yet there were some who criticized Tiberius for remaining in Rome, comparing his apparent inaction to Augustus, who frequently left the city to be closer to the war zone to receive reports and give guidance.[150] With a lifetime's experience in soldiering and war, Tiberius knew that respect for rank was the foundation of discipline. He had appointed his sons as legates with general instructions – 'he was to suit his measures to the emergency' – to quash the mutinies.[151] He had confidence in them to carry out their orders, and had to allow them leeway to do so. Both men had accomplished their missions, and both had remained loyal to him. With his legions and direct reports fully supporting him, Tiberius could now be sure his principate was secure.[152] He consented to improving the legionaries' pay.[153]

The memory of Augustus was honoured with the founding of the *Sodales Augusti*, an order of twenty-one priests chosen by lot; Tiberius, Drusus, Germanicus and his brother, Claudius, were among its members.[154] Separately, the *Ludi Augustales* were inaugurated on 12 October.[155] The first performance was marred by unseemly professional rivalry among the actors. Tiberius took great pains to prevent outbreaks of the populace and punished acts of public disorder with the utmost severity.[156] That it also happened on this occasion was a mark of disrespect against Augustus, which Tiberius would not tolerate. Despite their occasional differences, Tiberius revered his late father.

In the final decade of his life, Augustus had revived and expanded the scope of the laws on treason (*leges maiestatis*). Various pieces of legislation had been issued in years past under Marius, Sulla and Iulius Caesar covering 'betrayal of an army, seditious incitement of the populace – any act, in short, of official maladministration diminishing the "majesty of the Roman People".'[157] Augustus had added written libels, such as insulting attacks on him in works of satire, under their coverage. For Tiberius, the policy was, as stated in a reply to *praetor* Pompeius Macer, 'that the laws must be enforced'.[158] Roman justice relied on ordinary citizens bringing cases against criminal offenders to petition a *praetor* of a court which heard *crimina publica* ('crimes against the public').[159] The citizen would advise the defendant of his intention to bring an action (*editio actionis*) against him. Scope for abuse by the unscrupulous was built into the process. A senator might bring a charge of *maiestas* against a peer or a rival to settle a grudge or in the hope of securing political gain with Tiberius.[160] The litigants would appear before the *praetor*, who would decide if there was a case to hear. Where the alleged crime was against the state, a citizen might need some financial incentive to seek a prosecution, which led to accusers receiving a cash reward (*praemium*) if the case was won. To win meant gathering compelling evidence. This led to the rise of the professional prosecutor (*delator*), a private informer-cum-bounty hunter. A successful conviction might lead to the guilty party being fined or having their property confiscated; part of the proceeds went to the *delator*, which created an opportunity for bringing prosecutions. Failure to get a conviction, however, could result in the *delator* being punished, creating a high stakes game. The practice was well established before Tiberius assumed the principate. Tiberius even acknowledged it was necessary to reward *delatores* if the laws were to be enforced.[161]

In the basilicas of the *Forum Romanum*, Tiberius presided over courts in person – and sat in on cases adjudicated by other magistrates even when not invited.[162] He would permit the magistrates to sit in their regular places, while he took his usual seat on the bench facing them and as an *assessor* ('one who sits by the side of another'), hearing the case to ensure the law was properly applied and offering the magistrate advice he considered appropriate.[163] Two cases came before Tiberius which tested how far he would go in upholding the laws of treason. Charges of *maiestas* were brought against Falanius and Rubrius, two moderately wealthy *equites*.[164] Falanius was accused by a *delator* of acting against the divinity of Augustus by allowing a sleazy pantomime actor named

Cassius into a brotherhood devoted to the late *princeps*, who had also sold his house with a garden in which stood a statue of Augustus. Rubrius was charged for allegedly violating the divinity of Augustus by perjury. The *delator* hoped that Tiberius would find the men guilty, premised on his reverence for his divine father. However, Tiberius promptly dismissed the cases. In his opinion, he said it was not an act of sacrilege if the effigies of *Divus* Augustus, like other images of other gods, went with the property whenever a house or garden was sold. As for the perjury, it was on the same footing as if the defendant had taken the name of Jupiter in vain, adding that 'the gods must look to their own injuries'.[165]

Tiberius adjudicated in another case, heard in the Senate House, brought against one of its members. Granius Marcellus, proconsul of Bithynia, was accused of extortion by his *quaestor*, Caepio Crispinus, who added *maiestas* to bolster his chances of a conviction, with evidence gathered by Romanus Hispo.[166] An unpleasant man and a *delator*, Hispo claimed that Marcellus had made some disrespectful remarks about Tiberius. When the charges were read out and Tiberius heard that the proconsul had placed a statue of himself above those of Augustus and himself, he lost his temper and exclaimed that, 'in this case, he too would vote, openly and under oath'.[167] He was advised on a procedural point by Cn. Calpurnius Piso (II) that if he did so, his action would limit the freedom of the Conscript Fathers because, having voted first, the others would feel bound to vote the same way as him, while if he voted last, it would be unlikely that they would acquit the accused out of fear of appearing to condone the slanders. Regaining his composure and apologizing for his momentary lapse, he voted to acquit Marcellus of *maiestas*, and referred the charge of extortion to a commission of senators.

Any remaining threat to Tiberius' hold on power posed by his former wife, Iulia, ceased when she died in late 14 CE. She had been in Rhegium under house arrest since 4 CE, relocated there in an act of leniency by her father when the Roman People clamoured for her reinstatement.[168] She had outlived all her sons and seen her former husband restored to her father's favour – even as she lost hers. Tiberius had not been kind to Iulia, recently depriving her of the allowance and yearly income granted by Augustus under common law because he had made no provision for these in his will.[169] The cause of her death was reported as starvation.[170] In accordance with Augustus' instructions, her ashes were not placed in his mausoleum.[171] Her *familia* of slaves were freed and continued to live in Rhegium; on their gravestones they referred to her by her proper name, Iulia *Divi Augusti filia*.[172]

Towards the end of the year, the Tiber River flooded its banks.[173] After the inundation receded, several buildings had to be demolished in the interests of public safety. When Asinus Gallus proposed that they consult the Sibylline Books, Tiberius refused, instead setting up a commission, chaired jointly by

Aetius Capito and L. Arruntius, which was tasked with devising means to confine the river.[174] Among measures considered were diverting the Tiber or the lakes or streams feeding it. The commissioners consulted the civic leaders (*duoviri*) of the *coloniae* and *municipia* along the route of the Tiber and soon discovered that the proposals could seriously impact many communities.[175] Reviewing their findings, Calpurnius Piso (II) declared he would vote against the recommendations. Tiberius followed his lead, but appointed five senators, chosen by lot, to constitute a permanent commission to manage the river, so that it should maintain as even a flow as possible throughout the year.[176]

On 1 January, Drusus took his seat in the *Curia Iulia* as consul for 15 CE.[177] Tiberius was in Rome and perhaps attended the session later in the day to pledge himself separately to make his allegiance more conspicuous.[178] Now living permanently in the city, he needed a residence that befitted his status, yet one which provided him the privacy he craved. He had been at the Gardens of Maecenas on the Esquilinus Hill since 2 CE.[179] Conceivably, he could have lived in the ancestral home of the *Claudii Nerones* – the residence formerly owned by his deceased natural father (*Domus Tiberii*) on the Palatinus.[180] Appointed *pontifex maximus* from 10 March, Tiberius could, by rights, have lived in the *Domus Publica* ('Peoples' House') located within the Augustan compound on the south-west of the hill.[181] As his mother resided at the *Palatium*, he may have begun work on his own purpose-built house with all-new conveniences and interior decorations to his taste. This *Domus Tiberiana* was likely a house with an atrium and rooms arranged around a peristyle courtyard with a fishpond featuring niches in the south-east of the complex (map 11).[182] A library was one of the building's amenities.[183] It overlooked the *Velabrum* (the low valley between the Capitolinus and Palatinus hills), affording its imperial resident unobstructed views of the *Capitolium* on the hill opposite and of the *Forum Boarium* below – all while maintaining his distance from the people doing business there. The *Curia Iulia* was also within easy reach.

In Rome, Tiberius wrestled with domestic political and administrative matters. The workload of attending sessions of the Senate to discuss decrees, and meeting embassies, now consumed much of his time. He worked to ensure rules were followed, introducing a new one that proconsular governors who were vacating their positions at the end of their terms in office should be out by 1 June.[184] It had become common practice for many of those allotted governorships to linger in Rome and other parts of Italy instead of in their overseas postings, so that their predecessors continued in office beyond the appointed time. However, when Poppaeus Sabinus' term as his *Legatus Augusti Propraetore* of Moesia was due to end, Tiberius retained him in that post.[185] Achaea and Macedonia were reclassified as 'Provinces of Caesar' and added to Sabinus' portfolio.[186]

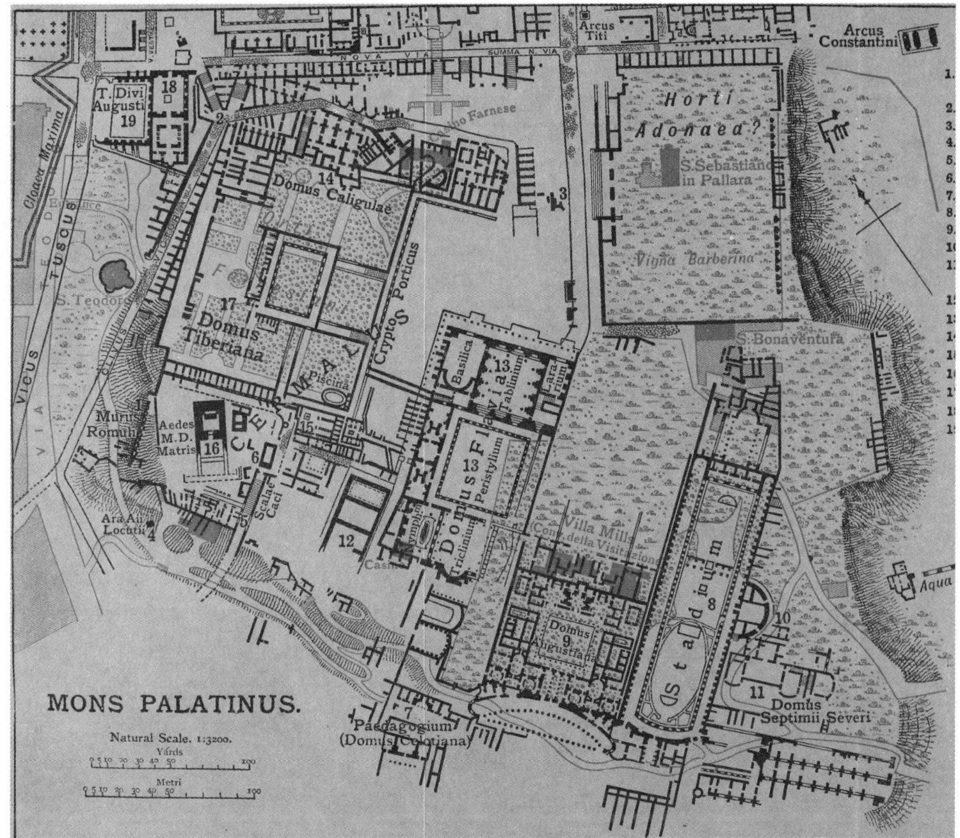


Map 11. Plan of the *Domus Tiberiana*, Rome.

Paying for the army through the duty of 1 per cent on auctioned goods, which had been imposed in 6 CE, was a cause of complaint by many people. Tiberius issued a declaration that 'the *Aerarium* was dependent on that resource; moreover, the *Res Publica* was not equal to the burden, unless the veterans were discharged only at the end of 20 years' service'.[187] The impromptu reform resulting from the mutinies of the troops the previous year, in which the legionaries had extorted from Drusus and Germanicus a maximum term of sixteen years, was cancelled and the longer term was reimposed.

Since 2 BCE, the nine *Cohortes Praetoriae* dedicated to protecting the *princeps* had been commanded by two tribunes appointed from the equestrian order.[188] L. Seius Strabo likely held the post alone shortly after the time of Augustus' passing.[189] Strabo then briefly shared the duty with his son, L. Aelius Seianus.[190] Seianus was related to Iunius Blaesus through his father's marriage to Blaesus' half-sister and was a favourite of wealthy gastronome M. Gabius Apicius.[191] When Strabo went to Egypt as *Praefectus Aegypti* (which entailed securing the grain supply), his son was appointed sole *Praefectus Praetorio*. Tiberius would come to rely on his cohort commander and develop a meaningful friendship with him.[192]

Drusus hosted gladiatorial games on behalf of himself and Germanicus; Tiberius did not attend.[193] Drusus was very fond of these bloodsports, being naturally inclined to violence with a quick temper. When he punched an equestrian on one occasion, he earned the nickname Castor after one of the popular gladiators of the day.[194] Taking after his father, he was also a heavy drinker.[195] When forced to lend aid with the *Praetoriani* to some people whose property was on fire and they begged them for water, he issued the order: 'Serve it to them hot!'[196] Drusus was a fan of actors too.[197] In October 15 CE, the *Ludi Augustales* were once again interrupted, but this time by a labour dispute when an actor refused to perform his role for the stipulated pay.[198] His fans showed their support, but others protested, and a riot broke out. There were casualties among the members of the audience. Several soldiers and a centurion were killed, and an officer of the Praetorian Cohorts was wounded, while attempting to repress the insults levelled at the magistrates from the crowd. The matter was later discussed in the Senate, with Tiberius present. Actors were ranked low on the social scale.[199] A proposal was presented to empower the praetors to use the lash (*scutica*) on them, but the tribune Haterius Agrippa vetoed it. The Conscript Fathers were reminded that Augustus had once remarked, in answer to a question, that actors were immune from the scourge (*flagrum* or *flagellum*) and that it would be blasphemy for Tiberius to contravene his words. Several measures were introduced to limit expenditures on entertainments and curb the extravagances of the supporters of the rival actors.[200] Among the measures were that no senator should enter the houses of the pantomimes; that if they came out into public, men of the *Ordo Equester* were not to gather, nor were their performances to be followed except in the theatre; and that the praetors were to be authorized to punish by exile any disorder among the spectators at such spectacles.

As supreme commander, executing a military strategy to ensure the security of Rome's dominions was the foremost of Tiberius' concerns. Illyricum had been pacified, but Germania was unfinished business. While his adopted son was in Rome, the two men doubtless considered options for his province, which was still smarting from recent setbacks. The defeat of Varus and his soldiers at *Saltus Teutoburgiensis* in 9 CE was unavenged and the ringleader, Arminius, was at liberty. Rome still had treaties with several Germanic nations. The loyal allies who had kept their word went unsupported, while those who had broken the terms went unpunished. It was a situation that needed a clear resolution: either win back the lost territory or abandon it as a lost cause. Tiberius' view was informed both by his personal experience of combat across the Rhine and by Augustus' last instructions. His counsel was clear: 'the restriction of the empire within its present frontiers.'[201] However, it was seemingly contradicted by the fact that 'Augustus Caesar had dispatched his grandson Germanicus to Germania to put an end to such traces of the war as still remained.'[202] With the morale of the Rhine legions restored from the attack on the Marsi the previous year, Germanicus was keen to lead a campaign across the river. Tiberius consented to his proposal. Returning to *Tres Galliae*, Germanicus issued instructions for the army to prepare. By the summer, the taskforce was ready. As Augustus had done when Tiberius was on active service, the *princeps* eagerly awaited regular reports from his legate. Unlike Augustus, he stayed in Rome, relying on the *cursus publicus* of mounted couriers (*stratores* or *speculatores*) stationed along the principal roads to deliver official correspondence.[203]

The hope for swift victory is represented on a cameo now called the *Gemma Tiberiana* or *Grand Camée de France*, which was exquisitely carved from sardonyx around 23 CE (plate 29). Jovian Tiberius bids farewell to Germanicus in his panoply, while *Divus* Augustus and Nero Drusus look on from above. The reality was somewhat different. From the war reports Germanicus had filed, Tiberius would have learned that, by the end of the campaign, the initial invasion had proceeded well but the return had ended in near disaster (map 12).[204] Germanicus, now aged 30, executed an operational plan replicating, in its key aspects, that of his father, Nero Drusus. He deployed his expeditionary army in two groups: he led his own by river from the Rhine, along the Dutch coast to the Ems River, while Caecina Severus marched inland from the Rhine.[205] Between them, they had engaged and defeated the enemy – Marsi, Bructeri, Chatti and Cherusci – with Arminius fleeing and his uncle, Inguiomerus, wounded in battle. They had rescued Arminius' father, Segestes, seized Arminius' pregnant wife, Thusnelda, and captured Segimerus, brother of Segestes. A significant achievement was the recovery of the *aquila* of *Legio* XIX. Yet tactical mistakes had led to unnecessary difficulties. Survivors of the massacre of 9 CE had guided the army to Teutoburg, where Germanicus led a solemn ceremony to bury the scattered and weathered bones of their brothers, but in doing so he committed a blasphemy, being that he was an *augur* and had touched dead men's bones.[206] On the return, Caecina had been pinned down by Arminius at the *Pontes Longi* before making a desperate escape, while Germanicus' fleet was shipwrecked off the coast of Frisia, with losses of men and matériel.[207] Meanwhile, his pregnant wife, Agrippina, had interjected herself into military matters to prevent the bridge over the Rhine at Vetera from being demolished so that the army could return.[208] Nevertheless, learning of the daring exploits, the communities of *Tres Galliae* rallied to replenish Germanicus' supplies.[209] Roman honour had been restored under the aegis of Tiberius. Germanicus had been acclaimed *imperator* for a second time, of which Tiberius approved.[210] Apronius, Caecina Severus and Silius were each awarded *ornamenta triumphalia*.[211] Arminius' son would soon be born in captivity among Romans. Tiberius, meanwhile, was himself blessed with another grandchild

Map 12. Military Operations in Germania, 14–16 CE.

when Agrippina gave birth to a daughter named Iulia Agrippina Minor in *Ara Ubiorum* on 7 November.[212]

The elections for the new consuls were held at the end of the year. Tiberius vetted the suitability of candidates, working with the exiting consuls to draw up the list to be put to the vote.[213] His written *commendatio* preferred those standing to have a track record of achievement in public service and he withheld their names so that a man's experience, rather than name recognition, was the basis of the free vote.[214] Tiberius continued to be actively involved in the daily affairs of the *Res Publica*, working with the Senate as a partner in government. One of the consuls was L. Scribonius Libo Drusus – the man allegedly hatching a plot against Tiberius.

In the spring of 16 CE, Germanicus once again took to the field, leading a third campaign across the Rhine.[215] With a rebuilt fleet, he launched an amphibious operation to the Ems River.[216] Meanwhile, Silius marched overland to engage the Chatti and Marsi to relieve a Roman outpost on the Lippe River.[217] Germanicus learned with dismay that the mound he had erected just the previous year at *Saltus Teutoburgiensis* had been desecrated. On the banks of the Weser River and again at Idistaviso, he fought the army of Arminius and forced the confederation of German nations to retreat. At Angrivarian Wall they clashed again one final time and the Romans claimed victory, although Arminius eluded capture once more.[218] The soldiers erected a trophy of captured arms and armour and attached a board to it bearing the words:

> AFTER THOROUGHLY CONQUERING THE NATIONS BETWEEN THE RHENUS AND THE ALBIS, THE ARMY OF TI[BERIUS] CAESAR, DEDICATED THIS MONUMENT TO MARS, JOVE, AND AUGUSTUS.[219]

The Angrivarii and Marsi had been punished, but there were errors of judgment that caused avoidable complications.[220] On the return, Germanicus' fleet was again damaged by storms. There was some good news, however. Upon reaching the Rhine, he sent Silius to engage the Chatti and led a group against the Marsi. During the surrender negotiations, a second *aquila* was recovered.[221]

Around this time, a Roman officer stationed in Germania Superior commissioned an armourer to make a special decorative piece for his kit. The so-called 'Sword of Tiberius', which is now displayed at the British Museum, consists of the iron blade of a *gladius* and its custom-made scabbard.[222] Though the scabbard is a typical design for the first century CE, it is an exceptional piece of equipment. The tinned and gilded detail is loaded with symbolism, with a medallion bearing the profile of Augustus mounted in the centre. The supporting bands of the scabbard are hammered to form the oak leaves of a *corona civica* – perhaps the awards received by the owner of the weapon. At the pointed end is a *lararium* (the shrine of the Roman household gods) and an Amazon (symbolizing wild barbarian enemies). In the upper panel, Tiberius sits semi-naked on a curule chair in the regal pose of Jove. His left hand rests on an *aspis* (the round shield of a Greek warrior) engraved with the words *FELICITAS TIBERI* ('Tiberius' Good Luck'). Standing behind him is winged Victoria, and in front of him the bearded Mars Ultor (the war god in the guise of vengeance).[223] The *princeps* is shown receiving a commander, who stands in full panoply and holds a *Victoriola* (a small figurine of Victory) in his left hand. The two men formally shake hands. This simple scene conveys the message that Germanicus went to war with the protection of Rome's gods under the aegis of the *princeps* and returned to him bringing the glory of victory.[224] In Germania Inferior, another military man erected a monument at Kelfkensbos, Nijmegen.[225] Originally standing some 7.5 metres (25½ft) high, the square profile column (plate 20) served as an orientation marker for vessels sailing on the River Waal. On its four sides are representations of Apollo, Bacchus, Ceres and Diana, once painted in bright colours. In one panel, a figure dressed in a tunic and *toga* is crowned with a wreath of leaves and a winged Victory, while he makes an offering. The altar beside him bears the inscription *TIBR CSAR*. It may have been erected to thank the gods for bringing Tiberius' victories over the Germani.

With the soldiers back in their winter camps, Germanicus wrote to Tiberius requesting another year to complete the project.[226] Politely, Tiberius refused, suggesting that Germanicus return to Rome to celebrate his triumph. Germanicus wrote again, but the answer was still 'no'. Tiberius' mind was made up – 'enough of success, enough of misfortune', he wrote.[227] He reminded his son that 'He himself had been sent nine times into Germania by *Divus* Augustus; and he had effected more by policy than by force.'[228] His son had already achieved much. Any further campaigning should be left to Drusus, so that he might have a chance at gaining some glory for himself. He added the inducement of a second consulship, and that he would be his partner as co-consul, for 18 CE.[229] Smartly, Germanicus relented and made his preparations to return home.

In Rome, Tiberius' friend, Vescuclarius Flaccus, had made discrete inquiries concerning the alleged plot to oust the *princeps*, gathering witness testimony, including statements from Libo's own slaves. He now pleaded with Tiberius to review what he had found. Tiberius declined, though he did not dismiss the allegation outright.[230] Indeed, he had invited Libo, while *praetor*, to dinner and conversed amiably with him, hoping to elicit more insight by himself. He took additional precautions – just in case. When Libo was offering sacrifice with him among the pontiffs, Tiberius had the usual iron knife (*secespita*) switched for one made of lead.[231] When Libo asked for a private interview, Tiberius would only agree to it if his son, Drusus, was present, and for the duration of the meeting he held Libo's right arm tightly, under the pretence of leaning on it as they walked together.[232]

Then the revelations spilled out. One of the witnesses, Iunius, gave information to Fulcinius Trio. A *delator* whose genius was famous among the professional informers, as well as his hunger for notoriety, Trio immediately went to the consuls and demanded an inquiry before the Senate. 'The Conscript Fathers were summoned,' writes Tacitus, 'to deliberate (it was added) on a case of equal importance and atrocity.'[233] In a panic, Libo went from friend to friend, hoping to find someone to speak for him, but to no avail.[234]

A year after first learning of rumours of the alleged plot, Tiberius presided over the hearing, which opened on 13 September.[235] Libo was so sick with anxiety that he had to be carried in a litter to the doors of the *Curia Iulia*.[236] Leaning on his brother for support, he appealed directly to Tiberius, with his hands raised like a supplicant. Tiberius, unmoved, proceeded to calmly read aloud the charges and accusers' names.[237] There were now four plaintiffs: Trio, Catus, Fonteius Agrippa and C. Vibius Serenus (I), each eager to lead the prosecution.[238] Libo, representing himself, refuted the charges, one by one. The accusations were 'extravagantly absurd', he said.[239] One accused him of inquiring of his astrologer if he would be rich enough to cover the *Via Appia* as far as Brundisium with money. A document in Libo's hand was produced by Vibius, listing the names of members of Tiberius' family and senators with odd markings against them – evoking the terrible days of the proscriptions during the Civil Wars when victims were selected this way. Libo denied every charge. It was resolved that his slaves, who recognized the handwriting, should be cross-examined under torture. However, an old decree prohibited a slave's examination in a case where it could affect the life of his master. In a novel and unprecedented move, Tiberius ordered the slaves to be sold individually to the treasury agent (*actor publico*); as property of the *Res Publica*, they could then be tortured. The accused asked for an adjournment to the next day and left for home, where he asked his relative, P. Sulpicius Quirinius, to make a final appeal to the *princeps*. Tiberius replied that Libo must address his petitions to the Senate. Soldiers were ordered to stand guard around his house.[240] Now desperate, Libo tried to have one of his slaves kill him; each in turn refused. During the evening, the wretched man stabbed himself to death.[241] The Senate met next day, as though Libo was still alive. In his summation, 'Tiberius declared on oath that, guilty as the defendant might have been, he would have interceded for his life, had he not laid an over-hasty hand upon himself.'[242]

The prosecutors each took a share of Libo's property as their reward and extraordinary praetorships were conferred on those of senatorial status.[243] Following the trial, various motions were proposed: by M. Aurelius Cotta Messallinus, that the effigy (*imago*) of Libo should not accompany the funeral processions of his descendants; by Cn. Cornelius Lentulus (II), that no member of the House of Scribonia should ever adopt the surname (*cognomen*) of Drusus; by Pomponius Flaccus, that days of public thanksgiving be agreed; by L. Piso, Asinius Gallus, Papius Mutilus and L. Apronius, that votive offerings be made to Jupiter, Mars and Concordia; and by all that 13 September, the anniversary of Libo's suicide, be observed as a festival day. The fallout did not end there. The *Senatus Consultum Libonianum* decreed that where a man's will was written out for him by another person, any disposition which it contained in the latter's favour should be void and taken as *pro non scripto* ('not written'), and be ignored by a court. It extended the *Lex Cornelia de Falsis*, the law on falsification, to punish the forgery of one dying in captivity.

The Senate then debated expelling astrologers and magicians (*mathematicis magisque*) from Italy. Supporting his father, Drusus argued for confiscation of property for offenders persisting in practicing these divinatory practices, but the Senate sided with Calpurnius Piso (II), who countered that citizens should not be punished, only for a tribune to veto the motion.[244] The expulsions of astrologers and magicians proceeded. One of those affected, L. Pituanius, was hurled from the Tarpeian Rock, while another, P. Marcius, was executed by the consuls outside the *Porta Esquilina* according to ancient custom and at the sound of a trumpet fanfare (*classicum*). In private, Tiberius continued to learn the art of divination from Thrasyllus.[245]

As the most powerful man in the Roman world, Tiberius could indulge his passion for art. He greatly admired a painting of Ephesus by Parrhasius, one of the three greatest painters of Ancient Greece. Pliny states that, according to Deculo, the *princeps* 'had it shut up in his bedroom, the price at which it was valued being HS 600,000'.[246] Also of great appeal to him was the *Apoxyomenos* ('Man using the Body-scraper') by the sculptor Lysippos of Sikyon, one of the three greatest sculptors of the Classical Greek era. It had been acquired by M. Agrippa, who placed it in front of his baths (*Thermae Agrippae*). Pliny relates that Tiberius initially restrained himself from seizing it, but eventually succumbed to the temptation and had the statue moved to his bedroom, replacing it with another statue at the baths.[247] The users of the public bathing facility strongly objected to this change, and loudly demanded its restoration during a theatre event. Despite Tiberius' personal fondness for the statue, he was compelled to return it because of the resolute opposition of the people.

On 15 September, the Senate discussed setting limits on conspicuous consumption. Q. Haterius, an ex-consul, and Octavius Fronto, an ex-*praetor*, led motions. One proposition approved by a vote prohibited the use of utensils made of gold to serve food, while another ruled that 'men should not disgrace themselves with clothes made of Chinese silk'.[248] Fronto moved to include restrictions on plate, furniture and household items. Asinius Gallus spoke against the motion, saying: 'With the expansion of the empire, private fortunes had also grown; nor was this new, but consonant with extremely ancient custom.'[249] He said that men should not be deprived of the pleasures they had worked hard to win. He won the argument, but Tiberius added that this was not the time for censorship.

During the debate, L. Calpurnius Piso (II) had lambasted the corruption of the courts, the bribery of judges and the cruel threats of the *delatores*, and concluded with a statement that he would be leaving Rome permanently for a country retreat.[250] Perturbed, Tiberius tried to convince him to stay, asking the old senator's relatives to intervene to stop his departure. Subsequently, when Piso sued Urgulania, whose friendship with Augusta had raised her station in society, the mother of the nation complained that she felt slighted. Urgulania defied the summons and went to the *Palatium* instead. An unexpected opportunity arose for Tiberius to improve his public image. He informed Augusta that he was going to the *praetor*'s court to support her friend. Carried in a litter with an armed guard following at a distance behind, he stopped to talk calmly with the people crowded around him. His delaying tactic resulted in Augusta giving orders for the sum in demand to be paid to Piso, which ended the dispute to everyone's satisfaction – it even helped Urgulania to earn a formidable reputation of her own.

In a later session of the Senate, members debated procedure and whether the body should be able to conduct its business without Tiberius being present.[251] Cn. Calpurnius Piso (II) spoke in favour of the Conscript Fathers having the option to discuss matters without him.[252] Asinius Gallus argued that debates would benefit from having the *princeps* chairing sessions. Tiberius listened quietly but adjourned the meeting when the discussion became testy. In a later session, Gallus and Tiberius argued about the election of key officials.[253] Gallus proposed that the elections should decide the magistrates for the next five years and that legionary legates, serving in that capacity before holding the praetorship, should immediately become praetors designate, with the *princeps* nominating twelve candidates each year. Tiberius replied that, 'It would try his moderation to have to elect so many and to put off so many.'[254] Annual elections already vexed many candidates, so how many more, he asked rhetorically, would be upset if they had to wait through an entire five-year cycle (*quinquennium*)? Gallus' proposal actually multiplied the number of magistrates fivefold, subverting the laws which had fixed the proper intervals for exercising the activity of candidates and for soliciting or securing office. Reporting the episode, Tacitus comments: 'With this speech, which seemed to have a favourable appearance, he [Tiberius] kept his hold upon the essentials of sovereignty.'[255] Responding to the shortage of quaestors to manage the provinces, Tiberius dispatched some from among those officials who had served the previous year to take up the vacant posts; this policy was implemented on other occasions too, as often as was necessary to meet the need.[256] He also picked three senators to oversee the copying of public records, which had either perished completely or at least become illegible with the passing of time, to preserve their contents.[257]

Tiberius increased the incomes of some senators. The financial qualification for a senator was HS 1 million, whereas for an equestrian it was HS 400,000.[258] Some men had fallen below the wealth threshold to remain in the Senate. As the late Augustus had done, Tiberius was prepared to assist men at risk of losing their privilege. The orator Hortensius had already benefited from such a grant from Augustus, so when his grandson, M. Hortalus, begged for another bursary so that his children in turn could qualify, Tiberius was irked. The *Res Publica* would be bankrupted, he said, if men kept coming forwarded asking for handouts to keep their positions in society. Industry would languish and idleness would be encouraged, he explained, if a man had nothing to fear, nothing to hope from himself, and then everyone, in utter recklessness, would expect relief from others, thus 'becoming useless to himself and a burden to us'.[259] The senators listened quietly or muttered under their breath. Sensing that he had been too harsh, Tiberius said in more conciliatory words that if the Senate thought it proper, he would present each of Hortalus' male children with HS 200,000. Hortalus remained silent. Tiberius never made the offer again.

Tiberius took his responsibilities very seriously, even at the cost of his health. According to Plutarch, when Tiberius entered the Senate House on one occasion, a member stood up and claimed that, as free citizens, they should speak their minds openly. Every senator, including Tiberius, sat in silence as the member stated that they all accused him of neglecting his own well-being, straining himself excessively for their sakes and not taking enough rest. As he continued his speech, the orator Cassius Severus remarked sarcastically that this level of candour would ruin Tiberius.[260] Tiberius despised sycophancy. Tacitus records:

> [A] tradition runs that Tiberius, on leaving the *Curia*, had a habit of exclaiming in Greek, 'These men! How ready they are for slavery!' Even he, it was clear, objecting though he did to public liberty, was growing weary of such grovelling.[261]

There was one last whisper of dissent against Tiberius' rule. Clemens, a slave of the late Agrippa Caesar, believed that his master's assassination had been arranged with Tiberius' knowledge, and he set out to avenge him.[262] Clemens had originally planned to rescue Agrippa from Planasia and to take him to Germania, where he trusted the army would champion his cause.[263] However, the merchant ship carrying him to the island was slow and arrived after his master was already dead and his body had been cremated. Clemens seized the urn containing the ashes and made for Cosa in Etruria. Growing his hair and beard, he came to resemble the unkempt appearance of Agrippa. Rumours thus began to spread throughout Italy that Agrippa Caesar was actually alive, and sightings of him were reported as Clemens went from town to town. He soon attracted a sizable number of followers, some of whom he met in Ostia and others in secret in Rome, allegedly among them senators and *equites*.[264] When Tiberius learned of his whereabouts, he entrusted Salustius Crispus with the task of catching the renegade. Pretending to be sympathizers, Crispus and two associates – perhaps soldiers – contacted and then arrested Clemens. They took him to the *Palatium* to be interrogated in person by Tiberius. Asked how he had become Agrippa, Clemens is reported to have replied: 'The same way you became Caesar!'[265] Even under torture, he refused to divulge the names of his accomplices.[266] Avoiding a public execution, Clemens was hauled away to a private part of the building and killed. That way the unwanted publicity it would attract to Tiberius could be averted.

In the last weeks of the year, a triumphal arch (*arcus*), erected near the Temple of Saturn, was opened to commemorate the recovery of the *aquilae* and *signa* by Germanicus, under the auspices of Tiberius.[267] The official line was clear: thanks to Germanicus, the Germans 'have been driven back from Gallia, after the military *signa* have been recovered and revenge has been taken for the defeat of the army of the Roman People through treachery, and after the status of the Gallic provinces has been given a firm order'.[268] The humiliation of the *Clades Variana* of 9 CE was finally and formally mitigated. In recognition of it, a temple was consecrated to *Fors Fortuna* (the goddess of luck associated with military conquest) beside the Tiber in the gardens which Iulius Caesar had bequeathed in his will to the Roman People; a chapel was dedicated to *gens Iulia*; and statues were erected at Bovillae to *Divus* Augustus.[269] Almost unnoticed, Tiberius quietly ended Augustus' practice of regularly publishing the accounts of the empire.[270]

# Chapter 6

# Enforcing Public Standards: 17–20 CE

When, on New Year's Day 17 CE, Tiberius (plate 8) was offered gifts of silver, he refused to accept them. He published an edict on this practice in which he used a word that was not in the Latin language. Suetonius and Dio relate the story that, after thinking about the matter over night, he sent for experts in the subject, because he was extremely anxious to speak without criticism.[1] Ateius Capito, an interpreter of sacred texts, declared: 'Even if no one has previously used this expression, yet now because of you we shall all cite it as an example of classical usage.' But one Porcellus replied: 'You, Caesar, can confer Roman citizenship upon men, but not upon words!'[2] Tiberius would not speak Greek on public occasions and especially avoided using it in the Senate.[3] In dealing with the People's business, his preference was always for Latin. In one recorded instance, before using the word *μονοπώλιον* ('*monopolion*'), he excused himself for having to use an imported word. Again, when the word *ἔμβλημα* ('*emblema*') was read in a decree of the Senate, he recommended that it should be changed for a Latin word and that if one could not readily be found, the concept should be expressed by several Latin words if necessary, or by periphrasis. In another situation, when a soldier was asked in Greek to give his testimony, Tiberius forbade him to answer except in Latin.[4]

Tiberius' patience was tried again when delators accused Appuleia Varilla of insulting *Divus* Augustus, Tiberius and Augusta in a series of scandalous conversations, and thus they argued she was guilty of *maiestas*.[5] Making the case scandalous was the fact that Varilla was the granddaughter of Augustus' sister. Adjudicating, Tiberius said that any words alleged to have been spoken against him or his mother should be disregarded from the inquiry and, as a result, she was acquitted of the charge of *maiestas*. However, it was decided that the *Lex Iulia de adulteriis et stupris* of 17 BCE did apply in her case. Tiberius suggested that, in accordance with established precedent, she ought to be handed over to her relatives and removed from Rome to a place beyond the 200th milestone. Her lover, Manlius, was banned from residing in Italy or Africa.

Upholding the good memory of Augustus was, nevertheless, sacrosanct to Tiberius. He either dedicated himself the statues and shrines then being erected to *Divus* Augustus, whether by communities or private individuals, or instructed one of the *pontifices* to do so.[6] Respecting the pact with the many ancient gods of Latium, during the year Tiberius reconsecrated temples that were variously dilapidated by age and neglect or damaged by fire or flood.[7] Augustus had begun the restoration of several buildings, but it was Tiberius who completed them. Although he paid for repairs to all these structures, he claimed none of them as his own work, instead using the names of the original builders.[8] Among them were the Temple to Liber, Libera and Ceres, and to Flora on the same site; a shrine of Ianus, built in the Herb Market; the Temple of *Spes* (Hope), which was dedicated by Germanicus; and the Temple of Vesta, destroyed during a fire.[9] Outside Rome still stands the lovely bridge made of white Istrian stone taking the *Via Aemilia* over the Marecchia River on five semicircular arches at Ariminum (the *Ponte di Tiberio* at Rimini). It was started by Augustus, but actually completed by Tiberius (fig. 20).[10] The inscription expressly notes it was given by both emperors.[11]

Tiberius expected members of the Senate to meet the stipulated financial requirements to retain their seats. He was, however, willing to assist some who struggled. To M. Aemilius Lepidus (II) he gave the property of Aemilia Musa, a wealthy woman who died intestate – on which the imperial treasury had a claim – because she appeared to belong to his family.[12] He gave to M. Servilius Nonianus the estate of Patuleius, a rich *eques* – though Tiberius was himself in part his heir – when he discovered his name in an earlier and unquestioned will.[13] Tiberius declined to accept a legacy from anyone unless he felt he had earned it by friendship.[14] However, he expelled 'spendthrifts whose vices had brought them to penury', including Appius Appianus, Cornelius Sulla, Marius Nepos, Vibidius Varro and Q. Vitellius.[15]

Figure 20. Schematic by Tommaso Temanza (1741) of the bridge at Rimini. It was begun by Augustus in 14 CE but completed by Tiberius in 21 CE. Two important Roman roads – the *Via Aemilia* towards Placentia and *Via Popilia-Annia* towards Aquileia – began here.

In Rome, a dispute arose between brothers Germanicus and Drusus and the Conscript Fathers of the Senate over which candidate should be elected as *praetor* to replace Vipstanus Gallus, who had died unexpectedly. Germanicus and Drusus supported Dec. Haterius Agrippa, a distant relation of Germanicus.[16] Many senators insisted that the deciding factor should be the number of a candidate's children, which was the legally correct position.[17] By just a few votes, Agrippa won. Tacitus writes: 'Tiberius was overjoyed to see the Senate divided between his sons and the laws.' It was evidence for him that the institutions of the *Res Publica* were working.[18]

On 26 May 17 CE, Germanicus stood proudly in a triumphal chariot in Rome.[19] Behind him, his legates – Apronius, Caecina Severus and Silius – rode horses and his troops marched on foot along the flagstones of the *Via Sacra*. Cheering crowds watched as the carts laden with spoils and floats carrying dioramas of scenes from the German War rolled by. The procession was notable for its non-Roman participants:

> [T]heir most famous men and women were led captive, I mean Segimundus, son of Segestes and chieftain of the Cherusci, and his sister Thusnelda, the wife of Arminius, the man who at the time of the violation of the treaty against Quintilius Varus was commander-in-chief of the Cheruscan army and even to this day is keeping up the war, and Thusnelda's three-year-old son Thumelicus; and also Sesithacus, the son of Segimerus and chieftain of the Cherusci, and Rhamis, his wife, and a daughter of Ucromirus chieftain of the Chatti, and Deudorix, a Sugambrian, the son of Baetorix the brother of Melo. But Segestes, the father-in-law of Armenius, who even from the outset had opposed the purpose of Arminius, and, taking advantage of an opportune time, had deserted him, was present as a guest of honour at the triumph over his loved ones. And Libes too, a priest of the Chatti, marched in the procession, as also other captives from the plundered tribes – the Caülci, Campsani, Bructeri, Usipi, Cherusci, Chatti, Chattuarii, Landi, Tubattii.[20]

Adding joy to the celebratory mood, Tiberius gave every man in the city HS 300.[21] The event marked the end of Tiberius' willingness for military adventures in Germania, heeding – at last – the sage advice of Augustus.

Domestic and border security still preoccupied Tiberius in 17 CE. Within the empire, there were pockets of discontent, which could turn violent if concerns were not addressed. In prosperous Africa Proconsularis, a Province of the People straddling the coast to the edge of the Sahara Desert, Tacfarinas started an uprising (map 13).[22] The cause is unclear, but it was likely related to land confiscations and taxation.[23] Tacfarinas, who had served as a Roman auxiliary soldier and then deserted, began recruiting bandits to plunder and steal

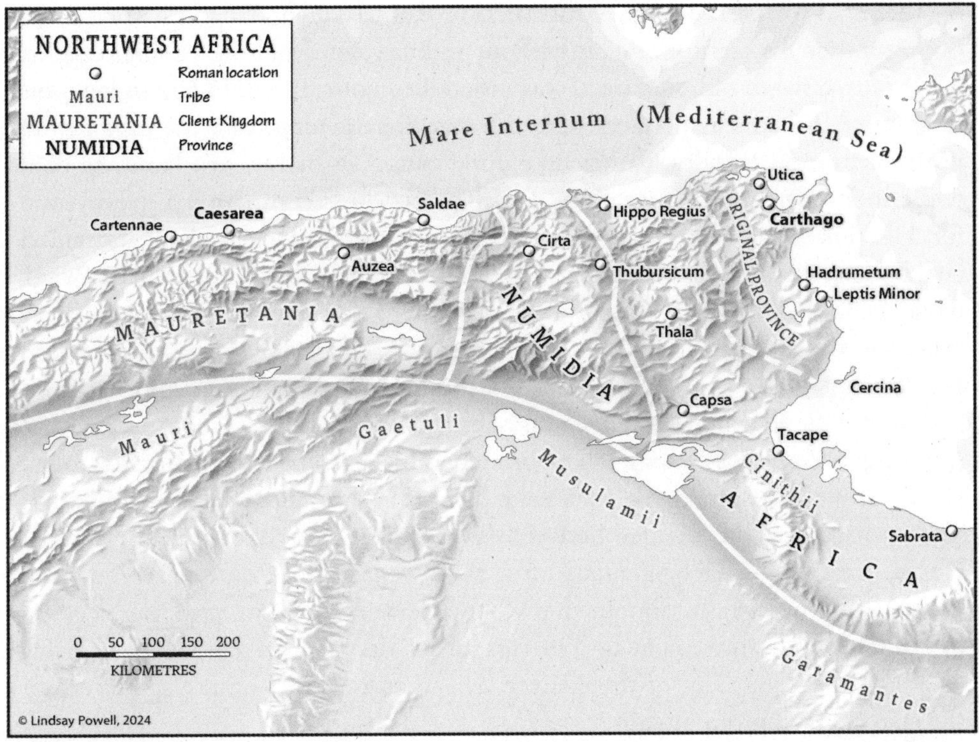


Map 13. Northwest Africa.

Roman assets. He organized his men into disciplined fighting units (*turmae*), each identified by flag standards (*vexilla*), in the manner the Roman Army had taught him. Eventually, Tacfarinas was recognized as the national leader of the entire Musulami people.[24] Living along the southern border of the province, the Musulami took up arms and drew the neighbouring Mauri people, led by Mazippa, into the conflict. Mazippa's army was more of a lightly armed band. They had then pressed the Cinithii to join them. It fell to M. Furius Camillus, proconsul of Africa, to bring an end to the rebellion; though not regarded as a soldier by inclination, he led *Legio* III *Augusta* and the auxiliaries stationed in his province into battle towards the massed enemy of Musulami, Mauri and Cinithii.[25] In textbook form, he placed the legion in the centre with the light infantry *cohortes*, and an *ala* of cavalry on each of the left and right flanks. When the two sides clashed, the Numidians were routed. Tiberius lauded Camillus' decisive victory in the Senate House; as one of their own, the Conscript Fathers voted him triumphal ornaments.[26]

Throughout the provinces in the East, there were cases of provincial maladministration (caused by feuds in the cities or by oppressive policies of their governors) and fiscal mismanagement (caused by over-taxation).[27] The provincials in Iudaea and Syria implored Tiberius for a reduction in the tribute imposed on them.[28] However, developments among Rome's client kingdoms presented opportunities for territorial gain without military intervention. In Cappadocia, Archelaus, now an old, sick man, was ordered to go to Rome to beg to keep his kingdom.[29] Tiberius had a deep-seated hatred for the king from the time he did not visit him on Rhodes. Either by natural causes or by his own hand, he died while in Rome.[30] The annexation of Cappadocia was considered a major coup for Tiberius – one achieved without recourse to war.[31] He asked for its capital city, Mazaca, to be called Caesarea.[32] In Commagene, King Antiochus had died, while in Cilicia, King Philopator too had died; in each case, the realm now passed to the Romans, to which some in those countries objected.[33] In Thrace, Raiskuporis – a loyal ally during the counterinsurgency in Illyricum (6–9 CE) – had been assigned the wilder western half of the kingdom by Augustus in 12 CE following the death of Roimetalkes, but when his attempt to oust Kotys (Cotys) II failed, he had since gone into exile at Alexandria and was put to death.[34] Thrace had been sub-divided between Roimetalkes and the two young sons of Kotys, overseen by Trebellienus Rufus, an ex-*praetor*, to ensure peace between the parties. There was a rumour that when a certain Mela, an *eques*, was accused of criminal mismanagement by Tiberius, in his despair he swallowed leek-juice weighing the equivalent of three silver *denarii* and expired on the spot without the slightest symptom of pain.[35]

Adding to the region's woes, a severe natural disaster struck the province of Asia in 17 CE. Pliny the Elder later described it as 'The greatest earthquake which has occurred in our memory.'[36] Along the western side of Anatolia, mountains shook, chasms opened, buildings collapsed and people were crushed in the rubble, all while shrouded in the darkness of night.[37] At least thirteen cities were devastated, including Ephesus, Mostene, Aegae, Hierocaesarea, Philadelphia, Tmolus, Temnus, Cymae, Myrhina, Apollonia Dia and Hyrcania.[38] Among them was Magnesia, lying below Mount Sipylus.[39] It was the news that Sardis was hardest hit, however, which deeply moved Tiberius; he immediately promised HS 10 million in cash to the afflicted community to aid in its recovery and went further, 'remitting for five years their payments to the national and imperial exchequers'.[40] Wise to potential political conflicts of interest over how the funds were to be apportioned in the affluent proconsular province, he set up a commission under ex-*praetor* M. Aetius, accompanied by five lictors 'so as to avoid the difficulties which might arise from the jealousy of two officials of similar standing'.[41] Ten other cities were also exempt from paying tribute and given funds from Tiberius' own savings, with the condition that a member of the Senate in Rome was to examine their actual condition and to relieve them.[42] Communities receiving the *princeps'* benefactions issued coins, Magnesia doing so with the legend, 'Tiberius Augustus, Founder'.[43] The mint in Rome, however, would wait five years – presumably for the work to be finished – before it issued a *sestertius* marking

Tiberius' liberality with the declaration, 'Cities of Asia Restored'.[44] Tiberius also reinstated to the people of Heliopolis an image carved in the naturally occurring volcanic glass Obsidian, which was an object of ceremonial worship to them. It had been found among the property left by one of the *praefecti Aegypti*.[45]

On the empire's eastern border, where divergent Roman and Parthian interests collided, there were unsettling political developments. Vonones, the oldest son of the late Phraates (Frahâta) of the Arsacid dynasty, had been a hostage under Augustus and then been returned to rule Parthia.[46] The choice of regent was unpopular with the people, who, in protest, summoned Artabanus and ousted Vonones.[47] Vonones fled to Armenia, usurping and executing the incumbent Artavasdes.[48] In years past, Tiberius had installed Tigranes in Armenia, but he did not last – though neither did Ariobarzanes, installed by Caius Caesar.[49] Now a fugitive, Vonones was living in exile in Cilicia under Creticus' close surveillance.[50] Vonones bribed his guards and tried to escape to Armenia.[51] By chance, he was captured by Vibius Fronto, a *praefectus equitum*; bound in chains, he was stabbed to death by Remmius, an enrolled prisoner.

As *princeps*, Augustus would regularly tour the empire in person to motivate the civic leaders in the cities and inspire his commanders in their bases. He had shared the duty with his right-hand man, M. Agrippa, following a pattern where one would remain in Italy while the other travelled, and later he had sent his adopted son, Caius, on a special mission. As *princeps*, Tiberius remained in Rome, preferring to work through his appointed deputies. To deal with the endemic problems in the East, Tiberius needed a trusted envoy who could travel there and act on his behalf. Tacitus writes:

> These circumstances, then, and the events in Armenia, which I mentioned above, were discussed by Tiberius before the Senate. 'The commotion in the East,' he added, 'could only be settled by the wisdom of Germanicus: for his own years were trending to their autumn, and those of Drusus were as yet scarcely mature.' There followed a decree of the [Conscript] Fathers, delegating to Germanicus the provinces beyond the sea, with overriding powers (*imperium proconsulare maius*), in all regions he might visit, those of the local governors holding office by allotment or imperial nomination.[52]

As 'Overseer of the East' (*praepositus Orienti*) – the title borne by C. Caesar in 1 BCE – his mission was 'in accordance with the authority of this order to settle overseas affairs'.[53] His powers were greater than the proconsuls of the provinces in the region – Achaea and Macedonia, Asia, Pontus-Bithynia, Cilicia, Cyprus and Crete/Cyrenaica – but subordinate to Tiberius.[54] It was stipulated that Tiberius' legates – principally for Syria – were to be adjutants (*adiutores*) to Germanicus on his special mission.[55] Tiberius' decision was hailed by Paterculus, who writes: 'With what honours did he send his beloved Germanicus to the provinces across the seas!'[56] To reach his new posting at Antiocheia on the Orontes in Syria would take several months, allowing him to explore the region for which he was now responsible.

Free Germania too was in turmoil. The coalition of tribes under Arminius was at war with the confederacy under Maroboduus. The Germani posed a constant threat to Roman interests and, even as a nominal ally, the Marcomanni could yet prove unreliable. The instability there risked the security of the Roman provinces along the Danube – Moesia, Pannonia, Noricum, Raetia – and Dalmatia and Italy too. Tiberius assigned oversight of the entire region to Drusus, investing him with *imperium proconsulare maius* to perform his duties.[57] Arriving in Dalmatia with his wife, Livilla, Drusus set to work.[58]

As Tiberius had intimated to Germanicus the previous year, Drusus would find glory in Germania, but not by direct intervention. The new border strategy was to engage foreign peoples indirectly through trade and proxy wars. Arminius was actively trying to overthrow his rival, Maroboduus.[59] A real opportunity now arose to destabilize the king's rule. A young man, Catualda of the Gotones nation, had been exiled by the king and sought revenge.[60] Assembling a group of supporters, he returned to Marcomannic territory and persuaded many of the chieftains to join him. With them he stormed Maroboduus' stronghold and entered the palace, where they discovered spoils of the Suebi and a number of sutlers and traders from the Roman provinces. Granted commercial privileges by Maroboduus, they had established business operations in the country and remained for the promise of increased profits. Maroboduus then fled.[61] Crossing the Danube with his retainers into Noricum, he urgently wrote to Tiberius. Appealing for his clemency, he stated that 'though many nations offered to welcome a king once so glorious, he had preferred the friendship of Rome'.[62] In his reply – preserved by Tacitus – Tiberius wrote that:

> 'he would have a safe and honoured seat in Italia, if he remained; but, should his interests make a change advisable, he might depart as securely as he had come.' He asserted, however, in the Senate that 'not Philip himself had been so grave a menace to Athens – not Pyrrhus nor Antiochus to the Roman People.' The speech is still extant, in which he emphasized 'the greatness of the man, the violence of the peoples beneath his rule, the nearness of the enemy to Italia, and the measures he had himself taken to destroy him.'[63]

Maroboduus was granted asylum and detained at Ravenna.[64] Whenever the Suebi became unruly on the border, the Romans raised the possibility of restoring him to Germania. For eighteen years, he lived in Italy. He grew into old age, his fame by the end much tarnished by enjoying too great a love of life.

A similar fate awaited Catualda. Shortly after having ousted Maroboduus, he was himself overthrown by the Hermunduri and their leader, Vibilius.[65] Catualda too received asylum from the Romans, but was detained at *Forum Iulii* in Gallia Narbonensis. In case the retainers of the two refugees intermingled with the local native Romanized populations and caused disruption, they were reassigned to King Vannius of the Quadi nation on the Danube.[66]

Arminius, meanwhile, faced threats to his own rule. A letter from Adgandestrius, war leader of the Chatti, was read in the *Curia*. He swore to kill Arminius if the Romans would provide him the poison to do so. Tiberius and the Conscript Fathers sent back the reply that 'it was not by deceit nor in secret but openly and in arms that the Roman People took vengeance on their foes'.[67]

En route to his posting in Syria, Germanicus met Drusus in Dalmatia, emphasizing the 'singular unanimity, unshaken by the contentions of their kith and kin' (map 14).[68] With him were his wife, Agrippina, and youngest son, Caius Caligula.[69] From there, Germanicus proceeded to Achaea. He sojourned at Nikopolis to view the battle site of Actium where, in 31 BCE, Augustus (his adoptive grandfather) had fought M. Antonius (his grandfather on his mother's side); he received confirmation of his second consulship here on 1 January 18 CE.[70] His colleague, Tiberius, resigned the consulship, yielding his curule chair to a suffect consul after just a few days.[71] Germanicus then stopped at Olympia and won first place in a race of four-horse chariots (*tethrippon*) in the 199th Olympiad.[72] At Lesbos, Agrippina gave birth to a daughter, named Iulia Livilla.[73] In the weeks following, he attended to his mission. He gave financial assistance to cities,[74] ruling that the Roman *as* should be the standard for calculating civic taxes rather than local currencies.[75] He also delivered new governors – Q. Veranius to Cappadocia and Q. Servaeus to Commagene – and personally crowned the pro-Roman Zenon as King Artaxias at Artaxata, Armenia, in a calculated move against Rome's nemesis, Parthia; these were celebrated as high achievements.[76] When news reached Rome that Germanicus had enthroned the king in Armenia, the Senate resolved that he and Drusus should each receive an ovation upon their return.[77] Additionally, triumphal arches bearing statues of the two Caesars were erected on either side of the Temple of Mars the Avenger.[78] Though a soldier for much of his life, 'Tiberius showed more pleasure at having kept the peace by diplomacy than if he had concluded a war by a series of stricken fields.'[79] Arriving in Antioch, Germanicus set up his home office in the suburb of Epidaphnae.[80]

Tiberius was in Rome for the duration of 19 CE. Maintaining peace at home preoccupied him. When the city's inhabitants complained bitterly about the punitive cost of wheat, he fixed a price to be paid by the consumer with the promise to add two *sestertii* on every peck (*modius*) for the traders.[81] Highly sensitive to the mischievous uses to which divination and prophecy could be turned, when shown a verse alleged to have come from the Sibylline Books, Tiberius denounced it as spurious.[82] He conducted an investigation into all the books that contained any prophecies, rejecting some as worthless and retaining others as genuine – though

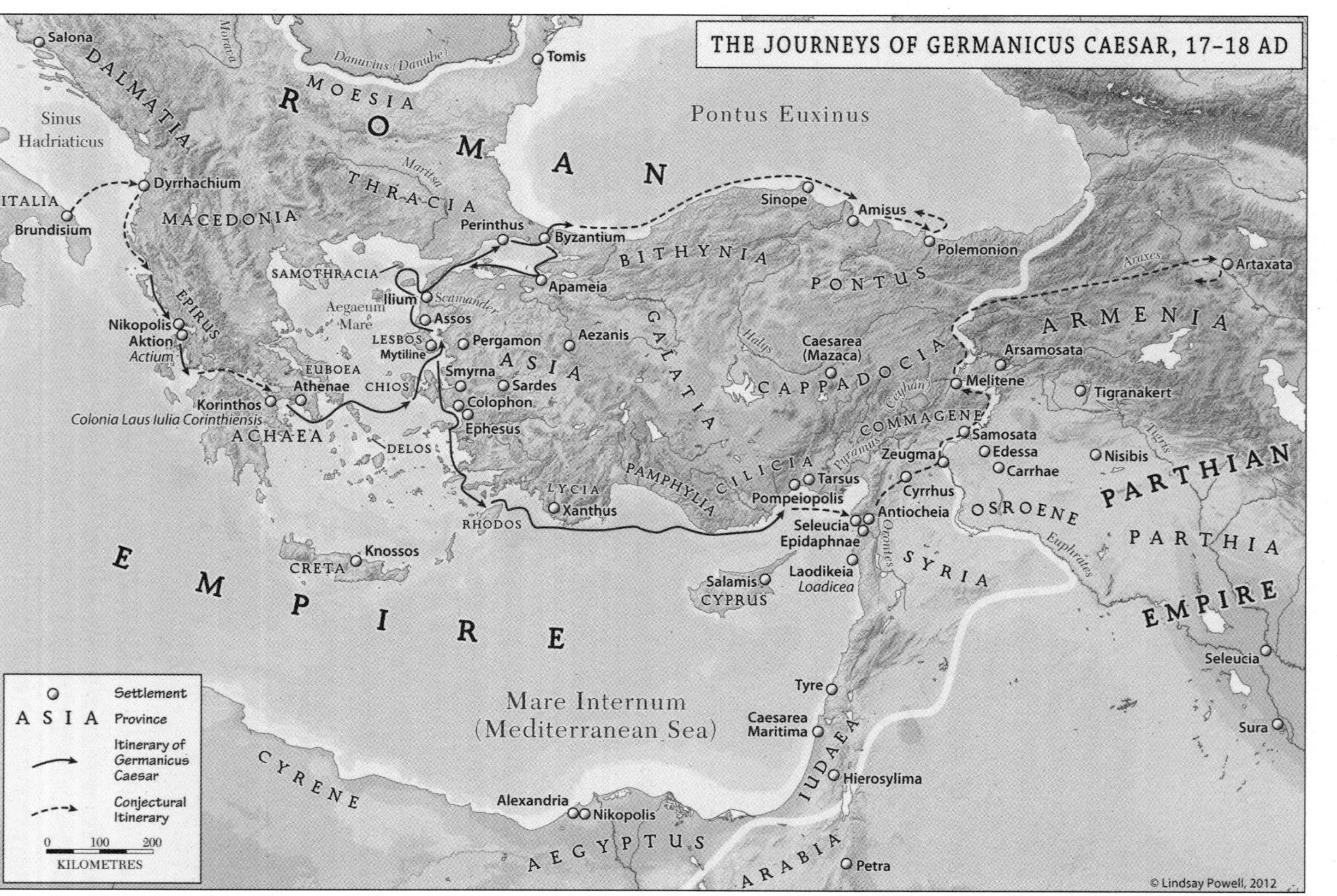


Map 14. The Journeys of Germanicus Caesar, 17–18 CE.

the sources do not specify the criteria he used to make the distinction. Foreign cults and religions (*externae caerimoniae*) spreading in Italy also attracted Tiberius' attention. Particularly concerning to him was the increasing numbers of Jews who were reported to be proselytizing in Rome. He perceived them as a source of potential unrest and took measures that banished most of them.[83] He ordered the freedmen of military service age to go to Sardinia, where they would help quell widespread banditry, with banishment or the threat of slavery for those not complying.[84] Followers of Egyptian rites, such as Isis, faced similar sanctions. He banished the astrologers too, but offered pardons to any who begged for indulgence and promised to give up their art.[85] In keeping with the general policy on clamping down on lax standards, an edict was issued clarifying who was banned from performing in public. Penalties could now be imposed on any senator or equestrian who took part in a performance, such as a pantomime – in addition to the *infamia* it would bring him. The prohibition also covered daughters, granddaughters and great-granddaughters who were under the age of 20 from senatorial or equestrian families who hoped to be recruited as gladiators (*gladiatrices*).[86] Another new decree of the Senate stipulated that 'no woman whose grandfather, father, or husband had been a Roman *eques* should get money by prostitution'.[87]

Tiberius then proposed the appointment of a new priestess to replace Occia, who had presided faithfully over the rites of Vesta for fifty-seven years.[88] Two men, Fonteius Agrippa and Domitius Pollio, proposed their own virgin daughters for the prestigious post of great antiquity and religious importance. Tiberius thanked each for their public-spirited rivalry. Pollio's daughter was preferred, simply because her mother was still living with the same husband, while Agrippa's divorce had blemished the reputation of his family. As a consolation (*solatium*) to the losing candidate, Tiberius presented her with a dowry of HS 500,000. His own family was enlarged this year with the birth of twin sons to Drusus and Livilla, named Ti. Iulius Caesar Nero (or familiarly Ti. Gemellus) and Germanicus Gemellus (plate 27).[89] The event, 'a rare felicity even in modest households,' writes Tacitus,

> affected the *princeps* with so much pleasure that he could not refrain from boasting to the Conscript Fathers that never before had twins been born to a Roman of the same eminence: for he converted everything, accidents included, into material for self-praise.[90]

In the summer of 19 CE, Germanicus chose to take a holiday in Egypt 'to study its antiquities' (map 15).[91] Disembarking at Alexandria, Germanicus was soon fêted by crowds of well-wishers, to whom he felt obliged to give a speech.[92] The 34-year-old Germanicus felt very comfortable in cosmopolitan Alexandria. He dressed in the Greek style and visited the city without his guards – lax behaviour that Tiberius did not much care for in his young representative.[93] Learning that famine afflicted the Egyptians, Germanicus responded by opening the granaries and reducing the price of wheat to feed the local population, despite not being authorized to do so. When Tiberius, who had never been to Egypt himself, was informed of these events, he was furious. He immediately wrote a letter in which he 'sharply censured' his son for his gross errors of judgment.[94] To prevent meddling with the corn supply was the reason an official from Rome was not to enter Egypt without first obtaining the express permission of the *princeps* – a practice established long before by Augustus – and it was an especially egregious offence when Tiberius was having to intervene to ameliorate the high prices Romans at home were paying.[95] Unaware of the letter, Germanicus then indulged himself in a cruise down the Nile, stopping off at famous landmarks, including the pyramids at Giza, Thebes and the Colossi of Memnon.[96] A visit to the Aspis Bull at Memphis did not go according to plan, when the sacred animal, believed to be able to see the future, refused to eat food from Germanicus' hand and turned away, which observers took to be a bad omen.[97] Reaching the island of Elephantine, he began his return journey.

Germanicus was urgently needed back in Syria. Tiberius had replaced Creticus Silanus, whose daughter was betrothed to Germanicus' son, Nero Caesar, with Cn. Calpurnius Piso (II).[98] Reports reached Germanicus that Piso was ignoring or even revoking his orders.[99] There had been friction between the two men on the outbound journey to the East: Piso had stirred up trouble for Germanicus during a stopover in Athens; Piso had refused to bring legions to Armenia when ordered; and there had been a less than amiable meeting between the two men in Syria.[100] Some altercations, however, were actively contrived by members of Germanicus' own support team:

> He [Germanicus] was indeed, as I have said, a kind-hearted man. But friends who knew well how to inflame a quarrel, exaggerated what was true and added lies, alleging various charges against Piso, Plancina, and their sons.[101]

Germanicus left Egypt in good spirits, but, arriving in Antioch on the Orontes, fell seriously ill. He may have taken a virus back with him to Syria, but rumours spread that Piso or his wife, Munatia Plancina, were implicated in a plot to poison him.[102] The sickness worsened. Initially he seemed to respond to treatment, but then he regressed and became weaker. Germanicus died on 10 October 19 CE.[103]

The tragic news of Germanicus' premature death reached Italy on or just before 8 December, when the Senate immediately declared a period of public mourning (*iustitium*).[104] Normal everyday life in Rome stopped: businesses shuttered their doors and the Senate went into voluntary recess.[105] Tiberius likely learned about it from Germanicus' general staff; Cn. Sentius had assumed the leadership position temporarily while awaiting instructions from Tiberius on the new appointment.[106] The general population may have learned of the death from crews aboard ships docking at Ostia, Brundisium and Tarentum, whence

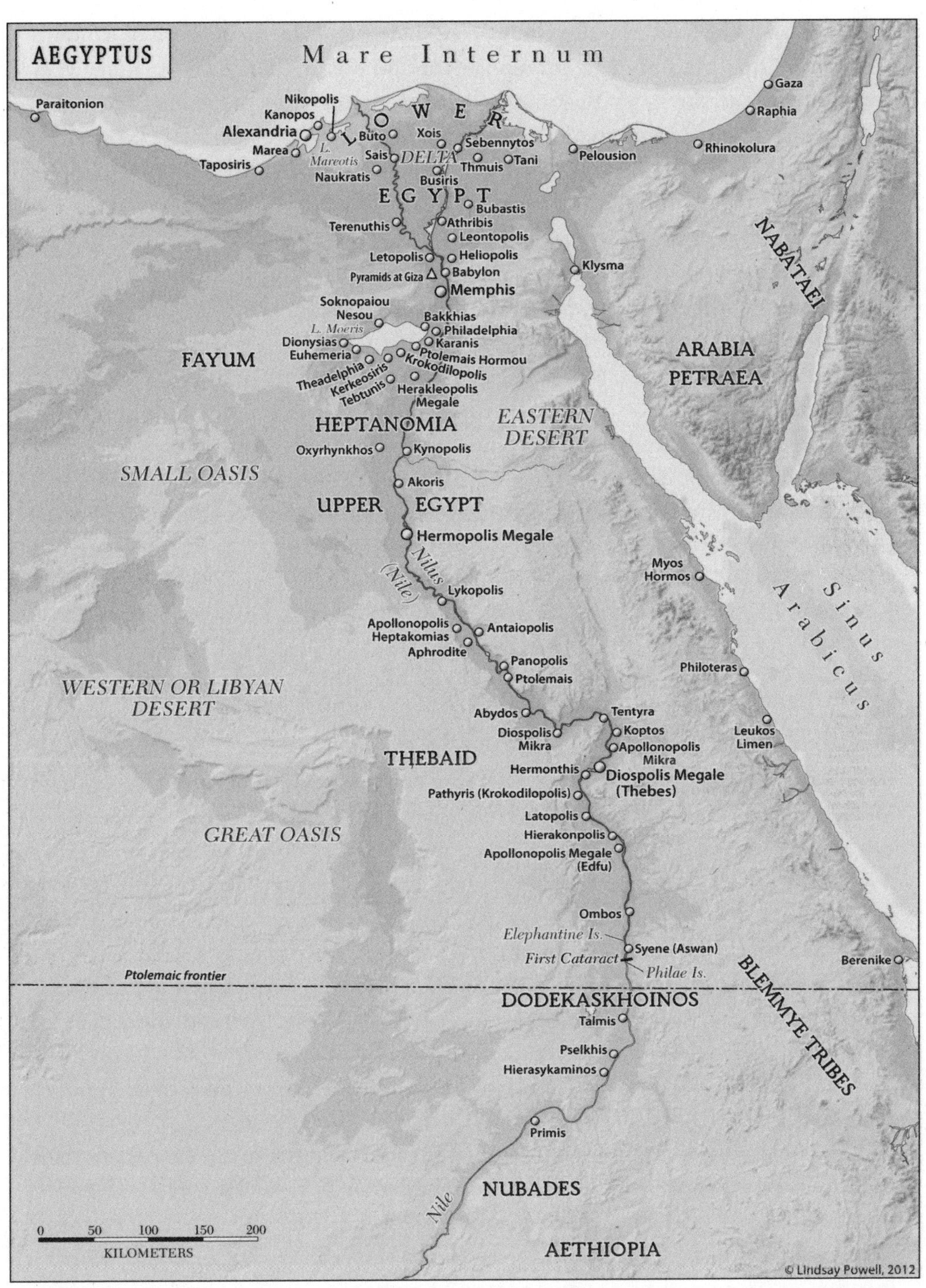


Map 15. Aegyptus.

it spread quickly, borne by travellers going by road.[107] In their distress, Romans expressed hope when they heard reports that he was, in fact, alive. At night they kept Tiberius awake in his Palatine home with their chants of 'Rome is safe! The Fatherland is safe! Germanicus is safe!'[108] When they discovered that those ships had set sail before he died, hope turned to abject despair.[109] Feeling abandoned by the gods, people protested at temples, some smashing altars, others throwing out the statuettes of their household gods.[110]

In Syria, Agrippina displayed the naked body of her husband in the *forum* at Antiocheia in order to show blue discolouration in his skin before consigning it to the flames of the funeral pyre.[111] Carrying the urn containing Germanicus' ashes, she then set out on the 2,250-kilometre (1,400-mile) journey by sea to Rome for the formal burial.[112] Meanwhile, Vitellius and Veranius sought to establish the cause of their commander's mysterious, lingering death. If by natural causes, it was to be much regretted, but if found to be murder, the person responsible had to be found, arrested, charged and punished. At the 'crime scene', they uncovered evidence of sorcery:

> It is a fact that explorations in the floor and walls brought to light the remains of human bodies, spells, curses, leaden tablets engraved with the name 'GERMANICUS', charred and blood-smeared ashes, and others of the implements of witchcraft by which it is believed the living soul can be devoted to the powers of the grave.[113]

Inquiries led them to a woman by the name of Martina, who was famed in Syria for her knowledge of poisons. Significantly for them, she was also a friend of Plancina. For the investigators, there was only one possible conclusion: Germanicus had been murdered. Tacitus records that they 'drew up the articles of indictment as though the case had already been entered'.[114] When they presented this 'evidence' to the new governor, Cn. Sentius, who was also a friend of Germanicus, without hesitation he ordered Martina apprehended and sent her to Rome for trial.[115] Her association with Plancina pointed the finger of accusation at her husband as the conspirator. Tacitus reports that Germanicus himself even believed that Piso (II) had given him poison and, in anger, had renounced his friendship with him.[116]

Convincing Vitellius and Veranius that Piso (II) was the prime suspect in their murder hypothesis were his own bizarre actions. A few days before 10 October, Piso and his wife had left Antiocheia on the Orontes, boarded a waiting ship and then sailed to Kos.[117] Discovering that he had been replaced as *legatus Augusti* by Sentius, at the urging of a friend named Domitius Celer and several centurions, but against the advice of his son, Marcus, Piso assembled an army of renegades, disgruntled legionaries and deserters – even commandeering a detachment of new legionaries in transit and requesting auxiliaries from client kings in Cilicia

– to retake his province.[118] He wrote to Tiberius 'accusing Germanicus of luxury and arrogance, and asserting that, having been driven away to make room for revolution, he had resumed the command of the army in the same loyal spirit in which he had before held it'.[119] When his troops under Domitius were defeated by legions from Syria led by Sentius at Celendris in Cilicia, Piso's reckless attempt at a coup failed.[120] Finally, he laid down his arms and heeded Marsus Vibius' advice to go to Rome and defend himself.[121] Piso sent his son, Marcus, ahead of him to Tiberius with a direct appeal. As the son of his old associate, Tiberius received him politely with what Tacitus describes as 'the liberality he was in the habit of showing to the cadets of noble families'.[122] Drusus attended the interview. His reply to the father, to be relayed through M. Piso, was that 'if the current imputations were true, his own resentment must rank foremost of all; but he preferred to believe they were false and unfounded, and that Germanicus' death involved the doom of no one'.[123] Eschewing secrecy, and any favouritism it might imply, the reply was published for all to read.

On 16 December 19 CE, the Senate passed a decree honouring the memory of Germanicus (*Senatus Consultum de honoribus Germanici decernendis*) with a slew of official distinctions.[124] Henceforth, his name was to be celebrated in the *Song of the Salii* (*Saliari Carmine*); chairs of state with garlands of oak leaves over them were to be set up in the places designated for the priesthood of the *Augustales*; his bust (*imago*), carved in ivory, was to lead the procession in the games of the Circus; and no *flamen* or *augur* – except when a member of *gens Iulia* – was to be chosen in the Room of Germanicus. Furthermore, triumphal arches were to be erected at Rome, on the banks of the Rhine and on Mount Amanus in Syria, with an inscription recording his achievements and how he had died in the service of the Roman People. A commemorative mound was to be raised at Epidaphnae, where he had died, and a cenotaph was to be built in Antiocheia on the Orontes, where the body was cremated. Numerous statues were also to be displayed in public places. To all of these, Tiberius willingly consented. However, when a golden shield (*clipeus*) of great size was voted to him as a 'leader among orators', Tiberius 'declared that he would dedicate to him one of the usual kind, similar to the rest, for in eloquence, he said, there was no distinction of rank, and it was a sufficient glory for him to be classed among ancient writers'.[125] The *equites* renamed the seats in the theatre known as 'The Juniors' as 'Germanicus' Benches' and agreed that their cavalry troop was to ride in procession behind his effigy in the *Transvectio equitum* on 15 July each year.[126] Tiberius paid Clutorius Priscus, an *eques*, to write a poem mourning Germanicus' death, which was widely read.[127] Tiberius' own remarks, possibly including a poem (*carmen* or *libellus*), were inscribed on plaques to be distributed across the empire.[128]

Crowds of mourners met Agrippina and Caius Caligula in respectful silence when they disembarked at Brundisium.[129] Tiberius had sent two Praetorian Cohorts to the port city to accompany her on her 542-kilometre (337-mile) journey by road to Rome.[130] He instructed the city magistrates of *coloniae* in Calabria, Apulia and Campania to pay the last honours to his son's memory. Preceded by standard bearers carrying unadorned *signa* and lictors bearing their *fasces* reversed to point downwards, the tribunes and centurions carried upon their shoulders the bier bearing Germanicus' urn. Passing through each town along the route, the inhabitants turned out dressed in black, the *equites* in their official robes, burning vestments and perfumes while displaying their grief by tears and wailing. Joining the procession at Tarracina (Terracina) were Drusus and Claudius with Germanicus' children, who had been at Rome. The new consuls, M. Valerius Messalla (II) and M. Aurelius Cotta Maximus Messalinus, and a great many ordinary people, thronged the *Via Appia* in scattered groups.[131]

The cortège finally reached Rome, probably in March 20 CE.[132] On the day of the funeral, Agrippina, her children, Drusus and Claudius processed with torches burning across the *Campus Martius* to the Mausoleum of Augustus. There were some who contrasted this simple ceremonial to mark Germanicus' passing with the full state funeral laid on for his father, Nero Drusus, years before.[133] Throughout this sorrowful time, Tiberius and Livia did not appear in public, preferring to remain inside the *Palatium*.[134] People speculated on Tiberius' motives for his conspicuous absence and with it, their criticism of him intensified.

People also continued to take to the streets of Rome to vent their fury and grief. There were growing demands for the culprit to face the consequences of his actions – and many blamed Tiberius personally for the loss of their national hero.[135] Tiberius knew that the *status quo ante* had to be restored in Rome – and quickly. He issued a proclamation in which he stated that,

> Many illustrious Romans had died for their country, but none had been honoured with such a fervour of regret: a compliment highly valued by himself and by all, if only restraint were observed. For the same conduct was not becoming to ordinary families or communities and to leaders of the *Res Publica* and to an imperial people. Mourning and the solace of tears had suited the first throes of their affliction; but now they must recall their minds to fortitude, as once *Divus* Iulius at the loss of his only daughter, and *Divus* Augustus at the taking of his grandchildren, had thrust aside their anguish. There was no need of examples from the past, showing how often the Roman People had patiently endured the defeats of armies, the loss of leaders, the total extinction of noble families. Statesmen were mortal, the *Res Publica* eternal. Let them return, therefore, to their usual occupations and – as the Megalesian Games would soon be exhibited – resume even their pleasures![136]

His appeal was heard; normal life resumed. With the city now calm, Drusus left Rome to continue his mission.[137]

In Africa, Tacfarinas and his confederation raised the standard of revolt again – initially by random raids, and later by destroying villages and pillaging on a larger scale. The violence culminated at a fort beside a river that was occupied by a cohort commanded by Decrius. Assembling the men in front of the camp, he addressed them and then led them into battle. The lines of Roman troops soon collapsed and Decrius was killed in the mêlée.[138] Learning of the embarrassing defeat, L. Apronius, who had succeeded Camillus as proconsul, decimated the dishonoured cohort, drawing by lot and flogging to death every tenth man (*decimatio*).[139] Word of the punishment spread to other units. When Tacfarinas' army assaulted Thala, it was soundly routed by a detachment of some 500 army veterans (*vexillum veteranorum*). During the engagement, one soldier, named Helvius Rufus, saved a Roman citizen's life, for which Apronius presented him with a collar (*torquis*) and spear (*hasta*); Tiberius later awarded Rufus the civic crown (*corona civica*), regretting, 'more in sorrow than in anger, that the proconsul had not exercised his power to award this further honour'.[140] Now sustaining losses, Tacfarinas resorted to guerrilla warfare. As long as the African rebel leader adhered to this strategy, 'he befooled with impunity the baffled and exhausted Roman'.[141] Then he made an error of judgment, moving from the interior of the country to the coast, where, encumbered by his train of booty which kept him near a fixed encampment, he was attacked. Apronius Caesianus – marching on his father's orders with the most mobile of the legionaries, reinforced by the cavalry and auxiliary cohorts – fought a successful engagement and drove Tacfarinas back into the desert.

Over decades, the number of children relative to other age groups in the Roman population had declined. Encouraging Roman families to marry and have children was the intended purpose of the unpopular *Lex Papia Poppaea* enacted by Augustus in 9 CE. However, it had failed, punitively impacting married couples unable to have children, as well as those deciding not to raise families.[142] The penalty imposed for breaches of the law, including confiscation of property, enabled *delatores* to spy on citizens, pry into their private lives and file prosecutions in the hope of financial gain. To study the issue and make recommendations leading to amendments of the comitial statute, Tiberius appointed a review board comprising five ex-consuls, five ex-praetors and five senators selected by lot.[143] While he awaited their findings, the law remained in effect.

In a high-profile case, Aemilia Lepida – the great-granddaughter of L. Cornelius Sulla and Cn. Pompeius Magnus – was accused of pretending to be a mother by P. Quirinus, who was a rich but childless man.[144] Charges of adultery, poisonings and of inquiries made through astrologers concerning the imperial house were levelled against her. She was defended in court by her brother, M'. Lepidus. Seeing how unyielding was Quirinus' enmity towards Lepida, the public began to sympathize with her. Tiberius first beseeched the Senate not to deal with the charges, and subsequently induced M. Servilius, an ex-consul, to divulge what he had apparently wished to deny. Tiberius surrendered Lepida's slaves, who were in military custody, to the consuls but would not allow them to be subjected to torture on matters relating to his own family. Her trial was interrupted, in the meantime, by games (*ludi*).[145] On one of the days, Lepida went into the Theatre of Pompeius with some notable women. In a dramatic public gesture, she appealed to her ancestors, rousing such sympathy that many in the audience shouted curses at Quirinus. Under torture, Lepida's slaves revealed her bad behaviour. Found guilty, a motion proposed by Rubellius Blandus was carried, leading to her being outlawed. While others had proposed a milder sentence, Drusus had supported Blandus. Scaurus, who had fathered a daughter by her, obtained as a concession that her property should not be confiscated. Tiberius then stated that he too had ascertained from Quirinius' slaves that Lepida had attempted to murder their master by poison.

Having taken a long, circuitous route from Cilicia, Piso (II) and Plancina finally arrived in Rome. They sailed their ship up the Tiber and berthed – provocatively – beside the Mausoleum of Augustus.[146] The couple held ostentatious dinner parties in their house on the Palatinus Hill. If their intention was to project confidence and unity, that would now be severely challenged. Also in Rome were Q. Veranius and P. Vitellius.[147] They now went to file the application with the consuls to bring an action for *maiestas* against Piso and his wife.[148] They soon discovered, however, that L. Fulcinius Trio, an *accusator* – one of the new cadre of legal professionals who made accusations to bring cases to court – had already asked them for permission to file the indictment. Trio was reproached by Veranius and Vitellius, who argued that Trio had no standing and, since they represented the deceased, it was *their* privilege to file, not his. Conceding the point, the *accusator* withdrew his application and sought, instead, to file a new charge based on Piso's financial mismanagement during his earlier career. Veranius and Vitellius went back to the consuls, who then asked Tiberius to take the case. Recognizing the difficulties such a case would pose, he called upon his close friends and advisers. He listened to the arguments presented by the prosecution and the defence, with Piso representing himself. The mood in the city was febrile. The mob demanded justice. Throughout the city, walls were daubed with the words 'GIVE US BACK GERMANICUS!'.[149]

Tiberius announced that he would attend the hearing in person, but *not* as the presiding judge.[150] He had long been dissatisfied by the way in which cases were being handled and chose to oversee them himself, a stance that was in keeping with his penchant for attending trials as an *assessor*. Acting for the prosecution were Q. Servaeus, Trio, Veranius and Vitellius. Drusus, now back from Dalmatia, postponed his *ovatio* to join his fellow advocates.[151] For his defence, Piso (II) had assembled a strong team comprising some of Rome's great names, including M. Aemilius Lepidus (II), Livineius Regulus (I) and his own brother, L. Calpurnius Piso (I).[152]

In a pre-trial arraignment hearing, Tiberius addressed the senators and the trial advocates.[153] He reminded them that Piso had been Augustus' legate and friend, but that he himself had picked Piso to govern Syria.[154] In deciding what happened between him and Germanicus, Tiberius said it was for the senators 'to make their determination with open [or unbiased] minds'.[155] He expressed his exasperation with the prosecution for circulating a story that Germanicus was killed by poison because it still required thorough investigation. That said, he would not prevent any evidence from being presented:

> If, however, a crime is discovered which ought to be punished, whoever the murdered man may be, it is for you to give just reparation both to the children of Germanicus and to us, his parents.[156]

On one important point Tiberius was adamant. 'Let the case be tried as simply as others,' he is reported to have said, 'let no one heed the tears of Drusus or my own.'[157] He specified that the trial would be held not in the *Forum*, as was normal practice, but in the *Curia Iulia*, 'not before a bench of judges, but before the Senate'.[158] Piso would be tried by his own peers. All sides agreed to allow two days for the prosecution to bring forward the indictments and, after an interval of six days, for the defence to have three days to present its case.[159]

On the first day of the trial in December, the *Curia* was packed. Over 300 senators stood or sat on seats arranged in rows facing each other.[160] At the far end of the high-ceilinged hall, on a raised dais, Tiberius sat on a curule chair between the two consuls, Valerius Messalla and Aurelius Cotta. Behind them stood the golden statue of Victoria carrying the *clipeus virtutis* inscribed with the famed virtues of Augustus.[161] Fulcinius Trio set up the prosecution's case by reminding the Senate about Piso's track record with accusations concerning intrigues and extortion during his administration of Hispania Tarraconensis.[162] Servaeus spoke next, followed by Veranius. According to Tacitus' account, Vitellius – the team's most eloquent speaker – exhorted the jury of his fellow senators,

> that out of hatred of Germanicus and a desire of revolution, Piso had so corrupted the common soldiers by licence and oppression of the allies that he was called by the vilest of them 'Father of the Legions' while on the other hand to all the best men, especially to the companions and friends of Germanicus, he had been savagely cruel.[163]

'Lastly,' Vitellius said,

> He had destroyed Germanicus himself by sorceries and poison, and hence came those ceremonies and horrible sacrifices made by himself and Plancina; then he had threatened the *Res Publica* with war, and had been defeated in battle, before he could be tried as a prisoner.[164]

The charges against Piso were thus much broader than just the murder of Germanicus.[165] The prosecution then enthusiastically presented the disquieting findings of their investigation at the house in which Germanicus had died.

The defence was overwhelmed by the torrent of accusations. They could not deny that Piso had interfered with the soldiers, nor that he had abandoned his province or that he had insulted his superior officer. Tacitus comments that, 'it was only the charge of poisoning from which he seemed to have cleared himself'.[166] Piso's advocates defended him vigorously, calling into question the credibility of the suggestion that the defendant had dropped a dose of poison into Germanicus' food. There were many people present during the meal, they argued, any of whom could have seen the deed performed. However, the senators 'could not be sufficiently convinced that there had been no treachery about the death of Germanicus'.[167] The prosecution was eager to show that Piso *had* administered poison during the dinner which allegedly caused Germanicus' death. To prove their case, they planned to present Martina as their star witness, but that line of attack was about to be frustrated. Mysteriously, she 'had suddenly yielded up the ghost at Brundisium; that poison had been concealed in a knot of her hair; and that no indications of self-murder had been found on the body'.[168] For lack of evidence, the charge of murder was dismissed.

Tiberius himself was much more interested in the grave allegation 'that war had been declared on a province'.[169] Tempers flared during the trial. 'The accusers and witnesses delivered their competing invectives,' writes Tacitus, 'without a voice to answer, [and] pity rather than anger began to deepen.'[170] Throughout the proceedings, Tiberius maintained an unemotional expression, listening carefully to each word.[171] Piso was seen to clutch a papyrus scroll – or so Tacitus recalled his elders saying when he was a youth.[172] At no time during the trial did Piso disclose the contents of this mysterious document. Many speculated that it was a letter from Tiberius, in which he gave Piso specific instructions regarding Germanicus. A demand for the correspondence to be read as evidence was rejected by Tiberius as well as by the defendant. Watching her husband's chances of acquittal fading fast, Plancina arranged for her defence to be handled separately.[173] She approached her friend, Augusta, and, in private, cut a deal with her – much to Tiberius' chagrin. It gave Plancina immunity from investigation and prosecution.

Outside the great bronze doors of the *Curia*, the crowd had become volatile. Some threatened the senators inside with violence if they let Piso go free; others took their anger out on statues of Piso. Having pulled the statues off their pedestals, they were preparing to throw them down the *Scalae Gemoniae* (the steep 'Gemonian Stairs').[174] Only Tiberius' direct intervention stopped the spread of mob violence.

In fear of his life, Piso went home borne in a litter, with a tribune of the Praetorian Cohorts following closely behind.[175] In his Palatine residence, Piso withdrew to his private office, where he wrote a letter. He sealed it using his personal signet ring and gave the document to one of his freedmen. Piso then relaxed with his wife. After she left his bedroom late that night, he ordered the doors to the room to be closed. At dawn, Piso's personal slave tapped on the door. Hearing no sound inside, he entered timidly. He found his master dead, laying on the floor in a pool of blood. His throat had been cut.[176] An army-issue *gladius* was found on the floor beside the body.[177] Rumours began to circulate that he been murdered by an operative working on the orders of Tiberius – or Seianus.[178]

Piso's death did not stop the trial, however. Tiberius solemnly read out Piso's letter – what amounted to his suicide note.[179] In it, Piso refuted the claims of his enemies, restated his loyalty to Tiberius and appealed for leniency for his son. The Senate continued hearing the case without the accused present. The defence team then gave its final statement. The magistrates presented their report (*relatio*) in the first instance to Aurelius Cotta, the consul.[180] To their proposals (*rogatio*), 301 senators assented.[181] The decree of the Senate (*Senatus Consultum de Cn. Pisone Patre*), dated 10 December 20 CE, records that Piso (II) was found guilty of flouting his authority, disobeying Germanicus' orders, colluding with Rome's enemies to provoke war with Armenia and Parthia, provoking civil war in a Roman province, illegally executing citizens, corrupting military discipline, openly rejoicing at the death of an enemy and violating the spirit of *Divus* Augustus.[182]

Cotta announced the punishment. In accordance with practice on *damnatio memoriae*, the name of Piso would be expunged from the records; additionally, one half of his property was confiscated, and the other made over to his son, Cn. Piso (who should change his first name). Furthermore, it was ruled that M. Piso should be stripped of his senatorial rank, and that he be relegated for a period of ten years with a gratuity of HS 5 million.[183] Exercising his *clementia*, Tiberius intervened to mitigate the harshest penalties.[184] On account of his firm policy position against pecuniary temptations, and the shame he felt at the acquittal of Plancina, he was lenient towards M. Piso. He absolved him from the charge of waging civil war, for 'the orders came from a father, and a son could not have disobeyed', and he saved him from ignominy.[185] He returned Piso's confiscated estate to the sons. Tiberius vetoed the proposals from Valerius Messalinus to erect a golden statue and from Caecina Severus to set up an altar to Vengeance in the Temple of Mars Ultor, stating that these 'should only be consecrated after victories abroad'.[186] It was a time for healing. 'Domestic calamities,' he said, 'called for sorrow and concealment.'[187] For avenging Germanicus, Messalinus had suggested that Tiberius, Augusta, Antonia, Agrippina and Drusus all ought to be officially thanked for their services, but in doing so he omitted Claudius, his devoted brother. Claudius' name was added after L. Asprenas demanded to know in the Senate if the omission was a deliberate act. Tiberius recommended that the Senate confer priesthoods on Vitellius, Veranius and Servaeus.[188] As an *accusator*, Trio would have hoped to receive a share of the estate as his *praemium*, but it was not to be in this case. Instead, by way of compensation, a few days after the trial, Tiberius promised him his personal support should he ever decide to stand as a candidate for public office – but he warned him not to precipitate the opportunity by his violent rhetoric.

To participate in the trial of Piso, Drusus had gone to Rome as a private citizen. Soon after the legal action ended, he returned to his military command in Dalmatia and, imbued with his *imperium*, officially re-entered Rome to celebrate his ovation.[189] As an additional reward, he was elected to be consul for 21 CE.[190] A few days later, his mother, Vipsania Agrippina, died; she was the woman – perhaps the *only* one – whom Tiberius truly loved.[191] Two other notables of Roman society passed away at the end of 20 CE: C. Sallustius Crispus, the confidant of Tiberius, and L. Volusius Saturninus, who had served Augustus as governor of Africa and Syria.[192] Arminius of the Cherusci also died, aged 37 years. Tacitus reports that after twelve years in power, he had become ever more autocratic, especially since the exile of Maroboduus. He was assassinated by one of his relatives.[193]

## Chapter 7

# Holding a Wolf by the Ears: 21–25 CE

In 21 CE, for the first time, Tiberius and Drusus served as consuls together in the same year.[1] It was Tiberius' fourth consulship and his son's second. Tiberius would be 62 on his next birthday, Drusus 35. The never-ending work of being 'First Man' was taking its toll on Tiberius. Needing a break from Rome – Tacitus cites restoring his health as the reason for respite – he decided to spend part of the year in Campania.[2] After just three months in office, Tiberius resigned the consulship, yielding his curule chair to Mamercus Aemilius Scaurus as suffect consul.[3] His departure from the city soon after allowed Drusus to exercise his authority independently of his father. One reported episode raised his popularity. The old and respected ex-*praetor* Domitius Corbulo complained to the Senate that L. Sulla, a young man of the *nobiles*, had not made room for him in the seating at recent gladiatorial games. When the arguing between each party's supporters became raucous, Drusus intervened to bring order. The uncle of Sulla apologized to Corbulo. In another debate, Corbulo complained that necessary road repairs were not being carried out in Italy because of dishonest contractors and negligent officials; Drusus himself took on the management of the task, in part paying for the work through confiscations of land and court convictions.

The House of Tiberius marked other family milestones. Germanicus' son, Nero Caesar, came of age and, at the urging of Tiberius, he was admitted into the *Vigintiviri* ('College of Twenty Men') before the legal age.[4] On the day of Nero's first official entry into the *Forum Romanum*, largesse was distributed to the plebeians.[5] Additionally, Seianus' rising favour with Tiberius was recognized with the binding of the two families through the marriage of the daughter of Seianus by Apicata to Claudius' son.[6]

By letter, Tiberius informed the Senate that Tacfarinas was active again in Africa.[7] He wrote 'that they must use their judgment in choosing as proconsul an experienced soldier of vigorous constitution, who would be equal to the war'.[8] Arguments ensued over two potential candidates' reputations, but the debate quickly digressed on to whether a governor of a province should take his wife (who could be a distraction) and who should govern Asia. In the event, Aemilius Lepidus (II) was chosen, but they could not agree on who should lead the counterinsurgency in Africa. Instead, the Senate chose to defer to Tiberius.

Evidently irritated, Tiberius replied in writing that he should not have to make every political decision which the Senate could perfectly well decide by itself. He proposed two men for the post. The Senate picked one of his two suggestions. Iunius Blaesus – uncle of Seianus – immediately left to take up his commission.[9] Paterculus describes Blaesus as 'no ordinary helper, a man whom one does not know whether to consider more useful in the camp or better in the *toga*'.[10]

Thrace too was in turmoil. Divided between Roimetalkes II and the sons of Kotys IV (under the supervision of T. Trebellienus Rufus), the parties objected to the imposition of Roman rules over their traditional ways.[11] Patriotic elements among the Coelaletae, Dii and Odrysae nations openly criticized Roimetalkes for not taking action and, in protest, they took up arms themselves; but rather than uniting against the Romans, they fought each other, blockading the king at Philippopolis. The nearest commander, P. Vellaeus, led cohorts of legionaries to liberate the king, while auxiliary cavalry and infantry confronted the Thracians who were pillaging the countryside.[12] The rebels were almost wiped out, with no casualties reported on the Roman side.

Meanwhile, a rebellion broke out among the supposedly pacified peoples of Belgica and Gallia Lugdunensis. Iulius Florus of the Treveri and Iulius Sacrovir of the Aedui were both aristocrats whose fathers or grandfathers had served Rome and been given citizenship.[13] They tapped into the widespread resentments among local communities towards the Romans over the seemingly unending tributes levied on them, the punitive rates of interest on loans they were charged, the cruelty and arrogance of the legates sent to govern them and the lingering sense of demoralization of the legionaries following the death of Germanicus.[14] The two men succeeded in assembling a coalition of disaffected Gallic tribes. The first to raise the standard of rebellion were the Andecavi and Turoni (in what are now respectively Anjou and Touraine).[15] Acilius Aviola, the *legatus Augusti Proptraetore* of Gallia Lugdunensis, took direct action. The Andecavi fell to the *Cohortis Urbanae* dispatched from *Colonia* Munatia,[16] while the Turoni succumbed to cohorts of legionaries sent by C. Visellius Varro of Germania Inferior, supported by units of several Gallic tribal leaders. Advised of the counterinsurgency measures, Tiberius apparently doubted the need for additional military intervention.[17] In the conflict, Sacrovir fought gallantly with his head bared so his men could see him. Florus convinced some troops of an *ala* of the Treveri to join him, together with a mob of the indebted who found common cause. The target of their ire was Roman businessmen.[18] They then made for the protective cover of the *Saltus* Arduenna (Ardennes Forest). On the way, they were intercepted by detachments of legions sent by the *legati Augusti* of Germania Inferior and Superior and led by Iulius Indus, a fellow Gaul but one who deeply despised Florus. Indus' army engaged the rebels, but in the ensuing rout Florus fled. Seeing no way to escape the encirclement by Roman soldiers, rather than surrender, he took his own life, thereby ending the revolt of the Treveri.

The Aedui continued with their struggle, however. Sacrovir occupied Augustodunum (Autun), the city founded by Augustus for this Gallic nation.[19] He took as hostages the sons of the Gallic aristocracy who were studying there to force their parents to join him. In preparation for the revolt, Sacrovir had arranged for weapons and equipment to be manufactured in secret.[20] His army numbered some 40,000; of these, 8,000 were heavily equipped like legionaries, but the majority just wielded spears and knives. Unusually, he had a small unit of men from the local gladiator school (*ludus*) who were training as *crupellarii*, a novel type of combatant for the arena who was fully encased in articulated plate armour, which made each man able to withstand direct hits, but at the cost of agility of movement.[21] After the Roman legates from the two Germanies argued over who should be in overall command, the younger and more experienced C. Silius assumed the leadership role. He sent auxiliaries to devastate the villages of the Sequani which adjoined Germania Superior and were neighbours of the Aedui.[22] Silius marched with two legions of highly motivated troops who were eager to fight, seeing the war as good as already won. Twelve miles outside Augustodunum, the opposing forces clashed. The professional Roman soldiers quickly crushed the amateur rebel army, resorting to axes and mattocks to hack down the gladiators encased in steel.[23] Sacrovir fled into the city to a house where he committed suicide; subsequently, the building was burned to the ground. His body was never found.

'And now at last a letter from Tiberius,' writes Tacitus, 'informed the Senate of the outbreak *and* completion of a war.'[24] In Rome, wild rumours had spread that the sixty nations of *Tres Galliae* were all in revolt, the tribes of Germania had joined them and the two Hispaniae were also at risk. Tiberius was severely criticized by people and senators alike for remaining in Italy and not going to direct the counterinsurgency operations in person. In his letter, Tiberius wrote that,

> the loyalty and courage of his *legati*, and his own policy, had won the day. At the same time, he added the reasons why neither Drusus nor himself had left for the war, insisting on the extent of the empire and on the loss of prestige to the sovereign if the disaffection of one or two communities could make him abandon the capital, which was the centre of government for the whole. However, now that fear was not the motive-force, he would go, view matters on the spot, and arrange a settlement.[25]

The Senate responded with vows for the *princeps*' safe return from Campania, various supplications and other excessive compliments; P. Cornelius Dolabella even proposed that he should enter the city with an ovation.[26] In his rescript, Tiberius replied that, 'after subduing some of the fiercest of nations, and receiving or rejecting so many triumphs in his youth, he was not so undistinguished as to crave a futile honour conferred for an excursion in the suburbs at his age'.[27]

Even as Roman armies were engaged in military action to re-establish order in the restless provinces, the Senate in Rome was enacting business of the political kind to uphold decency in public discourse in the mercurial homeland. People of all classes were discovering that they could insult and blame high-profile citizens yet avoid punishment just by grabbing something bearing Tiberius' image.[28] Even slaves and freedmen were scaring their former masters by speaking out or acting aggressively against them. C. Cestius Gallus commented on the disturbing trend. He acknowledged that leaders were, in some ways, like gods, but even gods only listened to fair requests. He pointed out that the laws seemed useless because someone he had proven guilty of fraud could openly threaten him in the *Forum*, using a picture of the ruler to shield him- or herself from a charge. Others shared similar or worse experiences, demanding that Drusus punish those who were causing trouble. To set an example, Drusus ordered the arrest of Annia Rufilla, who had been convicted of insulting the senator, and, after a trial, imprisoned her. Separately, Considius Aequus and Caelius Cursor, two *equites* who had accused *praetor* Magius Caecilianus of *maiestas*, were punished by the Senate for their false claims following Tiberius' directive.[29] The work of the *delatores* also continued unabated: Ancharius Priscus accused Caesius Cordus, who was proconsul of Creta and Cyrene, of wrongdoing, to which was added a charge of *maiestas*.[30] Antistius Vetus, a leading man from Macedonia, was acquitted of adultery, but Tiberius scolded the judges and brought him back for trial for having been involved in plotting with Raiskuporis to make war against Rome after the murder of Kotys IV.[31] Vetus was found guilty and sentenced to be banned from receiving the necessities of 'fire and water', and was kept on an island having no easy access to either Macedonia or Thrace.[32] Separately, Tiberius requested the Senate to grant a public funeral for P. Sulpicius Quirinus.[33] He was a noted soldier who had defeated the Homonadenses in Cilicia for Augustus, for which he earned a triumph, and was one of the few who had visited Tiberius while on Rhodes.[34]

Rome was constantly at risk from fire. A conflagration completely destroyed the Theatre of Pompeius (*Theatrum Pompei*) in the *Campus Martius*.[35] Arriving at the scene, Seianus took the initiative to prevent the fire from spreading further, likely rallying the men of the *Cohortes Vigilum* to assist. This organization, which trained for just such an eventuality, was commanded by a dedicated officer, the *praefectus vigilum*, under Tiberius.[36] The fire was extinguished, but the theatre was extensively damaged. Tiberius committed to restoring it.[37]

Towards the end of the year, C. Clutorius Priscus, who had written a poem mourning Germanicus' death, faced a distressing situation. A *delator* accused him of composing another set of verses while Drusus was sick and having planned to profit from it if the *princeps*' son died.[38] Boasting rather carelessly, Clutorius spoke of this in P. Petronius' house to Vitellia, his host's mother-in-law, with many high-ranking women present. When the informant filed a charge, most of the guests were scared into testifying – all except Vitellia, who claimed she had heard nothing. However, the witnesses with testimonies supporting the accusation were believed. Dec. Haterius Agrippa (the consul designate) pushed for the severest punishment. M. Aemilius Lepidus (II) objected, arguing that while Clutorius' words were plainly outrageous, the punishment should not exceed the severity of the crime.[39] He proposed confiscation of his property, exile and banning him from receiving 'fire and water'. Only one ex-consul, C. Rubellius Blandus, agreed with Lepidus; the rest voted for Agrippa's proposal, leading to Priscus' immediate imprisonment and swift execution.[40] In a written response, Tiberius praised the Senate for its loyalty in defending him from insults but criticized them for their haste in harshly punishing what was only a verbal slip. He praised Lepidus but did not blame Agrippa. The Senate agreed that, henceforth, death sentences would require a nine-day waiting period while the decree was registered at the *Aerarium*, and a person's case should not be made public within that time.[41]

With Tacfarinas still ravaging Africa, the consuls for 22 CE, Haterius Agrippa and C. Sulpicius Galba, saw to it that Blaesus' proconsular term was extended by a year.[42] In other business, they held debates about reining in overspending by people of means on opulent or lewd living – the extravagant banquets, flamboyant clothes worn by both men and women, lavish decorations of villas and enormous hordes of slaves.[43] The contrast with Tiberius' personal restraint had provoked fear of curbs imposed on others' excesses. 'In money matters he was frugal and close,' writes Suetonius, 'never allowing the companions of his foreign tours and campaigns a salary, but merely their keep.'[44] Leading by example, at formal dinners he often served meats left over from the day before or presented half of a boar, declaring that it had all the same good qualities of a whole one.[45] He was unabashedly pragmatic. When heavy rain fell during a festival he was attending, he took off his cumbersome *toga* and sensibly donned a dark woollen cloak.[46] He had been known to complain bitterly that the prices of Corinthian bronzes had risen to an immense figure and that three mullets had once been sold for H̶S̶ 30,000. Even his *familia* of slaves was modest.[47] In the Senate, C. Calpurnius Bibulus spoke for the *aediles* who argued that the law restricting expenditures was being largely ignored, that food prices were rising by the day and that the policy measures available to mitigate them were ineffective.[48] The Senate deferred the matter to Tiberius, who was still in Campania. In a rescript he replied that he could not force self-control upon these high-living individuals and asked to be excused from ruling on such an unpopular matter.[49] 'Something greater and loftier is expected of a *princeps*,' writes Tacitus in his version of the letter,

> and while everybody takes to himself the credit of right policy, one alone has to bear the odium of every person's failures … Such, Senators, are the anxieties which the *princeps* has to sustain, and the neglect of them will be utter ruin to the *Res Publica*.[50]

The *aediles* were then exempted from enforcing the law. Tiberius proposed that a limit be set on household furniture and that their prices in the market should be regulated each year at the discretion of the Senate.[51] The *aediles* were similarly instructed to impose restrictions on price increases at cook-shops and eating-houses (*popinas ganeasque*).

Tiberius subsequently wrote asking the Senate to grant Drusus tribunician power,[52] arguing that his son was now the same age as he had been when Augustus empowered him. The Senate responded with the usual offers of erecting statues of Drusus, altars to the gods, temples, arches and other honours.[53] When Haterius proposed that that the text of the decree itself should be inscribed with gold lettering into the walls of the *Curia Iulia*, some of the senators present laughed mockingly. In his rescript, Tiberius rejected the gold lettering outright, describing it as 'contrary to Roman custom'.[54] Drusus did receive the *tribunicia potestas*.[55]

The Senate was approached on several matters. The priest (*flamen*) of Jupiter, Servius Cornelius Lentulus Maluginensis, made an unusual request: he wanted the governorship of Asia.[56] Many interpreted – incorrectly, he asserted – that the law prohibited a *flamen* of Rome's chief god from leaving Italy on the basis that the schedule of religious rites could never be interrupted, yet when he had fallen ill other priests had taken his place without anyone complaining. Moreover, the *flamines* of Mars and Quirinus, who had the same status he enjoyed, *were* permitted provincial appointments. The matter was referred to the *Pontifex Maximus*. Tiberius then postponed his investigation into the legal standing of the *flamen*, blocking Maluginensis' request for the time being.[57]

During the year, the Senate discussed petitions received from the proconsular provinces.[58] Facing increasing numbers of abuses of the rights of sanctuary in which criminals and slaves were receiving asylum, often undeservedly, communities in the East were facing outbreaks of civil disorder. Delegations arrived in Rome from Crete and Cyrene, Cyprus, Ephesus, Hierocaesarea, Magnesia on the Meander and Sardis.[59] Overwhelmed by the number and complexity of the claims, the Conscript Fathers asked the consuls to study them and report back with their findings of fact and recommendations.[60]

Tiberius hurried back to Rome when he learned that his mother, now aged 81, was seriously ill. Although they still enjoyed good relations, a recent incident had stirred tension between them. While dedicating an image to *Divus* Augustus near the Theatre of Marcellus, Augusta placed Tiberius' name *after* hers in the official inscription.[61] This act, interpreted by many as undermining the *princeps*' imperial dignity, was believed to have troubled Tiberius, though if it did, he concealed his displeasure. The Senate then ordered special prayers and the Great Games (*Ludi Megalenses*) to be exhibited by the *pontifices*, the *augures* and the *Quindecemviri*, assisted by the colleges of the *Septemviri* and the *Sodales Augustales*. L. Apronius suggested that the *Fetiales* should oversee the Games, but Tiberius disagreed.

He argued that certain priesthoods had distinct privileges and cited precedents, specifically stating that the *Fetiales* did not hold such high prestige as the other colleges. He noted that the *Augustales* were only included because it was associated with the imperial family on the occasion in which their vows were being fulfilled.

Tiberius again had to watch the Senate to ensure that it scrupulously followed due process. In one case, C. Iunius Silanus was indited for extortion (*repetundae*) by the people of the province of Asia.[62] The charge was elevated to *maiestas* when former consul Mamercus Scaurus, Iunius Otho, a *praetor*, and Bruttedius Niger, an *aedile*, accused Silanus of both disrespecting Augustus' divinity and disregarding Tiberius' authority. The accusers had their own share of failings. Iunius Otho, a schoolteacher-turned-senator through Seianus' influence, showed his brazenness; Bruttedius, a man with ambitions, was impatient. Members of Silanus' staff – Gellius Publicola and M. Paconius, Silanus' former *quaestor* and legate respectively – joined the prosecution.[63] Few doubted that Silanus was guilty of cruelty and corruption. Lacking any legal expertise and hindered by fear for his life, Silanus stood alone, unable to fairly defend himself while facing hostile senators and several of the most skilled advocates from Asia. Tiberius himself undermined Silanus' case through his remarks, menacing looks and persistent questioning, leaving little room for the defendant to refute or evade questioning. His slaves were sold to the *Fiscus* so that they could be tortured to extract confessions.[64] No one came to his defence and the charges of *maiestas* compelled any who might to remain silent. Silanus requested a brief adjournment. Abandoning his defence, he wrote a personal petition to the *princeps*.

Tiberius sought to establish a clear precedent for his actions against Silanus. He recalled a past case involving L. Valerius Messalla Volesus (a former proconsul of Asia) in a letter written by Augustus and the decree sanctioned by the Senate, which he ordered read out.[65] L. Calpurnius Piso (I) suggested that Silanus be banned from receiving 'fire and water' and sent to the island of Gyarus, a proposal echoed by others, although Cn. Cornelius Lentulus (II) argued that Silanus' property derived from his mother's Atian line and should be restored to his son. Tiberius agreed.[66] P. Cornelius Dolabella, aiming to please him further, proposed barring any individuals with a scandalous life and wicked reputation from attaining provincial governorship positions, leaving all such decisions to the *princeps'* own discretion. Tiberius strongly disagreed. He was aware of the rumours concerning Silanus, he said, emphasizing that legal judgments should not be based on rumours. He argued against retroactive laws and autocratic decisions, advocating for due process. He suggested Cythnus was a more suitable place than Gyarus for Silanus' exile – a personal request made by Silanus' sister, Iunia Torquata.[67] This proposal was accepted without further debate.

The Senate received the accusation filed by Ancharius Priscus, proconsul of Crete and Cyrene, resulting in Caesius Cordus being found guilty of extortion, to which was added a supplemental charge of *maiestas*.[68] In contrast, when L. Ennius, a Roman *eques*, was accused of *maiestas* for allegedly melting down a small statue of the *princeps* for household purposes, Tiberius prohibited the trial from taking place. Ateius Capito, an authority on secular and religious law, protested. He emphasized that such a serious offence should not go unpunished, stating that while the ruler might be lenient toward personal grievances, Tiberius should not overlook the harm it did to the state. Tiberius foresaw the sinister implications of Capito's argument and resolutely rejected the case.[69]

Questions followed on religious matters. One was where to house the offering vowed by the *equites* to Fortuna-on-Horseback in fulfilment of a vow for Augusta's recovery.[70] Although there were many shrines to Fortuna in the city, none carried the specific epithet *equestri Fortunae*. They located a temple with that name at Antium, a place under the jurisdiction of Rome for all religious matters in Italian towns, and it was duly erected there. As *pontifex maximus*, Tiberius now addressed the postponed matter of the *Flamen Dialis*, Servius Cornelius Lentulus Maluginensis.[71] He presented a formal decree stating that if the *flamen* of Jupiter ever fell ill, he could be absent for more than two nights at the discretion of the *pontifex maximus*, but only on the conditions that it did not coincide with days designated for public sacrifice *and* that it occurred no more than two times in any given year. This ruling – dating from the time of Augustus – emphasized that a year-long absence thus made the *flamines* of Jupiter ineligible for governorships. Tiberius also referenced a past veto by the *pontifex maximus*, L. Caecilius Metellus, who had prevented the departure of the *flamen* A. Postumius.[72] Consequently, the consular next in seniority to Maluginensis was assigned to Asia.

Amid this flurry of legal actions, Tiberius showed his generosity by assuming responsibility for reconstructing at his own expense the Theatre of Pompeius destroyed by fire the previous year. He demonstrated his modesty by preserving the name of the original builder on the inscription affixed to the restored building.[73] He sincerely praised Seianus for preventing the fire from spreading further and received approval from the Senate to erect a statue of him inside the theatre in recognition of his good deed.[74] Thereafter, numerous private individuals erected images of Seianus and several speeches were given, praising him in public gatherings and before the Senate.[75] Prominent figures too, including the consuls, frequently visited his house early in the day for the *salutatio*. They not only conveyed their requests to be forwarded by him to Tiberius, but also discussed public affairs needing Seianus' personal attention. In this way, Seianus came to be involved in, or informed of, official matters.

When a large portico in Rome started to lean dangerously to one side, an unnamed architect managed to restore it to its original position in a remarkable manner. This architect strengthened the foundations and 'wrapped all the rest of the structure in fleeces and thick garments, binding it firmly together on all sides by means of ropes; then with the aid of many men and windlasses he raised it back to its original position'.[76] Tiberius admired his technical skill and rewarded him with money for his accomplishment. In Dio's opinion, Tiberius envied him too: he withheld the architect's name from the official records and banished him from the city. Later, goes the story, the exiled architect pleaded with Tiberius for forgiveness. He had a new invention to show Tiberius, a special, flexible glass. The man demonstrated this by purposely dropping a goblet made from his glass and, after finding it was dented, restored its shape just by the use of his fingers or a small hammer. Despite – or perhaps because of – the impressive demonstration, instead of granting him a pardon, Tiberius had the man's workshop destroyed (according to Pliny) 'in order to prevent the value of copper, silver, and gold, from becoming depreciated', or had him executed (according to Dio).[77]

The war to defeat Tacfarinas in Africa continued, steadily but surely, under Iunius Blaesus. His army had been augmented with the deployment of *Legio* VIIII *Hispana*.[78] Despite many tactical setbacks, Tacfarinas was still undefeated. He audaciously sent an embassy to Tiberius, demanding land for himself and his men and threatening a war without end if his terms were not met. Tiberius felt deeply and personally affronted. 'By all accounts,' writes Tacitus, 'no insult to himself and the Roman People ever stung the *princeps* more than this spectacle of a deserter and bandit aping the procedure of an unfriendly power.'[79] Even Spartacus, he recalled, had not been granted terms at the end of his revolt of gladiators and slaves, which caused significant turmoil and fear in Italy (in 73–71 BCE). Tiberius tasked Blaesus with persuading the rebels to put down their arms without consequence, but to ensure that Tacfarinas was captured by any means necessary. Many rebels readily accepted the amnesty they were offered. To beat their indefatigable leader, however, Blaesus adopted guerilla-style tactics similar to those used by the rebel chief himself.

Tacfarinas exploited the lightness and agility of his army deployed in small groups to ambush the Romans while on the march and raid their settlements.[80] Like Tiberius in Illyricum, Blaesus divided his army into three groups, which advanced upon the rebels simultaneously. Blaesus led the main force, setting up forts and entrenchments in the area. The second group, led by Blaesus' son, aimed to protect the settlements around Cirta.[81] *Legatus* Cornelius Scipio, leading the third army group, held the road by which the enemy had raided Leptis Minor (Lamta), and struck out against the Garamantes. Blaesus sub-divided the three army groups into smaller tactical units, each led by a battle-tested centurion.[82] Roman troops deployed across the province, often operating behind enemy lines and causing them significant losses. Rather than withdrawing for the winter, as was standard practice, Blaesus continued the campaign, establishing forts and relentlessly pursuing Tacfarinas as he moved from camp to camp in the Sahara Desert. In a significant success for the Romans, Tacfarinas' brother was taken alive. Tacfacrinas now abandoned the fight. Although there were some who felt the war was not yet over, Tiberius deemed the mission completed. He honoured Blaesus by allowing him to be acclaimed as *imperator* by his legions and awarded him triumphal honours – the first time in his reign.[83]

As the year ended, two prominent men passed away. One was Asinius Saloninus, son of Asinius Gallus and Vipsania (daughter of M. Agrippa and the first wife of Tiberius), who was to have married a daughter of Germanicus.[84] The other was jurist Ateius Capito. Exactly sixty-three years after the last Battle of Philippi (23 October 42 BCE), Iunia also died; she was the niece of Cato, and related to two leading assassins of Iulius Caesar, being the wife of C. Cassius Longinus and sister of M. Iunius Brutus.[85] In her will she left considerable wealth, mentioning almost every distinguished man in complimentary terms, except for Tiberius. He took the omission in good spirits and did not object to her funeral, which included a eulogy at the *Rostra Augusti*.[86] Effigies of twenty noble houses preceded her body to the family tomb, including members of Rome's distinguished clans, among them the *gentes Manlia* and *Quinctia*. However, the very absence of the portraits of Brutus and Cassius seemingly made their legacy shine even brighter in the eyes of many onlookers.

Tiberius remained in Rome through the following year, 23 CE. Germanicus Gemellus, one of the twin sons of Drusus, died.[87] Drusus Caesar, his grandson by Germanicus, now reached manhood and Tiberius distributed largesse to the plebeians.[88] As it had done for his brother, Nero Caesar, the Senate complimented the young man. On this important occasion, Tiberius spoke at the *Curia* and praised his own son, Drusus, noting how well disposed and kind he was to his nephews. He then raised the possibility that he might take a long-discussed tour of the provinces.[89] He observed that many soldiers' time in service had ended, and that conscription would be needed to raise sufficient numbers of new recruits to keep the army at full strength. He particularly noted that there was a shortage of good quality volunteers, remarking that 'those who did join willingly often lacked the courage and discipline shown by past generations because many of them were poor or homeless people'.[90] He recited the number of legions and the provinces in which they were stationed. They were the same deployments as in the last days of Augustus (Table 1) and he saw no reason to change the arrangement of troops.[91] Tiberius never did leave Italy.

In a related military matter – one that would come to have great consequence – Tiberius approved the construction of a permanent camp (*Castra Praetoria*) for the nine *Cohortes Praetoriae* on a high ridge just beyond the inhabited district of Rome to the far north-east.[92] Since the time of Augustus, the 10,000 men of the elite guard units, recruited from Etruria, Latium, Umbria and the long-established *coloniae*, had been dispersed around the city and across Italy.[93] Now, for the first time, they would be billeted together in purpose-built barracks, ready

Table 1: Disposition of the Legions, Summer 23 CE.

| Province | Units | Legions |
|---|---|---|
| Hispania Tarraconensis | 3 | IV *Macedonica*, VI *Victrix*, X *Gemina* |
| Germania Inferior | 4 | I *Germanica*, V *Alaudae*, XX *Valeria Victrix*, XXI *Rapax* |
| Germania Superior | 4 | II *Augusta*, XIII *Gemina*, XIV *Gemina*, XVI *Gallica* |
| Pannonia | 3 | VIII *Augusta*, VIIII *Hispana*, XV *Apollinaris* |
| Dalmatia | 2 | VII *Macedonica*, XI (later *Claudia*) |
| Moesia, Thracia-Macedoniaque, | 2 | IV *Scythica*, V *Macedonica* |
| Syria | 4 | III *Gallica*, VI *Ferrata*, X *Fretensis*, XII *Fulminata* |
| Aegyptus | 2 | III *Cyrenaica*, XXII *Deiotariana* |
| Africa | 1 | III *Augusta* |

Sources: Tac., *Ann.* 4.5; Hardy (1889), p.631; Lendering (Livius.org); Ritterling (1925); Syme (1933 and 1986).

to deploy at a moment's notice in the service of the *princeps* and his family. This decision to co-locate the units would also enable L. Aelius Seianus, who had been the *praefectus praetorio* since 14 CE, to curry favour among the ranks by getting to know the men personally, and even to appoint its tribunes and centurions by himself.[94] Additionally, the 6,000 men of the three *Cohortes Urbanae* – citizen paramilitaries dedicated to maintaining public order in the city under their own *Praefectus Urbanus* – were based here.[95]

In the seven years since Seianus' appointment, Tiberius had come to increasingly rely on him for advice and information.[96] He had since promoted him to *praetor*, 'an honour that had never yet been accorded to one of like class', and sometimes referred to Seianus as his *socius laborum* ('my ally in my labours').[97] Seianus is difficult to assess today. The accounts of Seianus and his deeds were all written long after he lived and often with prejudice. Thus, Tacitus describes him as

> a man hardy by constitution, fearless by temperament; skilled to conceal himself and to incriminate his neighbour; cringing at once and insolent; orderly and modest to outward view, at heart possessed by a towering ambition, which impelled him at whiles to lavishness and luxury, but more often to industry and vigilance – qualities not less noxious when assumed for the winning of a throne.[98]

If Tiberius and Seianus were good friends, the same could not be said of the Praetorian commander's relationship with Drusus who viewed Seianus as insinuating himself into becoming a colleague in his father's rule.[99] Drusus was a young man with a hot temper who was not above arguing with his father. On one occasion, Tiberius rebuked him with the remark, 'While I am alive you shall commit no deed of violence or insolence; and if you dare to try, not after I am dead, either.'[100] In a casual altercation with Seianus, Drusus raised his hand and struck him in the face.[101] The Praetorian commander did not hit back. In secret, Seianus began a serious affair with Drusus' wife, Livilla (Livia Iulia), sister of Germanicus.[102] The illicit lovers met frequently. To be more accessible, Seianus separated from his wife, Apicata, and their three children. Drusus began to suspect Seianus and his motives. A plot to remove the cuckold was suspected by her doctor and friend, Eudemus, but despite giving his advice to her, she continued to meet with Seianus. Drusus then fell ill. During his sickness, Tiberius dutifully attended sessions of the Senate.[103] On 14 September 23 CE, Drusus died; he was 36.[104] A rumour spread that he had been poisoned by accident.[105] It was alleged that the toxin had been administered by the eunuch Lygdus on the orders of Seianus, but some also surmised it was a botched attempt by Drusus to poison his father.[106]

While the body of his son was being prepared for burial, Tiberius continued to attend sessions of the Senate.[107] As a sign of mourning, the consuls sat on the ordinary benches of the *Curia*. Tiberius reminded them of their dignity and their proper place. Many of the senators present wept. Tiberius responded with consoling remarks. He recognized that he might be criticized for appearing before the Conscript Fathers so soon after having lost his son, but it was in serving the *Res Publica* that he found solace. He called for his grandsons (fig. 21), Nero Caesar and Drusus Caesar, to come before the assembled members. He implored the senators to take care of them and train them in their duties as good citizens, and spoke of his wish that the consuls or others would grasp the reins of governing the *Res Publica*. The memorials decreed for Germanicus were repeated in kind for Drusus, with notable additions.[108] The funeral procession included a parade of ancestral *imagines* – Aeneas, the entire dynasty of Alban kings and Romulus, followed by the Sabine nobles, Attus Clausus and the rest of the effigies

Figure 21. Nero Caesar and Drusus Caesar depicted on the reverse of a coin struck at the Caesaraugusta mint in Hispania Tarraconensis.

of the *gens Claudia*. From the *Rostra Augusti* in the *Forum Romanum*, Tiberius himself gave the funeral oration.[109] With Seianus standing by his side, he 'praised his son in front of him, and stood in front of the body, with the veil thrown only to hide the pontiff's eyes from the funeral, and though Roman People wept he held his features unmoved'.[110] The body was carried to the *Campus Martius*, where it was burned upon the pyre, and the urn containing Drusus' ashes was placed in the Mausoleum of Augustus.

The year brought another death – one almost as close to Tiberius as his son's. That was of Lucilius Longus, the only senator who had stayed with him at Rhodes, willingly putting friendship above widespread social censure.[111] Though regarded as a man of humble origin, the Senate decreed Longus a *censor*'s funeral and erected a statue of him in the *Forum Augustum* at the public's expense.[112] For Tiberius, who had few intimate friends, it was a deeply personal loss.

Tiberius immersed himself in his work. At his urging, the Senate issued decrees providing financial assistance to the cities of Aegium in Achaea and Cibyra in Asia, which had been devastated by earthquakes.[113] C. Vibius Serenus (I), the proconsul of Hispania Tarraconensis, was banished to the Greek island of Amorgus (Amorgos) for the violent way he treated his provincial subjects. Carsidius Sacerdos and C. Sempronius Gracchus were each acquitted of the charge of aiding Tacfarinas in Africa by supplying him grain. There were petitions and complaints. Samos and Kos petitioned for confirmation of their sanctuary rights.[114] Lucilius Capito, since appointed *procurator* of Asia, had been impeached by his province; he was now tried by his peers in the Senate. Tiberius strongly asserted 'that he had merely given the man authority over the slaves and property of the imperial establishments; that if he had taken upon himself the powers of a *praetor* and used military force, he had disregarded his instructions; therefore, they must hear the provincials'.[115] Capito was condemned. Gratified by this verdict, as well as by the sentence imposed on C. Iunius Silanus the previous year, the cities of the province of Asia voted to dedicate a temple to Tiberius, Augusta and the Senate.[116] The motion was granted and the cities were permitted to build the temple.

When Servius Maluginensis died, the post of priest of Jupiter became vacant. Tiberius proposed a new law – as Augustus had done where ancient rules were out of step with the needs of modern times – which relaxed the strict conditions regulating the eligibility of candidates for the position.[117] After a discussion of religious questions, the Senate decided that the institution of the male priests of Jupiter should remain unchanged. Maluginensis' son was chosen to succeed his father. However, a law was passed that the priestess, in regard to her sacred functions, was to be under the husband's control, yet retain the ordinary legal position of other women. A gift of HS 2 million was decreed to Cornelia, a Vestal

Virgin, chosen in the room of Scantia, and whenever Augusta entered the theatre to attend a show, she was to have a seat among the Vestals.

After various complaints by the praetors about the persistent bad behaviour of actors (*histriones*) performing in Atellan Farces, and their failed attempts to control them, Tiberius took up the issue and submitted a motion for a new regulation. 'They had often sought to disturb the public peace,' he said, 'and to bring disgrace on private families, and the old Oscan farce, once a wretched amusement for the vulgar, had become at once so indecent and so popular, that it must be checked by the Senate's authority.'[118] The Senate agreed with him and, with the passing of the decree, the players were banished from Italy.

Misunderstandings and frictions emerged among members of Tiberius' extended family in 24 CE. When the priests invoked blessings for Nero and Drusus Caesar during official prayers for the *princeps*' well-being, Tiberius was offended.[119] He was particularly irritated by the equal recognition given to the young men. In response, he called upon the priests and inquired whether their decision was influenced by Agrippina. They firmly denied the accusation. Tiberius reproached them, albeit mildly, because many of these priests were either Agrippina's relatives or influential figures in the *Res Publica*. Nonetheless, perhaps recalling Augustus' experience of raising Caius and Lucius Caesar, he cautioned the Senate against fostering arrogance in the young and impressionable minds of Nero and Drusus by offering them premature honours. Seianus too passionately argued that such actions were tearing the nation apart, claiming the existence of factions which aligned themselves with Agrippina. He warned that, unless this trend was curbed, more discord would emerge. He urged that one or two of the most ambitious leaders of the faction – some calling it 'Agrippina's Party' – should be suppressed as the only solution to the escalating conflict.[120]

Friends of Agrippina increasingly found themselves attacked by Seianus or his agents. C. Silius' loyalty was called into question when he boasted of how his legions did not mutiny in 14 CE, and of his success in the war with Sacrovir; his wife, Sosia Galla, was a close friend of Agrippina, which made her vulnerable.[121] Perceiving an opportunity to ingratiate himself to Seianus, the consul L. Visellius Varro led the prosecution against Silius, given impetus by his own father's feud against the accused man. The original charge of extortion was upgraded to *maiestas*. Silius avoided the ignominy of a trial by taking his own life.[122] His property was confiscated and his wife was banished on the motion of Asinius Gallus.[123] T. Sabinus was also suspected, but action against him was held back for the time being.[124]

L. Calpurnius Piso (II), the thoughtful and principled man who had in a previous year announced he would leave Rome, was charged with having engaged in a treasonable private conversation.[125] Q. Granius also alleged that Piso 'kept poison in his house and carried a sword whenever he came into the *Curia*'.[126]

Other charges were presented, but Piso died during the trial and the case was suspended. T. Cassius Severus, an aggressive and unprincipled man who had earlier been banished by the Senate to Crete, continued to rant in exile. More charges were levelled at him and, despite his talent as a public speaker, he was found guilty, removed to Seriphos (Serifos) and all his property in Rome was confiscated.[127] He lived out the rest of his life on the tiny, near-barren Greek island in the Aegean Sea.

Tiberius took personal interest in a remarkable criminal case, with *praetor* M. Plautius Silvanus accused of pushing his wife, Apronia, out of a window.[128] Tiberius was obliged to hear the case because Silvanus was connected to the family through his grandmother, Urgulania, the mother of Plautia Urgulanilla, the first wife of Claudius. When summoned by L. Apronius, his father-in-law, to stand before Tiberius, Silvanus responded incoherently. He claimed that he was in a deep sleep at the time and knew nothing, and argued that his wife must have chosen to end her own life. Tiberius immediately went to Silvanus' house to inspect the crime scene for himself and found evidence of her struggle and forced defenestration. He reported his observations to the Senate. As soon as judges were appointed, Urgulania sent him a dagger. Silvanus attempted to use it but failed, resorting instead to opening his veins. A short time after, his former wife, Numantina, was accused of causing her husband's insanity through magical incantations and potions. She was subsequently acquitted of the charge.

Beyond Rome, despite Blaesus' victory the previous year, the embers of conflict still smouldered in Africa. Tacfarinas' forces had since been bolstered by his allies among the Mauri nation.[129] Dissatisfied with life under Ptolemaeus (son of Iuba II), the Mauri chose to go to war. Tacfarinas also found support from the king of the Garamantes, who aided him in plundering settlements in the Roman province. His force comprised detachments of light troops, allegedly with a reputation that was greater than their actual effectiveness. Africa Proconsularis was now under the governorship of P. Cornelius Dolabella. He had previously administered Dalmatia – the littoral part of the former Illyricum – and overseen its pacification with a programme of road building from 14–20 CE, and was regarded by Paterculus as 'a man of noble-minded candour'.[130] After Blaesus' departure, however, *Legio* VIIII *Hispana* had been drawn down, leaving Dolabella with just one unit, *Legio* III *Augusta*, to ensure the region's security.[131] This represented an opportunity for Tacfarinas.[132] He began spreading rumours that nations were breaking away from the Roman Empire, insinuating that Roman soldiers were gradually withdrawing from Africa. This tactic allowed Tacfarinas to attract disaffected men to his forces. He established a new camp and laid siege to Thubuscum (likely Thubursicum located on a hilly site near modern Khamissa in eastern Algeria, map 13). In response to the threat, Dolabella gathered all available troops and, upon his arrival at the town, swiftly broke the siege. Dolabella then fortified strategic positions in Africa and executed several leaders of the Musulamii – Tacfarinas' own people – who were on the verge of rebelling.

Recognizing the futility of previous expeditions against Tacfarinas, Dolabella adopted a new strategy.[133] To increase the number of troops, he sought direct military assistance from Ptolemaeus in neighbouring Mauretania. Dolabella oversaw each military operation in person. He organized his combined army into four columns, variously under the command of his legionary legate and tribunes, with additional auxiliary units commanded by selected Mauri tribal leaders. Reports soon arrived that Tacfarinas' forces had established their base camp near a partially ruined fortress at Auzea – they had destroyed it by fire and now relied on its position, surrounded by extensive forests. Roman *cohortes* of infantry and *turmae* of cavalry were swiftly mobilized, each unaware of their destination yet moving at speed. At daybreak, to the sound of trumpets and blood-curdling shouts, the Romans surprised the half-asleep rebels, who were unable to get to their horses, which were either tethered or scattered across distant pastures. In tight formations, the Romans deployed for battle. The enemy, caught off guard, lacked arms, order or a plan, and were swiftly captured or slaughtered. Motivated by memories of their hardships and frustrations from previous conflicts, the Roman soldiers sought vengeance and blood. Throughout the ranks, the order spread that everyone should focus on capturing Tacfarinas. The ongoing war could only end when the enemy's leader was stopped. In the ensuing chaos of battle, Tacfarinas found himself surrounded, his guards defeated, his son taken captive and the Romans closing in on him from all directions. In a desperate but heroic move, he charged into a hail of missiles, meeting a death that spared him from captivity and humiliation.

His mission finally accomplished, Dolabella formally requested to be honoured with triumphal distinctions.[134] In a surprise decision, Tiberius declined. It was interpreted by some that, by not overshadowing the achievement of Blaesus, he was showing deference to his now-powerful nephew, Seianus.[135] However, Tiberius' judgement only served to increase Dolabella's fame. Despite leading a smaller army, Dolabella returned to Rome with distinguished prisoners and the glory of having killed the enemy's leader, concluding the war once and for all. In his entourage were envoys from the Garamantes, a rare sight in Rome. Fearing the repercussions of Tacfarinas' defeat, and being innocent of any hostile intentions, the Garamantes had sent the emissaries urgently to seek pardon from the Roman People. Recognizing King Ptolemaeus' devoted loyalty to Rome during the war, an ancient tradition was revived. A senator was dispatched to present Ptolemaeus with an ivory sceptre (*scipio eburneus*) and embroidered robe (*toga picta*) – traditional gifts only bestowed by the Roman Senate. Additionally, Ptolemaeus was granted the honorific titles of 'king, ally, and friend'.[136]

Hardly had the conflict ended in Africa when, in the summer of 24 CE, a certain T. Curtisius began fomenting rebellion among slaves in the heel of Italy. Remarkably, Curtisius was a former soldier of the Praetorian Cohorts, the most privileged units of the Roman Army. Tacitus, who is the only source for the events, does not give a reason for his grievance, writing only that, 'First at clandestine meetings in the neighbourhood of Brundisium and the adjacent towns, then by openly posted manifestoes, he kept summoning the fierce country slaves of the outlying ranches to strike for freedom.'[137] Curtius Lupus, the local *quaestor* responsible for managing the region of woodland who by coincidence was visiting, used his initiative. When three biremes, which accompanied passenger ferries and merchant ships crossing the Adriatic Sea, sailed into the nearby port, Lupus exercised his authority to take charge of the marines aboard the ships. Deployed on land, they soon 'broke up the seditious combination in its very first beginnings'.[138] Notified of the disturbances, Tiberius dispatched the tribune Staius with a detachment of soldiers. They seized Curtisius and his most daring followers and escorted them under armed guard to Rome for trial.[139] It was a wake-up call for Romans lulled into a false sense of social stability, as 'men already trembled at the vast scale of the slave-establishments, in which there was an immense growth, while the freeborn populace daily decreased'.[140] Tiberius knew these grim *ergastulae* only too well, having inspected them himself as a young *quaestor* – an experience which may have spurred his rapid response as *princeps*.[141] Thus, 'He stationed garrisons of soldiers nearer together than before throughout Italia.'[142]

The drudge of administration filled Tiberius' days, which he nevertheless undertook willingly and attentively.[143] He was present during the undignified showdown between a son and a father.[144] The father, Vibius Serenus (I), had been dragged from exile to Rome and now stood in chains in the *Curia*. Acting as both prosecutor and witness, Serenus (II) – the well-dressed son – pleaded for his father to be found guilty. He alleged that his father had plotted against the *princeps*, claiming that he had sent individuals to the *Tres Galliae* to incite rebellion. Additionally, he asserted that M. Caecilius Cornutus, an ex-*praetor*, had provided financial support for the conspiracy. In contrast, the accused father faced the situation with a proud, fearless spirit. Standing in his rags, he stared his son in the face, shook his heavy chains and appealed to the gods for vengeance. He demanded to be restored to his exile and expressed the hope that punishment might eventually reward his son. Additionally, the father vehemently protested the innocence of Cornutus, insisting that the allegation was completely unfounded. He argued that this would soon become apparent if other names were disclosed since he would not have conspired to assassinate Tiberius and foment a revolution with only one accomplice. Wrought by anxiety and perceiving the danger as equivalent to ruin, Cornutus had, in the meantime, taken his own life.

This alleged conspiracy greatly embarrassed Tiberius. The prosecutor cited two old and infirm senators, Cn. Cornelius Lentulus (II) and L. Seius Tubero – prominent Romans distinguished with war honours – who were also his close friends.[145] As Dio relates the same episode, Lentulus burst out laughing, sending the assembly into uproar.[146] 'I am no longer worthy to live,' Tiberius said, 'if Lentulus, too, hates me.'[147] The charge of plotting rebellious breach of the peace was immediately dismissed. As for Serenus (I), his slaves were subjected to torture, but the resulting testimonies did not support his son's claims. Consumed by remorse and frightened by the public outcry threatening him with imprisonment, being thrown from the Tarpeian Rock or the fate of a parricide, Serenus (II) fled Rome.[148] However, he was apprehended in Ravenna and prosecuted. The Senate then voted that Serenus (I) should be punished according to established precedent – death by flogging.[149] Tiberius intervened with his veto as tribune to stem public outrage. C. Asinius Gallus suggested confining Serenus (I) to Gyaros or Donusa, but the old man himself rejected the idea. He argued that both islands lacked sufficient water, and that someone spared from death should at least be granted the basic necessities of life. Consequently, Serenus (I) was taken back to Amorgus, where he died of old age later that year.[150]

After Cornutus' suicide, a proposal was submitted to withhold rewards from informers when a person accused of *maiestas* ended their own life before their trial ended.[151] The motion was about to be approved when Tiberius unexpectedly sided with the informers. He complained that, if passed, the laws would become invalid, and the *Res Publica* would soon be on the verge of ruin. 'Better,' Tiberius is reported to have said, 'to subvert the constitution than to remove its guardians.'[152] Whether or not there was ever any conspiracy, henceforth it would be harder for Tiberius to be struck down by the dagger of an assassin in the city now that the *Cohortes Praetoriae* were encamped as one body close to Rome. The privileged guards presented a public drill display.[153] This served as a not-so-subtle reminder to the senators that the ultimate authority behind the *princeps* was the massed swords of the Roman Army. They were in no doubt that the commander, Seianus, would enforce it.

When C. Cominius, an *eques*, was convicted of composing libellous verses against the *princeps*, Tiberius spared him.[154] The intercession of Cominius' brother, a senator, played a crucial role in Tiberius reaching this decision. In another case involving P. Suillius Rufus, a former *quaestor* to Germanicus, who was facing expulsion from Italy due to accusations of accepting money for a favourable judicial decision, Tiberius insisted on banishing him to an island – indeed, he felt so strongly about the matter that he swore an oath that the sentence was necessary for the public good.[155] Stern punishment was similarly meted out to Firmius Catus, a senator accused of falsely charging his sister with *maiestas*.[156] Tiberius argued against a sentence of exile but did not oppose his expulsion from the Senate. Tiberius now forbade those who were banned from receiving 'fire and water' to make a will, a custom that was still observed in Dio's time.[157] The historian also relates that Tiberius brought Aelius Saturninus before the Senate to face the charge of having recited some improper verses about him, and, upon his conviction, had him thrown down the Tarpeian Rock.[158]

The date 17 September 24 CE marked the tenth anniversary of Tiberius' principate. He did not ask for a vote for the Senate to renew his term, which Augustus had done each time his ten-year mandate expired.[159] Nevertheless, the *decennalia* festival was held in his honour (fig. 22).[160] He had accepted the leadership role in 14 CE under the proviso that, whenever the Senate deemed the time to be right, he would be allowed to retire.[161] The Senate never issued such an instruction. Instead, the Conscript Fathers adapted to working with their new head of state. Tiberius had well understood the demands of the position when he accepted it, and is reported to have remarked at the time: 'I have a wolf by the ears.'[162] Remarkably, he – like Augustus before him – managed the day-to-day affairs of state with the assistance of just a small team of domestic freedmen, who also ran his estates in Italy.[163] Following Augustus' example, he sought the counsel of trusted friends with whom he discussed matters before making his final decisions.[164]

In the year that followed, 25 CE, A. Cremutius Cordus was arraigned on a new charge. In his recently published *History*, he was said to have praised the conspirators in the murder of Iulius Caesar and called its ringleader, C. Cassius Longinus, 'the last of the Romans', which was considered sufficient to ruin him.[165] His accusers were Satrius Secundus and Pinarius Natta – both allies of Seianus. Facing a severe sentence, Cremutius resolved to end his life, but not before delivering a robust, public defence. He pointed out that other men of letters had written about these historic events and people, and that they had done so without censure.[166] By virtue of being a historian, he had preserved the memory of these men and their deeds. In fact, he argued, there was no crime. He then returned to his house, where he starved himself to death.[167] In compliance with a decree of the Senate, his books were burnt by the *aediles*. However, a few copies were concealed and later republished.

During the Latin Festival (*Feriae Latinae*) in April, when young Drusus Caesar received his credentials as *praefectus urbanus*, Calpurnius Salvianus brought charges against Sex. Marius.[168] Tiberius openly criticized this action, which resulted in Salvianus being banished. Separately, the people of Cyzicus in Mysia were accused of neglecting the worship of *Divus* Augustus and of committing acts of violence against Roman citizens.[169] In consequence, the city was stripped of the franchise it had earned during its war with Mithridates VI of Pontus (73 BCE), when its people bravely defended their city during a siege, assisted in their gallant resistance by L. Licinius Lucullus.

Figure 22. Statue of Tiberius seated from Privernum.

The former proconsul of Asia, Fonteius Capito, was finally acquitted when the charges brought against him by C. Vibius Serenus (II) were proven to be false. However, this exoneration did not harm Serenus (II), who already endured the animosity of the public at large.

Following the example of Asia, a deputation from Hispania Tarraconensis petitioned the Senate with a request to be allowed to erect a temple to Tiberius and Augusta. On this occasion, Tiberius, who was generally contemptuous of honours and flattery, now addressed the Senate to explain his reasons for denying the request:

> For myself, Conscript Fathers, I am mortal, performing human tasks, and it will be enough for me if I can adequately fill the position of *princeps*; I want you to vouch for this, and to have posterity remember it so. They will more

> than sufficiently honour my memory by believing me to have been worthy of my ancestry, watchful over your interests, courageous in danger, fearless of enmity, when the *Res Publica* required it. These sentiments of your hearts are my temples, these my most glorious and abiding monuments. Those built of stone are despised as mere tombs, if the judgment of posterity passes into hatred. And, therefore, this is my prayer to our allies, our citizens, and to heaven itself; to the last, that, to my life's close, it grant me a tranquil mind, which can discern alike human and divine claims; to the first, that, when I die, they honour my career and the reputation of my name with praise and kindly remembrance.[170]

This passionate speech may be Tacitus' own invention, but the sentiment and phrasing could plausibly be the authentic words of Tiberius himself. At any rate, from that time on he persisted in showing contempt for such fawning homage to himself by senators and provincials alike.

As the years passed, the influence of Seianus increased. With it, his confidence grew about his ambition for raising his social status. His devoted paramour, Livilla, now demanded that he marry her.[171] Seianus wrote a carefully worded letter to Tiberius making the case for a marriage, suggesting that if a husband was sought for Livilla, he hoped that the *princeps* would bear in mind a steadfast friend who would find his reward simply in the glory of the close family alliance. Tiberius replied that, in principle, he did not object. However, in a second letter he said there would likely be protests to an equestrian – even one so highly regarded – marrying a patrician.[172] However, should an opportunity present itself, either in the Senate or in a Popular Assembly, he would not be silent on the matter. Disappointed by the rebuff, Seianus now made it his objective to convince Tiberius to live some distance away from Rome.[173] Seianus would thus be able to control access to the *princeps*, from who visited him to what correspondence or reports he saw – all dutifully delivered by the soldiers under his direct control.

Tiberius was surprised to learn the truth of many senators' true feelings about him. During the trial of Votienus Montanus of Narbo for making offensive remarks about the *princeps*, the well-liked humourist tried to convince Tiberius that he should avoid attending Senate meetings in person.[174] The speeches at these assemblies, he explained, were often both true *and* offensive, and frequently directed at him. During the trial, a soldier named Aemilius, who was eager to prove the case, passionately recounted the entire story in minute detail amid bad-tempered clamour from the senators in the House. Hearing the insults directed at him that had been uttered in secret, Tiberius was visibly hurt and deeply upset.[175] He declared that he would either defend his good name immediately or before the end of the trial. The earnest pleas of friends and the flattery of the entire assembly hardly restored his composure. Votienus suffered the penalty for *maiestas*. Smarting from the humiliating experience, Tiberius doubled down on the severe way he sentenced accused individuals, about which he had just been criticized. He demanded that Aquilia be exiled for the crime of adultery with Varius Ligur. Cn. Cornelius Lentulus Gaetulicus (one of the consuls-elect for 26 CE) had suggested that the woman be condemned under the provisions of the *Lex Iulia*, but Tiberius insisted. Additionally, Apidius Merula was removed from the Senate register for failing to swear to obey the legislation of *Divus* Augustus.

In the weeks that followed, deputations arrived in Rome from overseas territories with questions for Tiberius and the Senate. Emissaries from Sparta and Messenia in the Peloponnesos (Achaea) argued over the dedication of the Temple of Diana in the Marshes.[176] The Spartans asserted that it had been dedicated by their ancestors and in their territory, but had been seized from them in wartime by Philip V of Macedonia, subsequently being restored to them by the decision of Iulius Caesar and M. Antonius. The Messenians alleged that the ancient division of the Peloponnesos among the descendants of Hercules, in which the territory of Denthelia (where the temple stood), had fallen to their king. Arbitrating in the dispute, first Roman commander L. Mummius, then the city of Miletus and most recently Atidius Geminus, *praetor* of Achaea, had decided in favour of the Messenians. The Senate agreed with their decisions. Separately, emissaries from Segesta petitioned for the restoration of the Temple of Venus at Mount Eryx in Sicilia, which had fallen into ruin.[177] They told the story of its origins dating back to antiquity, which delighted Tiberius. He undertook the work willingly, being himself related to the goddess by way of his Julio-Claudian roots. A petition was received from Massalia (Marseilles) in Gallia Narbonensis.[178] Volcatius Moschus, an exile banished to the city from Rome, had received citizenship from the community and left his property to his adopted home. The precedent was cited of P. Rutilius Rufus, who, having been legally banished from Rome, was adopted as a citizen by the people of Smyrna. Volcatius' bequest was confirmed.

News was received in Rome of a heinous crime committed in Hispania Tarraconensis. A peasant from the Termestini nation had attacked Tiberius' representative, the *legatus Augusti propraetore*, L. Calpurnius Piso (III).[179] The governor was travelling peacefully and unescorted at the time. Suddenly attacked, he was fatally wounded with a single blow. The assailant fled the scene on a swift horse, entering a wooded area where he parted ways with his steed and evaded pursuit in the rocky and impassable wilderness. When captured, the horse was led through nearby villages, resulting in the identification of its owner. He was apprehended and tortured to force him to reveal the names of his accomplices. Through the pain of the torturer's grim work, the assailant defiantly declared in his native language that questioning him would be in vain – even the most intense agony would not compel him to divulge the truth. The next day, while he was being hauled back to face another round of torture, he broke free from his guards and violently slammed his head against a rock, killing himself instantly. There were suspicions, however, that Piso was murdered with the support of many Termestini because he was investigating the embezzlement of public funds, and on account of his strict insistence on their full repayment proved too much for the patience of the local people.

In Rome, too, there was frustration with Tiberius, some of his critics resorting to verse to express their feelings. Suetonius preserves several stanzas penned by an anonymous writer:

> Obdurate wretch! too fierce, too fell to move
> The least kind yearnings of a mother's love!
> No *eques* thou art, as having no estate;
> Long suffered'st thou in Rhodes an exile's fate,
> No more the happy Golden Age we see;
> The Iron's come, and sure to last with thee.
> Instead of wine he thirsted for before,
> He wallows now in floods of human gore.
> Reflect, ye Romans, on the dreadful times,
> Made such by Marius, and by Sulla's crimes.
> Reflect how Antonius' ambitious rage
> Twice scar'd with horror a distracted age.
> And say, Alas! Rome's blood in streams will flow,
> When banish'd miscreants rule this world below.[180]

Regardless, Tiberius continued to faithfully execute his responsibilities as *princeps* despite what people thought of him. 'Let them hate me, provided they respect my conduct,' he is reported to have said from time to time.[181] Eighty-eight years before, when he found himself surrounded by enemies, then consul M. Tullius Cicero lamented, 'the preservation of the *Res Publica* no less than governing it – what a thankless task it is!'[182] It was a sentiment with which Tiberius would surely have agreed.

# Chapter 8

# Ruling as 'The Exile': 26–31 CE

In 26 CE, a rebellion threatened to consume the fragile peace in Thrace. Several clans of this allied client kingdom refused to supply men for service with the Roman Army, as the terms of their treaty required.[1] Under normal conditions, when they did provide men, the Thracians insisted on appointing their own leaders (whom they would obey capriciously) and then would only fight their neighbours. A rumour had circulated among them that the recruits were to be mixed with units made up of other nationals and then deployed to distant lands. Before taking up arms, they sent envoys to the Roman authorities to assure them of their friendship and loyalty as long as they were not burdened with additional demands. However, if destined for slavery as a conquered people, they declared their readiness to fight back with swords, young warriors and a spirit determined to be free or die. As the envoys spoke, they pointed towards fortresses (*castella*) among the rocky hilltops where they had installed their parents and wives for safety and issued a threat of a challenging, hard and bloody war if their demands were not met.

Tiberius' representative on the spot, C. Poppaeus Sabinus (consul in 9 CE), listened to the emissaries and gave them bland assurances.[2] Meanwhile, he made preparations for a military response, notifying the unit commanders reporting to him to be ready to mobilize and calling upon his colleagues and allies for assistance.[3] In such an emergency, a *legatus Augusti propraetore* was authorized to request the assistance of neighbouring governors.[4] Responding to the appeal, Pomponius Labeo arrived with a legion from Moesia and King Roimetalkes II came with reinforcements drawn from among his loyal subjects. Combining these forces with his own, Sabinus advanced towards the enemy, who were located in wooded defiles. Some of them emerged on to open ground. The Roman commander and his army approached in formation and easily overwhelmed them, yet caused only minimal casualties among the rebels, who then withdrew to a fortified hilltop in the Balkan Mountains. Sabinus quickly established a camp and seized control of a narrow, unbroken ridge. After inconclusive skirmishes, Sabinus blockaded the rebels with siegeworks of ditches and ramparts constructed over several days. He was able to starve them into action, provoking a final battle in which Roman military superiority in equipment, discipline and tactics won the day, and achieved the surrender of the rebels. With winter coming, other pockets of resistance in Thrace soon collapsed and Roman control was re-established. Sabinus had done exactly what Tiberius expected him to do and he was awarded triumphal insignia, which he celebrated the same year as his victory.[5]

In Rome, relations between Tiberius' extended family took a decided turn for the worse – a development from which they would never recover. Agrippina's second cousin, Claudia Pulchra, faced prosecution by Cn. Domitius Afer.[6] A *praetor* of modest standing, but eager for advancement through any means, Afer accused her of immorality. He alleged that a certain Furnius was her lover and charged her with attempting to harm the *princeps* by way of poison and sorcery. Agrippina immediately went to Tiberius, finding him in the middle of offering a sacrifice to his father and interrupted the proceedings. She exclaimed: 'It is not fitting for the same man to sacrifice to *Divus* Augustus *and* persecute his descendants!' He rebuked Agrippina with a Greek verse, reminding her that, 'She was not wronged because she was not a queen!'[7] Her intervention backfired. Both Pulchra and Furnius were condemned. Afer, recognized for his ability, received high praise from Tiberius, who acknowledged him as an advocate of natural genius. From that time on, whether acting as counsel for the defence or the prosecution, Afer gained fame for his eloquence rather more than for his virtue.[8]

Finding herself increasingly lonely, unwell and reportedly given to bouts of weeping, Agrippina went to Tiberius and implored him to arrange for her to have a new husband. Despite her insistence for a decision, he did not immediately respond.[9] Her anxiety and distrust were further heightened when Seianus involved his agents in mischief. Masquerading as friends, they warned her about an impending poisoning, advising her to avoid her father-in-law's table.[10] Uncertain of how to conceal her true feelings, she maintained both her facial expression and tone of voice as she sat beside him during dinner one evening. She refrained from touching any dish until Tiberius noticed her odd behaviour. He praised some fruit when it was served at the table and personally handed it to her to taste. This only intensified Agrippina's suspicions. She handed the morsel to a slave. Tiberius made no remarks in front of the assembled company, but he turned to his mother and whispered that it could not be considered surprising if he decided on harsh treatment for someone who implied he was a poisoner. He may have intended the remark to be darkly humorous, but subsequently, rumours began circulating that a conspiracy was afoot for Agrippina's demise.[11]

Tiberius attended the debates of the Senate, dedicating several days to hearing embassies from Asia over a dispute about the city in which a temple should be erected.[12] Eleven cities contended for the special honour, each emphasizing their antiquity and loyalty to Rome.[13] When the question was put up for a vote, the Senate gave preference to Smyrna.[14] C. Vibius Marsus moved that M. Aemilius Lepidus (II), to whom the province of Asia had been assigned as proconsul, should appoint a special commissioner to take charge of this new temple, but Lepidus declined to make the choice. To oversee the project, Valerius Naso, one of the ex-praetors, was chosen by lot and sent out.

The unrelenting pressure of governing the empire weighed heavily on Tiberius, taking a toll on him both emotionally and physically. This year, Tiberius would mark his 67th birthday. Tacitus claims that, as an older adult, Tiberius had become profoundly concerned by his deteriorating looks, which caused him to avoid attending public events whenever he could:

> There were those who believed that in his old age he had become sensitive also to his outward appearances. For he possessed a tall, round-shouldered, and abnormally slender figure, a head without a trace of hair, and an ulcerous face generally variegated with plasters.[15]

It was a dramatically different image to the one appearing on coins, which continued to show him with a full head of hair and an unblemished complexion (Appendix 2). Nevertheless, his physical health was still good and he was fully engaged with his work.

According to one account recorded by Tacitus, his mood was not helped by 'the imperious temper of his mother, whose partnership in his power he could not tolerate, while it was impossible to cut adrift one from whom he held that power in fee'.[16] The most powerful man in the Roman world now craved privacy above all else. If ever he needed solitude or planned to do something without interruption, his predecessor, Augustus, had a private room at the top of the *Palatium* to which he could escape for a while.[17] This approach did not work for Tiberius. The *Domus Tiberiana* was too exposed, the clamouring public in the *fora* below too close, for his comfort. Escaping Rome altogether was his desire. He decided to go on another tour through Campania. The public was advised that the purpose of the trip was to dedicate a temple to Jupiter at Capua and another to *Divus* Augustus at Nola, but it was really an opportunity for Tiberius to enjoy rest and relaxation.[18] Just as he had done when leaving for Rhodes years before, on this trip he was accompanied by a group of intimate friends. They included senator and legal scholar Cocceius Nerva, the very wealthy *eques* Curtius Atticus and a select few others – for the most part Greeks, all cultured men – in whose conversation he might find amusement. Joining them was his right-hand man, Seianus, with a contingent of the *Cohortes Praetoriae*.[19]

The imperial party sojourned at a retreat about halfway between Rome and Neapolis. Situated close to the shore, the complex had suites of rooms built around a central rectangular court (plate 34), with a gymnasium and even ponds for farming fish.[20] Away from the main building, the dining room (*tricilinium*) was set within a shallow, calming pool of water supplied along channels from the bay. However, it was the cavernous natural grotto (fig. 23) behind this room that

Figure 23. The cave at *Spelunca* was a unique feature of the villa complex owned by Tiberius. Diners in the building on the artificial island could view statues arranged in scenes from the legend of Odysseus' return to Ithaka inside the cave.

was the resort's spectacular feature and which gave the villa its name: *Spelunca* ('The Cave'). Inside stood enormous sculptures by highly regarded artists from Rhodes depicting scenes from Homer's *Odyssey*, as it was thought the legendary Greek hero had landed here on his way home to Ithaka.[21] The guests settled down on their couches to enjoy their tasty meal. Suddenly, part of the entrance to the cave collapsed, sending rocks falling, crushing some of the attendants beneath. Panic swept through the entire company and the guests tried to flee – everyone but Seianus. Without hesitation, he lunged over Tiberius, using his knee, face and hand to stop the falling stones striking him. It was in this posture that the security guards found him.

Tiberius was deeply grateful to Seianus, whose act of bravery thereafter earned the praetorian commander the *princeps*' unremitting trust. His influence over Tiberius grew ever stronger. For the family of the late Germanicus, this posed a particular danger, about which Tiberius seemed unaware.[22] Particularly at risk was Nero Caesar, the next in line for the throne. Though Nero possessed youthful modesty, he occasionally forgot the decorum or care his status required in some situations.[23] He was encouraged to show vigour and self-confidence by his freedmen and clients, who claimed it was what the Roman People and the army wanted to see. They asserted that Seianus would not dare to oppose him. Nero Caesar harboured no sinister intentions or ambitions, yet there were moments when he would unintentionally utter willful and thoughtless expressions. Seizing on these lapses, informers would notify Seianus.[24] They played mean-spirited games with the naive Caesar. One person would intentionally avoid meeting him, another would turn away after exchanging greetings and someone else would begin a conversation only to abruptly end it. Watching close by, Seianus' friends would stand and openly mock him. Reports of Nero's sleepless nights, dreams and sighs were all relayed by his wife to her mother, Livilla, and by her to Seianus.

Separately, Drusus Caesar had been lured into Seianus' wicked scheme with the promise of him becoming *princeps* after eliminating his already weakened older brother.[25] Drusus' hot temper, combined with a desire for power and the rivalry typical among high-status siblings, was further fuelled by his envy of his mother's apparent preference for Nero. Drusus Caesar did not seem to realize that Seianus was planning his eventual downfall too by exploiting the young man's impetuous nature.

Tiberius was still in Campania as 27 CE began. In the months ahead, two tragedies beset the people of Italy. Tiberius' unwillingness to pay for spectacles in the arena had created pent-up demand in the public to see bloody fights between men and beasts and duels between gladiators – one that could be lucratively satisfied by private impresarios (*editores*).[26] At Fidenae, located about 8 kilometres (5 miles) north of Rome on the *Via Salaria*, an enterprising freedman named Atilius had erected an amphitheatre. A purely for-profit venture, this former slave had taken extreme measures to reduce the cost of the building's construction. Tacitus reports that its foundations were not bedded into solid ground and that the wooden superstructure was not securely fastened to it, while Dio states it was crudely constructed of boards.[27] On the fateful day of the inaugural gladiator show, an enormous and enthusiastic audience packed the amphitheatre. The structure was not designed for the combined weight of the crowd and its flaws were quickly revealed: 'It collapsed, breaking inward or sagging outward, and precipitating and burying a vast crowd of human beings,' bringing death and despair to those in its tiered seating.[28] Suetonius states that 20,000 perished, while Tacitus sets the number of casualties – maimed or crushed to death – at 50,000.[29] In acts of generosity and kinship, Romans selflessly opened their homes to tend to the injured. Atilius was arrested, tried in court and banished. The Senate subsequently issued a decree that no one with a personal fortune of less than HS 400,000 could present a gladiatorial display, and that a new amphitheatre should only ever be built on ground of tried and tested solidity.[30] It was later said that 'the principate of Augustus had been made famous by the Varus Disaster, and that of Tiberius by the collapse of the amphitheatre at Fidenae'.[31]

Weeks later, a fire broke out in Rome. Several buildings on the *Mons* Caelius (Caelian Hill) were completely destroyed.[32] The public blamed Tiberius for the disaster. When advised of the destruction, Tiberius himself immediately came to the aid of the property owners by covering their losses and even encouraged unknown others to submit claims for compensation.[33] For his generosity and public spiritedness, he earned the goodwill of the Roman People. When the bust of Tiberius was found undamaged in the burned-out house of senator Iunius, a proposal was made to rename *Mons* Caelius as *Mons* Augustus.[34] Supporters of the motion referred to a similar episode in which the statue of Claudia Quinta twice survived fire; now considered sacred, it was placed in the Temple of the Mother of the Gods.[35] Indeed, people saw divine favour at work, saying, 'The Claudian clan was sacrosanct and acceptable to Heaven, and additional solemnity should be given to the ground on which the gods had shown so notable an honour to the *princeps*.'[36] Tiberius declined the honour.

In Iudaea, *praefectus* Pontius Pilatus, an *eques* appointed by Tiberius in 26 CE, had set up his office in the *praetorium* beside the seashore at Caesarea Maritima.[37] This was the administrative capital of the province, which encompassed the districts of Idumaea, Iudaea and Samaria. A busy port constructed by the late King Herodes, Caesarea was a cosmopolitan commercial centre where Latin- and Greek-speaking Romans mixed with Jews and other nationals.[38] Since the death of Herodes, his kingdom had been divided up among his sons, each ruling a tetrarchy, but this new arrangement led to unrest in the region and Augustus annexed the territories, appointing the new province's first *praefectus* in 6 CE.[39] Pilatus replaced Valerius Gratus after eleven years in the post. At some time

Figure 24. The *Praefactus Iudaeae*, Pontius Pilatus, erected a shrine to Tiberius at Caesarea. This is the only surviving inscription to mention the famous official by name.

during his tenure, Pilatus dedicated a *Tiberieum*, a shrine to Tiberius (fig. 24), in the city.[40] It was in Hierosolyma (Jerusalem), however, that he was to make mistakes that upset both the locals and Tiberius. Hierosolyma was the epicentre of Jewish culture, with its great Temple on the Mount rebuilt by Herodes and where the king had erected his principal residence. Philo tells the story of how Pilatus ordered gilded shields dedicated to Tiberius to be hung inside the palace.[41] The decorative items seemed innocuous enough to the Roman prefect, but the name of the dedicator was inscribed on them, which caused the Jews to protest. Pilatus refused to take them down. A delegation led by one of Herodes' sons was dispatched to Tiberius.[42] Upon hearing their complaint, Tiberius immediately issued instructions for Pilatus to move the shields to the Temple of *Divus* Augustus at Caesarea, thereby defusing a tense situation.[43] On another occasion, Pilatus ordered auxiliary troops into Hierosolyma by night; the following day there was consternation among devout Jews, who regarded the *signa* as bringing idolatry into the place where the Laws of Moses, rather than the Laws of the Twelve Tables, ruled.[44] In response, protestors demonstrated in Caesarea for six days, which only ended when Pilatus withdrew the troops and their military standards from the sacred city. In a third act seen as provocative, Pilatus authorized the construction of an aqueduct in Hierosolyma, which was paid for using Temple funds.[45] When a Jew accused of blasphemy was sent by the Sanhedrin (the supreme council of the Jews) to Pilatus for trial during *Pesach* ('Passover'), and finding his own loyalty to Tiberius was questioned, the *praefectus* sanctioned the execution of the man by crucifixion, the traditional punishment reserved for slaves, pirates, enemies of the state and seditionists.[46] The man's name was Yeshua Ben Yosef (Jesus of Nazareth).

In Rome every day, unscrupulous *delatores* continued to ply the streets in search of victims. Now Quinctilius Varus, a wealthy man and a relative of Tiberius, was suddenly served a summons by Domitius Afer, the same prosecutor who had successfully accused Claudia Pulchra, Varus' own mother, the previous year.[47] It surprised no one that Afer, a needy adventure-seeker who had quickly squandered his recent rewards, was now preparing to attack a fresh target. The involvement of P. Cornelius Dolabella in the prosecution was noteworthy, however, especially considering his illustrious ancestry, his friendship with Varus and willingness to destroy his own noble lineage and family. However, the Senate intervened and decided to await Tiberius' judgment, viewing it as the only way to avert an embarrassing spectacle. Around the same time, Votienus Montanus, the orator from Narbo, died in exile on the Balearic Islands, having been banished there in 25 CE.[48]

Before departing for Campania, Tiberius had taken the precaution of issuing an edict warning the public not to interrupt his peace and quiet.[49] Yet the crowds from the rural towns came anyway, all eager to see their *princeps* in the flesh, and they had to be kept at a distance from him by soldiers.[50] The disregard of his wishes enraged him; he had 'so intense a loathing for the *municipia*, the *coloniae*, and all things situated on the mainland' that he now decided to take decisive action to save his sanity.[51] He made up his mind once and for all: he would leave Rome *permanently*. For centuries, affluent Romans had villas in Campania – at Boscoreale, Herculaneum, Oplontis and Stabiae – where they spent weeks away from the hustle and bustle of the city. The trendy crowd flocked to the seaside resort of Baiae (Baia), which was notorious for partying and sexual licence.[52] To ensure his solitude, he needed an island home, but this time it was not to be Rhodes. Tiberius decamped from *Spelunca* and withdrew to Capreae (Capri).[53] The rocky island's form is still dramatic today, its isolation ever intimidating. Capri rises 589 metres (1,932ft) at its highest point out of the Tyrrhenian Sea, some 4.9 kilometres (3 miles) off the Sorrento Peninsula.[54] Perhaps the island's appeal to Tiberius was the exclusivity afforded by the difficulty of access – with its steep, rugged coastline of limestone and dolomite, encrusted with volcanic tuff 'accessible by only one small beach' – or by its compact size of just 10.4 square kilometres (4 square miles).[55] Tacitus speculates:

> The solitude of the place I should suppose to have been its principal commendation, as it is surrounded by a harbourless sea, with a few makeshift roadsteads hardly adequate for small-sized vessels, while it is impossible to land unobserved by a sentry. In winter, the climate is gentle, owing to the mountain barrier which intercepts the cold sweep of the winds; its summers catch the western breeze and are made a delight by the circling expanse of open sea; while it overlooked the most beautiful of bays.[56]

It was an idyll fit for a *princeps*. Capreae would be his forever home.

Crucially, rooms were available for Tiberius' immediate use. Years before, Augustus had acquired the island in an exchange of property with the city of Neapolis and had since 'ornamented it with numerous edifices'.[57] The properties included twelve villas dotted across the island.[58] Each was apparently named after one of the Olympian gods or minor divinities.[59] The island itself had an antiquity and mystery about it which would have greatly appealed to Tiberius. While Augustus' builders were laying the foundations of one of the palaces, Suetonius reports that they discovered 'the monstrous bones of huge sea monsters and wild beasts, called the "bones of the giants", and the "weapons of the heroes".'[60] Tiberius saw an opportunity here to create a personal 'Neverland' far away from the public gaze – somewhere he would come to regard as his place of refuge.[61]

The most impressive of these 'edifices' was the *Villa Iovis*, named after Jove (Jupiter, Zeus), or the *Villa Ionis*, after Io (the lover of Zeus).[62] It was perched precariously, but dramatically, on the far north-eastern tip of the island atop the 334 metre (1,096ft) high Monte Tiberio (plate 38).[63] This villa was the largest

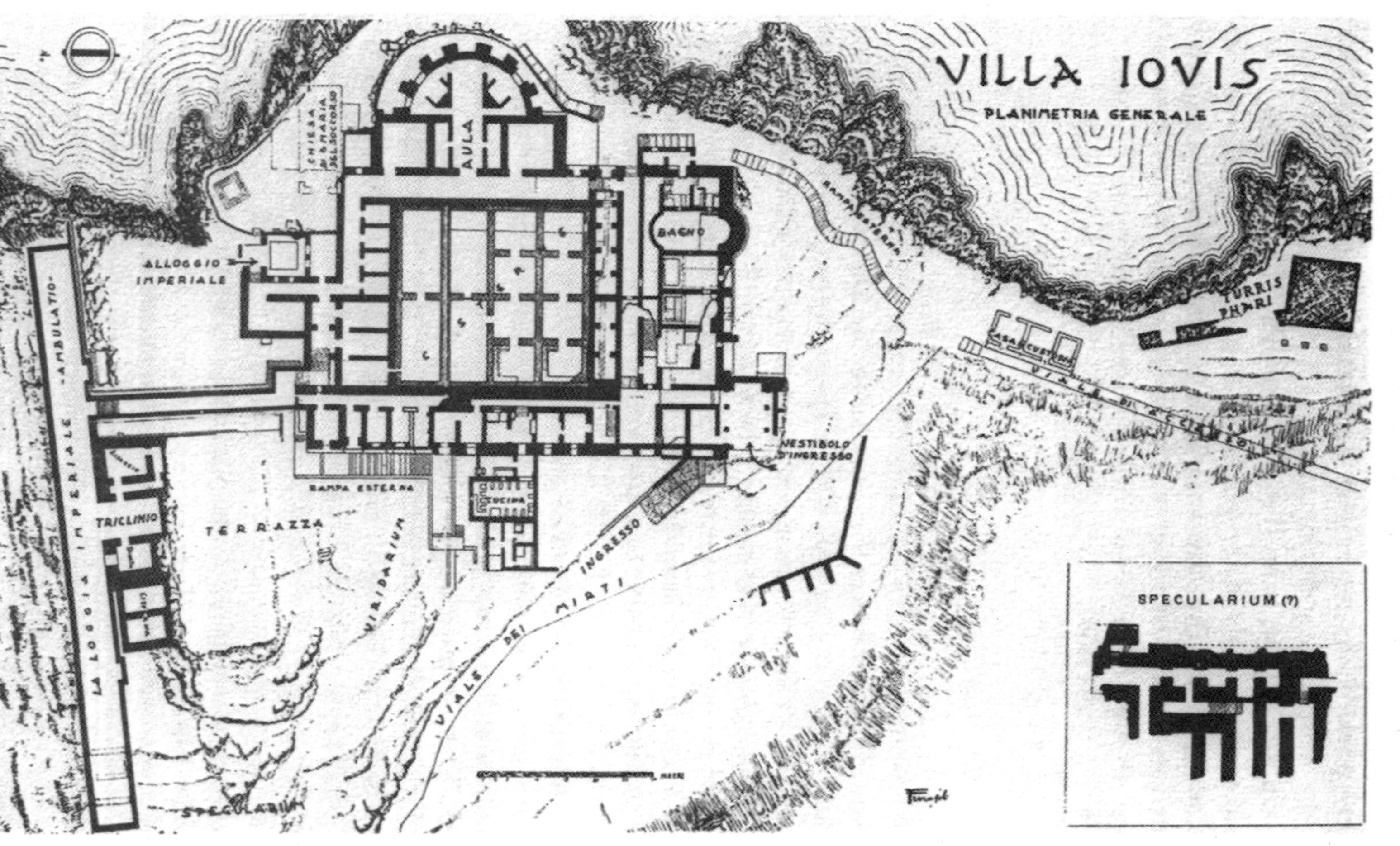

Map 16. Plan of the *Villa Iovis*, Capreae.

Figure 25. The exterior walls of the multi-storey *Villa Iovis* are constructed of *opus incertum* interspersed with courses of brick.

of the imperial residences on Capreae. The entire complex occupied an area of some 5,400 square metres (58,125 sq ft), making it about one-third the size of the *Domus Tiberiana* in Rome.[64] Excavations in modern times have revealed the layout of the main building (map 16).[65] It had a rectangular floorplan, measuring 75 metres (246ft) long by 50 metres (164ft) wide. Like the *Domus Tiberiana* in Rome, vaulted substructures were used throughout (plate 35). The building's thick, alternate brick and stone walls (*opus incertum*) could support several storeys (fig. 25). As the site sloped down away from the cliff edge by some 40 metres at its lowest point, there were likely three storeys above ground on the north side – the second of them possibly being a flat terrace roof designed as a peristyle – and as many as eight storeys on the west side.[66] The floors could be accessed via a staircase tower with ramps located on the south side.[67]

The interior architecture of the *Villa Iovis* resembled, in several key respects, a *praetorium* in an army camp – a highly appropriate design for Tiberius as the commander-in-chief. The residence of a Roman commander typically featured private rooms around a central courtyard, with amenities such as bedrooms (*cubicula*), a study (*tablinum*), dining room (*triclinium*), kitchen (*culina*), bathhouse (*thermae*) and latrine (*latrina*) for the exclusive use of the senior officer, his family and guests.[68] The location of the building on a high vantage point also reflected the preferences of other retired military men such as Marius, Pompeius Magnus and Iulius Caesar, who had their holiday or retirement homes on the mainland in Campania.[69] For his personal security, a detachment of the Praetorian Cohorts

Figure 26. The lighthouse of the *Villa Iovis* stands apart from the main complex.

Figure 27. Rooms of the *Villa Iovis* are connected by a corridor. The complex was equipped to provide for the needs of Tiberius, his guests and staff.

was stationed on the island; Seianus visited on extended stays.[70] There was also a lighthouse (*turris phari*, fig. 26) onsite to guide ships to Capreae.[71]

The villa was a place of work, rest and play.[72] The facilities were both luxurious and functional. The private rooms of Tiberius may have been located at the northern end of the building or on the now lost upper storeys.[73] It seems that he did not have 'a library in a garden', the essential amenity Cicero had recommended for a complete life.[74] Instead, two large rooms adjacent to the great audience hall (*aula*) may have been libraries, perhaps one for books in Latin and the other for books in Greek, which may have been managed by the director (*comes*), Ti. Iulius Pappus.[75] Alternatively, they may have been *triclinia*.[76] There was a long, T-shape walkway (*ambulatio*) for his enjoyment on the north side; on an incline, it offered a breathtaking view over the bay towards Misenum, Neapolis and Mount Vesuvius.[77] On the southern side of the building was a bath suite designed in the Roman fashion, comprising a warm room (*tepidarium*), hot room (*caldarium*) and cold room (*frigidarium*) equipped with plunge pool and toilets. An adjacent furnace (*praefurnium*) provided the heat, which flowed through the hypocaust system under the floors and through flues built into the walls.[78] In the centre of the villa, standing several storeys deep, was an array of four vaulted cisterns constructed of brick covered in waterproof cement; these immense tanks

Figure 28. View of the *Villa Damecuta* at Anacapri looking over to the Bay of Naples. Like the *Villa Iovis* it featured a semicircular *aula* and adjoining suites of rooms. It is located directly above the Blue Grotto.

collected rain from the top floor peristyle and roofs providing all the potable water to the site.[79] Hydraulic machinery likely fed faucets and fountains inside and outside the building.[80] On the western side, a range of rooms (fig. 27) for staff and storage, plus a kitchen with twelve stoves, indicate that supporting Tiberius' lifestyle was a large community of adjutants, craftsmen, freedmen and household slaves.[81]

To control access, there was a grand entrance with offices and guardrooms on the lowest level in the south-western corner of the *Villa Iovis*. Visitors permitted to enter would have been led down a corridor to the staircase tower to reach the upper floors. Exiting the stairs two flights up and turning right down another corridor, they might stop and enjoy a bath and, afterwards, returning to the stairs, they might rise another three levels to arrive at the floor with their assigned bedrooms and the *aula*.[82] Located on the eastern side of the Villa, this grand room (plate 36), covering an area of approximately 142 square metres (1,528 sq ft), featured an impressive, hemicycle bay window (*exedra*) with seven apertures, offering stunning views of the sunrise over the Sorrento Peninsula and across the bay during the day and evening.[83]

A similar semicircular *exedra* projecting from a large block of rooms is a feature of one of the other known Tiberian retreats on Capreae, the so-called *Villa di Damecuta* (named after the nearby promontory, fig. 28), located 6 kilometres (4 miles) away from the *Villa Iovis* at Anacapri in the north-west of the island.[84] This structure had a diameter of around 15 metres (49ft) and offered unobstructed panoramic views of the Bay of Naples, Misenum and the neighbouring island of Ischia. It was built 151 metres (495ft) above a smaller building (now called the *Villa di Gradola*) that stood directly above the Blue Grotto (*Grotta Azzurra*), which was used as a *nymphaeum*.[85] The main building of the *Villa di Damecuta* was linked by a porticoed *ambulatio*, some 80 metres (263ft) long with several niches for benches, to a small building erected on the east side reached by a steep staircase at the end. Fragments of wall plaster and mosaic flooring remain in the small *cubiculum*, in which the torso of a nude *ephebe* was found. Then as now, the grotto itself could only be accessed by boat.

In the *Villa Iovis*, plain white mosaics edged with black borders decorated the floors in the corridors; polished slabs of multicoloured marbles cut into hexagons and squares were laid elsewhere.[86] Throughout, rare marbles, alabasters and painted murals covered the walls.[87] Greek-inspired decorations and art likely adorned the interior spaces, enabling Tiberius to replicate here on the Italian island the contented life he had enjoyed on Rhodes two decades before.[88] To this end, joining him on Capreae was the group of friends who had accompanied him in Campania. Among such like-minded men, Tiberius could be happy. Additionally, there was a steady flow of family and invited guests – no doubt carefully vetted by Seianus – to distract him. It was far from being a life of solitude. It was, however, a life carefully regulated to suit the *princeps*' temperament.

Surrounding the complex, terraced gardens with statues and *nymphaea* provided tranquil beauty to the residents. Capreae had few natural agricultural sources to feed its inhabitants, beyond what livestock – such as goats – could be raised on the island or caught from fishing, so supplies were regularly shipped in from Misenum.[89] Pliny the Elder mentions that Tiberius grew his favourite fruit using a 'proto-greenhouse' for an ancient version of 'controlled environment horticulture':

> The *cucumis* [snake melon or 'Armenian cucumber'] belongs to the cartilaginous class of plants and grows above the ground. It was a wonderful favourite with the *princeps* Tiberius, and, indeed, he was never without it; for he had raised beds made in frames upon wheels, by means of which the cucumbers were moved and exposed to the full heat of the sun; while, in winter, they were withdrawn, and placed under the protection of frames glazed with *specularium* [mirror-stone].[90]

Within easy reach of the villa was a standalone structure, which may have been an observatory.[91] Here, Tiberius and Thrasyllus could perform their astronomical observations and astrological divinations to predict the future.[92] Curiously, other astrologers had failed to predict that Tiberius did not intend to live in Rome ever again.[93] People began to speak of their *princeps* as being an exile.[94] Tiberius had been called 'The Exile' before: his retreat to Rhodes, where he had 'put aside the garb of his country, took to the cloak and slippers', had caused consternation and derision in the capital city.[95] Once more, Romans found his decision peculiar and unsettling. 'It was a fatal year,' some said, 'and the *princeps*' decision to absent himself had been adopted under an evil star.'[96] Yet the incidents of 27 CE showed that, despite his intention to live and work away from Rome, the People could still count on Tiberius for support. His good deeds done, Tiberius could now settle in to the privacy of his island retreat – or so he may have hoped.

Returning to run affairs in Rome later in 28 CE, Seianus could freely promote his own agenda while appearing to act on Tiberius' orders. Former friends of Germanicus were easy targets of his spite. For this reason alone, T. Sabinus, an *eques* of the highest rank, was imprisoned.[97] Despite facing this same dire prospect, Sabinus continued to show Germanicus' widow and her children the respect due to them. Conspiring to attack Sabinus with the intention of securing the consulship for themselves – a position now only accessible with the blessing of Seianus – were Latinius Latiaris, M. Porcius Cato, Petitius Rufus and M. Opsius, all former praetors. To win Seianus' favour, they devised a plan where Latiaris, who had a passing acquaintance with Sabinus, would craft the plot, with the other conspirators as witnesses, leading to his prosecution. Latiaris set up his victim by casually praising Sabinus for not abandoning the House of Germanicus, to which he had been a loyal friend. He spoke highly of the late Germanicus and expressed compassion for Agrippina. Sabinus, moved by the hardship he faced, could not contain his emotions and criticized Seianus' cruelty, pride and ambition. Tiberius himself was not spared in Sabinus' diatribe. This supposedly confidential conversation seduced Sabinus into believing he had a close intimacy with Latiaris. In the following days, he actively sought out Latiaris, regularly visited his house and confided in him about his grievances, treating him as a most trusted friend. The other three senators hid themselves in the house, listening carefully to the conversations.[98] All this was dutifully reported by Seianus – with his spin – to Tiberius at Capreae. Tiberius would reply to his deputy by letter, relayed by messengers using the fast ships of the *Classis Misenensis* and swifter horses of the *cursus publicus*.[99]

Tiberius' response was read out to the Senate on 1 January 29 CE.[100] After offering the customary prayers for the New Year, his letter went on to discuss the matter of Sabinus. Tiberius castigated him in the strongest terms for having corrupted some of his freedmen and plotted against his life. In no uncertain terms, he demanded vengeance. The Senate agreed. Protesting as loudly and as best he could with his head covered, Sabinus was dragged away by the lictors. Sabinus was jailed that very day, and later perished without trial, his body being flung down the *Scalae Gemoniae* and cast into the river.[101] Dio records that the pet dog belonging to Sabinus accompanied him to the prison, then remained beside him at his death, finally leaping into the Tiber to be with his master's body.[102] Tiberius subsequently sent a letter in which he thanked the senators for having punished an enemy of the *Res Publica*.[103] He added that he had real anxieties and grounds for suspecting treachery from certain disaffected individuals, while mentioning no one specifically by name. When C. Asinius Gallus moved that Tiberius ought to explain these fears to the Senate, Seianus countered that the *princeps* should be given time to respond.

Many understood Tiberius' remark to refer to Agrippina and her son, Nero Caesar. Around this time, the extended imperial family lost Iulia Minor. The granddaughter of Augustus, she had been condemned of adultery by him and banished to Trimerus (Isole Tremiti), off the coast of Apulia, for twenty years.[104] She was 47 years old. Like her mother, her ashes were not placed in the Mausoleum of Augustus. Perhaps unbeknownst to Tiberius, she had been supported during her isolation with relief from Augusta. During the year, Tiberius bestowed the hand of his granddaughter Agrippina (Germanicus' daughter) on Cn. Domitius Ahenobarbus.[105] He directed that the marriage was to be celebrated in Rome. Domitius' family was a very old one and closely related to the Caesars.[106]

The *Pax Augusta* was shaken by reports that the Frisii in the far north-western corner of the empire were rebelling.[107] In 12 BCE, Nero Drusus had imposed on them the obligation to pay tribute in the form of ox hides for use by the Roman Army, a burden they had fulfilled for decades. The size or thickness of the hides had never been scrutinized rigorously until Olennius, a *primiplus* assigned to govern the Frisii, imposed the requirement of supplying hides of wild bulls as the acceptable standard. This was particularly intolerable for the Germanic nation, whose own domestic cattle were modest in size. Initially, they surrendered their herds, then their lands and finally their wives and children to bondage. When their protests yielded them no relief, they finally turned to war as the remedy. The soldiers tasked with collecting the tribute were seized by the Frisii and hanged. Anticipating their furious response, Olennius had already fled and sought refuge in the fort (*castrum*) of Flevum. Located beside the great canal of the *Fossa Drusiana*, the installation was garrisoned by a combined force of Roman citizen troops and allies, whose mission was to secure the shore along the North Sea.

Learning of this insurrection, L. Apronius, *Legatus Augusti Propraetore* of Germania Inferior, mobilized a vexillation of cohorts of *Legio* V *Alaudae* and *evocati* under the command of Cethegus Labeo from the neighbouring province of Germania Superior upriver, accompanied by allied and legionary cavalry units.[108] Quickly moving both armies down the Rhine, he confronted the Frisii, successfully lifting the siege of Flevum and dispersing the rebels. Apronius initiated the construction of roads and bridges over nearby estuaries to facilitate the movement of heavy troops to contain the rebels. Meanwhile, he directed the cavalry of the Canninefates and all the Germanic infantry allied with the Romans to attack the enemy from the rear. In the ensuing battle, the units arrived on the field in uncoordinated fashion and the Romans were repelled. Labeo requested the remaining cohorts of *Legio* V *Alaudae* to be sent and, with their arrival, the Frisii were finally overwhelmed. The Roman commander did not pursue vengeance or even bury the dead, despite the loss 'of many tribunes, prefects, and high-ranking centurions'.[109] Through the testimonies of deserters (*transfugae*), he discovered that 900 Romans had been slaughtered in an area known as Braduhenna's Wood, after continuing the fight into the following day. Another group of 400 men had taken refuge in the house of Cruptorix, a former soldier in the Roman Army; fearing betrayal, they had perished by killing each other. While the Frisii became famous in the region north of the Rhine, south of it, Tacitus comments critically that 'Tiberius kept our losses a secret, not wishing to entrust anyone with the war.'[110] No triumphal ornaments were granted to Apronius or Labeo.

In Rome, the Senate decreed an altar to *Clementia* ('Clemency') and another to *Amicitia* ('Friendship'), graced by statues of Tiberius and Seianus.[111] The Conscript Fathers invited both men to view the sacred monuments, but neither came to the city, travelling only from Capreae to Campania. Senators, *equites* and crowds from the local towns turned out to gawk at Seianus. Access to the *praefectus praetorio* was now particularly difficult, and then only though intrigue and by complicity with his aims. Those seeking an audience with him in Campania had to tolerate the arrogance of his staff, with most giving up and returning to Rome. Nevertheless, the Senate voted that the birthday of Seianus should be publicly observed.[112]

Tiberius returned to Capreae.[113] By this time, he had grown distant from his octogenarian mother.[114] During the three years after he left Rome, he saw her for one day only, and then for just a few hours.[115] When, shortly after his departure, she fell ill, he made no effort visit her. On 28 September of 29 CE, Augusta died (plate 26).[116] There was a delay of several days while people anticipated Tiberius' return to lay out the body, but the deteriorating condition of the corpse made it necessary to proceed with the funeral without him.[117] By letter, Tiberius arranged a simple affair for her – which he did not attend, citing the pressure of work – and the eulogy was delivered from the *Rostra Augusti* by her great-grandson, Caligula Caesar (youngest son of Germanicus).[118] Her ashes were placed in the Mausoleum of Augustus, as her husband had directed. Various distinctions were proposed, which Tiberius limited.[119] He absolutely forbade that his mother be deified or worshipped, which was in accordance with her own wishes.[120] The Senate ordered Roman women to mourn for her during the whole year, though Tiberius insisted that public business be conducted even at this time.[121] They voted her an arch – a distinction never before conferred upon a woman – 'because she had saved the lives of not a few of them, had reared the children of many, and had helped many to pay their daughters' dowries, in consequence of all which some were calling her *Mater Patriae* ("Mother of her Country").'[122] Rather than explicitly annul the decree, Tiberius did not allow the work to be done at public expense, promising to erect it himself at his own cost.[123] The arch was never built. Similarly, her will long remained unexecuted.[124] Augusta was, indeed, a true Roman institution. During her eighty-seven years, she had lived through the turmoil of civil wars and, in marrying Augustus, had assisted him in establishing his preeminent position in Roman society and politics; she had outlived him by fifteen years, during which she had seen her son succeed him.[125]

Tiberius regarded her as 'a headstrong [or overbearing] mother'.[126] In the letter he sent at the time of Augusta's death, Tiberius took a dim view of female friendships.[127] It was an indirect criticism of consul C. Fufius Geminus, who had risen-up the *cursus honorum* in part through Augusta's favour. Fufius knew how to flatter and win the affection of a woman. Considered witty by many, he often made barbed jokes that ridiculed Tiberius in words he was not likely to forget. Another letter was received by the Senate.[128] Widely believed to have been forwarded long before, but to have been held back, by Augusta, its contents were directed against Agrippina and Nero Caesar. Now read out in public, its words were personal and harsh. In no uncertain terms, the young man was accused of having sexual relations with other men. His mother was attacked for her insolent tongue and defiant spirit. The senators listened in stunned silence. Tiberius' intentions for criticising close members of his own family with such force were not clear, but M. Aurelius Cotta Maximus Messallinus rose and demanded that the matter be openly debated. Iunius Rusticus then stood and opposed the motion, fearing it would harm the living descendants of Germanicus.[129] Even as he was speaking, outside the *Curia*, crowds of protesters held up images of Agrippina and Nero. Praising Tiberius, they shouted that the letter was a forgery and that others were plotting to destroy his house. Inside the building, the senators decided their fates. Nero was banished to the island of Pontia (Ponza) in the Tyrrhenian Sea.[130] Agrippina was shipped to Pandataria, the same island to which Augustus had sent his daughter, Iulia.[131]

Soon after, copies circulated of anti-Seianus speeches, purportedly written by unknown ex-consuls.[132] Furious at the slanders, Seianus accused the Senate of ignoring the threats to Tiberius, while the disloyalty of the People, he said, risked the peace and security of the state. Tiberius wrote to the Senate repeating his denunciations of his grandson and daughter-in-law.[133] By edict, he reprimanded the People and complained that, by the duplicity of a single senator, his imperial majesty (*imperatoria maiestas*) had been publicly insulted. He insisted that the entire matter should be for him alone to decide. The senators declared that it was only the strong hand of the *princeps* that constrained their willingness to seek vengeance.[134]

By 30 CE, Seianus' authority (fig. 29) seemed to eclipse that of the *princeps* and his influence was felt right across the patrician class. Dio asserts that Seianus maintained illicit relations with the wives of nearly all the eminent men in Roman

Figure 29. The name of L. Aelius Seianus appears on the reverse of this coin minted at Bilbilis in Hispania Tarraconensis.

society, while holding out to them the promise of marriage.[135] During the ensuing pillow talk, he learned what their husbands were privately saying and doing. C. Asinius Gallus was now seeking to get close to Seianus, either because he believed the prefect would usurp Tiberius' position or perhaps by way of a plot to make Seianus an irritation to Tiberius and, by so doing, provoke his ruination.[136] Seianus knew there was a history between the two men. In 30 CE, Tiberius sent a letter about Gallus to the Senate, declaring, among other things, that this man was jealous of his friendship with Seianus, in spite of the fact that Gallus himself counted Vallius Syriacus – renowned as a cultured man – among his friends.[137] On the same day that Gallus was dining at Tiberius' house affirming his friendship with the *princeps*, he was being condemned by his peers in the *Curia*.[138] A *praetor* arrested him and led him away to execution, but Tiberius interceded, even though Gallus made his desire for death known as soon as he learned of the decree.[139] Tiberius instructed the Senate to hold Gallus in isolation, but without chains, until he himself could reach the city. This was done, it was inferred, not to prevent his escape, but to prevent his death.[140] Syriacus was executed just because he was a friend of Gallus.[141] Tiberius allegedly did the same thing to several other individuals. In one instance, Tiberius imprisoned one of his companions, and then, when his execution was mooted, he remarked that he had not yet made his peace with his erstwhile friend.[142] Seianus' influence was similarly felt across the imperial family. He made a false accusation against Drusus Caesar through his wife, yet Tiberius seemed not to take the claim seriously and merely sent Drusus to Rome. Fearing that Tiberius might change his mind about prosecuting Drusus, Seianus persuaded Cassius Longinus to propose some other action against him.[143] As a result, Drusus Caesar was confined 'in a lower floor room in the *Palatium*'.[144]

In Rome, C. Fufius Geminus was accused of *maiestas* against Tiberius. Fufius took his will into the *Curia*.[145] Reading it aloud to his peers, he disclosed that he had left his inheritance in equal parts to his children and to the *princeps*. When accused of cowardice, he went home before the vote was taken and, upon learning that the *quaestor* had arrived to escort him to his execution, he stabbed himself; exposing the fatal wound to the magistrate, Fufius demanded that the official report to the Senate state that such was the manner in which this Roman died.[146] When a complaint was subsequently filed about his wife, Mutilia Prisca, she entered the Senate House and stabbed herself with a dagger she had hidden in her clothing.[147]

After sixteen years of friendship, Tiberius began calling Seianus the 'Sharer of his Cares' and often repeated the phrase 'My Seianus', using it in letters addressed to the Senate and Roman People.[148] The two men seemed inseparable in the eyes of the public. Gold-covered bronze statues were being erected everywhere to both men, their names were inscribed together in the public records and gilded chairs were brought into the theatres in their honour.[149] People now sacrificed to the images of Seianus, just as they did to those of Tiberius.[150] Seianus' rise culminated with his election, for the first time, to the consulship for 31 CE, which he would share with Tiberius himself – indeed, it was voted that he and Tiberius should be made consuls together every five years and that a group of citizens should go out to greet them whenever they entered Rome.[151] Tiberius had since added 'Partner in the Consulship' to his list of unofficial titles for Seianus.[152] Tiberius also welcomed him into his family by agreeing to let him marry Livia Iulia, the 23-year-old daughter of Drusus and Livilla.[153]

On 1 January 31 CE, Seianus proudly took his curule chair in the Senate House. However, he sat alone on the dais at the north-eastern end of the *Curia Iulia*. His co-consul – Tiberius' fifth time in this high office – was absent, instead residing at Capreae.[154] Tiberius had earlier indicated to him that he would join him in Rome but, excusing himself as being sick, he did not come.[155] Instead, he sent letters concerning his wellbeing both to Seianus and to the Senate, advising them that he was in bad health and almost at the point of death, writing some days later that he was fully recovered and that he would arrive in Rome soon.[156] In one letter he would heartily praise his colleague, only to criticize him in another, or would honour some of Seianus' friends while disgracing others. In May, Tiberius resigned the consulship, yielding his curule chair to a suffect consul, Faustus Cornelius Sulla, a direct descendant of the notorious dictator.[157] Seianus did likewise, being replaced by Sex. Tedius Valerius Catullus.[158]

Tiberius was beginning to have serious doubts about his right-hand man. There are clues in the extant texts about what he knew of his friend's intentions. He had learned that the Senate now respected Seianus rather more than its *princeps*.[159] According to one story, he had received a letter from Antonia Minor, delivered to him at Capreae by her freedman, Pallas, in which she reported a plot to overthrow Tiberius being hatched by Seianus; she had been contacted by Herod Agrippa, who had been informed of the conspiracy by his incarcerated freedman, Eutychus.[160] Since he greatly respected the widow of his brother, he took the matter very seriously. The more likely source was Satrius Secundus, from whom he learned of the plot to replace him, even perhaps to kill him.[161] In this planned coup, P. Vitellius was to unlock the *Aerarium*, as its comptroller, to fund the revolution.[162] If true, it was a terrible betrayal. Tiberius' instinct was to do nothing hasty or rashly in thwarting it. He knew he was vulnerable. Partly by the benefits he granted, partly by the hopes he inspired and partly by intimidation, Seianus had established complete control over the Praetorian Cohorts, and he had also secured the favour of many of the senators.[163] All of Tiberius' associates were now his friends and Seianus could rely on them to report to him anything and everything the *princeps* said or did. In contrast, isolated on his island, no one informed Tiberius of what Seianus said or did. It was not the kind of 'retirement' he had imagined for himself.

Tiberius' response was to use patience and process to regain his respect. During the year, Tiberius appointed Seianus and his son to the priesthood, but he did the same for his 19-year-old grandson.[164] Seianus also received the *imperium proconsulare*, and the Senate voted that, hereafter, the consuls of each year should emulate him in their conduct while holding the office.[165] However, when Seianus asked permission to go to Campania, on the basis that his betrothed was ill, Tiberius advised him to remain in Rome, because he himself was going to arrive there very soon. Caius Caligula was appointed *augur* in place of his brother, Drusus Caesar, and then advanced to the office of pontiff.[166] Caius then joined Tiberius on Capreae, where he celebrated his coming of manhood by wearing the all-white *toga virilis* and shaving his beard for the first time.[167] The news of Tiberius' favour towards the youngest son of Germanicus greatly pleased the general population, who still revered his father's memory.[168] The move improved Tiberius' image too. It also had the desired effect of alienating Seianus.[169] The mixed messages in his official correspondence only served to confuse him further about Tiberius' true feelings towards him.

An opportunity for Tiberius to reassert his authority arose when a case was heard in the Senate involving a man who was a known enemy of Seianus.[170] He had been chosen to govern Baetica ten years before. Under the consul's influence, certain charges were now brought against him. Tiberius moved to quash the indictment. As a consequence of this particular case, Tiberius granted a general immunity to officials from such suits, applicable during the interval before taking office and to all who were designated to govern provinces or to perform any other public business. Soon after, in a letter to the Senate he mentioned the death of Nero Caesar, aged 24, and referred to Seianus merely by his name, omitting the other titles.[171] He did not stop there. Knowing that sacrifices were being offered to Seianus, Tiberius prohibited offerings to be made to any living human being. Additionally, renewing his earlier injunction, since many public honours were being voted for Seianus, Tiberius banned consideration of any measure that proposed honours for himself as *princeps*, thus precluding them for his associate too.[172]

It was now becoming clear to many that Seianus' special relationship with Tiberius was unravelling. Tiberius had been working on a clandestine plan to remove the former favourite altogether. He let it be known that he would be granting Seianus the *tribunicia potestas*.[173] He secretly appointed Naevius Sertorius Macro as *praefectus praetorio*. Then he sent a letter addressed to the Senate to be delivered in person by Macro, with whom he had shared his plan. On a pre-agreed day, Macro entered Rome by night.[174] There, he met P. Memmius Regulus (suffect consul since 1 October 31 CE) and Graecinius Laco, *praefectus vigilum*.[175] The Senate was due to host a meeting at the Temple of Apollo on the Palatinus on 18 October.[176] At dawn that day, Macro made his way to the temple, where he chanced upon Seianus, who had not yet entered the building. Seianus was anxious because he had received no letter from Tiberius about him receiving the tribunician power. Macro took him aside and told him in confidence that he was bringing the official notice of his grant and that Seianus should go on ahead. Delighted by this news, Seianus confidently strode into the room to take his seat among the senators.[177] To the *Praetoriani* who were there to guard Seianus, Macro showed the insignia of his authority, indicating that he was now their commander. Declaring that he carried a letter from Tiberius which promised them cash rewards, he ordered the men back to camp. Replacing them were men of Laco's *Vigiles*. After deploying the nightwatchmen around the temple, Macro entered the chamber.[178] Once inside, he delivered Tiberius' letter to the consuls and then withdrew before a word of it was read.[179] Outside, he instructed Laco to keep guard while he himself hurried to the *Castra Praetoria* to prevent any trouble among the cohorts.

At the time, the senators were cheerfully discussing Seianus' anticipated award.[180] Called to order, Tiberius' letter was now read to the assembled members. Opening with a matter of some minor importance, he proceeded to the main subject.[181] He began his critique of Seianus with a slight censure of his conduct and proceeded, little by little, to raise further objections about him, leading to a wholesale denunciation of the man formerly known as 'the partner in his labours'. He beseeched the senators to send one of the consuls to bring him, 'a lonely old man', under military escort into their presence.[182] In closing, he wrote that two senators – who were among his intimate associates – must be punished and that Seianus himself must be kept under armed guard. Careful to avoid any public disorder, Tiberius refrained from giving the explicit order to put him to death.[183]

Hearing a very different message than the one they had expected, the senators were at first perplexed.[184] Then they felt dejection. Some of those seated nearest to Seianus stood up and left, wishing to physically distance themselves from the man whom they had valued as their friend. Then praetors and tribunes surrounded Seianus to prevent him from leaving.[185] Instead, he remained in his seat. Regulus told him to stand.[186] Seianus stayed seated:

> Raising his voice and pointing at him, Regulus called a second and a third time. 'Seianus,' he demanded, 'come here!' 'Me?' replied Seianus, 'you are calling me?' When, at last, Seianus stood up, Laco, who had since returned, stood beside him. After the last word of the letter had been read, the senators with one voice denounced and threatened him.[187]

The situation had quickly become volatile. Fearing resistance, since Seianus still had many important relatives and friends, Regulus did not put the vote to the Senate or propose the death penalty.[188] Instead, he asked a single senator if Seianus should be imprisoned and, when that senator agreed, Laco dragged him out of the temple to the Tullianum (Mamertine) prison in the *Forum Romanum*.

Witnessing the arrest of Seianus, the public's reaction was swift. With glee and jubilation, they tore down the ubiquitous statues of Seianus from their plinths, venting their fury as they attacked them and cursed his name.[189] The prisoner could hear all this in his dark, dank cell below street level. Later the same day, the Senate gathered again, but this time in the Temple of Concordia – a potent and symbolic choice of venue located just feet away from the jail.[190] Observing the rampaging mob outside and noting the complete absence of the Praetorian Cohorts, they voted to condemn Seianus to death. By decree of the Senate, he was strangled, and his body was thrown down the *Scalae Gemoniae*.[191] Lying bruised, bloodied and broken, the rabble abused the traitor's corpse for three whole days and then tossed what remained of it into the Tiber.

Chaos then reigned in the city, with gangs lynching anyone they believed to have been an ally of Seianus.[192] Even the *Praetoriani* now joined in the disturbance by burning and plundering property; they were angry at having been implicated in the crimes of the disgraced *praefectus praetorio* and because Tiberius had shown preference to the *Vigiles* over them in exposing their former commander.[193] The senators who had been associated with Seianus were terrified by thoughts of the coming retribution. In acts of conciliation, the Senate voted to erect a statue of *Libertas* (Liberty) in the *Forum* and for a festival – in a first of its kind – to be held under the auspices of all the magistrates and priests, Furthermore, the senators voted to celebrate the day on which Seianus had died each year with horse-races and wild beast-hunts (*venationes*) – in another first of its kind – under the direction of the members of the four priesthoods and the *Sodales Augustales*.[194] They recognized Macro and Laco, awarding them each large sums of money; additionally, they gave Macro the rank of an ex-*praetor* and Laco that of an ex-*quaestor*, and allowed them to witness the games in their company and to wear the purple-bordered *toga praetexta* at the votive festivals.[195] The two men, however, declined these honours.[196] Similarly, Tiberius refused any of the many honours that were voted him, principally the title *Pater Patriae* and the proposal that his birthday should be marked by ten horse-races and a banquet of the senators. To emphasize the point, he gave notice again that no one should introduce such motions before the Senate.[197]

Tiberius waited anxiously for news from Rome, 'constantly watching from a high cliff for the signals which he had ordered to be raised afar off as each step was taken, for fear the messengers should be delayed'.[198] Had the ploy failed, and Seianus then occupied Rome and moved against him at Capreae, Tiberius had prepared ships to make his escape. In the event of an armed revolt, his 'Plan B' required that Macro bring Drusus Caesar before the Senate and People and declare him the new commander-in-chief (*dux*).[199] The original plan had not only worked, but had been executed flawlessly. Tiberius was relieved and overjoyed when he learned of Seianus' death. Later, in his biography, he would write 'that he had punished Seianus because he found him venting his hatred on the children of his son Germanicus'.[200] However, he refused to receive the embassy of senators and *equites* that was sent from Rome to congratulate him.[201] He even spurned suffect consul Regulus, who had always been a supporter of his interests and had come at the *princeps*' own request to ensure his safe return to the city.[202] For the next nine months, Tiberius would remain on Capreae at the *Villa Iovis*.[203] He had made his point. No one now doubted who was *princeps*: it was mission accomplished.

During the weeks that followed, a frenzy of retribution was visited upon associates of Seianus and old scores were settled. Regulus was attacked by Fulcinius Trio (one of the suffect consuls from 1 July 31 CE) for not having dealt with Seianus' cronies sooner, to which Regulus countered that Trio should be investigated in case he was himself implicated in the alleged plot.[204] Tiberius insisted that any accused should stand before his peers in the Senate and, if found guilty, be sentenced by them – it would *not* be his decision.[205] The fact of having been a friend of Seianus was often enough to bring a man to trial.[206] Some were tried for deeds which had caused envy years before among those now seeking their condemnation.[207] Others acquitted of charges in the past were retried and found guilty because it was Seianus who had protected them the first time. To try and save themselves, friends accused former friends, yet they perished nevertheless, partly for being liable to face the same charges on which they were prosecuting the others, and also for betraying their friends and revealing their own guilt.[208] Only Tiberius' favour could save them now.[209] While many defended themselves, several committed suicide before their trials so that their children might inherit their property, since a voluntary death rarely led to confiscation.[210] This was the fate of P. Vitellius, comptroller of the *Aerarium*, who opened a vein with a small knife.[211] Those found guilty either paid the penalty in jail or were hurled from the Capitolinus Hill by the tribunes or the consuls, their bodies then tossed as rubbish into the Tiber. One was Seianus' uncle, Q. Iunius Blaesus.[212] The property of the guilty was confiscated, leaving little or nothing for their accusers.[213] P. Pomponius Secundus – a man of refined manners and high intellect – was accused of sheltering his friend, Aelius Gallus, in his garden after Seianus has been executed; he decided to bear his unfavourable predicament with resignation and went on to outlive Tiberius.[214] Seianus' property was to be transferred from the Treasury to Tiberius.[215] He accepted every inheritance that was bequeathed to him, and in this atmosphere of recrimination and retaliation, nearly everybody began leaving him something in their wills. He also raised a particular tax – presumably levied on inheritances – by 0.5 per cent to a full 1 per cent.[216]

By the end of the year, the popular rage against Seianus and his accomplices had begun to wane.[217] Tiberius issued an amnesty.[218] There remained, however, the issue of what to do about Seianus' family. His wife, Apicata, was spared capital punishment.[219] However, the Senate decreed that his three children were to be put to death.[220] In late October, when the *praetor* and lictors arrived, his son knew what awaited him, but his little sister did not understand what she had done wrong and protested. Since it was unlawful for a freeborn Roman virgin to be executed, the girl (who was betrothed to the son of Claudius) was first raped by the public executioner.[221] Then both siblings were strangled with a noose.[222] This dreadful desecration of innocent victims devastated Apicata. After seeing their mangled bodies at the base of the *Scalae Gemoniae*, she would have her revenge.

Apicata returned to her house, where she composed a detailed statement about what she knew of the death of Tiberius' son, Drusus.[223] She explained that Livilla, his wife, had been the cause of a quarrel between herself and her husband, resulting in their separation. What had been passed off as death by natural causes was actually murder by poison.[224] She sent this document to Tiberius. Then, eight days after her husband's death, she took her own life. By this means, Tiberius came to learn the truth of his son's fate.[225] The revelation devastated him. At the time, Tiberius had channelled his grief into his work, but now he spent days obsessively investigating the matter.[226] When advised of the arrival of a host of his from his time in Rhodes, whom he had invited to Rome in an amiable letter, he had him tortured immediately, presuming that he was a witness who had come forward and whose testimony was important for this case. Discovering his mistake, Suetonius reports, he had the man executed to keep him from going public about the wrong done to him. The prosecution of Livilla became his top priority. Some forty-four speeches were delivered in the Senate about her punishment.[227] She was given the death sentence.[228] The manner of her last moments is unclear. Dio writes: 'I have, indeed, heard that he [Tiberius] spared Livilla out of regard for her mother Antonia, and that Antonia herself of her own accord killed her daughter by starving her.'[229]

In this moment of heightened public anxiety, there were rumours of sightings of Drusus Caesar on the Cycladic Islands and on the Greek mainland.[230] There was a young man of the same age and appearance as Drusus about whom some of Tiberius' freedmen were circulating the story that he had escaped from custody in Rome and was on his way to the armies of his late father, Germanicus, with the intention of invading Egypt or Syria.[231] When many young men started to flock to him, Poppaeus Sabinus, governor of Achaea and Macedonia, then heard of the matter.[232] To pre-empt any danger this development might pose, Sabinus sent out agents who ascertained that the man, after questioning, had said that he was the son of M. Silanus, and that he had embarked on a ship going to Italy. Sabinus sent his report to Tiberius. Nothing more is known of the affair, but it was a reminder of the potential for trouble that an imposter could cause with an impressionable crowd.

In another incident, men of a *Cohors Vigilum* raced to Ostia to extinguish what they thought was a major fire. As they moved ever closer to the seaport town, they began to realize that the intense, red glowing in the night sky was not caused by flames engulfing buildings on earth, but it was an atmospheric phenomenon creating the effect that the heavens were burning.[233]

# Chapter 9

# Aging Disgracefully: 32–37 CE

The impact of Seianus' denouncement and death was still felt the following year. Breaking with the recently established practice for just one of the members of the Senate to take the oath of loyalty on New Year's Day on behalf of the entire body, on this 1 January 32 CE they swore separately and individually, as if this act would make them more committed to their pledge.[1] On Togonius Gallus' motion, they also voted that Tiberius should be allowed to select as many men from their membership as he liked and then employ twenty of them – to be chosen by lot and armed with daggers – as personal bodyguards whenever he entered the *Curia*.[2] Since the *princeps* already had a detail from the Praetorian Cohorts, which would be deployed around the perimeter of the Senate House, their resolution appeared to be directed against themselves, implying that they were his enemies.[3] Tiberius wrote to thank the Senate for its consideration but declined their offer as being without precedent. 'Were they always to be the same, or was there to be a succession?' he replied, as reported by Tacitus:

> Were they to be men who had held office or youths, private citizens or officials? Then, again, what a scene would be presented by persons grasping their swords on the threshold of the *Curia*? His life was not worth much if it had to be defended by arms.[4]

Writing again later, Tiberius asked the Senate to allow Macro and a number of military tribunes to escort him into the Senate House, should he decide to go, advising that this bodyguard would suffice for his needs.[5] The senators themselves acknowledged this and attached a clause to their decree – passed the following year – providing that they should be searched upon entering to ensure that no one hid a dagger in his clothing.[6]

He did not go. Instead, Tiberius awarded honours to the men of the *Cohortes Praetoriae* in the form of recognitions and cash donatives.[7] However, when Iunius Gallio, a retired guardsman, proposed that veteran *Praetoriani* – men who had been honourably discharged from the service – should be given the privilege of watching the games from the fourteen rows of seats reserved for the *equites*, Tiberius was incandescent with fury.[8] Gallio had crossed an important 'red line'. Tiberius demanded to know what *he* had to do with the soldiery, whose duty it was to receive the commander's orders or his rewards from the *princeps* himself as the commander-in-chief. Had Gallio really discovered something which *Divus* Augustus had not foreseen?[9] Tiberius expelled Gallio from the Senate and banished him from Italy on the specific charge that he was attempting to induce soldiers to be loyal to the *Res Publica* rather than to him, to whom they swore the *sacramentum*. When he learned that Gallio was departing for Lesbos, with all its attractions and comforts, he arranged for him to be taken into the custody of the magistrates upon his arrival and returned to Rome, where he was kept under house arrest.[10]

Figure 30. Portrait bust of Caius (often called by his nickname Caligula) as a young man.

In the same letter to the Senate, Tiberius attacked Sextius Paconianus, to the great satisfaction of the senators present.[11] Sextius, an ex-*praetor*, was a daring, mischievous man, who had made it his business to know everyone else's secrets. He had been picked by Seianus to be his agent in his scheme against Caius Caligula (fig. 30). When this was revealed, a wave of long-concealed hatreds was unleashed. Sextius would have been given a death sentence had he not himself begun informing on others – on Lucanius Latiaris in particular, who had been instrumental in bringing down Titius Sabinus.[12] A series of debates ensued in which recriminations were voiced. Dec. Haterius Agrippa heavily criticized the consuls of 31 CE, who now sat in complete silence. Regulus replied that he was waiting to discuss the matter with Tiberius. Q. Sanquinius Maximus, one of the ex-consuls, implored the Senate not to add to the *princeps*' problems, as he was competent to provide solutions. Thus, Regulus was saved. In another dispute, M. Aurelius Cotta Maximus Messallinus was accused of questioning Caligula's sexuality in a private conversation, and of describing an entertainment with the priests on Augusta's birthday – at which he was present – as a funeral party. When complaining about the influence of M. Aemilius Lepidus (II) and L. Arruntius, he had reportedly said, 'They will have the Senate's support; I shall have that of my *Tiberiolus* ['little Tiberius].'[13] Exasperated, Tiberius wrote a letter to the Senate, opening with this admission:

> If I know at this moment what to write to you, Conscript Fathers, or how to write it, or what, in short, to leave unwritten, may all the gods and goddesses visit me with more destruction than I feel that I am daily suffering.[14]

He said that Cotta's words had been misconstrued and urged the members not to turn the freedom of table talk into a crime. The senators failed to convict him on all the charges.[15] The Senate was given authority to decide the case of C. Caecilianus, one of its members, who was the chief witness against Cotta. It was agreed that he should be given the same penalty that was imposed on Aruseius and Sanquinius, the accusers of L. Arruntius.[16]

There were more cases against friends of Seianus in which Tiberius intervened. He denounced Q. Servaeus (an ex-*praetor*, who had been a friend of Germanicus) and Minucius Thermus (an *eques*) as criminals and requested C. Cestius Gallus to share with the Senate what he had communicated to him by letter.[17] Cestius undertook the prosecution. Upon being condemned, Minucius and Servaeus defected to the prosecution. Iulius Africanus of the Gallic Santones nation and Seius Quadratus were similarly condemned.[18] In another case, M. Terentius called out his colleagues who, he said, had hypocritically repudiated their friendship with Seianus but only after he was dead.[19] Terentius had associated himself with Seianus, he argued, because the now disgraced man had been highly honoured by Tiberius himself.[20] Tiberius agreed. Terentius' speech led to his accusers being sentenced to banishment or death.[21] Similarly, Tiberius dismissed the charge against *praetor* L. Caesianus.[22] In the story told by Dio, Caesianus, who was attending the *Floralia*,

> had seen to it that all the merry making up to nightfall was done by bald-headed men, in order to poke fun at the *princeps*, who was then bald, and at night had furnished light to the people as they left the theatre by torches in the hands of five thousand boys with shaven pates. Indeed, Tiberius was so far from becoming angry with him that he pretended not to have heard about it at all, though all bald-headed persons were thenceforth called *Caesiani*.[23]

A letter was received from the *princeps* concerning Sex. Vestilius, an ex-*praetor*; as he was a close friend of his brother, Nero Drusus, Tiberius had admitted him into his own circle.[24] Vestilius was accused of writing a personal attack on Caius Caligula for his alleged profligacy. For this act, Vestilius was henceforth excluded from Tiberius' entourage. Full of remorse, Vestilius tried to cut a vein to end his life, but quickly bound up the bleeding wound after deciding instead to beg Tiberius to pardon him, only to open the vein once more when he received the *princeps*' damning reply. Many senators were charged with *maiestas*, among them the highly distinguished C. Annius Pollio, C. Appius Iulius Silanus, Mamercus Aemilius Scaurus, C. Calvisius Sabinus and L. Annius Vinicianus, along with his father, C. Annius Pollio. Celsus, tribune of a *Cohors Urbanae* and now one of the prosecutors, saved Appius and Calvisius from standing trial. Tiberius postponed the cases of Pollio, Vinicianus and Scaurus, intending to try them himself with the Senate. Women too and even close friends of Tiberius faced prosecution. Vitia, an aged woman, was executed for weeping upon hearing of the death of her son, C. Fufius Geminus.[25] Two of Tiberius' oldest friends, Vescularius Atticus and Iulius Marinus, who had been his companions on Rhodes and Capreae, were executed. Vescularius was Seianus' broker in the plot against M. Scribonius Libo Drusus, while Marinus' co-operation had enabled Seianus to ruin Curtius Atticus.[26]

With so many cases being heard in the Senate, Tiberius felt he must attend in person. He boarded his trireme and sailed from Capreae along the Campanian coast, heading north.[27] On his mind was whether he should enter Rome, as he had not set foot there in six years. He disembarked at points within reach of the city, sometimes visiting gardens beside the Tiber – one near an artificial lake created for sea battles (*naumachiae*) – after first posting a guard detail along the banks of the river to keep away the crowds who came out to meet him.[28] He finally decided that he would return to the solitude of the seashore.[29] On this occasion, Tacitus ascribes his reticence to go into Rome to being 'ashamed of the crimes and lusts into which he had plunged so unrestrainedly, that in the fashion of a despot he debauched the children of free-born citizens'.[30] Repeating what happened when he withdrew to Rhodes, Tiberius' total absence from Rome had created a dangerous vacuum for wild speculations of a life of extreme vice (*vitium*) to rush in:

> It was not merely beauty and a handsome person which he felt as an incentive to his lust, but the modesty of childhood in some, and noble ancestry in others. Hitherto unknown terms were then for the first time invented, derived from the abominations of the place and the endless phases of sensuality. Slaves too were set over the work of seeking out and procuring, with rewards for the willing and threats to the reluctant, and if there was resistance from a relative or a parent, they used violence and force, and actually indulged their own passions as if dealing with captives.[31]

Rumours circulated about grotesque sexual perversions practiced on the island:

> On retiring to Capreae he devised *Sellaria* for his secret orgies: teams of wantons of both sexes, selected as experts in deviant intercourse and dubbed *spintriae*, copulated before him in triple unions to excite his flagging passions. Its bedrooms were furnished with the most salacious paintings and sculptures, as well as with an erotic library, in case a performer should need an illustration of what was required. Then in Capreae's woods and groves he arranged a number of nooks of venery where boys and girls, dressed up as Pans and Nymphs, solicited outside bowers and grottoes: people openly called this 'the Old Goat's Garden', punning on the island's name.[32]

Suetonius delights in recounting that:

> He acquired a reputation for still grosser depravities that one can hardly bear to tell or be told, let alone believe. For example, he trained little boys, whom he termed *pisculos* to crawl between his thighs when he went swimming and tease him with their licks and nibbles; and unweaned babies he would put to his organ as though to the breast, being by both nature and age rather fond of this form of satisfaction.[33]

Titillating details are offered:

> Left a painting of Parrasius' depicting Atalanta pleasuring Meleager with her lips on condition that if the theme displeased him he was to have a million *sestertii* instead, he chose to keep it and actually hung it in his bedroom. The story is also told that once at a sacrifice, attracted by the acolyte's beauty, he lost control of himself and, hardly waiting for the ceremony to end, rushed him off and debauched him and his brother, the flute-player, too; and subsequently, when they complained of the assault, he had their legs broken.[34]

Suetonius tells fantastical stories, not just of alleged sexual depravity, but of wanton cruelty:

> How grossly he was in the habit of abusing women even of high birth is very clearly shown by the death of a certain Mallonia. When she was brought to his bed and refused most vigorously to submit to his lust, he turned her over to the informers, and even when she was on trial he did not cease to call out and ask her 'whether she was sorry'; so that finally she left the court and went home, where she stabbed herself, openly upbraiding the ugly old man for his obscenity. Hence a stigma put upon him at the next plays in an Atellan farce was received with great applause and became current, that 'the old goat was licking the does'.[35]

Then there is the tale of the fisherman:

> A few days after he reached Capreae and was by himself, a fisherman appeared unexpectedly and offered him a huge mullet; whereupon in his alarm that the man had clambered up to him from the back of the island over rough and pathless rocks, he had the poor fellow's face scrubbed with the fish. And because in the midst of his torture the man thanked his lucky stars that he had not given the *princeps* an enormous crab that he had caught, Tiberius had his face torn with the crab also. He punished a Praetorian soldier with death for having stolen a peacock from his preserves. When the litter in which he was making a trip was stopped by brambles, he had

> the man who went ahead to clear the way, a centurion of the first cohorts, stretched out on the ground and flogged half to death.[36]

Romans hearing such lurid stories were left to ponder that there was no smoke without fire, yet they had no means to validate the veracity of them. Only those able to sail to the island, guided there by the flames of its lighthouse, would know the truth.

In the event, Tiberius did not enter Rome on this excursion.[37] He would continue to conduct business with the Senate by letter. When a motion was presented in the Senate by Quintilianus, a tribune of the People, about a Sibylline Book, Tiberius sent a rescript in which he gently censured the magistrate because of his youth and lack of knowledge on the subject. In contrast, he scolded L. Caninius Gallus, a member of the *Quindecemviri*, who had brought the matter to a poorly attended Senate, without first getting the informed opinion of the College or having the verses read and critiqued. Tiberius himself doubted their authenticity. He also reminded Gallus that, as many such documents purporting to have been produced by the Sibyl were forgeries, Augustus had assigned a day within which they should be deposited with the *Praetor Urbanus*, after which it was unlawful for any private person to knowingly hold a copy. The book in question was then referred to the *Quindecemviri* to scrutinize.

That year, the plebs in Rome took to the streets to complain about the high price of corn for their bread. For several days there were noisy demands, with unusually unrestrained language directed at Tiberius in what authorities saw as potentially seditious behaviour.[38] Learning of the unrest, Tiberius castigated the magistrates and Senate in writing 'for not having used the authority of the *Res Publica* to put down the people' and so restore public order.[39] Having himself been *quaestor* with responsibility for the *annona* in his late teens, he was well-aware of the need to ensure adequacy of supply of food to the poor in Italy, yet the price increases made little sense to him because he had imported more corn than Augustus had before him.[40] The Senate and consuls issued strongly worded decrees. Yet by not making his frustration publicly known, Tiberius' apparent silence on the matter, rather than taken as a proof of his patriotism, was seen by the plebs instead as evidence of his pride.[41] To avoid any interruption in the supply of grain, when the *praefectus Aegypti*, Vitrasius Pollio, died, Tiberius temporarily appointed a certain Hiberus, an imperial freedman, pending the formal designation of A. Avillius Flaccus of equestrian rank to govern the province.[42] Keeping the peace in the city was paramount, so when *praefectus urbi* Piso died, Tiberius appointed L. Lamia, whom he had already assigned to govern Syria but was detaining in Rome awaiting a final decision.[43] He also honoured Piso with a funeral at the public expense, a distinction that he also granted to other deserving individuals.[44]

In the closing weeks of 32 CE, C. Geminius, Iulius Celsus and Pompeius, all *equites*, were each arraigned on the charge of conspiracy.[45] Geminius had been a friend of Seianus on account of his opulent and effeminate lifestyle, but had not committed any serious offences. While in confinement, tribune Celsus loosened his chain, twisted it around his neck and, by yanking it, killed himself. Rubrius Fabatus, in despair at the state of affairs in Rome under Tiberius, was placed under surveillance on the suspicion that he might defect to the Parthians. He was stopped near the Strait of Sicily, and, when dragged back to the city by a centurion, could offer no plausible reason for his long journey. Nevertheless, Fabatus lived on unpunished because, it is reported, he had been simply forgotten by his accusers.

Family matters again occupied Tiberius' thoughts at the start of 33 CE. He had to pick suitable men to be husbands for his granddaughters, Iulia Livilla and Drusilla by Germanicus.[46] After some consideration, he selected L. Cassius Longinus and M. Vinicius.[47] Both were respectable individuals, raised by accomplished fathers, and he made a passing reference to them in his letter to the Senate. He excused his decision not to enter Rome – without specifying any particular reason – and raised the matter of having an armed escort should he ever enter the *Curia*; the Senate then enacted its decision of the previous year.[48]

Tiberius sailed back to Capreae for the winter. 'The incessant and constant cares of empire, coming from all sides,' notes Plutarch, 'did not make that island repose of his pure and complete.'[48] The situation in Italy, which had begun with complaints about inflation in the price of food staples, continued to deteriorate. Tiberius was sufficiently troubled that he returned again to the mainland. A serious financial crisis was now impacting Rome's patrician class. The cause was not a debasing of the coins; Tiberius' mint at *Colonia* Munatia kept the purity of the silver at the same level as his predecessor.[50] The roots of the crisis reached back over forty years. Usury had long been a problem in Italy. The Twelve Tables prohibited anyone from exacting more than 10 per cent interest on loans. Subsequently, interest was reduced to half that amount, and finally compound interest was forbidden by a law brought by the tribunes.[51] Iulius Caesar had sought a remedy by passing a law requiring that creditors invest two-thirds of their capital in Italian land as collateral to lend at interest.[52] The law had since been unenforced, but it remained on the statute books. After the civil wars, Augustus spent his spoils lavishly on professionalizing the army, establishing colonies for veterans and building public infrastructure. He had minted coin to pay for it, much of it going to the frontier provinces under his direct care.[53] His largesse and expenditures were known to have driven up price inflation.[54] In comparison, Tiberius had been relatively frugal, even being widely considered stingy.[55] The result was a net outflow of money from Italy, leaving ready cash in short supply. Money lenders began to ratchet up interest rates on loans. In 33 CE, the law on usury was revived by the Senate.[56] Tacitus writes:

> The lenders, however, called in the full amounts, and the borrowers could not in honour refuse to answer the call. Thus, at first there were hurryings to and fro, and appeals for mercy; then a hum of activity in the praetor's court; and the very scheme which had been devised as a remedy – the sale and purchase of estates – began to operate with the contrary effect, since the usurers had withdrawn their capital from circulation in order to buy land. As the glutting of the market was followed by a fall in prices, the men with the heaviest debts experienced the greatest difficulty in selling, and numbers were ejected from their properties. Financial ruin brought down in its train both rank and reputation.[57]

It was thus the loss of *dignitas* that finally prompted the Senate to act to avert a full-blown economic crisis – potentially a recession on a scale not seen since 66 BCE, when entire family fortunes in Rome were devastated.[58] A man named Nerva starved himself to death because Tiberius had reaffirmed the laws on contracts enacted by Caesar, which he was sure would result in great loss of confidence and financial confusion; despite Tiberius repeatedly urging him to eat, Nerva ignored the *princeps*' advice.[59]

If the Senate's aim had been to stimulate the circulation of cash and to allow the debtors to pay in land, it failed spectacularly.[60] Tiberius responded as the lender of last resort. He distributed HS 100 million of his own funds to the *Fiscus* for distribution throughout the banks (*mensarii*) and allowed them the freedom to borrow without interest for three years, provided that the borrower gave security to the *Fiscus* in the form of land worth double the amount.[61] 'The latter also was to relieve a condition of great hardship,' remarks Suetonius.[62] In the interests of expediency, the purchase of estates was not carried out according to the strict letter of the Senate's decree. In this way, credit and confidence were finally restored. Responding positively to the policy, private lenders gradually returned to the market.[63]

Tiberius' quick and decisive actions had averted a financial catastrophe. Throughout the crisis, he steadfastly refused to enter Rome, residing at a villa just 4 miles beyond the city walls.[64] Nevertheless, Tiberius' presence was felt. Without him ever attending in person, the Senate met and decided judicial cases. He encouraged them to follow a strict working day, insisting that its members should not arrive later, or depart earlier, than the appointed times.[65] He also sent many injunctions to the consuls, and once ordered that statements be read aloud by them.[66] These included not only the documents given him by *delatores*, but also the confessions Macro had extracted from people under torture, leaving the Senate to vote for or against their condemnation.

The number of cases of *maiestas* rose again. One was levelled against Considius Proculus, who was happily celebrating his birthday when he was hurriedly brought before the Senate, condemned and put to death.[67] On the accusation of Q. Pomponius, Proculus' sister, Sancia, was also outlawed. Pomponius was motivated to win favour with the *princeps* in order to alleviate the dangers facing his brother, Pomponius Secundus. The lady Pompeia Macrina was sentenced to banishment. Cases against her husband, Argolicus, and her father-in-law, Laco – both leading men of Achaea – had ruined them. Now her father, an illustrious *eques*, and her brother, an ex-*praetor*, were found guilty because their great-grandfather, Theophanes of Mitylene, had been one of the close friends of Pompeius Magnus and some Greek flatterers had deified him. Rather than face the executioner's garrotte, they killed themselves. Sex. Marius – reputed to be the richest man in Baetica – is reported to have been accused of committing incest with his daughter, though *maiestas* is much more likely; condemned, he was thrown headlong from the top of the *Scalae Gemoniae*.[68] Marius' wealth derived from gold mines in the Iberian Peninsula, which were forfeited to the Roman state after his execution.[69]

To stem the waves of legal actions, Tiberius issued an order that the most notorious of those bringing accusations against others should be executed in a single day.[70] However, when a retired centurion attempted to submit information against someone, Tiberius prohibited him and anyone else who had served in the army from doing so, although senators and *equites* were still permitted to.[71] Tiberius was widely praised for these acts, especially because he declined the numerous honours that were voted him.[72]

In the meantime, Tiberius appointed Caius Caligula (plate 13) to the office of *quaestor* and promised to advance him to the other public service positions five years earlier than was customary – this despite, on a previous occasion, having urged the Senate not to make the young man conceited by offering him several or premature honours.[73] By arrangement, Caligula was married to Iunia Claudilla, a daughter of M. Iunius Silanus, and Tiberius was in Antium to celebrate it.[74] Caligula accompanied Tiberius back to Capreae, joining a now diminished circle of the *princeps'* closest friends.[75] He had grown into a man who, Tacitus writes,

> masked a savage temper under an artful guise of self-restraint, and neither his mother's doom nor the banishment of his brothers extorted from him a single utterance. Whatever the humour of the day with Tiberius, he would assume the like, and his language differed as little. Hence the fame of a clever remark from the orator Passienus, that 'there never was a better slave or a worse master'.[76]

Suetonius reports that, while on the island, at night Caius Caligula enjoyed revelling, dancing and singing disguised in a wig and long robe. Tiberius willingly indulged him in the hope that these unconventional activities would tame his wild nature.[77] The biographer alleges Tiberius used to say, now and then, that 'to allow Caius to live would prove the ruin of himself and of all men, and that he was rearing a viper for the Roman People, and a Phaethon for the world'.[78]

It was becoming increasingly evident to all that Caligula was being marked out as Tiberius' legitimate successor.[79] If Tiberius was to preserve the dynasty envisaged by Augustus, his options were now few. He may have feared that if he sought a new *princeps* from outside his family, it would slight the memory of *Divus* Augustus and the name of Caesar.[80] As a son of Germanicus, Caligula was certainly popular with the Roman People. Germanicus' brother, Ti. Claudius, was 43 years old and, with a limp and stammer, was regarded by many as a fool.[81] Even his own mother, Antonia, often called him 'a monster of a man, not finished but merely begun by Nature'.[82] Aware of his challenges, Augustus had discussed with Tiberius about what to do with Claudius at the *Ludi Martiales* in 12 CE, suggesting he should be kept from public view.[83] Though known for his kind nature and liberal culture, he seemed an unsuitable candidate as *princeps*. Tiberius had a 14-year-old grandson, Ti. Gemellus. As he was still a child, and suspecting that he was not the son of Drusus, the *princeps* overlooked him.[84] Dio suggests that Tiberius was certain that the boy would one day be murdered by Caligula.[85] He records that, during an argument, Tiberius told his grandson: 'You will kill him, and others will kill you.'[86]

The comment may have been intended to be darkly humorous. Similarly, interrupting someone who had just asked him if he remembered something, he said: 'I do not remember what I was.'[87] Tiberius' mood is reported as often sombre during these days. He would say that old Priamos (Priam), the last King of Troy, was fortunate because he consumed both his country and his throne in his own utter destruction.[88] On frequent occasions, he is said to have uttered the line from a Greek tragedy, 'When I am dead, let fire o'erwhelm the earth.'[89] Tiberius, with his love of Hellenic culture, may have uttered it for no more than melodramatic effect.

As Caligula's importance grew, his older brother, Drusus Caesar, died under appalling circumstances.[90] Locked in a room of the *Palatium*, he had sustained himself for eight days on barely edible food, even chewing the stuffing of his mattress, before succumbing to death by starvation.[91] There had been rumours of a reconciliation between Tiberius and his grandson, but events proved otherwise. In his letter to the Senate, Tiberius was scathing about Drusus Caesar, accusing him of immorality, conspiracy and sedition.[92] He ordered that a daily journal of all that the young man had said and done be read in public.[93] There was much to disclose. Throughout his life, spies had recorded his every word and deed. The latest journal included the reports compiled by Attius, a centurion, and Didymus, a freedman, which listed the names of slaves who had either struck or scared

Drusus as he tried to leave his room. Attius had shamelessly recorded his own language in all its unedited ferociousness, as well as the dying man's last words cursing Tiberius.

Then came the shocking news of the death of Caligula's mother, Agrippina, at the age of 46.[94] There had been rumours of a reconciliation between Tiberius and her too, but by 33 CE relations between them had been bad for too long. Tiberius noted that Agrippina 'died on the same day on which Seianus had paid the penalty of his crime two years before' and stipulated that the fact be formally recorded.[95] Tiberius also pointed out that she had not been strangled by the halter and flung down the *Scalae Gemoniae*.[96] However, the manner of her death was almost as terrible. On Pandataria, a centurion had beaten her until one of her eyes was destroyed.[97] It was alleged that, when she resolved to die of starvation, the same centurion had her mouth pried open and food forcibly crammed into it, resulting in her choking to death – although Tacitus doubts the story, describing it as 'a concocted fiction'.[98] The Senate gave a vote of thanks to Tiberius and decreed that on every 18 October thereafter, an offering be consecrated to Jupiter.[99] Dio claims that Tiberius ordered the remains of Drusus Caesar and his mother be hidden somewhere underground so carefully that they could never be found, while Suetonius reports that the remains of both mother and son were so scattered that it was only with difficulty that they could ever be collected.[100] In fact, the *stela* marking the place of Agrippina's funerary urn – erected by Caius Caligula seventeen years later – still survives, casting doubt on the versions of events of the historian and the biographer.[101]

Tiberius had not foreseen these events, despite indulging his passion for astrology. Having reviewed a chart, Tiberius sent for C. Sulpicius Galba, who was then consul. After discussing a variety of topics, he finally told him in Greek: 'You too, Galba, will someday have a taste of power.'[102] While he delved into the futures of people around him, about this time he looked back on his own life and wrote his biography (*commentarius*), which Suetonius describes as 'sketchy and brief'.[103] His life story would inspire a future emperor and become his favourite reading matter.

Among the notable deaths of prominent Romans at this time was C. Asinius Gallus, who had been found guilty and imprisoned three years before.[104] In his mid-70s, he died of starvation – though whether of his own choice or by compulsion was a question many pondered.[105] Asked whether he would allow him to be buried, Tiberius consented, adding his regret that he had not himself investigated the charge. He had never forgiven Gallus for marrying his first love, Vipsania.[106] In acts of *damnatio memoriae*, his name was scratched out from public inscriptions, such as boundary markers in Rome.[107] Munatia Plancina, the widow of Cn. Calpurnius Piso (II), tried for plotting the death of Germanicus and *maiestas*, faced a new murder charge supported by Tiberius. No longer shielded by Augusta, she was found guilty and took her own life.[108] M. Cocceius

Nerva, the jurist, decided to end his life, despite being in good health and under no threat of violence. As soon as he learned of his friend's intentions, Tiberius sat with him, inquiring to know his reasons, pleading with him not to carry out his wish and, finally, protesting that it would be a burden on his conscience and a blot on his reputation if the most intimate of his friends was to die without any cause for his death.[109] Nevertheless, Nerva was resolved. He firmly refused Tiberius' pleas and declined all food. Those who knew his mind said that the closer he peered into the current state of affairs, the more Nerva preferred to choose, in anger and alarm, an honourable death on his own terms. L. Aelius Lamia became *Praefectus Urbanus* in 33 CE, only to die in office of natural causes just months into his new role.[110] Before this, Tiberius had appointed him to govern Syria in 20 CE, but had not allowed him to leave Rome and carry out his duties in the province.[111] His life was celebrated with the honours of a censor's funeral. His successor to the post of *legatus Augusti propraetore* in Syria, Flaccus Pomponius, also died unexpectedly this year. In frustration, Tiberius wrote a letter to the Senate in which he complained that 'all the best men who were fit to command armies declined the service, and that he was thus necessarily driven to entreaties, by which some of the ex-consuls might be prevailed upon to accept provinces'.[112] He seemed to have completely forgotten that L. Arruntius had been detained in Rome for ten years and that he was being prevented from taking up his posting in Hispania Tarraconensis, forcing him to perform his duties remotely.[113]

It appeared to some that Tiberius was remiss about his primary responsibility of ensuring the security of the Roman People and their dominions. Suetonius writes that, leaving the mainland and returning to Capreae,

> he utterly neglected the conduct of the *Res Publica*, from that time on never filling the vacancies in the *decuriae* [groups of ten cavalrymen], nor changing the *tribuni militum* and the *praefecti*, nor the governors of any of his provinces. He left Hispania and Syria without consular legates for several years, suffered Armenia to be overrun by the Parthi, Moesia to be laid waste by the Daci and Sarmatae, and the Gallic provinces by the Germanic tribes, to the great dishonour of the empire and no less to its danger.[114]

On the contrary, concerns about provincial governance *did* preoccupy Tiberius' thoughts. In 34 CE, Abudius Ruso, who had been an *aedile*, was condemned and banished from Rome for seeking to imperil Cn. Cornelius Lentulus Gaetulicus, under whom he had commanded a legion, by alleging that he had betrothed his daughter to one of the sons of Seianus.[115] At the time, Gaetulicus commanded the army of Germania Superior and had won its affection and loyalty as a man of kindliness and forbearance; he was even popular with the army in neighbouring Germania Inferior under L. Apronius, his father-in-law. His past friendship with Seianus was contentious. A rumour circulated persistently affirming that

Gaetulicus had sent Tiberius a letter in which he reminded him that his alliance with Seianus was not made of his own choice, but on the advice of Tiberius. He had been deceived, just as Tiberius had been. It would be unjust, then, if Tiberius were to be regarded as innocent, while others were guilty of a capital offence. He reminded Tiberius that he would remain steadfastly loyal so long as there was no plot against him. Gaetulicus proposed a compact be agreed between them, by which he would retain his province and Tiberius would be master of all else. Tiberius would seem to have consented, as alone of those formerly connected with Seianus, Gaetulicus lived in safety and high favour.

In a letter to the Senate, Tiberius intervened in the case of Pomponius Labeo, who was accused of maladministration and other crimes in Moesia.[116] He had governed the province for eight years but was indicted, together with his wife, for taking bribes.[117] Labeo dreaded facing the executioner, and as the condemned, besides having his property confiscated, would be deprived of a proper burial; alternatively, if he committed suicide, his body would be interred and the terms of his will would be respected. He cut his veins first, then his wife, Paxaea, followed his example. Tiberius argued in a letter to the Senate that whenever the ancestors terminated a friendship, it had been their practice to forbid the person their house. While Labeo could be said to have complied, he had tried to hide his guilt from the grave charges filed against him by groundlessly alarming his wife, who, though herself guilty by association, was still free from danger.

The date 17 September 34 CE marked the twentieth anniversary of Tiberius' principate. He did not enter the city but sojourned close by in the vicinity of the Alban Hills and Tusculum.[118] Consuls Paullus Fabius Persicus and L. Vitellius honoured the completion of Tiberius' second *decennium* and voted to grant him another decade as leader, as the Senate had done automatically in the past for Augustus. As they were celebrating the occasion at the *Decennalia* festival, however, the two consuls were convicted of conspiracy, based on evidence in papers in the possession of Tiberius and in statements obtained under torture by Macro. It was widely believed that the real reason why Tiberius stayed away from Rome that day was to avoid the public embarrassment of being present when the sentences were pronounced.

On 16 November, Tiberius reached his 75th birthday. There is no mention of how he celebrated it – if he did at all. He generally eschewed public appearances, especially now as an older adult. He insisted on having his privacy. When he learned that there was a newly written play which alluded to him as a tyrant, he felt insulted. The playwright was the distinguished senator and talented advocate, Mamercus Aemilius Scaurus. His tragic drama, called *Atreus* after the legendary king of Mycenae, was written in the grand style of Euripides.[119] Macro discovered the play and dutifully informed the *princeps*.[120] Tiberius deduced that Scaurus had intended the main character to allude to him, claiming that he was

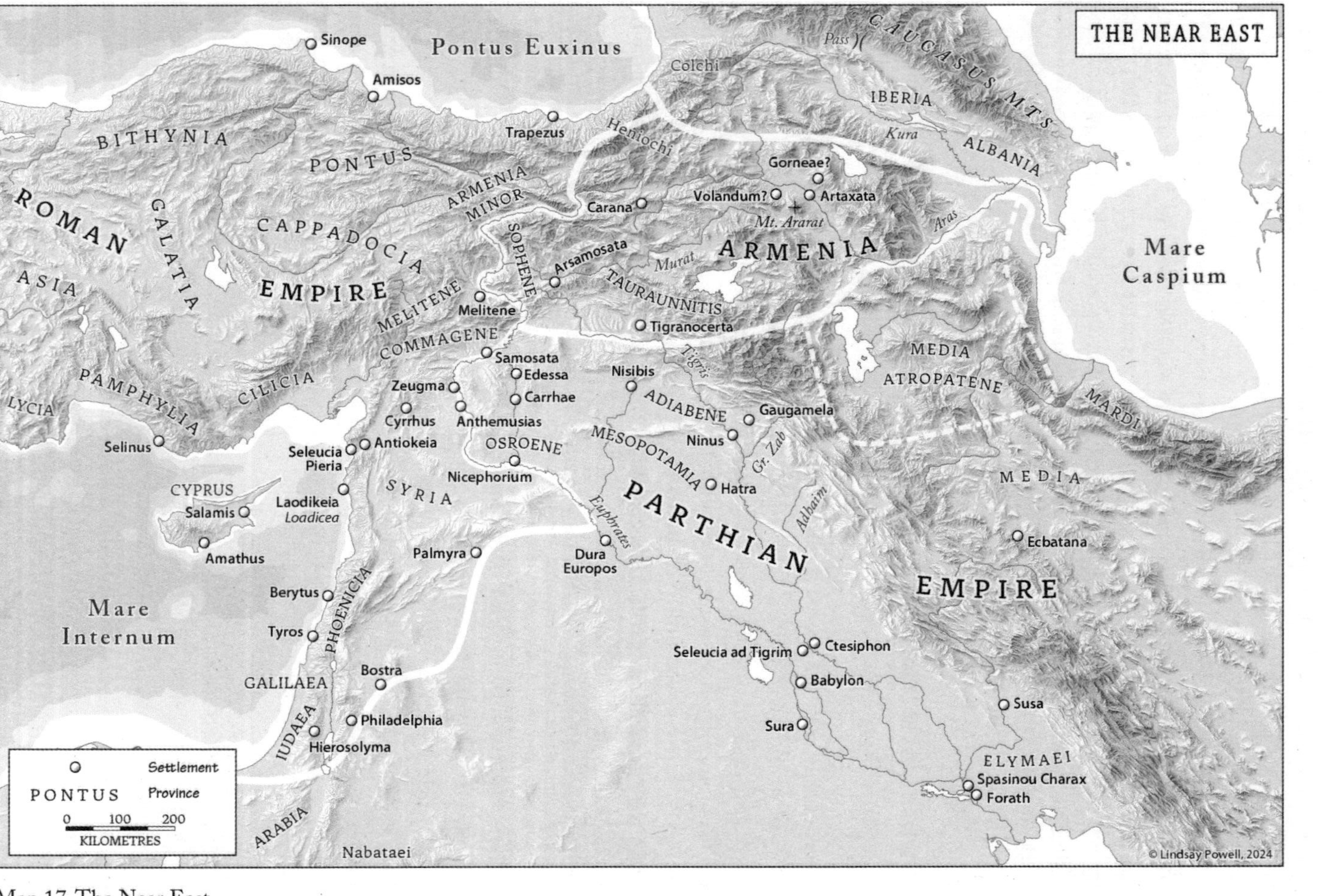


Map 17. The Near East.

Figure 31. In 35 CE, Artabanus II of Parthia, 'Great King of Kings', attempted to conquer Armenia and assert his son, Arsaces I, as its king. Tiberius responded with military force.

Atreus because of his supposed bloodthirstiness. In Dio's account, Tiberius said, 'I will make *him* Ajax' and compelled Scaurus to commit suicide.[121] It was likely all a dramatic deflection. The actual accusation made by the delators, Servilius and Cornelius, concerned Scaurus' alleged adultery with Livilla, involving the practice of magical rituals.[122] Persuaded by his wife, Sextia, Scaurus took his own life, and she followed suit. Bringing down Scaurus made Servilius and Cornelius notorious. Later, for having taken money from Varius Ligur in return for dropping a prosecution, they were outlawed and transported to faraway islands.[123] That was the stuff of Greek tragedy.

Conflict with Rome's nemesis would dominate foreign policy for the next two years. The frontier with Parthia had been largely peaceful since the failed expedition led by Caius three decades before (map 17).[124] In the years following, Artabanus II, King of Parthia (fig. 31), began to assert his influence in the region. Growing ever more confident and ambitious, he envisioned a new, larger Parthian Empire, one that even reclaimed lands once conquered by Alexander the Great. With the death of Artaxias III, he annexed Armenia and installed his son, Arsaces, upon the nation's throne.[125] He boldly demanded from the Romans the treasure that exiled King Vonones I had deposited in Cilicia and Syria. Without his knowledge, in 34 CE, a secret delegation of Parthians, supported by noblemen Sinnaces and led by the eunuch Abdus, arrived in Rome. As most of the royal Arsacid family had been murdered by Artabanus II, or was too young to rule, the clandestine emissaries requested that Phraates, son of King Phraates IV, should return from Rome – where he presently resided as a hostage – to Armenia.[126] To make the plan to install their own man work, they only needed two things: the name of a scion of the House of Arsaces, who would show himself on the banks of the Euphrates River, and Tiberius Caesar's authorization. Always preferring diplomacy over war to achieve policy objectives, Tiberius agreed.[127] He gave Phraates what he needed to assume his father's sovereignty, and the emissaries then departed.

In Parthia, Artabanus II learned about the secret diplomatic mission and was furious.[128] Upon his return to Parthia, Abdus was murdered and Sinnaces was put off by pretexts and presents. Arriving in Syria, Phraates assumed Parthian dress and manners, but, unable to adjust to the customs that were now foreign to him, and picking up an infection from which he had no immunity, he died. Despite these setbacks, Tiberius did not give up on the mission. He threw his support behind Tiridates III, a man from the same nation as Artabanus II. Separately, Mithridates, King of Iberia and an ally of the Romans, reconciled with his brother, Pharasmanes, in the Caucasus.[129] A clash between the two empires was now inevitable.

Tiberius assigned the execution of his eastern border policy to L. Vitellius, *legatus Augusti propraetore* in Syria with four legions under his command.[130] Though he had a bad reputation in Rome, in the administration of provinces, Vitellius acted with the honour and integrity that Romans valued in earlier times. At Tiberius' request, Mithridates persuaded his brother to lead the campaign to take Armenia.[131] Arsaces was murdered by assassins paid in gold. The Iberian army then marched into Armenia and seized the capital city of Artaxata.[132] With the situation becoming ever more uncertain, Artabanes II sent another of his sons, Orodes, with soldiers to eradicate the opposition forces. Pharasmanes recruited more troops from his allies among the Albani and Sarmatae and brought them to Armenia.[133] With this enlarged army, he was ready to challenge Orodes. In the ensuing battle, Orodes was badly wounded in the head but not killed.[134] Assuming his son to be dead, Artabanus retaliated by moving his entire army against Pharasmanes. However, he could not secure a decisive victory. Separately, Vitellius led his army towards Mesopotamia.[135] Unwilling to risk losing his capital at Ctesiphon, and with it his empire, Artabanus withdrew his troops from Armenia to fend off the invading Romans.[136] Sinnaces convinced his father, Abdagaeses, to rebel, opening another front for Artabanes to deal with. With defections, the Parthian king's army was rapidly reduced in size. Seeing that he had no hope of winning, he abandoned his troops and fled to the border with Scythia.

Vitellius now told Tiridates III to grasp his chance at securing the throne.[137] After offering sacrifices to their respective Roman and Parthian gods, a pontoon bridge was constructed over the Euphrates and the troops marched across it. First to show his loyalty to Tiridates was Ornospades, a Parthian auxiliary unit leader (*auxiliator*) who brought several thousand cavalrymen. Formerly an exile from his nation, Ornospades had provided Tiberius with much-needed assistance that helped him end the Batonian War (6–9 CE), for which he had been rewarded with Roman citizenship. Sinnaces arrived with reinforcements and Abdagaeses came with the royal treasure. Vitellius believed it was sufficient to have displayed the military might of Rome and, after advising Tiridates to remember his grandfather, Phraates, and foster-father, Ti. Caesar, he returned with the legions to Syria. For Tiberius, the outcome – a pro-Roman ally on the eastern border installed without loss of Roman life – could not have been better.

Far to the west, in Rome, notorious *delator* L. Fulcinius Trio himself now faced a crowd of accusers.[138] Before taking his own life, and to have the last word, he inserted in his will several withering statements. Some concerned Macro and the *princeps'* principal freedmen, but he also attacked Tiberius personally by referring to his 'mental deterioration brought on by old age and continuous absence in exile'.[139] Though Trio's heirs tried to have the will suppressed, Tiberius ordered it, along with the insults, to be read in public.[140] By doing this, he hoped to demonstrate his tolerance of free speech and indifference to what others thought of him.[141] More senators fell to the charge of *maiestas*. Granius Marcianus, accused by C. Sempronius Gracchus, ended his own life, while the ex-*praetor*, Tarius Gratianus, was condemned under the same law and sentenced to death. T. Trebellenus committed suicide, and Sextius Paconianus was strangled in prison for having written some lampoons about the *princeps*.[142] His proximity to Rome meant Tiberius could both receive and respond to senatorial questions within a day.

The year 36 CE was filled with human drama of all kinds. Former king Tigranes IV of Armenia was impeached; the fact that he had a royal title did not mean he could escape the punishment of an ordinary Roman citizen.[143] When the wealth of the Blaesi dwindled from the recent financial crisis, access to the priesthoods, traditionally filled by their family, was now denied them by Tiberius, who opened the vacant offices to other families. C. Sulpicius Galba (consul 22 CE) had squandered the greater part of his fortune, but as a proconsul he would hope to enrich himself at the expense of the provincials.[144] When Tiberius denied him participation in the annual draw by lot for provincial appointments, Galba left Rome and took his own life.[145] Two sons of Q. Iunius Blaesus – cousins of Seianus – committed suicide. After an action against him, Vibulenus (or Vibullius) Agrippa, an *eques*, swallowed poison contained in his ring and collapsed in the *Curia*.[146] Regardless, a semi-conscious Vibulenus was hurried away to prison by the lictors, where he was strangled with the executioner's halter. Aemilia Lepida, widow of Tiberius' son, Drusus, became a victim of the *delatores* when she was accused of adultery with a slave; her guilt was not doubted and, without even attempting a defence, she committed suicide. Thrasyllus, Tiberius' long-serving, loyal and most trusted friend, also died this year.[147] Tiberius' mentor in divination, there were some who thought that the astrologer cleverly 'handled' the *princeps* in much bigger issues too.[148]

Overseas, the Clitae, a nation subject to King Archelaus of Cappadocia, refused to submit an accounting of their revenues and to agree to paying tribute.[149] Instead, they retreated to Mount Taurus, where they defended themselves against the king's troops. Responding to a request for assistance from the king, Vitellius dispatched his *legatus legionis*, M. Trebellius, from Syria with 4,000 legionaries and some picked auxiliaries. They surrounded with entrenchments two hills occupied by the Clitae, then waited. Any daring to sally out from their position, the Romans cut down. The rest were forced to surrender through thirst and starvation.

In Parthia, Artabanus II re-emerged as a threat to Tiridates III. With the consent of the Parthians, Tiridates had occupied the Mesopotamian cities of Nicephorium, Anthemusias and others founded by Alexander the Great or his successors, and the Parthian towns of Halus and Artemita.[150] Their inhabitants detested Artabanus for his cruel treatment of them and hoped to find in Tiridates a kindlier ruler on account of his Roman education and training. The city of Seleucia, in particular, welcomed its new king having suffered under Artabanus.[151] Two of Tiridates' satraps, Phraates and Hiero, requested a delay in the scheduling of the king's coronation. They were working secretly to restore Artabanus.[152] With the aid of his Scythian allies, Artabanus took to the field.[153] Taken by surprise, Tiridates, who had since been crowned in Ctesiphon, hesitated. Heeding Abdagaeses' counsel, Tiridates retreated west, losing men from defections to his opponent along the way.[154] He crossed the Euphrates into Syria and the protection of the Roman Empire. Meanwhile, Mithridates, the son of Mithridates the Iberian, became King of Armenia, while his uncle, Pharasmanes, became King of the Iberians after him.[155] Tiberius' proxy had failed in taking Parthia and Artabanus II remained in power, but the Roman ally had secured Armenia.

While in Rome, Herod Agrippa learned something he believed he ought to share with the *princeps*. In the autumn of 36 CE, he crossed the Bay of Naples to meet with Tiberius on Capreae. He brought with him an accusation about his grandfather, Herod Antipas, tetrarch of Galilee.[156] The specifics are unclear. It might have concerned an intrigue about Seianus and Artabanus II, but whatever it was, Tiberius decided not to press charges.[157] Herod Agrippa had become a friend of Caius Caligula, who was on the island. During a dinner with him, Herod Agrippa said, with hands outstretched, that he 'openly wished that Tiberius might die, and that he might quickly see him [Caius Caligula] emperor of the world'.[158] Informed by one of Herod Agrippa's own domestics, Tiberius 'became very angry, and ordered Agrippa to be bound, and had him very ill-treated in the prison for six months'.[159]

According to an early Christian tradition, Pontius Pilatus notified Tiberius of the man now being referred to as *Christus* ('Christ') in his province of Iudaea. This individual had been crucified during his prefecture.[160] Pilatus wrote of how he was already regarded by his many followers – called *Chrestiani* or *Christiani* – to be a god because they believed he had risen from the dead.[161] It is claimed that, in his eighteenth year as *princeps* (36 CE), Tiberius petitioned the Senate for the consecration (*consecratio*) of *Christus* and to add his name to the pantheon of Roman gods.[162] The Senate refused to sanction the motion, on the basis that it had sole legal authority to make such a ruling and that it had not properly assessed the petition on its merits.[163] The Senate proposed to eject the followers of the cult from Rome, but according to this tradition, Tiberius 'stood to his resolution, and issued severe penalties against all who should accuse the *Christiani*', even issuing an edict to enforce it.[164]

In November 36 CE, a fire broke out in Rome. Part of the *Circus Maximus* was burnt down, along with buildings on *Mons* Aventinus (the Aventine Hill).[165] As he had done nine years before in response to the fire on the Caelius, Tiberius compensated property owners who had suffered the loss of their homes or tenement blocks up to a total of HS 100 million, which was widely regarded as a very generous sum in comparison to the modest budgets he allocated for his own public projects. To administer the claims and disbursements, he established a commission – four husbands of his grand-daughters, with a fifth commissioner nominated by the Senate.[166] Many honours and recognitions were proposed for Tiberius in gratitude.[167]

The following year, there were more bizarre antics among the senatorial class.[168] Dec. Laelius Balbus, known for his savage eloquence, accused Acutia, ex-wife of P. Vitellius, of *maiestas*. The tribune of the people, Iunius Otho, vetoed the reward being voted to her prosecutor – hence a feud arose between Vitellius and Otho, ending in Otho's banishment. Albucilla, wife of Satrius Secundus, was charged with disloyalty towards the *princeps*.[169] Notorious for the number of her lovers, Cn. Domitius Ahenobarbus, C. Vibius Marsus and L. Arruntius were named as accomplices who had shared her bed. As there was no letter from Tiberius against the defendants, many suspected that the charge was invented to satisfy Macro's well-known enmity towards Arruntius.[170] The accused men approached their predicaments differently: Domitius prepared his defence; Marsus decided to starve himself to death; and Arruntius protested in the Senate, slitting his wrist as he concluded his speech.[171] As for Albucilla, she stabbed herself, but the wound was not fatal and, by the Senate's order, she was hauled off to prison.[172] Sex. Papinius threw himself off a building when he could no longer cope with his mother's extravagant lifestyle.[173] She appeared before the Senate, lay prostrate and pleaded for mercy, but she was banned from Rome for ten years – long enough for her youngest son to grow up without suffering her bad influence.

While his mind was still sharp, Tiberius was physically weaker now. Macro's influence over him had grown, but he was increasingly looking to Caligula. Tiberius taunted him for 'forsaking the setting sun and looking to the rising sun'.[174] Macro's relationship with Caligula had, indeed, become closer; it is reported that he even persuaded his wife, Ennia, to seduce the young man and propose that they marry.

Caligula and Macro were with Tiberius as he toured the mainland. Suetonius records that after seeing a distant view of Rome's city walls, without ever going close to them, he left because he was alarmed by a portent.[175] He had a pet snake, and when he was going to feed it from his own hand – as he usually did – he discovered, to his dismay, that it had been devoured by ants, which he took as a warning to beware of the power of the crowd.[176] As the snake was a symbol of health, luck and prosperity in Roman culture, its death was interpreted as foretelling impending doom. He hurried to Campania, moving from place-to-place and intending to return to Capreae.[177] While at Astura, he fell ill.[178] Having made a slight recovery, he travelled on to Circeii (modern San Felice Circeo). To avoid giving rise to any suspicion of his weakening condition, Tiberius attended the games of the soldiers (*castrensibus ludis*); a boar had been let lose into the arena, and he threw darts at it from his seat in the imperial box.[179] He immediately felt a pain in his side. Exposed to a draught during the performance and subsequently running a temperature, his illness worsened. Later, upon reaching Misenum (plate 37), he settled into the villa once owned by L. Licinius Lucullus.[180] The distinguished physician, Charicles, had meanwhile offered to help and joined the party for dinner. Before leaving the occasion, Charicles took Tiberius' hand to kiss it out of respect.[181] Tiberius, believing that he was trying to feel his pulse, withdrew his hand and urged the physician to remain and take his place again. Tiberius insisted that the dinner continue, and it went on to a late hour. As each guest departed, he stood in the middle of the dining-room (*triclinium*) with a lictor by his side and addressed the guests by name as they said their farewells. Tiberius remained behind and read the report of proceedings from the Senate (*Acta Senatus*).[182] Its contents infuriated him, since it was an accusation brought by a *delator* and the case was dismissed without a hearing. He resolved to return to Capreae at any cost. A depression now settled now over the bay, bringing with it bad weather.[183] The lighthouse at Capreae was reportedly damaged by an earthquake.[184] The increasing severity of Tiberius' illness detained him and his associates at the villa in Misenum.[185] Examining the imperial patient, Charicles advised Macro that Tiberius' breath was failing and that he would likely not last more than two days.[186] Preparations were hurriedly made. The senior officials at Misenum met in conference, and despatches were made ready to send to the legates of the provinces and their armies.

On 'the seventeenth day before the Kalends of April', Tiberius died.[187] He had lived seventy-seven years, four months and nine days, and had led the *Res Publica* as *princeps* for twenty-two years, seven months and seven days.[188] What exactly happened on 16 March 37 CE is unclear.[189] Just as mystery accompanied his birth, so it shrouded his demise.

Tiberius' death may have been by entirely natural causes, perhaps connected with the pains and fever he had suffered in the days before. According to the earliest account by Seneca (which is preserved by Suetonius),

> conscious of his approaching end, he [Tiberius] took off the ring, as if to give it to someone, but held fast to it for a time; then he put it back on his finger, and clenching his left hand, lay for a long time motionless; suddenly he called for his attendants, and on receiving no response, got up; but his strength failed him and he fell dead near the couch.[190]

In Josephus' version too, sickness was the culprit.[191]

Suetonius cites other unsubstantiated versions in circulation at the time, each alleging a conspiracy.[192] In the first, Caligula had given Tiberius a slow and wasting poison. No proof is offered. In the second, during his convalescence from an attack of fever, Tiberius was refused food when he asked for it. This version echoes the earlier one of Seneca. In the third, a pillow was thrown upon his face, and then, when he regained consciousness and demanded his ring, which had been taken from him during a fainting fit, he was smothered again until he expired. Who did the deed is not disclosed. Suetonius adds the ominous detail that

> the ashes from the glowing coals and embers in the brazier, which had been brought in to warm his *triclinium*, after they had died out and been for a long time cold, suddenly blazed up in the early evening and glowed without stopping until late at night.[193]

As for a motive, Caligula himself was later reported to have confessed that he had once entered the bedroom where Tiberius was sleeping, holding a dagger,

> to avenge the death of his mother and brothers; but that, seized with pity, he threw down the dagger and went out again; and that though Tiberius knew of this, he had never dared to make any inquiry or take any action.[194]

If the anecdote is true, it reveals that Caligula held his adoptive grandfather, not Seianus, personally responsible for the destruction of his family.

In Tacitus' version, Caligula left the room, believing Tiberius to have expired, and announced the sad news to a crowd which had gathered at the villa.[195] The guests were congratulating him on his accession, when suddenly a report came that Tiberius had recovered his voice and sight, and was calling for someone to bring him food to revive him from his feeling of faintness. Panic ensued, those present either feigning grief or ignorance, while Caligula stood in silence from shock. Macro, however, calmly and clearheadedly ordered the old *princeps* to be smothered under a huge heap of bedclothes and then left alone.

In Dio's version, Caligula feared that Tiberius might recover.[196] He refused Tiberius' requests for something to eat on the basis that it would harm him, and then, pretending that he needed to be kept warm, wrapped him up in many thick clothes and smothered him, aided in the task by Macro.

Tiberius' body was prepared for the final journey. When the funeral procession left Misenum, many along the roadside shouted that the corpse ought to be carried to Atella and half-burned in the amphitheatre.[197] In Rome, many welcomed the news with rejoicing. Some were so glad that they ran about the streets shouting, 'Tiberius to the Tiber!'[198] Others turned to *Terra Mater* ('Mother Earth') and the *Manes* (the divine dead), praying for them to confine the deceased man's spirit among the Damned. There were yet others who threatened to throw his corpse down the *Scalae Gemoniae*. Meanwhile, the cortège, led by Caligula and escorted by soldiers, proceeded up the *Via Appia*. It entered Rome on 29 March 37 CE at night, and the body was laid out at dawn.[199]

Two years before his death, Tiberius had made two exact copies of his will, one written in his own hand and the other in that of a freedman.[200] Now the will was read by Macro in the *Curia*.[201] In it, Tiberius named his grandsons, Caius Caligula, son of Germanicus, and Ti. Gemellus, son of Drusus, as heirs to equal shares of his estate, with each to be sole heir in the case of the other's death. He also gave legacies to several other individuals, including the Vestal Virgins. His public legacy was modelled after that of Augustus. Tiberius left to the Roman People HS 45 million and, in addition, the HS 240 apiece which they had failed to receive when he received the *toga virilis*, together with interest in the amount of HS 60.[202] He paid HS 1,000 to each man of the *Cohortes Praetoriae*.[203] To each of the men of the *Cohortes Urbanae*, the *Vigiles*, the regular soldiers outside of Italy and to any other army of citizens that was in the smaller forts, and all the other military installations, he gave HS 300.[204] Tiberius left the *Res Publica* solvent, with HS 2,700 million in the *Fiscus*.[205] By prior agreement with Caligula, the consuls annulled the will, declaring Tiberius to have not been of sound mind when he wrote it, yet they still authorized the cash payouts.[206]

The state funeral of Tiberius took place on 3 April. Caligula delivered the eulogy, with many tears, but actually said little in praise of Tiberius, instead reminding the Roman People of Augustus and Germanicus and commending himself to them.[207] Tiberius' body was solemnly carried to the *Campus Martius*, where, with the required public rituals, it was reduced to ashes and the urn containing them was formally placed in the Mausoleum of Augustus.

When official letters bearing the news of Tiberius' death and of Caligula's accession were received at the army camps, there were no mutinies. The transfer of power was peaceful, as Tiberius would have wished. Tiberius had not wanted to be deified, but his successor demanded that the Senate grant it, along with the same distinctions it had accorded Augustus. In the event, Caligula accepted the offer of the funeral, but the process for Tiberius' deification was never initiated.[208] Within months, Caligula had Ti. Gemellus murdered, just as Tiberius had predicted.[209] Another of his forecasts also proved to be correct: Galba did become *princeps* – albeit very briefly.[210]

# Chapter 10

# Remembering Tiberius: 38 CE–1453

Dio writes that on 1 January 38 CE,

> The regular oaths to support the act of Tiberius were not taken and for this reason are not in use nowadays, either; for no one reckons Tiberius among the emperors in connection with this custom of the oaths.[1]

Just months after the death of Tiberius, the process of shaping the narrative of Rome's second *princeps* had already begun.

Of the surviving texts by writers contemporary with Tiberius, the majority are positive in their assessments of him.[2] Foremost of them is Paterculus (M. – or C. – Velleius Paterculus, *c.* 20/19 BCE–31 CE).[3] What distinguishes him from other writers is that he knew Tiberius personally: he served with him on military campaigns, and in other civil roles during his principate. According to his own account, Paterculus began his eventful career as a soldier, serving as *tribunus militum* in Thracia Macedoniaque under P. Silius and the father of M. Vincius.[4] Assigned to the away team of Augustus' adopted son, he accompanied Caius to Achaea, Asia and the eastern border provinces, commenting that 'it is not without feelings of pleasure that I recall the many events, places, peoples, and cities'.[5] It was on an island in the Euphrates that he witnessed in person the momentous peace conference between Rome and Parthia (1 CE). He served for nine years (4–12 CE) as *praefectus equitum* in Germania (a position once held by his father), where he notes: 'I was a spectator of his [Tiberius'] superhuman achievements, and further assisted in them to the extent of my modest ability.'[6] Paterculus' civil career was interrupted in 6 CE when he took part in the mobilization for the Batonian War in Pannonia (Illyricum) as an equestrian-rank commander, 'and led from the city [of Rome] to Tiberius a portion of the army which was entrusted to me by Augustus'.[7] In 4 CE, he accepted the post of *praefectus equitum* in Germania under Tiberius.[8] He and his brother, Magius Celer Velleianus, participated in Tiberius' triumph on 23 October 12 CE in recognition of their service during the Batonian War in Illyricum.[9] Both brothers were praetors-designate in 14 CE, posts they filled the following year, earning them 'the distinction of being the last to be recommended by Augustus and the first to be named by Tiberius Caesar'.[10] Paterculus was still alive in 30 CE, the year that saw publication of his book which he dedicated to M. Vinicius.[11] He then disappears from history and is presumed to have died in 31 CE.[12]

Velleius Paterculus' *Roman History* (*Historia Romanae*) begins with Greek mythology and climaxes with the principate of Tiberius.[13] He covers the first fifteen years of Tiberius' twenty-seven-year reign.[14] His writing imitates the oratorical styles of Sallust and Cicero, with antithesis and point often in long sentences. His use of successive rhetorical questions and exclamations evocative of panegyric has led some twentieth-century historians to be disdainful or dismissive of his account, seeing it as uncritical sycophancy biased entirely in favour of his senior battlefield commander.[15] By way of an example:

> What public buildings did he construct in his own name or that of his family! With what pious munificence, exceeding human belief, does he now rear the temple to his father! With what a magnificent control of personal feeling did he restore the works of Cnaeus Pompeius when destroyed by fire! For a feeling of kinship leads him to protect every famous monument. With what generosity at the time of the recent fire on the Caelius Hill, as well as on other occasions, did he use his private fortune to make good the losses of people of all ranks in life! And the recruiting of the army, a thing ordinarily looked upon with great and constant dread, with what calm on the part of the People does he provide for it, and without any of the usual panic attending conscription![16]

He declares that Tiberius was a new ruler who had 'no need of arms either to defend the good or to restrain the bad'.[17]

*Roman History* may indeed have elements of style that derive from the orator's or poet's repertoire; however, in Paterculus' writings they surely reflect the evident patriotism of his post-civil war times when the *princeps* was the focus of national leadership.[18] The only historian to have survived in the decades after Livy (T. Livius, 59 BCE–17 CE) – whose own account ended with the premature death of Tiberius' younger brother in 9 BCE – and to have lived before the next generation of great historians, was Velleius Paterculus.[19] Moreover, because he is a direct link to Tiberius, he cannot be easily dismissed.[20] Through his writings, we witness – albeit through the uncritical eyes of an admirer – Tiberius as a diplomat in the East and an active battlefield commander in Germania and Illyricum, observe his preparations for war against Maroboduus, and follow his domestic and foreign policy actions as *princeps*, alone and in association with Seianus.

After Tiberius' death, there were no calls for *damnatio memoriae*.[21] The buildings he had dedicated were maintained, the inscriptions were left undamaged, the statues of him remained standing and the coins minted under his aegis continued in circulation. When Strabo (Strabon of Amasia, 64/63 BCE–*c.* 24 CE) writes in his *Geography* (*Geographika*) 'the present government', 'in his times' or 'in our times', he is referring to Tiberius.[22] In describing Italy, he praises the regime for its careful government of the Roman world:

> We now see Italia, which has frequently been torn by civil war even since it came under the dominion of the Romans, nay, even Rome herself, restrained from rushing headlong into confusion and destruction by the excellence of her form of government and the ability of her emperors. Indeed, it was hard to administer the affairs of so great an empire otherwise than by committing them to one man as a father. For it would never have been in the power of the Romans and their allies to attain to a state of such perfect peace, and the enjoyment of such abundant prosperity, as Augustus Caesar afforded them from the time that he took upon himself the absolute authority; and which his son Tiberius, who has succeeded him, still maintains, who takes his father for a pattern in his government and ordinances. And in their turn his sons, Germanicus and Drusus, who are exercising the functions of government under their father, take him for their model.[23]

The theme of peace is repeated elsewhere, such as in the description of Lusitania in which Strabo writes:

> Tiberius, who succeeded Augustus Caesar, carried out his intention of placing a military force of three legions in these parts, by which means he has not only preserved peace, but introduced amongst some of them a civil polity.[24]

Strabo notes Tiberius' direct intervention in the aftermath of a devastating earthquake in Asia: 'Sardes, and many other cities which participated in this calamity about the same time, have been repaired by the provident care and beneficence of Tiberius the present ruler.'[25]

Similarly, in *Memorable Deeds and Sayings* (*Factorum et Dictorum Memorabilium*), Valerius Maximus (writing around 30 CE) describes Tiberius as 'our leader and *princeps*' and 'beneficial *princeps*', representing 'the surest security for our country' against the outbreak of civil war.[26] He was presented as a man of compassion too. Other than Castor and Pollux, Maximus knew of no other exemplar of filial love than that displayed by the two Claudian brothers.

With hindsight, many thought Tiberius to have been a wise and respectful ruler.[27] Philo (Philon, *c.* 20 BCE–*c.* 40/50 CE), a Greek-speaking philosopher born into a prominent Jewish family in Alexandria, writes in his *Embassy to Caius* (*Legatio ad Gaium*) – an account of his diplomatic mission to Rome to meet the third emperor – that Tiberius was called 'The Old Man' as a mark of respect because of his wisdom.[28] For Philo, by praising Tiberius he was able to emphasize the contrast between him and Caius Caligula's troubling behaviour. He recognized Tiberius' innate talents, describing him as a person excelling in intelligence and sharpness of mind.[29] Philo particularly noted his wisdom and goodness.[30] He observed that Tiberius strongly disliked any youthful displays of wit used purely for amusement, as he himself had been serious and solemn since his early years.[31]

Around the same time, Seneca the Elder (L. Annaeus Seneca, *c.* 54 BCE–*c.* 39 CE) wrote a history of Rome which has been nearly completely lost, except for a fragment (*PHerc.* 1067), which, by chance, mentions the name of Tiberius.[32] The book was a source for at least one of the historians who followed him, whose work *has* substantially survived. The Stoic philosopher Seneca the Younger (L. Annaeus Seneca, *c.* 4 BCE–65 CE) writes in his *On Clemency* (*De Clementia*), addressed to Emperor Nero (r. 54–68 CE), that 'no one any longer speaks of the good times of the late Emperor Augustus, or the first years of the reign of Tiberius'.[33] Thus, just two decades after his passing, a popular view had emerged of the life of Tiberius in terms of 'the good years' and 'the bad years'. In his *On Benefits* (*De Beneficiis*), Seneca also recounts a brief exchange between Tiberius and another:

> Someone approached Tiberius Caesar and started to say, 'Do you remember…?' before he uttered several remarks of old familiarity. 'I do not remember,' he [Tiberius] said, 'what I was'.[34]

From this introspective moment, Seneca asks rhetorically:

> Why should benefit not be reaped from this? Oblivion was to be desired; he eschewed the knowledge of all his friends and contemporaries, and looked upon that alone as his present fortune, that alone he wished to be thought of and told of. He had an old friend, 'the Inquisitor'![35]

It is Pliny the Elder (C. Plinius Secundus, 23/24 CE–79 CE) who characterizes Tiberius as *tristissimus hominum* ('the saddest [or gloomiest] of men').[36] Yet in the *Natural History* (*Naturalis Historia*), which he completed in 77 CE, there are fascinating facts about Tiberius that humanize the man. His 'sad man' comment is made in this observation:

> Why is it that we salute a person when he sneezes, an observance which Tiberius Caesar they say – the saddest of men, as we all know – used to exact when riding in his carriage even?[37]

He records Tiberius' momentary ability to see clearly at night, his love of *cucumis*, his nickname for Apion the Grammarian as *Cymbalum mundi* ('Trumpeter of the World') and his land speed record for distance covered in a single day and night.[38] Among other things, we learn that, 'It is said that when it thundered, *princeps* Tiberius was in the habit of putting on a wreath of laurel to allay his apprehensions of disastrous effects from the lightning' and that 'Tiberius used also to observe the changes of the moon for cutting his hair.'[39] Pliny records:

> It was only in the principate of Tiberius Caesar that this disease made its appearance [in Italia], the *princeps* himself being the first to be attacked by it; a circumstance which produced considerable mystification throughout the City, when it read the edict issued by that emperor excusing his inattention to public business, on the ground of his being laid up with a disease, the very name of which was till then unknown.[40]

He also preserves this fact:

> One variety [of pear] is known as the *Tiberiana*, from its having been a particular favourite with the *princeps* Tiberius; it is more coloured by the sun, and grows to a larger size, otherwise it would be identical with the Licerian variety.[41]

Memorable is this story of a talking bird:

> In the reign of Tiberius, one of a brood of ravens that had bred on the top of the Temple of Castor, happened to fly into a shoemaker's shop that stood opposite: upon which, from a feeling of religious veneration, it was looked upon as doubly recommended by the owner of the place. The bird, having been taught to speak at an early age, used every morning to fly to the *Rostra*, which look towards the *Forum*; here, addressing each by his name, it would salute Tiberius, and then the Caesars Germanicus and Drusus, after which it would proceed to greet the Roman populace as they passed, and then return to the shop: for several years it was remarkable for the constancy of its attendance.[42]

Of the histories written in Tiberius' day or shortly after, which might have informed us of his life and deeds, all are long gone. Foremost would be the *History* (*Historia*) and *German War* (*Bellum Germanicum*) of Aufidius Bassus, a man admired for his eloquence.[43] They could also have included the works of Servilius Nonianus, M. Cluvius Rufus and Fabius Rusticus, who variously wrote about the times of Caius Caligula, Claudius and Nero.[44] Memory of Tiberius inevitably faded as the years passed. His eccentric successors shaped the principate into a hereditary, imperial autocracy. The extinction of the Julio-Claudian dynasty with Nero's suicide marked the beginning of a period of close re-evaluation of the state of the *Res Publica* by educated Romans.

Under the Flavian (69–96 CE) and Nerva-Antonine emperors (96–192 CE), historians tried to explain what had happened to the city their ancestors knew – and to their allies too. In telling the story of the Jewish people, historian Josephus (Yosef Ben Matityahu, Flavius Iosephus, 37–*c.* 100 CE) wrote of relations between the ruling elite in Iudaea and Tiberius. In *Antiquities of the Jews* (*Ioudaike Archaiologia*), published in 93/94 CE, Josephus relates that Herod the Tetrarch built Tiberias on the shores of the Sea of Galilee in 28 CE in recognition of the favour in which the emperor held him; he shows how Tiberius actively worked to maintain order in the province yet banished the Jews from Rome; he describes Tiberius' nature as 'dilatory' and tells a story of how Tiberius kept Herod Agrippa in chains on Capreae while he decided what to do with him; he then reveals Agrippa's reaction to the news of Tiberius' demise with the words 'The lion is dead!'[45] In his summary, Josephus writes:

> Tiberius had brought a vast number of miseries on the best families of the Romans: since he was easily inflamed with passion in all cases: and was of such a temper, as rendered his anger irrevocable, until he had executed the same, although he had taken a hatred against men without reason. For he was by nature fierce in all the sentences he gave and made death the penalty for the lightest offences. Insomuch that when the Romans heard the rumour about his death gladly, they were restrained from the enjoyment of that pleasure by the dread of such miseries as they foresaw would follow, if their hopes proved ill grounded.[46]

It was in the interests of the Flavian emperors to present themselves as steady and sensible, in contrast with their predecessors as capricious and corrupted. As a client of Vespasian and Titus, Josephus was happy to represent history in a way that was favourable to them.[47] Already, by his time, portraying Tiberius as an irascible tyrant had become established practice by historians. Nevertheless, Titus (r. 79–81 CE) saw prestige in reissuing coins of his imperial predecessors in 80 or 81 CE, with two copper *ases* in the series bearing the likeness of Tiberius

Figure 32. During his principate, Titus reissued an earlier coin of Tiberius out of respect for his Julio-Claudian antecedent.

Figure 33. Domitian was a great admirer of Tiberius and in honour of him reissued an earlier coin of Rome's second *princeps* during his reign.

(fig. 32) and his titles.[48] His brother Domitian (r. 81–96) continued the project the following year (fig. 33).[49] Regarding Rome's second *princeps* as a role model, he 'read nothing except the memoirs and transactions of Tiberius Caesar'.[50] It was in this era that the legend of Tiberius became established and was elaborated.[51] Perhaps this was when an unknown writer published a biography of Tiberius portraying him as a suspicious and cruel tyrant, like Domitian, that influenced later writers.[52]

In 105 CE, Tacitus (P. or C. Cornelius Tacitus, *c.* 56 CE–*c.* 120 CE) published the first books of a history called *The Annals* (*Annales*).[53] Tiberius appears in five out of the original six books, most of Book 5 and part of Book 6 being lost, meaning the years 29–31 CE are missing. He drew on a variety of sources, including archived copies of the *Acta Senatus*, the speeches of Tiberius and contemporary historians, notably Pliny the Elder.[54] He recognized that their accounts differed, writing: 'I can hardly venture a single definite assertion – so conflicting is the evidence, not of the authors alone, but of the *princeps*' own speeches.'[55] Referring to witnesses who told him that Piso carried letters from Tiberius to his trial, and that his death was not suicide, he writes, 'it was my duty not to suppress a version given by contemporaries who were still living in my early years'.[56] He states that he followed 'the consentient testimony of historians'.[57] By his day, much of that historical consensus was negative towards Tiberius.[58] The resulting story he crafted from this material has been profound for Tiberius' legend and legacy.

At the start of his *Annals*, he introduces Tiberius by quoting the gossip circulating by a majority of people about him before he became *princeps*:

> Tiberius Nero was of mature years, and had established his fame in war, but he had the old arrogance inbred in the Claudian family, and many symptoms of a cruel temper, though they were repressed, now and then broke out. He had also from earliest infancy been reared in a reigning house; consulships and triumphs had been heaped on him in his younger days; even in the years which, on the pretext of seclusion he spent in exile at Rhodes, he had had no thoughts but of wrath, hypocrisy, and secret sensuality.[59]

For Tacitus, Tiberius inherited the distinctive traits and drives that defined him. His obituary of Tiberius is longer and more nuanced:

> And so died Tiberius, in the seventy-eighth year of his age. Nero was his father, and he was on both sides descended from the *gens Claudia*, though his mother passed by adoption, first into the Livian, then into the Iulian family. From earliest infancy, perilous vicissitudes were his lot. Himself an exile, he was the companion of a proscribed father, and on being admitted as a stepson into the House of Augustus, he had to struggle with many rivals, so long as Marcellus and Agrippa and, subsequently, Caius and Lucius Caesar were in their glory. Again, his brother Drusus enjoyed in a greater degree the affection of the citizens. But he was more than ever on dangerous ground after his marriage with Iulia, whether he tolerated or escaped from his wife's profligacy. On his return from Rhodes, he ruled the *princeps*' now heirless house for twelve years, and the Roman world, with absolute sway, for about twenty-three. His character too had its distinct periods. It was a bright time in his life and reputation, while under Augustus he was a private citizen or held high offices; a time of reserve and crafty assumption of virtue, as long as Germanicus and [son] Drusus were alive. Again, while his mother lived, he was a compound of good and bad [or evil]; he was infamous for his cruelty, though he veiled his debaucheries, while he loved or feared Seianus. Finally, he plunged into every wickedness and disgrace, when fear and shame being cast off, he simply indulged his own inclinations.[60]

At first glance, Tacitus is even-handed and keeps to the known facts. The text is cleverly constructed, however: in his framing, each period of Tiberius' life ends worse than the previous one, and with a friend or relative dying.[61] With devastating effect, in the last clause he repeats the unsubstantiated tales of vice that have ever-after stained his reputation. Tacitus' is a moral tale in the mould of Sallust (C. Sallustius Crispus, 86–35 BCE); Tiberius Caesar is his exemplar of turpitude caused by the corrupting effects of power concentrated in one man.[62] In Tacitus' hands, it is the tragic story both of Tiberius *and* of Rome.

Right at the start of his First Book, Tacitus boldly claims to write about events *sine ira et studio*:

> The histories of Tiberius, Caius, Claudius, and Nero, while they were in power, were falsified through terror, and after their death were written under the irritation of a recent hatred. Hence my purpose is to relate a few facts about Augustus – more particularly his last acts, then the reign of Tiberius, and all which follows, without either bitterness or partiality, from any motives to which I am far removed.[63]

In practice, Tacitus was not impartial – especially so in the case of Tiberius.[64] Indeed, Tacitus later confesses:

> My purpose is not to relate at length every motion, but only such as were conspicuous for excellence or notorious for infamy. This I regard as history's highest function, to let no worthy action be uncommemorated, and to hold out the reprobation of posterity as a terror to evil words and deeds. So corrupted indeed and debased was that age by sycophancy that not only the foremost citizens who were forced to save their grandeur by servility, but every ex-consul, most of the ex-praetors and a host of inferior senators would rise in eager rivalry to propose shameful and preposterous motions. Tradition says that Tiberius as often as he left the *Curia* used to exclaim in Greek, 'How ready these men are to be slaves!' Clearly, even he, with his dislike of public freedom, was disgusted at the abject abasement of his creatures.[65]

'Tradition' is not necessarily truth. Tacitus' portrait of Tiberius is notable for its focus on infamy, rather than on excellence. Modern historians tend to be sceptical of his account of Tiberius' principate, seeing it as unremittingly hostile and explicitly biased against Rome's second emperor.[66]

A senator and a consular who venerated the 'good old days' of the Roman Republic, Tacitus saw in Augustus a paradoxical figure, one who had rescued the Commonwealth from utter destruction, but had done so at the cost of concentrating power in his own person as *princeps*, which meant sacrificing the hard-won *libertas* of the Roman Senate and People.[67] As Augustus' successor, he saw Tiberius as an autocrat who had finally succumbed to the worst temptations that holding supreme power enabled. Through oratorical and literary techniques and by selectively using facts and inserting innuendo into his narrative, Tacitus disparaged his imperial subject in pursuit of a higher purpose.[68] This was that hereditary tyranny – a return to the *dominatio* of the kings in all but name – was an evil imposition upon the *Res Publica*. The very words he uses to mark the beginning of Tiberius' principate are, 'At Rome, however, consuls, senators, and knights were rushing into *servitum* [slavery]. The more exalted the personage, the grosser his hypocrisy and his haste.'[69]

The result is that Tacitus sees negative intent in almost everything Tiberius does.[70] To convince his reader of his thesis, Tacitus downplays Tiberius' personal achievements on the battlefield and his respect for Roman law and tradition, and instead exaggerates his faults and alleged crimes. The contrast between Tiberius and Germanicus is a case in point.[71] He asserts that Tiberius sent Germanicus to the East in 17 CE, 'where he would be vulnerable at once to treachery and chance'.[72] Recounting rumours, he implicates Tiberius in the subsequent death of Germanicus, blaming him for persecutions of Agrippina and her sons, and causing the prosecution of senators in treason trials.[73] Tacitus also dwells on Tiberius' reliance on Seianus, who 'inflamed and exacerbated his jealousies; and, with his expert knowledge of the character of Tiberius, kept sowing the seed of future hatreds'.[74] Compared to Augustus, Tiberius is presented by Tacitus as the weaker man – indeed, a cruel, depraved and hypocritical one. His Tiberius firmly anchors his authority in Augustus' achievement – he has Tiberius cite his predecessor's speeches and deeds as marks of his devotion to him and his memory – and by doing so he implicitly calls into question his own legitimacy.[75] However there are contradictions. Tacitus alleges 'wickedness and disgrace', yet elsewhere reports that Tiberius 'brought forward a motion [with the Senate's authority] about the licentious behaviour of the players' on stage, citing them for a breach of the peace, disgracing eminent families and indecency, then banned them from Italy – hardly the response of someone allegedly partial to lewdness.[76] Tacitus even criticizes Tiberius for not expanding the Roman Empire through military campaigns like his predecessors, lamenting, 'Mine is an inglorious labour in a narrow field.'[77] The remark reveals that, for Tacitus, Tiberius' authorization of wars of necessity to sustain the empire consistent with Augustus' instructions was prudent, but just less interesting to him as an historian.

For Tacitus, particularly worth reporting, however, was the accusation of *maiestas* directed at A. Cremutius Cordus. A senator and historian like Tacitus himself, Cordus' alleged crime was writing a history in which he had praised M. Brutus and called C. Cassius 'the last of the Romans', remarks which Seianus' informers understood to defame Augustus and Tiberius.[78] Tacitus points out that it was 'a new charge, now for the first time heard'.[79] Having rejected the charge before the Senate presided over by Tiberius in person, Cordus went home, where he starved himself to death.[80] He may have seen a parallel with his own times. Tacitus had lived through the reign of Domitian (81–96 CE). In his *Agricola*, a biography of his father-in-law Cn. Iulius Agricola, Tacitus portrays a time in which Romans kept their political views silent out of fear of being monitored and reported by paid informers.[81] Books critical of the emperor were seized and destroyed, and their authors were murdered or exiled. His recollection of these experiences – both his own and of others – of living under Rome's eleventh *princeps* may, however, have prejudiced his presentation of Rome's second when writing his *Annals*.[82] As a literary creation, Tacitus' Tiberius is a brilliant study of a reluctant tyrant, but as an accurate portrait of the real historical figure it is deeply flawed. The result is a caricature.

That great biographer of famous men, Plutarch (L. Mestrios Ploutarchos, *c.* 46 CE–after 119 CE), composed a *Life of Tiberius* in Greek half a century or more after the emperor's death as part of a series of portraits of Rome's rulers from Augustus through to Vitellius.[83] Just two fragments from it are preserved and they both discuss Tiberius' self-imposed exile on Rhodes.[84] Around the same time, Suetonius (C. Suetonius Tranquillus, *c.* 69 CE–after 122 CE) wrote his *Life of Tiberius* (*Vita Tiberi*) in a much larger collection of portraits published as *Lives of the Caesars* (*De vita Caesarum*).[85] Fortunately, most of it survives. Organizing his findings by category (*per specie*), Suetonius groups topics relating to his subject not chronologically but thematically: the man's ancestry, his career before accession, public actions, private life, physical appearance, personality and the manner of his death.[86] His biography of Tiberius is a compilation of factoids and stories, real or rumoured, and it is not always clear which is which. Suetonius delights in reporting the man's foibles and peculiarities. He frequently presents biographical information prefaced by statements like 'it is said that', 'it is commonly believed' or 'some think'.[87] Similarly, in discussing Tiberius' alleged sexual peccadilloes, the report is prefaced with the comment, 'He acquired a reputation for still grosser depravities that one can hardly bear to tell or be told, let alone believe.'[88] Such phrasings imply that they are not facts at all; having mentioned them, he often proceeds to refute them:

> But after all I cannot be led to believe that an emperor of the utmost prudence and foresight acted without consideration, especially in a matter of so great moment. It is my opinion that, after weighing the faults and the merits of Tiberius, he [Augustus] decided that the latter preponderated, especially since he took oath before the People that he was adopting Tiberius for the good of the country, and alludes to him in several letters as a most able general and the sole defence of the Roman People.[89]

The stories he reported had been passed down; in transmission, they could have been edited, embellished or entirely invented. Similarly, there were the salacious but likely spurious tales of tour guides:

> At Capreae they still point out the scene of his executions, from which he used to order that those who had been condemned after long and exquisite tortures be cast headlong into the sea before his eyes, while a band of marines waited below for the bodies and broke their bones with boathooks and oars, to prevent any breath of life from remaining in them. Among various forms of torture he had devised this one: he would trick men into loading themselves with copious draughts of wine, and then on a sudden

> tying up their private parts, would torment them at the same time by the torture of the cords and by stopping them urinate.[90]

Suetonius published them regardless.[91]

While gossip, hearsay and rumour were as much the currency in which the Roman biographer deals as incontrovertible facts, he was capable of delivering insights into Tiberius' personality. Holding three positions under Hadrian (r. 117–138 CE) as *a studiis*, *a bibliotecis* and *ab epistulis* – keeper of the archives, controller of the Roman libraries, and supervisor of the emperor's correspondence – Suetonius had access to original documents, both state and private, of his subjects.[92] Suetonius' *Life* is the only extant source quoting text of letters written by Augustus to Tiberius, though sadly not any replies from him, though his letter to the Senate is included.[93] Additionally, he also drew upon the writings of others, notably Theodorus of Gadara (citing a quotation from him apparently revealing the cruel streak of Tiberius) and directly from Seneca's account (for one of the three scenarios of Tiberius' death).[94] He would have studied earlier histories of Tiberius' life and times, likely the same ones as Tacitus, which were hostile towards his subject.[95]

If there is a common narrative thread linking the parts of the *Vita Tiberi*, it is how Tiberius withdrew from the public into his private space, then returned and withdrew again – a migration which the biographer considers negatively.[96] The more that politics intruded into his private life, the more disconsolate and anxious Tiberius became. Even the lines of classic works that Suetonius has Tiberius quote from infer that the emperor was paranoid.[97] 'Once relieved of fear,' he writes, 'he at first played a most unassuming part, almost humbler than that of a private citizen.'[98] Yet, the overall sense from reading the Roman biographer's account is of Tiberius' failure to live up to people's high expectations in his apparent negligence of public affairs; they are worsened by allegations of increasing cruelty and depravity in the last decades of his life, all enabled by his isolation on Capreae.[99]

A century after Tacitus and Suetonius, Cassius Dio (L. Cassius Dio, *c.* 155/163 CE–*c.* 235 CE) wrote an epic *Roman History* covering from 753 BCE–211 CE in eighty volumes. Tiberius appears in Books 52–58. Dio has a very particular opinion of Tiberius – and it is not a good one.[100] After the death of Augustus, he writes, 'when they [the Roman People] found his successor Tiberius a different sort of man, they yearned for him who was gone'.[101] His character sketch is worth quoting in full:

> Tiberius was a patrician of good education, but he had a most peculiar nature. He never let what he desired appear in his conversation, and what he said he wanted he usually did not desire at all. On the contrary, his words indicated the exact opposite of his real purpose; he denied all interest in

> what he longed for and urged the claims of whatever he hated. He would exhibit anger over matters that were very far from arousing his wrath and make a show of affability where he was most vexed. He would pretend to pity those whom he severely punished and would retain a grudge against those whom he pardoned. Sometimes he would regard his bitterest foe as if he were his most intimate companion, and again he would treat his dearest friend like the veriest stranger. In short, he thought it bad policy for the sovereign to reveal his thoughts; this was often the cause, he said, of great failures, whereas by the opposite course far more and greater successes were attained. Now if he had merely followed this method quite consistently, it would have been easy for those who had once come to know him to be on their guard against him; for they would have taken everything by exact contraries, regarding his seeming indifference to anything as equivalent to his ardently desiring it, and his eagerness for anything as equivalent to his not caring for it. But, as it was, he became angry if anyone gave evidence of understanding him, and he put many to death for no other offence than that of having comprehended him. While it was a dangerous matter, then, to fail to understand him – for people often came to grief by approving what he said instead of what he wished – it was still more dangerous to understand him, since people were then suspected of discovering his practice and consequently of being displeased with it. Practically the only sort of man, therefore, that could maintain himself – and such persons were very rare – was one who neither misunderstood his nature nor exposed it to others; for under these conditions men were neither deceived by believing him nor hated for showing that they understood his motives. He certainly gave people a vast amount of trouble whether they opposed what he said or agreed with him; for inasmuch as he really wished one thing to be done but wanted to appear to desire something different, he was bound to find men opposing him from either point of view, and therefore was hostile to the one class because of his real feelings, and to the other for the sake of appearances.[102]

In summing up the life of Tiberius, Dio writes: 'Thus Tiberius, who possessed a great many virtues and a great many vices, and followed each set in turn as if the other did not exist, passed away in this fashion on the twenty-sixth day of March.'[103]

Dio was a proud member of the senatorial class, becoming consul (probably for 222 CE), and thus one of the Roman elite of the third century CE.[104] He perceived the world, and wrote its history, applying the traditional ideals and values of his class. Living 200 years after Augustus and Tiberius, he understood that the imperial monarchy they had established was the only practical means for

Rome to achieve stability in governing an empire. While Tiberius' unwillingness to undertake wars of choice aligned with Dio's own opposition to military expansion, nevertheless, his portrait of the emperor is far from flattering.[105]

Dio explicitly states at the start of the *Roman History* that his desire was to write a history of all the Romans' memorable achievements in peacetime as well as wartime so that nobody should have to search for the essential facts:

> Although I have read pretty nearly everything about them that has been written by anybody, I have not included it all in my history, but only what I have seen fit to select. I trust, moreover, that if I have used a fine style, so far as the subject matter permitted, no one will on this account question the truthfulness of the narrative, as has happened in the case of some writers; for I have endeavoured to be equally exact in both these respects, so far as possible.[106]

Parts of the extant *Roman History* are actually excerpts by Xiphilinus (Ioannis Xiphilinos), a monk of Constantinople of the eleventh century CE. Thus, some of Dio's original text is missing and what survives through the epitimator's work may be faulty.[107]

Written in Attic Greek, Dio's book is arguably modelled on the famous work of Thucydides (Thoukudides, *c.* 460–*c.*400 BCE), which gave primacy to politics, statecraft, power and war; indeed, Dio's writing shows that he relished discussing aspects of Roman administration and government.[108] Each year in his *History* begins with the names of the consuls, establishing a clear historical timeline. The reporting includes the most significant events in each year, but it is affairs in Rome that dominate Dio's narrative of the reign of Tiberius.[109] There are occasional digressions, such as the disposition of the legions.[110] He includes trivia, such as the consul of 19 CE with a trumpet-playing habit, and many of the sayings of Tiberius.[111] Consistent with ancient chronicling practice, Dio includes omens and portents as they were witnessed at the time of major crises. Dio's annalistic account of the man and events he lived through helpfully validates or fills in the gaps in the earlier Roman historians' works. Like them, he used a variety of sources and recognized that some contradicted others. In the case of delaying news of the death of Augustus to wait for Tiberius, he writes:

> This, at any rate, is the statement made by most writers, and the more trustworthy ones; but there are some who have affirmed that Tiberius was present during the emperor's illness and received some injunctions for him.[112]

Comparing the extant sources, Paterculus wrote a celebratory history, Tacitus a moralistic history, Suetonius a popular biography and Cassius Dio a chronicle. There are inherent problems with all of these ancient historians and their approaches. They each include or exclude information according to their needs. One issue is *what* sources they used, which, for the most part, are obscure to us. The authors may have based their accounts on some of the same written sources, such as the *Acta Senatus* and official correspondence.[113] Seneca the Elder may have been a source for Tacitus, Suetonius and Dio. Tacitus cites Pliny the Elder, and Dio may have referred to him too, as well as Cluvius Rufus or Aufidius Bassus.[114] Whether Suetonius read Tacitus, or Dio read Tacitus or Suetonius, is debated.[115] Anyone with personal knowledge of the events would have long since died, depriving each of these writers of the opportunity to interview witnesses, with the sole exception of Paterculus. Then there is the matter of *how* they used their sources, as the Roman authors interpreted and presented material according to their purposes.

The four Roman writers describe the debate in the Senate House on 17 September 14 CE in broadly similar terms, but with considerable variation in tone and use of detail, enabling them to make specific points for or against Tiberius.[116] The perspectives of each of these authors are crucial to our understanding of him. Paterculus' Tiberius is a hero who puts country above self. The Tiberius of Tacitus is an unwilling national leader who dissimulates and bears personal grudges. Suetonius' Tiberius is dishonest and a schemer, while that of Dio is a manipulative political operator with a knack for the quick retort who will punish his enemies. Differences in treatment can be found in other episodes too, such as the end of the mutiny of the legions on the Rhine in 14 CE and the events of 33 CE.[117] Establishing whose portrayal is closest to the real Tiberius is the fundamental challenge facing the modern biographer and historian.

This variation is also a characteristic of Christian histories. Tiberius had lived in the same period as Jesus of Nazareth (Yeshua Ben Yosef). In the four Gospels – Matthew, Mark, Luke and John, which are generally agreed to have been written between 70 and 110 CE – Tiberius is a remote, godfather-like figure. He is mentioned only once by name.[118] He was the Caesar in 'Render to Caesar the things that are Caesar's, and to God the things that are God's'.[119] He was also responsible for appointing Pontius Pilatus, who sentenced Jesus to death by crucifixion.[120] The non-canonical New Testament *Apocrypha*, an assortment of parabiblical literature, have their own histories and issues of acceptance.[121] The *Cure for the Health of Tiberius* (*Cura Sanitatis Tiberii*) in the Gospel of Nicodemus tells the tale of the second Roman emperor, facing his own death, travelling to Jerusalem in search of the miraculous healing power of the Jewish physician named Jesus.[122] The *Letter of Pilate to Tiberius* (*Epistola Pilati ad Tiberium*) and *Letter of Tiberius to Pilatus* (*Epistola Tiberii ad Pilatum*) were actually written in Medieval or Renaissance Latin and are, therefore, complete fictions.[123]

Early writers of Christian faith specifically mention Tiberius and his alleged view of the Christians. Tertullian of Carthage (Q. Septimius Florens

Tertullianus, *c.* 155–*c.* 220 CE), writing in Latin in the early third century CE, states in his *Apology* (*Apologeticum*) that Pontius Pilatus, 'who in his conscience was a Christian, sent Tiberius Caesar an account of all these proceedings relating to Christ'.[124] Tiberius responded by proposing to recognize Christ's divinity, but faced resistance:

> By virtue of this old decree, it was that Tiberius, in whose reign Christianity came into the world, having received intelligence from Syria Palaestina about the miracles of Christ, proposed it to the Senate, and used his prerogative for getting Him enrolled among the number of their gods. The Senate, indeed, refused the proposal, as having not maturely weighed His qualifications for a deity; but [Tiberius] Caesar stood to his resolution, and issued out severe penalties against all who should accuse the worshippers of Christ.[125]

The Romans had plenty of gods; adding a new one would be nothing out of the ordinary. The accusers, however, would likely be the monotheistic Jewish authorities in Iudaea, since the Romans were not actively persecuting Christians at this period.[126]

This story is repeated by bishop Eusebius (Eusebius Pamphilius, 265–339 CE). Writing in *Ecclesiastical History* (*Historia Ecclesiastica*) in Greek in the late third/early fourth century CE, he builds on Tertullian's story that Tiberius had read a report, sent to him by Pontius Pilatus 'in order that no event might escape his notice', of the resurrection of Christ, news of which was known throughout the province, and 'how he was already believed by many to be a god, in that, after his death, he had risen from the dead'.[127] In this version of events, Tiberius 'kept the opinion which he had formerly held and made no wicked plans against the teaching of Christ'.[128] Referring to Tertullian, Eusebius explains the law on deifications, adding that Tiberius, in defiance of the Senate, 'continued in his own opinion and threatened death to the accusers of the Christians'.[129]

In his *History Against the Pagans* (*Historiarum Adversum Paganos*), written in Latin in the fifth century CE, Christian historian Paulus Orosius (385–420 CE) paraphrases Eusebius, adding the detail that Seianus was a dissenting voice. Despite both the Senate and his right-hand man standing in opposition to his request, Tiberius adamantly supports the Christians:

> The Senate therefore refused to deify Christ and issued an edict that the Christians should be banished from the City. There was also the special reason that Seianus, the prefect of Tiberius, was inflexibly opposed to the recognition of this religion. Nevertheless, in an edict Tiberius threatened denouncers of Christians with death.[130]

The veracity of the story of Tiberius' *consecratio* is highly questionable.[131] Significantly, it is not reported by Tacitus, Suetonius or Cassius Dio. Indeed, it might be purely an invention of Tertullian, from whom the other Christian chroniclers inherited and embellished the story. Why did they portray Tiberius as an ally? In all of their accounts, it is the Roman Senate that refuses to consecrate Christ as a god. Furthermore, Tiberius is presented as an active enabler of the new faith. Eusebius gives three reasons for his pivotal role: firstly, it was in Tiberius' time that the name 'Christian' came into this world; secondly, for his advocacy for threatening death to the accusers of the Christians; and lastly, for assisting the spread of the Gospel across the world.[132] Whereas Tertullian wrote a polemical treatise demanding legal toleration for Christianity in the empire, Orosius rewrote Roman history itself to diminish the achievements of pagan Romans and celebrate the attainments of the followers of Jesus Christ. The Christian chroniclers each emphasize the humanity and sincerity of the emperor's opinion; they present Tiberius as a good man because he assisted the first Christians.

Orosius' contemporary, Jerome (Eusebius Sophronius Hieronymus, 342/347–420 CE), translated and augmented Eusebius' *Chronicle* of key incidents in each year of the principate of Tiberius. In his own *Chronicles* (*Chronicon*), Christ's ministry is the central event of the reign: 'Tertullian, in that book which he wrote against the Jews, affirms that Christ was born in the 41st year of Augustus' – that is, 2 BCE.[133] His life and death are set in the context of verifiable historical events.[134] He was crucified 'in the 18th year of Tiberius', 32 CE.[135] It is from Jerome's chronology that we learn that the rejection of Christ's divinity by the Roman Senate, first described by Tertullian, occurred in 36 CE – that is, four years after the crucifixion.[136]

Yet the narrative about Tiberius established by earlier historians endured. In a letter to statesman and philosopher Themistius, the Emperor Julian (Flavius Claudius Julianus, 361–363 CE), called the Apostate by Christians, wrote of 'the harsh and naturally cruel tyrant Tiberius'.[137] Julian wrote a skit for the Saturnalia holiday of 361 CE in which he described a contest between the emperors in the presence of the Olympian gods. In it, he lampooned Tiberius along with all the other Caesars:

> The third to hasten in was Tiberius, with countenance solemn and grim, and an expression at once sober and martial. But as he turned to sit down his back was seen to be covered with countless scars, burns, and sores, painful welts and bruises, while ulcers and abscesses were as though branded thereon, the result of his self-indulgent and cruel life. Whereupon Silenus cried out, 'Friend, you appear far different now, than before,' [Homer, *Od.* 16.181] and seemed more serious than he had wont.
>
> 'Pray, why so solemn, little father?' said Dionysus.
>
> 'It was this old satyr,' he replied. 'He shocked me and made me forget myself and introduce Homer's Muse.'

'Take care,' said Dionysos. 'He will pull your ear, as he is said to have done to a certain grammarian [Seleucus].'

'Plague take him,' said Silenus, 'in his little island!' (He was alluding to Capreae). 'Let him scratch the face of that wretched fisherman!'[138]

The fisherman story comes straight out of Suetonius.[139]

By the time historian Zosimus (Zosimos, 490s–510s CE) was recounting events in his *New History* (*Istoria Nea*) in Constantinpole, the capital of the Roman Empire in the East, the wicked exiled Tiberius was *de facto* truth. 'The tyranny of Tiberius,' he writes, 'was so severe as to be intolerable to his subjects, who expelled him to an island, where he secreted himself for some time and then died.'[140]

Yet Roman parents named their boys Tiberius for centuries after his death. Indeed, it was the *praenomen* of four men who became emperors of the Eastern Roman (or Byzantine) Empire.[141] Long after the fall of the Roman Empire in the West, handwritten copies of Tertullian's and Orosius' books informed readers in the Medieval Age that Tiberius was the Caesar who had lived at the time of the crucifixion of Jesus. One of these, Gerald of Wales (Gerald de Barri, *c.* 1146–*c.* 1223), while chancellor of the cathedral of Lincoln, wrote his *Instructions for a Ruler* (*De Principis Instructione*) in Latin. In it, he included Tiberius as one of the Romans worthy of study.[142] Gerald includes him in his chapter on 'The Bloody Ends of Tyrants' – along with Caligula – but omits him from 'The Praiseworthy Life and Death of Chosen Princes'.[143] Gerald wrote one of the first post-Roman era texts in the West to emphasize the negative of aspects Tiberius' life.

# Chapter 11

# Reimagining Tiberius: 1454 – Present Day

Monks copied out ancient texts in Latin by hand for hundreds of years, yet before the 1450s the works of Suetonius and Tacitus were hardly known in Western Europe outside a few monasteries.[1] In the wake of the end of the Roman Empire in the East with the capture of Constantinople by an Ottoman army on 6 April 1453, refugees fleeing to the Christian West brought with them books by Roman authors writing in Greek. They included Cassius Dio in versions made by Zonaras, private secretary to Emperor Alexis I, as well as Xiphilinus and the *Suda* (*Souda*), a tenth-century Byzantine encyclopaedia or lexicon of the Ancient World. The invention of the printing press with movable type by Johannes Gutenberg (*c.* 1398–1468) made copies of both Greek and Latin works available to a public eager to read the Classics for themselves. Tacitus' *Annals* was first printed in a Latin edition by Vindelinus de Spira in Venice about 1471–72, and the books featuring Tiberius in 1515.[2] An English translation by Richard Greenway appeared in London in 1598 – even England's Queen Elizabeth I (r. 1558–1603) attempted a translation of it.[3] Derivative works soon followed: Virgilio Malvezzi's *Discorsi sopra Cornelio Tacito* was published by Ginammi in Venice in 1535, then as *Discourses Upon Cornelius Tacitus* in London in 1642. One of the earliest editions in Latin of Suetonius' *Lives of the Caesars* was printed by Johann Prüss in Strassburg (Strasbourg) around 1520.[4] An English translation by Philêmon Holland was published in London in 1606. With each new printing, the life and times of Tiberius came to be better known by generations whose only knowledge of him up until then had been as the Caesar mentioned in the New Testament during the life of Christ or the *Chronicles* of Jerome.[5]

The availability of printed books enabled scholars to study the ancient texts for insights and wisdom that could be applied to their own day. The Italian Niccolò Machiavelli (1469–1527) mentions Tiberius only once in his *Discourses on the First Decade of Titus Livius* (*Discorsi sopra la prima deca di Tito Livio*, published posthumously in 1531), and that was as the victim of Seianus' conspiracy.[6] Curiously, Tiberius himself is not mentioned at all in his more famous *The Prince* (*Il Principe*, published in 1532), though many notable Romans are.[7] Nevertheless, Tiberius was among the names revived in Italy – as Tiberio – in the fifteenth and sixteenth centuries, when it was the fashion to adopt Roman names.

Figure 34. Tiziano Vecellio's popular paintings of the *Eleven Caesars* were favourite subjects for scaled-down etchings and engravings on paper. This image of Tiberius was produced in the 1620s in a set by Aegidius Sadeler (1570–1629).

Figure 35. An etching and engraving on paper of Tiberius by Hubert Quellinus (1619–1687) published in Antwerpen between 1646 and 1670.

Figure 36. An etching and engraving on paper of Tiberius by Andries Vaillant (1665–1693) after the painting by Tiziano Vecellio.

Figure 37. Etching and engraving on paper of a Chalcedony cameo of Tiberius by Friedrich Kibler (1747–1816), published in 1788.

The pages of monochrome text were often enlivened by illustrations printed off woodcuts or engraved copper plates. The sources for the images were works by contemporary artists. The Italian Tiziano Vercellio (Titian, 1488/90–1576) painted eleven *Cesari* ('Caesars') for Frederico Gonzaga, first Duke of Mantua, in the mid-1530s.[8] They were more fantasy-art than faithful reproductions of the emperors' likenesses. Tragically, all of the *Cesari* were destroyed when the palace in Madrid caught fire in 1734. Titian's *Tiberio* is, however, known from a copy bought by Abraham Darby IV, though it was mis-sold to him as an original.[9] Tiberius is shown standing with his left shoulder towards the viewer, his head side-on, the aquiline nose in profile, the dark brown hair tumbling down his neck. The emperor's visage is serious, the eyes gazing at some object to the left beyond the frame of the painting. It is a good study of a powerful man, but it is not a good representation of the historical Tiberius. Titian's *Cesari* were also reproduced as a series of black-and-white prints by Aegidius Sadeler II (1570–1629), an enterprising Flemish painter and engraver who, in the 1620s, spotted an opportunity to sell mass-produced, reasonably priced prints (fig. 34) to those seeking to decorate their homes with fine art, just as the nobility did their palaces.[10] Others imitated Sadeler (fig. 35) hoping for quick sales. Tiberius Caesar was copied in various poses wearing Roman panoply (fig. 36). They were reproduced and adapted for use in books about Ancient Rome and the Caesars published over the next two centuries, becoming ever-better likenesses (fig. 37) as antiquaries, who sought empirical evidence of the past, uncovered statues and coins of Tiberius from the earth.

In 1620, there was great excitement among scholars and art lovers. The French antiquary, Nicolas-Claude Fabri de Peirsec, working in the Treasury of the Sainte-Chapelle in Paris, discovered a Roman cameo of exquisite design. Known both as *Le Grand Camée de France* and the *Gemma Tiberiana*, De Peirsec determined that it showed Germanicus bidding Tiberius and Augusta farewell before leaving on a mission. To help publish the find as part of a book on carved Roman gems, De Peirsec approached celebrated Flemish painter Peter Paul Rubens (1577–1640). Himself interested in ancient artworks, Rubens agreed to undertake the project. In 1626, he delivered to the Frenchman a magnificent painting that he entitled *L'Apothéose de Germanicus* ('The Apotheosis of Germanicus'). While not an exact representation of the cameo, it was the artist's interpretation of its classical beauty, adding warmth to the cold stone and endowing the human figures with graceful naturalism and intensified expressions.[11] As in the original, Tiberius is presented as a Jovian figure, naked except for an embroidered cloak covering his waist and legs, with a laurel crown upon his head but a more natural facial expression.[12] The painting of the cameo was itself turned into etchings (fig. 38).

As artists became more familiar with the life of Tiberius, certain events in it became subjects for their canvases. Tiberius' journey to Rhodes in 6 BCE provided

Figure 38. Etching and engraving on paper of the *Gemma Tiberiana* ('L'Apothéose de Germanicus') by Cornelis Galle the Elder (1576–1650) after the painting by Peter Paul Rubens. The image is reversed (compare to plate 29).

French artist Félix-Joseph Barrias (1822–1907) with the idea for a painting while at the Académie de France in Rome. *Les Exilés de Tibère* ('The Exiles of Tiberius', plate 39) depicts a group of people aboard a small boat.[13] In the centre stands Tiberius in his *toga*, accompanied by a woman and a child, each looking back to the land they are departing. Behind them, crouching in their shadows, are two figures, one holding a box and appearing to swoon. Seated beside Tiberius is a hooded woman dressed in black, staring down at the sea. Opposite her is a young woman wearing bright clothes and clutching a baby, who looks directly at the viewer. The woman in black could be the personification of grief, the other a representation of hope. Oarsmen and a steersman propel the boat, while a guard in a chain mail shirt with a sheathed *gladius*, who is seated upon the bow, stares nonchalantly ahead.

In 1881, the Polish painter Henryk Hektor Siemiradzki (1843–1902), renowned for his monumental art, painted *Orgia na Capri* ('Orgy on Capri').[14] At the time, those sections of Suetonius' *Vita Tiberi* describing the alleged erotic escapades on Capreae were considered too outrageous to be translated and were often left in the original Latin. Siemiradzki's evocation takes place on a rocky shoreline beneath a stormy evening sky, some time after 27 CE. In the centre, female revellers dance semi-naked, led by a young man in a dark blue tunic. Dangers lurk. On the left, a sheet hangs from a tree branch, beneath which two naked individuals lie, their garlands strewn upon the ground, while a third is sprawled close by. Have they passed out from their exertions? Or does the blood from their head wounds suggest executions – perhaps by falling from the clifftop above? An old white-haired man in a long tunic follows the group and looks at the bodies from a distance: this must be Tiberius himself. The light from a burning torch carried by a staring girl illuminates the violent scene on land while, on the far right, the light of the Pharos warns ships of perils at sea.

A few years earlier, in 1864, Jean-Paul Laurens (1838–1921) painted *La Mort de Tibère* ('The Death of Tiberius', plate 40).[15] The French artist presents an intimate but disturbing scene from 37 CE, in which, Tiberius, dressed in his *toga* and covering his head as a priest, lies on the floor, partly leaning against his bed. A younger, bearded man in a red embroidered cloak leans down beside him. His left knee rests against Tiberius' abdomen, his left hand seemingly pressing against Tiberius' chest. Tiberius' right hand reaches up to him, clasping his right hand. The bearded man could be Macro, the Praetorian Cohort commander or perhaps he is the emperor's personal slave or freedman, or the physician Charicles.[16] The action is ambiguous: is the younger man helping the older, or is he ensuring that Tiberius is dying?

Writers too have explored the complexity of Tiberius Caesar's character and the essentially tragic arc of his life to create plays, screenplays and novels. One of the earliest playwrights of the Modern Age to realize the potential was Benjamin 'Ben' Jonson (1572–1637), a contemporary and rival of William Shakespeare – who curiously never wrote about Rome's second emperor.[17] *Sejanus: His Fall* was first performed by the King's Men company of actors in 1603. It tells the tale of Tiberius' trusted deputy, 'Associate of our labours, our chief helper', and the consequences of his betrayal – his denunciation before the Senate by a letter from Tiberius, ending in his execution.[18] Tiberius is almost a bit part in the play, but at his first appearance he delivers a long speech to the Senate. It is Jonson's interpretation, set to verse, of the speech of 25 CE reported by Tacitus:

For our part,
We here protest it, and are covetous
Posterity should know it. We are mortal;
And can but deeds of men: 'twere glory enough,
Could we be truly a prince. And, they shall add
Abounding grace unto our memory,
That shall report us worthy our forefathers,
Careful of your affairs, constant in dangers,
And not afraid of any private frown
For public good. These things shall be to us
Temples and statues, reared in your minds,
The fairest, and most during imagery:
For those of stone or brass, if they become
Odious in judgment of posterity,
Are more contemn'd as dying sepulchres,
Than ta'en for living monuments. We then
Make here our suit, alike to gods and men;
The one, until the period of our race,
To inspire us with a free and quiet mind,
Discerning both divine and human laws;
The other, to vouchsafe us after death,
An honourable mention, and fair praise,
To accompany our actions and our name:
The rest of greatness princes may command,
And, therefore, may neglect; only, a long,
A lasting, high, and happy memory
They should, without being satisfied, pursue:
Contempt of fame begets contempt of virtue.[19]

The action is dominated throughout by the Praetorian prefects, Sejanus (Seianus) and later Macro. Jonson's Tiberius is magisterial, but respectful, a proud patriot, but modest in manner. Speaking to the Senate, Tiberius says:

The burden is too heavy I sustain
On my unwilling shoulders; and I pray
It may be taken off, and reconferred
Upon the consuls, or some other Roman,
More able, and more worthy.[20]

Another of the memorable lines spoken by Tiberius:

For myself
I know my weakness, and so little covet,

Like some gone past, the weight that will oppress me,
As my ambition is the counter-point.[21]

There is advice for attentive rulers too:

The prince that feeds great natures, they will slay him;
Who nourisheth a lion must obey him.[22]

The public's response to the play in 1604 at The Globe Theatre on London's Southbank was, however, unfavourable, with the audience heckling and hissing at the cast in at least one performance. *Sejanus: His Fall* was not performed again until 1928. It was next staged by the Royal Shakespeare Company in 2005, to critical acclaim. One reviewer wrote, 'you should not read *Sejanus*. You need to see it. Only by seeing it can you really appreciate the shocking fact that Tiberius is not physically present in Act Five', the point in the play where Sejanus is denounced by the emperor's letter.[23] It found an audience again during the lockdown imposed in response to the Covid-19 pandemic, with a streamed performance from the Red Bull Theater on New York's Broadway.[24]

Compared to Jonson's play, the emperor has a substantially larger role in *The Tragedie of Claudius Tiberius Nero, Rome's Greatest Tyrant* (or *The Tragicall Life and Death of Claudius Tiberius Nero*) by an anonymous writer. The title makes the playwright's view of Tiberius plain to see. Published in 1607, it tells a version of events from his reign firmly based on Tacitus' account, from his accession to his murder by Caligula; the conspiracy to poison Germanicus, the fall of Seianus and the rise of Caligula are sub-plots. There is little to endear the audience to the Tiberius in this portrayal. He schemes to kill the children of his adopted son, Germanicus. He kills his own son, Drusus, and with his death extinguishes his own natural line of succession. In a deranged frenzy, he stabs a group of messengers, lays a burning crown on Seianus' head and finally causes the deaths of Agrippina, Nero and Drusus. Reflecting on Cocceius Nerva's death, the now vengeful Tiberius exclaims:

Well vertue go with him, vice stay with me,
Till I have massacred my prisoners.
And rooted out all this conspiracie.[25]

Even on his deathbed, as he suffers in pain, Tiberius still rages, threatening to 'burne even all the Temples of the Gods, That cannot help the Romaine Emperour'.[26] In the end, the 'monster tyrant' even abandons the gods of Rome.[27] Whether the play was ever performed is not known.

Across the English Channel, French dramatists of the eighteenth and nineteenth centuries were particularly drawn to Rome's second emperor as a means to comment on their own times. *Tibère* ('Tiberius') was written by Marseille-born poet and playwright Abbé Simon-Joseph Pellgrin (1663–1745).

The tragedy, composed in rhyming verse, was performed for the first time on 13 December 1726 at the Théâtre de la rue des Fossés, Saint-Germain, during the time of Louis XV (Louis *le Bien-Aimé*, 'the Beloved', r. 1715–1774). The play is set in the immediate aftermath of Augustus' death at Nola in 14 CE. Tiberius' accession hangs in the balance when Agrippa Caesar unexpectedly asserts his right to his inheritance, and thus becomes a serious rival to Tiberius. 'But I was not born for this excess honour,' Tiberius says, letting his modesty momentarily overwhelm him.[28] The rivals meet. Agrippa protests that *he* is the rightful heir to Augustus. Supporters press their cases for their respective candidates. But Agrippa is dispatched; Tiberius succeeds as *princeps* – as the revered Augustus had willed it.

The French Revolution, which began in 1789 with cries of '*liberté, égalité, fraternité*' ('liberty, equality, fraternity'), had beheaded Bourbon king Louis XVI (r. 1774–92) by guillotine; it established France as a republic inspired by the Roman model. When Napoléon Bonaparte (1769–1821) became *Premier Consul* ('First Consul') from 1799, and then *Empereur des Français* ('Emperor of the French') from 1804–1815 and again in 1815, those promises were, in the opinion of many, betrayed. French playwrights looked to Ancient Rome for stories of the corruption of autocrats. Tiberius provided the subject. *Tibère: Tragédie* by Marie-Joseph De Chénier (1764–1811) dramatized the version of key events reported in Tacitus' *Annals*. The play's criticism of the *nouveau tyran* ('new tyrant') was too overt and led to Napoléon banning the play. Five years after Napoléon's death in exile, Chénier's *Tibère* appeared in print in 1819. Poet and playwright Népomucène Lemercier (1771–1840) called it a masterpiece, 'the best [tragedy] he [Chénier] has done'.[29]

A new Bourbon king was crowned in 1814, making France a constitutional monarchy. Criticism of the conservative-leaning King Charles X (r. 1824–1830) soon grew, and discontent arose at all levels of French society about so much power again being in the hands of one individual. In these unsettled times, the tragedy *Le Dernier Jour de Tibère: tragédie en cinq actes et en vers* ('The Last Day of Tiberius: tragedy in five acts and in verse') by Lucien Émile Arnault (1787–1863) was performed for the first time at the Théatre-Français, Paris, on 2 February 1828.[30] This play takes place in the Palace of Macron (Macro) in Rome. Tiberius is suffering with pain. Chariclès, his doctor, confides in Galba that, after twelve years in exile, Tiberius is approaching death. Galba wants to see an end to the tyranny of the emperors, but Chariclès sees only his patient, a sick man. Cayus (Caius Caligula) is eager for power and seeks Macron's support, but Galba has sought his help too. Tiberius, lamenting the futility of his reign, considers who should succeed him. Senators gather and discuss the succession with Macron. Given the choice of governing the Roman state or continuing the *status quo*, the Senate opts to support Cayus. In the final act, Tiberius falters, realizing too late that he has been poisoned by Chariclès. He cries out – with effort – for the Praetorians to surround him:

> Under a perfidious plot
> I fall, but I reign; and the gods by your arms
> Are ready to punish the vilest of ungrateful people.[31]

Everyone present, pointing at Cayus, replies 'Yes!' Tiberius then hands Cayus the laurel crown from his own head, as Macron utters the words, 'The world will obey', and Cayus replies, 'Macron will be judged'.[32] Tiberius expires for the last time.

When the new French king placed restrictions on press freedoms and elections, urban mobs rioted in Paris in July 1830. Charles abdicated and hurriedly left for England. The monarch having fled, Victor Faguet staged his *Tibère à Caprée* in 1838. Tiberius' self-imposed exile and his supposed immoral life on Capreae enabled by his isolation from the people provided the material for playwrights during the ensuing Second French Republic, which was established in 1848 with the February Revolution that overthrew King Louis-Phillipe I (r. 1830–1848). Louis-Napoléon Bonaparte was elected President in 1848. Staging a *coup d'état*, Bonaparte proclaimed himself Napoléon III, *Empereur des Français* (r. 1852–1870) and initiated the Second French Empire. French playwrights again looked to Roman history for the dangers inherent in imperial autocracy. Bernard Campan's *Tibère à Caprée* was performed in 1847. Tiberius' death on Capri in these plays is factually incorrect, of course, as he died at Misenum, but situating the death scene on the island for dramatic effect quickly became *de facto* for later playwrights.

During the Third Republic (1870–1940), political disruptions and the surrender of France to Prussia led to new constitutional laws in 1875. Crises and scandals plagued the *République*. Once more, Ancient Rome offered warnings from the past. The action in *Tibère: Drame en cinq actes (huit tableaux)* by Ferdinand Dugué (1881) takes place on Capri and in Rome, and even features lions, gladiators and a follower of a new religion. The theatre critic Jules Lemaître writes:

> This drama is fun; it is, in some respects, remarkable. … There is a Christian (already!): Blandine, daughter of Nerva. Nerva having conspired, Tiberius seizes Blandine, and first wants to dishonour her by delivering her to a slave. She gets out of this mess. Tiberius, then, condemns her to the lions because she has blasphemed the gods of the empire. And, in the fourth act, she avenges herself on the tyrant by saving his life.[33]

In the drama, Caligula is a central character, a young man eager for power, who hatches a plot. Each day he has to prove his loyalty to the suspicious emperor, who has laid traps for him.[34] In the dramatic climax of the play, a Gallic slave, priests and druids attempt to assassinate Tiberius. He survives it, vowing to slaughter all Gauls in Rome, only to die in the final scene by some dark magic, having named Caligula his successor.[35] 'A very beautiful drama', wrote the critic, describing the character of Tiberius as 'clearly and vigorously drawn' and 'lively'.[36]

*Tibère à Caprée*, a passionate work written in French by the Polish Count Stanislas Rzéwuski, also portrayed Tiberius as a corrupt despot in the Tacitean manner.[37] One reviewer wrote,

> Mr. Rzéwuski has made of him [Tiberius] a hypochondriac nihilist that a hideous experience and the perfect contempt for humanity, joined to the vertigo of omnipotence, and also to a dreadful satiety which excludes neither the fear of death nor the terror of losing what he is nevertheless satisfied with, have made him partly monstrous.[38]

Performed at the Théâtre de la Porte-Saint-Martin, Paris, on 4 May 1894, Tibère (played by Paul Félix Joseph Tailliade) discovers the treachery of Séjan (Seianus, Philippe Garnier) and his involvement in killing his son. In a grandiose scene, Séjan is denounced by letter in the Senate House. Tiberius has him executed; but the prefect's death is not enough for the betrayed emperor, who seeks vengeance: he wants to torture Séjan's soul too. Mortified by events, Tiberius lives on, bored but in agonizing pain. Seeking a cure, they find a Christian in the hope that she can administer one of Jesus' legendary miracles. Caligula cohabits with his uncle but lives impatiently, waiting for his turn to rule. The healer calms the emperor and, while he sleeps, Caligula stabs the visitor and then smothers Tiberius. The old man resists, crying out for help, and momentarily thinks to disinherit the assassin:

> but soon he changes his mind, because his hatred of the human race is stronger than the concern for his personal revenge, and he expires monstrously happy to bequeath to the Romans a master capable of making them miss Tiberius.[39]

The play was critically received. 'This drama, full of obscurity, length and interest, … is honourably performed by M. M. Taillade, [his] Tiberius tainted with romanticism,' wrote one reviewer.[40] 'There is, in this *Tibère à Caprée*, a very beautiful drama,' wrote another, 'but too many things surrounding it', urging that it should be edited for length and content.[41] Referring to the earlier plays about Tiberius, he asks:

> As for Mr. Rzéwuski's meetings with Ben Johnson, Arnault, Victor Séjour, Marie-Joseph Chénier and M. Ferdinand Dugué, were they not inevitable? And is it really worth talking about?[42]

1. Portrait bust of an older woman identified as Tiberius' mother, Livia Drusilla, given the honorific title Augusta after September 14 CE.

2. Portrait bust of Imp. Caesar *Divi Filius* Augustus as *pontifex maximus* with his head covered while conducting a sacrificial ritual.

3. Portrait bust of a togate and velate young man, possibly Tiberius or Nero Claudius Drusus.

4. Portrait bust of Tiberius as a young man.

5. Portrait bust of Tiberius in middle age.

6a. View of the left side of the portrait bust of Tiberius in middle age.

6b. View of the right side of the portrait bust of Tiberius in middle age.

7. Rear view of the portrait bust of Tiberius in middle age.

8. Portrait bust of Tiberius in middle age; the nose is a modern repair.

9. Bronze statue of Tiberius as *pontifex maximus* with his head covered while conducting a sacrificial ritual.

10. Portrait bust of Nero Claudius Drusus, brother of Tiberius.

11. Portrait bust of Drusus Iulius Caesar, son of Tiberius, as a young man.

12. Portrait bust of Germanicus Iulius Caesar, nephew of Tiberius, as a young man.

13. Portrait bust of Caius Caligula, great nephew and heir of Tiberius, as a young man.

14. View of the hill fort of Monte Bernorio, which was besieged during the Cantabrian and Asturian War, 29–19 BCE.

15. An island in the Euphrates River at Dura Europos, which may have been the location where the peace treaty was negotiated with the Parthians by Tiberius in 20 BCE or Caius in 1 CE.

16. View of Bodensee (Lake Constance) looking towards Bregenz, Austria (ancient Brigantium), with the Allgäu Alps in the distance.

17. View of Moravia near Rýmařov, Czech Republic (ancient Bohaemium), the homeland of the Marcomanni.

18. View from Kuk Fortress, Solin, Croatia (ancient *Colonia* Martia Iulia Salonnae in Illyricum).

19. View of terrain around Šišák, Croatia (ancient Siscia in Illyricum).

20. View of a section of the reconstructed Roman fort at LWL-Römermuseum Haltern am See, Germany.

21. Two soldiers (presumed to be Tiberius and Nero Drusus) offering branches in celebration of victory in the Alps on a *denarius* of Augustus.

22. The great altar to Roma et Augustus at Condate-*Colonia* Munatia (modern Lyon) on the reverse of a *dupondius* of Tiberius.

23. The frontage of the Temple of Concordia on a *sestertius* of Tiberius, who paid for its reconstruction.

24. *Divus* Augustus on the reverse of an *aureus* of Tiberius.

25. Tiberius in his chariot during the triumph of 12 CE on the reverse of an *aureus* of Augustus.

26. *Pax* or Augusta seated on the reverse of an *aureus* of Tiberius.

27. The twins Tiberius Gemellus and Germanicus Gemellus on the reverse of a *sestertius* of Tiberius.

28. The *Gemma Augustea* is interpreted to show enthroned Augustus receiving Tiberius, who is descending from a triumphal chariot as Germanicus watches.

29. *Le Grand Camée de France* is interpreted to show enthroned Tiberius receiving Germanicus returned victorious from war as a young Caius Caligula watches.

30. Side profile of Tiberius on a cameo carved from chalcedony.

31. Side profile of Tiberius in military panoply on a cameo carved from chalcedony.

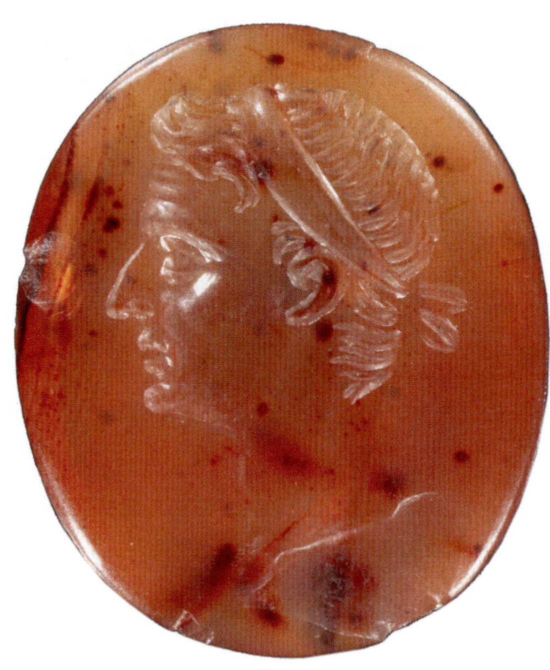

32. Side profile of Tiberius on an engraved gem, likely from a finger ring.

33. Monument erected to honour Tiberius, with winged goddess Victoria holding a laurel crown over his head and a laurel branch in her other hand.

34. View of Tiberius' villa at Sperlonga (*Spelunca*), Campania, overlooking the Bay of Naples.

35. View of the *Villa Iovis* towards the central block of the palatial building containing cisterns for fresh water.

36. View of the *aula* of the *Villa Iovis* looking towards the north coast of Capreae.

37. View of Capo Miseno, base of the *Classis Misenensis* and the location of the Villa of L. Licinius Lucullus where Tiberius died.

38. Imaginative reconstruction of the *Villa Iovis* on Capreae by architect and illustrator Jean-Claude Golvin.

39. *Les Exilés de Tibère* ('The Exiles of Tiberius') by Félix Joseph Barrias (1850).

40. *La Mort de Tibère* ('The Death of Tiberius') by Jean-Paul Laurens (1864).

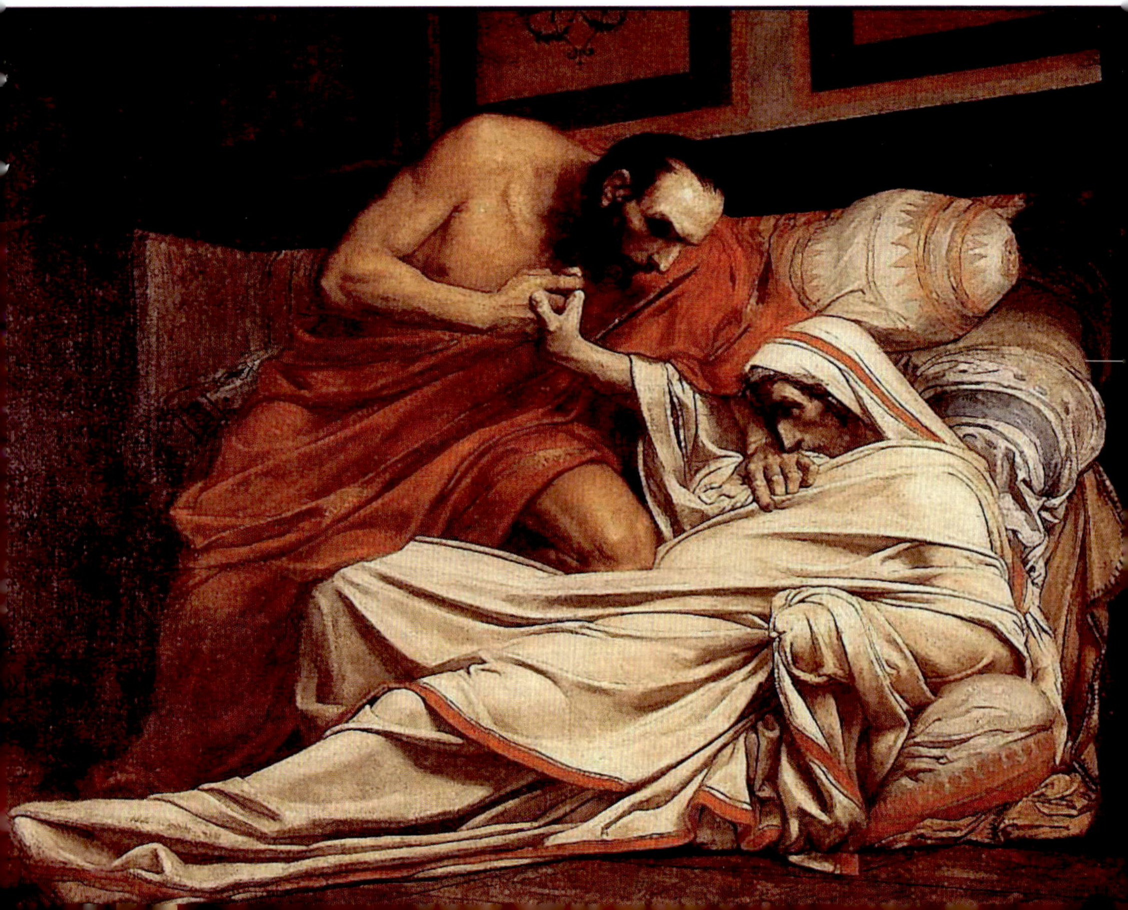

For four centuries, British and French audiences had been shown versions of Tiberius as a tyrant and a monster, inspired by Tacitus. An English poet living in Australia, Francis Williams Lauderdale Adams (1862–1893), crafted an unapologetically sympathetic portrayal of Rome's second emperor in *Tiberius: A Drama* (1894). In the Introduction to the published text of the play, critic and writer William M. Rosetti (1829–1919) explains:

> But it is not on the man and emperor Tiberius that Adams, who might herein have followed the lead of Tacitus and many other historians, fastens these anti-social offences; he fastens them, on the contrary, on the Roman aristocracy, and regards Tiberius as the destined and conscious avenger of the misdeeds. Tiberius, according to his dramatist, accepts power and administers government with the express purpose of rooting out the tyrant aristocrats in the interest of the suffering populations, and is so far a public benefactor, though a ruthless sovereign. He labours to effect from above an upheaval of social forces, such as the 'Army of the Night' are now, as by a clarion-cry, incited to battle for from below. That the general drift of recent historical investigation has been to take a much less dark and indignant view of the character of Tiberius than of old is a fact sufficiently well known.[43]

Adams, a radical socialist, saw Tiberius as a man of the people. His Tiberius is noble, thoughtful and principled, speaking these words upon becoming emperor:

> Sejanus,
> There stands between the peace and power of the world
> A gang of old assassin-thieves, these ruthless,
> Greedy, lustful Roman aristocrats!
> Augustus held them down; his moderation
> Seemed more than mercy to their guilty dread.
> Now they take heart again. The stake is huge.
> I see their eyes aglitter, and, when his hand
> Is raised, they make their last most tigerish leap
> To thrust the Emperor from his armoured watch
> And seize the world again, their helpless prey
> For robbery and crime. They shall never do it!
> Sejanus, there is but one word for them.
> That word's extermination! Man by man
> Calmly and coldly we will cull them out
> As we would weeds – unwearied trap and slay them
> As we would vermin! They are the world's curse.[44]

'"Spoiled by power" seems to be the ruling idea in the drama of Tiberius,' noted Rosetti.[45] Sadly, it seems that it was never performed.[46] Covering the years 11 BCE (when Tiberius was 31) through to 37 CE (when he was 77), and with a cast of twenty-seven characters plus 'priests, priestesses, soldiers, slaves, people', the play was considered difficult to stage. Just 250 copies of the play were printed in London, and then only after the playwright's suicide.

The nineteenth and twentieth centuries saw interest grow in historical fiction. One of the earliest to feature Tiberius as a central character was *Villa Jovis: Tibère à Caprée* by Bogdan Bosławita (the pseudonym of Josef-Ignacy Kraszewski, 1812–1887). Published in Paris in 1902, it was a translation in French of the original Polish edition of 1881 and was, perhaps, an extract from *Caprea i Roma: Obrazy z pierwszego wieku t. I–II* ('Caprea and Roma: Images of the First Century Vol. I–II', 1859). The story had appeared in serialized episodes in *Gazeta Warszawska* in 1859 and was published in book form the following year. Kraszewski was forced to leave Warsaw in 1863 by Count Aleksander Wielopolski (1803–1877), the head of the civil government within the Russian Empire, whom he had offended in an editorial.

Famous for his autobiography *Good-bye to All That* (1929), British poet and writer Robert Graves (1895–1985) forever changed novels in English set in Ancient Rome, elevating the genre to high literary art. The reader is introduced to Tiberius in *I, Claudius* (1934) as the writer's uncle, who was one of the bad members of the Claudian clan.[47] Subtitled 'From the Autobiography of Tiberius Claudius. Emperor of the Romans. Born B.C. X. Murdered and deified A.D. LIV', Graves created a delicious pastiche concocted from the writings of Suetonius and Tacitus, blended with dollops of his own imagination. The Tiberius of the novel is described by its imperial author as gloomy, aloof, harsh and not-at-all well-liked.[48] Livia is the villain of Graves' story: by her hand, her eldest son's rivals are steadily eliminated until Tiberius alone is left to inherit the powers Augustus had spent a lifetime accumulating – even poisoning her husband to ensure the handover is secured. As emperor, Tiberius becomes the monster depicted in *The Annals*. He suspects Germanicus of disloyalty. With his mysterious death, Agrippina and her children are bullied and tormented with the willing help of Sejanus. Groomed by Tiberius on Capri, and eager for power, the last of Germanicus' sons discovers his own talent for cruelty and debauchery. The novel ends with the accession of Caius Caligula and the terrors Claudius endures under his nephew's fickle will. The book proved so popular that Graves rushed out a sequel, *Claudius the God*, in 1935. With the introduction of lower-cost paperback editions of books, sales of historical novels took off. Graves' novels benefited from this technological change after he signed an agreement with Penguin Books, a pioneering publisher of books in the format, which released both volumes in 1941.[49] Through this work of literary fiction, Tiberius was lifted out of the dusty tomes of academe and brought to the attention of an entirely new generation of casual readers seeking to be entertained.

The real Tiberius wrote a personal memoir, which is now entirely lost.[50] What if, by some extraordinary good luck, it had survived and been found – what would it reveal of the man? This was the conceit which Scottish journalist and novelist Allan Massie explored in *Tiberius: The Memoirs of the Emperor* (1990). It followed the success of his *Augustus: A Novel* (1986).[51] In *Tiberius*, the emperor looks back on his own life, candidly examining episodes in his childhood, youth and adulthood. He recognizes that his introvert personality, social awkwardness and impatience with superficiality have limited the number of intimate relationships he has enjoyed. He reflects on how he wrestled with the demands of his ambitious, overbearing mother and his politically motivated stepfather. Massie's Tiberius is bisexual, enjoying intimacy with both young men and women. His illicit sexual flings with Augustus' daughter, Iulia, his marriage to Vipsania, his anguish at divorcing her and having to marry Iulia, his military career where he finds happiness among soldiers, his retirement to Rhodes, his travails as *princeps* and the wrenching betrayal by Seianus are all described from the first-person perspective. The Tiberius who emerges from the pages of Massie's novel is one with whom the reader empathizes and even comes to like. Yet it is the autobiographical story of a man living an achingly lonely life, which one reviewer described as 'an examination of the appalling solitude of power'.[52] The success of the two novels convinced Massie to write a series of reconstructed autobiographies or biographies of Roman leaders.[53] *Tiberius* is, arguably, the best of them.

Tiberius attracted the attention of a dissident in Poland whose medium for criticism of his nation's regime was historical fiction. Living under the strict hegemony of the Polish Communist Party, Jacek Bocheński (b. 1926) had already written two books of a planned trilogy set in Ancient Rome. Considered an anti-government writer, his tales of Julius Caesar and the poet Ovid were scrutinized by apparatchiks before publication. He started work on the third book, *Tyberiusz Cezar* (*Tiberius Caesar*), in 1970; however, struggling with how to tell his tale, he put the project aside until 2005 – well after Poland had established its democracy – and finished it four years later. The narrator-cum-protagonist of this 'essayistic novel' is Tiberius, a tourist on a journey in time, guided through places associated with Rome's second emperor. The English translator of the book summarizes Bocheński's Tiberius as 'A moral, intellectual, emotional zero whose only skill in life was to grab power and hang onto it. At any cost. There is nothing inside.'[54] He writes that compared to the Polish author's other works, the book is 'terrifying'. It is an overly bleak assessment. Rather, Bocheński's *princeps* is worthy of the reader's sympathy, not disdain like the monster of Tacitus or Suetonius – extracts of whose texts he cites as something to be critiqued. Tiberius is presented as having been born into the most powerful Roman family and destined to rule, but against his own free will, and who is ensnared by imperial politics. He escapes from the grubby business of the city to his island palaces to cling on to what little privacy he has, yet – as a consequence – is doomed to be a loner.

The age of mass media of the late twentieth century, when families sat together at home in the evening in front of the television, drove the need for new audio-visual content. The story of Tiberius and his time – or fictionalized versions of it – was told in made-for-television plays. The first of its type, *The Caesars*, appeared on British screens in 1968 in a drama series written and produced by Granada TV's Head of Drama, Philip Mackie (1918–1985). A studio-based production, it was directed by Derek Bennett (b. 1930) and shot in black and white. André Morell (1909–1978) sympathetically played Tiberius as a sober, intelligent, yet ultimately tragic figure. The series of six, 55-minute episodes focused on politics and power, and how power perverts politics.[55] Advertisements for the series inserted in the *Financial Times, The Times*, and *Sunday Telegraph* featured the following headline in a large font in white letters against a black background: 'SOME COUNTRIES WILL PAY ANY PRICE FOR INTERNAL SECURITY'. The body copy explained:

> The Romans knew all about terror as an instrument of government; they had generations of practice. This is the world of the Caesars, when government was a court, the laws made by fratricide and assassination. In the name of the common good, of course.[56]

The series had particular resonance for audiences at the time: these were the days of the Cold War (1947–1991) and the Vietnam War (1955–1975). Tiberius, not Augustus, is the central figure of this series. One reviewer wrote:

> Tiberius dominates four and [one-third] of the six episodes of *The Caesars*. That's almost but perhaps not quite enough to have the whole series named after Tiberius. Mackie could have called it *Tiberius and Friends*. Or, more accurately, *Tiberius and No Friends*.[57]

Morell's Tiberius carries the burdens of empire reluctantly, avoiding violence and war whenever possible and mulling over the succession to ensure the stability of the Roman Commonwealth. He does not enjoy ruling. In a scene with his friend M. Cocceius Nerva (played by Donald Eccles), they discuss what it is to be a 'good ruler':

> Tiberius: 'The management of men, which we call politics, is a contemptable business.'
>
> Nerva: 'Ruling is politics, politics are dirty. Every good ruler yet has been in muck up to his elbows and enjoyed it.'
>
> Tiberius: 'You're right, I'm not a good ruler.'[58]

The series enjoyed good reviews at the time and was reissued as a DVD set in 2006.

Tiberius came to life again on television in 1976, this time in colour, when Jack Pulman (1925–1979) wrote the script for an adaptation of Robert Graves' Claudius novels. Where *The Caesars* was a serious historical drama about the politics of autocratic rule, *I, Claudius* was a popular drama about one of history's most dysfunctional ruling families.[59] Herbert Wise (1924–2015) directed twelve, 55-minute episodes for BBC TV. The series borrowed much from the TV soap opera format. Unlike the big-budget Hollywood epics, with their grand outdoor sets and thrilling battle scenes or chariot races, the action in *I, Claudius* centred around Augustus' extended family, all taking place in studio. George Baker (1931–2011) starred as Tiberius and appeared in eight of the episodes. Then aged 45, the role required Baker to play Tiberius from age 18 to 77. His interpretation showed his character as a military man never quite able to get over the loss of his first wife and younger brother, becoming increasingly frustrated by politics and, above all, by his mother. Baker's Tiberius variously sulks and rages. One reviewer wrote that formerly a tough-but-fair Roman field general, 'Tiberius has been reduced to a resentful urban errand boy for Augustus, confined to a royal court he detests, and helpless against his mother's murderous plans for his advancement within it.'[60] Suspecting Nero Drusus as harbouring Republican sympathies, she favours his brother to succeed Augustus. In a memorable scene, Augustus (Brian Blessed) and Livia (Sîan Phillips) meet with a petulant Tiberius as he departs Rome for Germania. Augustus offers his good wishes and some last peremptory instructions before leaving. Tiberius is exasperated by the exchange and gets in a strop with his mother. Livia reminds him of the chicken that prophesied his destiny for greatness. Tiberius is dismissive of her claim and prepares to depart:

> Livia: 'Do well on the Rhine. Your brother is covering himself with glory in Illyricum. We mustn't fall behind.'
>
> Tiberius: 'Well, have I ever?'
>
> Tiberius: 'No. When it comes to the less imaginative arts, you are certainly to be relied upon.'[61]

Aired in the USA on PBS, according to the broadcaster's webstore 'this Emmy®-winning BBC series is one of the most popular and acclaimed dramas in Masterpiece Theatre history'. The series was reissued as a DVD set in 2002. When the entire series was aired again on BBC TV in the summer of 2023, one newspaper declared that it 'should by rights be the broadcast sensation of the year', calling *I, Claudius* 'the BBC's greatest-ever drama'.[63]

A new adaptation of Graves' *I, Claudius* was written for BBC Radio 4 by Robin Brooks (b. 1961) and broadcast in 2010. Tiberius was the subject of the second episode in a series of six 60-minute episodes, with Tim McInnerny – perhaps best known as Lord Percy and Captain Darling in the *Black Adder* (1983–89) comedy series – in the lead role. Directed by Jonquil Panting (b. 1966), it was released as a BBC Audiobook the following year and won the 2012 Audie Award in the 'Audio Dramatization' category.

In the made-for-TV film *Imperium: Augustus* (or *Augustus: The First Emperor*, 2003), directed by Roger E. Young (b. 1942) and featuring Peter O'Toole (1932–2013) in the lead role, Tiberius was played by Michele Bevilacqua. Like many a 'sword and sandals' movie before it, and despite an impressive cast, *Augustus* was a low budget production with serious shortcomings. It took the form of flashbacks, which simplified historical events to fit them into two hours and fifty-eight minutes.

A curious Biblical tale was the subject of a theatrical piece by John Wolfson, first performed as a radio play on BBC Radio 4 and then staged at the Sam Wanamaker Playhouse in London in 2016. Wolfson took the *Cura Sanitatis Tiberii* and developed it into a stage play. In *The Inn at Lydda: A Meeting of Caesar and Christ*, a frightened and frightening Tiberius (played by Stephen Boxer) is disappointed to discover – during a brief stop in the city of Lydda (Lod) – that Jesus was crucified three days prior on the orders of Pontius Pilatus. Tiberius has Pilatus executed, but is drawn into the centre of an incredible, life-altering encounter. The emperor's eyes are opened to better understanding life, power and madness. In the finale, he gazes upon the face of Jesus (Samuel Collings) – the point being that, if someone was condemned to death but should happen to see their face, it was ancient custom that he would be spared from his condemnation. This fantasy piece, directed by Andy Jordan, received mixed reviews from critics at the time; the *Financial Times* described it as 'An audacious, fitfully successful staging of a New Testament story', *The Guardian* called it 'deeply flawed' and the *Church Times* declared, 'what a muddle! It is wildly uneven in tone.'[64]

TV critics found much to gripe about in *Barbaren* (2020, 2022 and 2023), created and written by Andreas Heckmann for Netflix. While the producers invested in remarkably accurate replicas of Roman arms and armour, they resorted to the old nineteenth-century tropes of 'dirty, smelly', fur-wearing barbarians living in dark forests.[65] The Romans speak Latin with modern Italian accents, while the Germans speak *Hochdeutsch*, thus achieving two anachronisms in one conceit. Tiberius (Giovanni Carta) appears in Season 2. The grey-haired commander is an affable diplomat, who can converse with ease in German with Roman ally Marbod[uus] (Murathan Muslu), reminding him that, 'As Caesar [Augustus] says, there are neither allies nor enemies, only common interests.'[66] Yet he becomes impatient at the slow progress of Germanicus' (Alessandro Fella) punitive operations in Germania to capture or kill Arminius (Laurence Rupp). The storyline tells of treachery and shifting alliances. While the battle scenes are convincing, Tiberius is shown personally involved in the war in ways that are not in recorded history; he tests the loyalty of Marbod and executes Thusnelda's parents in front of her, even seizing her child.[67]

Initially, there was also a critical reception for *Domina*, a multi-episode historical drama created and written by Simon Burke for MGM+ (formerly Epix) and Sky Studios (2021 and 2023). Livia Drusilla (Nadia Parkes, then Kasia Smutniak) is the hero of the series, a woman able to hold her own among Rome's strong men. In a depressingly dark city, and an even darker family home, young Tiberius (Earl Cave, then Benjamin Isaac) seems troubled. Raised on-the-run in wartime, as a teenager he is rather serious for his age; he is bullied by cousin Marcellus and his friends, worried about his lost pet terrapin (deliberately killed by his cousin), then patiently plans his revenge. He is always close to, and protective of, his playful but less intellectually gifted brother, Drusus (Ewan Horrocks). Tiberius observes the power-hungry Julio-Claudian family at work and play, learning about politics and war from Caius (Octavian/Augustus, played by Matthew McNulty), Agrippa (Ben Batt) and Maecenas (Youssef Kerkour). Tiberius is secretly fixated on his mother. Yet Livia's plan to re-establish the Republic involves Drusus as leader. She prefers him over Tiberius, of whom she says, 'he has no ambition, and nobody likes him; he's the last person who will ever succeed Caius'.[68] Her eldest son's talents for schemes and stratagems gradually become evident, and even Caius notices them. Later in the same episode, her attendant Antigone tells her: 'Tiberius is as smart as you.' Livia replies: 'I know.' 'Then show it,' says Antigone. When, in a subsequent episode in the family tomb, where Livia's family are gathered, she reveals her plan of restoring the *Res Publica* and demands that Tiberius supports Drusus, but he adamantly refuses – as it puts his brother at grave risk and because he is a 'fool'.[69] Livia denounces him. Stunned and heartbroken, Tiberius runs away. Drusus tracks him down to a brothel, only to find he has strangled the prostitute, having projected onto her his own mother. The dark secret of Tiberius' personality is revealed. Later, his senses having returned, he vows to his mother to help Drusus. Tiberius was thereafter established as a pivotal character in the dramatic tale.[70] The planned third season of *Domina* was cancelled.

Trying to make sense of the 'evidence' that exists for the life and times of Tiberius has been a long line of modern historians. Several biographies of him and general histories of Rome appeared during the eighteenth, nineteenth and early twentieth centuries, often illustrated with engraved plates and line drawings (fig. 39).[71] A new treatment of Tiberius appears in English roughly every twenty years. There are texts in other languages too – in Dutch, French, German, Italian and Spanish. Each biographer has produced a fine profile of the Claudian who became a Caesar. Yet, as Dame Mary Beard acknowledged in her Sather Lecture of 2021, modern historians tend to 'take ancient historians, sieve out bits we don't

Figure 39. The discovery and early excavation of the *Villa Iovis* prompted artists to recreate its original appearance. This imaginative reconstruction by Carl Weichardt illustrates the lavish book *Das Schloss des Tiberius und andere Roemerbauten auf Capri*, published in 1900 (compare to plate 38).

like and join the dots to make a picture we *do* like'.[72] A book's title or subtitle sometimes reveals the biographer's angle – or the commissioning editor's variant, with potential readers in mind. Tiberius is variously presented as: 'Emperor of Rome' (George P. Baker, 1929), 'le Second César' (Catherine Salle, 1985), and 'De opvolger' (Willemijn van Dijk, 2017); or 'the Politician' (Barbara Levick, 1976), 'El republicano en el trono de los Césares' (José María Arbizu, 2018), 'La Forza Irresistible Del Dispotismo' (Lidia Storoni Mazzolani, 2006), 'the Tyrant' (John Charles Tarver, 1902); but also as 'I'l *princeps* inquieto' (Marco Busetta, 2017), 'L'imperatore che non amava Roma' (Antonio Spinosa, 1993), 'Kaiser ohne Volk' (Holger Sonnabend, 2021), 'L'empereur mal-aimé' (Christophe Burgeon, 2022), 'Principe indesiderato, imperatore per forza' (Antonio Fumagalli, 2021), 'The Resentful Caesar' (Gregorio Marañon, 1956), 'Der traurige Kaiser' (Zvi Yavetz, 1999) and even as 'Grausamer Kaiser – tragischer Mensch' (Ute Schall, 2018). One subtitle epitomizes 2,000 years of vituperation in the author's choice of 'sadist, murderer and tyrant' (Ernst Mason, 1960), the cover of which was illustrated by a suitably suggestive artwork (fig. 40) in a later reprint. This writer chose 'From Masterly Commander to Masterful Emperor of Rome'.[73] Subtitled 'Roman Grand Strategy under Tiberius', 'Iron *Imperator*' (Iskander Rehman, 2024) even attempts to apply insights gleaned from a study of his key conflicts to contemporary security challenges and modern-era global defence policy.

Figure 40. The cover art produced by illustrator Michael Leonard for the 1969 reprint of Ernest Mason's *Tiberius* reflects the widely held stereotype of the sex life of Rome's second emperor.

The Tiberius many think they know today is the composite of interpretations and reinterpretations, as well as representations and misrepresentations. The resulting largely negative press, which began to appear in Roman accounts just decades after his death, has come to dominate the narrative. It has been said, 'When the legend becomes fact, print the legend.'[74] Yet it has not completely expunged all vestige of positive reputation earned by Rome's second *princeps*. In 1985, the city of Bregenz, the capital of the state of Vorarlberg in Austria, celebrated the second millennium of its Roman connection. In 15 BCE, it was a military camp during the war in Raetia prosecuted by Tiberius and Nero Drusus, which became the town of Brigantium. Commemorative bronze and silver medallions were struck to mark the occasion. One in bronze showed the profile of Augustus surrounded by the legend '*2000 Jahre Bregenz*' on the obverse, with finely engraved portraits of the Claudian brothers on the reverse (fig. 41). The second issue in bronze showed the profile of Tiberius alone within the legend '*Tiberius Claudius Nero Brigantium 15 v. Chr*' on the obverse, and the coat of arms of the city on the reverse. The portrait depicts Tiberius wearing a *corona civica* with his head tilted and his eyes gazing down. It is a twentieth-century tribute from the proud community on the south-eastern shore of Lake Constance to its soldier-founder in the first century. He was known to his contemporaries for his *virtus*, *clementia* and *moderatio* – and two millennia later, he still deserves respect for them.

Figure 41. For its *2000 Jahre* celebrations in 1985, the Austrian town of Bregenz struck this medallion. It features naturalistic portraits of Augustus, Tiberius and his brother, Nero Drusus.

# Chapter 12
# Assessment

Ti. Caesar *Divi* Augusti *filius Divi* Iuli *nepos* Augustus (né Ti. Claudius Nero) presents us with a conundrum.[1] His legend in death has obscured his truth in life – they have become one and the same. Separating the two is crucial to any attempt at telling his story. A fair and balanced assessment of his life and achievements hinges on a critical examination and understanding of the source material, combined with insights from archaeology, architecture, epigraphy, iconography, numismatics and statuary in their historical context. The real Tiberius who emerges from it is far more interesting than the parody of later historians.

## Tiberius' Character and Personality

The Tiberius described in the ancient sources is not an appealing figure. Raised in a time of civil strife, as a young man he had an intense, brooding manner, yet grew up to be a brave warrior and a bold and fearless Roman patriot; but he was unlucky in love and, for reasons not well understood, suddenly withdrew to a life in exile on Rhodes before returning to become the loyal right-hand man and surprise successor of Augustus. As Imperial Rome's second *princeps*, he was a monstrous, mean and cruel tyrant who foolishly relied on an ambitious and scheming deputy, a hypocrite and dissembler intent upon settling old scores; he again lived in exile, this time on Capreae, where he indulged in sexual depravity and used astrology to predict the future. This is the composite caricature presented in the contradictory profile of Suetonius, the ambivalent report of Tacitus and disdainful chronicle of Cassius Dio, all of whom wrote decades after their subject died. They may have drawn upon a now-lost work of an earlier biographer or historian of unknown identity who was definitively anti-Tiberian.[2] The pro-Tiberian account of his contemporary Velleius Paterculus and the positive remarks of others, including the Christian historians, have been largely disregarded as sycophantic or fallacious.

Suetonius' biography preserves several details about Tiberius' appearance in his 20s or 30s. He depicts a healthy individual with an athletic build living an active lifestyle. His mannerisms, with his stern look, forward lean and fast gait, were considered so odd that Augustus felt he had to apologize for his stepson to others. This image suits the purpose of Suetonius in writing a salacious account of an arrogant and socially awkward man. Velleius Paterculus, who knew Tiberius in his 40s, comments on his handsome features and seemingly limitless energy. His depiction is flattering. Tacitus, however, portrays Tiberius in his late 60s. His profile depicts an individual with a slender, old man's body with rounded shoulders. He is bald, his skin blotched and face covered with plasters to hide ulcers.[3] Tacitus' portrayal is as much an evocation of Tiberius' supposed morally corrupt inner life as a description of his decaying outer appearance. In contrast, the public image of Tiberius replicated on coins (Appendix 2(a)) and statue busts (fig. 42) hardly changes from decade to decade, with only slight variations to the hairstyle.[4] They show him (plates 5, 8 and 9) with a full head of hair, a blemish-free complexion and a prominent nose, creating the impression of an eternally youthful ruler in the tradition of *Divus* Augustus.

Figure 42. The fine portrait bust of Tiberius found at Gabii in 1792 is featured in Alfred von Domaszewski's *Geschichte der Romischen Kaiser*. The sculpture is now in the collections of the Musée du Louvre (Ma 1239).

Some ancient writers assumed that a man's character was fixed at birth, though others accepted that a man could change during his lifetime.[5] In his obituary, Tacitus described the life of Tiberius in five stages, in which vice and cruelty were always deeply ingrained in his character, but he hid them hypocritically behind a veneer of virtue.[6] Only after Germanicus, Drusus and finally his mother died did he reveal his true nature, though his fear of Seianus sublimated his alleged sexual yearnings and fostered his cruelty until his deputy was executed. Tacitus' depiction of Tiberius' life of decline aligns with his narrative of Imperial Rome's supposed waning greatness. Suetonius is more matter of fact in providing a catalogue of examples illustrating his subject's temperament and temptations, predilections and prejudices.

Where other writers saw a man who fell to Earth, Velleius Paterculus witnessed a rising star. Among Tiberius' accepted virtues was his talent for military command. His soldiers respected his aptitude for leadership and responded with obedience. They considered his enforcement of discipline as firm but fair. Paterculus remarks on his personal charisma and ability to remain calm under pressure. Tiberius took his responsibilities for the welfare of his fellow citizens very seriously. He was concerned to mitigate the harm his men would encounter through detailed planning and by making thorough preparations. Only then would he commit them to danger. On the battlefield, he even made his own medic available to aid wounded troops in their recovery. The soldiers who served with him made jokes about his drinking and put him in his place, but they lifted him up when times got tough – acclaiming him many times – and cheered him even as veterans.[7]

Reducing risk extended to a deep need to know, and to control, the future.[8] He learned Chaldaean mathematics from Thrasyllus in order to divine events both in his own life and in the lives of others. It was not such an odd skillset to master for the times. Astrologers were widely consulted across all classes of Roman society, including by Augustus as well as many followers of Stoic philosophy, of which Tiberius may have been one.[9] Lives could be changed by horoscopes.[10] Ancient scientific theory of the universe was predicated on knowledge that the stars, sun, planets and living creatures are all connected as a rational being with plans and impulses of its own (fig. 43).[11] Its intentions could be discerned through close study of astronomical phenomena and predictions could be made by preparing charts. It could be said that these astrological charts were the means for this *princeps* to predict outcomes two millennia ago just as statistical models and scenario planning are tools for forecasting used by a prime minister or president today. It may, however, suggest Tiberius had a deeper anxiety about avoiding an uncertain fate. His sensitivity to, or concerns about, others having access to his own chart led him to ban astrologers from Italy. He was certainly receptive to portents. Suetonius suggests it was the ominous discovery of his pet snake having been eaten by ants that upset him profoundly and that he immediately left the environs of Rome for Misenum, where he died days later.

Tiberius was famous for his many moral virtues. On the battlefield or in the courtroom, he showed his *virtus* ('manliness' or 'courage') in meeting his opponent face to face.[12] In exercising restraint in his personal ambition or self-importance, or

Figure 43. The globe and a rudder on the obverse of this coin symbolizes Rome's – and by association Tiberius' – control over the land and sea.

in curbing his power with the Senate or Roman People, he revealed his *moderatio* ('self-control').[13] In mitigating a harsh sentence given to the condemned in a trial, he showed his *clementia* ('mildness').[14] The Senate consecrated an altar to this virtue in 29 CE. His work ethic (*industria*) was second to none.[15] Regardless of his circumstances or whereabouts, Tiberius took his work with him. There was no time right up to the night of his death when he was not fully engaged in the affairs of the *Res Publica*. Even ensconced on Capreae, Tiberius was still part of the world.[16] In expressing his devotion or respect for the natural order – whether social, political or religious – he demonstrated his *pietas* ('dutifulness'). In public and in private, he demonstrated his *frugalitas* ('thriftiness') by personally eschewing an opulent lifestyle, such as serving leftovers to dinner guests, and allowing his travel companions only to claim expenses but not a full salary.[17]

Philo reports that Romans recognized in Tiberius an old head on young shoulders.[18] His sharp intellect was honed by respected Greek teachers, who numbered Nestor and Theodoros of Gadara. As a student, he enjoyed putting his tutors on the spot to probe how well they knew their subjects. His fluency in Latin and Greek, which he used both as a public speaker and writer of poems, and possibly the translator of Aratus' *Phaenomena*, were noted by Suetonius. His preference was for *diritas*, blunt or plain speaking.[19] His dry and economical form of oratory, modelled on M. Valerius Messalla Corvinus (I), who was known for his affected style, was difficult for some listeners to follow. His rehearsed erudition and cultivated *gravitas* with his excessive mannerisms and obscure words might confuse them. Analysis of extracts in Tacitus do indeed suggest that Tiberius' speeches were peppered with words that had long fallen out of common usage.[20] In using them, he was asserting 'Roman-ness', but Tacitus and Cassius Dio may have interpreted this to portray his intentions as dissembling and deliberately ambiguous.[21] Displaying *dissimulatio* ('dissimulation'), *ira* ('rage') or harbouring *invidia* ('grudges') were archetypal characteristics of the tyrant in Roman rhetoric.[22] In speeches he delivered in the Senate House, he was pedantic about the use of correct terminology and insisted on native Latin words over Greek imports, even if it meant using several words to explain the point.[23] Tacitus remarks that Tiberius balanced his words to the point of being intentionally obscure. This sounds like a professional politician speaking, one practiced in the art of making reassuring appeals while avoiding specific commitments. Audiences better understood Tiberius when he made unprepared remarks and spoke with his authentic voice. His humour was dry and often self-deprecating. Tacitus notes that Tiberius enjoyed combining jesting and seriousness in the same statements. The extracts of his speeches preserved by Tacitus and Cassius Dio do, indeed, reveal something of his wit and wisdom (Appendix 1). Far from dour, Tiberius had a keen sense of humour, uttering quips on many recorded occasions.[24]

Roman historians were skilled practitioners of rhetorical and storytelling techniques. They delighted in framing arguments which would convince a reader of their particular presentations of people and events. Their descriptions of Tiberius as mean, licentious and cruel were consistent with *vituperatio*, the use of personal attack on an opponent, which was accepted as standard practice in Roman courts.[25] As suited their purpose, they could present Tiberius as behaving beyond accepted norms. Suetonius cites Tiberius' taste for wine and drinking to excess in the punning nickname his soldiers coined for him, Biberius Caldius Mero. The clue is in the name Mero, which relates to *merum*, undiluted wine causing the consumer to get 'drunker than the drunken grape'.[26] At a dinner party (*convivio*) in a formal dining room setting, conversation and conviviality with the host were encouraged and the wine was mixed with water to weaken its effects, but in a drinking session (*commissatio*) where food was not part of the occasion, toasting and getting drunk was the expectation.[27] Consuming cups of *merum* in quick succession was not acceptable behaviour in polite society.[28] Habitual intoxication was believed to so weaken the mind that its consequences were felt long after the act of drinking had stopped.[29] Observed psychological and physical effects of chronic drunkenness were memory loss, narcissistic self-indulgence, antisocial behaviour, impaired speech and vision among many symptoms, including an early death.[30] By exposing this trait, Tiberius is shown as weak and unable to control himself.

A more serious blot on his character was the allegation of sexual depravity (*libidinis*). By dwelling on this trait, Tiberius is depicted as a monster or a creep. The anecdotes of lewd behaviour are presented in the form of 'He acquired a reputation for…' or 'The story is also told…'. The reports seem credible on account of the specific details offered, yet no witnesses or sources are disclosed. Tiberius was not the first man to be character-assassinated this way. Suetonius recorded that Iulius Caesar had been attacked for 'shameless vice and for adultery', adding, 'But to remove all doubt that he had an evil reputation both for, I have only to add that the elder Curio in one of his speeches calls him "every woman's man and every man's woman".'[31] M. Tullius Cicero accused M. Antonius in his youth of having an affair with the same C. Scribonius Curio, as well as having intimate relations with other men.[32] Augustus, too, had been attacked for selling himself for sex as a youth, notably with Iulius Caesar, which Antonius said explained how he came to be adopted.[33] Even in old age, Augustus could not shake off 'the charge of lustfulness, and they say that even in his later years he was fond of deflowering maidens, who were brought together for him from all quarters, even by his own wife' – a wild accusation that also implicates Augusta.[34] In terms of his sexual preference, Tiberius is always depicted enjoying the company of women; he was only interested in Vipsania and after the divorce and subsequent failed marriage to Iulia, no other women are mentioned. There is no evidence of homosexuality in his life.

Romans were accustomed to public nudity in art, bathing and religious festivals, and prostitution was generally accepted.[35] Neither Strabo nor Seneca mention anything unusual about Tiberius in this regard. The lurid stories about him only appear in reports of later writers when they describe his residency at Capreae, but not before. Thus, they may be complete fictions. Yet in an era where slavery was accepted, in which consent was not required between owner and owned, and a man with absolute power could do as he wished in the privacy of his home, it *was* entirely possible that Tiberius could have engaged in taboo sex that others might find distasteful, even depraved.[36] (There were certainly Romans who enjoyed it.) As the contemporary Warren Cup shows, slaves were often present to assist.[37] At the very least, the stories reported by Suetonius and Tacitus do reveal what some Romans were willing to believe about their former national leader. In his own lifetime, however, personal attacks did not seem to bother Tiberius, who was remarkably tolerant of being lampooned, considering it a right of free speech consistent with every citizen's entitlement to *libertas* ('freedom').[38] Rather, Tiberius felt deeply and personally affronted by Tacfarinas in 22 CE. 'By all accounts,' writes Tacitus, 'no insult to himself and the Roman People ever stung the *princeps* more than this spectacle of a deserter and bandit aping the procedure of an unfriendly power!'[39]

A plausible explanation is that what went on at Capreae was misinterpreted by the unknown source for Suetonius and Tacitus who had recorded garbled information. The origin of the lewdness they report may actually lie in traditional theatrical spectacles set in gardens of allusion, which were popular with Ancient Rome's elite.[40] Tiberius was not the inventor of the format. Respectable Roman masters, matrons and guests reversed roles and played judgement-free in temporary, private brothels, the first recorded example of which was set up by Metellus Scipio in 52 BCE.[41] The privacy afforded by the island and its rustic setting allowed Tiberius to give free rein to his imagination. He was a cultured man, and despite his patriotism, he was a lover of all things Greek.[42] Tiberius particularly enjoyed the myth of Odysseus, and perhaps he identified with the wandering hero of the Homeric epic through his own sojourns in Rhodes and *Spelunca*, and finally at his permanent residence at Capreae.[43] There, he could make art and legend come alive for his indulgence and pleasure.[44] He created indoor and outdoor spaces (*sellaria*) – in effect, Tiberius' 'home theatre' – with stages and seating where young, good-looking, well-born males and females called *spintriae* performed together in *tableaux vivants* or masques of mythical tales of Pans and Nymphs.[45] One of these pretty boys was alleged to be A. Vitellius, who would become emperor in 69 CE.[46] The erotic artworks in the rooms and grounds of the *Villa Iovis* and other locations on the island would have provided inspiration for the actors and guests in this sex-positive idyll.[47] Tiberius reportedly treated the performers in their costumes and makeup as prostitutes. It proved a popular distraction. Caius Caligula took full advantage of the facilities while living on the island, and he would later build a mock brothel in Rome for the entertainment of himself and his friends.[48]

Depicting Tiberius as a drunkard or sexual pervert was unflattering, but more damaging to his character was the allegation of wanton cruelty (*saevitia*), wilfully causing pain or suffering to others or feeling no concern about it. Suetonius declares that Tiberius had a cruel streak from a young age – first detected by Theodoros of Gadara – which became more evident as he grew older.[49] It was not a quality he approved of in his son, however. In the biographer's view, the execution of Seianus marked the point of no return, exacerbated by the revelations of how Drusus died. A few examples given of his cruelty include acts of pettiness intended to humiliate victims, like the *eques* named Pompeius, or holding men in prison without trial for long periods to increase their misery; other acts were meant to cause real harm, as in the case of Paconius, who was later charged with *maiestas*.[50] Like any Roman magistrate, however, Tiberius' *tribunicia potestas* included *coercitio*, the authority to compel others to comply with orders by force or the threat of force, and this could include imposing time in prison.[51] The veracity of other examples may be doubted. The unfortunate fisherman on Capreae whose face was savagely scraped (*lacerari*), first with a mullet and then with a crab, or the cheeky jester at Augustus' funeral, or the interview and execution of the imposter Clemens, may be complete inventions, even retellings of older folkloric tales.[52] Nevertheless, the impulsive jailing of Herod Agrippa or the thoughtless execution of a man from Rhodes due to a mistaken identity late in his reign, if indeed true, are shocking. The fact he did not use his much-vaunted *clementia* to pardon either Drusus Caesar or Nero Caesar is surprising. Seneca, who was around 40 and in Rome when Tiberius died, recalls the *princeps* as cruel, unfeeling and unfriendly in his last days.[53] By emphasizing this trait, Tiberius is shown as lacking in basic humanity. Yet, while fully capable of acts of cruelty and vindictiveness by himself, many more were committed by others presuming to carry them out in his name.

In dealing with change, loss or stress, he could be anxious, emotional, impatient and insistent. His response to Augustus' refusal to let him retire to Rhodes was impassioned verging on hysterical, culminating in him going on hunger strike, but once he had made his mind up there was no changing it.[54] When, several years into his retirement, he realized his mistake, he wrote frequently to his mother, pleading for her to make a representation on his behalf. A much humbler man returned to Rome, living a lower-profile existence to show his contrition in accordance with Augustus' terms. He wished to be shown respect, reciprocating good manners, but he despised sycophancy, refusing to be called *dominus* or by other honorific titles. He could also be cautious or suspicious. When attending a ritual sacrifice with L. Scribonius Libo, who was suspected of plotting against Tiberius, he arranged for the iron knife used to be swapped for one of lead, and he insisted that Drusus was with him in a private interview with the man. In case the arrest of Seianus failed, Tiberius had a ship moored at Capreae ready to take him to safety. Rather than paranoia, these were the sensible precautions of a statesman looking to ensure his personal security. Tiberius was, after all, the *princeps* and needed to be constantly alert to assassins or usurpers. As a soldier, he understood danger, indeed he had faced 'the first danger from childhood'.[55] He only had to look at his own family: Iulius Caesar had been murdered, and even Augustus had been the target of several assassination attempts.[56]

With few interruptions, from 14–26 CE, Tiberius personally attended sessions of the Senate to discuss laws or adjudicate in trials. The pressure of work was unrelenting. In his letter to the Senate of 22 CE, Tiberius remarked that he alone had to shoulder the blame for everyone's failures, but accepted it was part of the job of being *princeps*.[57] Ten years later, in the immediate aftermath of Seianus' downfall, recriminations dominated conversations. Tiberius wrote to the Senate, clearly in some distress, that he was suffering every day with the consequences.[58] Tiberius' response that he did not remember what he was when asked a question if he recalled something is genuinely poignant.[59] In 21 CE, he took a much-needed break in Campania. It did him good and he would return there for respite in 26 and 27 CE (when he stayed at *Spelunca*). After relocating to Capreae, he returned to Campania in 29, 32, 36 and finally 37 CE on his way to and from Rome. On these occasions, he made it known that he did not wish for crowds to turn out, even deploying troops to act as a cordon. His privacy came to be the thing he most prized. If the Senate expected him to serve as *princeps*, at least on his island home, he could live his life as an older adult on his own terms.

Writing about Tiberius, Pliny the Elder describes him as the gloomiest of men.[60] When Caius Caligula presented Tiberius' will, the Senate rejected it because they felt the late *princeps* was not of sound mind or body when he wrote it. That decision was based on political expediency, not a medical assessment. In modern times, attempts at a psychiatric assessment of Tiberius have been made on the presumption that he was mentally ill. One study used psychotherapy to diagnose Tiberius as suffering with resentment.[61] Another determined that Tiberius suffered from a premorbid Axis II Obsessive-Compulsive Personality Disorder (OCPD), which is commonly associated with depression, with a later onset of Axis I, Major Depressive Disorder, Substance Abuse (alcohol) and Event-caused Persecutory Delusional Disorder, and Axis III Myocardial Infarction (heart-attack).[62] Some have seen paranoia in his responses to perceived threats.[63] Extreme Post-Traumatic Stress Disorder (PTSD) has been suggested to explain the alleged multiple sex sessions as a form of self-medication.[64] The problem with all these diagnoses is the dataset upon which they were made. Their authors relied on interpreting the biased writings of men who had neither observed Tiberius' behaviours with their own eyes nor interviewed him in person. A diagnosis cannot be made in absentia. Applying scientific language merely perpetuates the caricatures formed in the minds of the Roman writers; it does not validate them. In 35 CE, contemporary Fulcinius Trio, who had known Tiberius personally for decades, accused the then 76-year-old of displaying psychological frailty associated with aging, but even that eyewitness' judgment was biased by grievance.

## Tiberius' Relationships with Family and Friends

In Roman society, family lineage and reputation mattered. Tiberius was born into the *gens Claudia*, with its rich heritage and outsize reputation. 'It is notorious besides that all the *Claudii* were aristocrats and staunch upholders of the prestige and influence of the patricians,' writes Suetonius.[65] Tiberius lived his life in that family tradition. It was a lot to live up to. His grandfather and father before him had risen to prominent positions in the *Res Publica* and made their impacts at crucial times in its history. Tiberius resided with his father until he died, delivering the *laudatio funebris* in the *Forum* when he was aged 9. Later, he honoured the memory of his grandfather and father with separate games in expressions of his *pietas*.

Following his father's death, Tiberius moved into the *Palatium* to be raised in the House of Augustus by his mother, Livia Drusilla. Her family, the *Livii Drusi*, was proud of its lineage, with its own list of high achievers. The relationship between mother and son, as portrayed by the Roman historians, was close but complicated.[66] As her first born, she had carried him during the travails and traumas of civil war and returned to Rome only when peace was declared. Soon thereafter, she divorced Ti. Nero for the victor in the conflict. She noted omens prophesying a glorious future for her son and, perhaps inspired by them, was a staunch advocate for him throughout his life. Allegations that she conspired behind the scenes to promote her son by removing rivals – Marcellus, Caius and Lucius Caesar – or perceived threats to her ambitions – Nero Drusus and Germanicus – are fanciful inventions of novelists or conspiracy theorists, however. Loved and respected by Augustus as strong and shrewd, Livia's influence over him was great. When Tiberius felt abandoned on Rhodes, it was to her that he turned to intercede with Augustus to allow him to return to Rome. As Augustus' widow, Tiberius respected his mother, allowing her the honorific title 'Augusta' voted by the Senate in 14 CE, but he did insist that protocol was observed when she hosted a party in Augustus' honour at her home by hosting it himself. Her ambiguous position in the *Res Publica* was down to Augustus not making it explicit during his lifetime, and Tiberius inherited an insoluble problem after his

Figure 44. Tiberius' mother represents *SALVS AVGVSTA*, the personified Roman deity of health and prosperity, on the obverse of this coin.

death.[67] Tacitus reports that Tiberius regarded her as overbearing, yet he did not resent the numerous recognitions she received from people across the empire and the high status they accorded her.[68] The issue was that women were not supposed to be so highly visible in the male-dominated Roman political system.[69] When she used her own abundant influence to help her friends and strayed into affairs of state, Tiberius would remind her to not interfere, a position which was in keeping with his interpretation of the role of a *princeps*.[70] Her protection of Plancina in the trial of Calpurnius Piso (II) was particularly galling to him. In the civil dispute over money owed to Piso by Augusta's friend, Urgulania, in 16 CE, Tiberius said he would go to court on his mother's behalf but contrived to delay his progress in the street, resulting in his mother giving orders for the sum in demand to be paid. There were fractious moments, such as when she placed her name before Tiberius' in the official inscription at the Theatre of Marcellus in 22 CE, coming so soon after he had been told she was sick and he had travelled to join her.[71] Nevertheless, that year she appeared on a bronze *dupondius* – the first time her image was struck on the coinage – with the legend *SALVS AVGVSTA* (fig. 44) to mark her full recovery.[72] As a matter of policy, Tiberius dismissed any charges involving people accused of slandering him *or* his mother. Though they lived separately, they remained in contact right through to her death, aged 86 or 87, and while he (then himself 72 years old) did not attend her funeral, he made the necessary arrangements; her *laudatio funerbris* was given by Caius Caligula. Tiberius refused her several posthumous honours awarded by the Senate, considering them excessive.[73] Despite casting her as having her own political agenda, Tacitus recognized Augusta's many strengths in his obituary of her.[74]

Tiberius loved his brother, Nero Claudius Drusus, who was younger than him by four years.[75] Collaborative rather than competitive siblings, they combined their talents for military strategy and leadership during the wars in the Alps in 15 BCE, when, in co-ordinated moves, they conquered Raetia, Vindelicia and Noricum.[76] Gold and silver coins were minted showing the two men offering branches to Augustus seated on a tribunal, and Horace immortalized their achievement in poetic form in his *Ode* IV. Hearing of Nero Drusus' fatal fall at the end of the German War in 9 BCE, Tiberius raced to the solemn camp – in the process setting a land speed record – just in time to hear his brother's last words. In another act of *pietas*, he accompanied the body on the road all the way to Rome, earning him a place in Valerius Maximus' *Memorable Sayings and Deeds*. In the *Forum Romanum*, he delivered the oration and then accompanied his remains to the Mausoleum of Augustus. Nero Drusus' premature death at 29 was a tremendous personal loss to Tiberius. Many had seen the two Claudian brothers as the living Castor and Pollux (rather than Romulus and Remus) of legend.[77] Tiberius expressed that sentiment by rededicating both the Temples of Castor and of Concordia in their joint names in 6 CE and 10 CE respectively.[78] Tacitus remarks that Nero Drusus enjoyed greater affection among the citizens than his older brother.[79] His politics were believed to favour a return to the joint rule of Senate and Roman People, meaning the removal of Augustus as *princeps*, a view that his older brother may not have shared; the incident when his letter to Tiberius was read by Augustus is recorded only by Suetonius.[80] Nero Drusus' popularity, which endured long after his death, was in large part because he died young and before he could disappoint.[81] His death also removed any potential for later rivalry with Tiberius.[82] He left a widow, Antonia, who had Tiberius' enduring respect and trust. It is unlikely that he learned of Seianus' alleged conspiracy through her, however.

Regret would characterize Tiberius' fateful relationship with his first wife, Vipsania Agrippina. Daughter of M. Agrippa by his marriage to Pomponia Caecilia Attica, Tiberius found love and fulfilment with his wife. His marriage of some nine years was only foreshortened at the personal request of Augustus. Ironically, the death in 12 BCE of Tiberius' father-in-law, who up to that time was Augustus' son-in-law and best friend, left his daughter, Iulia, a widow. Augustus insisted, despite Tiberius' protests. The ensuing divorce from Vipsania deeply hurt Tiberius.[83] He may never have fully recovered from the imposed separation from his romantic soulmate. When Augustus learned that, after being married to Iulia, Tiberius had met Vipsania, he reprimanded him and took measures to ensure it would not happen again. When she subsequently married C. Asinius Gallus in 11 BCE, Tiberius harboured a grudge against the man that lasted three decades. She died some time around 20 CE. Ten years later, at Tiberius' request, the Senate imprisoned Gallus and he died in solitary confinement in 33 CE.

The marriage with Iulia was strained from the start. To his credit, Tiberius did try to make the relationship work.[84] They slept together and a child was expected in their first year. When the baby was still born, the marriage quickly fell apart. Tiberius immersed himself in his military campaigns in Illyricum, leaving his wife behind in Rome. Her happiness was overlooked by both Tiberius and Augustus. Apparently, everyone knew that Iulia was having sex with multiple partners in public – all except Augustus. When he found out in 2 BCE, he disowned her. Invoking the *Lex Iulia de adulteriis coercendis*, he banished her to Pantadria where she lived with her mother. Her behaviour, however, may have been intended as a protest against the moral straitjacket imposed upon her by Augustus' return to traditional family values.[85] Already several years into his elective retirement on Rhodes, Tiberius wrote to his father-in-law to appeal for mercy, but notification of his divorce from Iulia was the response. Tiberius let her keep their wedding gifts. As *princeps*, Tiberius was tough on his ex-wife. Seeing no provision made for her in Augustus' will, he cut her annual allowance (*peculium*), since Augustus had left everything to Tiberius and Augusta.[86] When she died at Rhegium in 14 CE, Tiberius did not attend her funeral, but he honoured *Divus* Augustus' request not to let her ashes be placed in his mausoleum.

Tiberius' relationship with Iulia's sons by M. Agrippa, Caius and Lucius, was dutiful rather than affectionate.[87] Adopted by Augustus by arrangement with their father, Agrippa, in 17 BCE, Tiberius was a small part of their upbringing. He was appointed to mentor Caius on an expedition across the Rhine into Germania in 8 BCE, a task which he completed successfully and for which he received an imperatorial acclamation. The social prominence of the two boys exposed them to adulation by rich and poor, leading them to grow up to be rather spoiled and entitled. Augustus embarked on corrective action by sending his adopted sons on separate military assignments. Caius seems to have been offended that Tiberius' *tribunicia potestas* was extended for five years.[88] One of the reasons cited for Tiberius' withdrawal from public life in 6 BCE was to give the two boys space to grow into their roles as future leaders in the *Res Publica*, in the belief it would be better achieved if Augustus' stepson was out of the away. This seems credible. Entrusted with leading the mission to Armenia, Caius was accompanied by M. Lollius, a man who bore a deep grudge against Tiberius, likely going back to his ousting as governor of the *Tres Galliae* in 16 BCE. On Caius' outbound journey, Tiberius felt compelled – even as a private citizen – to pay his personal respects to Caius, sailing to meet him on Samos. Under Lollius' negative influence, however, that encounter proved awkward. Only when Lollius was exposed as a traitor did Caius warm to Tiberius, in fact agreeing, when consulted by Augustus, for him to return from Rhodes to Rome in 2 CE. When Lucius died on his way to Hispania Tarraconensis in the same year as his step-uncle's return, Tiberius composed a lament for the young man, a fact preserved by Suetonius. He did not do the same for Caius upon his death two years later.

Tiberius' marriage to Vipsania Agrippina produced a son, whom he named after his brother.[89] Drusus grew up to be a strong-willed youth who enjoyed partying with actors, yet revealed moments of real cruelty. Again, Augustus interfered in this father-son relationship, insisting that, following the deaths of Caius and Lucius, Tiberius should adopt Germanicus as his son. The move was intended to create a line of succession two generations deep, but it eclipsed the prominence of his natural son. Nevertheless, as brothers, Drusus and Germanicus enjoyed a fraternal friendship of 'surpassing harmony' (*egregie concordes*).[90] In an indication of his respect for his deceased brother, he met Agrippina bearing the ashes at Tarracina, and in the trial of 20 CE in which Cn. Calpurnius Piso (II) was charged with murdering Germanicus by poison in Antiocheia, Drusus presented the case for the prosecution. Tiberius subsequently positioned Drusus to succeed him, seeing him elected consul for 15 CE and again in 21 CE, the second time sharing it with his son. He also negotiated with the Senate for him to receive the tribunician power in 22 CE. He proved a faithful deputy, negotiating the end of the mutiny of the legions in Pannonia in 14 CE and leading campaigns there and in Germania in later years.[91] Tiberius had occasionally to rein-in his son in moments of recklessness, issuing a tirade that Drusus would commit no act of violence or insolence while he was alive, or after his death, yet there can be no doubt about his paternal love for his son.[92] Drusus' death in 23 CE, the ninth year of his reign, was another emotional hammer blow for Tiberius. Believing he had succumbed to sickness, Tiberius' way to deal with the loss of his son was to invest himself fully in his work. He had memorials and statues erected in honour of him; a few of those busts of Drusus grace the collections of museums today.[93] When, years later, he learned from Apicata that Drusus had been murdered in a conspiracy engineered by her former husband, L. Aelius Seianus – who had been in a love pact with, and possibly already married to, Livilla – Tiberius was brokenhearted, mourning his son's death a second time.[94] In Tacitus' presentation of history, the death of Drusus marked a turning point for the worse in Tiberius' principate.[95]

Tiberius' relationship with Germanicus was sentimental and respectful.[96] Germanicus was, after all, his deceased brother's son and, on account of it, he held his nephew in high affection and fond regard. Suetonius reports that Livia dissuaded Augustus from adopting Germanicus directly, and he took her advice, leading to his adoption by Tiberius. Intentionally or unintentionally, there were times when Tiberius did favour his adopted son over his natural son, but these may have been based on the fact that Germanicus was simply a year older and thus eligible sooner for promotions. Germanicus proved a quick student and a loyal deputy.[97] In the Batonian Revolt (6–9 CE), he arrived in theatre with his volunteer cohorts and accomplished his first mission admirably. As the counteroffensive moved forward, Tiberius devolved greater responsibilities to him, and Germanicus proved up to each challenge. As *legatus Augusti propraetore* of the *Tres Galliae* at the time the legions mutinied in Germania Inferior and Superior in 14 CE, he remained steadfast and his devotion to Tiberius was never in doubt.[98] Initially sent by Augustus to campaign across the Rhine, upon his accession, Tiberius arranged for his *imperium* to be levelled up to match his seniority and authorized Germanicus to capture or kill Arminius. His campaigns in 15 and 16 CE met with limited success, however, succeeding only in recovering two of the three legionary eagles lost by Varus, rescuing endangered Roman ally Segimerus and capturing Arminius' wife, Thusnelda, and their child.[99] Tiberius politely but firmly declined his request for a troop surge for 17 CE, enticing Germanicus with the gift of a full triumph and a consulship in 18 CE. Tiberius now faced the question of what to do with a popular, energetic and ambitious 'successor in waiting' who still needed to gain more experience before he was ready to undertake the role of *princeps* when the time came.[100] Germanicus was only 33 when Tiberius promoted him to oversee the provinces in the East and restore order to them, in a similar capacity to M. Agrippa and Caius before him. Germanicus' lack of wisdom and judgement were revealed when he arrived in Egypt without authorization and, worse, opened the granaries to the starving population there. Tiberius had to remind Germanicus that he was in breach of the regulations set by Augustus.

Tacitus interpreted Tiberius' decision to send Cn. Calpurnius Piso (II) to Syria as a means to manage Germanicus, on the spurious basis that he might pose a threat as a challenger. The terms of his command preserved in the *Senatus Consultum de Cn. Piso Patre*, however, expressly gave Germanicus *imperium maius* over subordinates, which included Piso, but his power was below that of the *princeps*, completely undermining Tacitus' interpretation.[101] This arrangement giving Germanicus superiority over all other legates and proconsuls in the region did not sit well with Piso. His refusal to send troops to Armenia when Germanicus requested them, and his general belligerent and uncooperative attitude towards him, were insubordinate and unprofessional. Indeed, Tiberius knew very well how independent-minded and problematic Piso could be from having served with him as consul in 7 BCE, and he may have actually sent his faithful son Germanicus to oversee *him*.[102] It would test his ability to manage troublesome deputies. The unforeseen complete breakdown in relations between Germanicus and Piso led to the *legatus Augusti* quitting his appointment and leaving his province. By then, Germanicus had fallen gravely ill and, when he died, the rumours of a conspiracy to poison him by Piso and his wife, Placina, spread, in part propagated by Germanicus' own team of adjutants. Death by poison is the verdict of Josephus, but the cause of Germanicus' death was never proved in the court case held in 20 CE, and Tacitus himself disbelieved it; an unidentified virus or disease likely killed him.[103] Tacitus also recalled a story that Piso had letters written by Tiberius with instructions which he brought to the *Curia Iulia* that were never given in evidence so their contents remain a mystery. Tacitus implied those unseen instructions were to cause Germanicus mischief. The verdict of the Senate was to find Piso guilty of several crimes, including *maiestas* and incitement to cause civil war. By then Piso was already dead, though whether by suicide or the blade of an assassin sent by Seianus cannot be determined with certainty – notably he did leave a note imploring Tiberius to be kind to his children. Significantly, in a show of *clementia Caesaris*, Tiberius intervened to mitigate the harshest sentences given to Piso's sons.[104] His wife, Plancina, finally took her own life in 33 CE when facing a separate murder charge.

Tiberius' response to others' grief could appear unsympathetic.[105] The news of the death of Germanicus in late 19 CE plunged the Roman People into despair. Memorials, including triumphal arches, statues and other honours, were decreed for Germanicus. When the prolonged period of mourning declared by the Senate began to negatively impact the city's work, Tiberius publicly expressed his sorrow, but pointed out that everyone faced loss of a loved one at some time and issued a polite but firm request for a return to normal business. The People complied. Months later, they assembled on the *Campus Martius* to witness the return of his ashes, brought from Syria by his widow, Agrippina. That day, however, Tiberius and Augusta surprised the crowd by their decision to remain at home. Their apparent disinterest in the ceremony upset many.[106] Most likely, Tiberius interpreted the funeral as already having taken place in Antiocheia, where his wife had prepared and burned Germanicus' body on a pyre in the marketplace with the customary rites. He considered placing the urn in Augustus' Mausoleum as a private matter for his wife and children. It was a misreading on his part of the mood of the People, who recalled the pomp of his brother's funeral and regarded Tiberius' absence in his adopted son's memorial ceremony as a heartless snub of a popular and beloved member of the imperial household.

Tiberius' relationship with Agrippina, granddaughter of Augustus, was once cordial. After Germanicus' death, for which she blamed Tiberius, it broke down irretrievably.[107] As a widow, she was devoted to keeping alive his memory and to protecting his sons. She brought his ashes to Rome in melodramatic style. Her grief seems to have unhinged her. Her pride and independence, impertinent tongue and defiant spirit irked Tiberius as inappropriate behaviours.[108] She once interrupted a solemn religious ceremony led by Tiberius to intercede for a friend accused of a charge. Behind this friction was Seianus. When she approached Tiberius to ask his permission to remarry, he simply refused to answer and left.[109] Forewarned by Seianus in his twisted scheme to eliminate her family, she became suspicious of Tiberius, refusing to eat fruit at a dinner, fearing it had been poisoned.[110] Her sons were followed, abused and reported on by Seianus' agents. Tired of her antics, in 29 CE Tiberius denounced Agrippina and banished her. Her last days on Pandateria were miserable and her death horrible. Tiberius did not weep when he was told of her passing. In Tacitus' account, Agrippina was a character through which the historian could show Tiberius as lacking in compassion and having difficulties with strong-willed women.

Tiberius' relationships with the sons and daughter of Germanicus and Agrippina were initially paternalistic. He followed Nero Caesar and Drusus Caesar on their journeys through childhood, distributing largesse to the plebeians when they reached manhood, and encouraged them in their progression on the *cursus honorum*, allowing them to be selected for offices before the stipulated ages. When Drusus died, he tearfully implored the senators to nurture them and to train them in their duties as good citizens. The demise each suffered was clearly the crooked work of Seianus.[111] He exploited the seeming naïveté of Nero Caesar and the jealous ambition of his younger brother, Drusus Caesar. Nero was maligned as homosexual and banished to the island of Pontia. Similarly, Drusus was falsely accused of an unspecified crime and confined in the *Palatium*. Yet Tiberius must have seen potential in the younger boy because, had the plot to arrest Seianus failed, his 'Plan B' required Macro to bring Drusus Caesar before the Senate and People and to declare him *dux*, the new commander-in-chief who would lead the counter-revolution.[112] Neither brother survived into their thirties. Tiberius' last close companion was his nephew, Caius Caligula, who reached manhood on Caprea, where he was permitted to indulge in the pleasures of dancing and cavorting with his *spintriae* in the hope it would tame his wild inclinations.[113] If the anecdote reported by Suetonius is correct, Caius blamed Tiberius, not Seianus, for the destruction of his family. As for Livilla, Tiberius welcomed her as the wife of his son, Drusus. He was thrilled at the birth of his twin grandsons, Ti. Gemellus and Germanicus Gemellus, a happy occasion widely seen to be fortuitous. When Drusus died, Tiberius was resistant to allowing Seianus to marry Livilla. Tiberius was mortified to learn of her role in murdering his son, in which she had willingly conspired to keep the affections of Seianus. Yet he spared her from execution out of respect for her mother, Antonia.

Beyond the extended family, there were cherished friendships. Although perhaps inclined to introversion, Tiberius deeply enjoyed the companionship of a small number of intimate – and exclusively male – friends for conversation and Greek-style *symposia*.[114] He was certainly no loner. Living with him on Rhodes were Licilius Longus, a senator of humble background, and Vescularius Flaccus and Iulius Marinus, who were two of his oldest friends. There he met Thrasyllus, who became a lifelong confidant and teacher. All followed him to Capreae. On that island they were joined by the wealthy Curtius Atticus, jurist M. Cocceius Nerva and Ti. Iulius Pappus, who managed his library. When, in 33 CE, Nerva later announced he was taking his own life, Tiberius did all he could to convince him otherwise, but in this he was unsuccessful. Flaccus and Marinus were

Table 2: Tiberius' Military and Political Career.

| Year | Position/Powers | Theatre |
|---|---|---|
| 26–25 BCE | *Tribunus Militum Laticlavius* | Asturia and Cantabria |
| 23 | *Quaestor* | Rome and Italy |
| 20 | Special Envoy of Augustus (with *Imperium proconsulare*?) | Parthia |
| 19 | *Ornamenta Praetoria* | |
| 16–15 | *Praetor* (*Urbanus*?) | Rome |
| 15 | *Legatus Augusti Pro Praetore* | *Tres Galliae* |
| 13 | *Legatus Augusti Pro Praetore* | Raetia and Noricum ('Alpine War') with Nero Drusus |
| 13 | Consul [I] with P. Quinctilius Varus | |
| 12–9 | *Legatus Augusti Pro Praetore* | Illyricum ('Pannonian War') |
| 11 | *Imperium proconsulare* | Illyricum ('Pannonian War') |
| 8 | *Legatus Augusti Pro Praetore* | Germania |
| 7 | Consul [II] with Cn. Calpurnius Piso | |
| 6–5* | *Tribunicia Potestas* [I] for 5 years | |
| 4–5* CE | *Tribunicia Potestas* [VI] for 5 years | |
| 5 | *Legatus Augusti Pro Praetore* | Germania |
| 6–9 | *Legatus Augusti Pro Praetore* | Illyricum ('Batonian War'/'Dalmatian War') |
| 10–11 | *Legatus Augusti Pro Praetore* | Germania |
| 13 | *Imperium proconsulare maius* | |
| 13–14* 12? | *Tribunicia Potestas* [XVI] | |
| 14–37 | *Sodalis Augustalis* | |
| 14–37 | *Princeps* | |
| 15 | *Pontifex Maximus* | |
| 18 | Consul [III] with Germanicus | |
| 22–23* | *Tribunicia Potestas* [XXIIII] | |
| 23 | Consul [IV] with Drusus | |
| 24 | First *Decennalia* | |
| 31 | Consul [V] with L. Aelius Seianus | |
| 34 | Second *Decennalia* | |
| 36–37* | *Tribunicia Potestas* [XXXVIII] | |

* The *tribunicia potestas* was effective from 26 June, ending 25 June the following year. Renewed for Tiberius each year after 5 CE. Hammond (1938); Woytek (2017).

executed in 33 CE after Tiberius discovered their treachery in assisting Seianus in the downfall of prominent Romans. Thrasyllus died a natural death; some thought he had had too much influence over Tiberius with his horoscopes and divinations.

## *Princeps* and *Senatus*, Prosecutions and Seianus

The most consequential person in Tiberius' life was Augustus. When Tiberius entered the *Palatium* to join his mother, he was still a young man, at just 9 years old. Every step of his political and military career would need the approval of his stepfather (Table 2). His advancement exposed him to how the Roman system worked – or failed to work – in addressing real world issues. Only in the last decade of that relationship would Augustus come to rely completely on Tiberius. It would take an extraordinary – and unfortunate – series of fatal mishaps for Tiberius to become the leading candidate to take over as *princeps*.

At the start of his career, the immensely talented M. Agrippa was Augustus' life-long right-hand man.[115] The same age as the *princeps*, in the event of the premature death of Augustus, Agrippa was widely seen as his heir, but in that role he would be more of a temporary caretaker while a younger talent was trained. Indeed, M. Claudius Marcellus, son of Octavia, was the protégé in the *Domus Augusta*.[116] His premature death in 23 BCE prompted Augustus to adopt Agrippa's sons, Caius and Lucius, in 17 BCE. Fast-tracked into the *cursus honorum*, they were still young and unproven when Agrippa died in 12 BCE. Seemingly operating in their shadows, meanwhile, Livia's sons performed their assigned duties with vigour and distinction.[117] Even then, the slight evidence we have suggests that of the two men, Nero Drusus, rather than Tiberius, was Augustus' favourite. His death in 9 BCE, and those of Lucius in 2 CE and Caius in 4 CE, left Augustus with few options, since Germanicus and Agrippa Caesar were too young and inexperienced.

Augustus had relied on his best friend, M. Agrippa, for three decades.[118] Agrippa and Tiberius were alike in many ways. Both were strong personalities; both were patriots; both shared a natural talent for leadership in warfare and administration; both were self-motivated and bashful (though Tiberius gladly celebrated his triumphs, whereas Agrippa declined his); and both were temperamental and plain speaking. Above all, both men were unswervingly loyal to Augustus. At his bidding, they were linked through Tiberius' marriage to Vipsania. They were, however, different in a fundamental respect. Agrippa came from humble origins, the absence of consuls in his family tree making him a *novus homo*, a 'new man' despised by the elite families whose ancestors had reached the pinnacle of the *Res Publica* many times; Tiberius was from one of those prestigious families. It was through necessity that Tiberius was elevated to being the indispensable helper and next-in-line for Augustus' curule chair.[119] Tiberius could not have had a better role model to prepare for it than Agrippa. By then, his stepfather had forgiven Tiberius his aberrant decision to retire to Rhodes in 6 BCE and the chastened stepson had a new-found acceptance of his place in Rome eight years later. On 27 June 4 CE, Augustus made it known that he was adopting Tiberius for reasons of state.[120] He was, without doubt, the best man available to support Augustus in his final years – indeed, a surrogate Agrippa.[121] Tiberius had established a formidable reputation of his own. Then 45 years old, he was an accomplished statesman and Rome's most successful living commander. He had contributed directly and disproportionately to establishing the peace which bore his adoptive father's name: *Pax Augusta*. Augustus may have felt he sometimes needed to apologize for Tiberius' odd mannerisms, but the letters preserved by Suetonius reveal his active interest in his son's work, even a genuine concern for his wellbeing. He trusted the maturity and judgement of 'The Old Man'. By 14 CE, Tiberius' political powers were equal to the *princeps'*. No one knows what Augustus and Tiberius talked about in their last private conversation in Nola, and while a plan for the days and months after his death would seem most likely, the dying *princeps* did not make his wishes publicly known. He could not be seen to nominate Tiberius as his successor because Rome was not a monarchy.

Augustus' *principatus* ('national leadership' status) derived from his wartime command as *dux* of the army fighting against Kleopatra and her associate, M. Antonius (31–30 BCE), during which all of Italy had sworn an oath to him, and his subsequent recognition as *princeps Senatus* (since 23 BCE) with its privileges in the House. He defined his leadership thereafter as taking 'precedence of all in rank, but of power I possessed no more than those who were my colleagues in any magistracy'.[122] There was no 'central magistracy', no elected 'proconsul of the Roman Empire' for him to pass on to Tiberius.[123] Augustus hoped that individual enterprise and circumstances would produce future generations of leaders. With that in mind, his own *Forum Augustum* displayed statues and inscriptions of *viri triumphales*, exemplars of great men 'who had raised the estate of the Roman People from obscurity to greatness'.[124] In 2 BCE, he issued the proclamation, 'I have contrived this to lead the citizens to require me, while I live, and the *principes* [First Men] of later times as well, to attain the standard set by those worthies of old.'[125]

Through survival of the fittest, Tiberius emerged as such a leader. The same process had revealed Agrippa Caesar, Agrippa's posthumously born son, to be a man fundamentally unfit to be a *princeps*. Augustus abdicated his adoption, stripping him of his Julian name and reverting him to *gens Vipsania*.[126] Thus, prior to his death, Augustus (possibly with his wife's support) made the arrangements for Agrippa Caesar to be killed so that there would be no one to challenge the man he had marked out to lead the Roman Senate and People.[127] Augustus hoped to avoid an internal civil war. It was cold, political calculus. Tiberius did not know about the execution until informed that it had already happened. His first act was to give the watchword to the prefects of the Praetorian Cohorts, and to inform the provincial governors and the commanders of the Roman Army of the situation in Nola. Significantly, Tiberius did not claim to be *princeps*.[128]

Augustus had solved the conundrum of how to rule Rome as an autocrat without being assassinated for doing so. A work in progress, the evident problem with Augustus' novel form of *Res Publica* was that there was no precedent for how to manage the peaceful transition from one *princeps* to another.[129] Tiberius was the one now having to work this out. On 4 September 14 CE, Tiberius made arrangements for the funeral and oversaw the reading of Augustus' will in the Senate House. When some senators proposed a vote for Tiberius to become *princeps* and take the title *Augustus*, he adamantly refused. It was inappropriate, disrespectful even in his eyes, to discuss the matter at that moment; this was a time for mourning. The Senate met again on 17 September. Paterculus mentions the 'trepidation of the Senate'.[130] During the meeting, he states that the Senate struggled 'to induce him [Tiberius] to succeed to the position of his father, while he on his side strove for permission to play the part of a citizen on a parity with the rest rather than that of a *princeps* over all'.[131] Reason prevailed and Tiberius acceded to the will of the Senate and People. Paterculus rejoices that, 'He is the only man to whose lot it has fallen to refuse the principate for a longer time, almost, than others had fought to secure it.'[132] Tacitus, in the longest account of this event, quotes an extract from Tiberius' speech to the Senate in which he sought to rule the empire jointly with the Conscript Fathers. Tacitus remarks critically, 'A speech in this tenor was more dignified than convincing', casting doubt on the sincerity of Tiberius by highlighting his diction, the meaning of which the historian determined to be deliberately confusing.[133] He moves on to the undignified overtures by some senators for Tiberius to accept the principate, leading to readings of documents prepared by Augustus, and to a pointed exchange between the new ruler and Asinius Gallus. Gallus then tried to appeal to Tiberius' better nature, recalling his past military successes in the name of peace. 'He [Gallus] failed, however,' Tacitus observes, 'to soothe the imperial anger: he had been a hated man ever since his marriage to Vipsania.'[134] The tortuous debate continued, with several senators being considered as candidates for the principate, when, 'Wearied at last by the universal outcry and by individual appeals, he [Tiberius] gradually gave ground, up to the point, not of acknowledging that he assumed the sovereignty, but of ceasing to refuse and to be entreated.'[135] Suetonius describes the same occasion in nearly farcical terms, accusing Tiberius of 'barefaced hypocrisy' for adamantly refusing the title of *princeps* in the face of dramatic appeals by several senators, even though he did 'not hesitate at once to assume and to exercise *dominatio* ['mastery' or 'tyranny']', having already assigned himself a bodyguard *before* attending the assembly.[136] Dio's account of the meeting focuses on a fractious debate in which one senator sarcastically suggests that Tiberius be given a guard detail, seeing he already had one, followed by discussion on how to divide up management of the empire, involving a terse argument between Tiberius and Asinius Gallus. The scene ends with the historian's barbed observation, 'For Gallus had married the former wife of Tiberius and claimed Drusus as his son, and he was consequently hated by the other even before this incident.'[137]

What really happened that day? Better than anyone alive, Tiberius fully understood the challenges the *Res Publica* now faced. With this new duty would come great personal sacrifice. Tiberius was an insider who had witnessed Augustus making decisions. Augustus was unique, a man with the intellect to grapple with the complex issues of state, the deft touch to negotiate with many different constituencies and the ability to manage their competing interests without resort to overt threat. Tiberius paid tribute to his consummate skills in his funeral oration on 6 or 8 September. There was no one else like him. On 17 September, Tiberius' instinct was again to decline the Senate's request for him to assume the same leadership role Augustus had undertaken. Tiberius did not know the political system of his father's or grandfather's time:

> There were magistrates with the same titles; there was a younger generation, sprung up since the victory of Actium, and even many of the older men had been born during the civil wars. How few were left who had seen the *Res Publica*![138]

He could only reflect on what he had been told about the system in the time before Augustus or could read about it in the history books and the proceedings of the Senate. Perhaps his instincts, like those of his younger brother, were in favour of a genuine attempt to restore the *Res Publica* of a previous but unspecified time that his ancestors fought and died to uphold.[139] He had seen Augustus struggle with the quandary of how to manage an empire within a constitution formulated by and for an evolving small city-state, which had led the Senate to recognize him as *princeps*. The *Res Publica* of the previous two centuries was never totally open to new talent or new ways. The great families, with their moral authority grounded in *mos maiorum* ('tradition' or 'ways of the ancestors'), were able to field candidates descended from praetors and consuls and they expected to receive the same appointments, making the Senate effectively a quasi-hereditary body.[140] These *nobiles* were resistant towards electing *novi homines* ('new men') like Cicero or M. Agrippa. The failure of many prominent men to live by the *mos maiorum* in the first century BCE was a contributing factor in the rise of Sulla, Crassus and Iulius Caesar and the ensuing civil wars which created the conditions for Augustus to emerge. Now the Senate was asking Tiberius – himself one of these privileged nobles – to continue Augustus' hybrid model of governance.

Tiberius' response was to advise the Conscript Fathers that Rome needed a *group* of men to share the awesome responsibility. Rather than rise to the occasion, however, the assembled body panicked.[141] Asinius Gallus tried to engage him in an exchange about which role and responsibilities Tiberius wanted in this proposed division of power, but he refused to be drawn into the argument. The Senate now begged Tiberius; it was intent on picking one man. Their deal was all or nothing. Tiberius, however, was still negotiating his terms of acceptance. Rather than yield to a less qualified individual than himself, he finally relented. The consuls led the chamber in swearing the oath of loyalty to him. The Senate voted him *imperium* without setting a time limit on it.[142] Augustus had had to formally ask the Senate to renew his *imperium* every five or ten years; it would not be so for Tiberius. Neither Augustus nor Tiberius had intended the transition to go this way.[143] Tiberius also told the Senate on 17 September that when they felt the time was right, he would step down from his leadership role and, by implication, he looked to them, and not the Roman People, to make that determination.[144] Tiberius did not formally adopt the appellation *Augustus* and made a point of refusing the title of *Pater Patriae*.[145] He could not abide sycophancy anyway, but the clear inference is that Tiberius considered his role as temporary and did not intend to hold it unto death. Tacitus and Dio see hypocrisy in Tiberius' negotiating, but there is no reason to doubt that Tiberius was sincere.[146] Thus, it would fall to Tiberius with active participation of the Senate to refine the operating procedures they had not fully developed with Augustus. For this second iteration of the *Res Publica* with a *princeps* to function successfully, Tiberius chose to adhere to precedent set by Augustus and to long-established legal principles.[147] He believed in the rule of law and the legacy of *Divus* Augustus (fig. 45), stating in his address to the Senate in 25 CE: 'I who respect as law all his actions and sayings.'[148] He would make the point again and again that senators must respect the laws of Augustus: it was fundamental – the baseline – to sustaining this new Principate form of the Roman Commonwealth. There were real consequences for non-compliance. Apidius Merula was removed from the Senate register for failing to swear to obey the legislation of *Divus* Augustus in 25 CE. Taking their cue from Tiberius, who was also sensitive to criticism of Augustus or idolizing of Caesar's assassins, the Senate heard a case against Cordus the historian in 25 CE.

Figure 45. This coin minted by Tiberius shows *DIVVS AVGVSTVS PATER* and a profile of 'Father Divine Augustus' in a radiate crown on the obverse. The eagle clutching the globe symbolizes Jupiter's – and by association Rome's – possession of the world.

Keeping the peace and driving procedural efficiencies were Tiberius' legislative priorities. Reviewing the body of edicts, laws and decrees issued during the second principate (Table 3) reveals Tiberius' interests lay in ensuring public order, ridding Roman society of disruptive elements (whether they be astrologers, cults or actors), controlling prices and conspicuous consumption, and interrogating household slaves for court cases. They were typically enacted after incidents like the riots in the theatre in 15 CE or the collapse of the amphitheatre at Fidenae in 27 CE. Older statutes could be clarified or augmented. In 19 CE, a *Senatus Consultum* extended the *Lex Iulia de Adulteriis* of Augustus to repress forms of non-marital sexual relations considered unacceptable by Roman society. In 19 CE, the Senate issued a decree protecting women from exploitation in low-grade professions. To streamline the law-making process, in 14 CE, the *Comitia Centuriata* or *Tributa* ('Peoples' Assembly') was relieved of its right of proposing laws (*leges*) and thereafter the Senate took on this responsibility.[149] The last *lex* was voted in 24 CE, with none attested after that year.[150] In the meantime, Tiberius frequently consulted a small group of friends as trusted advisors on a range of matters before making his final decision.

Important to Tiberius was that the laws must be enforced. He took an active and personal interest in the application of the law, both sacred and secular. He was renowned for his mastery of it, having spoken in defence of Archelaus of Cappadocia in 26 BCE, advocated for the people of Tralles in Asia in 25 BCE, participated as prosecuting counsel in a treason trial in 23 BCE and served as a *praetor* – likely *praetor urbanus* – in 16 BCE.[151] Inscriptions honoured Tiberius as *iustissimus princeps* ('most just *princeps*').[152] On coins he promoted *iustitia*, an appeal to 'justice' in the sense of uprightness or fairness. He took pride in being regarded as *senator et iudex* ('a statesman and a judge'), exercising judicial functions in concert with his peers.[153] He would sit conspicuously in public court cases as an *assessor*, ostensibly proffering the presiding magistrate advice, but his presence also lent the hearings gravitas and kept the proceedings honest. In the same way, he sat in the *Curia* keeping the discussions on the straight and narrow, ensuring that points were rooted in sound interpretations of the law. He would argue against retroactive laws and autocratic decisions, advocating for due process. In the case of C. Iunius Silanus, he argued that legal judgments should not be based on rumours. In the trial of Cn. Calpurnius Piso (II), who faced multiple charges, Tiberius was present as an observer, but not as an *assessor*. He was emphatic about ensuring that his relationship to Germanicus and his feelings as a father should have no bearing on the case: he counselled the prosecution and defence to make their cases, and the senators in their role as a jury to reach their verdict independently of him. In 32 CE, his written response to discovering that an illegal copy of the Sibylline Books was in circulation found fault with L. Caninius Gallus and the Senate, who had failed in their due diligence; one thing he could

Table 3: Edicts, Senatorial Decrees and Laws Issued Under Tiberius.

| Legal Instrument | Date Issued CE |
|---|---|
| Rescript of Tiberius on indictment of magistrates | ? |
| *Senatus Consultum* (?) on convicts' wills | ? |
| *Senatus Consultum* on consulting soothsayers | ? |
| *Senatus Consultum* on limitation of furniture, prices, etc | ? |
| *Senatus Consulta* regulating actors' conduct | 15 |
| *Senatus Consultum* restricting luxury | 16 |
| *Senatus Consultum Libonianum* extending *Lex Cornelia de Falsis* | 16 |
| *Senatus Consultum* on expulsion of astrologers and magicians from Italy | 16/17 |
| *Lex Cornelia de Falsis* extended | 16/20/29 |
| *Praefectura Urbis* | 17 |
| *Lex* approving *imperium maius* and mission to Germanicus in the East | 17 |
| Edicts of Germanicus on army deserters | Before 19 |
| *Senatus Consultum* extending *Lex Iulia de Adulteriis* | 19 |
| *Lex Iulia de Adulteriis*, extended | 19 |
| *Senatus Consultum* banning elite Romans from performing on stage, in arena* | 19 |
| *Senatus Consultum* on expulsion of Jews | 19 |
| *Senatus Consultum* on expulsion of the cult of Isis | 19 |
| *Senatus Consultum de honoribus Germanici decernendis*** | 19 |
| *Senatus Consultum* on responsibility of governor for his wife's acts | 20 |
| *Senatus Consultum de Cn. Pisone Patre* | 20 |
| *Lex Papia Poppaea*, amended | 20 |
| *Senatus Consulta* extending *Lex Cornelia de Falsis* | 20/29 |
| *Senatus Consultum* on criminal trial of slaves | 20 |
| *Senatus Consultum* on asylum of emperor's image | 21 |
| *Senatus Consultum* on ten days' interval between conviction and execution | 21 |
| *Senatus Consultum* suppressing Druidical priesthood | 21? |
| *Senatus consulta* on the right of asylum | 21–23 |
| Edict of Tiberius on sumptuary law | 22 |
| *Senatus Consultum* on expulsion of actors | 23 |
| *Senatus Consultum* on use of gold ring | 23 |
| *Lex Visellia* regulating the activities of freedmen | 24 |
| *Senatus Consultum* on speculative building and hosting gladiatorial shows | 27 |
| Edict of Tiberius on public order | 29 |
| *Senatus Consultum* on indictment of *legatus* | 31 |
| *Senatus Consultum* (?) on sacrifices to human beings | 31 |
| Edicts of magistrates on public order | 32 |
| *Senatus Consultum* on public disorder | 32 |
| *Senatus Consultum* reaffirming Caesar's investment law | 33 |
| *Senatus Consultum* granting Tiberius armed escort | 33 |
| *Senatus Consultum Persicianum* 60+-year-old men exempt from penalties of *caelibatus* | 34 |

Source: Cooley (2023); González (1999); Harries (2013); Powell (2013), pp.220–25; and Rogers (1935), p.216. **Tabula Larinas* ***Tabula Hebana/Tabula Siarensis*

not abide was incompetence. He would frequently throw out frivolous cases against individuals for committing offences of sacrilege against him or Augusta, dismissing the cases of Falanius and Rubrius for allegedly defaming the gods in 15 CE. He resolutely upheld the principle of *Deorum injuriae Diis curae.*[154]

With the tribunician power, which gave him the responsibility for the *ius auxilii* and the *imperium* to execute it, Tiberius could take the prerogative to intercede on behalf of citizens aggrieved by magisterial injustices.[155] In the case of Vibius Serenus (I), he intervened with his veto as tribune to spare the old man a death by flogging; instead, he was sent back into exile and died a natural death. As *pontifex maximus*, charged with maintaining the *pax deorum* ('peace with the gods'), he gave advice to the magistrates, after collecting and interpreting the omens. The potent combination of these temporal and religious powers gave Tiberius unmatched *auctoritas* ('influence'). Indeed, there were some in the Senate who advocated that the body could not conduct its business at all without his guidance. Ever mindful of his weighty responsibilities, he was cautious and conscientious in applying his prestige and influence:

> He even introduced a semblance of free government by maintaining the ancient dignity and powers of the Senate and the magistrates; for there was no matter of public or private business so small or so great that he did not lay it out before the senators.[156]

Out of respect for the members, 'He always entered the *Curia* alone; and when he was brought in once in a litter because of illness, he dismissed his attendants.'[157]

Tiberius did not always get the balance right. In the eyes of later writers such as Tacitus, it was Tiberius' enforcement of the laws on *maiestas* that would come to harm his reputation.[158] Tiberius did not create the body of law on *maiestas*, however; it already had a long history.[159] Cases brought under *maiestas* law were actively prosecuted under Augustus, who extended its scope.[160] That fact seems to have been forgotten by later writers such as Pliny, who, in his *Panegyricus* to Trajan, asserts the ridiculous idea that Tiberius became *princeps* in order to pursue cases of *maiestas*.[161] As a committed follower of Augustus, Tiberius was bound by his word to enforce his laws, including those on *maiestas*. The noun is often translated into English as 'treason'. Nowadays it refers to the crime of betraying one's own country, especially by attempting to kill or overthrow the sovereign or government. However, to a Roman of the time of Augustus or Tiberius, *maiestas* could include inciting rebellion as well as committing libel or even adultery if it affronted 'the majesty of the Roman People'.

A troubling issue in Tiberius' day was the abuse of the law by *delatores*, the informers who brought cases to court in the hope of winning them for a significant share of the condemned's estate.[162] Men like Romanus Hispo and Fulcinius Trio were motivated by money, and their work practices verged on unethical in pursuit of it. The absence of a body to enforce the law and defend the interests of the *Res Publica* – equivalent to a justice department, state attorney or the Crown Prosecution Service – meant this route was increasingly used to bring such cases to court. Under Tiberius, the Senate began to exercise its jurisdictional power over *maiestas* on a greater scale than previously, finally replacing the courts (*quaestiones*) of the praetors in trying these offences. The exact tally of cases of *maiestas* litigated under Tiberius is not known, but based on those reported by Tacitus, the number of individuals impacted by these charges was relatively small. During the entirety of Tiberius' principate, no more than fifty-two people were accused of *maiestas*.[163] Of them, nearly half were *not* found guilty of the charge. Moreover, the four people who were innocent but still condemned were not the victims of Tiberius' wrath but of the Senate's fervour. Contrary to the impression left by Dio and Tacitus, the alleged rivers of blood ran shallow. Eight of the twelve individuals who were executed at his request were clearly guilty.[164] Shocked by the speed with which the Senate issued its guilty verdict and carried out the sentence of death on the poet Clutorius Priscus in 21 CE, whom he might have pardoned if given the chance, Tiberius initiated the *Senatus Consultum* requiring an interval of ten days between conviction and execution. These prosecutions largely impacted the members of the senatorial class, who resented Tiberius for it and whose descendants wrote the histories with that prejudice. Tiberius' assertion that it was better to subvert the constitution than to remove its guardians explained why he personally supported rewarding *delatores* after the trial of C. Vibius Serenus (I) in 24 CE. However, it served only to encourage more scurrilous prosecutions.

Better yet would have been to apply higher standards to admissible evidence for probable cause before *delatores* could bring charges. Some changes were, indeed, made. A *Senatus Consultum* extending the *Lex Cornelia de Falsis* covering the forgery and suppression of wills was issued in 16, 20 or 29 CE, and the decree on the criminal trial of slaves and use of their testimony was published in 20 CE. Faced with accusations of *maiestas*, the law on inheritance incentivized those with a weak defence to commit suicide in order to protect their estates by allowing them to be passed down to family rather than confiscated. Tiberius recognized that the Roman legal system was deeply flawed in cases of *maiestas*: to reduce the number of legal actions without merit, Tiberius issued an order in 33 CE that the most notorious of the *delatores* should be executed in a single day, which earned him praise from members of the Senate.

Nevertheless, corrupt officials – especially those indulging in *repetundae* – discovered that they worked under a regime willing to hold them to account. Tiberius set a high standard of performance for himself, and was keen for all those working in the service of the Roman People to similarly give of their best. Using his non-binding *commendatio*, Tiberius often proposed the best-qualified candidates for election; invariably, the Senate followed his lead and voted them into office, though there were others to choose from.[165] Tiberius was resistant to Asinius Gallus' proposal to elect praetors five years in advance, among other ideas, on the basis that it would destroy the existing – and fully functional – system, but also because it would put him in the uncomfortable position of affronting potential candidates.[166] The sentence of exile was frequently imposed on offending citizens, and a new rule disallowing them to write wills was established, but as in the case of Volcatius Moschus he respected legal precedent. Tiberius believed that the punishment should fit the crime. For example, he demanded the return of Iunius Gallio to Rome to be kept under house arrest because his destination of exile, Lesbos, was considered too luxurious. However, he was quite willing to offer his *clementia*, as in the trial of Cn. Piso (II), where he intervened to save the condemned man's son from the harshest of penalties since he was not to blame for his father's poor judgment. This virtue was paired with his widely recognized quality of *moderatio*.[167]

It was tricky for Tiberius to navigate the line between encouraging and intervening in the independence of the Senate. Aware of the impact of his influence, he often refused to vote first, as was his privilege as *princeps Senatus*, lest it bias subsequent votes. He was genuinely delighted that there was disagreement over which candidate should be elected as *praetor* to replace Vipstanus Gallus in 17 CE, seeing it as evidence that the Senate was becoming a deliberative body as it used to be. But this was a brief moment of autonomy. Tiberius was even prepared to assist men at risk of losing their senatorial privilege, helping M. Hortalus with cash. To his great dismay, the Senate seemed unwilling to fully grasp the chance to regain its historical role as the preeminent law-giving body of the *Res Publica*.[168] Tiberius worked in earnest with the Senate and approached the institution with respect. He was genuinely hurt when he learned of the insults directed at him in secret which were revealed in the testimony of Aemilius during the trial of Votienus Montanus of Narbo in 25 CE. His instinctual response was to defend his good name and subsequently to lash out by issuing harsh sentences in other cases. Yet if the Senate was to be allowed to make its own independent determinations, that meant accepting it would make mistakes and sometimes be disrespectful to him.

In the first years of Tiberius' principate, it seemed there was a real prospect that he could resign as *princeps* and finally retire. He was actively mentoring Germanicus for *principatus*. Authorizing him to conduct wars in Germania and later posting him to the East in the role of an overseer of the governors, these were assignments consistent with broadening the younger man's experience. Had Germanicus lived, it is possible that Tiberius might have abdicated in favour of his adopted son a decade later, when Germanicus would have been in his early 40s. His premature death in 19 CE created the opportunity for his own son, Drusus, to assume the preeminent position as national leader. Again, it is possible that Tiberius might have abdicated in favour of his natural son when Drusus would have been in his early 40s. His murder in 23 CE left Tiberius with the sons of Germanicus – Nero Caesar, Drusus Caesar and Caius Caligula – and two twin grandsons who were still babies. Then aged 64, he faced never being able to withdraw from government, a realization that must have been crushing.

Tiberius made his decision to leave Rome permanently three years later, being encouraged to do so by L. Aelius Seianus.[169] Promoting Seianus to the rank of *praetor* and then treating him as his *socius labrorum* was a practical, and initially non-political, way for Tiberius to manage the unending flow of administrative work generated by a worldwide empire. Tiberius trusted him above all others to carry out his instructions in his absence.[170] As a military man like himself, and briefed by his network of informers, Seianus could give him reliable information on a range of matters. Seianus had been associated with the imperial family as commander of the *Cohortes Praetoriae* providing personal security for Drusus to the Danube during the mutiny of 14 CE, and even physically protecting Tiberius when rocks fell on him in the cave at *Spelunca* in 26 CE. He had also used his initiative to stop the spread of fire in Rome in 21 CE. Seianus was Tiberius' partner for seventeen years, during which time his power and influence grew. From the mid-20s CE, Seianus increasingly had the role of a gatekeeper in Tiberius' life, controlling what he was told and by whom. Eventually, Seianus was seen by many in the Senate as the primary decision maker in Rome, eclipsing Tiberius himself. Seianus clearly enjoyed wielding power. Whether Tiberius was aware of his deputy's manipulations is unclear, and some now doubt there was ever a conspiracy conceived by him to oust Tiberius.[171] He may have been trying to position himself for *principatus*, intending to follow after his commander. Coming from an old family, Tiberius could sometimes be a snob. When Seianus asked the hand of Tiberius' niece, Drusilla, in marriage, he was politely refused, yet the marriage in 21 CE of Seianus' daughter by Apicata to Claudius' son brought him into the imperial family. The impression created by Tacitus, however, is that Seianus was so ambitious for power that he became a traitor. The evidence, such as it is, does point to Seianus being behind the downfall of Drusus Caesar and Nero Caesar, along with their mother. When Tiberius discovered Seianus' conspiracies against the family of Germanicus, as he wrote in his biography, he rationally and meticulously planned – in the usual way he prepared his military operations – to defeat and capture his opponent.[172] The Senate, not Tiberius, took the decision to execute him. The later revelation of Seianus' complicity in the death of his son, nevertheless, must have been deeply painful to Tiberius.

Matters of state demanded Tiberius' attention, and he responded to them. Despite leaving for Capreae, he could never retire from public life, a fact noted by Plutarch. He would occasionally return to the mainland with the intention of going to Rome. Following the demise of Seianus, the Senate took steps to ensure his personal safety so that he could attend sessions without fear. In 36 CE, he stayed at a villa just 4 miles from the city. Letters now passed between him and the Senate in just hours. Yet something prevented him from crossing the *pomerium*. It was surely not his personal security. Perhaps, having moved to his island home, he had become accustomed to operating remotely, a workstyle which afforded him the luxury of time to consider issues, discuss them with his friends and carefully formulate his written responses. Perhaps, having worked ceaselessly and thanklessly for years on end, he may simply have decided to prioritize his own wellbeing and assert what has come, in our times, to be called 'work-life balance'. Having a private life was vitally important to Tiberius. In his final attempt to force the Senate to function independently of him, in 33 CE, he insisted on set 'office hours' when senators were expected to conduct their business. However, in practice its workflow was interrupted by pauses while it waited for Tiberius' rescripts. In constant fear of actions brought by *delatores* and traumatized by years of terror under Seianus and the brutal reprisals which followed, senators were no longer willing to take risks. Inadvertently, under Tiberius, the Senate became an even more subservient institution than it was under Augustus.[173]

Just as Augustus had wrestled with the question of who would lead the Roman People after him, so Tiberius faced the same dilemma. By 33 CE, his best candidates (Germanicus and Drusus) *and* his next-best (Nero Caesar and Drusus Caesar) were all dead. He likely never wanted to be an autocrat and have to daily balance his own authority and that of the Senate.[174] Acting out of *pietas*, he was unwilling to look beyond the family of Augustus. This left him with two choices: his grandson by Drusus, Ti. Gemellus, and his adopted grandson by Germanicus, Caius Caligula. His solution was to name them in his will as joint heirs with equal shares of his estate, the implication being they could rule *together* just as did the two annually elected consuls. However, neither young man had the training or experience to be *princeps*, shortcomings that were largely down to Tiberius himself. Supported by Macro, the ambitious *praefectus Praetorio*, Caligula seized the initiative in Misenum. The Senate obsequiously acknowledged him in Rome. If restoring the *Res Publica* was predicated on the consuls having their traditional powers of government, as Tiberius indicated on several occasions he wished to see, he did not fully reinstate them; but if Tiberius had hoped the consuls would find the courage to grab back control *after* his death, he would have been disappointed.[175] Within a year, Ti. Gemellus was dead, either by suicide or assassination – the ancient sources give differing accounts. The son of Germanicus now ruled without a rival and he was popular, at least for a while. Thus, Tiberius' decision unintentionally affirmed Rome as a dynastic autocracy. Remarkably, it would endure for centuries.

## Tiberius' Domestic and Foreign Policies

Key to understanding Tiberius is to see him first and foremost as a soldier, and specifically as a deputy of Augustus. For decades, Tiberius served him as a military commander with total commitment and selfless dedication, and in that role he thrived. His instincts were those of an officer. When he issued an order, he expected it to be executed, and in the chaos of battle he relied on his officers to use their initiative to complete their mission. He brought the insights of military leadership to his role as *princeps*, but his challenge was to work in concert with the civil institutions and to negotiate with their often antagonistic constituents.

Mutinies among citizen legions stationed in Germania Inferior and Pannonia inaugurated his principate in September 14 CE, when he was most vulnerable. It was an inauspicious start. As *legatus Augusti propraetore* recently imbued by Tiberius with *imperium proconsulare*, Germanicus sped to the bases of the legions on the Rhine to face down the mutineers. Responding to the governor's call for assistance, Tiberius sent Drusus to the camps on the Danube. The cause of the discontent in both cases was abuse of their terms and conditions of employment by their officers.[176] Men were serving well beyond their contracted years of service. Active campaigning, with its potential for war spoils, had given way to pacification duties and boredom. Heavy-handed enforcement of discipline caused resentment in the ranks. Both sons of Tiberius proved their unswerving loyalty to him and negotiated settlements with the troops. Their actions de-escalated the protests and restored discipline and morale. Civil war was averted. Tiberius consented to improving the legionaries' pay, but later rescinded the reduction in years of service.

Tiberius understood the highs and lows of military life. As a life-long soldier, he won the respect and loyalty of the rank and file. In military matters, disciple was key. At Andetrium in 9 CE, his troops were demoralized, but he addressed them, giving out rebukes and admonitions, and, with their old discipline restored, he led them to victory. He enforced his rules on packing light for the crossing into Germania the following year, inspecting each soldier's baggage before letting them proceed. Stern but fair, his men loved him for it. Paterculus was witness to the enthusiastic reception Tiberius received from veterans who had served with him. They had seen first-hand how concerned he was about their welfare, even providing his carriage to ferry wounded men from the battlefield. Army life suited his temperament. Among professional soldiers, he felt he belonged. Between 26 BCE and 14 CE, Tiberius learned, then proved, his capabilities as a field commander. Augustus could count on him to get the job done, in whichever theatre of war he sent him. By the time Tiberius became *princeps*, he had spent over half of his life on active campaign (Table 2).[177] Most of those years were spent on counterinsurgency or pacification operations – wars of necessity rather than of choice. These experiences shaped how he determined military strategy and policy as supreme commander. He had begun his career as a *tribunus militum* 'of the broad stripe' in the Cantabrian-Asturian War when just 16 years old. In this position, Tiberius had the opportunity to learn the arts of war by observing the legates, prefects, centurions and soldiers. That was the Roman way. The next time he took a military assignment, he was 20 years old, when Augustus assigned him the extraordinarily high-profile responsibility as leader of a mission negotiating for the return of Roman insignia and prisoners from the Parthians. M. Agrippa may have done the detailed groundwork, but sealing the deal still required deftness and maturity. Tiberius accomplished the task with distinction. From this adventure he learned that diplomacy, backed by military force, could in some instances achieve policy objectives. As *princeps*, it would be his preferred approach. 'Tiberius showed more pleasure at having kept the peace by diplomacy than if he had concluded a war by a series of stricken fields,' writes Tacitus.[178]

In the Alps, in 15 BCE, he worked in collaboration with his brother, Nero Drusus, and together they seized Raetia, Noricum and Vindelicia, to great acclaim.[179] For Tiberius it was a valuable hands-on lesson, both in the value of meticulous planning before a campaign and in deploying combined military operations. In 12 BCE, in Agrippa's footsteps, Tiberius went to Illyricum on what would be the first of many tours of duty in the region, with the task of pacifying peoples presumed conquered. Mountainous terrain limited the scope for set-piece battles, disadvantaging Tiberius' army. Guerilla warfare would test the 30-year-old, but he was prepared, having seen it years before in Asturia or Cantabria. There were victories for the Romans and, as in Raetia, forced relocations of men of military age for the defeated, while others were enrolled in auxiliary units. When Nero Drusus died on campaign in 9 BCE, Augustus appointed Tiberius to finish the conquest of Germania. He spent several years of his third decade in action across the Rhine and Danube rivers attempting to subjugate the many adversarial nations, while maintaining the loyalty of Rome's few remaining allies there. Forests and rivers made progress difficult. His tenacity would earn Tiberius two imperatorial acclamations. In January 7 BCE, Tiberius' achievement in Germania was recognized with an ovation. He would return to Germania in 4 CE to defeat the rebellious Bructeri and re-enforce the alliance with the wavering Cherusci. A year later, he was marching deep into Germania and was one of the few Romans ever to gaze across the Elbe River.

More complex was the mission to neutralize Maroboduus, a former ally turned threat. Tiberius conceived an elaborate three-pronged invasion of Bohaemium in 6 CE with a taskforce that was one of the largest ever assembled by Rome. The columns of troops had just crossed the Danube when they were halted by a revolt in Illyricum. Once again, Tiberius returned to the Western Balkans to lead counterinsurgency operations. Germanicus would also take part, embarking on the first miliary campaign of his career. The war was another test of Tiberius' mettle. It started off badly; he was trapped in Siscia for almost two years and forced to rely on army groups from neighbouring provinces which were free to move around and engage with the enemy. Four years passed before the men of Illyricum finally succumbed. When dealing with revolts in Germania and Illyricum, Tiberius employed violence to enforce submission in the quest for a more perfect union between Roman and subject. When the people there rose up, he fought back hard. Counterinsurgency operations did not break the resistance, however, and year after year the people of the Balkans rebelled. Heavy-handed treatment by the Romans failed to produce the desired results. Eventually, Tiberius realized the futility of this policy. Bato of the Daesidiates told him in a farming metaphor that the Romans themselves were to blame for the uprising because they had sent wolves to protect their flocks, not sheepdogs or shepherds.[180] To finally pacify the region, it took a willingness on the part of Tiberius to pivot his view and see the natives as partners, rather than as adversaries. Showing his *clementia* by pardoning Bato in 9 CE was the turning point. He decided that a light touch was now prudent, even advising his legates in a line echoing Bato: 'It is the part of a good shepherd to shear, not flay, his sheep.'[181] It proved good advice. In time, Illyricum, through its derivatives Dalmatia and Pannonia, would become prosperous, producing agricultural products, iron, silver and gold, as well as hardy men for the legions – and even emperors.[182]

In military matters, Tiberius was never impulsive or rash. In the aftermath of the *Clades Variana* of 9 CE, he bided his time. In 10 and 11 CE, he led an expeditionary force over the Rhine. The goal was not reconquest, however, but rather to assert that Romans could still enter the region at will. To emphasize the point, games were held on German soil in honour of Augustus' birthday. Again, a show of force was deployed rather than actual violence. He would never again take to the field. When a revolt broke out in the *Tres Galliae* in 13 CE, Germanicus was already in command of the army on the Rhine and able to squash the uprising. Germania beyond the Rhine remained problematic, however.

As *princeps*, Tiberius focused on sustaining what he had inherited, in keeping with Augustus' wise counsel. For the majority of his principate, Augustus was absorbed in extending Roman power and influence beyond the border (*finis*) of its empire, and pacifying the lands within it; indeed, it was the stated justification for position in the *Res Publica*, and how he held on to power.[183] It was for Augustus that the poet Vergil coined the phrase *imperium sine fine* ('empire [or power] without a border [or end]').[184] Only in his final years, after decades of spilled blood and squandered treasure, did he advocate for containment. Before his death, Augustus had offered the counsel (*consilium*) 'advising the restriction of the empire within its present frontiers'.[185] Tacitus explains: 'The ocean and remote rivers were the boundaries of the empire – the legions, provinces, fleets, all things were linked together.'[186] For Tiberius, the guiding principle (*praeceptum*) – in effect, the grand strategy – was *imperium cum fine*. It was a much less exciting task offering little glory to its new imperial guardian, but it was one with which he was familiar. It had been the recurring theme of his military career. Ever the armchair general, Tacitus accuses Tiberius of being 'a *princeps* indifferent [or careless] about enlarging the empire'.[187] It is a mischaracterization. Tiberius understood military might, but he also understood the limits of military might. Tiberius followed the spirit of Augustus' *consilium*, even if he did not always follow the letter of it. He was a realist.

Tiberius certainly knew about conquest, but he understood containment. Deterrence was a strategy later memorably articulated by Vegetius Renatus as 'who desires peace, prepares for war'.[188] To that end, Tiberius sustained Augustus' standing army. He continued to pay for it through a 5 per cent tax on inheritances and bequests and a 1 per cent duty on auctioned goods, which had been imposed in 6 CE, even though it was a cause of protest by many people.[189] He maintained the deployments of the twenty-five legions virtually unchanged from 14 CE, where they defended the border delineated by the Rhine, Danube, Euphrates, Nile and Sahara Desert (Table 1).[190] On a network of high-quality roads, soldiers could march anywhere to deal with a crisis, as demonstrated in the wars in Illyricum (6–9 CE) or Africa Proconsularis (17–24 CE). Maintaining discipline and readiness for action were paramount. Crucially, Tiberius respected the chain of command as the basis of enforcing that discipline. He rebuked several proconsuls in command of armies because they did not present their reports (*res gestae*) to the Senate.[191] He appreciated the power of rewards and distinctions, having received seven acclamations of *imperator* (Table 4) himself and earned three curule triumphs (Table 5). He was greatly annoyed with his legates who failed to use their authority to recognize individual troops for acts of valour and instead referred to him for permission.[192] In the provinces, his deputies were semi-autonomous, imbued with the power to command (*imperium*) derived from his that came with their rank. Each led professional army units – legions and auxiliaries – with which to carry out his duty (*provincia*). As commander-in-chief, Tiberius did not take to the field in person; he did not need to. His handpicked legates were expected to fight his wars for him, just as Tiberius had done for his commander-in-chief, Augustus. Tiberius told the Senate before he was appointed *princeps* that the soldiers who accompanied him to the *Curia* did not belong to him personally, but to the *Res Publica*.[193] Suetonius notes that Tiberius consulted the Senate 'about levying and disbanding the soldiers, and the disposal of the legionaries and auxiliaries; [and] finally, about the extension of military commands and appointments to the conduct of wars'.[194] These were budgetary and manpower issues. Overturning a concession, which was key to ending the mutinies of the legions on the Danube

Table 4: Tiberius' Imperatorial Acclamations

| Acclamations | Year | Campaign | Notes |
|---|---|---|---|
| I | 10/9 BCE | Illyricum ('Pannonian War') | Declined, 1 |
| II | 8 | Germania | |
| III | 5 CE | Germania | |
| IV | 8 | Illyricum ('Batonian War') | |
| V | 9 | Illyricum | 1 |
| VI | 11 | Germania | |
| VII | 13 | Germania | 1 |
| VIII | 16 | Germania | 1 |

Sources: Dio; Suetonius; Tacitus; Swan (2004), p.365; Vervaet (2020).
Notes: 1. Sandys & Campbell (1927), p.235, argue for (I) 9 BCE, (V) 10–11 CE, (VII) 14 CE and (VIII) 21 CE.

and Rhine in 14 CE, the following year Tiberius mandated that legionaries must serve twenty years to qualify for honourable discharge (*honesta missio*); this was because the *Aerarium* could not afford the cost of shorter careers. It was out of frustration in 33 CE that he wrote to the Senate complaining that all the men suited for military command were refusing to serve, and that he was forced to plead with them to reconsider.[195] There were also legates and military tribunes for the legions and prefects of the auxiliary units who Tiberius had to personally appoint, as Augustus had done.

However, he would not tolerate interference in matters of security, which he regarded as his domain. It was offensive to Tiberius because it disregarded the chain of command. He discontinued Augustus' practice of publishing the accounts of the empire, which included the disposition of the army, ensuring he had control of it.[196] These were strategic issues for which he and his legates were responsible. In 23 CE he was again concerned about replacing troops leaving the army; finding the new recruits from among volunteers to be both insufficient in number and of poor suitability, he proposed conscription. Iunius Gallio's request

Table 5: Tiberius' Triumphal Ornaments, Ovations and Triumphs.

| Year | Date | Campaign | Award |
|---|---|---|---|
| 12 BCE (declined by Augustus) | ? | Illyricum | *Ornamenta* |
| 11 BCE | ? | Illyricum | *Ornamenta* |
| 9 BCE | ? | Illyricum | *Ovatio* |
| 7 BCE | 1 January | Germania | *Triumphus* |
| 7 CE | 1 January | Germania | *Triumphus* |
| 9 CE, postponed to 12 CE | 23 October | Illyricum ('Batonian War') | *Triumphus* |

Sources: Dio; Suetonius; Tacitus; Vervaet (2020).
Notes: Jer., *Chron.* mentions a triumph in 10 BCE for victories over the Pannonii and another in 6 BCE for the Raeti, Vindelici, Armeniae and Pannonii.

for special treatment of veterans of the Praetorian Cohorts in 32 CE hit a raw nerve, and the ex-soldier was severely reprimanded. The *Praetoriani* had done very well under Tiberius. Continuing Augustus' policy, their pay was higher than the regular legionaries received, their length of service was shorter and they were based in Italy – indeed, these were contributing factors in causing the mutinies of 14 CE. Whereas there had been two commanders of the *Cohortes Praetoriae* under Augustus, under Tiberius there was just one. An unforeseen consequence of this decision was that the *praefectus praetorio* would come to exert great influence in deciding who would be the future leaders of Rome, beginning with Caius Caligula. In 22 CE, Tiberius acceded to Seianus' recommendation of co-locating in a single *castrum* the Praetorians, previously billeted around the city, with the *Cohortes Urbanae*. A measure to improve operational efficiency, it also meant that a strong military presence was now highly visible close to Rome. The *Vigiles*, for practical reasons, continued to be dispersed in each of the city's fourteen *vici*.

Wherever Tiberius was based, that was the *praetorium* from which he could administer all aspects of military matters and public affairs. After 27 CE, Capreae was the *de facto* strategic high command headquarters. The location of the *Villa Iovis* on Capraea and its adjacent lighthouse looking towards Misenum suggest that Tiberius intended to be accessible, not disconnected. Swift Liburnians of the nearby *Classis Misenensis* continually brought letters and reports detailing the concerns of the empire to his island retreat, even if they were first filtered by his deputy (up to October 31 CE). His rescripts could be delivered to a legate anywhere via this fleet, which could reach any port in the Mediterranean, thence overland by road, relayed by *cursus publicus* at the speed of a galloping horse.[197]

Guarding the empire's borders was not a passive activity. There were allies to sustain, some located beyond the border, and threats to contain. The Romans had turned enemies into friends for centuries, making them *socii* ('allies') or *clientes* ('clients') under their patronage.[198] Suetonius notes that, 'Kings who were ill-affected towards him, he kept in subjection, more by menaces and remonstrances, than by force of arms.'[199] The Roman Army did not have to be located in these places to have an impact. There were notable achievements with this approach. Under Tiberius, the former allied kingdoms of Cappadocia and Commagene became provinces. The pro-Roman monarch, Artaxias, was installed on the throne of Armenia. Maroboduus upheld his treaty obligations, keeping the Marcomanni out of conflict with the Romans. Raiskuporis of Thrace provided Tiberius with military assistance during the uprising in the Western Balkans. To retake the lands across the Rhine carelessly lost by Varus, Tiberius permitted Germanicus to try and capture Arminius. After two seasons of active campaigning, he assessed that the costs of this war of choice outweighed the benefits. At the end of 17 CE, when Germanicus requested a troop surge, Tiberius refused. Having spent several years of his own life in combat there, the commander-in-chief knew better than anyone the futility of expending additional effort. The Suebi and Sugambri no longer representing an existential thread to the security of the *Tres Galliae* and less powerful tribes now taking their places on the border, and treaties with the powerful Batavi and Marcommani remaining in force, Tiberius calculated that the Germanic tribes could be largely left to resolve their own internal disputes without direct Roman intervention. Germania was thus quietly abandoned, although Rome would still exert its influence across the Rhine through proxy wars and trade. However, when the Frisii (allies since Nero Drusus negotiated a treaty in 12 BCE) rebelled against increased tribute demands in 28 CE and killed a cohort of soldiers, the commander of *Legio* V *Alaudae* dealt with it, albeit at the cost of many casualties. Tiberius' preference was always for diplomacy, or as his critic writes, he was 'faithful to his rule of manipulating foreign affairs by policy and craft without a resort to arms'.[200] Diplomacy with Artabanus of Parthia established peace in the East until it was briefly interrupted in 34 CE. As circumstances changed, Tiberius was willing to adapt to uphold Rome's security interests. On Rome's international border with Armenia and Parthia, L. Vitellius engaged in a war of choice (35–36 CE) authorized by Tiberius. As soon as the campaign was successfully executed and Mithridates of Iberia was installed, Vitellius withdrew. His victory restored the *status quo ante* between the two superpowers, going back to the time when, over half a century earlier, Tiberius himself had received the military insignia lost during several failed Roman expeditions against Parthia.

Maintaining Rome's control *within* the borders of the Roman Empire often entailed the unpleasant, and sometimes inglorious, work of pacification. There were several violent uprisings during Tiberius' principate. Cn. Calpurnius Piso (II)'s bizarre attempt to seize back control of Syria with an army of renegades in 19 CE was dealt with both on the battlefield and in the *Curia*. To inform future generations, a copy of the Senate's ruling on the trial in bronze was sent to every major city and army base in the empire.[201] The counterinsurgency operations against Tacfarinas in Africa (17–24 CE) took four different *legati* (three recognized with triumphal honours approved by the Senate), but concluded with the bonus addition of Numidia to Mauretania within the *imperium* of the Roman People. Similarly, the war in Illyricum (6–9 CE) required the direct assistance of several legates and their armies from neighbouring provinces working together in co-ordinated combat operations to stamp out the rebellion. In both the Western Balkans and Northwest Africa Tiberius' commanders had to adapt the standard Roman military doctrine of deploying large formations in campaigns of successive set-piece battles, by breaking their legions and auxiliaries into smaller tactical units to overcome their adversaries fighting guerilla style in multiple, concurrent skirmishes or sieges. The combined revolt of the Aedui led by Sacrovir ('Holy Man', perhaps a druid) and the Belgae by Iulius Florus (21 CE), the levies in

Thracia (25–26 CE) and the Clitae (36 CE) all required significant military intervention, but order was restored. In Hispania Tarraconensis, the peasant from the Termestini nation who, operating alone, had attacked Tiberius' *legatus Augusti propraetore*, was eventually captured through basic police work.[202] In Italy, the remarkable attempt at a revolt by slaves led by a recalcitrant Praetorian guardsman in 24 CE was quashed by the swift action of local officials faithfully carrying out their civic duties. When they asked for military assistance, Tiberius unhesitatingly dispatched it.

The result of Tiberius' policy was that under his aegis, the Roman Empire was more secure than ever. It was quite a feat. Far from 'indifferent' or 'careless', as Tacitus would have it, Tiberius was heedful, indeed, *careful*. His successors would try again to expand the limits of Roman power through conquest, and some were successful.[203] It was Hadrian, the other great student of Augustus, however, who saw the folly of this and restored the first emperor's policy upon his accession almost exactly a century after Tiberius.[204]

Tiberius delegated war fighting to his hand-picked *legati Augusti*. Imperative for Tiberius was to choose the best men for the job. He held his deputies to high standards of conduct and enforced Rome's laws to ensure good governance. *Imperium* came with responsibility. The trials against corrupt officials show that he was willing to prosecute in the public interest. Unlike Augustus, who rotated his *legati* in his provinces every three years, Tiberius retained his deputies in position for extended terms. The logic of a short tenure was that a man took the first year to learn the job, the second year to perform it and the final year to prepare his return to Rome, thus providing insufficient opportunity for the politically ambitious to plot against the *princeps*. Tacitus, always reading sinister intent into the policy of Tiberius, writes:

> Various reasons are given for this. Some say it was the weary dislike of recurring trouble which caused him to treat a decision once made as eternally valid; others that he grudged to see too many men enjoying promotion. There are those who believe that as his intellect was shrewd, so his judgment was hesitant; for, on the one hand, he did not seek out preeminent virtue, and, on the other, he detested vice. The best he feared as a private danger, the worst as a public scandal. In the end, this vacillation carried him so far that he assigned provinces to men whom he had no intention of allowing to leave Rome.[205]

The reality was more prosaic: there was a shortage of men qualified for key government positions. In 16 CE, Tiberius had to dispatch some ex-quaestors who had already served the previous year to take up still-vacant posts. Tiberius was a pragmatist. A long tenure gave a governor more time to build deeper relationships with local communities, while making it less likely that he would cheat them, resulting in greater stability in his province.[206] P. Cornelius Dolabella was in charge of Dalmatia for nearly six years (14–19 CE), L. Apronius in Germania Inferior for a decade (28–37 CE), C. Calvisius Sabinus in Pannonia for almost twenty-two years while C. Poppaeus Sabinus governed Achaea-Macedonia-Moesia for twenty-four years (15–35 CE).[207] Tiberius-appointee Valerius Gratus (15–26 CE) had served eleven years as *Praefectus Iudaeae* before being replaced by Pontius Pilatus (26–36 CE, fig. 46).[208] Though increasing the risk of creating a challenger with an army to back him, in practice no usurpers emerged to confront Tiberius during his principate. Even Lentulus Gaetulicus, who had a tight hold on the officers and men of the legions stationed in Germania Superior (29–39 CE), turned to Tiberius when threatened by accusers in 34 CE; Tacitus suggests a *quid pro quo* was involved, with the arrangement suiting both men.[209] Confidence in the commander-in-chief was the crucial factor, and it was felt in the lowest ranks too. The *nautae* – a unit of auxiliary marines of the fleet or boatmen on the Seine River – erected a pillar in Lutetia (modern Paris) in a devotional display of loyalty to Jupiter Optimus Maximus *and* Tiberius.[210]

Trust (*fides*) extended beyond the military into the civic space. As *princeps*, his duty required him to work with diverse peoples and communities which were under Rome's sway. For a Roman citizen living in the provinces facing a capital charge, he was the last court of appeal. For a non-Roman, he was the ultimate arbitrator. Tiberius despised corrupt or incompetent officials – like Lucilius Capito (Asia), Caesius Cordus (Creta and Cyrene), C. Vibius Serenus (I) (Hispania Tarraconensis) and Pomponius Labeo (Moesia) – and held them to account. Deputations and petitions from Achaea, Cyprus, Gallia Narbonensis, Kos and Sicilia sought Tiberius' advice on a range of issues, from

Figure 46. The names of Tiberius Caesar and Pontius Pilatus appear in Greek letters on this *prutah* minted in Hierosolyma (Jerusalem), Iudaea.

Figure 47. Tiberius' virtue of *MODERATIO* – 'self-restraint' – is celebrated on the reverse of this coin.

disputes over temple dedications to appeals from exiles, each community trusting in the impartiality and wisdom of their *princeps*. Public messaging supported and encouraged this belief. The mint in Rome struck coins drawing attention to Tiberius' virtues or topical themes (Appendix 2(a)). During the first decade of his principate, coins celebrated his *MODERATIO* (fig. 47), *CLEMENTIA* (fig. 48) and *IVSTITIA* (fig. 49). Tiberius' foresight was acknowledged on coins bearing the legend *PROVIDENTIA* (fig. 50) on the reverse with *Divus* Augustus *Pater* on the obverse, implying, as his antecedent had done decades before, that he was the son of a god. His *PIETAS* (fig. 51) was recognized in connection with respect for tradition, Augustus and his brother. Issued in low denominations, these coins circulated at relatively high velocity via cash transactions at markets

Figure 48. Tiberius' virtue of *CLEMENTIA* – 'mildness' – is celebrated on the reverse of this coin.

Figure 49. Tiberius' mother represents *IVSTITIA*, the personified Roman deity of justice, on the obverse of this coin.

and bars, ensuring that people saw them in their hands. Some types were replicated in communities across the empire, spreading the messaging far and wide (Appendix 2(b)).

Tiberius knew the value of money. Suetonius writes that 'there was no matter of public or private business so small or so great that he did not lay it out before the senators, consulting them about revenues and monopolies, constructing and restoring public buildings.'[211] Tiberius did not skimp on key expenditures. He was acutely aware, as a former *quaestor*, that feeding the poor people of Rome their daily bread was essential to maintaining public order, and he worked to increase supply. When, in 19 CE, the price of a *modius* of wheat rose, he introduced a subsidy of HS 2.[212] Germanicus' unauthorized visit to Egypt that year and his

Figure 50. The obverse shows *DIVVS AVGVSTVS PATER* and a profile of 'Father Divine Augustus' in a radiate crown. *PROVIDENT[IA]* alludes to the foresight of his son Tiberius as well of the Roman gods.

Figure 51. Tiberius' mother represents *PIETAS*, the personified Roman deity of duty to one's country or parents or other blood relations, on the obverse of this coin.

opening of the granaries to starving Alexandrians put the supply chain of the *annona* at risk and earned him a sternly worded reprimand from Tiberius. When the Tiber burst its banks in 15 CE, flooding the warehouses where the grain was stored, Tiberius established a commission to investigate ways to prevent future inundations. The Senate voted against its recommendations after assessing the impact on towns along the Tiber. It was too important an issue to leave to chance. Tiberius then set up a permanent commission to manage the river.

On the occasions of his accession, triumphs or when male members of his extended family reached manhood, Tiberius was generous in his cash *donativa* ('gifts') and edible *prandia* ('lunches') to the people. However, he despised frivolity and detested waste. He was not a fan of men wearing Chinese silks. In helping communities in Asia damaged by earthquakes in 17 CE to rebuild, however, he exhibited his *munificentia* ('generosity') and *liberalitas* ('kindness'). In recognition of it, the *augustales* of Puteoli (Pozzuoli) offered him their thanks by raising a statue.[213] He generously compensated people after fire destroyed their homes on the Caelius in Rome in 27 CE and the many victims hurt in the collapse of the amphitheatre at Fidenae in the same year, for which he was rightly praised, and he did so again when fire afflicted *Mons* Aventinus nine years later. In terms of public order, he knew that providing entertainment was as essential as bread, even if he did not sponsor many events himself.[214] Thus, he restored public buildings, such as the Theatre of Pompeius damaged by fire in 21 CE and the *Circus Maximus* when it burned in 36 CE. Following Tiberius' example, future Roman emperors would show their willingness to offer financial assistance to their fellow citizens in times of natural disaster, demonstrating their solidarity with the People and patronage of them.[215] Tax collecting was still the responsibility of *procuratores* in the Provinces of Caesar, but *equites* operated as licenced *publicani* ('tax farmers') in the Provinces of the People since senators were barred from commercial activities.[216] Tiberius was mindful of abuses which might arise. The heavy-handed way higher-quality hides were demanded from the Frisii, seemingly on the whim of a centurion, was costly in lives and upset an ally.

Tiberius' apparent frugality in public spending was in contrast to his predecessor, who claimed he had left him a city of marble.[217] The many wars of Augustus brought in new capital – material and human – as well as flows of tax revenue and tribute. He and his deputies spent money building aqueducts, forums, libraries, roads, temples and theatres.[218] Waging war was much less of a feature of Tiberius' principate. The implied relative cut in spending on infrastructure and entertainments may have been a factor culminating in the financial turmoil of 33 CE.[219] The other was that Italy had become a net importer of goods, which pulled money out of the local economy to pay for them. Augustus' high expenditures, and those of the ultra-rich, contributed to price inflation. Tiberius imposed limits on price increases on furniture and bar food in 22 CE, a policy which was passed to the Senate to regulate. Over the next decade, liquidity became tight and money lenders started to raise interest rates on loans. The Senate's decision to reaffirm Iulius Caesar's investment law in 33 CE provoked a full-blown economic crisis. Tiberius' solution was to provide cash secured by land in Italy as collateral, with himself standing as lender of last resort. Reflecting the return of confidence, a survey of the number of inscriptions for buildings in Italy suggests they reached a peak under Tiberius.[220]

He also finished many constructions left incomplete by Augustus, such as temples in Rome and the bridge at Ariminum. Generally, he refrained from putting his name on them. The exceptions were the Temple of Castor and the Temple of Concordia, which Tiberius rebuilt, paid for from his share of proceeds from war spoils. Both were very fine examples of public architecture.[221] He liked fine art. In the Temple of Concordia, he installed his own collection of paintings and sculpture for the enjoyment of the Roman People. His interest in architecture extended to private projects too, beginning the tradition of emperors constructing their own purpose-built imperial homes. The *Domus Tiberiana* on the Palatinus and *Villa Iovis* on Capreae were intended for his own use. After Tiberius' death, the *Domus Tiberiana* was repurposed by Claudius for his habitation, with supporting vaults subsequently added to expand its size by Nero, Hadrian and Antoninus Pius.[222] The *Villa Iovis* and the other properties on Capreae, however, were abandoned, eventually falling into decay to be claimed by Nature, until rediscovered in a later millennium.[223]

A very small portion of the population was in regular contact with Tiberius. Beyond the elite in Rome, to other Romans in Italy and in the provinces, he was always a remote figure. They knew him from his profile on the coins and statues, from the dates when he was one of the consuls and the inclusion of his name in liturgies. To him they owed their increasing confidence for transacting their business in a world free of civil strife.[224] In Herculaneum in 37 CE, L. Mammius Maximus willingly erected a statue of Tiberius 'with his own money'.[225] The abundance of coins bearing the portrait of Tiberius minted in *coloniae* and towns in Africa, Asia, Baetica, Hispania Tarraconensis, Macedonia, Syria and elsewhere also illustrates the eagerness of local civil magistrates to associate with the great leader in Rome (Appendix 2(b)). From T. Caecilius Lepidus and C. Aufidius Gemellus, the *duoviri* of *Colonia* Caesaraugusta in Hispania Tarraconensis, to Kleon Agapetos at Apamea in Asia, and from L. Rusticelius Cordus, the *duovir quinquennalis* of *Colonia* Iulia Augusta Diensis in Macedonia, to Megalokles, the *strategos* of the *koinon* of Thessaly, Tiberius was esteemed by many of his aspirational contemporaries in the provinces. The client states, too, were keen to associate with Tiberius; men like Aspurgus I, King of Bosporus on the northern Black Sea – who even bore the Roman name Ti. Iulius Aspurgus Philoromaios ('Lover of Rome'). They were not obligated to, but they chose to. Similarly, intaglios of finger rings (fig. 52, plate 32), cameos (plates 30 and 31) and coins drilled with holes to attach a cord to be worn around the neck, each bearing likenesses of Tiberius, suggest that many individuals sufficiently appreciated him that they wore his image as jewellery.[226] In Egypt, on the island of Philae, the image of Tiberius in the art style peculiar to the country was carved into a wall on the western side of the temple forecourt dedicated to Hathor-Isis in honour of the birth of her son, Horus. It shows Tiberius striking down the enemies before Ha, Isis, Horus and Hathor.[227] The presence of a cult devoted to Tiberius in Baetica and Lusitania, and also a temple dedicated to him in Asia and the request to erect one in Hispania Tarraconensis, illustrate the extent to which some communities were invested in ensuring the well-being of their national leader and courted his blessing. While encouraging the worship of *Divus* Augustus, Tiberius expressly refused divine honours for himself and Augusta in Italy.[228] As he requested, he was never deified.

Figure 52. Impression in modelling clay of the engraved image, which may be the profile of Tiberius, on a gemstone (see plate 32).

Tiberius was not particularly devout. He established the *sodales Augustales* in 14 CE to administer the sacred rites of the cult of *Divus* Augustus and *gens Iulia* to shore up political support for his regime by association as much as for the veneration of the new god through religious worship. While he was tolerant of religious faiths, and delighted in adjudicating over the dedications of historic temples in Asia and Greece, he was sceptical of foreign cults and malevolent influences which could threaten public order. After the revolt of 21 CE, he suppressed the druids of *Tres Galliae*.[229] Two years earlier, followers of the Egyptian mystery cult of Isis and Jews faced expulsion from Rome.[230] The ancient sources seem to conflate these two communities or the events. A Roman woman was tricked by priests dressed as Anubis, and once exposed they were punished, their temple was torn down and the statue of the goddess was tossed into the Tiber. The separate incident of the conversion of the wealthy lady Fulvia to Judaism, in which she was also tricked by four fraudsters from Iudaea, was seen as 'un-Roman'. Some 4,000 Jewish men who bravely refused to reject their faith were shipped to fight bandits in Sardinia to comply with another decree of the Senate, which may have been issued as a collective punishment for the misdemeanours of the four recalcitrants. Seianus is blamed for the removal of Jews, but the only source for his alleged anti-semitism is Philo.[231] Perhaps on account of the antiquity of their religion, Tiberius was generally favourable towards Jews, so long as they did not proselytize outside their social order.[232] Philo reports that, responding to complaints from Jewish residents involving gilded shields placed inside the palace of Herodes in Hierosolyma, Tiberius reprimanded Pilatus and insisted he take them down.[233] The likely cause of the offence were the words referring to the deified Augustus (part of Tiberius' official name), which were written on the shields.[234] The authors of the New Testament texts are generally more predisposed towards the famous Roman prefect appointed by Tiberius than Philo or Josephus.[235] For historians of the emerging sect of Christians, Tiberius was considered a benign figure, the Caesar in whose reign *Christus* had lived and died – and was resurrected.

### *Summa Cum Laude*

Tiberius might not have been the perfect fit temperamentally for the position Augustus created to lead the *Res Publica*, but he was *credible*.[236] In addition to his extensive professional experience and abundant credentials, he displayed the most cherished of Roman virtues, all of which were valuable qualities for a leader whose primary task was to sustain 'the great cycle of ages born anew' established by his predecessor.[327] Continuity was what mattered now. Bar none, Tiberius was the right man for the job at the right time. He used his proven skills in military and diplomatic affairs to avoid war whenever possible. He respected the Senate's independence and recruited competent public administrators. 'It was, in fact, not so much popularity in the present for which he cared as for appreciation in the future,' writes Tacitus.[238] It was just as well, as news of Tiberius' death was met with rejoicing by some people.

'To rule as a Caesar,' writes one modern historian, 'was to stand as an actor upon the great stage of the world.'[239] Visibility was essential to establishing *principatus* in the new *Res Publica*. Augustus understood this and grew into the star role as he aged, frequently attending public events, spending years touring the empire and meeting his fellow citizens, both civilian and military. In contrast, as *princeps*, Tiberius rarely attended public entertainments, preferring to attend to his work, and, despite promising that he would, he never visited the provinces.[240] Tiberius was not a tyrant. For him, national leadership was never about popularity or absolute power; it was always about service, to Augustus and to the *Res Publica*. His primary objective as *princeps* was to enable the machinery of government to function, where necessary enforcing the rules through prosecutions of officials accused of transgressions, even if that made him unpopular with the patrician class. Tiberius was not a reluctant *princeps*. He kept his public and private lives separate, preferring seclusion, conversing with close friends or studying horoscopes, yet he was actively engaged in governing the Roman Commonwealth right to the end.[241]

Concluding his sweeping *Roman History*, a grateful Velleius Paterculus called upon the gods to 'guard, preserve, protect the present state of things, this peace which we enjoy, this *princeps*'.[242] Valerius Maximus appealed for the 'tranquility of our epoch, which there was never a happier, by prolonging the safety of our leader and saviour to the longest limits allowed to human condition'.[243] His contemporary, Philo, praised the *princeps* too, noting his profound prudence for dispensing peace and its benefits to the end of his life.[244] Even Tacitus had to admit that 'this was an age of peace unbroken or half-heartedly challenged'.[245] During his twenty-two years as *princeps*, Tiberius persevered to accomplish his final mission. When he died, the Roman People were prosperous and the Treasury was solvent.[246] The army remained loyal and the curved trumpets of war were silent.[247] True to his nature as a soldier, he had fulfilled his duty. A natural actor on the world stage he may not have been, but he gave the performance of a lifetime. For that, Tiberius deserves a standing ovation.

For myself, Conscript Fathers, I am mortal, performing human tasks, and it will be enough for me if I can adequately fill the position of *princeps*; I want you to vouch for this, and to have posterity remember it so.

*Ego me, Patres Conscripti, mortalem esse et hominum officia fungi satisque habere si locum principem impleam et vos testor et meminisse posteros volo.*

Tiberius' address to the Senate in 25 CE, quoted in Tacitus, *Annals* 4.38.

Figure 53. The modern sculptor of this Janiform herm in the Summer Garden, St Petersburg, Russia, chose a Greek philosopher or playwright to look back to the past and Tiberius to look forward to the future.

# Appendix 1

# The Wit and Wisdom of Tiberius

The extant accounts preserve examples of Tiberius' wit and wisdom. A well-read man with experience of life in all its aspects, he could express his insights pithily and eruditely, often with dry humour and self-deprecation. This sampling is representative.

Until I come to the time when it may seem right to you to grant an old man some repose.
*Dum veniam ad id tempus, quo vobis aequum possit videri dare vos aliquam senectuti meae requiem.*
Suet., *Tib.* 24.2. *Addressing the Senate on 17 September on accepting the role of* princeps.

How can the same man both make the division and choose?
*Πῶς οἷόν τέ ἐστιν' εἶπεν 'τὸν αὐτὸν καὶ νέμειν τι καὶ αἱρεῖσθαι?*
Dio 57.2.6. *Referring to a discussion on dividing of the empire.*

The condition of holding power [or command] is that an account cannot be balanced unless it be rendered to one person.
*Eam condicionem esse imperandi, ut non aliter ratio constet quam si uni reddatur.*
Tac., *Ann.* 1.6. *Responding to Livia about meddling in the running of the empire.*

The soldiers do not belong to me, but to the *Res Publica*.
*Οἱ στρατιῶται οὐκ ἐμοὶ ἀλλὰ δημόσιοί εἰσι.*
Dio 57.2.3. *Responding to criticism Tiberius already had a bodyguard while attending the Senate on 4 September 14 CE when requesting one.*

No one man could bear the whole burden without a colleague, or even several colleagues.
*Quando universae sufficere solus nemo posset nisi cum altero vel etiam cum pluribus.*
Suet., *Tib.* 25.2. *When asking the Senate for help to rule the empire.*

The business of the *Res Publica* would be more easily carried out by the joint efforts of a number.
*Plures facilius munia rei publicae sociatis laboribus exsecuturos.*
Tac. *Ann.* 1.11.1. *Tiberius' eulogy at Augustus' funeral.*

All human affairs are uncertain, and the higher I have climbed the more slippery my position.
*Cuncta mortalium incerta, quantoque plus adeptus foret, tanto se magis in lubrico dictitans.*
Tac., *Ann.* 1.72. *Tiberius refusing a vote in 15* CE *on the taking of an oath to obey his enactments.*

If I had been giving my views, I should have proposed this or that.
*Ελεγεν ὅτι 'εἰ γνώμην ἐποιούμην, τὰ καὶ τὰ ἂν ἀπεδειξάμην.*
Dio 57.7.4. *On permitting others the freedom to express their honest views.*

I am master of the slaves, commander of the soldiers, and chief of the rest.
*Δεσπότης μὲν τῶν δούλων, αὐτοκράτωρ δὲ τῶν στρατιωτῶν.*
Dio 57.8.2. *On how he should be addressed, either Caesar or Germanicus.*

Nobody willingly submits to being ruled, but a man is driven to it against his will; for not only do subjects delight in refusing obedience, but they also enjoy plotting against their rulers.
*Ιὐδεὶς ἑκὼν ἄρχεται ἀλλ' ἄκων εἰς τοῦτο συνελαύνεται: μὴ μόνον γὰρ μὴ πειθαρχεῖν τοὺς ἀρχομένους ἡδέως, ἀλλὰ καὶ ἐπιβουλεύειν τοῖς ἄρχουσι.*
Dio 57.19.1b. *When chastising persons accused of any offence.*

While I am alive you shall commit no deed of violence or insolence; and if you dare to try, not after I am dead, either.
*Ζῶντος μέν μου οὐδὲν οὔτε βίαιον οὔθ' ὑβριστικὸν πράξεις: ἂν δέ τι καὶ τολμήσῃς, οὐδὲ τελευτήσαντος.*
Dio 57.13.2. *Rebuking his son Drusus.*

I want my sheep shorn, not shaven.
*Κείρεσθαί μου τὰ πρόβατα, ἀλλ' οὐκ ἀποξύρεσθαι βούλομαι.*
Dio 57.10.5. *Advising Aemilius Rectus,* Praefectus Aeqypti *not to over tax the provincials.*

Go tell the truth to my father.
*Patri meo verum referre.*
Suet., *Tib.* 57.2: *Apocryphal story told of Tiberius ordering the execution of a jester watching the funeral cortege of Augustus who called aloud to the corpse to let Augustus know that the legacies which he had left to the Roman People were not yet being paid.*

The gods must look to their own injuries.
*Deorum iniurias dis curae.*
Tac., *Ann.* 1.73. *Dismissing the cases of Falanius and Rubrius for defaming the gods in 15* CE, *referring to a principle of Roman law (*Deorum injuriae Diis curae*) about where legal responsibility for damages should lie when there has been an accident, or a breached contract, or a natural disaster.*

It was not by deceit nor in secret but openly and in arms that the Roman People took vengeance on their foes.
*Non fraude neque occultis, sed palam et armatum populum Romanum hostis suos ulcisci.*
Tac. *Ann.* 2.88: *Tiberius responding to a request from Adgandestrius, war leader of the Chatti, for poisons to kill Arminius.*

It is better to correct them privately in some way or other than to inflict any public punishment upon them.
*Οτι ἄμεινόν ἐστιν ἰδίᾳ τρόπον τινὰ αὐτοὺς σωφρονίζειν ἢ κοινήν σφισι*
Dio 57.13.3. *Referring to punishing people accused of loose living.*

What will you do, then, if there are thirteen Caesars?
*Τί' ἔφη 'ποιήσετε, ἂν δεκατρεῖς Καίσαρες γένωνται?*
Dio 57.18.1 Xiph. *Responding to a motion to name November after him.*

These men! How ready they are for slavery!
*O homines – ad servitutem paratos!*
Tac., *Ann.* 3.65. *Commenting on the sycophantic behaviour of senators as he left the* Curia Iulia.

I have a wolf by the ears.
*Lupum se auribus tenere.*
Suet., *Tib.* 25: *Reflecting on his predicament as* princeps.

Let them hate, provided they respect [my conduct].
*Oderint, dum probent*
Suet., *Tib.* 59.2: *Tiberius responding to public criticism, adapting the line* Oderint, dum metuant! *('Let them hate so long as they fear') in L. Accius' play* Atreus.

You also shall one day taste of the sovereignty.
*Καὶ σύ ποτε τῆς ἡγεμονίας γεύσῃ.*
Dio 57.19.4 Xiph. *Addressing Ser. Sulpicius Galba at his betrothal ceremony. (Galba became emperor for three months in 68–69* CE.*)*

If I were consul, I should not have done so.
*Τοὺς ὑπάτους συναγορεύειν τισὶν ἐκώλυσεν, εἰπὼν ὅτι 'εἰ ὑπάτευον.*
Dio 57.21.1 Xiph. *Commenting on consuls attempting to advocate for clients in trials.*

I am no longer worthy to live, if Lentulus, too, hates me.
*Αξιός εἰμι, εἴγε καὶ Λέντουλός με μισεῖ.*
Dio 57.24.8. *Commenting on an assassination attempt by Lentulus in 24* CE.

Such honours ought to be conferred only on those of tried character and mature years.
*Non debere talia praemia tribui nisi expertis et aetate provectis.*
Suet., *Tib.* 54.1. *Referring to the inclusion of vows on 1 January each year for the safety of Germanicus and Drusus Minor.*

Something greater and loftier is expected of a *princeps*, and while everybody takes to himself the credit of right policy, one alone has to bear the odium of every person's failures.
Such, Conscript Fathers, are the anxieties which the *princep*s has to sustain, and the neglect of them will be utter ruin to the *Res Publica*.
*Maius aliquid et excelsius a principe postulatur; et cum recte factorum sibi quisque gratiam trahant, unius invidia ab omnibus peccatur.*
*Patres Conscripti, curam sustinet princeps; haec omissa funditus Rem Publicam trahet.*
Tac., *Ann.* 3.53–54. *Tiberius' letter to the Senate in 22* CE.

My ally in my labours.
*Socius laborum.*
Tac., *Ann.* 4.2. *Tiberius' description of L. Aelius Seianus.*

Better to subvert the constitution than to remove its guardians.
*Subverterent potius iura quam custodes eorum amoverent.*
Tac., *Ann.* 4.30. *Tiberius explaining why he supported rewarding informers after the trial of Vibius Serenus in 24* CE.

I have not yet made my peace with him.
*Οὐδέπω αὐτῷ διήλλαγμαι.*
Dio 58.3.6 Xiph. *Referring to the imprisonment and imminent execution of a companion.*

He has been too terribly outraged to live with honour.
*Εἰπὼν ὅτι χαλεπωτέρως ὕβρισται ἢ ὥστε καλῶς δύνασθαι ζῆν.*
Dio 58.3.7 Xiph. *On the execution of a brutally tortured man found to be unjustly charged.*

You will kill him, and others will kill you.
*Σύ τε τοῦτον ἀποκτενεῖς καὶ σὲ ἄλλοι.*
Dio 58.23.3. *Addressing Caius Caligula.*

When I am dead, let fire o'erwhelm the earth.
*Αναφθέγξασθαι τοῦτο δὴ τὸ ἀρχαῖον ἐμοῦ θανόντος γαῖα μιχθήτω πυρί.*
Dio 58.23.4. *A line Tiberius often quoted from a Greek tragedy, perhaps Euripdes'* Bellerophon *or* Sisyphus.

I will make *him* Ajax.
*Εγὼ οὖν Αἴαντ' αὐτὸν ποιήσω.*
Dio 58.24.4 *citing a line from Euripdes'* Atreus *in which Atreus (the character Tiberius identified with) intends Ajax (here Mamercus Aemilius Scaurus) to commit suicide.*

You do well, indeed, to abandon the setting sun and hasten to the rising sun.
*Non abdita ambage occidentem ab eo deseri, orientem spectari exprobravit.*
Tac., *Ann.* 6.46. *Referring to a liaison set up by Macro between his wife and Caius Caligula, as the* Praefectus Praetorio *sought favour with the heir apparent.*

I do not remember what I was.
*Non memini quid fuerim.*
Sen., *Ben.* 5.25.2: *Interrupting someone who asked him if he remembered something.*

# Appendix 2

# The Coins of Tiberius

Compared to his predecessor, Tiberius used coins sparingly to propagate policy messages during his principate. The mint at the Temple of Iuno Moneta in Rome produced the low denomination bronze, brass, and copper coins (*sestertius, dupondius, as, semis, quadrans*), stamped 'S C' as having been issued under *senatus consultum*, a lawful decree of the Senate. After 15 BCE production of gold (*aureus, quinarius*) and silver (*denarius, quinarius*) coins had moved entirely from Rome to *Colonia* Copia Felix Munatia (*Colonia* Munatia or Lugdunum). The early issues relate to the memory of *Divus* Augustus, clearly establishing Tiberius' connection to the god, but thereafter mostly depict a laureate portrait of himself on the obverse and Livia seated on a throne on the reverse. Coins remained in circulation for decades, meaning that his issues comingled with coins minted under Augustus and Julius Caesar. The cumulative effect reinforced the primacy of Tiberius, but also the place of his mother with her great prestige as 'Iulia Augusta'. For discussions of coins in imperial policy and their often-vague meanings see Bay (1972), Brunn (1999), Calomino (2015), Butcher & Ponting (2009), Levick (1999), Romer (1978), Sutherland (1941b, 1942, 1978), and Wallace-Hadrill (1986). For depictions of buildings see Tameanko (1999).

In contrast, mints across the empire – particularly Alexandria, and cities in Asia, Baetica, and Hispania Taraconnensis – produced a very wide variety of coins (*tetradrama, didrachmon, drachma, sestertius, dupondius, as, semis, chalkon, dichalkan, obol*) bearing the image and name of Tiberius, or members of his family, indicating the loyalty of their communities and elected magistrates to him. In Galatia the mint of the *legatus Augusti propraetore* issued *dupondii*, in Iudaea the mint of the *Praefectus Iudaea* issued *perutot*. For surveys of provincial issues see Ashton (2003), Burnett (2011), and Grant (1950b).

Coins often appeared with slight variations owing to the skills of individual die makers, and dies could be replaced when one or both halves wore out, so that several versions of the same type might be struck. The same dies were often used to strike both the gold and the silver coins of a particular issue. This catalogue is selective, including only the important types produced as they relate to Tiberius during the period 14 BCE–37 CE. For a comprehensive survey of coins struck under Tiberius see Grant (1950a), and for an analysis of the fineness of the metal used in the *denarii* see Butcher and Ponting (2005 and 2011).

# Abbreviations

AV *Aurum*: gold.
AR *Argentum*: silver.
AE *Aes*: brass (*orichalcum*), bronze or leaded bronze, or copper.
*ANS* Grant, M., *Aspects of the Principate of Tiberius.*
BI *Billion*, alloy of silver.
*BMC* *British Museum Catalogue*
*BMCRE* Mattingly, H. & Carson, R. A. G., *Coins of the Roman Empire in the British Museum. Volume 1.*
*Calicó* Calicó, E. X., *The Roman Avrei, Volume 1: From the Republic to Pertinax. 196 BC–193 AD*
*CBN* Giard, J.-B., *Catalogue des Monnaies de l'Empire Romain.*
Cohen Cohen, H., *Description Historique des Monnaies frappées sous l'Empire Romain.*
*FAB* Fernando Álvarez Burgos, *Catálogo general de la moneda hispánica. Volume 1.*
*RCV* Sear, D., *Roman Coins and Their Values. Volume 1.*
*RIC* Sutherland, C. H. V., *Roman Imperial Coinage. Volume 1.*
*RPC* Burnett, Andrew M., Amandry, Michel & Ripollès, Pere Pau, *Roman Provincial Coinage (44 BC–AD 9). Volume 1.*
*SNG* *Sylloge Nummorum Graecorum.*

**(a) Imperial Mints**

AV *aureus*. *Colonia* Munatia-Lugdunum mint. Struck 15–13 BCE. Obverse: AVGVSTVS – DIVI F, bare head of Augustus right. Reverse: IMP X in exergue, two cloaked soldiers each with *parazonium* offering branches to Augustus seated left on platform. (Numismatic references: *RIC* I 164a; *BMC* 443; *CBN* 1370; and variant with head of Augustus facing left *RIC* I 164b).
*The figures likely represent Tiberius and his brother Nero Claudius Drusus after successfully concluding the Alpine War, 15 BCE.*

AR *denarius*. *Colonia* Munatia-Lugdunum mint. Struck 15–13 BCE. Obverse: AVGVSTVS – DIVI F, bare head of Augustus right. Reverse: IMP X in exergue, two cloaked soldiers each with *parazonium* offering branches to Augustus seated left on platform. (Numismatic references: *RIC* I 165; *BMC* 445; *CBN* 1366; Cohen 133).
Plate 21. *Silver version of aureus above.*

AV *aureus*. *Colonia* Munatia-Lugdunum mint. Struck 13–14 CE. Obverse: CAESAR AVGVSTVS DIVI F PATER PATRIAE, laureate head of Augustus right. Reverse: TI CAESAR AVG F TR POT XV, togate, laureate Tiberius standing right in triumphal *quadriga*, holding eagle-tipped sceptre in left hand and laurel branch in right. (Numismatic references: *RIC* I 221; *BMC* 511; *BN* 1685–6; Calicó 294; Lyon 89).
*This* aureus, *struck in the final months of Augustus' life, bears the portrait of Augustus. The reverse is dedicated to Tiberius, who is shown in a four-horse chariot celebrating his victories in Germania and Illyricum, while the legend announces that his* tribunicia potestas *had been renewed for the fifteenth time. The minting of this coin might indicate that Augustus now looked to Tiberius to succeed him.*

AR *denarius*. *Colonia* Munatia-Lugdunum mint. Struck 13–14 CE. Obverse: CAESAR AVGVSTVS DIVI F PATER PATRIAE, laureate head of Augustus right. Reverse: TI CAESAR AVG F TR POT XV, bare head of Tiberius right. (Numismatic references: *RIC* I 226; *RSC* 2 (Tiberius and Augustus); *BMC* 507; *RIC* I 226).
*This is the only coin from an imperial mint struck while Augustus was alive which shows the heads of both the* princeps *and Tiberius. The minting of this coin might indicate that Augustus now looked to Tiberius to succeed him.*

AV *aureus*. *Colonia* Munatia-Lugdunum mint. Struck 14–15 CE. Obverse: TI CAESAR DIVI AVG F AVGVSTVS, laureate head of Tiberius right. Reverse: TR POT XVI, Tiberius, holding branch and sceptre, driving triumphal *quadriga* right, IMP VII in exergue. (Numismatic references: *RIC* I 1; *BMC* 1).
Plate 25. *This* aureus, *struck after Augustus' death and deification, bears the portrait of Tiberius with his new imperial titles. The reverse shows Tiberius in a four-horse chariot celebrating his victories in Germania and Illyricum, while the legend announces that his* tribunicia potestas *had been renewed for the sixteenth time.*

AV *aureus*. *Colonia* Munatia-Lugdunum mint. Struck 14–16 CE. Obverse: TI CAESAR DIVI – AVG F AVGVSTVS, laureate head of Tiberius right. Reverse: DIVOS AVGVST – DIVI F, laureate head of Augustus right, six-pointed star above. (Numismatic references: *RIC* I 24. *BMC* 29; *CBN* 1; Calicó 311; Cohen 3).
Plate 24. *Augustus was deified upon his death in 14 CE by decree of the Senate. The star may relate to an actual comet appearance.*

AR *denarius*. *Colonia* Munatia-Lugdunum mint. Struck 15–16 CE. Obverse: TI CAESAR DIVI AVG F AVGVSTVS, laureate head of Tiberius right. Reverse: TR POT XVII, Tiberius, holding branch and sceptre, driving triumphal *quadriga* right, IMP VII in exergue. (Numismatic references: *RIC* I 4; Lyon 122; *RSC* 48).
*Version of RIC* I 1; *BMC 1 above in silver.*

AE *dupondius* or *as*. *Colonia* Munatia-Lugdunum mint (?). Struck 14–21 CE. Obverse: TI CAESAR DIVI AVG F AVGVSTVS, laureate head of Tiberius right. Reverse: ROM ET AVG, front elevation of the Altar at Condate-*Colonia* Munatia-Lugdunum, decorated with the oak wreath (*corona civica*) between laurels and stylized figures; Victories standing on columns. (Numismatic references: *RIC* I 31 and variant *RIC* I 32).
Plate 22. *For a discussion of the imperial cult centre see Fishwick (1999).*

AR *quinarius*, *Colonia* Munatia-Lugdunum mint. Struck 15–16 CE. Obverse: TI DIVI F – AVGVSTVS, laureate head of Tiberius right. Reverse: TR POT – XVII, Victory seated right on globe, holding wreath with both hands. (Numismatic references: *RIC* I 93, 5; *BMC* 121, 12 and pl. 22, 4 (these dies); Cohen 49; and variant *RIC* I 8; *BMC* 16; Cohen 52).

AE *as*. Rome mint. Struck 15–16 CE. Obverse: TI CAESAR DIVI AVG F AVGVST IMP VII, bare head of Tiberius left. Reverse: PONT MAXIM TRIBVN POTEST XVII, S C across field, draped female seated right, holding *patera* and sceptre, feet on footstool; ornate chair legs. (Numismatic references: *RIC* I 34; *BMC* 68; Cohen 18; and variant *RIC* I 36).

AE *as*. Rome mint. Struck 15–16 CE. Obverse: TI CAESAR DIVI AVG F AVGVSTVS IMP VII, bare head of Tiberius right. Reverse: PONT MAXIM TRIBVN POTEST XVII, draped female seated right, holding patera and sceptre, S C in fields. (Numismatic reference: *RIC* I 35 and variant *RIC* I 33).

AE *as*. Rome mint. Struck 15–16 CE. Obverse: DIVVS AVG – VSTVS PATER, radiate head of Augustus left; star above, thunderbolt before. Reverse: Seated female figure right, feet on stool, holding patera and sceptre. (Numismatic references: *RIC* I 71; C. 244; *BMC* 151).
Divus *Augustus* Pater *consecration issue by Tiberius. For a discussion see Sutherland (1941b and 1942).*

AE *as*. Rome mint. Struck 15–16 CE. Obverse: DIVVS AVGV - STVS PATER, radiate head of Augustus left; star above, thunderbolt before. Reverse: Seated female figure right, feet on stool, holding *patera* and sceptre. (Numismatic references: *RIC* I 72; Sutherland, *Divus* 2).
Divus *Augustus* Pater *consecration issue by Tiberius. For a discussion see Sutherland (1941b and 1942).*

AE *as*. Rome mint. Struck 15–16 CE. Obverse: TI CAESAR DIVI AVG F AVGVSTVS IMP VII, bare head of Tiberius left. Reverse: PONT MAXIM TRIBVN POTEST XVII, draped female figure seated right, holding *patera* and sceptre, S C in fields. (Numismatic references: *RIC* I 36; Cohen 17).

AE *dupondius*. Rome mint. Struck 16–22 CE. Obverse: TI CAESAR DIVI AVG F AVGVST IMP VIII., laureate head of Tiberius left. Reverse: CLEMENTIAE, small bust of Tiberius within laurel wreath; all in the centre of a large, round shield with palmettes and raised petals, S C in fields. (Numismatic references: *RIC* I 38; *BMC* 85; *CBN* 127; Cohen 4).
*The coin promotes Tiberius'* clementia.

AE *as*. Rome mint. Struck 16–22 CE. Obverse: TI CAESAR DIVI AVG F AVGVST IMP VIII, laureate head of Tiberius left. Reverse: MODERATIONIS, S C across field, small bust of Tiberius within laurel wreath; all in the centre of a large round shield with palmettes and raised petals. (Numismatic references: *RIC* I 40; *BMC* 90 var. (MODERATIONI); *BN* 128; Cohen 6; and variant *RIC* I 39; *BMC* 90; Cohen 5).
Fig. 47. *The coin promotes Tiberius' celebrated virtue of* moderatio.

AV *quinarius*. *Colonia* Munatia-Lugdunum mint. Struck 18–19 CE. Obverse: TI DIVI F – AVGVSTVS laureate head of Tiberius right. Reverse: TR POT XX, Victory seated right on globe, holding wreath with both hands. (Numismatic references: *RIC* I 6; *BMC* 14. Cohen 50. King 2).

AV *aureus*. *Colonia* Munatia-Lugdunum mint. Struck 18–37 CE. Obverse: TI CAESAR DIVI AVG F AVGVSTVS, laureate head of Tiberius right. Reverse: PONTIF MAXIM, Livia (as Pax) seated right, holding olive-branch and long vertical sceptre; ornate legs to chair. (Numismatic references: *RIC* I 29; *BMC* 46; *BN* 26; Cohen 15; and variants *BMC* 46–47).
Plate 26. *This design was probably the most minted reverse of Tiberius' reign.*

AR *denarius*. *Colonia* Munatia-Lugdunum mint. Struck 18–37 CE. Obverse: TI CAESAR DIVI AVG F AVGVSTVS, laureate head of Tiberius right. Reverse: PONTIF MAXIM, Livia, as Pax, seated right, holding olive-branch and long vertical sceptre; ornate legs to chair. (Numismatic references: *RIC* I 30; *BMC* 48; *RSC* 16a; and many variants of this type).
*This is the silver version of the* aureus. *This* denarius *was probably the most minted silver coin of Tiberius' reign. Numismatists have examined the coins and see stylistic differences in pieces produced in 18, 18–35, 36–37 and 36–37 CE. It is often called the 'Tribute Penny' by collectors, referring to the story in Matthew 22:20–21.*

AE *dupondius*. Rome mint. Struck 21–22 CE. Obverse: PIETAS, veiled, diademed, and draped bust of Pietas right. Reverse: DRVSVS CAESAR TI AVGVSTI F TR POT ITER, around large S C. (Numismatic reference: *RIC* I 43).
Fig. 51. *The coin promotes Tiberius' virtue of* pietas.

AE *sestertius*. Rome mint. Struck 22–23 CE. Obverse: Crossed cornucopia, each surmounted by the bust of a boy, face-to-face; winged caduceus in between.

Reverse: DRVSVS CAESAR TI AVG F DIVI AVG N PONT TR POT II, large S C across fields. (Numismatic references: *RIC* I 42; *BMC* 95; *Cohen* 1). Plate 27. *The boys are presumed to be Ti. Gemellus and Germanicus Gemellus.*

AE *dupondius*. Rome mint. Struck 22 CE. Obverse: TI CAESAR DIVI AVG F AVGVST IMP VIII, laureate head of Tiberius left. Reverse: CLEMENTIAE, small bust of Tiberius within laurel wreath, all set in the centre of a large, round shield with palmettes and raised petals, S C in fields. (Numismatic references: *RIC* I 38. *BMC* 85; *CBN* 127; Cohen 4).
Fig. 48. *This issue may celebrate the awarding of a 'Shield of Valour'* (Clipeus Virtutis) *by the Senate to Tiberius in 22 CE. The coin promotes Tiberius'* clementia.

AE *dupondius*. Rome mint. Struck 22–23 CE. Obverse: DIVVS AVGVSTVS PATER, radiate head of Augustus left. Reverse: S C, hexastyle temple with ornate conical roof surmounted by figure; calf and lamb standing on bases flanking. (Numismatic references: *RIC* I 74; *BMC* 142; Cohen 251; *MIR* 2, 55–5).
Divus Augustus Pater *commemorative issue by Tiberius. For a discussion see Sutherland (1941b and 1942).*

AE *as*. Rome mint. Struck 22–23 CE. Obverse: DRVSVS CAESAR TI AVG F DIVI AVG N, bare head Drusus Minor left. Reverse: PONTIF TRIBVN POTEST ITER, around large S C. (Numismatic references: *RIC* I 45; *BMC* 134, 99; Cohen 2).

AE *dupondius*. Rome mint. Struck 22–23 CE. Obverse: DIVVS AVGVSTVS PATER, radiate head of Augustus left. Reverse: S C, hexastyle temple with ornate conical roof surmounted by figure; calf and lamb standing on bases flanking. (Numismatic references: *RIC* I 74; *MIR* 2, 55–5; *BMC* 142; Cohen 251).
Divus *Augustus* Pater *commemorative issue by Tiberius. For a discussion see Sutherland (1941b and 1942).*

AE *dupondius*. Rome mint. Struck 22–23 CE. Obverse: IVSTITIA, draped bust of Iustitia right, wearing stephane. Reverse: TI CAESAR DIVI AVG F AVG P M TR POT XXIIII, around large S C. (Numismatic references: *RIC* I 46; Vagi 498).
Fig. 49. *This coin promotes* iustitia *meaning 'justice', 'rightness' or 'fairness'. The portrait of the woman may be Antonia Minor or Agrippina Maior.*

AE *sestertius*. Rome mint. Struck 22–23 CE. Obverse: CIVITATIBVS ASIAE RESTITVTIS, togate, laureate Tiberius seated on curule chair left feet on stool, holding *patera* and sceptre. Reverse: TI CAESARI DIVI AVG F AVGVST P M TR POT XXIIII, around large S C. (Numismatic reference: *RIC* I 48).

*This coin publicises measures undertaken by Tiberius to provide relief for cities in Province Asia which had been devastated by earthquake in 17* CE.

AE *dupondius*. Rome mint. Struck 22–23 CE. Obverse: SALVS AVGVSTA, bare-headed and draped bust of Iulia Augusta (Livia Drusilla) in the guise of 'Salus Augusta' right. Reverse: TI CAESAR DIVI AVG F AVG P M TR POT XXIIII around large S C. (Numismatic references: *RIC* I 47; *BMC* 81–4; *BN* 63–7; Cohen 5).
Fig. 44. *This coin promotes* salus *meaning 'safety', 'salvation' or 'welfare' and alludes to the recovery of Augusta after a bout of sickness.*

AE *sestertius*. Rome mint. Struck 22–23 CE. Obverse: SPQR IVLIAE AVGVST, ornamented *carpentum* drawn right by pair of mules. Reverse: Legend around large SC. (Numismatic references: *RIC* I 51; *BMC* 76; Cohen 6.).
*Alludes to Iulia Augusta, the wife of Augustus and mother of Tiberius.*

AE *dupondius*. Rome mint. Struck 22–26 CE. Obverse: DIVVS AVGVSTVS PATER, radiate head of Augustus left. Reverse: Large S C in oak wreath. (Numismatic references: *RIC* I 79; *BMC* 143; Cohen 252).
Divus *Augustus* Pater *commemorative issue by Tiberius. For a discussion see Sutherland (1941b and 1942).*

AE *as*. Rome mint. Struck 22–30 CE. Obverse: DIVVS AVGVSTVS PATER, radiate head of Augustus left. Reverse: PROVIDENT in exergue, S C across field, ornate altar enclosure with double panelled door. (Numismatic references: *RIC* I 81; *BMC* 146; Cohen 228).
Fig. 50. Divus *Augustus* Pater *commemorative issue by Tiberius. For a discussion see Sutherland (1941b and 1942).*

AV *quinarius*. *Colonia* Munatia-Lugdunum mint. Struck 28–29 CE. Obverse: TI DIVI F – AVGVSTVS, laureate head of Tiberius right. Reverse: TR POT – XXX, Victory seated right on globe, holding wreath with both hands. (Numismatic references: *RIC* I 14; *BMC* 505; *BN* 1679–80; Lyon 80; Bahrfelt 229).

AV *quinarius*. *Colonia* Munatia-Lugdunum mint. Struck 30–31 CE. Obverse: TI DIVI F – AVGVSTVS laureate head of Tiberius right. Reverse: TR POT – XXXII, Victory seated right on globe, holding wreath with both hands. (Numismatic references: *RIC* I 16; Lyon 136).

AV *quinarius*. *Colonia* Munatia-Lugdunum mint. Struck 32–33 CE. Obverse: TI DIVI F – AVGVSTVS, laureate head of Tiberius right. Reverse: TR POT – XXXIIII, Victory seated right on globe, holding wreath with both hands. (Numismatic references: *RIC* I 18; *BMC* 24; *RCV* 1761 var.)

AV *quinarius*. *Colonia* Munatia-Lugdunum mint. Struck 33–34 CE. Obverse: TI CAESAR DIVI – AVG F AVGVSTVS, laureate head of Tiberius right, Reverse: TR POT – XXXV, Victory seated right on globe, holding wreath with both hands. (Numismatic references: *RIC* I 19; *BMC* 25).

AE *as*. Rome mint. Struck 34–35 CE. Obverse: TI CAESAR DIVI AVG F AVGVST IMP VIII, laureate head of Tiberius left. Reverse: PONTIF MAX TR POT XXXVI around, S C flanking ship's rudder superimposed vertically across a banded globe; a small globe at base of the rudder. (Numismatic references: *RIC* I 52. *BMC* 104. *CBN* 89. Cohen12 (misdescribed)).

AE *as*. Rome mint. Struck 34–35 CE. Obverse: TI CAESAR DIVI AVG F AVGVST IMP VIII, laureate head of Tiberius left. Reverse: PONTIF MAXIM TRIBVN POTEST XXXVI around S C flanking a winged *caduceus* placed vertically. (Numismatic references: *RIC* I 53; Cohen 21).
*The* cauduceus, *a recognized symbol of commerce and negotiation, represents the god Mercury and the trades, occupations, or undertakings associated with him.*
Fig. 43.

AE *as*. Rome mint. Struck 34–37 CE. Obverse: DIVVS AVGVSTVS PATER, radiate head of Augustus to left. Reverse: S C, winged thunderbolt. (Numismatic references: *RIC* I 83; *BMC* 157; *BN* 141; Cohen 249).
Fig. 45. Divus *Augustus* Pater *commemorative issue by Tiberius. For a discussion see Sutherland (1941b and 1942).*

AE *as*. Rome mint. Struck 34–37 CE. Obverse: DIVVS AVGVSTVS PATER, radiate head of Augustus left. Reverse: S C, eagle standing facing on globe, head right. (Numismatic references: *RIC* I 82; *BMC* 155; Cohen 247).
Divus *Augustus* Pater *commemorative issue by Tiberius. For a discussion see Sutherland (1941b and 1942).*

AE *sestertius*. Rome mint. Struck 35–36 CE. Obverse: DIVO AVGVSTI SPQR, OB/CIVIS/SER in three lines across shield bordered by oak wreath; round shield supported by two capricorns set on globe. Reverse: TI CAESAR DIVI AVG F AVGVST PM TR POT XXXVII, around large S C across field. (Numismatic references: *RIC* I 63; *BMC* 109; Cohen 303; *MIR* 2, 54–4; and variants: *RIC* I 63; *BMC* 109; Cohen 303; MIR 2, 54–4; and *RIC* I 69; *BMC* 139, 129).
*Commemorates the award of a crown of oak leaves* (corona civica) *by the Senate to Augustus in 27 BCE for 'rescuing all his fellow citizens', which was celebrated on coins during his principate (e.g. see RIC I 77a; BMC 378; RSC 208).*

AE *sestertius*. Rome mint. Struck 35–36 CE. Obverse: Empty horse-drawn *quadriga* right, its side panels decorated with Victory and captives. Reverse: TI

CAESAR DIVI AVG F AVGVST P M TR POT XXXVII around large S C. (Numismatic references: *RIC* I 60; *BMC* 113; *BN* 91; Cohen 66).
*The empty* quadriga *may allude to the military campaign led by L. Vitellius against Artabanus of Parthia, 36* CE.

AE *sestertius*. Rome mint. Struck 35–36 CE. Obverse: DIVO AVGVSTO S P Q R, *quadriga* of elephants with riders driving them walking left pulling a four-wheeled cart (decorated with shields?) bearing the figure of Augustus radiate seated on a *sella* left holding laurel-branch and a long sceptre. Reverse: TI CAESAR DIVI AVG F P M TR POT XXXVII around large S C. (Numismatic reference: *RIC* I 62).
*The obverse depicts the ceremonial vehicle featured in the* pompa circensis *('circus parade'), which was the procession preceding the official games in honour of Augustus (*ludi Augustales*) held annually on 12 October in the* Circus Maximus *as part of the religious festival established by Tiberius (Tac.,* Ann. *1.54). The processional route started from the Temple of Mars Ultor in the* Forum Augustum.

AE *sestertius*. Rome mint. Struck 36–37 CE. Obverse: DIVO AVGVSTO S P Q R, *quadriga* of elephants with riders driving them walking left pulling a four-wheeled cart (decorated with shields?) bearing the figure of Augustus radiate seated on a *sella* left holding laurel-branch and a long sceptre. Reverse: TI CAESAR DIVI AVG F P M TR POT XXXIIX around large S C. (Numismatic reference: *RIC* I 68).
*The obverse depicts the ceremonial vehicle featured in the* pompa circensis *('circus parade'), which was the procession preceding the official games in honour of Augustus (*ludi Augustales*) held annually on 12 October in the Circus Maximus as part of the religious festival established by Tiberius (Tac.,* Ann. *1.54). The processional route started from the Temple of Mars Ultor in the* Forum Augustum.

AE *sestertius*. Rome mint. Struck 36–37 CE. Obverse: The Temple of Concordia: goddess Concordia seated left on throne, holding *patera* and sceptre, above altar within hexastyle façade set on podium; entrance flanked by statues of Hercules and Mercury; pediment decorated with statues of Jupiter, Juno, Minerva, and Victories in *acroteria*; wings of transverse *cella* with windows behind; pediments decorated with statues. Reverse: TI CAESAR DIVI AVG F AVGVST P M TR POT XXXIIX, legend around large S C. (Numismatic references: *RIC* I 62; MIR 2, 58–4; *BMC* 133; Cohen 70 corr. (Temple of Divus Augustus)).
*Rebuilt by Tiberius between 7* BCE *and 10* CE*, the temple was rededicated on the 16 January 10* CE *as the Temple of Concordia of Augustus* (Aedes Concordiae Augustae). *Here Tiberius exhibited his personal collection of statues, which he had acquired during his extended sojourn on Rhodes. The temple was used for meetings, notably the one in which Aelius Seianus was denounced.*

**(b) Provincial Mints**

**Achaea**

AE *chalkon*. Thessaly mint. Struck 14–37 CE. Obverse: ΤΙΒΕΡΙΣ ΣΕΒΑΣΤΗΩ, bare head of Tiberius right. Reverse: ΘΕΣΣΑΛ Ω ΜΕΓΑΛΟΚΛΕΟΥΣ, laureate head of Apollo or Iulia Augusta right. (Numismatic references: *RPC* I 1429). *Megalokles was* strategos *of the* koinon *of Thessaly.*

**Africa Proconsularis**

AE *as*. Carthago mint. Struck 10 CE. Obverse: TI CA F IMP V, bare head of Tiberius right. Reverse: P I SP D V SP IIVIR C I C around P P in upper field and D D in lower field.
(Numismatic references: *RPC* I 748).
*D V SP and P I SP were the* duoviri *elected to the 'Commission of Two Men' of Carthago.*

AE *dupondius*. Lepti Minus mint. Struck 10 CE. Obverse: TI CAE AVG F IMP V; bare head of Tiberius, right. Reverse: ΛΕΠΤΙC, B (under the bust); bust of Hermes with petasus and caduceus, left. (Numismatic references: *RPC* I 789; Müller, Afrique 18, Alexandropoulos 74).
*Lepti Minus (Lamṭah) was a small Carthaginian city located 16 km (10 miles) from Ruspinum (modern Al-Munastīr in Tunisia).*

AE *dupondius*. Utica mint. Struck 27–28 CE. Obverse: TI CAESAR DIVI AVG F AVGVST IMP VIII, bare head of Tiberius left. Reverse: C VIB MARSO PR COS NE CAE Q PR A M GEMELLVS F C, D D in upper field, P P in lower field; Iulia Augusta, veiled, seated right. (Numismatic references: *RPC* I 732).
*When the coin was minted,* C. *Vibius Marsus was in the first year of his proconsulship of Province Africa, A M Gemellus was* praetor *and Nero Caesar* quaestor.

AE *dupondius*. Utica mint. Struck 29–30 CE. Obverse: TI CAESAR DIVI AVG F AVGVST IMP VIII, bare head of Tiberius left. Reverse: C VIBIO MARSO PR(O)COS III C CASSIVS FELIX A IIVIR around D D in upper field, P P in lower field; Iulia Augusta, veiled, seated right, holding sceptre and phiale. (Numismatic references: *RPC* I 742; *SNG* Copenhagen 442).
*When the coin was minted, Vibius Marsus was in the third year of his proconsulship of Province Africa, while C. Cassius Felix was one of the* duoviri *elected to the 'Commission of Two Men' of Utica. The remains of the city are located near the mouth of the Medjerda River into the Mediterranean Sea.*

**Asia**

AE *as*. Aezani (Phrygia) mint. Struck 19–23 CE. Obverse: ΣΕΒΑΣΤΟΣ, bare head of Tiberius, right, sometimes *lituus*. Reverse: ΑΙΖΑΝΙΤΩΝ ΕΠΙ

ΜΕΝΑΝΔΡΟ(Υ), Zeus of Aezani standing, left, with eagle and sceptre, (Numismatic references: *RPC* I 3068; *BMC* 50).
*Menandros (without title) was magistrate of Aezani of the* Conventus *of Sardis. Aezani was a Greek city situated astride the River Penkalas, in what is now the district of Çavdarhisar in Kütahya Province of Turkey.*

AE *as*. Aezani (Phrygia) mint. Struck 19–23 CE. Obverse: ΚΑΙΣΑΡ ΕΠΙ ΜΕΝΑΝΔΡΟΥ, bare head of Tiberius, right. Reverse: ΣΕΒΑΣΤΗ ΑΙΖΑΝΙΤΩΝ, draped bust of Livia, left. (Numismatic references: *RPC* I 3071).
*Menandros (without title) was magistrate of Aezani of the* Conventus *of Sardis. Aezani was a Greek city situated astride the River Penkalas, in what is now the district of Çavdarhisar in Kütahya Province of Turkey.*

AE *as*. Aezani (Phrygia) mint. Struck 19–23 CE. Obverse: ΚΑΙΣΑΡ ΕΠΙ ΜΕΝΑΝΔΡΟΥ, bare head of Tiberius, right. Reverse: ΔΡΟΥΣΟΣ ΑΙΖΑΝΙΤΩΝ, draped bust of Drusus Minor, left. (Numismatic references: *RPC* I 3072).
*Menandros (without title) was magistrate of Aezani of the* Conventus *of Sardis. Aezani was a Greek city situated astride the River Penkalas, in what is now the district of Çavdarhisar in Kütahya Province of Turkey.*

AE *as*. Apamea (Bithynia-Pontus) mint. Struck 14–19 CE. Obverse: ΤΙΒΕΡΙΟΣ ΚΑΙΣΑΡ, bare head of Tiberius right. Reverse: ΓΑΙΟΣ ΙΟΥΛΙΟΣ ΚΑΛΛΙΚΛΗΣ ΑΠΑΜΕΩΝ, eagle standing left on a thunderbolt, head right, with wings spread; monogram to left. (Numismatic references: *RPC* I 3133; *BMC* 142).
*C. Iulius Kallikles was city magistrate of Apamea of the* Conventus *of Apamea. The remains of Apamea on the right bank of the Orontes River are visible at Afamia, Syria.*

AE *as*. Apamea (Bithynia-Pontus) mint. Struck 15 BC–19 CE. Obverse: ΓΕΡΜΑΝΙΚΟΣ ΚΑΙΣΑΡ, bare head of Germanicus right. Reverse: ΙΟΥΛΙΟΣ ΚΑΛΛΙΚΛΗΣ ΑΠΑΜΕΩΝ, stag standing right on meander pattern. (Numismatic references: *RPC* I 3134; *SNG* von Aulock 3488).
*C. Iulius Kallikles was city magistrate of Apamea of the* Conventus *of Apamea. The remains of Apamea on the right bank of the Orontes River are visible at Afamia, Syria.*

AE *as*. Herakleia Salbake (Caria) mint. Struck 14–37 CE. Obverse: ΣΕΒΑΣΤΟΣ, bare head of Tiberius right. Reverse: ΑΠΟΛΛΩΝΙΟΣ ΑΠΟΛΛΩΝΙΟΥ ΗΡΑΚΛΕΩΤΩΝ, Heracles walking, left, with arm extended and club. (Numismatic references: *RPC* I 2856; *BMC* 15).
*Apollonios Apolloniou (without title) was likely city magistrate of Herakleia Salbake in the* Conventus *of Alabanda, the site of which is located near Vakıf, Turkey.*

AE *as*. Apollonia Salbake (Caria) mint. Struck 14–37 CE. Obverse: ΣΕΒΑΣΤΟΣ, bare head of Tiberius right. Reverse: ΑΠΟΛΛΩΝΙΑΤΩΝ ΚΑΛΛΙΠΠΟΣ

ΑΡΤΕΜΙΔΩΡΟΥ, Apollo standing left, holding raven and laurel branch. (Numismatic references: *RPC* I 2864).

*Kallippos (without title) and Artemiodoros (without title) were likely city magistrates of Apollonia Salbake in the* Conventus *of Alabanda, the site of which is located near Medet, Turkey.*

AE *as*. Apollonoshieron (Lydia) mint. Struck 14–37 CE. Obverse: ΤΙΒϹΡΙΟϹ ΚΑΙϹΑΡ, laureate head of Tiberius right. Reverse: ΑΠΟΛΛωΝΙϹΡΙΤωΝ, lyre. (Numismatic references: *RPC* I 3044).

*Apollonoshieron was a harbour city in the* Conventus *of Sardis. It is located at the village Yenicekent near Bulladan, Turkey.*

AE *as*. Magnesia ad Sipylum (Lydia) mint. Struck after 17 CE. Obverse: ΤΙΒϹΡΙΟΝ ϹϹΒΑϹΤΟΝ ΚΤΙϹΤΗΝ, laureate head of Tiberius, right. Reverse: ΜΑΓΝΗΤΩΝ ΑΠΟ ϹΙΠΥΛΟΥ, the emperor Tiberius raising Tyche of Magnesia. (Numismatic references: *RPC* I 2451).

*The city of Magnesia (modern Manisa) was damaged during the earthquake of 17 CE, second only in severity to Sardis. It was rebuilt with financial assistance from Tiberius.*

AE *as*. Neocaesarea (Lydia) mint. Struck 14–37 CE. Obverse: ΤΙΒΕΡΙΟΝ ϹϹΒΑϹΤΟΝ, bare head of Tiberius right. Reverse: ΝΕΟΚΕϹΑΡΕΙΣ (or ΝΕΟΚΑΙϹΑΡΕΙϹ), winged thunderbolt. (Numismatic references: *RPC* I 3017; *GRPC* 150).

*The city of Philadelphia was damaged during the earthquake of 17 CE. It was rebuilt and renamed Neocaesarea under Tiberius. Its remains can be seen at Alaşehir, Turkey.*

AE *as*. Sardis (Lydia) mint. Struck 14–37 CE. Obverse: ΣΕΒΑΣΤΟΣ ΚΑΙΣΑΡΕΩΝ ΣΑΡΔΙΑΝΩΝ, togate figure of Tiberius raising kneeling figure of Tyche of Sardis Reverse: ΣΕΒΑΣΤΗ ΙΟΥΛΙΟΣ ΚΛΕΩΝ ΚΑΙ ΜΕΜΝΩΝ, Livia seated right on throne, holding sceptre and grain ears. (Numismatic references: *RPC* I 2991; *SNG* Copenhagen 515; *SNG* München 505; *BMC* 98).

*Ioulios Kleon (without title) and Memnon (without title) were likely city magistrates of Sardis, the site of which is located at Sart, Turkey.*

AE *as*. Sardis (Lydia) mint. Struck 14–37 CE. Obverse: ΚΑΙΣΑΡ ΣΕΒΑΣΤΟΥ ΥΙΟΣ, bare head of Tiberius. Reverse: ΣΑΡΔΙΑΝΩΝ ΟΠΙΝΑΣ ΑΚΙΑΜΟΣ, city name in three lines within wreath. (Numismatic references: *RPC* I 2989; *BMC* 102).

*Opinas (without title) and Akiamos (without title) were likely city magistrates of Sardis, the site of which is located at Sart, Turkey.*

AE *as*. Sardis (Lydia) mint. Struck 28/29 CE. Obverse: ΔΡΟΥΣΟΣ ΚΑΙ ΓΕΡΜΑΝΙΚΟΣ ΚΑΙΣΑΡΕΣ ΝΕΟΙ ΘΕΟΙ ΦΙΛΑΔΕΛΦ(ΟΙ), togate figures

of Drusus Minor and Germanicus seated, left, on curule chairs, one holding out *lituus*. Reverse: ΓΑΙΩ ΑΣΙΝΝΙΩ ΠΟΛΛΙΩΝΙ ΑΝΘΥΠΑΤΩ surrounding wreath, ΚΟΙΝΟΥ ΑΣΙΑΣ inside wreath. (Numismatic references: *RPC* I 2995; *BMC* 106).
*Coin was restruck by Asinius Pollio,* proconsul. *Drusus and Germanicus are called 'brother-loving new gods'. The* Koinon *(Leagues) in the Empire – in this case Asia – were primarily concerned with the Imperial Cult.*

AE *as*. Pergamum (Mysia). Struck 14–37 CE. Obverse: ΣΕΒΑΣΤΟΙ/ΕΠΙ ΠΟΠΠΑΙΟΥ, laureate heads of Augustus and Tiberius facing each other. Reverse: ΣΕΒΑΣΤΗΝ ΠΕΡΓΑΜΗΝΩΝ ΜΗΝΟΓΕΝΗΣ, Iulia Augusta seated right on throne, holding sceptre and grain ears. (Numismatic references: *RPC* I 2368; *BMC* 251–2).
*Poppaeus (proconsul) and Menogenes (magistrate). The remains of Pergamum are located northwest of Bergama, Turkey.*

AE *as*. Pergamum (Mysia) mint. Struck 14–37 CE. Obverse: CΕΒΑCΤΟΙ ΕΠΙ ΠΕΤΡΩΝΙΟΥ ΤΟ Ϛ, draped bust of Livia and laureate head of Tiberius facing each other. Reverse: ΘΕΟΝ CΕΒΑCΤΟΝ ΠΕΡΓΑΜΗΝΟΙ, tetrastyle temple containing statue of *Divus* Augustus holding spear. (Numismatic references: *RPC* I 2369; *SNG* I 2039; *BMC* 253).
*The precinct and temple of* Divus *Augustus was one of the first to be erected in Asia. The remains of Pergamum are located northwest of Bergama, Turkey.*

AE *as*. Eumeneia (Phrygia) mint. Struck 14–37 CE. Obverse: ΣΕΒΑΣΤΟΣ, bare head of Tiberius right. Reverse: ΟΥΑΛΕΡΙΟΣ ΖΜΕΡΤΟΡΙΞ ΕΥΜΕΝΕΩΝ, butting bull right. (Numismatic references: *RPC* I, 3144; BMC 35; *SNG* Tübingen 4013).
*Valerius Zmertorix (without title) was likely magistrate of Eumeneia in the* Conventus *of Apamea, the site of which is near Civril, Turkey.*

AE *as*. Eumeneia (Phrygia) mint. Struck 14–37 CE. Obverse: ΣΕΒΑΣΤΟΣ, laureate head of Tiberius right. Reverse: ΚΛΕΩΝ/ΑΓΑΡΗΤΟC/ΕΥΜΕ-ΝΕΩΝ in three downward lines the first two on the right, the last on the left; Zeus standing facing, head left, wearing himation, phiale in right hand, resting left hand on sceptre, star above crescent with horns up on left.
(Numismatic references: *RPC* I 3147; *SNG* München 206; *SNG* Copenhagen 391; *SNG* von Aulock 3589; *BMC* 37).
*Kleon Agapetos (without title) was likely magistrate of Eumeneia in the* Conventus *of Apamea, the site of which is near Civril, Turkey.*

AE *as*. Laodicea ad Lycum (Phrygia) mint. Struck 14–37 CE. Obverse: ΣΕΒΑΣΤΟΣ, bare head of Tiberius right. Reverse: ΛΑΟΔΙΚΕΩΝ ΠΥΘΗΣ

ΠΥΘΟΥ, Zeus Laodikeos standing left, with eagle and staff; to left. and right, *pilei* with star. (Numismatic references: *RPC* I 2901; *BMC* 138).
*Pythes Pythou (without title) was likely city magistrate of Laodicea ad Lycum in the* Conventus *of Cibyra, the site of which is located near Denizli, Turkey.*

AE *as*. Laodicea ad Lycum (Phrygia) mint. Struck 14–37 CE. Obverse: ΛΑΟΔΙΚΕΩΝ, laureate head of Apollo right; lyre to right. Reverse: ΠΥΘΗΣ ΠΥΘΟΥ, *cista mystica* with serpent emerging left and surmounted by headdress of Isis. (Numismatic references: *RPC* I 2903).
*Pythes Pythou (without title) was likely city magistrate of Laodicea ad Lycum in the* Conventus *of Cibyra, the site of which is located near Denizli, Turkey.*

AE *as*. Laodicea ad Lycum (Phrygia) mint. Struck 14–37 CE. Obverse: ΣΕΒΑΣΤΟΣ; bare head of Tiberius right. Reverse: ΛΑΟΔΙΚΕΩΝ ΠΥΘΗΣ ΠΥΘΟΥ ΤΟ ΔΕΥΤΕΡΟΝ, Zeus Laodikeos standing left, holding eagle in right hand and sceptre in left; caps of Dioskouroi surmounted by stars in left field. (Numismatic references: *RPC* I 2908; *BMC* 140).
*Pythes Pythou (in office for the second time) as magistrate of Laodicea ad Lycum in the* Conventus *of Cibyra, the site of which is located near Denizli, Turkey.*

AE *as*. Prymnessus (Phrygia) mint. Struck 14–37 CE. Obverse: ΣΕΒΑΣΤΟΣ, laureate head of Tiberius right. Reverse: ΚΑΙΚΙΛΙΟΣ ΠΛΟΚΑΜΟΣ ΠΡΥΜΝΗΣΣΕΩΝ, Dikaiosyne advancing left, with scales and two ears of corn; in exergue monogram. (Numismatic references: *RPC* I 3202; *SNG* von Aulock, Phrygiens II 990–8 (Augustus)).
*Caecilius Plokamos, (without title) was likely magistrate of Prymnessus in the* Conventus *of Synnada, the site of which is located near Sülün, Turkey.*

**Baetica**
AE *as*. Italica mint. Struck 14–37 CE. Obverse: TI CAESAR AVGVSTVS PONT MAX IMP, bare head of Tiberius right. Reverse: MVNIC ITALIC PERM DIVI AVG, altar inscribed PROVIDENTIAE AVGVSTI. (Numismatic references: *RPC* I 65. *SNG* Copenhagen 417).
*The remains of Italica lie north of modern-day Santiponce, Spain.*

AE *as*. Italica mint. Struck 14–37 CE. Obverse: PERM DIVVS AVGVSTVS PATER, head of Augustus radiate head right, star above, thunderbolt right. Reverse: IVLIA AVGVSTA MVN ITALIC, Iulia Augusta (Livia Drusilla) seated left, holding *patera* and cornucopia.
(Numismatic references: *RPC* I 67).
*For a discussion see Sutherland (1941b and 1942).*

AE *semis*. Italica mint. Struck 16–19 CE. Obverse: GERMANICVS CAESAR TI AVG F, bare head of Germanicus right. Reverse: MVNIC ITALIC, PER AVG, legionary *aquila* with *vexillum* between two *signa*. (Numismatic references: *RPC* I 70).

AE *semis*. Italica mint. Struck 19–23 CE. Obverse: DRVSVS CAESAR TI. AVG. F, bare head of Drusus Minor right. Reverse: MVNIC ITALIC, PER AVG, legionary *aquila* with *vexillum* between two *signa*. (Numismatic references: *RPC* I 71).

AE *as*. Romula mint. Struck 14–37 CE. Obverse: PERM DIVI AVG COL ROM, laureate head of Tiberius left. Reverse: CAESAR GERMANICVS DRVSVS CAESAR, bare heads of Germanicus and Drusus Minor, facing each other. (Numismatic references: *RPC* I 74).
Colonia *Romula is on the site of modern Sevilla, Spain.*

AE *dupondius*. Romula mint. Struck 14–37 CE. Obverse: PERM DIVI AVG COL ROM, head of Augustus radiate head right, star above, thunderbolt right. Reverse: IVLIA AVGVSTA GENETRIX ORBIS, Iulia Augusta (Livia Drusilla) head left on globe, crescent above.
(Numismatic references: *RPC* I 73).

**Cilicia**

AE *chalkon*. Anazarbus mint. Struck 14–37 CE. Obverse: laureate head of Tiberius, right. Reverse: ΚΑΙϹΑΡΕΩΝ ΤΩΝ ΠΡΟϹ ΑΝΑΖΑΡΒ, three ears of corn. (Numismatic reference: *RPC* I 4058A).
*Anazarbus (Caesarea ad Anazarbus) is now Ağaçli in Turkey. For a discussion see Ziegler (1998/99), 102.*

AE *chalkon*. Rhosus mint. Struck Year 61 or 71 (19/20 CE or 29/30 CE). Obverse: ΤΙΒΕΡΙΟΥ ΚΑΙΣΑΡΟΣ ΣΕΒΑ[, laureate head of Tiberius, right. Reverse: ΡΩΣΕΩΝ ΕΤ Α[, wolf, left (Numismatic reference: *RPC* I 4078).
*Rhosus is now Arsuz in Turkey. For a discussion see Levante (1985), 242.*

**Commagene**

AE *dupondius*. Uncertain mint in Commagene. Struck 19–20 CE. Obverse: TI CAESAR DIVI AVGVSTI F AVGVSTVS, laureate head of Tiberius right. Reverse: PONT MAXIM COS III IMP VII TR POT XXI, winged caduceus between crossed cornucopias. (Numismatic references: *RPC* I 3868; *RIC* I 89; *BMC* 175).
*Germanicus sent Q. Servaeus to organise the new province in 18 CE.*

**Cappadocia**

AR *drachma*. Caesaraea-Eusebia mint. Struck 18–37 CE. Obverse: ΤΙΒΕΡΙΟΣ ΚΑΙΣΑΡ ΣΕΒΑΣΤΟΣ, laureate head of Tiberius right. Reverse: ΘΕΟΥ ΣΕΒΑΣΤΟΥ ΥΙΟΣ, Mount Argaeus surmounted by a naked statue of Helios holding globe and sceptre. (Numismatic references: *RPC* I 3620; *BMC* 11; Sydenham, Caesarea 42).

*Germanicus sent Q. Veranius to organise the new province in 18 CE.*

AR *drachma*. Caesaraea mint. Struck 32–33 CE. Obverse: TI CAES AVG P M TR P XXXIV, laureate head of Tiberius right. Reverse: DRVSVS CAES TI AVG F COS II TR P IT, bare head of Drusus Minor left. (Numismatic references: *RPC* I 3621; *RIC* I 84, 85).

*The Latin inscription contrasts with the Greek text on earlier coins.*

AR *drachma*. Caesaraea mint. Struck 33–34 CE. Obverse: TI CAES AVG P M TR P XXXV, laureate head of Tiberius right. Reverse: RVSVS CAES TI AVG COC II TR P, bare head of Drusus Minor left. (Numismatic references: *RPC* I 3622A; *BMC* I 171 corr.; *RIC* I 86, 87, 88).

**Egypt**

AE *dichalkon*. Alexandria mint. Struck 17/18 CE. Obverse: Σ E, bare head of Tiberius right. Reverse: TI/L Δ ('Year 4') within wreath. (Numismatic references: *RPC* I 5076; Köln 46; Dattari (Savio) 94; K&G 5.3; Emmett 68).

AE *obol*. Alexandria mint. Struck 18/19 CE. Obverse: Bare head of Tiberius right. Reverse: ΤΙΒΕΡΙΟΥ, LE ('Year 5'?), hippopotamus standing. (Numismatic references: *RPC* I 5082).

AR *tetradrachma*. Alexandria mint. Struck 20–21 CE. Obverse: ΤΙΒΕΡΙΟΣ ΚΑΙΣΑΡ ΣΕΒΑΣΤΟΣ, LZ ('Year 7'), laureate head of Tiberius right. Reverse: ΘΕΟΣ ΣΕΒΑΣΤΟΣ, radiate head of Augustus. (Numismatic reference: *RPC* I 5089).

AR *drachma*. Alexandria mint. Struck 27–28 CE. Obverse: ΤΙΒΕΡΙΟΣ ΚΑΙΣΑΡ ΣΕΒΑΣΤΟΣ, LIΔ ('Year 14'), laureate head of Tiberius right. Reverse: ΘΕΟΣ ΣΕΒΑΣΤΟΣ, radiate head of Augustus. (Numismatic reference: *RPC* I 5090).

**Galatia**

AE *dupondius*. Apollonia Moridaeum mint. Struck 14–37 CE. Obverse: ΤΙΒΕΡΙΟΣ ΣΕΒΑΣΤΟΣ, laureate head of Tiberius, right. Reverse: ΑΠΟΛΛΩΝΙΑΤΩΝ ΚΟΡΝΟΥΤΟΣ ΕΥΕΡΓΕΤΗΣ, head of Cornutus, bound with taenia, right. (Numismatic reference: *RPC* I 3528).

*Apollonia Moridaeum in Psidia (Uluborlu in Turkey) was located on the via Sebaste. For a discussion see Grant (1950b).*

AE *dupondius*. Koinon of Galatia mint. Struck c. 30/31 CE or 35/37? CE. Obverse: TIBEPIOC K[AI]CAP; bare head of Tiberius, right; all in wreath. Reverse: EΠI BACIΛ ΠPEC CEBACTOC, temple with six columns. (Numismatic reference: *RPC* I 3549).
*The coin was struck by T. Helvius Basila (*Legatus Augusti Propraetore*) from 30 CE or 37 CE.* EΠI indicates control by the governor. *For a discussion see Grant (1950b).*

AE *dupondius*. Koinon of Galatia mint. Struck Year 50 (25 CE or 28/30 CE). Obverse: TIBEPIOΣ KAIΣAP ΣEBAΣTOΣ; laureate head of Tiberius, left. Reverse: MHTHP ΘEωN ETEI N, turreted and draped bust of Cybele, left. (Numismatic reference: *RPC* I 3554).
*The coin was struck by T. Helvius Basila (*Legatus Augusti Propraetore*) from 30 CE or 37 CE. For a discussion see Grant (1950b).*

AE *dupondius*. Koinon of Galatia mint. Struck 18 CE or 21/23 CE. Obverse: TIBEPIOΣ KAIΣAP, bare head of Tiberius, left. Reverse: EΠI ΠPEIΣKOΥ MHN, ΓM (in field), head of Mên wearing cap on crescent, left. (Numismatic reference: *RPC* I 3554A).
*The coin was struck by Priscus, presumably* Legatus Augusti Propraetore *about whom little is known. For a discussion see Grant (1950b).*

**Hispania Tarraconensis**

AE *as*. Augusta Bilbilis mint. Struck 31 CE. Obverse: TI CAESAR DIVI AVGVSTI F AVGVSTVS, laureate head of Tiberius right. Reverse: MVN AVGVSTA BILBILIS TI CAESARE V L AELIO SEIANO, laurel wreath containing COS. (Numismatic references: *RPC* I 398; *SNG* Copenhagen 620). Fig. 29. *In some specimens the name of Seianus is stamped out in* damnatio memoriae.

AE *semis*. Caesaraugusta mint. Struck 14–37 CE. Obverse: TI CAESAR DIVI AVG F AVGVSTVS, laureate head of Tiberius left. Reverse: C C A (across field), SEX AEB[VTIVS L LVC]RETIUS II VIR, legionary *aquila* between two *signa*. (Numismatic references: *RPC* I 353; *SNG* Copenhagen 560).
*Sex. Aebutius and L. Lucretius were* duoviri *elected to the 'Commission of Two Men' of* Colonia *Caesaraugusta. The Roman colony is now Zaragoza in southeastern Spain.*

AE *semis*. Caesaraugusta mint. Struck 14–37 CE. Obverse: TI CAESAR DIVI AVG F AVGVSTVS, laureate head of Tiberius right. Reverse: C C A, bull standing right, with 'pediment' above head. (Numismatic references: *RPC* I 334).

AE *semis*. Caesaraugusta mint. Struck 14–37 CE. Obverse: TI CAESAR DIVI F AVG F AVGVSTVS, laureate head of Tiberius right. Reverse: CLEMENS ET LVCRETIVS, legionary *aquila* between two *signa*, C C A between the standards, II VIR in exergue. (Numismatic references: *RPC* I 354).

*Clemens and Lucretius Rufus were elected* duoviri *elected to the 'Commission of Two Men' of* Colonia *Caesaraugusta.*

AE *as*. Caesaraugusta mint. Struck 14–37 CE. Obverse: TI CAESAR DIVI AVG F AVGVSTVS, laureate head of Tiberius right. Reverse: T CAECILIO LEPIDO ET C AVFIDIO GEMELLO II VIR, around large C C A. (Numismatic references: *RPC* I 365; *FAB*-363).
*T. Caecilius Lepidus and C. Aufidius Gemellus were* duoviri *elected to the 'Commission of Two Men' of* Colonia *Caesaraugusta.*

AE *as*. Caesaraugusta mint. Struck 14–37 CE. Obverse: TI CAESAR DIVI AVGVSTI F AVGVSTVS, laureate head of Tiberius right. Reverse: C C A NERO CAESAR DRVSVS CAESAR II VIR, heads of Nero Caesar and Drusus Caesar facing each other. (Numismatic references: *RPC* I 343; *ACIP* 3069).
Fig. 21. *Nero Caesar and Drusus Caesar were sons of Germanicus. The* duoviri *of* Colonia *Caesaraugusta are not named.*

AE *as*. Calagurris (Nassica) Iulia mint. Obverse: TI AVGVS DIVI AVGVSTI F IMP CAESAR, laureate head of Tiberius right. Reverse: L SATVRNINO L FVL SPARSO, bull standing right. (Numismatic references: RPC I 448; *FAB* 429).
*L. Fulvius Sparsus and L. Saturninus were* duoviri *elected to the city's 'Commission of Two Men'. The remains of Calagurris lie in modern-day Calahorra in north-eastern Spain.*

AE *semis*. Carteia mint. Struck 14–37 CE. Obverse: GERMANICO ET DRVSO, head of Fortuna wearing mural crown (*corona muralis*) right. Reverse: CAESARIBVS IIII VIR CART, ship's rudder. (Numismatic references: *RPC* I 123).
*The remains of* Colonia *Libertinorum Carteia lie in modern-day San Roque (Cádiz) in southern Spain. The remains of* Colonia *Libertinorum Carteia lie in modern-day San Roque (Cádiz) in southern Spain.*

AE *semis*. Carthago Nova mint. 26 BCE-before 4 CE. Obverse: C HELVI POLL PR TI NERONE QVI, bare head of Tiberius right. Reverse: HIBERO PRAEF, Military elements: *simpulum*, *securis*, *aspergillum*, and *apex*. (Numismatic references: *RPC* I 166).
*The use of the name Ti. Nero suggests the mintage was before his adoption by Augustus. C. Helvius Pollio and Q, Varius Hiberus were both* praefecti *of Carthago Nova, modern Cartagena (Murcia), Spain. Other commanders featured on coins minted under Hiberus include Augustus (*RPC *I 162 and 166) and M. Agrippa (*RPC *I 164).*

AE *semis*. Carthago Nova mint. Struck 14–37 CE. Obverse: TI CAESAR DIVI AVGVSTI F AVGVSTVS P M, bare head of Tiberius to the left. Reverse: C V I N C NERO ET DRVSVS CAESARES QVINQ, heads of Nero Caesar and Drusus Caesar facing each other. (Numismatic references: *RPC* I 179, 180, 181; *FAB*-607).
*Nero Caesar and Drusus Caesar were sons of Germanicus.*

AE *semis*. Carthago Nova mint. Struck 33–37 CE. Obverse: TI CAESAR DIV(I) AVG(V) F AVG(VST)(V) P M, laureate head of Tiberius to the left. Reverse: C CAESAR TI N QVIN(Q) IN (or C) V I N K(AR), bare head of Caius (aka Caligula) left. (Numismatic references: *RPC* I 182; *SNG* Copenhagen 502).
*Caius was the youngest son of Germanicus.*

AE *as*. Celsa mint. Struck 14–37 CE. Obverse: TI CAESAR AVGVSTVS, laureate head of Tiberius right. Reverse: C V I CEL BAGG FRONT (or FRO(N)) CN BVCCO II VIR II, bull standing right, head facing. (Numismatic reference: *RPC* I 279).
*Baggius Front[o or -inus?] and Cn. Bucco were* duoviri *elected to the 'Commission of Two Men' for a second term in Celsa. Typically, the* cognomen *of Baggius appears as FRONT but, in a few cases, it has been recorded as FRON. The ruins of Celsa are located near the modern town of Velilla de Ebro (Zaragoza) in northern Spain.*

AE *as*. Cascantum mint. Struck 14–37 CE. Obverse: TI CAESAR DIVI AVG F AVGVSTVS, laureate head of Tiberius right. Reverse: Bull to right, above MVNICIP, below CASCANTVM. (Numismatic reference: *RPC* I 425, and variants 426, 427, and 428).
*Cascantum is Cascante (Navarra) in northern Spain.*

AE *as*. Clunia Sulpicia mint. Struck 14–37 CE. Obverse: TI CAESAR AVG F AVGVSTVS IMP, laureate head of Tiberius right. Reverse: CLVNIA; C AEM METO (or MET) T COR MATE (or MAT) L CAEL PRES C CAEL CAND (or CAN) IIII VIR, bull standing left. (Numismatic reference: *RPC* I 454).
*C. Aemilius Meto, C. Caelius Cand[?], L. Caelius Pres[?], and T. Cor[?] Mate[?] were* quattuorviri *elected to the city's 'Commission of Four Men'. The remains of* Colonia *Clunia Sulpicia are located at Alto de Castro (Burgos) in northern Spain.*

AE *as*. Ercavica mint. Struck 14–37 CE. Obverse: TI CAESAR DIVI AVGVSTI F AVGVSTVS, laureate head of Tiberius right. Reverse: II VIR C COR FLORO L CAEL ALACRE, bull standing right, head facing, above legend MVN ERCAVICA. (Numismatic reference: *RPC* I 462).
*C. Corne[lius] Florus and L Caeli[us] Alacr[is] were* duoviri *elected to the city's 'Commission of Two Men'. The remains of Ercavica are at Santaver near Cañaveruelas (Cuenca) in central Spain.*

AE *as*. Graccurris mint. Struck 14–37 CE. Obverse: TI CAESAR DIVI AVG F AVGVSTVS, laureate head of Tiberius right. Reverse: MVNICIP GRACCVRRIS, bull standing right, head facing right, temple pediment on horns. (Numismatic reference: *RPC* I 429; *SNG* Copenhagen 595–596).
*Graccurris was a* municipium*; it is modern day Alfaro (La Rioja) in northern Spain.*

AE *as*. Graccurris mint. Struck 14–37 CE. Obverse: TI CAESAR DIVI AVGVSTI F, laureate head of Tiberius right. Reverse: MVNICIP GRACCVRRIS, bull's head facing forward. (Numismatic reference: *RPC* I 430).
*Graccurris was a* municipium. *It is modern Alfaro (La Rioja) in northern Spain.*

AE *as*. Ilercavonia-Dertosa mint. Struck 14–37 CE. Obverse: TI CAESAR DIVI AVG F AVGVSTVS, laureate head of Tiberius right. Reverse: DERT M H I ILERCAVONI(A), merchant ship under sail left. (Numismatic reference: *RPC* I 207).
*The* municipium *of Ilercavonia-Dertosa is Ilercavonia (Tortosa) in northeastern Spain.*

AE *as*. Ilici mint. Struck 14–37 CE. Obverse: TI CAESAR DIVI AVG F AVG(VSTVS) P M, bare head of Tiberius, left. Reverse: C I I A L TER LON L PAP AVIT II VIR Q; two togate figures standing with hands clasped over *thymiaterion*, below IVNCTIO. (Numismatic reference: *RPC* I 198).
*L. Papirius Avitus and L. Terentius Longus were* duoviri *elected to the city's 'Commission of Two Men'. Ilici was a former* oppidum *in the southeast of the Iberian Peninsula which became an affluent city.*

AE *semis*. Osca mint. Struck 14–37 CE. Obverse: TI CAESAR DIVI AVG F AVGVSTVS, laureate head of Tiberius right. Reverse: M AEL MAXVMO Q AEL PROCVLO / II VIR OSCA. (Numismatic reference: RPC I 292).
*M. Aelius Maxumus and Q. Aelius Proculus were duoviri elected to the city's 'Commission of Two Men'. Urbs Victrix Osca was a* municipium. *It is modern Huesca (Huesca) in northeastern Spain.*

AE *as*. Osicerda mint. Struck 14–27 CE. Obverse: TI CAESAR AVGVSTVS, laureate head of Tiberius right. Reverse: MVN OSICERDA, bull standing right. (Numismatic reference: *RPC* I 468).
*Urbs Victrix Osca was a* municipium. *It is modern Huesca in northeastern Spain.*

AE *as*. Osicerda mint. Struck 14–27 CE. Obverse: TI CAESAR AVGVST, laureate head of Tiberius right. Reverse: above MVN, below OSIC. (Numismatic reference: *RPC* I 469).
*Oscicerda was a* municipium. *It is modern La Puebla de Híjar (Baja Aragón turolense) in northeastern Spain.*

AE *as*. Saguntum mint. Struck 14–37 CE. Obverse: TI CAESAR DIVI AVG (F) AVG(VS), bare head of Tiberius right. Reverse: L SEMP GEMIN(O) L VAL SVRA II VIR, navy bireme/trireme under oars right, SAG above. (Numismatic reference: *RPC* I 202).
*L. Sempronius Geminus and L. Valerius Sura were* duoviri *elected to the city's 'Commission of Two Men'. The remains of Saguntum are at Sagunto (Valencia) in eastern Spain.*

AE *as*. Segobriga mint. Struck 12–14 CE. Obverse: TI CAESAR DIVI AVG F AVGVS F IMP VIII, bare head of Tiberius left. Reverse: Laurea, inside SEGOBRIGA. (Numismatic reference: *RPC* I 474 and variants 475, 476, 477).
*Segobriga is on a hill near the modern town of Saelices (Cuenca) in central Spain.*

AE *as*. Tarraco mint. Struck 4–14 CE. Obverse: IMP CAES AVG TR POT PON MAX P P, laureate head of Augustus right. Reverse: TI CAESAR C V T, bare head of Tiberius right. (Numismatic reference: *RPC* I 215).
Colonia *Urbs [Triumphalis] Tarraco (CVT) is the modern city of Tarragona (Catalonia) in northeastern Spain.*

AE *sestertius*. Tarraco mint. Struck 15–37 CE. Obverse: DIVVS AVGVSTVS PATER, radiate head of Augustus left. Reverse: C V T T, altar decorated with garlands in the shape of a round shield, palm tree above. (Numismatic reference: *RPC* I 218).
*For a discussion see Sutherland (1941b and 1942).* Colonia *Urbs Triumphalis Tarraco (CVTT) is the modern city of Tarragona (Catalonia) in northeastern Spain.*

AE *as*. Turiaso mint. Struck 14–37 CE. Obverse: TI CAESAR AVGVST F IMPERAT, laureate head of Tiberius right. Reverse: MVN TVR C CAEC SER[E] M VAL QVAD II VIR bull, right (Numismatic reference: *RPC* I 417).
*C. Caecilius Serenus and M. Valerius Quadratus were* duoviri *elected to the city's 'Commission of Two Men'. The* municipium *of Turasio is the modern city of Tarazona (Aragón) in northern Spain.*

AE *as*. Turiaso mint. Struck 14–37 CE. Obverse: TI CAESAR AVGF IMP PONT M, laureate head of Tiberius right. Reverse: MVN TVR L CAEC AQVIN M CEL PALVD II VIR, bull standing right, head facing. (Numismatic reference: *RPC* I 419; *FAB* 2459).
*L. Caec[ilius] Aquinus and M. Cel[ius] Palud[us] were* duoviri *elected to the city's 'Commission of Two Men'. The* municipium *of Turasio is the modern city of Tarazona (Aragón) in northern Spain.*

AE *as*. Turiaso mint. Struck 14–37 CE. Obverse: TI CAESAR AVGVSTVS, laureate head of Tiberius right. Reverse: DIVVS AVGVSTVS MVN

TVR[IASO], radiate head of *Divus* Augustus right. (Numismatic reference: *RPC* I 423; *ACIP* 3297).

*The* municipium *of Turasio is the modern city of Tarazona (Aragón) in northern Spain.*

**Iudaea**

AE *perutah*. Caesarea or Jerusalem mint. Struck 16 CE. Obverse: ΙΟΥ/ΛΙΑ in two lines within wreath. Reverse: L-Γ ('Year 3') across field, three lillies. (Numismatic reference: Hendin 1335).

*Valerius Gratus was* Praefectus Iudaeae *(15–26 CE) who succeeded Annius Rufus. For a discussion see Jacobson (2019).*

AE *perutah*. Caesarea or Jerusalem mint. Struck 29 CE. Obverse: TIBEPIOY KAICAPOC and date LIϚ ('Year 16') surrounding *simpulum*. Reverse: IOYLIA KAICAPOC, three bound heads of barley, the outer two heads drooping. (Numismatic reference: *RPC* I 4967; Meshorer 21; Hendin 1341).

Fig. 46. *Pontius Pilatus was* Praefectus Iudaeae *(26–36 CE) who succeeded Valerius Gratus. For a discussion see Jacobson (2019).*

AE *perutah*. Caesarea Paneas mint. Struck 30–31 CE. Obverse: ΣΕΒΑΣΤWN, jugate heads of Tiberius (?) and Iulia Augusta. Reverse: ΕΠΙ ΦΙΛΙΠΠΟϒ ΤΕΤΡΑΡΧΟϒ, tetrastyle temple with central round design (shield?). (Numismatic reference: *RPC* I 4951; Meshorer 100a; Hendin 1229a; Howgego 457 and 690).

*The coin was minted 'In the time of (Herod) Philipp the Tetrarch' (4 BCE–34 CE). The building depicted is the* Augusteum *of Panias (Caesarea Philippi). Its ruins lie within the Hermon Stream (Banias) Nature Reserve at the foot of Mount Hermon, north of the Golan Heights.*

**Lusitania**

AE *as*. Emerita mint. Struck 14–37 CE. Obverse: DIVVS AVGVSTVS PATER, radiate head of Augustus right, star above, thunderbolt in front. Reverse: AVGVSTA EMERITA across attic of double-arched city gate between two towers; continuation of crenellated city walls above. (Numismatic reference: *RPC* I 21, and variants 22, 25, and 27).

*For a discussion see Sutherland (1941b and 1942).* Colonia *Augusta Emerita was founded in 25 BCE for veterans of legions (V* Alaudae, *X* Gemina, *and possibly XX* Valeria Victrix*), who fought in the Cantabrian and Asturian Wars. It is present day Mérida (Badajoz) in western Spain.*

AE *as*. Emerita mint. Struck 14–37 CE. Obverse: DIVVS AVGVSTVS PATER, radiate head of Augustus left. Reverse: COL AVGVSTA EMERITA, double-

arched city gate between two towers; continuation of crenellated city walls above. (Numismatic reference: *RPC* I 26 and variants 20, 23, 24, and 26).
*For a discussion see Sutherland (1941b and 1942).*

**Macedonia**
AE *chalkon* or *as*. Amphipolis mint. Struck 14–37 CE. Obverse: ΤΙ ΚΑΙΣΑΡ ΣΕΒΑΣΤΟΣ, laureate head right. Reverse: ΑΜΦΙΠΟΛΙΤΩΝ, Artemis Tauropolos on bull right. (Numismatic reference: *RPC* I 1632).

AE *chalkon* or *as*. Edessa mint. Struck 14–37 CE. Obverse: ΤΙ ΚΑΙΣΑΡ ΣΕΒΑΣΤΟΣ, laureate head of Tiberius right. Reverse: ΣΕΒΑΣΤΗ ΕΔΕΣΣΑΙΩΝ, bare head of Iulia Augusta right, star behind. (Numismatic reference: *RPC* I 1526; *BMC* 18).

AE *as*. Philippi (?) mint. Struck 14–37 CE. Obverse: TI AVG, bare head of Tiberius right. Reverse: Two priests ploughing right. (Numismatic reference: *RPC* I 1657; *SNG* Copenhagen 283 (Parium)).

AE *dupondius* or *as*. Dium mint. Struck 14–37 CE. Obverse: PIETAS, veiled of Pietas (or Iulia Augusta) right. Reverse: L RVSTI / CELIVS / CORDVS / [III] VIR / QVINQ / D D in six lines. (Numismatic reference: *RPC* I 1543).
*L. Rusticelius Cordus was* duovir quinquennalis, *one of the 'Commission of Two Men' of the* Colonia *Iulia Augusta Diensis. The site is now Dion in Central Macedonia, Greece. For a discussion see Sutherland (1941a).*

AE *dupondius* or *as*. Uncertain mint. Struck 14–37 CE. Obverse: TI CAESAR AVG F AVGVSTVS, bare head of Tiberius right. Reverse: P BAEBIVS / P F L RVSTICELIVS / BASTERNA / IIVIR QVINQ / D · D in five lines. (Numismatic reference: *RPC* I 1537).
*C. Baebius P. f. and L. Rusticelius Basterna were the* duoviri quinquennalis, *the two members of the 'Commission of Two Men' of their city. For a discussion see Sutherland (1941a).*

**Sicily**
AE *as*. Panormus mint. Struck 14–37 CE. Obverse: PANORMITANORVM, bare head of Tiberius right. Reverse: AVGVS(TVS), veiled head of Iulia Augusta (as Demeter) left. (Numismatic reference: *RPC* I 643 and variant 642; *CNS* I 38).

AE *as*. Panormus mint. Struck 14–19 CE. Obverse: DRV, bare head of Drusus Minor right. Reverse: GER, bare head of Germanicus right. (Numismatic reference: *RPC* I 5452).
*For a discussion see Frey-Kupper (1991).*

**Syria**

AE *chalkon*. Aegae mint. Struck 14–37 CE. Obverse: ΤΙΒΕΡΙΟΥ ΚΑΙCΑΡΟC CΕΒΑCΤΟΥ, laureate head of Tiberius left. Reverse: ΕΠΙ ΚΟΥΛΕΩΝΟC ΑΙΓΕΑΙΩΝ ΔΗΜΑΝ, inscription in five lines in wreath. (Numismatic reference: *RPC* I 4030).
*Culleo was* demarchos, *a largely symbolic office supervising public religious acts and festivals in Aegae.*

AR *tetradrachma*. Antioch on the Orontes mint. Struck 14–37 CE. Obverse: ΤΙΒ ΚΑΙΣΑΡ ΣΕΒΑΣΤΟC, laureate head of Tiberius, right. Reverse: ΑΝΤΙΟΧΕΩΝ ΜΗΤΡΟΠΟΛΕΩC, ΔΠ (in field), Tyche of Antioch seated right, with palm branch, before the river god Orontes. (Numismatic reference: *RPC* I 4162).
*Tyche was the goddess of luck/fortune and the counterpart of the Roman Fortuna. The image of the goddess reproduces the cult statue made by Eutychides of Sicyon in Corinthia (c.335–c.275 BCE), which stood inside her temple, the Tychaion, at Antioch. She sits on a rock (representing Mount Sipylus), has one foot on a swimming figure (the Orontes River), and holds several ears of grain in her hand (symbolising the city's fertility and prosperity). She wears a mural crown, representing a walled city (Antioch, now Antakya in Turkey).*

AE *chalkon*. Antioch on the Orontes mint. Struck '[Actian] Year 45', 14–15 CE. Obverse: ΣΕΒΑΣΤΟΣ ΣΕΒΑΣΤΟΥ ΚΑΙΣΑΡ, bare head of Tiberius, right. Reverse: Α ΕΠΙ ΣΙΛΑΝΟΥ ΑΝΤΙΟΧΕΩΝ ΕΜ, inscription within a laurel wreath of eight leaves. (Numismatic reference: *RPC* I 4270, *BMC* Galatia 150–1, McAlee 214).
*Minted under Q. Caecilius Metellus Creticus Silanus (*legatus Augusti pro praetore*).*

AR *tetradrachma*. Tarsus mint. Struck 35–37 CE. Obverse: ΤΙΒΕΡΙΟΥ ΚΑΙΣΑΡΟΣ ΣΕΒΑΣΤΟΥ, laureate head of Tiberius right. Reverse: ΣΕΒΑΣΤΗΣ ΙΟΥΛΙΑΣ ΗΡΑΣ ΜΗΤΡ, Iulia Augusta as Hera on throne right, holding ears of corn and poppies; to right, ΤΑΡ. (Numismatic reference: *RPC* I 4005).
*For a discussion see Butcher & Ponting (2009).*

**(c) Client States**

AV *stater*. Uncertain mint in Bosporus. Struck 30 CE. Obverse: Bare head (of Augustus? or Tiberius?) right. Reverse: ΒΑΡ (ligatured) ΖΚΤ ('Year 327') on two lines, bare head of man. (Numismatic reference: *RPC* I 1894).
*Ti. Iulius Aspurgus Philoromaios ('Lover of Rome') was monarch of the Kingdom of Bosporus Kingdom, a client state of Rome from 14 CE.*

AE *as*. Uncertain mint in Bosporus. Struck 30-? CE. Obverse: ΤΙΒΕΡΙΟΥ ΚΑΙΣΑΡΟΣ, laureate head of Tiberius right. Reverse: ΒΑΡ (ligatured) ΙΒ on two lines, diademed head of man. (Numismatic reference: *RPC* I 1903).

*Ti. Iulius Aspurgus Philoromaios ('Lover of Rome') was monarch of the Kingdom of Bosporus Kingdom, a client state of Rome from 14* CE.

**(d) Later Issues**

**Nero**

BI *tetradrachma*. Alexandria mint. Struck 66–67 CE. Obverse: ΝΕΡΩ ΚΛΑV ΚΑΙΣ ΣΕΒ ΓΕΡ AV, radiate head of Nero with *aegis* left, LΙΓ ('Year 13') below chin. Reverse: ΤΙΒΕΡΙΟΣ ΚΑΙΣΑΡ, laureate head of Tiberius right. (Numismatic reference: *RPC* I 5295; Dattari (Savio) 185; Emmett 134).
*Billion* tetradrachma *struck by the principal mint in Egypt.*

**Titus**

AE *as*. Rome mint. Struck 80–81 CE. Obverse: TI CAESAR DIVI AVG F AVGVST IMP VIII, bare head of Tiberius left. Reverse: IMP T CAES DIVI VESP F AVG REST around large S C. (Numismatic reference: *RCV* 2591).
*Restoration issue struck under Titus, the second Flavian emperor.*

AE *as*. Rome mint. Struck 80–81 CE. Obverse: TI CAESAR DIVI AVG F AVGVST IMP VIII, bare head left. Reverse: IMP T CAES DIVI VESP F AVG PM TRP PP COS VIII RESTITVIT in two lines around large S C. (Numismatic reference: *RIC* II 433; Cohen 73; *BMC* (Titus) 284; Sear 2595).
Fig. 32. *Restoration issue struck under Titus, the second Flavian emperor.*

**Domitian**

AE *as*. Rome mint. Struck 81–82 CE. Obverse: TI CAESAR DIVI AVG F AVGVST IMP VIII, bare head of Tiberius left. Right: IMP D CAES DIVI VESP AVG REST around large S C. (Numismatic reference: *RIC* II 826; *BMC* (Domitian) 509; Sear 2895).
Fig. 33. *Restoration issue struck under Domitian, the third and last Flavian emperor, who was a fan of Tiberius.*

# Glossary

| | |
|---|---|
| *HS* | *Sestertius*, sesterce. |
| *IIIvir* | *Triumvir*, member of a commission of three political leaders (*triumviri* pl.). |
| *Accusator* | A legal professional who made accusations to bring cases to court. |
| *Acies quadratum* | Dense, defensive square formation. |
| *Aedilis* | Magistrate in charge of public works, regulating state festivals and enforcing public order. |
| *Aes* | 'Copper'. |
| *Ala* | 'Wing', legionary cavalry on wings of battle formation (*alae* pl.). |
| *Amicitia* | 'Friendship'. |
| *Amphora* | Tall jar in which olive oil, fish sauce, wine and other products were carried and stacked in the holds of ships (*amphorae* pl.). |
| *Annona* | Personification of the grain supply of Rome. |
| *Aquila* | 'Eagle', the eagle standard of a legion. |
| *Ara* | Altar. |
| *As* | 'Copper', Roman coin worth half one *dupondius* (*aes, asses* pl.). |
| *Assessor* | Advisor hearing a case to ensure the law was properly applied and offering the presiding magistrate advice he considered appropriate. |
| *Augur* | Soothsayer specialising in interpretation of bird flight. |
| *Augustus* | 'Revered One', honorific title voted to Imp. Caesar |
| *Divi filius* | (Octavian) and his successor Tiberius. |
| *Aureus* | 'Gold', highest denomination gold coin worth 25 *denarii* (*aurei* pl.). |
| *Auxilia* | 'Helpers', professional support troops formed of allies or non-Roman citizens (*auxiliae* pl.). |
| *Ballista* | Artillery weapon throwing bolts or stones (*ballistae* pl.). |
| *Caliga* | Openwork military boot worn by Roman soldiers (*caligae* pl). |

| | |
|---|---|
| *Campus Martius* | 'Field of Mars', a large park and recreation ground in northwest Rome. |
| *Capitolium* | Temple of Iuppiter *Optimus Maximus* in Rome. |
| *Carru triumphali* | Decorated chariot used in a triumph. |
| *Castra Praetoria* | Fort in Rome of the *Cohortes Praetoriae* and *Cohortes Urbanae.* |
| *Censor* | Magistrate in charge of the *census.* |
| *Census* | Assessment of taxable assets carried out every five years (*lustum*). |
| *Centuria* | 'Century', unit of eight *contubernia* or eighty men; sixty centuries formed a *legio.* |
| *Centurio* | 'Centurion', officer in charge of a *centuria.* |
| *Clades* | 'Disaster', a devastating military defeat associated with *infamia.* |
| *Clementia* | 'Clemency' or 'mildness', a Roman virtue. |
| *Coercitio* | 'Coertion', force or punishment. |
| *Cohors* | 'Cohort', unit of six centuries or twelve in a First Cohort (*cohortes* pl.). |
| *Cohortes Praetoriae* | 'Praetorian Cohorts', Praetorian Guard. |
| *Cohortes Urbanae* | 'Urban Cohorts', para-military police force in Rome. |
| *Cohortes Vigilum* | Cohorts of *Vigiles,* Rome's firefighting service. |
| *Cohortres Voluntariorum* | 'Volunteer Cohorts', units formed of conscripted Roman citizens or freedmen. |
| *Colonia* | 'Colony', city founded for retired legionaries where citizens lived tax-free. |
| *Comitia Centuriata* | 'Centuriate or Peoples' Assembly' |
| *Comitia Tributa* | 'Tribal (or People's) Assembly. |
| *Commendatio* | 'Recommendation', excellence or worth. |
| *Commissatio* | Drinking session or revel. |
| *Consilium* | Advice, counsel or policy. |
| *Consecratio* | Consecration; dedication; making sacred; deification; devoting person to a god. |
| *Consulis* | One of the two highest magistrates of the *res publica,* elected annually. |
| *Contio* | 'Meeting', an address by a magistrate to the people or the commander to his troops to present a proposal. |
| *Convivio* | Meal and conversation in a formal dining room setting. |
| *Curia Iulia* | Senate House. |
| *Cursus honorum* | Competitive career ladder leading to entry into the Senate. |
| *Decimatio* | 'Decimation', execution by flogging of every tenth man. |

| | |
|---|---|
| *Decursio* | Military exercise performed as a pageant on special occasions. |
| *Deditio* | 'Surrender', capitulation. |
| *Delator* | 'Informer' or 'denouncer', usually in a case of *maiestas* (*delatores* pl.). |
| *Denarius* | Silver coin, worth 4 *sestertii* (*denarii* pl.). |
| *Dictator* | Extraordinary term-limited magistracy granted *imperium* over all other officials and magistrates during a national crisis, but limited to several months. |
| *Dilectus ingenuorum* | Levy of civilians into *cohortes voluntariorum.* |
| *Dominatio* | 'Mastery', tyranny of imperial authority. |
| *Dupondius* | Bronze coin, worth 2 *asses* or one half a *sestertius* (*dupondii* pl.). |
| *Dux* | 'Leader', chief, commander. |
| *Editor* | Sponsor of *ludi* or *munera* (*editors* pl.). |
| *Eques* | 'Knight', the commercial class of Roman society (*equites* pl.) forming the *Ordo Equester.* |
| *Ergastulum* | 'Prison', especially for slaves (*ergastula* pl.). |
| *Evocatus* | 'Recalled' or reservist, an honourably discharged *miles gregarius* available for recall on the orders of a consul or military commander (*evocati* pl.) |
| *Exercitus* | 'The Army'. |
| *Exilium* | 'Exile'. |
| *Expeditio* | 'Taskforce'. |
| *Fasces* | The tied bundle of rods around an axe carried by *lictores* as a symbol of the consul's or *praetor*'s high office. |
| *Feria* | Public holiday and festival day (*feriae* pl.). |
| *Flamen* | Priest (*flamines* pl.). |
| *Frater* | 'Brother', a familiar form of address used by soldiers (*fratres* pl.). |
| *Frugalitas* | 'Thriftiness', a Roman virtue. |
| *Forum Romanum* | Roman *Forum* in central Rome. |
| *Gladius* | Short stabbing and thrusting weapon used by legionaries (*gladii* pl.). |
| *Haruspex* | Soothsayer specialising in interpreting animal entrails. |
| *Hasta* | Javelin used by Roman *auxilia* and cavalry. |
| *Humanitas* | 'Humanity', the Roman virtue associated with being cultured from having a good education. |
| *Ianus* | 'Arch', triumphal arch. |
| *Imago* | Mask of wax made during the lifetime of a Roman citizen; military standard bearing a small statue bust of the *princeps*. |

| | |
|---|---|
| *Impedimenta* | Baggage train. |
| *Imperator* | 'Commander', a title shouted by Roman troops to a victorious leader. |
| *Imperium* | Legal power vested in a Roman magistrate. |
| *Imperium proconsulare* | Legal power to govern territories beyond Italy, including the right to wage war. |
| *Imperium proconsulare maius* | 'Supreme power', originally given to consuls, including the right to wage war. |
| *Industria* | 'Industry', Roman virtue of working hard. |
| *Infamia* | 'Shame', disgrace. |
| *Iustitia* | 'Justice', fairness. |
| *Kalendae* | 'Calends', first day of the month. |
| *Latrocinium* | Brigandage. |
| *Laudatio* | 'Eulogy'; *laudatio funebris*, funeral oration. |
| *Legatus Augusti pro praetore* | Governor of one of the Provinces of Caesar (propraetorian provinces). |
| *Legatus Legionis* | Commander of a *legio* 'delegated' the *imperium* by Augustus. |
| *Legio* | Unit of 10 *cohortes*, approximately 6,000 men (*legiones* pl.). |
| *Lex* | Law (*leges* pl.) |
| *Libertas* | Roman virtue of independence, freedom of speech. |
| *Libertus* | 'Freedman', ex-slave (*liberti* pl.). |
| *Liburna* | 'Liburnian', type of ship, usually with two rows of oarsmen. |
| *Lictor* | Bodyguard of a senior magistrate: a *consul* had twelve, a *praetor* six, a *propraetor* five and an *aedile* two (*lictores* pl.). |
| *Ludi* | Roman blood games, held for religious observance and increasingly used to further political ends. |
| *Lustrum* | Period of five years. |
| *Maiestas* | 'Majesty', treason caused by an affront to the majesty of the Roman People. |
| *Medicus* | 'Medic', doctor (*medici* pl.). |
| *Merum* | Undiluted or neat wine. |
| *Miles* | Common soldier, *miles gregarius* (*milites* pl.). |
| *Moderatio* | 'Self-control' or 'self-restraint', Roman virtue of restraint from excess. |
| *Modius* | Measure of grain equivalent to a third of an *amphora*. |
| *Mos maiorum* | 'The ways of the elders', traditional values and forms of worship. |

| | |
|---|---|
| *Munera* | Roman blood games held for political and entertainment purposes. |
| *Municipium* | Chartered provincial Roman city, typically in Italy. |
| *Natio* | 'Nation', community or tribe (*nationes* pl.). |
| *Nobiles* | 'Nobles', high-born families with consuls or praetors in their history. |
| *Novus homo* | 'New man', a man born of non-Roman aristocracy. |
| *Obses* | 'Hostages'. |
| *Officium* | 'Service', the staff – office – responsible for record keeping. |
| *Oppidum* | 'Stronghold', a town or defensible settlement often on a hill. |
| *Ovatio* | Lower form of triumph awarded to a victorious commander who was permitted to ride on a horse or walk through the streets of Rome. |
| *Palatium* | Augustus' house on the *Palatinus.* |
| *Parazonium* | Sword of a commander. |
| *Pater* | 'Father'. |
| *Pater Patriae* | 'Father of the Fatherland'. |
| *Paterfamilias* | Legal master of the household. |
| *Pax Augusta* | 'Augustan Peace', subjugation of an enemy achieved by military victory (often called *Pax Romana*). |
| *Pax Deorum* | 'Peace of the Gods'. |
| *Pietas* | 'Dutifulness', Roman virtue of respect for the natural order of things. |
| *Pilum* | Roman javelin, missile thrown by legionaries (*pila* pl.). |
| *Pompa* | Procession in a religious rite or funeral. |
| *Pompa triumphalis* | Full triumph in which the *triumphator* rode in a chariot followed by floats displaying the captive and spoils of war. |
| *Pontifex Maximus* | 'Chief Bridge Builder' (from *pons*, Latin for 'bridge'), chief priest responsible for maintaining *Pax Deorum.* |
| *Praeceptum* | 'Precept', dogma, order or maxim. |
| *Praefectus* | 'Prefect', senior officer or magistrate. |
| *Praefectus Aegyptii* | 'Prefect of Egypt', the governor of province Aegyptus. |
| *Praefectus Castrorum* | 'Prefect of the Camp', third in command of a *legio.* |
| *Praefectus Equitum* | 'Prefect of Horse', senior officer in command of a *turma.* |
| *Praefectus Praetorio* | 'Prefect of the Headquarters' (*Cohortes Praetoria*). |
| *Praefectus Vigilum* | 'Prefect of the Vigiles' (*Cohortes Vigilum*). |
| *Praepositus* | 'Overseer', special envoy or governor general. |

*Praetor* — Senior magistrate responsible for administering law, the *ludi* and *feriae.*

*Praetor Urbanus* — 'Urban Prefect', chief *praetor* in charge of administration of law in Rome.

*Praetorium* — 'Praetor's building', house of the *legatus* or senior officer of a unit in a fort, or the official residence of a provincial commander.

*Primipilus* — 'First javelin', the most senior *centurio* of a *legio*; (also *primus pilus*).

*Princeps* — 'First Man', the title adopted by Augustus to describe his leadership position.

*Princeps Praetorii* — Officer in charge of the army unit's *officium.*

*Principatus* — 'Commander-in-chief', head of state.

*Principia* — Headquarters building in a Roman fort.

*Proconsulis* — 'Ex-consul', governor of a senatorial province.

*Propraetor* — 'Ex-*praetor*', governor of an imperial province.

*Quaestiones* — Courts.

*Quaestor* — Junior magistrate in charge of law courts and public financial accounting.

*Repetundae* — 'Extortion', abuse of provincials.

*Res Gestae* — 'Things Done', the title of Augustus' autobiography.

*Res Publica* — 'Public Thing', the commonwealth of the Roman state.

*Rostra* — Tribunal, speaker's platform in *Forum Romanum.*

*Rostrum* — Bronze ram fitted to the front of a warship (*rostra* pl.).

*Sacerdos* — Priest (*sacerdotes* pl.).

*Saeculum* — A period estimated to be the lifetime of a man, approximately 100 years.

*Saevitia* — 'Cruelty', ferocity, rage.

*Salutatio* — Morning visit by clients to the patron.

*Semis* — Roman coin worth half one *as.*

*Senatus Consultum* — Decree of the Senate.

*Sestertius* — Brass coin, equal in value to one-quarter *denarius* (*sestertii* pl.).

*Signum* — Unit standard (*signa* pl.).

*Socius* — 'Ally', associate (*socii* pl.)

*Suffectus* — A consul replacing another who had resigned during his term in office.

*Toga praetexta* — White *toga* with a broad purple stripe along the curved edge.

*Toga pura* — 'Manly gown', the all-white *toga* worn by Roman adult men.

| | |
|---|---|
| *Toga virilis* | 'Manly gown', the all-white *toga* worn by Roman adult men. |
| *Transfugae* | 'Deserters'. |
| *Tresvir* | 'Three Man', a member of a board responsible for a state function, e.g. *tresviri monetales* who were responsible for managing the coin supply. |
| *Tribunus* | Tribune: *tribunus plebis*, a representative of the people elected annually; *tribunus militum*, 'military tribune'; *tribunus laticlavius*, the second in command of a *legio* was accompanied by five junior *tribuni angusticlavii.* |
| *Triumphator* | The military commander awarded an *ovatio* or *pompa triumphalis.* |
| *Triumvir* | Member of a commission of three political leaders (*triumviri* pl.). |
| *Tropaeum* | 'Trophy' made of captured weapons (*tropaea* pl.). |
| *Ustrinum* | Crematory in the Mausoleum of Augustus. |
| *Vexillum* | Flag standard. |
| *Via Appia* | 'Appian Way' connecting Rome to Brundisium. |
| *Via Flaminia* | 'Flaminian Way' connecting Rome to Ariminum. |
| *Via Praetoria* | 'Front Way', cross road in a Roman camp leading to *principia.* |
| *Via Principalis* | 'Principal Way', main street of a Roman camp. |
| *Via Sacra* | 'Sacred Way', the main road running through the *Forum Romanum.* |
| *Vicus* | One of the 265 districts of Rome, a village outside a fort (*vici* pl.). |
| *Virtus* | 'Manliness', Roman virtue of courage. |
| *Vituperatio* | Use of personal attack on an opponent. |

# Place Names

| **Cities and Towns** | |
|---|---|
| Actium | Aktion |
| Alexandria | Alexandria |
| Aliso | *Anreppen or Haltern-am-See* |
| Andetrium | Muč |
| Antiocheia | Antakya |
| Apollonia | Pojani |
| *Ara* Ubiorum | (after 1 CE) Cologne, Köln |
| Arausio | Orange |
| Argentorate | Strasbourg |
| Ariminum | Rimini |
| Artaxata | Artashat |
| Asciburgium | Asberg |
| Athenae | Athens, Athenai |
| *Augusta* Treverorum | Trier |
| Baiae | Baia |
| Batavodurum | Kops Plateau, Nijmegen |
| Brigantium | Bregenz, Austria |
| Brigantium | Briançon, France |
| Brundisium | Brindisi |
| Burnum | Roman camp near modern Kistanje, Croatia |
| Caesaraugusta | Zaragoza |
| Caesarea Maritima | Caesarea National Park, Israel |
| Carnuntum | Roman fortress located east of Vienna |
| *Colonia* Caesaraugusta | Zaragoza |
| *Colonia* Copia Felix Munatia (before mid-first century CE) | Lyon (Fourvière) |
| *Colonia* Iulia Augusta Diensis | Olympus |
| *Colonia* Martia Iulia Salonnae | Solin |
| Confluentes | Koblenz |
| Fectio | Vechten |

| | |
|---|---|
| Fidenae | Now a district in northeast Rome |
| Gadara | Umm Qais |
| Hierosolyma | Jerusalem |
| Lugdunum | (after mid-1st Century CE) Lyon |
| Massalia | Marseille |
| Misenum | Miseno |
| Mogontiacum | Mainz |
| Mutina | Modena |
| Mytilene | Mytilini |
| Nemausus | Nîmes |
| Narbo | Narbonne |
| Nikopolis | 'Victory City', Preveza, Greece |
| Novaesium | Neuss |
| *Oppidum* Ubiorum | (prior to 1 CE) Cologne, Köln |
| Perusia | Perugia |
| Puteoli | Pozzuoli |
| Ravenna | Ravenna |
| Rhegium | Reggio di Calabria |
| Roma | Rome, Roma |
| Salona | Solin, alternative name for *Colonia* Martia Iulia Salonnae |
| Segisama | Sasamón |
| Sirmium | Mitrovica |
| Siscia | Šišák |
| Tarraco | Tarragona |
| Ticinum | Pavia |
| Tilurium | Gardun near Trilj, Croatia |
| Tridentum | Trento |
| Vetera | Xanten |

**Islands**

| | |
|---|---|
| Amorgus | Amorgos |
| Capreae | Capri |
| Gyarus | Gyaros, Gioura |
| Pandateria | Ventotene |
| Planasia | Pianosa |
| Pontia | Ponza |
| Rhodos | Rhodes |
| Seriphos | Serifos |
| Siciliae | Sicily |
| Trimerus | Isole Tremiti |

**Mountains**

| | |
|---|---|
| *Mons* Alma | Fruska Gora |
| *Mons* Aventinus | Aventine Hill, Rome |
| *Mons* Caelius | Caelian Hill, Rome |
| *Mons* Capitolinus | Capitoline Hill, Rome |
| *Mons* Claudius | Papuk Hills |
| *Mons* Esquilinus | Esquiline Hill, Rome |
| *Mons* Medullus | *Peña Sagra?* |
| *Mons* Palatinus | Palatine Hill, Rome |
| *Mons* Quirinalis | Quirinal Hill, Rome |
| *Mons* Viminalis | Viminal Hill, Rome |
| *Mons* Vindius | *Peña Santa?* |

**Rivers**

| | |
|---|---|
| Albis | Elbe |
| Amisia | Ems |
| Arar | Saône |
| Bathinus | Bosna |
| Danuvius | Danube, Donau |
| Ister | Danube, Donau |
| Kolops | Kulpa |
| Lupia | Lippe |
| Moravus | Morava, March |
| Mosella | Moselle, Mosel |
| Minius | Miño, Minho |
| Moenus | Main |
| Nilus | Nile |
| Padus | Po |
| Rhenus | Rhine, Rhein |
| Rhodanus | Rhône |
| Savus | Sava, Save, Száva |
| Visurgis | Weser |

**Seas**

| | |
|---|---|
| *Mare* Aegaeum | Aegean Sea |
| *Mare* Germanicum | North Sea |
| *Mare Internum* | 'Internal (or Our) Sea', Mediterranean Sea |
| *Oceanus* | Atlantic Ocean |
| *Pontus* Euxinus | Black Sea |
| *Sinus* Arabicus | Red Sea |
| *Sinus* Hadriaticus | Adriatic Sea |

# Notes

## ABBREVIATIONS

**Ancient**

| | |
|---|---|
| Agath., *Hist.* | Agathias, *Historiae* |
| Ael. Don., *Vita Verg* | Aelius Donatus, *Vita Vergiliana* |
| Aul. Gell., *Noc. Att.* | Aulus Gellius, *Noctes Atticae* |
| Amm. Marc., *Res. Gest.* | Ammianus Marcellinus, *Res Gestae* |
| App., *Bell. Civ.* | Appian, *Bellum Civile* |
| Arat., *Phaen.* | Aratus, *Phaenomena* |
| Aug., *Res Gest.* | Augustus, *Res Gestae* |
| Caes., *Bell. Civ.* | Caesar, *Commentarii de Bello Civili* |
| Caes., *Bell. Gall.* | Caesar, *Commentarii de Bello Gallico* |
| *Cat., Carm* | Catullus, *Carmina* |
| Cic., *Ad Att.* | Cicero, *Ad Atticum* |
| Cic., *Cat.* | Cicero, *In L. Catilinam Oratio* |
| Cic., *Fam.* | Cicero, *Ad Familiares* |
| Cic., *Phil.* | Cicero, *Orationes Philippicae* |
| Dio | Cassius Dio, *Romaike Historia* |
| Diog. Laert. | Diogenes Laertius, *Bion kai Gnomon ton en Philipsophiai Eudokimesanton* |
| Euseb., *Hist. Eccl.* | Eusebius, *Historia Ecclesiastica* |
| Eutrop. | Eutropius, *Breviarium Historiae Romanae* |
| *Fast. Ost.* | *Fasti Ostienses* |
| *Fast. Praen.* | *Fasti Praenestini* |
| Florus | Florus, *Epitome* |
| Front., *Strat.* | Frontinus, *Stategemata* |
| Fronto, *Epist.* | Fronto, *Epistulae* |
| Hor., *Carm. Saec.* | Horace, *Carmen Saeculare* |
| Hor., *Odes* | Horace, *Carmina* |
| *Inst. Ius.* | Justinian, *Institutiones* |
| Jer., *Chron.* | Saint Jerome, *Chronicon* |
| Jos., *Ant. Iud.* | Josephus, *Antiquitates Iudaeicae* |
| Jul., *Ad Themist.* | Julian, *Epistula ad Themistium* |
| Jul., *Sat.* | Julian, *Saturnalia* |
| Just., *Digest.* | Justinian, *Digesta* |
| Juv., *Sat.* | Juvenal, *Satires* |
| Livy, *AUC* | Livy, *Ab Urbe Condita* |
| Livy, *Peri.* | Livy, *Periochae* |
| Macrob., *Sat.* | Macrobius, *Saturnalia* |
| Man., *Astro.* | Manlius, *Astronomica* |
| Nic., *Vit. Caes.* | Nicolaus of Damascus, *Vita Caesaris* |
| Oros., *Pagan.* | Orosius, *Historiae Adversus Paganos* |

| | |
|---|---|
| Ovid, *Fast.* | Ovid, *Fasti* |
| Ovid, *Pont.* | Ovid, *Epistulae ex Ponto* |
| Ovid, *Trist.* | Ovid, *Tristia* |
| Philo, *Flacc.* | Philo, *In Flaccum* |
| Philo, *Leg.* | Philo, *Legatio ad Gaium* |
| Pliny, *Nat. Hist.* | Pliny, *Naturalis Historia* |
| Plut., *Ant.* | Plutarch, *Antonius* |
| Plut., *Brut.* | Plutarch, *Brutus* |
| Plut., *Caes.* | Plutarch, *Caesar* |
| Plut., *Moral.* | Plutarch, *Moralia* |
| Plut., *Reg. et imp. Apophth.* | Plutarch, *Regum et Imperatorum Apophthegmata* |
| Polyb., *Hist.* | Polybius, *Historia* |
| Prop., *Eleg.* | Propertius, *Elegiae* |
| Ptol., *Geog.* | Ptolemy, *Geographia* |
| Ptol., *Tetra.* | Ptolemy, *Tetrabiblos* |
| Quint., *Instit. Orat.* | Quintilian, *Institutio Oratoria* |
| *SCPP* | *Senatus Consultum de Cn. Pisone Patre* |
| Sen., *Ben.* | Seneca, *De Beneficiis* |
| Sen., *Clem.* | Seneca, *De Clementia* |
| Sen., *Consol. Marc.* | Seneca, *Consolatio ad Marciam* |
| Sen., *Controv.* | Seneca, *Controversiae* |
| Sen., *Ep.* | Seneca, *Epistulae* |
| Sen., *Suas.* | Seneca, *Susaoriae* |
| Strabo | Strabo, *Geographika* |
| Suet., *Caius* | Suetonius, *Vita Cai* |
| Suet., *Div. Aug.* | Suetonius, *Vita Divi Augusti* |
| Suet., *Div. Claud.* | Suetonius, *Vita Divi Claudi* |
| Suet., *Div. Iul.* | Suetonius, *Vita Divi Iuli* |
| Suet., *Gramm.* | Suetonius, *De Grammaticis* |
| Suet., *Nero* | Suetonius, *Vita Neronis* |
| Suet., *Tib.* | Suetonius, *Vita Tiberi* |
| Suet., *Vit.* | Suetonius, *Vita Vitelii* |
| Tac., *Agr.* | Tacitus, *Agricola* |
| Tac., *Ann.* | Tacitus, *Annales* |
| Tert., *Apol.* | Tertullian, *Apologia* |
| Tibull., *Eleg.* | Tibullus, *Elegiae* |
| Ulpian, *Dig.* | Ulpian, *Digesta* |
| Val., *Anthol.* | Vettius Valens, *Anthologia* |
| Val. Max. | Valerius Maximus, *Factorum et Dictorum Memorabilium* |
| Vell. Pat. | Velleius Paterculus, *Historiae Romanae* |
| Veg., *Milit.* | Vegetius, *De Rei Militare* |
| Ver., *Aen.* | Vergil, *Aeneid* |
| Ver., *Ecl.* | Vergil, *Eclogues* |
| Vict., *Caes.* | Aurelius Victor, *De Caesaribus* |
| Zos., *Hist. Nova* | Zosimus, *Historia Nova* |

**Modern**

| | |
|---|---|
| *CIL* | *Corpus Inscriptionum Latinarum* |
| *EJ* | V. Ehrenberg & A. H. M. Jones, *Documents Illustrating the Reigns of Augustus and Tiberius* (Oxford: Oxford University Press, 1955, Second Edition) |

| | |
|---|---|
| *ILS* | *Inscriptiones Latinae Selectae* (ed. H. Dessau) |
| *Inscr. Ital.* | *Inscriptiones Italiae* |
| *P.Oxy.* | *Oxyrhynchus Papyri* |
| *Tab. Heb.* | *Tabula Habana* |
| *Tab. Siar.* | *Tabula Siarensis* |

## PREFACE

1. Suet., *Tib.* 61.1.
2. Consul: Suet., *Tib.* 61.6; Cordus: Tac., *Ann.* 4.34–35; Fenestella: Pliny, *Nat. Hist.* 33.146 [52] and Jer., *Chron.* A19.
3. Tac., *Ann.* 1.81.
4. Luke 3:1.
5. Mark 12:17 and Matthew 22.21: *Ἀπόδοτε οὖν τὰ Καίσαρος Καίσαρι καὶ τὰ τοῦ Θεοῦ τῷ Θεῷ.*
6. Steven Saylor, 'Ancient Rome's Short-Lived Teen Emperor: Practical Joker, Drag Queen, Transgender?', *The History Reader*, 29 June 2021.
7. Banner (2021), p.8.
8. Banner (2021), p.10.
9. Shawn McCreesh, 'The Journalist and the Billionaire: What did an old Establishment guy like Walter Isaacson learn writing Elon Musk's biography?', *New York Magazine*, 11 September 2023.
10. Banner (2021), p.269.
11. Edward Gibbon, *Decline and Fall of the Roman Empire*, Volume 1, Chapter 20.
12. Tac., *Ann.* 1.17.
13. *CIL*, IV, 1679, graffito at the Bar of Hedone or Colepius, Pompeii.
14. Tac., *Ann.* 1.1: *sine ira et studio.*

## CHAPTER 1: GROWING UP IN TURBULENT TIMES

1. Dio 55.12.1; Suet., *Tib.* 9.1.
2. At least two cohorts would accompany a member of Augustus' family on an assignment out of Italy: Tac., *Ann.* 1.24.2, 2.20.
3. Balmaceda (2014), p.340. It is not clear if his *praenomen* was Caius or Marcus.
4. Vell. Pat., 2.104.3.
5. Vell. Pat. 2.114.3.
6. Adapted from Vell. Pat., 104.3–4: *At vero militum conspectu eius elicitae gaudio lacrimae alacritasque et salutationis nova quaedam exultatio et contingendi manum cupiditas non continentium protinus quin adiicerent, 'videmus te, imperator? Salvum recepimus?' Ac deinde 'ego tecum, imperator, in Armenia, ego in Raetia fui, ego a te in Vindelicis, ego in Pannonia, ego in Germania donatus sum' neque verbis exprimi et fortasse vix mereri fidem potest.* Vell. Pat. 2.114.3 observes that Tiberius preferred to ride a horse rather than take a carriage.
7. Dio 54.13.2, 54.27.5.
8. Suet., *Tib.* 5.1: *Tiberium quidam Fundis natum existimaverunt secuti levem coniecturam, quod materna eius avia Fundana fuerit et quod mox simulacrum Felicitatis ex s. c. publicatum ibi sit. Sed ut plures certioresque tradunt, natus est Romae in Palatio XVI. Kal. Dec. M. Aemilio Lepido iterum L. Munatio Planco conss. per bellum Philippense. Sic enim in fastos actaque in publica relatum est. Nec tamen desunt, qui partim antecedente anno, Hirti ac Pansae, partim insequenti, Servili Isaurici [L.]que Antoni consulatu, genitum eum scribant.* Fundi is modern Fondi in southern Lazio, Italy. Kornemann (1960), p.13, and Seager (1972), p.7, agree on Rome; Van Wijk (2019), p.18, picks the birthplace as Perusia (Perugia); Baker (1929), Levick (1976), p.14, Shotter (1992) and Tarver (1902) opt not to say.

9. For Tiberius' interest in astrology and his bans on others practicing divination, see: Dio 55.11.1, 57.15.8, 57.19.3–4; Suet., *Tib.* 36.1, 69.1; and Hayes (1959).
10. The Battle of Philippi was fought in Macedonia on two separate days, 3 and 23 October 42 BCE.
11. 15 March 44 BCE. App., *Bell. Civ.* 2.117; Dio 44.8.4, 44.15–19; Jer., *Chron.* B44; Livy, *Peri.* 116.3; Suet., *Div. Iul.* 82; Plut., *Caes.* 66.
12. Vell. Pat. 2.75.1: *Ti. Caesaris pater, magni vir animi doctissimique et ingenii.*
13. Suet., *Tib.* 4.1; Dio 42.40.6.
14. Polyb., *Hist.* 6.12.
15. Caes., *Bell. Alex.* 25.3. Overcoming the Alexandrians, Caesar declared Kleopatra VII queen with her brother Ptolemy XIV Philopator.
16. It was popularly known as *Provincia*, preserved in the modern name Provence. Among these settlements were Iulia Paterna Arelatensium Sextanorum (modern Arles) for men of *Legio* VI *Ferrata* and Narbo Martius (Narbonne) for *Legio* X *Equestris*; both communities went on to thrive. Some *evocati* ('recalled' veterans) from *Legio* X *Equestris* later formed the core of Imp. Caesar's *Legio* X *Gemina* ('Twin') reconstituted by M. Aemilius Lepidus in 44/43 BCE; other veterans were recruited in Capua, Dio 45.12.1–5. For unit histories, see Parker (1993), pp.267–269 and Powell (2018), pp.296, 299.
17. Chase (1897), p.154.
18. Suet., *Tib.* 1.2: *Deinceps procedente tempore duodetriginta consulatus, dictaturas quinque, censuras septem, triumphos sex, duas ovationes adepta est.* On the magistracies of the *Res Publica*, see Polyb., *Hist.* 6.12–14.
19. Suet., *Tib.* 2.4: *Praeterea notatissimum est, Claudios omnis, … optimates adsertoresque unicos dignitatis ac potentiae patriciorum semper fuisse.*
20. Suet., *Tib.* 3.1: *Quae familia, quanquam plebeia, tamen et ipsa admodum floruit octo consulatibus, censuris duabus, triumphis tribus, dictatura etiam ac magisterio equitum honorata.*
21. Tarver (1902), p.103.
22. Barrett (2002), p.11.
23. App., *Bell. Civ.* 2.5[35]; Caes., *Bell. Civ.* 1.9; Dio 41.4.1; Suet., *Div. Iul.* 31.2.
24. Dio 41.6.1, 4.7.3.
25. Seager (1972), p.7.
26. Suet., *Tib.* 4.1: *Tamen Caesare occiso, cunctis turbarum metu abolitionem facti decernentibus, etiam de praemiis tyrannicidarum referendum censuit.*
27. Dio 45.14.1; Nic., *Vit. Caes.* 28; Suet., *Div. Iul.* 85.1.
28. App., *Bell. Civ.* 3.3[24].
29. App., *Bell. Civ.* 3.4[27]; Dio 45.35.2; Suet., *Div. Aug.* 10.2.
30. Plut., *Brut.* 22.1–22.3; Suet., *Div. Aug.* 7.1; Vell. Pat. 2.59.1–2.
31. Dio 45.3.1; Suet., *Div. Aug.* 10.1, 94.12; Vell. Pat. 2.59.3–4.
32. Nic., *Vit. Caes.* 7; Vell. Pat. 2.59.5.
33. Suet., *Div. Aug.* 7.2; Nic., *Vit. Caes.* 30.
34. Aug., *Res Gest.* 1; Cic., *Ad Fam.* 11.20.1; Suet., *Div. Aug.* 12.1; Nic., *Vit. Caes.* 28; Vell. Pat. 2.61.3.
35. Aug., *Res Gest.* 1; Dio 46.35.4; Suet., *Div. Aug.* 10.3. For a discussion of the Battle of Forum Gallorum and Mutina, see Powell (2014a).
36. Dio 46.47.1–2.
37. Suet., *Div. Aug.* 12.1; Vell. Pat. 2.62.6.
38. Aug., *Res Gest.* 4; Suet., *Div. Aug.* 26.1. He would go on to be elected consul thirteen times during his career, Suet., *Div. Aug.* 26.2–3.
39. Dio 46.53.1–54.1.

40. Suet., *Div. Aug.* 10.1, 29.2.
41. Aug., *Res Gest.* 1, 7; Suet., *Div. Aug.* 27.1.
42. Dio 46.55.4–56.2.
43. Vell. Pat. 2.70.1.
44. Aug., *Res Gest.* 2; Suet., *Div. Aug.* 9.1, 13.1, 29.2; Vell. Pat. 2.70.2–4.
45. Suet., *Tib.* 4.3; Tac., *Ann.* 5.1.
46. Vell. Pat. 2.75.3: *Livia … genere, probitate, forma Romanarum eminentissima.*
47. Tac., *Ann.* 5.1: *sanctitate domus priscum ad morem, comis ultra quam antiquis feminis probatum, mater impotens, uxor facilis et cum artibus mariti, simulatione filii bene composita. funus eius modicum, testamen tum diu inritum fuit.*
48. Tarver (1902), p.104.
49. Suet., *Tib.* 4.3.
50. Suet., *Tib.* 5.1.
51. On Roman practices concerning clear assertion of *pater potestas*, see Balsdon (1969), p.90, and Carcopino (1940), pp.77–78.
52. Suet., *Tib.* 4.3.
53. Suet., *Tib.* 4.1; Tac., *Ann.* 5.1.
54. Suet., *Div. Aug.* 9.1, 14.1, 96.2.
55. Suet., *Div. Aug.*15.1; *cf.* Tac., *Ann.* 6.51.
56. Suet., *Tib.* 4.2; Vell. Pat. 2.74.3.
57. Vell. Pat. 2.75.1: *Per eadem tempora exarserat in Campania bellum, quod professus eorum, qui perdiderant agros, patrocinium ciebat Ti. Claudius Nero.*
58. Dio 48.15.3; Suet., *Tib.* 4.2; Vell. Pat. 2.73.1–3, 2.75.3.
59. Dio 48.17.1–4.
60. Dio 48.15.3; Suet., *Tib.* 4.3.
61. Suet., *Tib.* 6.1–2: *Infantiam pueritiamque habuit laboriosam et exercitatam, comes usque quaque parentum fugae; quos quidem apud Neapolim sub inruptionem hostis navigium clam petentis vagitu suo paene bis prodidit, semel cum a nutricis ubere, ite[ru]m cum a sinu matris raptim auferretur ab iis, qui pro necessitate temporis mulierculas levare onere temptabant. Per Siciliam quoque et per Achaiam circumductus ac Lacedaemoniis publice, quod in tutela Claudiorum erant, demandatus, digrediens inde itinere nocturno discrimen vitae adiit flamma repente e silvis undique exorta adeoque omnem comitatum circumplexa, ut Liviae pars vestis et capilli amburerentur.*
62. Suet., *Tib.* 6.3: *Munera, quibus a Pompeia Sex. Pompei sorore in Sicilia donatus est, chlamys et fibula, item bullae aureae, durant ostenduntur que adhuc Baiis.* The *bulla* was worn around the neck by a young freeborn Roman boy from childhood until his rite of passage into manhood.
63. Dio 48.29.1–48.30.1.
64. Dio 48.36.1–48.38.3.
65. Tac., *Ann.* 5.1; Suet., *Tib.* 4.1; Vell. Pat. 2.77.3.
66. Dio 48.44; Suet., *Aug.* 62.2; Suet., *Tib.* 4.3; Vell. Pat. 2.79.2; Tac., *Ann.* 5.1.
67. Suet., *Aug.* 63.1.
68. Suet., *Aug.* 62.2: *'pertaesus,' ut scribit, 'morum perversitatem eius'*; *cf.* Suet., *Div. Aug.* 69.1.
69. *Fasti Ver.* (*EJ.* p.46).
70. Suet., *Div. Claud.* 11.3, stating it was the same day as the birthday of M. Antonius, 14 January; *cf.* Ovid, *Fasti* 1.597–598, stating it was 13 January. For a discussion about the date, see Powell (2011), pp.1–3.
71. Suet., *Div. Claud.* 1.1.
72. Suet., *Div. Claud.* 1.1; Suet., *Tib.* 4.1. For a biography of the life of Dec. (later Nero) Claudius Drusus, aka Drusus Maior or Drusus the Elder, see Powell (2011).

73. Suet., *Tib.* 6.4. Shotter (1992), p.7, puts the funeral in 32 BCE.
74. Suet., *Tib.* 7.1.
75. Suet., *Tib.* 7.1: *rudiariis quoque quibusdam revocatis auctoramento centenum milium. Rudiarii* were champion-level gladiators who had each been given a *rudis*, a wooden sword which granted them their liberty. On the Theatre of Statilius Taurus, see Suet., *Div. Aug.* 29.5. Grandfather Ti. Claudius Nero was *praetor* in *c.* 67 BCE, the year in which he served under Cn. Pompeius Magnus during the War Against the Pirates fought in Cilicia.
76. Suet., *Tib.* 7.1.
77. Suet., *Aug.* 72.1; Dio 53.26.5, 53.16.5. On what is known of the *Palatium*, see Wiseman (2019), pp.5–10, 19–29.
78. Octavia Minor's children by C. Claudius Marcellus: Claudia Marcella Maior, Claudia Marcella Minor and M. Claudius Marcellus; by M. Antonius: Antonia Maior and Antonia Minor.
79. Macrob., *Sat.*: Julia's Wit 2.5.1–10.
80. Suet., *Div. Aug.* 64.2.
81. Suet., *Tib.* 71.1.
82. Suet., *Tib.* 70.3: *Maxime tamen curavit notitiam historiae fabularis usque ad ineptias atque derisum; nam et grammaticos, quod genus hominum praecipue, ut diximus, appetebat, eius modi fere quaestionibus experiebatur: 'Quae mater Hecubae, quod Achilli nomen inter virgines fuisset, quid Sirenes cantare sint solitae'.*
83. Vell. Pat. 2.63.1. For Lepidus' career, see Syme (2016) and Welch (1995).
84. Dio 48.31.3.
85. For the Atropatene campaign, see Dio 49.19.1–33.4. For the so-called Donations of Alexandria of Autumn 32 BCE, see Dio 49.41.1–3 and Plut., *Ant.* 54.3–4.
86. Dio 49.1.1–14.6, 49.17.1–18.7, 49.34.1–38.4; Suet., *Div. Aug.* 19.2; Vell. Pat. 2.78.2.
87. Dio 49.33.3–34.1.
88. Dio 46.47.4–8, 49.41.6; Plut., *Ant.* 55.1–2.
89. Imp. Caesar *Divi Filius* was the form he used after *c.* 38 BCE: Dio 52.41.3 (*cf.* Suet., *Div. Iul.* 76.1). Iulius Caesar was declared a god on 1 January 42 BCE.
90. For the Actian War and the Battle of Actium, see Tarn (1931, 1932 and 1938), Lange (2009b and 2011) and Powell (2015), pp.75–99, and the Alexandrian War and siege of Alexandria, see Powell (2018), pp.21–25.
91. Day 1 (13 April 29 BCE) the Illyrian War; Day 2 (14 April) the Actian War; and Day 3 (15 April) the Alexandrian War. Aug., *Res Gest.* 4; Dio, 51.21.6–8; Plut., *Ant.* 86.8; *Fasti Tr. Barb.* (*EJ* p.35); *Fasti. Ant.* (*EJ* p.50).
92. Dio 51.21.7.
93. Suet., *Tib.* 6.4. Tiberius' brother, Nero Drusus, and stepsister, Iulia, 9 and 10 years old respectively, may have ridden in the chariot: see Beard (2007), p.224.
94. Thorburn (2008), p.441; Vervaet (2011).
95. Vervaet (2010).
96. Dio 53.12.1–16.3; Strabo 17.3.25; Suet., *Aug.* 47.1. The Provinces of the Senate and People were Africa, Numidia, Asia, Achaia, Epirus, Illyricum, Sicily, Crete and the Cyrenaic portion of Libya, Bithynia and Pontus, Sardinia and Baetica; the Provinces of Caesar were Hispania Citerior, the Three Gallic provinces of Aquitania, Gallia Comata (also known as Celtica) and Belgica, Narbonensis (also known as Provincia), Coele-Syria, Syria, Cilicia, Cyprus and newly acquired Aegyptus.
97. Dio 53.12.2: *ἀλλὰ τὰ μὲν ἀσθενέστερα ὡς καὶ εἰρηναῖα καὶ ἀπόλεμα ἀπέδωκε τῇ βουλῇ, τὰ δ' ἰσχυρότερα ὡς καὶ σφαλερὰ καὶ ἐπικίνδυνα καὶ ἤτοι πολεμίους τινὰς προσοίκους ἔχοντα ἢ καὶ αὐτὰ καθ'.* On whether Augustus had a grand strategy, see Powell (2018), pp.174–184.

98. Dio 53.16.6–8 *ἀλλὰ Αὔγουστος ὡς καὶ πλεῖόν τι ἢ κατὰ ἀνθρώπους ὢν ἐπεκλήθη: πάντα γὰρ τὰ ἐντιμότατα καὶ τὰ ἱερώτατα αὔγουστα προσαγορεύεται*; *cf.* 53.18.2.
99. *Fasti Prae.* (*EJ* p.48); *Inscr. Ital.* XIII, ii, 131.
100. Suet., *Tib.* 6.3; on the Roman coming of age ceremony and celebrations, see Balsdon (1969), p.120.
101. Suet., *Tib.* 6.4. The event was also called the *Lusus Troiae* and *Troiae Decursio*, and was intended to represent an exercise introduced by Aeneas and the Trojans after their landing in Italy; see: Suet., *Div. Iul.* 39.2, Dio 49.43.3, 51.22.4.
102. *Cf.* Dio 49.43.3. In 28 BCE, Ti. Claudius Nero, then 14 years old, was *ductor turmae puerorum maiorum*, commanding a group of the biggest boys (Suet., *Tib.* 6.1).
103. Suet., *Div. Aug.* 43.1: *Sed et Troiae lusum edidit frequentissime maiorum minorumque puerorum, prisci decorique moris existimans clarae stirpis indolem sic notescere.*
104. Suet., *Div. Aug.* 43.2: presumably L. Nonius Asprenas who, nevertheless, became suffect consul in 6 CE.
105. Vell. Pat 2.92.2.
106. Suet., *Tib.* 70.1, 71.1.
107. Nestor: Levick (1976), p.16. Theodoros: Suet., *Tib.* 57.1; *Suda*, 151.
108. DuPont (1992), p.128.
109. Suet., *Tib.* 70.1. Corvinus lived 64 BCE–8 or *c.* 12 CE and was consul for 31 BCE. For his life and achievements see Syme (1986), pp.200–216; for his rhetoric see Kenty (2017).
110. *ILS* 5990 records Corvinus as the owner of the famed Gardens of Lucullus (*Horti Luculliani*) located on the Pincian Hill, where the Villa Borghese gardens are today.
111. Cicero's town treatise on public speaking survives as *Orator ad M. Brutum*.
112. Quint., *Instit. Orat.* 10.1.60.
113. Philo, *Leg.* 142.
114. Quint., *Instit. Orat.* 11.3.100.
115. Suet., *Tib.* 70.1: *Sed adfectatione et morositate nimia obscurabat stilum, ut aliquanto ex tempore quam a cura praestantior haberetur.*
116. Tac., *Ann.* 13.3.2: *Tiberius artem quoque callebat, qua verba expenderet, tum validus sensibus aut consulto ambiguus.*
117. Suet., *Div. Aug.* 86.2: *Sed nec Tiberio parcit et exoletas interdum et reconditas voces aucupanti.*
118. Dio 57.1.1: *ταῦτα μὲν κατὰ Αὔγουστον ἐγένετο, Τιβέριος δὲ εὐπατρίδης μὲν ἦν καὶ ἐπεπαίδευτο, φύσει δὲ ἰδιωτάτῃ ἐκέχρητο. οὔτε γὰρ ὧν ἐπεθύμει προσεποιεῖτό τι, καὶ ὧν ἔλεγεν οὐδὲν ὡς εἰπεῖν ἐβούλετο, ἀλλ' ἐναντιωτάτους τῇ προαιρέσει τοὺς λόγους ποιούμενος πᾶν τε ὃ ἐπόθει ἠρνεῖτο καὶ πᾶν ὃ ἐμίσει προετείνετο: ὠργίζετό τε ἐν οἷς ἥκιστα ἐθυμοῦτο, καὶ ἐπιεικὴς ἐν οἷς μάλιστα ἠγανάκτει.*
119. Tac., *Ann.* 6.2: *ludibria seriis permiscere solitus.*
120. Dio 53.22.5.
121. Dio 53.22.5: *καὶ τὰ τούτων ἀκατάστατα ἔτι, ἅτε τῶν ἐμφυλίων πολέμων εὐθὺς ἐπὶ τῇ ἁλώσει σφῶν ἐπιγενομένων, ἦν.*
122. Dio 53.25.2, 53.25.3–8.
123. Livy, *AUC* 2.12.10: *facere et pati fortia Romanum est.*
124. On the organization of the legion under Augustus, see Powell (2018), pp.288–289.
125. Suet., *Div. Aug.* 38.2, 46.1.
126. On the duties of a *tribunus militum*, see Polyb., *Hist.* 6.12.
127. The First Cohort is believed to have been of double size.
128. Dio 53.15.2. Powell (2018), p.288.
129. Suet., *Tib.* 9.1. The legions to which they were assigned are not now known.
130. For a survey of archaeological evidence from the Roman campaigns in Asturias and Cantabria, see Fernández-Götz & Roymans (2024), pp.31–45.
131. Dio 51.20.5, 53.25.2.

132. Flor. 2.33. *Cf.* Strabo 3.3.8.
133. Dio 56.43.3.
134. Dio 53.25.5; Flor. 2.33; Strabo 3.4.5; Suet., *Div. Aug.* 20, 21. For the *Bellum Cantabricum et Asturicum*, see Powell (2018), pp.41–45, Colmenero (1979) and Morillo (2011), pp.13–15. For a survey of the sites in the region explored by archaeologists, see Fernández-Götz & Roymans (2024), pp.31–46.
135. Powell (2018), Order of Battle 1, p.42. Known to have taken part were *Legiones* I *Augusta*, II *Augusta*, IIII *Macedonica*, V *Alaudae*, VI *Victrix*, VIIII *Hispana*, X *Gemina* and XX. For a discussion of the number and whereabouts of units present, see Syme (1934a), pp.298–301. Curchin (1995), p.69. They were supported by auxiliary cavalry from *Ala Augusta, Ala* II *Gallorum*, *Ala Parthorum* and *Ala* II *Thracum Victrix Civium Romanorum*; and auxiliary infantry from *Cohors* II *Gallorum* and *Cohors* IV *Thracum Aequitata*. Curchin (1995), pp.71–72, casts doubt on the presence of *Cohors Thracum*.
136. For the legates with Augustus, see Powell (2018), p.42 and Syme (1934a), pp.301–302. Flor. 2.33 mentions that M. Agrippa was involved, which is problematic since he was certainly in Rome at this time. Magie (1920), p.335, suggests that Florus may have compressed three different campaigns into a single statement.
137. Flor. 2.33; Oros., *Pagan.* 6.21.6–7; Dio 53.25.7–8; Vell. Pat. 2.90.4.
138. App., *Bell. Civ.* 5.111.1; Flor. 2.33; Oros., *Pagan.* 6.21.10; Dio 53.25.8, 54.5.1–2. See Syme (1934a), pp.315–316.
139. Dio 53.25.6.
140. Flor. 2.33.
141. Attica/Velica: Dio 53.25.6, Oros., *Pagan.* 6.2.5; Bergida: Flor. 2.33.
142. Dio 53.25.7. Flor. 2.33; Oros. 6.21. *Mons* Vindius may have been one of the mountains in the Cordillera Cantábrica.
143. Oros., *Pagan.* 6.21.4.
144. For the siege of Monte Bernorio, see Torres-Martínez & Fernández-Götz (2017).
145. Flor. 2.33: *quasi quadam cogebat indagine.*
146. Dio 53.27.5.
147. Dio 53.25.7; Suet., *Div. Aug.* 81.1: *cum etiam destillationibus iocinere vitiato ad desperationem redactus contrariam.*
148. Dio 53.25.7; Flor. 2.33; Suet., *Div. Aug.* 81.1.
149. Dio 53.30.1–2.
150. Flor. 2.33; Oros., *Pagan.* 6.21. The Miño is the longest river in Galicia, Spain, with an extension of 340km. For the whereabouts of *Mons* Medullus, see Magie (1920), pp.334–345.
151. Flor. 2.33 says 18 miles; Oros., *Pagan.* 6.21.7 says 15 miles.
152. *RIC* I 1, a silver *quinarius*, shows Victory crowning a trophy while *RIC* I 4, a *denarius*, shows the trophy itself. Both, minted at Emerita Augusta, bear the legend *P CARISIVS LEG AVGVSTI PRO P.*
153. Suet., *Div. Aug.* 81.
154. Dio 53.30.4.
155. Dio 53.29.1.
156. Dio 53.28.3: *τῷ τε Μαρκέλλῳ βουλεύειν τε ἐν τοῖς ἐστρατηγηκόσι καὶ τὴν ὑπατείαν δέκα θᾶττον ἔτεσιν ἤπερ ἐνενόμιστο αἰτῆσαι, καὶ τῷ Τιβερίῳ πέντε πρὸ ἑκάστης ἀρχῆς ἔτεσι τὸ αὐτὸ τοῦτο ποιῆσαι ἐδόθη.*
157. Suet., *Div. Aug.* 59.
158. Suet., *Tib.* 8.1; Vell. Pat. 2.94.1 confirms this occurred 'in his nineteenth year', *undevicesimum annum.*
159. Agath., *Hist.* 2.17; Suet., *Tib.* 8.1; Strabo 12.8.18. King Archaelus: Dio 57.17.3.

160. Suet., *Tib.* 8.1: *varia quosque de causa.*
161. Suet., *Tib.* 8.1.
162. The term was sufficiently ambiguous that it was used to prosecute any form of treason, revolt or failure in public duty. Little is recorded about the case beyond Dio 54.3.4–8, who writes that the accused men actually did not stand trial and were convicted by default since they represented a flight risk; see Stockton (1965).
163. Dio 54.3.6.
164. Strabo 14.5.4. Athenaeus wrote a treatise on machines and dedicated it to 'Marcellus', who scholars identify as Augustus' deceased son-in-law.
165. Dio 54.3.5.
166. Dio 54.3.5.
167. Tac., *Ann.* 3.56. Levick (1976), p.23.
168. Dio, 53.12.7. Augustus returned Cyprus and Gallia Narbonensis to the care of the Senate and took Illyricum in exchange. For a discussion of Augustus' *imperium proconsulare maius*, see Ehrenberg (1953), Gruen (2005) and Jones (1951).
169. Dio 54.12.2–4. For a discussion of Agrippa's *imperium*, see Gray (1970) and Kornemann (1930).
170. Tac., *Ann.* 1.1: *nomine principis sub imperium accepit*; *cf.* Aug., *Res Gest.* 7. Gruen (2005), p.35, stresses this important point.
171. Suet., *Div. Aug.* 79.1–2: *Oculos habuit claros ac nitidos, quibus etiam existimari volebat inesse quiddam divini vigoris, gaudebatque, si qui sibi acrius contuenti quasi ad fulgorem solis vultum summitteret; sed in senecta sinistro minus vidit; dentes raros et exiguos et scabros; capillum leviter inflexum et subflavum; supercilia coniuncta; mediocres aures; nasum et a summo eminentiorem et ab imo deductiorem; colorem inter aquilum candidumque; staturam brevem – quam tamen Iulius Marathus libertus et a memoria eius quinque pedum et dodrantis fuisse tradit – sed quae commoditate et aequitate membrorum occuleretur, ut non nisi ex comparatione astantis alicuius procerioris intellegi posset.*
172. Suet., *Div. Aug.* 80.1.
173. Suet., *Div. Aug.* 81.1–2.
174. Suet., *Div. Aug.* 20.1–22.1, 24.1–25.3, 28.1–3, 37.1–38.1–2.
175. Suet., *Div. Aug.* 33.1.
176. Suet., *Div. Aug.* 36.1, 39.1, 41.1, 49.2, 81.1–2.
177. Suet., *Div. Aug.* 84.2.
178. Suet., *Div. Aug.* 54.1, 66.2.
179. Suet., *Div. Aug.* 31.4, 93.1, 94.7–12, 96, 97.1–98.4.
180. Suet., *Div. Aug.* 90.1–92.1.
181. Suet., *Div. Aug.* 21.2–3, 27.4, 51.1–2, 66.1–2.
182. Suet., *Tib.* 8.1.
183. For the origin, role and responsibilities of the *quaestor Ostiensis*, see Chandler (1978).
184. Vell. Pat. 2.94.3.
185. Suet., *Div. Aug.* 51.3: *Tiberio quoque de eadem re, sed violentius apud se per epistulam conquerenti ita rescripsit: 'Aetati tuae, mi Tiberi, noli in hac re indulgere et nimium indignari quemquam esse, qui de me male loquatur; satis est enim, si hoc habemus ne quis nobis male facere possit.'*
186. Suet., *Tib.* 8.1. Tac., *Ann.* 4.27 remarks on 'the vast scale of the slave-establishments, in which there was an immense growth', *multitudinem familiarum quae gliscebat immensum.*
187. Suet., *Tib.* 8.1; *cf.* Suet., *Div. Aug.* 32.1. For the *ergastula*, see Fitzgibbon (1976).
188. Dio 53.30.4.
189. Suet., 63.1; Tac., *Ann.* 1.3; Vell. Pat. 2.93.2.
190. Dio 53.30.5.

191. Dio 53.30.6. Iulius Caesar had cleared the space for the structure before 44 BCE; the theatre was completed in 13 BCE and formally inaugurated by Augustus in 12 BCE. Parts of the building still stand.
192. Dio 53.30.6.
193. Dio 53.30.1.
194. Dio 53.31.1–2.
195. Dio 54.6.5.
196. Dio 53.30.2.
197. Dio 53.31.4–53.32.1.
198. Dio 53.32.1.
199. For Agrippa's trip to Lesbos as a secret diplomacy mission in the East, see Magie (1908).
200. For Agrippa's *imperium proconsulare*, see Gray (1970) and Kornemann (1930).
201. Dio 54.6.1; Vell. Pat. 2.94.4.
202. Dio 54.7.1.
203. Aug., *Res Gest.* 15.
204. Dio 51.3.1, 51.3.5.
205. Dio 54.1.3–4; Suet., *Div. Aug.* 52. For the powers of dictator and the Roman People, see Yakobson (2021).
206. Dio 54.1.4; Suet., *Div. Aug.* 37.1, *cf.* 40.2, 41.2–3.
207. Dio 54.6.1–2.
208. Dio 54.6.2–3.
209. Ball (2023), pp.29–30.
210. For Augustus' reception in Athens, see Hoff (1989), p.269, interpretating Dio 54.7.2–3.
211. Aigina: Plut., *Reg. et imp. Apophth.* 207 f.; Samos: Dio 54.7.4.
212. Dio 54.7.4.
213. Dio 54.9.2–3.
214. Dio 54.9.4; Jos., *Ant. Iud.* 15.105.
215. Vell. Pat. 2.94.4.
216. Dio 54.9.5.
217. Suet., *Tib.* 9.1; Vell. Pat. 2.94.4 called the new regent by the name Artavasdes. For Tiberius' mission to Armenia, see Chaumont (1992).
218. Vell. Pat. 2.94.4: *tanti nominis fama territus*.
219. Eutrop. 7.9.; Strabo 6.4.2; Vell. Pat. 2.94.4. Dio 54.9.5 is less than flattering about Tiberius' contribution, asserting that he assumed a lofty bearing, especially after sacrifices had been voted to commemorate what he had done, as though he had accomplished something by valour.
220. Strabo 6.4.2: *καὶ παῖδας ἐπίστευσε Φραάτης τῷ Σεβαστῷ Καίσαρι καὶ παίδων παῖδας ἐξομηρευσάμενος θεραπευτικῶς τὴν φιλίαν.*
221. Dio 54.8.2–3: *καὶ αὐτοὺς ἐκεῖνος ὡς καὶ πολέμῳ τινὶ τὸν Πάρθον νενικηκὼς ἔλαβε: καὶ γὰρ ἐπὶ τούτοις ἐφρόνει μέγα, λέγων ὅτι τὰ πρότερόν ποτε ἐν ταῖς μάχαις ἀπολόμενα ἀκονιτὶ ἐκεκόμιστο.*
222. Dio 54.9.7–10.
223. Ael. Don., *Vita Verg.* 35.
224. Dio 54.10.4.
225. Dio 54.10.4: *cf.* Suet., *Div. Aug.* 53.2.
226. Dio 54.10.4, *cf.* 53.28.3 and Suet., *Tib.* 9.3.
227. Dio 54.10.5. Some commentators question if Dio misunderstood and accurately reported the array of honours, citing Aug., *Res Gest.* 6, which claims these powers in 18 BCE. Syme (1986), p.42 notes the twelve *fasces* denoted a proconsul's *imperium* outside Rome and that conceding the right to display the insignia within the *pomerium* of the city from 19 BCE and thereafter was a visible change.

228. Aug., *Res Gest.* 29.
229. Dio 54.10.2.
230. Aug., *Res Gest.* 11; *Fast. Amit. ad IV Id. Oct. et ad XVIII Kal. Ian*; *Fast. Cum. ad XVIII Kal. Ian.*; Prop., *Eleg.* 4.3.71; Dio 54.10.3. It is depicted on a *denarius*: *BMC* 4; *RIC* I 322.
231. Dio 54.8.3: *καὶ προσέτι καὶ ἐπὶ κέλητος ἐς τὴν πόλιν ἐσήλασε καὶ ἁψῖδι τροπαιοφόρῳ ἐτιμήθη*. This triumphal parade was an *ovatio*.
232. The silver coins bear the legend *SIGNIS RECEPTIS: RIC* I[2] 86b (*Colonia* Patricia). The same mint issued a *denarius* the following year showing on the obverse a *toga picta* over *tunica palmate* between *aquila* on the left and wreath on the right, and the legend *SPQR PARENT* (above) *CONS SVO* (below), and on the reverse a triumphal *quadriga* facing right, ornamented with two Victories and surmounted by four miniature galloping horses, and the legend *CAESARI* (above) *AVGVSTO* (below): *RIC* I 99.
233. Aug., *Res Gest.* 29. *Cf.* Dio 54.8.3.
234. Most modern historians avoid dating the wedding. The Chronology in Seager (1972) places it in 20 BCE with a '(?)'.
235. Seager (1972), p.14.
236. Many of these letters survive.
237. Suet., *Tib.* 7.2.

## CHAPTER 2: COUNTING LOVES AND LOSSES

1. Suet., *Tib.* 70.2. Klooster (2017).
2. Only six of Rhianos' epigrams survive in *Μοῦσα Παιδική*, *The Boyish Muse*, a compilation of man–boy love poetry initially compiled by Straton of Sardis in the second century CE. Tiberius might even have met Parthenios, who may have still been alive and living in Rome at the time. Parthenios was taken captive in the Mithridatic Wars (88–63 BCE) and was transported to Rome in 72 BCE. The composer of *Ἐρωτικὰ Παθήματα*, *Of the Sorrows of Love*, lived to 14 CE.
3. For whether the Greek into Latin translation was the work of Tiberius or Germanicus, see Baldwin (1981), Gain (1976), pp.17–20, and Powell (2016), pp.30–31.
4. Possanza (2012), p.73, comparing Arat., *Phaen.* (Greek) lines 545–549 with *Phaen.* (Latin) 532–564.
5. Dio 54.26.3.
6. Suet., *Div. Aug.* 34.1.
7. Dio 54.18.2.
8. Hor., *Carm. Saec.* 65–67: *si Palatinas videt aequos aras / remque Romanam Latiumque felix / alterum in lustrum meliusque semper prorogat aevum.*
9. Dio 54.18.1.
10. Suet. *Div. Claud.* 1.5: *ut coheredem semper filiis instituerit, sicut quondam in senatu professus est.*
11. Flor. 2.30.24: *Inde validissimas nationes Cheruscos Suebosque et Sicambros pariter adgressus est, qui viginti centurionibus in crucem actis hoc velut sacramento sumpserant bellum, adeo certa victoriae spe, ut praedam in antecessum pactione diviserint.* *Cf.* Dio 54.20.4.
12. Strabo 7.1.4: *ἤρξαντο δὲ τοῦ πολέμου Σούγαμβροι πλησίον οἰκοῦντες τοῦ Ῥήνου.*
13. Strabo 7.1.4: *Μέλωνα*; his name is spelled Maelo in Aug., *Res Gest.* 32.
14. They were nations who had been looking for new homelands a half-century before in Iulius Caesar's times: Caes., *Bell. Gall.* 4.4, 4.7.
15. Dio 54.20.5.
16. Suet., *Div. Aug.* 20.1.
17. Tac., *Ann.* 1.10.
18. Suet., *Div. Aug.* 20.1.

19. Dio 54.20.6.
20. Aug., *Res Gest.* 19; Dio 54.19.4.
21. Dio 54.19.5.
22. Dio 50.3.2, 50.24.3–5; Plut., *Ant.* 31.2–3. For a biographical study of Antonia, see Kokkinos (2002).
23. Plut., *Ant.* 31.2. For depictions of Antonia in Roman art, see Karin (1973).
24. This is Germanicus. For the debate about birth years, see Levick (1966), pp.238–240, and Powell (2013), p.4 and n.24, who pick 16 BCE.
25. The omens were meticulously recorded by Dio 54.19.7.
26. Dio 54.20.6; Livy, *Peri.* 134.2.
27. Livy, *Peri.* 134.2.
28. Dio 54.21.2–8.
29. Caes., *Bell. Gall.* 1: *Gallia est omnis divisa in partes tres.*
30. Dio 53.12.4. Gallia Narbonnenis was returned to the Senate in 22 BCE (Dio 54.4.1).
31. Strabo 4.3.2.
32. Strabo 4.3.1. *Colonia* Copia Felix Munatia is shown on a coin struck at the foundation of the colony. Issac (1971) suggests the formal title of the city was *Colonia* Munatia Triumphalis and later *Colonia* Copia Claudia Augusta. In this book, the form *Colonia* Munatia is used.
33. The building has been identified and excavated in Lyon. For a full description of the *Palatium* and environs, see Powell (2011), pp.50–51.
34. Dio 53.13.5. For the *imperium* of Augustus, see Jones (1951), Drogula (2015), pp.355–356, and Powell (2018), pp.36–37.
35. Dio 53.13.6. Caes., *Bell. Civ.* 3.51: 'The duties of a legate and of a commander are different: the one ought to do everything under direction, the other should take measures freely in the general interest', *Aliae enim sunt legati partes atque imperatoris: alter omnia agere ad praescriptum, alter libere ad summam rerum consulere debet.*
36. Ulpian, *Dig.* 1.18.13pr: *pacata atque quieta.*
37. The word *provincia* originally meant 'appointment' or 'task', and outside of Rome it was applied to the responsibilities of proconsuls, propraetors and quaestors: Lintott (1993), p.22.
38. The locations of the camps of *Legiones* I, XIII *Gemina*, XVII, XIIX and XIX in Aquitania and V *Alaudae* in Belgica at this time is not known.
39. Drinkwater (1983), p.108; Goudineau (1996), p.488.
40. Dio 54.25.1.
41. Tac., *Ann.* 3.41. See also *CIL*, IX, 1617 = *ILS* 2117; *CIL*, XIII, 1833 = *ILS* 2116; and *CIL*, VI, 531 = *ILS* 3729 (238–44).
42. Dio 53.13.8.
43. Dio 54.20.5.
44. For the Battle of Vercellae (30 July 101 BCE), see Powell (2011b).
45. Strabo 4.1 (Narbonensis), 4.2 (Aquitania), 4.3 (Lugdunensis) and 4.4 (western Lugdunensis and Belgica).
46. The so-called fort 'Neuss A' was a 6.5-hectare fort with a double ditch: see Wells (1972), pp.127–128, fig. 6; *cf.* Rüger (1996), p.525.
47. The Ubii were culturally Iron Age Celtic rather than Germanic and were resettled at *Oppidum* Ubiorum by M. Agrippa in 39–38 or 20–19 BCE: see Powell (2015), p.139; Wells (1972), pp.134–136.
48. The Treveri were culturally Germanic and were resettled by M. Agrippa in 39–38 or 20–19 BCE: see Boatman (1970), p.36; Wells (1972), p.26. The first Roman bridge across the Moselle has been dated to 18/17 BCE.

49. Dio 54.21.1–2.
50. Strabo 4.3.3, 4.6.8.
51. Strabo 4.3.3, 4.6.8–9.
52. For the various options for birth years, see Levick (1966), pp.236–238, who picks 13 BCE. If Drusus had served as a *tribunus militum* as a teenager, as Tiberius had done, it is nowhere documented in the extant sources.
53. Vell. Pat. 2.97.2–3: *dulescenti tot tantarumque virtutum, quot et quantas natura mortalis recipit vel industria perficit. Cuius ingenium utrum bellicis magis operibus an civilibus suffecerit artibus, in incerto est: 3 morum certe dulcedo ac suavitas et adversus amicos aequa ac par sui aestimatio inimitabilis fuisse diciiur; nam pulchritudo corporis proxima fraternae fuit.*
54. Livy, *Peri.* 140.2. For Tiberius' and Drusus' campaign of 15 CE, see Powell (2011a), pp.26–48.
55. Vell. Pat. 2.95.1: *Quippe uterque e diversis partibus Raetos Vindelicosqueadgressi.*
56. Dio 54.22.4: *ἐσβαλόντες οὖν ἐς τὴν χώραν πολλαχόθεν ἅμα ἀμφότεροι, αὐτοί τε καὶ διὰ τῶν ὑποστρατήγων.*
57. *CIL*, V, 8003: *Viam Claudiam Augustam Quam Drusus Pater Alpibus Bello Patefactis Derexerat.* For the full text of the inscriptions on the milestones, see Powell (2011a), pp.166–167.
58. Dio 54.22.3.
59. Caes., *Bell. Gall.* 1.6.
60. Strabo 4.3.3 mentions that part of the territory in which the Raeti and Vindelici lived was marshland and near a lake that fed the Rhine. Rageth & Zanier (2010) report on excavations of the contemporary battle site at Crap Ses Gorge in the Julier Pass of southeastern Switzerland where several lead sling stones (*glandes*) have been found imprinted with the legionary stamps 'L•III', 'LEG•X' and 'L•XII', which may have served under Tiberius or Nero Drusus in this campaign; some 2,500 hobnails from Roman soldiers' boots (*caligae*) and fragments of military equipment were also found scattered about the battlefield.
61. Vell. Pat. 2.95.2.
62. Dio 54.22.4 simply mentions that Tiberius crossed 'the lake' without naming it: the footnote in the Loeb translation on page 339 identifies this as *Lacus* Venetus, Lake Garda, which puts the site of the battle back in the vicinity of Tridentum. The earliest extant record of *Lacus* Venetus is Pomponius Mela, writing his *Chorographia* ('Description of the World') around 43 CE. However, other commentators associate Dio's location with Bodensee, better known as Lake Constance to the Americans and British, but equally if he had been following the course of the Rodanus (River Rhône) from Lugdunum it would have taken him to Lake Geneva; Lake Geneva is the largest natural freshwater lake in Western Europe at 582km$^2$. All that can safely be said is that the ancient sources are too obscure to make a definite identification of the lake in question.
63. Strabo 7.1.5 refers to an island in the lake, which Tiberius used as a base of operations in his naval battle with the Vindelici. Strabo 4.6.8 mentions the stronghold at Brigantium. Jer., *Chron.* B15, asserts that Tiberius made Vindelicia a Roman province. On the Roman archaeology of Bregenz, see Lewis (1907). Strabo 7.1.5 writes that Tiberius then proceeded just a day's journey from this lake and saw for himself the source of the Danube.
64. Vell. Pat. 2.95.1: *multis urbium et castellorum oppugnationibus*; Dio 54.22.5. For known units of *Cohortes Alpinorum* and *Cohortes Raetorum*, see Walser (1994), pp.35–43 and Powell (2018), pp.306 and 309.
65. Cunliffe (1997), p.218: the remains lie in Zollfeld in the Austrian state of Carinthia.
66. Dio 54.22.5. For known *alae* and *cohortes* of the Raeti, Norici and Vindelici, see Powell (2018), pp.77, 309, 310.

67. Livy, *Peri.* 138.1; Strabo 4.6.8 notes they were still pacified at the time he was writing his *Geography* thirty-three years later.
68. Aug., *Res Gest.* 26: *Alpes a regione ea, quae proxima est Hadriano mari, ad Tuscum pacari feci. Cf.* Suet., *Div. Aug.* 21.1.
69. For Tiberius and Nero Drusus as exemplars of Augustan heroism, see Vervaet (2020).
70. Gold *aureus*: *RIC* I 164a, Cohen 132, *BMC* 443; silver *denarius*: *RIC* I 165b, Cohen 135, *BMC* 448. The branches look like cuttings from pine trees, which would be appropriate for the Alps.
71. Syme (1978), p.154.
72. Hor., *Odes* 4.73–76: *Nil Claudiae non perficient manus / quas et benigno numine Iuppiter / defendit et curae sagaces / expediunt per acuta belli.*
73. Dio 54.25.1.
74. *Legiones* I, V *Alaudae*, XIV *Gemina*, XVI *Gallica*, XVII, XII and XIX: Powell (2018), pp.82–84.
75. Wells (1972), p.148.
76. *Fossa Drusiana* or *Fossae Drusinae*: Powell (2011), pp.64–66. *Classis Germanica*: Powell (2018), p.311.
77. There were twenty-eight legions at this time.
78. Aug., *Res Gest.* 12; Dio 54.25.1.
79. Dio 54.28.1.
80. Suet., *Div. Aug.* 29.5; Tac., *Ann.* 3.72; Dio 54.25.2; Pliny, *Nat. Hist.* 5.5, 36.12.60; Vell. Pat. 2.51.3.
81. Dio 54.25.5–6.
82. Dio 54.25.3.
83. Dio 54.27.8–9.
84. Dio 54.27.1.
85. This is Nero Claudius Drusus, aka Drusus Minor or Drusus the Younger, later renamed Drusus Iulius Caesar: Suet., *Tib.* 7.2; Suet., *Div. Claud.* 1.1. For the various birth years see Levick (1966), pp.236–238, who picks 13 BCE. Tiberius and Vipsania may well have had others who died in childhood, as was the case with Drusus Maior and his son, Germanicus, but it is not recorded.
86. Suet., *Tib.* 1.2.
87. Dio 54.28.2.
88. Dio 54.28.3.
89. Vell. Pat. 2.96.1; Tac., *Ann.* 3.56.3; Livy, *Peri.* 138.2; Pliny, *Nat. Hist.* 7.46.
90. Dio 54.28.4.
91. Dio 54.28.5.
92. For the Greek transcript of the original Latin *laudatio funebris* found in Fayum (now called P. Köln Inv. 04701 + 04702, *Recto: Laudatio funebris des Augustus auf Agrippa*), see Koenen (1970), and for its implications on Varus' relationship with Agrippa see Reinhold (1972).
93. Powell (2015), pp.181, 202.
94. Marcellus and now M. Agrippa.
95. Though it bears Agrippa's name on the frieze, the concrete-domed Pantheon, which stands today, is not Agrippa's but Hadrian's complete rebuild following its destruction by fire.
96. Dio 54.29.1.
97. Vell. Pat. 2.94.2–3: *innutritus caelestium praeceptorum disciplinis, iuvenis genere, forma, celsitudine corporis, optimis studiis maximoque ingenio instructissimus, qui protinus quantus est, sperari potuerat visuque praetulerat principern.*

98. Philo, *Leg.* 142: *Γέρος.*
99. *Industria*: see Marsh (1931), p.127. *Moderatio*: see Levick (1976), p.253 n.29.
100. Suet., *Tib.* 68.1–2: *Corpore fuit amplo atque robusto, statura quae iustam excederet; latus ab umeris et pectore, ceteris quoque membris usque ad imos pedes aequalis et congruens; sinistra manu agiliore ac validiore, articulis ita firmis, ut recens et integrum malum digito terebraret, caput pueri vel etiam adulescentis talitro vulneraret. Colore erat candido, capillo pone occipitium summissiore ut cervicem etiam obtegeret, quod gentile in illo videbatur; facie honesta, in qua tamen crebri et subiti tumores, cum praegrandibus oculis et qui, quod mirum esset, noctu etiam et in tenebris viderent, sed ad breve et cum primum e somno patuissent; deinde rursum hebescebant.*
101. Suet., *Tib.* 68.3–4: *Incedebat cervice rigida et obstipa, adducto fere vultu, plerumque tacitus, nullo aut rarissimo etiam cum proximis sermone eoque tardissimo, nec sine molli quadam digitorum gesticulatione. Quae omnia ingrata atque arrogantiae plena et animadvertit Augustus in eo et excusare temptavit saepe apud senatum ac populum professus naturae vitia esse, non animi.*
102. Suet., *Tib.* 68.3–4: *Valitudine prosperrima usus est, tempore quidem principatus paene toto prope inlaesa, quamvis a tricesimo aetatis anno arbitratu eam suo rexerit sine adiumento consiliove medicorum.*
103. Tac., *Ann.* 4.57.
104. Suet., *Tib.* 42.1: *In castris tiro etiam tum propter nimiam vini aviditatem pro Tiberio 'Biberius', pro Claudio 'Caldius', pro Nerone 'Mero' vocabatur.* Plin., *Nat. Hist.* 14.8 [64] records that Tiberius disliked *Surrentinium*, which doctors prescribed for invalids, likening it to vinegar.
105. Aug., *Res Gest.* 13: *parta victoriis pax.*
106. For recent archaeological and literature surveys, see: Demicheli (2017); Džino (2005, 2008a, 2008b, 2009, 2010, 2012, 2016 and 2017); Džino and Kunić (2018); Kos (2010, 2011, 2012, 2014a, 2014b, 2015, 2017 and 2022); and Kovács (2017 and 2018).
107. Dio 54.34.3: *πολεμῶν τε ἅμα ἀμφοτέροις, καὶ τοτὲ μὲν τῇ τοτὲ δὲ τῇ μεθιστάμενος.*
108. Dio 54.34.4: *κἀκ τούτου καὶ ἡ Δελματία τῇ τοῦ Αὐγούστου φρουρᾷ, ὡς καὶ ὅπλων τινῶν ἀεὶ καὶ δι' ἑαυτὴν καὶ διὰ τὴν τῶν Παννονίων γειτονίαν δεομένη, παρεδόθη.*
109. Suet., *Tib.* 7.1.
110. Suet., *Tib.* 7.2: *cum et Agrippinae consuetudine teneretur et Iuliae mores improbaret, ut quam sensisset sui quoque sub priore marito appetentem, quod sane etiam vulgo existimabatur.*
111. Dio 54.35.4; Suet., *Tib.* 7.2.
112. Suet., *Tib.* 7.3: *Sed Agrippinam et abegisse post divortium doluit et semel omnino ex occursu visam adeo contentis et [t]umentibus oculis prosecutus est, ut custoditum sit ne umquam in conspectum ei posthac venire.*
113. Suet., *Tib.* 7.3.
114. Livy, *Peri.* 140.2. On the identity of which Octavia, see Singer (1948).
115. Dio 54.35.4–5.
116. For a survey of the sites in the region explored by archaeologists, see Fernández-Götz & Roymans (2024), pp.46–61.
117. For the German War of Nero Drusus, see Powell (2011), pp.70–105.
118. Dio 54.36.4.
119. Dio 54.36.3.
120. Suet., *Div. Claud.* 2.1. This is Claudius, who will become Rome's fourth emperor.
121. Suet., *Tib.* 50.1: *Odium adversus necessitudines in Druso primum fratre detexit, prodita eius epistula, qua secum de cogendo ad restituendam libertatem Augusto agebat.*
122. Suet., *Div. Claud.* 1.4.
123. Suet., *Tib.* 7.3.

124. Dio 54.36.2.
125. Dio 54.36.2–4.
126. Dio 54.36.4.
127. Dio 54.1.4.
128. For the design of the *Ara Pacis Augustae*, see Momigliano (1942), Rossini (2007) and Toynbee (1961).
129. For interpretations of scenes and figures represented on the *Ara Pacis*, see Galinsky (1966), Grummond (1990), Holliday (1990), Kleiner (1978), Rehak (2001), Spaeth (1994) and Weinstock (1960).
130. For the sacrificial aspect of the altar, see Elsner (1991).
131. On the south side, Tiberius S-33(?) stands about two-thirds the way down the line, well behind Augustus S-15, Agrippa S-27 and Julia S-31, but ahead of Antonia S-35, Germanicus S-37 and Drusus S-38. For the figures and their identifications, see Rose (1990), Ryberg (1949) and Stern (2006 and 2023).
132. Front., *Strat.* 2.1.15: *Ti. Nero adversus Pannonios, cum barbari feroces in aciem oriente statim die processissent, continuit suos passusque est hostem nebula et imbribus, qui forte illo die crebri erant, verberari. Ac deinde, ubi fessum stando et pluvia non solum sed et lassitudine deficere animadvertit, signo dato adortus superavit.* The text appears in the section *De Tempore ad Pugnam Eligendo*, 'On Choosing the Time to Fight'.
133. Dio 54.33.5. Tac., *Ann.* 3.74 explains that the acclamation as *imperator* was 'a time-honoured tribute to commanders who, after a successful campaign, were acclaimed by the joyful and spontaneous voice of a conquering army. Several might hold the title simultaneously, nor did it raise them above an equality with their colleagues. It was awarded in a few cases even by Augustus' (*prisco erga duces honore qui bene gesta re publica gaudio et impetu victoris exercitus conclamabantur; erantque plures simul imperatores nec super ceterorum aequalitatem. concessit quibusdam et Augustus*). For the tally of acclamations given to Augustus and Tiberius, see Barnes (1974), p.26.
134. Suet., Tib. 9.2: *triumphalibus ornamentis honoratus, novo nec antea cuiquam tributo genere honoris.* The phrase *ut quidam putant* ('as some think') indicates that Suetonius was not sure about the veracity of the honour or its date. Dio 55.2.4, *cf.* 54.33.5; Jer., *Chron.* B10.
135. Dio 55.2.4.
136. Dio 55.2.5.
137. Val. Max. 5.5.3; *cf.* Suet., *Div. Aug.* 20.
138. Dio 55.2.2–3.
139. Flor. 2.30.23–24; Dio 55.2.3; Ptol., *Geog.* 2.10.
140. Strabo 7.1.3.
141. Livy, *Peri.* 142.2.
142. Dio 55.2.4; Pliny, *Nat. Hist.* 7.20 [84].
143. Dio 55.2.1; Livy, *Peri.* 142.3; Val. Max. 5.5.3.
144. Val. Max. 5.5.3: *barbariam Antabagio duce solo comite*, perhaps from Germania, Noricum or Raetia; Pliny, *Nat. Hist.* 7.20 [84] mentions the use of a *vehiculis.*
145. Val. Max. 5.5.3.
146. Pliny, *Nat. Hist.* 7.20 [84]: *cuius rei admiratio ita demum solida perveniat, si quis cogitet nocte ac die longissimum iter vehiculis Tib. Neronem emensum festinantem ad Drusum fratrem aegrotum in Germaniam. ea fuerunt CC passuum.* It is confirmed by Val. Max. 5.5.3.
147. Dio 55.1.4–5; Suet., *Div. Claud.* 1.5.
148. Val. Max. 5.5.3.
149. Livy, *Peri.* 142.2.
150. Vell. Pat. 2.97.3: 'in his thirtieth year', *agentem annum tricesimum.* For the possible cause of Nero Drusus' death, see Powell (2011), pp.109–110.

151. For the events after Nero Drusus' death, see Powell (2011), pp.111–114.
152. Sen., *Consol. Marc.* 3.1.
153. Suet., *Tib.* 7.3: *cuius corpus pedibus toto itinere.*
154. Dio 55.2.1.
155. Suet., *Div. Claud.* 1.3; Dio 55.2.1.
156. Suet., *Div. Claud.* 1.3.
157. Suet., *Div. Claud.* 1.3.
158. Dio 55.2.1. Nothing of the speech survives.
159. Suet., *Div. Claud.* 1.5.
160. Suet., *Div. Claud.* 1.5; Dio 55.2.3.
161. Tac., *Ann.* 2.41.3: *reputantibus haud prosperum in Druso patre eius favorem vulgi.*
162. For the honours awarded posthumously to Nero Drusus, see Powell (2011), pp.114–119.
163. Suet., *Div. Claud.* 1.3.
164. Suet., *Div. Claud.* 1.3. The remains of the tower are now called the Eichelstein or Drususstein in Mainz.
165. Dio 55.2.5; Sen., *Consol. Marc.* 3.1.

## CHAPTER 3: PAYING THE PRICE FOR DISLOYALTY

1. Dio 55.6.1.
2. Dio 55.6.5; Vell. Pat. 2.97.4.
3. Dio 55.6.4.
4. Dio 55.6.2. The Sugambri were resettled around Vetera where they became known as Ciberni, Cuberni or Cugerni. For known units of *Cohortes Sugambrorum*, see Powell (2018), pp.310–311.
5. Dio 55.6.3.
6. Vell. Pat. 2.97.4: *quod is sua et virtute et fortuna administravit peragratusque victor omnis partis Germaniae sine ullo detrimento commissi exercitus, quod praecipue huic ,duci semper curae fuit, sic perdomuit eam, ut in formam paene stipendiariae redigeret provinciae.*
7. For Roman policy on the German frontier at this time, see Powell (2018), p.106, citing Külhorn (2004), p.29 and Wells (1972), pp.163–211.
8. Dio 55.6.5.
9. Dio 55.6.4.
10. Dio 55.6.5; Suet., *Tib.* 9; Vell. Pat. 2.97.4, 2.99.1.
11. Dio 55.6.5.
12. Dio 55.8.1. The *Curia* was a room used for occasional meetings of the Senate within the *Portico Octaviae*, an enclosure erected by Octavia in memory of her son, Marcellus, in 33 BCE.
13. For a biography of Cn. Calpurnius Piso, see Powell (2018), p.244. His presence in Hispania is inferred in Tac., *Ann.* 3.16.4.
14. Tac., *Ann.* 2.43: *Cn. Pisonem, ingenio violentum et obsequii ignarum, insita ferocia a patre Pisone.* For the Calpurnii Pisones, see Syme (1986), pp.367–381.
15. Tac., *Ann.* 2.43: *vix Tiberio concedere, liberos eius ut multum infra despectare.*
16. Dio 55.8.2; Suet., *Tib.* 20.
17. Dio 55.8.1.
18. Kuttner (1995), p.148.
19. The two so-called Boscoreale Cups were part of a hoard of precious items found in 1895. They were placed in an empty cistern in the wine cellar of the *villa rustica* at Boscoreale, situated on the south-eastern slopes of Vesuvius, apparently when its owners fled before the eruption of 79 CE.

20. Designated 'BR II' or 'Tiberius Cup': see Kuttner (1995), pp.4–5. For the triumphal procession shown on BR II, see Kuttner (1995), pp.143–154.
21. Laurel: Aul. Gell, *Noc. Att.* 5.6; Ovid, *Pont.* 2.2.81; Tibull. 1.7.7; Pliny the Elder, *Nat. Hist.* 15.39 [127]. Gold: Pliny the Elder, *Nat. Hist.* 33.4.11 [12]. As the procession advanced, the *servus publicus* would remind the *triumphator* of his mortality and dependence on other men, speaking the words, *Respice post te; hominem te esse memento*, 'Look behind you; remember you are only a man' – see Beard (2007), p.82.
22. Dio 55.8.3.
23. Dio 55.9.1: *ἐν γὰρ δὴ τῇ Γερμανίᾳ οὐδὲν ἄξιον μνήμης συνέβη*. The Sugambri continued to cause problems for the Romans even after, and likely because of, the arrest of their envoys in 8 BCE (Dio 55.6.3): see Swan (2004), p.75.
24. *Quaestor*, *praetor*, *propraetor*, consul and proconsul.
25. Dio 55.9.4; Vell. Pat. 2.99.1.
26. Vell. Pat. 2.99.1.
27. Granted in 18 BCE and renewed in 13 BCE.
28. Livy, *AUC* 2.33.1, 3.55.1–7, 13–15.
29. Polyb., *Hist.* 6.12.1, 6.16.4–5. On the history of the power of veto, see Watson (1987), pp.401–402.
30. Dio 55.9.4.
31. For Tiberius' powers, see Levick (1972).
32. Suet., *Tib.* 10.1.
33. Dio 55.9.1.
34. Dio 55.9.1: *τῷ δὲ ὑστέρῳ, ἐν ᾧ Γάιός τε Ἀντίστιος καὶ Λαίλιος Βάλβος ὑπάτευσαν, ἰδὼν ὁ Αὔγουστος τόν τε Γάιον καὶ τὸν Λούκιον αὐτούς τε μὴ πάνυ, οἷα ἐν ἡγεμονίᾳ τρεφομένους, τὰ ἑαυτοῦ ἤθη ζηλοῦντας ʽοὐ γὰρ ὅτι ἁβρότερον διῆγον, ἀλλὰ καὶ ἐθρασύνοντο.*
35. Dio 55.9.2.
36. Dio 55.9.4.
37. Dio 55.9.5.
38. Dio 55.9.5–8; Suet., *Tib.* 10.1–2; Vell. Pat. 2.99.2. Levick (1972a).
39. Suet., *Tib.* 10.2; Vell. Pat. 2.99.2.
40. Suet., *Tib.* 10.1.
41. Vell. Pat. 2.99.2: *commeatum ab socero atque eodem vitrico adquiescendi a continuatione laborum petiit.*
42. Suet., *Tib.* 10.2: *honorum satietatem ac requiem laborum.*
43. Vell. Pat. 2.99.2; Suet., *Tib.* 10.2.
44. Dio 55.9.5, 55.11.5. When Agrippa left Rome in 23 BCE, the move had led many to speculate on the state of his friendship with Augustus, some seeing it as a protest that Marcellus was gaining favour at Agrippa's expense.
45. Suet., *Tib.* 10.2.
46. Suet., *Tib.* 10.2: *aut vitrico deseri se etiam in Senatu conquerenti veniam dedit.*
47. Suet., *Tib.* 10.2: *cibo per quadriduum abstinuit.*
48. Dio 55.9.5: *ἀμέλει καὶ ἐς Ῥόδον ὡς καὶ παιδεύσεώς τινος δεόμενος ἐστάλη.*
49. Suet., *Tib.* 10.2: *Facta tandem abeundi potestate, relictis Romae uxore et filio confestim Ostiam descendit, ne verbo quidem cuiquam prosequentium reddito paucosque admodum in digressu exosculatus.* About Iulia's whereabouts, see Dio 55.9.7.
50. Dio 55.9.5–8: *καὶ τήν τε ὁδὸν ἰδιωτικῶς ἐποιήσατο… καὶ ἐς τὴν νῆσον ἐλθὼν οὐδὲν ὀγκηρὸν οὔτε ἔπραττεν οὔτε ἔλεγεν. ἡ μὲν οὖν ἀληθεστάτη αἰτία τῆς ἐκδημίας αὐτοῦ τοιαύτη ἐστί, λόγον δέ τινα ἔχει καὶ διὰ τὴν γυναῖκα τὴν Ἰουλίαν, ὅτι μηκέτ᾽ αὐτὴν φέρειν ἐδύνατο, τοῦτο ποιῆσαι: κατέλιπε γοῦν αὐτὴν ἐν τῇ Ῥώμῃ. οἱ δὲ ἔφασαν χαλεπῆναι αὐτὸν ὅτι μὴ καὶ Καῖσαρ ἀπεδείχθη οἱ δὲ ὑπ᾽ αὐτοῦ τοῦ Αὐγούστου ὡς καὶ τοῖς παισὶν αὐτοῦ ἐπιβουλεύοντα ἐκβληθῆναι. ὅτι μὲν γὰρ οὔτε παιδείας ἕνεκα οὔτ᾽*

*ἀβουλήσας τὰ δεδογμένα ἀπεδήμησε, δῆλον ἔκ τε τῶν ἄλλων ὧν μετὰ ταῦτα ἔπραξε, καὶ ἐκ τοῦ τὰς διαθήκας αὐτὸν εὐθὺς τότε καὶ λῦσαι καὶ τῇ μητρὶ τῷ τε Αὐγούστῳ ἀναγνῶναι, ἐγένετο: κατεικάζετο πάνθ' ὅσα ἐνεδέχετο.* (Xiph. 100.18–30; Exc. 5.177; Zon. 10.35.) *Cf.* Manlius, *Astronomica* 4.474–76: 'Rhodes, the sojourn of him who was one day to rule the world, / and in very truth the Sun's abode at that time when / the lamp of the universe, in the person of our Caesar, was within her gates.'; *Rhodos, hospitium recturi principis orbem, / tumque domus uere Solis, cui tota sacrata est, / cum caperet lumen magni sub Caesare mundi.*

51. For the meaning of exile, see Braginton (1944) and Kelly (2006).
52. On exile and banishment, see Drogula (2011).
53. Suet., *Tib.* 11.1: *Ab Ostia oram Campaniae legens inbecillitate Augusti nuntiata paulum substitit. Sed increbrescente rumore quasi ad occasionem maioris spei commoraretur, tantum non adversis tempestatibus Rhodum enavigavit.*
54. Suet., *Tib.* 11.1: *Ab amoenitate et salubritate insulae iam inde captus cum ad eam ab Armenia rediens appulisset.*
55. Dio 55.11.1.
56. Tac., *Ann.* 2.28, 4.15, 6.10.
57. Tac., *Ann.* 4.57: *et Rhodi secreto vitare coetus, recondere voluptates insuerat.*
58. Dio 55.9.6.
59. Suet., *Tib.* 11.1.
60. Suet., *Tib.* 13.1.
61. Suet., *Tib.* 11.3.
62. *Cf.* Dio 55.9.6; Vell. Pat. 2.99.4.
63. Suet., *Tib.* 11.2.
64. Whether out of morbid curiosity or genuine concern is not recorded.
65. Suet., *Tib.* 11.2: *tandem singulos circuit excusans factum etiam tenuissimo cuique et ignoto.*
66. Vell. Pat. 2.99.4: *ut omnes, qui pro consulibus legatique in transmarinas sunt profecti provincias, visendi eius gratia Rhodum deverterint atque eum convenientes semper privato, si illa maiestas privata umquam fuit, fasces suos summiserint fassique sint otium eius honoratius imperio suo.*
67. Tac., *Ann.* 3.48.
68. Tac., *Ann.* 2.42 explains that intimate friends of Augustus thought it unwise to visit Rhodes because Caius was his deputy in the region.
69. Jos., *Ant. Iud.* 17.9.5, 17.10.1–2.
70. Vell. Pat. 2.117.2: *quam pauper divitem ingressus dives pauperem reliquit.*
71. Suet., *Nero* 4: *Verum arrogans, profusus*; Dio 55.10a.2.
72. Dio 55.9.9.
73. Dio 55.9.10.
74. Dio 55.10.12.
75. Dio 55.10.13.
76. Suet., *Tib.* 10.1: *dubium uxorisne taedio quam neque criminari aut dimittere auderet neque ultra perferre posset.*
77. Dio 55.10.14.
78. Dio 55.10.15.
79. Suet., *Tib.* 11.4.
80. Suet., *Tib.* 11.5.
81. Suet., *Tib.* 12.1.
82. Suet., *Tib.* 12.1.
83. Suet., *Tib.* 12.2.
84. Dio 55.10.18; Suet., *Tib.* 12.2.
85. Dio 55.10.19 mentions Chios.

86. Suet., *Nero* 4.1: *omni parte vitae detestabilem*. Domitius was father of the later emperor, Nero.
87. Suet., *Tib.* 12.2.
88. Suet., *Tib.* 12.3.
89. Suet., *Tib.* 12.1.
90. Suet., *Tib.* 13.1. The robust cloak and boots of a Roman officer were quite distinct from a Greek mantle and felt slippers.
91. Suet., *Tib.* 13.2.
92. Dio 55.10a.4.
93. Dio 55.13.2.
94. Suet., *Tib.* 12.2: *comes et rector*; Tac., *Ann.* 3.48; Vell. Pal. 1.102.1.
95. Pliny, *Nat. Hist.* 9.58; Vell. Pat. 2.102.1.
96. Suet., *Nero* 4.1.
97. Dio 55.11.1: *ὑτός τε γὰρ ἐμπειρότατος τῆς διὰ τῶν ἄστρων μαντικῆς ὤν.*
98. Suet., *Tib.* 69: *quippe addictus mathematicae plenusque persuasionis cuncta fato agi*. Velleius Paterculus never mentions his interest in astrology, or Tacitus his awareness of omens.
99. Many astrologers in Tiberius' lifetime still followed the Babylonian zodiac of thirteen signs by including Orphiuchus, 'the serpent bearer' (29 November to 17 December), which would place Tiberius under the natal sign of Libra (30 October to 23 November). Though Manlius writes about the twelve-sign zodiac, he specifically mentions a Caesar born under the sign of Capricorn, which would be Augustus, and one born under Libra (4.548-52), which would likely be Tiberius who was then reigning (4.736–37, 5.510–20). A century later, Claudius Ptolemy rejected the inclusion of Orphiuchus, fixing the zodiac at twelve signs, which is the form still in use. The dates of the astrological sign Scorpio, the eighth in the zodiac of twelve signs, are 23 October to 21 November. For Tiberius and Libra as his natal sign, see Housman (1913), Mac Gregor (2004) and Steele (1931).
100. Their works survive. Man., *Astrono.* 2, 3, 4; Valens, *Anthol.* 1.2[10.P]; Ptol., *Tetra.* 1.11–16.
101. Val., *Anthol.* 1.2[10.P].
102. Suet., *Tib.* 14.4: *Thrasyllum quoque mathematicum, quem ut sapientiae professorem contubernio admoverat, tum maxime expertus est affirmantem nave provisa gaudium afferri.* Thrasyllus is mentioned once in Valens, *Anthol.* 9.10.
103. Tac., *Ann.* 6.20. On preparing horoscopes, see Valens, *Anthol.* 2.6, 5.5, 6.9.
104. Tac., *Ann.* 6.21.
105. Dio 55.11.2.
106. Dio 55.11.3; Suet., *Tib.* 14.4.
107. Tac., *Ann.* 6.21.
108. For Tiberius' interest in divining the future, see Hayes (1959).
109. Suet., *Tib.* 14.4: *Praegnans eo Livia cum an marem editura esset, variis captaret ominibus, ovum incubanti gallinae subductum nunc sua nunc ministrarum manu per vices usque fovit, quoad pullus insigniter cristatus exclusus est. Ac de infante Scribonius mathematicus praeclara spopondit, etiam regnaturum quandoque, sed sine regio insigni, ignota scilicet tunc adhuc Caesarum potestate. Et ingresso primam expeditionem ac per Macedoniam ducente exercitum in Syriam, accidit ut apud Philippos sacratae olim victricium legionum arae sponte subitis conlucerent ignibus; et mox, cum Illyricum petens iuxta Patavium adisset Geryonis oraculum, sorte tracta, qua monebatur ut de consultationibus in Aponi fontem talos aureos iaceret, evenit ut summum numerum iacti ab eo ostenderent; hodieque sub aqua visuntur hi tali.*
110. Pliny, *Nat. Hist.* 10.41[76] asserts that eagles are not native to Rhodes; *cf.* Suet., *Tib.* 14.4.

111. Suet., *Tib.* 14.4.
112. Dio 55.13.2.
113. Dio 55.15.1. On the life of Maecenas, see Dio 55.7.1.
114. Suet., *Tib.* 15.1.
115. Rogers (1943), pp.93–94. Drusus remained in Rome while his father was on Rhodes.
116. Dio 55.10a.9; Vell. Pat. 2.102.3.
117. Dio 55.12.1.
118. Suet., *Tib.* 70.1.
119. Dio 55.10a.4–5.
120. Dio 55.10a.6.
121. Dio 55.10.19, 55.10a.7.
122. Dio 55.10.8.
123. Dio 55.10.9; Vell. Pat. 2.102.3. Limyra is now an archaeological site.
124. Dio 55.12.1.
125. Dio 55.13.1a.
126. Vell. Pat. 2.103.1–2.
127. Dio 55.13.2; *Inst. Ius.* 1.11.11; Suet., *Tib.* 15. For the adoptions and the legal context, see Levick (1966).
128. Suet., *Caius* 4.1; Tac., *Ann.* 4.57.
129. Dio 55.13.1a; Vell. Pat. 2.103.2.
130. Suet., *Div. Aug.* 65.1. For the procedure, see Aul. Gell, *Noc. Att.* 5.19. For the *Saepta Iulia*, see Dio 53.21.1–2.
131. Vell. Pat. 2.104.1 quoting Augustus' exact words (*his ipsis Caesaris verbis*). *Cf.* Suet., *Tib.* 21.3.
132. Suet., *Tib.* 15.2: *Nec quicquam postea pro patre familias egit aut ius, quod amiserat, ex ulla parte retinuit. Nam neque donavit neque manumisit, ne hereditatem quidem aut legata percepit ulla aliter quam ut peculio referret accepta.*
133. Rogers (1943), p.95; Levick (1966), p.234.
134. Dio 55.13.1a; Suet., *Tib.* 15.2; Vell. Pat. 2.104.1. This M. Agrippa, born in 12 BCE, is commonly named Agrippa Postumus by modern historians. The name is shown as Agrippa Caesar on coins, such as *RPC* I 1141a and 1141b, and is used in this text.
135. Vell. Pat. 2.103.2. Suet., *Tib.* 15.2 says *quinquennium* (five years); Dio 55.13.1a states ten years.
136. Tac., *Ann.* 1.10: *etenim Augustus paucis ante annis, cum Tiberio tribuniciam potestatem a patribus rursum postularet, quamquam honora oratione quaedam de habitu cultuque et institutis eius iecerat, quae velut excusando exprobraret. Cf.* Suet., *Tib.* 68.3.
137. Tac., *Ann.* 3: *illuc cuncta vergere: filius, collega imperii.*
138. Suet., *Tib.* 16.1; *cf.* Aug., *Res Gest.* 31.
139. Vell. Pat. 2.104.2.
140. Suet., *Div. Aug.* 29.2. For a plan of the *Forum*, see Powell (2018), p.116, Map 17.
141. Suet., *Tib.* 16.1: *delegatus pacandae Germaniae status*; Dio 55.13.1a; Vell. Pat. 2.103.3, 2.104.2.
142. Vell. Pat. 2.104.3–4.
143. Vell. Pat. 2.114.3: *Adiciam illud, quod, quisquis illis temporibus interfuit, ut alia, quae retuli, agnoscet protinus: solus semper equo vectus est, solus cum iis, quos invitaverat, maiore parte aestivarum expeditionum cenavit sedens; non sequentibus disciplinam, quatenus exemplonon nocebatur, ignovit; admonitio frequens, interdum et castigatio, vindicta tamen rarissima, agebatque medium plurima dissimulantis, aliqua inhibentis.*
144. *CIL*, XIII, 3570 (Bagacum): *Ti(berio) Caesari Augusti f(ilio) divi nepoti, adventu(i) eius sacrum, Cn(aeus) Licini[us] C(ai) f(ilius) Vol(tinia) Navos*; 'To Tiberius Caesar, son of

Caesar Augustus, grandson of the divine Caesar, on the occasion of his visit, has Cn. Licinius Navos, son of Caius, of the Voltinian district, dedicated this.' The inscription is now lost, having been destroyed during the Second World War.

145. Dio 55.13.2.
146. Vell. Pat. 2.105.1: *cum omnem partem asperrimi et periculosissinu belli Caesar vindicaret sibi, iis, quae minoris erant discriminis, Sentium Saturninum, qui iam legatus patris eius in Germania fuerat.*
147. Vell. Pat. 2.105.1. Legions stationed in Germania at this time were I, V *Alaudae*, XVII, XIIX and XIX; Powell (2018), Table 2, p.128.
148. Powell (2018), pp.125–128.
149. Suet., *Tib.* 19.1: *Disciplinam acerrime exegit animadversionum et ignominiarum generibus ex antiquitate repetitis atque etiam legato legionis, quod paucos milites cum liberto suo trans ripam venatum misisset, ignominia notato. Proelia, quamvis minimum fortunae casibusque permitteret, aliquanto constantius inibat, quotiens lucubrante se subito ac nullo propellente decideret lumen et extingueretur, confidens, ut aiebat, ostento sibi a maioribus suis in omni ducatu expertissimo.*
150. Vell. Pat. 2.107.1–3: *Non tempero mihi quin tantae rerum magnitudini hoc, qualecumque est, inseram. Cum citeriorem ripam praedicti fluminis castris occupassemus et ulterior armata hostium virtute fulgeret, sub omnem motum conatumque nostrarum navium protinus refugientium, unus e barbaris aetate senior, corpore excellens, dignitate, quantum ostendebat cultus, eminens, cavatum, ut illis mos est, ex materia conscendit alveum solusque id navigii genus temperans ad medium processit fluminis et petiit, liceret sibi sine periculo in eam, quam armis tenebamus, egredi ripam ac videre Caesarem. Data petenti facultas. Tum adpulso lintre et diu tacitus contemplatus Caesarem, 'nostra quidem', inquit, 'furit iuventus, quae cum vestrum numen absentium colat, praesentium potius arma metuit quam sequitur fidem. Sed ego beneficio ac permissu tuo, Caesar, quos ante audiebam, hodie vidi deos, nec feliciorem ullum vitae meae aut optavi aut sensi diem'. Impetratoque ut manum contingeret, reversus in naviculam, sine fine respectans Caesarem ripae suorum adpulsus est. Cf.* Suet. *Tib.* 19.1.
151. Vell. Pat. 2.105.1.
152. Vell. Pat. 2.105.3. For Roman policy on the German frontier at this time, see Powell (2018), pp.125–28.
153. Dio 55.27.5: *τά τε γὰρ τῶν πολέμων ἅμα διῴκει, καὶ ἐς τὴν πόλιν, ὁπότε παράσχοι, συνεχῶς ἐσεφοίτα, τὸ μέν τι πραγμάτων τινῶν ἕνεκα, τὸ δὲ δὴ πλεῖστον φοβούμενος μὴ ὁ Αὔγουστος ἄλλον τινὰ παρὰ τὴν ἀπουσίαν αὐτοῦ προτιμήσῃ.*
154. Powell (2018), p.130.
155. Dio 55.28.5. For the route taken, see Swan (2004), p.194.
156. Vell. Pat. 2.106.3: *Et eadem mira felicitate et cura ducis, temporum quoque observantia, classis, quae Oceani circumnavigaverat sinus, ab inaudito atque incognito ante mari Qumine Albi subvecta, cum plurimarum gentium victoria parta cum abundantissima rerum omnium copia exercitui Caesarique se iunxit.* The fleet likely sailed from the Roman base at Vechten: see Swan (2004), p.194.
157. Vell. Pat. 2.106.2 *Fracti Langobardi, gens etiam Germana feritate ferocior.*
158. Vell. Pat. 2.106.2 *Fracti Langobardi, gens etiam Germana feritate ferocior; denique quod numquam antea spe conceptum, nedum opere temptatum erat, ad quadringentesimum miliarium a Rheno usque ad flumen Albim, qui Semnonum Hermundurorumque fines praeterfluit, Romanus cum signis perductus exercitus.* Paterculus' claim overstates the achievement: Nero Drusus had reached the Elbe River in 9 BCE (see Ch. 2 n.138); Domitius Ahenobarbus had crossed the Elbe River without opposition in 3 BCE (see Ch. 3 n.71).

159. Vell. Pat. 2.106.1: *Pro dii boni, quanti voluminis opera insequenti aestate sub duce Tiberio Caesare gessimus! Perlustrata armis tota Germania est, victae gentes paene nominibus incognitae, receptae Cauchorum nationes: omnis eorum iuventus infinita numero, immensa corporibus, situ locorum tutissima, traditis armis una cum ducibus suis saepta fulgenti armatoque militum nostrorum agmine ante imperatoris procubuit tribunal.*
160. Dio 55.28.5: *οὐ μέντοι καὶ ἀξιομνημόνευτόν τι τότε γε ἐπράχθη.*
161. Dio 55.28.6–7.
162. *Greek Anthology* 16.16: *Ἀντολίαι, δύσιες, κόσμου μέτρα: καὶ τὰ Νέρωνος / ἔργα δι' ἀμφοτέρων ἵκετο γῆς περάτων. / ἥλιος Ἀρμενίην ἀνιὼν ὑπὸ χερσὶ δαμεῖσαν / κείνου, Γερμανίην δ' εἶδε κατερχόμενος. / δισσὸν ἀειδέσθω πολέμου κράτος: οἶδεν Ἀράξης / καὶ Ῥῆνος, δούλοις ἔθνεσι πινόμενοι.*
163. Strabo 7.1.4. Ober (1984), pp.309–310, interprets Strabo's statement to mean Augustus forbade the Roman Army to cross the Elbe River, at least temporarily, so that they could focus on other regions of higher strategic importance.

## CHAPTER 4: FIGHTING FOR THE *PAX AUGUSTA*

1. Dio 55.26.1.
2. Jer., *Chron.* A6: 27.5 *denarii.*
3. Dio 55.26.1.
4. Dio 55.26.2–3.
5. Dio 55.27.1–2.
6. Dio 55.27.3.
7. Dio 55.26.4; Strabo 5.3.7; Suet., *Div. Aug.* 25.2; Tac., *Ann.* 13.27.1. For the *Vigiles*, see Powell (2018), p.313.
8. Dio 55.26.5. On the *vici* of Rome, see Goodman (2020).
9. Dio 55.27.3.
10. Dio 55.27.4.
11. Vell. Pat. 2.107.3.
12. Dio 55.27.4.
13. Dio 54.18.2; *cf.* Suet., *Div Aug.* 30.1. Powell (2018), pp.69–70.
14. For the ground plan and a reconstructed elevation of the *Arcus Augusti*, see Holland (1946), fig. 1, p.52, and fig. 3, p.56.
15. The temple had suffered damage in the past and had already been rebuilt twice before, in 117 BCE and 73 BCE.
16. On the date, see Seager (1972) p.39, n.6.
17. Suet., *Tib.* 69: *Circa deos ac religiones neglegentior.*
18. Livy, *AUC* 3.20.5: *Sed nondum haec quae nunc tenet saeculum neglegentia deum venerat.*
19. The podium measures 32m × 49.5m (105ft × 162ft), and 7m (23ft) in height. Gartrell (2021), p.33, notes that the distinctive feature of the temple is 'the very high podium'.
20. Suet., *Tib.* 20: *Dedicavit … aedem, item Pollucis et Castoris suo fratrisque nomine de manubiis.* Ovid, *Fast.* 1.707–08.
21. Dio 55.27.4: *τοῦτό τε γὰρ αὐτοὺς ἐπὶ τῇ τοῦ Δρούσου μνήμῃ παρεμυθήσατο, καὶ ὅτι τὸ Διοσκόρειον ὁ Τιβέριος καθιερώσας οὐ τὸ ἑαυτοῦ μόνον ὄνομα αὐτῷ, Κλαυδιανὸν ἑαυτὸν ἀντὶ τοῦ Κλαυδίου διὰ τὴν ἐς τὸ τοῦ Αὐγούστου γένος ἐκποίησιν ὀνομάσας, ἀλλὰ καὶ τὸ ἐκείνου ἐπέγραψε.* For restorations of the inscription, see Gartrell, pp.166–171.
22. For a discussion of the parallels between the two Claudian brothers and the Dioscuri, see Champlin (2011a) and Gartrell (2021), pp.163–166.
23. Gartrell (2021), p.145, explains that the twins were popular divinities, credited with rescuing ordinary folk – travellers and sailors – in times of crisis, and their temple was where the standards for weights and measures were kept. On 15 July each year, 5,000 *equites*, led by two impersonators of the heroes who commemorated the victory at the

Battle of Lake Regillus (499, 496 or 493 BCE), rode on horseback along the *Via Sacra* to the temple in a cavalry parade (*transvectio*). The Senate frequently met in the temple as an alternative venue to the *Curia Iulia*. Sumi (2009) argues that the rededication was part of a broader process taking place under Augustus through which the historical memories associated with the temple contributed to shaping the ideology of his own Principate.

24. Aug., *Res Gest.* 17; Dio 55.25.2.
25. Dio 55.25.3.
26. Dio 55.25.5.
27. Dio 55.25.6.
28. Dio 56.28.1–4. For a full listing of conflicts, see Powell (2018), pp.131–133.
29. Dio 55.28.7.
30. Suet., *Div. Aug.* 25.4: *Ἀάσφαλὴς γάρ ἐστ ' ἀμείνων ἢ θρασὺς στρατηλάτης* is a line from Euripides, *Phoenissae* 598. Armand D'Angour, Professor of Classics at Oxford University, offered me this translation: 'I'd prefer a cautious leader to a rash one any day' as it 'preserves sense and imitates the rhythm [Trochaic tetrameter catalectic]', 23 October 2023.
31. Suet., *Div. Aug.* 25.4: *Proelium quidem aut bellum suscipiendum omnino negabat, nisi cum maior emolumenti spes quam damni metus ostenderetur. Nam minima commoda non minimo sectantis discrimine similes aiebat esse aureo hamo piscantibus, cuius abrupti damnum nulla captura pensari posset.*
32. The fortress encompassed an area of 37 hectares: Powell (2018), map 19, p.130; Pietch, Timpe and Wamser (1991); Pietch (1993); von Schurbein (2000 and 2004), pp.34–35 and fig. 26.
33. The fortress encompassed an area of 58 hectares: Powell (2018), p.376, n.48; Erlich (2016), fig. 5 on p.248. Cf. Vell. Pat. 2.110.1.
34. Strabo 7.1.3; Vell. Pat. 2.108.1.
35. Dio 55.10a.2.
36. Vell. Pat. 2.108.1: *in interiora refugiens incinctos Hercynia silva campos incolebat.* For the Hercynian Forest see Strabo 7.1.5.
37. Strabo 7.1.3; Vell. Pat. 2.108.2.
38. Vell. Pat. 2.108.2, 2.109.2.
39. Vell. Pat. 2.109.1: *fastigium gerebatque se ita adversus Romanos, ut neque bello nos lacesseret, et si lacesseretur, superesse sibi vim ac voluntatem resistendi ostenderet.*
40. Vell. Pat. 2.109.2.
41. Vell. Pat. 2.109.1.
42. Vell. Pat. 2.108.1, 2.109.4.
43. Vell. Pat. 2.108.1: *Nihil erat iam in Germania, quod vinci posset, praeter gentem Marcomannorum.*
44. Vell. Pat. 2.109.5.
45. Erdrich (2016), p.247; Musilová (2016), p.231.
46. Powell (2018), p.136. Examples include Nero Drusus' use of boats in his German Wars of 12–9 BCE and Trajan's in the Dacian Wars of 101–102 CE and 105–106 CE.
47. Vell. Pat. 2.110.1–2: *Praeparaverat iam hiberna Caesar ad Danubium admotoque exercitu non plus quam quinque dierum iter a primis hostium aberat, legionesque quas Saturninum admovere placuerat, paene aequali divisae intervallo ab hoste intra paucos dies in praedicto loco cum Caesare se iuncturae erant.*
48. Vell. Pat. 2.110.3: *in interiora exercitu vacuam.*
49. Dio 55.29.1. Vell. Pat. 2.112.2 calls Messallinus *Praepositus Illyrico* ('Overseer of the Illyrici').
50. Vell. Pat. 2.112.2: *vir animo etiam quam gente nobilior dignissimusque.*

51. Dio 55.29.1.
52. Dio 55.29.2.
53. Dio 56.16.3.
54. Dio 55.29.2.
55. Vell. Pat. 2.110.6.
56. Vell. Pat. 2.110.4.
57. Vell. Pat. 2.110.3–4: *parentis acerrimis ac peritissimis ducibus.*
58. Dio 55.28.7.
59. Vell. Pat. 2.110.4.
60. Vell. Pat. 2.110.1: *Rumpit interdum, interdum moratur proposita hominum fortuna.*
61. Dio 55.30.1.
62. Vell. Pat. 2.110.3: *necessaria gloriosis praeposita.*
63. Erdrich (2016), p.246. There was a steady trade in amber and slaves as well as tribute moving from the north to the south, with manufactured goods in pottery, bronze and silver as well as wine moving from the south to the north: see Wells (1972), p.46.
64. Dio 55.28.7; Vell. Pat. 2.110.3.
65. Dio 55.29.2.
66. Vell. Pat. 2.112.2: *praepositus Illyrico subita rebellione cum semiplena legione vicesima circumdatus hostili exercitu amplius viginti milia fudit fugavitque et ob id ornamentis triumphalibus honoratus est.* The legion may have earned its *cognomen* '*Valeria Victrix*' in this battle.
67. Dio 55.30.2.
68. Dio 55.29.4.
69. Auxiliary units did not usually have artillery per Campbell (1986).
70. Dio 55.30.4.
71. Dio 55.29.3; Vell. Pat. 2.110.4.
72. Dio 55.29.3.
73, Dio 55.29.2.
74. Dio 55.30.4. Seager (1972) p.40.
75. Dio 55.30.5: *καὶ ἐς μὲν χεῖρας, καίπερ τοῦ Τιβερίου πλησιάσαντός σφισιν, οὐκ ἦλθον αὐτῷ, ἄλλοσε δὲ καὶ ἄλλοσε μεθιστάμενοι πολλὰ ἐπόρθησαν: τῆς τε γὰρ χώρας ἐμπείρως ἔχοντες καὶ κούφως ἐσκευασμένοι, ῥᾳδίως ὅπῃ ποτὲ ἐβούλοντο ἐχώρουν.*
76. Dio 55.30.5.
77. Vell. Pat. 2.110.6.
78. The legions were stationed in Augustus' *provincia* and Africa Proconsularis: Dio 53.12.2, 55.23.1–7.
79. Vell. Pat. 2.111.2: *Audita in Senatu vox Principis, decimo die, ni caveretur, posse hostem in urbis Romae venire conspectum.*
80. Suet., *Tib.* 16.1: *gravissimum omnium externorum bellorum post Punica.* For the wars with Carthage, see Powell (2023).
81. Vell. Pat. 2.111.2: *Itaque ut praesidium ultimum Res Publica ab Augusto ducem in bellum poposcit Tiberium.*
82. For Tiberius' activities in Illyricum, see Kos (2017).
83. Vell. Pat. 2.111.1.
84. Dio 55.31.1.
85. For the *Cohortes Voluntariorum*, see Powell (2013), pp.41–43.
86. Dio 55.31.1.
87. For the *Cohortes Voluntariorum* under Augustus, see Powell (2018), p.312.
88. Dio 55.32.1.
89. Dio 55.32.2.

90. Dio 55.32.2; Tac., *Ann.* 1.3.4.
91. Suet., *Div. Aug.* 65.4. Braginton (1944), pp.395–396.
92. On the ramifications of his involuntary abdication, see Levick (1972b).
93. Vell. Pat. 2.113.1 states 'in a word a greater army than had ever been assembled in one place since the civil wars', *tanto denique exercitu, quantus nullo umquam loco post bella fuerat civilian*, i.e. since the Actian War (31 BCE) and Alexandrian War (30 BCE). Powell (2018), p.133.
94. Vell. Pat. 2.113.1: *tantum in bello ducem, quantum in pace vides principem. Iunctis exercitibus, quique sub Caesare fuerant quique ad eum venerant, contractisque in una castra decem legionibus, septuaginta amplius cohortibus, decem alis et pluribus quam decem veteranorum milibus, ad hoc magno voluntariorum numero frequentique equite regio, tanto denique exercitu, quantus nullo umquam loco post bella fuerat civilia.* The king providing the cavalry was Roimetalkes of Thrace.
95. Vell. Pat. 2.113.2.
96. Vell. Pat. 2.113.3.
97. Dio 55.112.3. *Mons* Claudius has been identified as either the mountain range near the modern city of Varaždin on the Drava River in Croatia, or the Papuk near the city of Požega in eastern Croatia.
98. Dio 56.12.1.
99. Suet., *Tib.* 20.1. This incident is not dated but would make sense at this juncture.
100. Dio 53.37.3. For the location of Tiberius' ditch in Siscia, see Radman-Livaja & Vukelić (2018).
101. Vell. Pat. 2.112.4–5.
102. Vell. Pat. 2.112.5: *ex insperato victoriam vindicaverunt.* McDermott (1970), pp.190–191, describes the life of L. Caesius Bassus, a legionary of the time of Tiberius who fought in Illyricum, from the inscription preserved on his tombstone, *CIL*, III, 2014.
103. Dio 55.32.3.
104. Dio 55.32.3. Powell (2013), pp.45–46.
105. Dio 55.32.3.
106. Suet., *Div. Aug.* 25.4: *sat celeriter fieri quidquid fiat satis bene.*
107. Dio 55.31.1: *μαθὼν οὖν ταῦτα ὁ Αὔγουστος, καὶ ὑποπτεύσας ἐς τὸν Τιβέριον ὡς δυνηθέντα μὲν ἂν διὰ ταχέων αὐτοὺς κρατῆσαι, τρίβοντα δὲ ἐξεπίτηδες ἵν' ὡς ἐπὶ πλεῖστον ἐν τοῖς ὅπλοις ἐπὶ τῇ τοῦ πολέμου προφάσει ᾖ.*
108. Dio 53.35–37; Suet., *Div. Aug.* 20.1.
109. Suet., *Tib.* 21.3: *ut peritissimum rei militaris utque unicum p. R. praesidium prosequatur.*
110. Suet., *Tib.* 21.4: *Vale, iucundissime Tiberi, et feliciter rem gere, ἐμοὶ καὶ ταῖς μούσαις στρατηγῶν. Iucundissime et ita sim felix, vir fortissime et dux νομιμώτατε, vale.* The reference may be to Tiberius' literary tastes; *cf.* Horace, *Odes* 3.4.37ff; *Epist.* 1.3. For use of Greek expressions in Augustus' letters, see Elder & Mullen (2019).
111. Suet., *Tib.* 21.5: *Ordinem aestivorum tuorum ego vero [laudo], mi Tiberi, et inter tot rerum difficultates καὶ τοσαύτην ἀποθυμίαν τῶν στρατευομένων non potuisse quemquam prudentius gerere se quam tu gesseris, existimo. [H]ii quoque qui tecum fuerunt omnes confitentur, versum illum in te posse dici: unus homo nobis vigilando restituit rem. Cf.* Enn., *Ann.* 370 V[2].
112. Suet., *Tib.* 21.6: *Sive quid incidit de quo sit cogitandum diligentius, sive quid stomachor, valde medius Fidius Tiberium meum desidero succurritque versus ille Homericus: Τούτου γ' ἑσπομένοιο καὶ ἐκ πυρὸς αἰθομένοιο / Ἄμφω νοστήσαιμεν, ἐπεὶ περίοιδε νοῆσαι. Iliad*, 10.246 f.
113. Suet., *Tib.* 21.6: *Attenuatum te esse continuatione laborum cum audio et lego, di me perdant nisi cohorrescit corpus meum; teque oro ut parcas tibi, ne si te languere audierimus, et ego et mater tua expiremus et summa imperi sui populus R. periclitetur.*
114. Suet., *Tib.* 21.6: *Nihil interest valeam ipse necne, si tu non valebis.*

115. Suet., *Tib.* 21.6: *Deos obsecro, ut te nobis conservent et valere nunc et semper patiantur, si non p. R. perosi sunt.*
116. Jer., *Chron.* A7.
117. Dio 55.34.3; Suet., *Div. Aug.* 20.
118. Dio 55.33.1.
119. Dio 55.33.2. The text breaks off at this point in the story.
120. Dio 55.34.4–5.
121. Dio 55.34.6.
122. Dio 55.34.7.
123. Vell. Pat., 2.114.4: *Hiems emolumentum patrati belli contulit, sed insequenti aestate omnis Pannonia reliquiis totius belli in Delmatia manentibus pacem petiit. Ferocem illam tot milium iuventutem, paulo ante servitutem minatam Italiae, conferentem arma, quibus usa erat, apud flumen nomine Bathinum prosternentemque se universam genibus imperatoris, Batonemque et Pinnetem excelsissimos duces, captum alterum, alterum a se deditum iustis voluminibus ordine narrabimus, ut spero.*
124. Dio 55.34.6.
125. Suet., *Tib.* 17.1: *praetextatus et laurea coronatus*. Comparing Suetonius' text to Dio's in 56.1.1, Swan (2004), p.224, argues convincingly that this *adventus* refers to Tiberius' return in 9 CE for his victories in Illyricum (Pannonia) in 8 CE. For Germanicus being in Rome, see Swan (2004), pp.239–240, citing Suet., *Div. Aug.* 34.2.
126. For the *Suburra*, see Paoli (1963), p.13, citing Martial 12.28.2, Juvenal 11.51 and *CIL*, VI, 9284.
127. Suet., *Tib.* 17.1. Powell (2018), p.156, erroneously states *Forum Romanum*.
128. *Cf.* Suet., *Div. Aug.* 34.2 and *Tib.* 17.2. The temples were like the ones on the *Capitolium*.
129. Vell. Pat. 2.114.5, 2.125.5.
130. Vell. Pat. 2.116.1.
131. Dio 56.11.1–2.
132. Dio 56.11.3–7. For Raetinum see the gravestone of Andes, an *eques* of *ala* Claudia *ILS* 2504 = *CIL*, XIII, 7023 in Mainz.
133. Dio 56.12.1.
134. Dio 56.12.2.
135. Vell. Pat, 2.115.2: *cum difficultate locorum et cum vi hostium luctatus, magna cum clade obsistentium excisis agris, exustis aedihciis, caesis viris.*
136. Dio 56.12.3.
137. Vell. Pat. 2.115.4: *Illa aestas maximi belli consummavit effectus: quippe Perustae et Desidiates Delmatae, situ locorum ac montium, ingeniorum ferocia, mira etiam pugnandi scientia et praecipue angustiis saltuum paene inexpugnabiles.* Swan (2004), pp.239, 243, believes the source text is corrupted and argues for a reading of three nations, see Appendix 9, pp.372–374.
138. I accept here the sequence of events placing the fighting against the Perustae before the siege of Andetrium proposed by Swan (2004), pp.236–239. Wilkes (1992), p.190, identifies Andetrium with Muć.
139. Dio 56 12.4; *cf.* Strabo 7.315 also calls Andetrium a stronghold. For a discussion of fortified native settlements, see Wilkes (1992), pp.190–192.
140. Dio 56.12.5: *ὥστε τὸν Τιβέριον, πολιορκεῖν σφας δοκοῦντα, αὐτὸν τὰ τῶν πολιορκουμένων πάσχειν.* The Roman supply dump was likely at Salonnae.
141. Dio 56.13.1.
142. Dio 56.13.1.
143. Dio 56.13.1; *cf.* Vell. Pat. 2.114.3.
144. Dio 56.13.3.

145. Dio 56.13.4.
146. Dio 56.14.1.
147. Dio 56.14.2.
148. Vell. Pat. 2.114.1.
149. Vell. Pat. 2.114.2: *Erat desiderantibus paratum iunctum vehiculum, lectica eius publicata, cuius usum cum alii tum ego sensi; iam medici, iam apparatus cibi, iam in hoc solum uni portatum instrumentum balinei nullius non succurrit valetudini; domus tantum ac domestici deerant, ceterum nihil, quod ab illis aut praestari aut desiderari posset.*
150. Dio 56.14.3–4.
151. Dio 56.14.5.
152. Dio 56.14.6.
153. Dio 56.14.7: *κρυπτομένους ἀνευρόντες ὥσπερ θηρία ἀπέκτειναν.*
154. Dio 56.15.1.
155. Dio 56.15.2.
156. Postumius: Vell. Pat. 2.116.2; Dio 56.15.3 has him as Postumus. Apronius: Vell. Pat. 2.117.3.
157. Such as the Boscoreale Cup BR II: see Ch. 3, n.19 and 20.
158. Dio 56.16.1.
159. Dio 56.16.2–3: *ἐπὶ βήματος αὐτῷ καθημένῳ προσαχθεὶς ὑπὲρ μὲν ἑαυτοῦ οὐδὲν ἐδεήθη, ἀλλὰ καὶ τὴν κεφαλὴν προέτεινεν ὥστ᾽ ἀποκοπῆναι, ὑπὲρ δὲ τῶν ἄλλων πολλὰ ἀπελογήσατο. καὶ τέλος ἐρωτηθεὶς ὑπὸ τοῦ Τιβερίου 'τί ὑμῖν ἔδοξε καὶ ἀποστῆναι καὶ ἐπὶ τοσοῦτον ἡμῖν χρόνον ἀντιπολεμῆσαι;' ἔφη ὅτι 'ὑμεῖς τούτων αἴτιοί ἐστε: ἐπὶ γὰρ τὰς ἀγέλας ὑμῶν φύλακας οὐ κύνας οὐδὲ νομέας ἀλλὰ λύκους πέμπετε.'.*
160. Suet., *Tib.* 20; Suetonius places the gift giving scene at his triumph in 12 CE.
161. Dio 56.17.1. On the tally of acclamations given to Augustus and Tiberius, see Barnes (1974), p.26.
162. Vell. Pat. 2.115.4: *non iam ductu, sed manibus atque armis ipsius Caesaris tum demum pacati sunt, cum paene funditus eversi forent.*
163. Aug., *Res Gest.* 30.
164. Suet., *Tib.* 16.2: *per quindecim legiones paremque auxiliorum copiam triennio gessit.* There were twenty-eight legions at this time, meaning fully 54 per cent of the citizen army were committed to the war.
165. Dio 56.16.4: *ὁ μὲν οὖν πόλεμος τοῦτο τὸ τέλος ἔσχε, πολλῶν μὲν καὶ ἀνδρῶν, πλείστων δὲ δὴ καὶ χρημάτων ἀπολομένων: πάμπολλά τε γὰρ ἐς αὐτὸν στρατόπεδα ἐτράφη καὶ λεία ἐλαχίστη.* In contrast, according to Vell. Pat. 2.115.2, Lepidus met Tiberius 'victorious and laden with booty' (*laetus victoria praedaque*) during his operations in 9 CE.
166. Vell. Pat. 2.116.1–3; Dio 56.17.1–2. Only Dio mentions the arches; their locations are not known.
167. Suet., *Tib.* 17.2: *Sed de cognomine intercessit Augustus, eo contentum repromittens, quod se defuncto suscepturus esset.* Vervaet (2021), pp.192–194, argues that Augustus saw the motion as excessive and moderated the award of honours in general to his stepsons in deference to practice during the Late Republic, and by dutifully accepting his decision, they, as 'mouthpieces and instruments of Augustus' will', propagated 'Augustus' new triumphal framework'.
168. Dio 56.17.3.
169. Dio 56.18.1; Vell. Pat. 2.117.1 is specific about the number of days.
170. Dio 56.22.3; Vell. Pat. 2.120.3.
171. Varus was proconsul of Africa (8–7 BCE) with *Legio* III *Augusta* under his command, and then *legatus Augusti propraetore* of Syria (6–4 BCE) in charge of *Legiones* III *Gallica*, VI

*Ferrata*, X *Fretensis* and XII *Fulminata* and with them had put down a revolt in Iudaea in 4 BCE.

172. Vell. Pat. 2.117.3–4: *quique gladiis domari non poterant, posse iure mulceri. Quo proposito mediam ingressus Germaniam velut inter viros pacis gaudentes dulcedine iurisdictionibus agendoque pro tribunali ordine trahebat aestival.*
173. Vell. Pat. 2.117.3: *corpore et animo immobilior, otio magis castrorum quam bellicae adsuetus militiae.*
174. Vell. Pat. 2.117.3: *vir ingenio mitis, moribus quietus.*
175. Suet., *Div. Aug.* 23.1 and *Tib.* 17.1.
176. Vell. Pat. 2.117.1. For the size of Varus' army and casualties see Powell (2014), p.28 and Powell (2018), p.152.
177. Pliny, *Nat. Hist.* 7.46.
178. Dio 56.23.1.
179. Suet., *Div. Aug.* 23.2: *Adeo denique consternatum ferunt, ut per continuos menses barba capilloque summisso caput interdum foribus illideret, vociferans: 'Quintili Vare, legiones redde!' diemque cladis quot annis maestum habuerit ac lugubrem. Cf.* Dio 56.23.1.
180. Pliny, *Nat. Hist.* 7.45 [150]; Suet., *Div. Aug.* 23.1, who pairs it with the *clades Lolliana* (17 BCE); *cf* Tac., *Ann.* 1.3, 1.10. Ball (2023), p.223, questions the extent of Varus' culpability and suggests that he was scapegoated by Roman historians to deflect blame away from Augustus.
181. Vell. Pat. 2.120.3.
182. Dio 56.23.3; Suet., *Tib.* 17.2; Vell. Pat. 2.120.1.
183. Suet., *Tib.* 17.2: Suetonius may be conflating his separate arrivals in the spring and summer of 9 CE.
184. Dio 56.23.1. The fear of invasion by Germanic tribes reached back to the Cimbri and Teutones who had beaten the Romans at Arausio on 6 October 105 BCE in what was their worst military defeat ever; they recovered with their victory at Vercellae on 30 July 101 BCE under Marius: see Powell (2011b).
185. Dio 56.23.1.
186. Dio 56.23.2–3: *ὅμως δ' οὖν τά τε ἄλλα ὡς ἐκ τῶν παρόντων παρεσκευάσατο, καὶ ἐπειδὴ μηδεὶς τῶν τὴν στρατεύσιμον ἡλικίαν ἐχόντων καταλεχθῆναι ἠθέλησεν, ἐκλήρωσεν αὐτούς, καὶ τῶν μὲν μηδέπω πέντε καὶ τριάκοντα ἔτη γεγονότων τὸν πέμπτον, τῶν δὲ πρεσβυτέρων τὸν δέκατον ἀεὶ λαχόντα τήν τε οὐσίαν ἀφείλετο καὶ ἠτίμωσε. καὶ τέλος, ὡς καὶ πάνυ πολλοὶ οὐδ' οὕτω τι αὐτοῦ προετίμων, ἀπέκτεινέ τινας. ἀποκληρώσας δὲ ἔκ τε τῶν ἐστρατευμένων ἤδη καὶ ἐκ τῶν ἐξελευθέρων ὅσους ἠδυνήθη, κατέλεξε.*
187. Suet., *Div. Aug.* 24.1. The incident is undated yet seems apposite under these extreme circumstances of 9 CE, but seems unlikely because the man was a Roman citizen.
188. Dio 56.23.1.
189. Vell. Pat. 2.119.5.
190. Ball (2023), p.205. Syme (1986), p.328 remarks 'Varus had had bad luck.'
191. Ovid, *Fast.* 1.647–48; Degrassi, *Inscr. Ital.* 13.2: *Fast. Praen.* 115.
192. Dio 56.25.1. Suet., *Tib.* 20 infers 12 CE.
193. *RIC* I 62; *MIR* 2, 58–4; *BMC* 133; Cohen 70 corr. Appendix 2(a). For a description of the temple, see Kellum (1993).
194. For a specimen of the cornice of the *Aedes Concordiae*, see Carandini (2017), Vol. 1, pl.33.
195. See n.12. above.
196. Carandini (2017), Vol. 1, p.170. Additional land was acquired from the adjacent Basilica Opimia.
197. They included statues of: a Leto as Nursing Mother with the infants Apollo and Artemis in her arms by Euphranor; an Apollo and a Hera by Baton; a Hermes, a Diskobolos and a Man Sacrificing a Ram by Naucydes; a Wrestler Winded by Naucerus; an Asclepis and

a Hygieia by Nikeratos; a Demeter, a Zeus and an Athena by Sthennis; and a Marsyas Bound by Zeuxis: Pliny the Elder, *Nat. Hist.* 34.73, 77, 80, 89, 90. Among the paintings were a Father Liber (or Dionysus) by Nikias and a Casandra by Theoros: Pliny, *Nat. Hist.* 35.66, 35.131, 35.144, 35.196. Pliny, *Nat. Hist.* 37.4 relates the curious story of an engraved sardonyx, once owned by Polykrates of Samos (*c.* 540 BCE), which he cast into the sea as an offering to Fortuna in gratitude for his prosperity, but it was then eaten by a fish that was caught and served up as dinner to the king; set in a golden horn, 'It was presented by the Augusta and is ranked almost last in a collection containing many gems that are valued more highly', *in Concordiae delubro cornu aureo Augustae dono inclusam et novissimum prope locum praelatis multis optinentem.*

198. Suet., *Tib.* 18.1; Dio 56.24.6.
199. Vell. Pat. 2.118.1.
200. Vell. Pat. 2.118.2.
201. For a detailed review of events based on extant sources, see Powell (2014), pp.28–40, and Powell (2018), pp.152–156.
202. Ovid, *Tris.* 4.2.29–38; Man., *Astr.* 1.899–900; Vell. Pat. 2.117.1.
203. Dio 56.22.4; Front., *Strat.* 3.15.4; Vell. Pat. 2.117.1; Tac., *Ann.* 1.61 mentions survivors later guiding Germanicus Caesar to the site of the final massacre in 15 CE, while Tac., *Ann.* 12.27 mentions a few survivors of the Varian disaster being liberated from their slavery after forty years.
204. Dio 56.24.1.
205. Tac., *Ann.* 1.31, 4.73.
206. Tac., *Ann.* 1.31, 1.37, 3.41, 4.73. Powell (2018), p.158, erroneously switches the units stationed at *Ara* Ubiorum and Vetera.
207. Suet., *Tib.* 18.1: Varus, *temeritate et neglegentia ducis accidisse*; Tiberius, *Curam quoque solito exactiorem praestitit.*
208. Suet., *Tib.* 18.1: *Traiecturus Rhenum commeatum omnem ad certam formulam adstrictum non ante transmisit, quam consistens apud ripam explorasset vehiculorum onera, ne qua deportarentur nisi concessa aut necessaria.*
209. Suet., *Tib.* 18.2: *Trans Rhenum vero eum vitae ordinem tenuit, ut sedens in caespite nudo cibum caperet, saepe sine tentorio pernoctaret, praecepta sequentis diei omnia, et si quid subiti muneris iniungendum esset, per libellos daret; addita monitione ut, de quo quisque dubitaret, se nec alio interprete quacumque vel noctis hora uteretur.*
210. Suet., *Tib.* 19.1: *Disciplinam acerrime exegit animadversionum et ignominiarum generibus ex antiquitate repetitis atque etiam legato legionis, quod paucos milites cum liberto suo trans ripam venatum misisset, ignominia notato.*
211. Dio, 56.24.6 [Zon. 10.37] states that 'Tiberius did not see fit to cross the Rhine, but kept quiet, watching to see that the barbarians did not cross. And they, knowing him to be there, did not venture to cross in their turn'; *ὁ δὲ Τιβέριος διαβῆναι τὸν Ῥῆνον οὐκ ἔκρινεν, ἀλλ' ἠτρέμιζεν ἐπιτηρῶν μὴ οἱ βάρβαροι τοῦτο ποιήσωσιν. ἀλλ' οὐδ' ἐκεῖνοι διαβῆναι ἐτόλμησαν γνόντες αὐτὸν παρόντα.* On views pro and contra, see Swan (2004), p.275, Syme (1978b), p.58, and Woodman (1977), 2.120.1–2. On the balance of the evidence, I believe he campaigned in both years.
212. Vell. Pat. 2.121.1.
213. Tac., *Ann.* 1.34.
214. His son, Drusus, was accompanied by two Praetorian Cohorts to the legions on the Danube in 14 CE, Tac., *Ann.* 1.24.2.
215. Suet., *Tib.* 19: *Sed re prospere gesta non multum afuit quin a Bructero quodam occideretur, cui inter proximos versanti et trepidatione detecto tormentis expressa confessio est cogitati facinoris.*
216. Tac., *Ann.* 1.50.

217. Vell. Pat. 2.121.1.
218. Dio 56.25.2.
219. Dio 56.25.2–3: *οὐ μέντοι οὔτε μάχῃ τινὶ ἐνίκησαν ʽἐς γὰρ χεῖρας οὐδεὶς αὐτοῖς ᾔει οὔτε ἔθνος τι ὑπηγάγοντο: δεδιότες γὰρ μὴ καὶ συμφορᾷ αὖθις περιπέσωσιν, οὐ πάνυ πόρρω τοῦ Ῥήνου προῆλθον, ἀλλὰ αὐτοῦ που μέχρι τοῦ μετοπώρου μείναντες καὶ τὰ τοῦ Αὐγούστου γενέθλια ἑορτάσαντες καί τινα ἱπποδρομίαν ἐν αὐτοῖς διὰ τῶν ἑκατοντάρχων ποιήσαντες ἐπανῆλθον.* Paterculus is silent on this year's campaign.
220. Barnes (1974), p.26. Powell (2018), p.159, erroneously states this was Augustus' twenty-first acclamation.
221. Dio 56.26.1.
222. Dio 56.26.2.
223. Dio 56.26.2–56.27.1.
224. Dio 56.27.2–3: *ἐπειδή τε συχνοὶ φυγάδες οἱ μὲν ἔξω τῶν τόπων ἐς οὓς ἐξωρίσθησαν τὰς διατριβὰς ἐποιοῦντο, οἱ δὲ καὶ ἐν αὐτοῖς ἐκείνοις ἁβρότερον διῆγον, ἀπηγόρευσε μηδένα πυρὸς καὶ ὕδατος εἰρχθέντα μήτε ἐν ἠπείρῳ διατρίβειν μήτε ἐν νήσῳ τῶν ὅσαι ἔλαττον τετρακοσίων ἀπὸ τῆς ἠπείρου σταδίων ἀπέχουσι, πλὴν Κῶ τε καὶ Ῥόδου Σάμου τε καὶ Λέσβου: ταύτας γὰρ οὐκ οἶδ' ὅπως μόνας ὑπεξείλετο. ἐκεῖνά τε οὖν αὐτοῖς προσέταξε, καὶ τὸ μήτε περαιοῦσθαί ποι ἄλλοσε, μήτε πλοῖα πλείω φορτικοῦ τε ἑνὸς χιλιοφόρου καὶ κωπήρων δύο κεκτῆσθαι, μήτε δούλοις ἢ καὶ ἀπελευθέροις ὑπὲρ εἴκοσι χρῆσθαι, μήτ' οὐσίαν ὑπὲρ δώδεκα καὶ ἡμίσειαν μυριάδα ἔχειν, τιμωρηθήσεσθαι καὶ αὐτοὺς ἐκείνους καὶ τοὺς ἄλλους τούς τι παρὰ ταῦτα συμπράξαντάς σφισιν ἐπαπειλήσας.* Swan (2004), pp.289–290, determines the vessels to be an *oneraria* (cargo-carrying freighter) and two *actuariae* (oared galleys suitable for carrying passengers) based on the definitions in *Dig.* 49.15.2 (Marcellus). The sum of 125,000 *drachmai* was equivalent to HS 500,000.
225. Agrippa Caesar: Jameson (1975); Powell (2013), p.41, erroneously cites Surrentum instead of Planasia. Ovid: Ovid, *Trist.* 2.207, and *Pont.* 2.9.72, 3.3.72.
226. Suet., *Caius* 1.1, 8.1–3. He will grow up to be Caligula, Rome's third *princeps.*
227. Dio 56.17.1–2; Vell. Pat. 2.121.1–2.
228. Vell. Pat. 2.121.3: *Quippe omnis eminentissimos hostium duces non occisos fama narravit, sed vinctos triumphus ostendit; quem mihi fratrique meo inter praecipuos praecipuisque donis adornatos viros comitari contigit.*
229. Suet., *Tib.* 20. Bato disappears from history hereafter.
230. Suet., *Tib.* 20: *Ac prius quam in Capitolium flecteret, descendit e curru seque praesidenti patri ad genua summisit.*
231. Suet., *Tib.* 20.
232. *Aureus*: *BMC* 1, *RIC* I 1. *Denarius*: *BMC* 512, *RIC* I 222.
233. Vell. Pat. 2.121.1: *ut aequum ei ius in omnibus provinciis exercitibusque esset, quam erat ipsi, decreto complexus est.*
234. Augustus' *imperium*: Dio 56.28.1. Tiberius' *imperium*: Suet, *Tib.* 21.1; *cf.* Dio 55.13.2n.
235. Dio 56.28.2.
236. Suet., *Div. Aug.* 85.1: *Rescripta Bruto de Catone.* In 46 BCE, M. Iunius Brutus the assassin published a eulogy of M. Porcius Cato Uticensis; *cf.* Cic., *Ad Att.* 12.21.
237. Dio 57.3.1.
238. Suet., *Caius* 8.3; *Tab. Siar.* 1.12; Vell. Pat. 2.123.1. Syme (1978), p.58 and n.5, 6.
239. Syme (1978), pp.58–61.
240. Vell. Pat. 2.123.1: *Quippe Caesar Augustus cum Germanicum nepotem suum reliqua belli patraturum misisset in Germaniam.*

## CHAPTER 5: FOLLOWING IN AUGUSTUS' WAKE

1. Vell. Pat. 2.123.1: *Tiberium autem filium missurus esset in Illyricum ad firmanda pace quae bello subegera*; Suet., *Div. Aug.* 98.5.

2. It is still called Illyricum in 14 CE: *CIL*, III, 1741 (Ragusae) = *ILS* 938, and Vell. Pat. 2.125.5. For the evidence for the administrative division of Illyricum, see Kos (2010, 2011, 2015 and 2022).
3. Vell. Pat. 2.125.4.
4. *Cf. ILS* 2280 = *EJ* 265.
5. Tac., *Ann.* 1.16, 1.23, 1.30.
6. Suet., *Div. Aug.* 97.3, 98.1.
7. Suet., *Div. Aug.* 98.2–3. *Epheboi* were Greek-speaking youths between the ages of 18 and that of full citizenship, who enjoyed regular gymnastics training as a part of their overall education; once common in Greek Italy (Magna Graecia), the training now survived in Capreae.
8. Suet., *Div. Aug.* 98.4.
9. Suet., *Div. Aug.* 98.5.
10. Suet., *Div. Aug.* 98.5; Vell. Pat. 2.123.1.
11. Suet., *Div. Aug.* 97.3; Vell. Pat. 2.123.1.
12. Suet., *Div. Aug.* 98.5, 100.1; Vell. Pat. 2.123.1.
13. Suet., *Div. Aug.* 98.5; Vell. Pat. 2.123.1.
14. Vell. Pat. 2.123.2.
15. Tac., *Ann.* 1.5.3; *cf.* Suet., *Div. Aug.* 98.5 and *Tib.* 21.1.
16. Vell. Pat. 2.123.2: *commendans illi sua atque ipsius opera. Cf.* Suet., *Div. Aug.* 98.5.
17. Suet., *Tib.* 21.2: *Scio vulgo persuasum quasi egresso post secretum sermonem Tiberio vox Augusti per cubicularios excepta sit: 'Miserum populum R., qui sub tam lentis maxillis erit.'*
18. Suet., *Div. Aug.* 99.1; *cf.* Dio 56.30.3.
19. Dio 56.30.3: *τέλος ἔφη ὅτι 'τὴν Ῥώμην γηίνην. Cf.* Suet., *Div. Aug.* 28.3. For the veracity of the claim see Powell (2024).
20. Suet., *Div. Aug.* 99.1: *εἰ δέ τι / Ἐπεὶ δὲ πάνυ καλῶς πέπαισται, δότε κρότον / Καὶ πάντες ἡμᾶς μετὰ χαρᾶς προπέμψατε.*
21. Suet., *Div. Aug.* 99.2.
22. Suet., *Div. Aug.* 99.1: *Livia, nostri coniugii memor vive, ac vale!*
23. Suet., *Div. Aug.* 100.1; Dio 56.30.5.
24. Dio 56.30.5.
25. The accounts of Dio, Suetonius and Tacitus differ greatly. For a well-reasoned reconstruction of the historical chronology of August to October 14 CE, see Mallan (2020), Appendix II, pp.309–310.
26. Dio 56.31.1.
27. Tac., *Ann.* 1.7; Dio 57.2.1, 66.23.2.
28. Aug., *Res Gest.* 25.2; Dio 57.3.2; Tac., *Ann.* 1.7.2. The only soldiers in Italy were the *Cohortes Praetoriae*.
29. Vell. Pat. 2.124.1.
30. Dio 56.30.2; *cf.* Tac., *Ann.* 1.5.1.
31. Suet., *Caius* 2.1: *Obiit autem, ut opinio fuit, fraude Tiberi, ministerio et opera Cn. Pisonis.*
32. Dio 56.30.1; Tac., *Ann.* 1.5.1–2.
33. Tac., *Ann.* 1.6.
34. Suet., *Tib.* 22.1.
35. Though banished, Agrippa Caesar was still a Roman citizen.
36. Vell. Pat. 2.124.1: *Id solum voce publica dixisse satis habeo: cuius orbis ruinam timueramus, eum ne commotum quidem sensimus, tantaque unius viri maiestas fuit, ut nec pro bonis neque contra malos opus armis foret.*
37. Dio 56.31.2.

38. Dio 56.31.2; *cf.* Suet., *Div. Aug.* 100.2; *cf.* Dio 55.2.1, 54.25.3–4. The body likely arrived between midnight and dawn.
39. For calculations of the number of days taken to travel the route, see Swan (2004), p.306.
40. Dio 56.34.2n.
41. Tac., *Ann.* 1.7.3; Suet., *Tib.* 23; Dio 56.28.1n.
42. Tac., *Ann.* 1.7.3: *verba edicti fuere pauca et sensu permodesto: de honoribus parentis consulturum, neque abscedere a corpore, idque unum ex publicis muneribus usurpare.*
43. Dio 56.31.3.
44. Tac., *Ann.* 1.8.1.
45. For a reconstruction of the order of business, see Mallan (2020), Appendix III, p.365.
46. Suet., *Tib.* 23.
47. Dio 56.31.3, 56.32.1; Suet., *Div. Aug.* 101.1. Suet., *Div. Aug.* 50 notes that Augustus used a ring with an intaglio featuring an engraved phoenix, later a profile of Alexander the Great by Dioskurides.
48. Dio 56.32.1; *cf.* Suet., *Iul.* 83.2; *Caius Inst.* 2.104. The imperial freedman read the will as it was deemed improper for a senator to read a dead man's will.
49. Suet., *Tib.* 23: '*Quoniam atrox fortuna Gaium et Lucium filios mihi eripuit, Tiberius Caesar mihi ex parte dimidia et sextante heres esto.*'
50. Suet., *Div. Aug.* 101.2.
51. Dio 56.32.1.
52. Augustus' heirs in the second degree were his grandsons through adoption, Drusus and Germanicus, his three natural great-grandsons, children of Germanicus and Agrippina; in the third degree were friends and relatives (Suet., *Div. Aug.* 101.2), among them Claudius (later Rome's fourth *princeps*), who received HS 800,000 (Suet., *Div. Claud.* 4.7.).
53. Dio 56.32.2, 57.14.2 paid in 15 CE. The thirty-five tribes (*tribus*) of plebeian residents of Rome also received HS 3,500,000 (Suet., *Div. Aug.* 101.2); *cf. plebi* in Tac., *Ann.* 1.8.3. The sums paid to the soldiers are confirmed in Tac., *Ann.* 1.8.2. The *Vigiles* who were recruited from *liberti* are not mentioned in either Dio or Tacitus.
54. Suet., *Div. Aug.* 101.4: *Tribus voluminibus, uno mandata de funere suo complexus est, altero indicem rerum a se gestarum, quem vellet incidi in aeneis tabulis, quae ante Mausoleum statuerentur, tertio breviarium totius imperii, quantum militum sub signis ubique esset, quantum pecuniae in aerario et fiscis et vectigaliorum residuis.* Confirmed in Tac., *Ann.* 1.8.3; *cf.* Dio 56.33.1–6 mentions four books. Suet., *Div. Aug.* 101.1 remarks that the will, composed in 13 CE, was written in part in Augustus' own hand and part in those of his ex-slaves, Polybius and Hilarion.
55. Dio 57.47.1.
56. Tac., *Ann.* 1.8.1; Dio 57.2.1; Suet. *Div. Aug.* 101.1.
57. Dio 57.2.2. Presumably Tiberius was asking for Praetorian Cohorts. At this first meeting following Augustus' death, he may have had men of the *Germani Corporis Custodes* who had since returned to Rome (Tac., *Ann.* 1.24).
58. Dio 57.2.3: '*οἱ στρατιῶται οὐκ ἐμοὶ ἀλλὰ δημόσιοί εἰσι*'.
59. Tac., *Ann.* 1.8.3.
60. Dio 56.43.1.
61. For the date of the funeral, see Swan (2004), p.320.
62. App., *Bell. Civ.* 1.105–106.
63. Tac., *Ann.* 1.10.
64. Dio 56.34.2.
65. Dio 56.34.2–3.
66. Dio 56.34.4; *cf.* Polyb., *Hist.* 6.54.1–2.

67. Dio 56.34.2; *cf.* 56.35.1 and Suet., *Div Aug.* 100.3. Galinsky (2012), p.179, notes the significance of the location since Caesar's statue could not be included in the procession as he was already a god.
68. Dio 56.34.1–41.9; Tac., *Ann.* 1.11.1; Suet., *Div. Aug.* 100.3. Dio's speech is his own invention; Swan (2004), pp.325–339.
69. Suet., *Div. Aug.* 100.2–3; *cf.* Tac., *Ann.* 3.76.2; Arce, *Funus* 46–47.
70. Dio 56.34.2.
71. Dio 56.42.2; Strabo 5.3.8.
72. For different interpretations of Dio 56.42.2, see Swan (2004), pp.341–342.
73. Dio 56.42.3 states that an eagle was released at this moment, but the story is problematic: neither Suetonius nor Tacitus mention it in their accounts. Instead, Suet., *Div. Aug.* 100.2: 'a man of praetorian rank affirmed upon oath, that he saw his spirit ascend from the funeral pile to heaven', *nec defuit vir praetorius, qui se effigiem cremati euntem in caelum vidisse iuraret.* For a discussion of this episode, see Swan (2004), pp.343–344.
74. Dio 56.42.4; *cf.* Suet., *Div. Aug.* 100.4. The ashes of Augustus joined those of M. Claudius Marcellus (Dio 53.30.5), Octavia (54.35.4), Nero Claudius Drusus Germanicus (54.28.5) and M. Agrippa (55.2.3).
75. Suet., *Div. Aug.* 100.4; Vell. Pat. 2.124.3, 2.126.1; Tac., *Ann.* 1.10.8; Dio 56.46.2 names the witness as Numerius Atticus.
76. Dio 56.46.1–56.47.5; *cf.* Tac. *Ann.* 1.10.8, 1.54.
77. Tac., *Ann.* 1.14. For Livia's place in the Roman Imperial Cult, see Grether (1946).
78. Dio 57.12.4; Suet., *Tib.* 50.2–3; Tac. *Ann.* 1.14. The titles proposed included *Patriae* ('Parent of the Fatherland') and *Mater Patriae* ('Mother of the Fatherland'), and she was declined a *lictor*: see Chapter 7, n.61.
79. Vell. Pat. 2.124.2: *Una tamen veluti luctatio civitatis fuit, pugnantis cum Caesare senatus populique Romani, ut stationi paternae succederet, illius, ut potius aequalem civem quam eminentem liceret agere principem.*
80. Tac., *Ann.* 1.11: *plures facilius munia rei publicae sociatis laboribus exsecuturos.*
81. Tac., *Ann.* 1.11. The second reading took place two weeks after the first. For an assessment of different historians' views on the *breviarum totius imperii* and when it was read, see Swan (2004), pp.314–319. *Cf.* Suet., *Div. Aug.* 28.1 and Suet., *Caius* 16.1 state that Augustus had submitted such a report to the Senate before.
82. Dio 56.33.5–6: *γνώμην τε αὐτοῖς ἔδωκε τοῖς τε παροῦσιν ἀρκεσθῆναι καὶ μηδαμῶς ἐπὶ πλεῖον τὴν ἀρχὴν ἐπαυξῆσαι ἐθελῆσαι: δυσφύλακτόν τε γὰρ αὐτὴν ἔσεσθαι, καὶ κινδυνεύσειν ἐκ τούτου καὶ τὰ ὄντα ἀπολέσαι ἔφη. τοῦτο γὰρ καὶ αὐτὸς ὄντως ἀεί ποτε οὐ λόγῳ μόνον ἀλλὰ καὶ ἔργῳ ἐτήρησε: παρὸν γοῦν αὐτῷ πολλὰ ἐκ τοῦ βαρβαρικοῦ προσκτήσασθαι οὐκ ἠθέλησε. Cf.* Aug., *Res Gest.* 26, 27.
83. Aug., *Res Gest.* 17; Dio 54.25.2–6.
84. Tac., *Ann.* 1.11.
85. Dio 57.2.4–5: *ἔπειτα δὲ κοινωνούς τέ τινας καὶ συνάρχοντας, οὔτι γε καὶ πάντων καθάπαξ ὥσπερ ἐν ὀλιγαρχίᾳ, ἀλλ᾽ ἐς τρία μέρη νέμων αὐτήν, ᾔτει, καὶ τὸ μὲν αὐτὸς ἔχειν ἠξίου, τῶν δὲ ἑτέρων ἄλλοις παρεχώρει. ἦν δὲ ταῦτα ἓν μὲν ἥ τε Ῥώμη καὶ ἡ ἄλλη Ἰταλία, ἕτερον δὲ τὰ στρατόπεδα, καὶ ἕτερον οἱ λοιποὶ ὑπήκοοι.* Since 27 BCE, Italy was managed by annually elected praetors, the 'Provinces of the People' by the Senate and the 'Provinces of Caesar' by the *princeps*: see Mallan (2020), pp.108–109.
86. *Cf.* Dio 57.2.5: *Ἀσίνιος δὲ δὴ Γάλλος παρρησίᾳ ἀεί ποτε πατρῴᾳ καὶ ὑπὲρ τὸ συμφέρον αὐτῷ χρώμενος 'ἑλοῦ' ἔφη 'ἣν ἂν ἐθελήσῃς μοῖραν'.*
87. Dio 57.2.6: *καὶ Τιβέριος 'καὶ πῶς οἷόν τέ ἐστιν' εἶπεν 'τὸν αὐτὸν καὶ νέμειν τι καὶ αἱρεῖσθαι'*. On Tiberius' alleged plans to divide the empire, see Schrömbges (1992).
88. Dio 57.2.6.
89. Tac., *Ann.* 1.13.

90. Tac., *Ann.* 1.13: '*quo usque patieris, Caesar, non adesse caput rei publicae?*'
91. Tac., *Ann.* 1.13: *non ut fateretur suscipi a se imperium, sed ut negare et rogari desineret.* Whether this is the moment he became *princeps* (*dies imperii*) is not clear. His contemporaries accepted a 'start date': Ovid, *Pont.* 4.13.27–8; Vell. Pat. 2.124.1–2. Gruen (2005). Swan (2004), Appendix II, p.361, argues for a date in late October 14 CE.
92. Tac., *Ann.* 1.7.
93. Tac., *Ann.* 1.7: *Nam Tiberius cuncta per consules incipiebat, tamquam vetere re publica et ambiguus imperandi.*
94. Tac., *Ann.* 1.72.
95. Dio 57.8.1. Similarly, Augustus: see Suet., *Div. Aug.* 53.1.
96. Tac., *Ann.* 1.72.
97. Dio 57.8.2.
98. For a detailed examination of Tiberius' use of titles on coins, see Grant (1950), pp.41–49.
99. Dio 57.8.2. In the sources he is most often addressed as Caesar.
100. Tac., *Ann.* 14.3.
101. Suet., *Tib.* 25.1; Dio 57.15.4. For a discussion of the case of Scribonius Libo, see Pettinger (2012).
102. Scribonia, Augustus' first wife, had been his great-aunt. Hallett (1984), p.159; Seager (1972), p.90.
103. Tac., *Ann.* 2.27, 6.10.
104. Seager (1972), p.90.
105. Suet., *Tib.* 25.1.
106. Tac., *Ann.* 1.18–19.
107. Tac., *Ann.* 1.31, 1.37.
108. Tac., *Ann.* 1.24. Drusus had spoken at the funeral on 6 or 8 September.
109. Tac., *Ann.* 1.31, 1.37–39, 1.45.
110. Tac., *Ann.* 1.34.
111. Mallan (2020), Appendix II, p.360; Kos (2014b).
112. Tac., *Ann.* 1.18–19.
113. Tac., *Ann.* 1.17.
114. Tac., *Ann.* 1.18–20.
115. Tac., *Ann.* 1.21–2.
116. Tac., *Ann.* 1.23.
117. Tac., *Ann.* 1.23.
118. Vell. Pat. 2.125.4: *prisca antiquaque severitate usus ancipitia.*
119. Tac., *Ann.* 1.25.
120. Tac., *Ann.* 1.26.
121. Tac., *Ann.* 1.27.
122. Tac., *Ann.* 1.28. On the eclipse, see Salomon (1968), p.127, and Woodman (2006b), pp.307, 315, 318.
123. Tac., *Ann.* 1.28–29.
124. Tac., *Ann.* 1.30.
125. For a full account of the mutiny in Germania, see Powell (2013), pp.71–84.
126. Tac., *Ann.* 1.31, 1.37–39, 1.45.
127. Tac., *Ann.* 1.35.
128. Tac., *Ann.* 1.36.
129. Tac., *Ann.* 1.34.
130. Tac., *Ann.* 1.35.
131. Tac., *Ann.* 1.36. Conditions would include serving as *evocati* when called back.

132. Tac., *Ann.*1.31: *vernacula multitudo, nuper acto in urbe dilectu.* From them it had spread to the other legions. *Cf.* Dio 57.5.4. These *Cohortes Voluntariorum* would be the units founded by Germanicus in 6 CE or Tiberius in 9 CE.
133. Dio 57.5.3; Tac., *Ann.* 1.37.
134. Tac., *Ann.* 1.35; Suet., *Tib.* 25.2.
135. Tac., *Ann.* 1.39.
136. Suet., *Caius* 9.1.
137. Tac., *Ann.* 1.39.
138. Dio 57.5.6; Tac., *Ann.* 1.39.
139. Tac., *Ann.* 1.39.
140. Tac., *Ann.* 1.41; Suet., *Caius* 9.1.
141. Dio 57.5.7; Tac., *Ann.* 1.44.
142. Tac., *Ann.* 1.48–49.
143. Woodman (2006), p.324, interprets this to be a form of collective madness among the soldiers.
144. Tac., *Ann.* 1.49.
145. Tac., *Ann.* 1.50.
146. Tac., *Ann.* 1.51.
147. Tac., *Ann.* 1.31, 1.37.
148. Tac., *Ann.* 1.40.
149. Suet., *Caius.* 4.1.
150. Tac., *Ann.* 1.46; Suet., *Tib.* 38.1.
151. Tac., *Ann.* 1.24: *nullis satis certis mandatis.*
152. Mallan (2020), Appendix III, p.363, suggests this moment as the starting date of Tiberius' principate in Dio 57.7.1.
153. Dio 57.4.2, 57.6.4–5; Tac., *Ann.* 1.52.
154. Tac., *Ann.* 1.54.
155. Tac., *Ann.* 1.54.
156. Suet., *Tib.* 37.2.
157. Tac., *Ann.* 1.72: *si quis proditione exercitum aut plebem seditionibus, denique male gesta re publica maiestatem populi Romani minuisset.* The body of law included the *Lex Apuleia* of 91 BCE, *Lex Cornelia* of 81–80 BCE and *Lex Iulia* of 48 BCE.
158. Tac., *Ann.* 1.72: *exercendas leges esse re spondit.*
159. Tac., *Ann.* 4.19. For procedures in Roman courts, see Powell (2013), pp.57–58.
160. Flower (2006), pp.132–133.
161. Tac., *Ann.* 4.30.
162. Dio 57.7.6.
163. Tac., *Ann.* 1.75; *cf.* Pliny, *Ep.* 20, 6.11, 10.19; Aul. Gell., *Noc. Att.* 1.22. Bablitz (2009) stresses that Tiberius did not position himself to appear superior to the presiding magistrate but sat at ground level, either nearby or across the courtroom, so that his attendance would not unduly influence the decision.
164. Tac., *Ann.* 1.73.
165. Tac., *Ann.* 1.73: *deorum iniurias dis curae.* Cf. Suet., Tib. 58. *Cf.* Suet., *Tib.* 58.
166. Tac., *Ann.* 1.74.
167. Tac., *Ann.* 1.74. *proclamaret se quoque in ea causa laturum sententiam palam et iuratum.*
168. Suet., *Div. Aug.* 65.3; Tac., *Ann.* 1.53, 3.24; Dio 57.18.1a. Levick (1966 and 1976b) argues that Augustus consented to her relocation from Pandateria to Rhegium when he agreed for Tiberius to return to Rome from Rhodes; and Linderski (1988) sees Iulia and Livia in a contest over whose son should succeed Augustus.
169. Suet., *Tib.* 50.1.

170. Dio 57.18.1a.
171. Suet., *Div. Aug.* 101.3.
172. Two inscriptions set up by ex-slaves Thiasos and Celos were found at Rhegium: see Gardener (1988) and Linderski (1988).
173. The river frequently flooded. During his own lifetime, Tiberius would have known floods in 32 BCE (Dio 50.8.3), 27 BCE (Dio 53.20.1), 23 BCE (Dio 53.33.5), 22 BCE (Dio 54.1), 13 BCE (Dio 54.25.2), 5 CE (Cassiodorus, *Chron.* 604; Dio 55.22.3) and 12 CE (Dio 56 27.4). For a full survey of floods in Ancient Rome, see Aldrete (2007).
174. Tac., *Ann.* 1.76; *cf.* Dio 57.13.7. Iulius Caesar and Augustus had also set up commissions to consider engineering solutions.
175. Tac., *Ann.* 1.79.
176. Dio 57.13.8.
177. Dio 57 List of Consuls and 57.14.1.
178. Dio 57.8.5–6.
179. Dio, 55.15.1.
180. Carandini (2017), Vol. 1, p.236.
181. *Pontifex Maximus*: Taylor (1929), p.89, n.7. *Domus Publica*: Carandini (2017), Vol. 1, p.272, n.286. The *Domus Publica* was originally on the *Via Sacra* in the *Forum Romanum* but was moved to its new location on the Palatinus by Augustus in 12 BCE.
182. Bruce (1986), p.520; Carandini (2017), Vol. 1, plate 63 show remains of the excavated pool; on p.236 he notes that after Tiberius' death, Caius Caligula refused to live at the *Domus Tiberiana.* It was substantially modified by Claudius, Nero and Hadrian during their reigns. P. Clodius Pulcher had constructed the earliest vaults on the site as a substructure for a peristyle and walking track (*ambulatio*). The existing vaults of brick and cement, which are Neronian or Hadrianic in date, were reopened to the public in 2023. See also Wiseman (2019), p.35.
183. Bruce (1986), p.520, citing Fronto, *Epist.* 4.5 and Aul. Gell, *Noc. Att.* 13.20.1.
184. Dio 57.14.5.
185. Tac., *Ann.* 1.80.
186. Dio 60.24.1; Suet., *Tib.*, 25.4–5; Tac., *Ann.* 1.76, 1.80.
187. Tac., *Ann.* 1.78: *centesimam rerum venalium post bella civilia institutam deprecante populo edixit Tiberius militare aerarium eo subsidio niti; simul imparem oneri rem publicam, nisi vicesimo militiae anno veterani dimitterentur.*
188. Dio 55.10.10.
189. Dio 57.19.6; Tac., *Ann.* 1.7.
190. Dio 57.19.5–6; Vell. Pat. 2.127.3.
191. Apicius (*c.* 25 BCE–*c.* 37 CE) is associated with the recipe book *De Re Coquinaria.* According to Dio 57.19.5, Apicius committed suicide when he realized that his fortune of HS 10 million might not be enough to sustain his extravagant lifestyle into old age.
192. Vell. Pat. 2.128.4.
193. Dio 57.14.3; Tac., *Ann.* 1.76.
194. Dio 57.14.9.
195. Dio 57.14.10.
196. Dio 57.14.10: *θερμόν σφισιν ἐγχέαι κελεῦσαι*. See Chapter 2, n.104.
197. Dio 57.14.10.
198. Tac., *Ann.* 1.77; Dio 57.14.10, 56.47.2. *Cf.* Dio 57.14.4; Suet., *Tib.* 34.
199. Balsdon (1969), pp.278–280.
200. *Cf.* Suet., *Tib.* 34.1.
201. Tac., *Ann.* 1.11: *consilium coercendi intra terminos imperii.*

202. Vell. Pat. 2.123.1: *Quippe Caesar Augustus cum Germanicum nepotem suum reliqua belli patraturum misisset in Germaniam.*
203. Suet., *Div. Aug.* 49.
204. For Germanicus' campaign of 15 CE, see Powell (2013), pp.85–97.
205. Sen., *Suas.* 1.15; Tac., *Ann.* 1.55–60.
206. Tac., *Ann.* 1.61–62.
207. Tac., *Ann.* 1.61–68.
208. Tac., *Ann.* 1.69.
209. Tac., *Ann.* 1.70–71.
210. Tac., *Ann.*1.58.5. For the significance of this, see Syme (1978), p.61, and Syme (1979), pp.322–323, noting that Tiberius did not add this acclamation to his own titulature, and his declining of it may be seen as an act of 'admonition, still amicable'. Germanicus is recorded as *Imp. II* on *ILS* 176 *ff* erected after his death.
211. Tac., *Ann.* 1.72.
212. Barrett (1996), p.xix; Freisenbruch (2010), p.100.
213. Tac., *Ann.* 1.81.
214. Levick (1967), pp.209–214.
215. For Germanicus' campaign of 16 CE, see Powell (2013), pp.98–118.
216. Tac., *Ann.* 2.5–6.
217. Tac., *Ann.* 2.7.
218. Tac., *Ann.* 2.8. For the battles at Weser River, Idistaviso and Angrivarian Wall, see Powell (2014), pp.41–70.
219. Tac., *Ann.* 2.22: *debellatis inter Rhenum Albimque nationibus exercitum Tiberii Caesaris ea monimenta Marti et Iovi et Augusto sacravisse.* For Roman war trophies, see Powell (2016).
220. Tac., *Ann.* 2.8.
221. Tac., *Ann.* 2.25: it is not clear whether this *aquila* belonged to *Legio* XVII or XIIX. The eagle standard of *Legio* XIX had been found by L. Stertinius and recovered from the Bructeri the previous year (Tac., *Ann.* 1.60).
222. The sword and scabbard were found in Mainz, Germany, and are now in the collections of The British Museum, London (inventory number GR 1866.0806.1; Bronze 867).
223. The British Museum interprets the figures to be Augustus receiving Tiberius. Zanker (1988), p.233, argues for Tiberius receiving Germanicus or Drusus.
224. Zanker (1988), p.233.
225. Pillar of the Gods was found; it is now in the collections of the Valkhof Museum, Archeologisch Depot Gelderland (inventory number PDB.2008.194.NIJM.182).
226. Tac., *Ann.* 2.26.
227. Tac., *Ann.* 2.26: *satis iam eventuum, satis casuum.*
228. Tac., *Ann.* 2.26: *se novies a divo Augusto in Germaniam missum plura consilio quam vi perfecisse.*
229. Tac., *Ann.* 2.42.
230. Tac., *Ann.* 2.28.
231. This *secespita* had a long, sharp point and a double-edged blade, with a handle of ivory ornamented with gold and silver inlays.
232. Suet., *Tib.* 25.3.
233. Tac., *Ann.* 2.28: *Et vocantur patres, addito consultandum super re magna et atroci.*
234. Tac., *Ann.* 2.28.
235. Suet., *Tib.* 25.1; Tac., *Ann.* 2.28.
236. Dio 57.15.4.
237. Tac., *Ann.* 2.29.
238. Tac., *Ann.* 2.30.

239. Tac., *Ann.* 2.30: *inerant et alia huiusce modi stolida vana.*
240. Tac., *Ann.* 2.31.
241. Dio 57.15.5.
242. Tac., *Ann.* 2.31: *iuravitque Tiberius petiturum se vitam quamvis nocenti, nisi voluntariam mortem properavisset. Cf.* Vell. Pat. 2.130.3; Dio 57.15.5.
243. Tac., *Ann.* 2.32.
244. Dio 57.15.8–9; Tac., *Ann.* 23.2.5.
245. Dio 57.15.7–8.
246. Pliny, *Nat. Hist.* 35.37[70]: *ut auctor est Deculo, HS |LX| aestimatam cubiculo suo inclusit.*
247. Pliny, *Nat. Hist.* 34.19[62].
248. Tac., *Ann.* 2.33: *ne vestis serica viros foedaret. Cf.* Dio 57.15.1–2.
249. Tac., *Ann.* 2.33: *auctu imperii adolevisse etiam privatas opes, idque non novum, sed e vetustissimis moribus.*
250. Tac., *Ann.* 2.34.
251. Tac., *Ann.* 2.35.
252. Dio 57.15.9.
253. Tac., *Ann.* 2.36.
254. Tac., *Ann.* 2.36: *Grave moderationi suae tot eligere, tot differre.*
255. Tac., *Ann.* 2.36: *favorabili in speciem oratione vim imperii tenuit.*
256. Dio 57.16.1; *cf.* 53.15.1. Strabo 17.3.25 states that Tiberius observed the division of the empire into 'Provinces of Caesar' and 'Provinces of the People' according to the agreement reached between Augustus and the Senate of 27 BCE; to the former Tiberius appointed *legati* and procurators from men of consular or praetorian rank or equestrians, to the latter he sent praetors or proconsuls. Dio 57.14.4 cites Crete as an example of a proconsul being superseded by a *quaestor*. During his reign, Augustus required that magistrates should not be sent to the provinces immediately after their term in office expired (Suet., Div. Aug. 36.1).
257. Dio 57.16.2.
258. Mattingly (1937).
259. Tac., *Ann.* 2.36: *sibi ignavi, nobis graves.*
260. Plut., *Moral*: Flatterer from Friend 18. Tac., *Ann.* 1.72, calls Cassius Severus, who had been banished to Crete by Augustus in 8 or 12 CE a slanderer who 'had blackened the characters of men and women of repute in his scandalous effusions', *qua viros feminasque inlustris procacibus scriptis diffamaverat.*
261. Tac., *Ann.* 3.65: *memoriae proditur Tiberium, quoties curia egrederetur, Graecis verbis in hunc modum eloqui solitum 'o homines ad servitutem paratos!' scilicet etiam illum qui libertatem publicam nollet tam proiectae servientium patientiae taedebat.*
262. Suet., *Tib.* 25.1, 25.3.
263. Tac., *Ann.* 2.39.
264. Tac., *Ann.* 2.40.
265. Tac., *Ann.* 2.40: '*quo modo tu Caesar*'.
266. Dio 57.16.3.
267. Tac., *Ann.* 2.41.
268. *Tab. Siar.* Frag. 1, 12–18: *Senatum populumque Romanum id monum[entum aeternae dedi] casse memoriae Germanici Caesaris cum i{i}s Germanis bello superatis [et ... longissime ?] / a Gallia summotis receptisque signis militaribus et vindicata frau[dulenta clade] / exercitus p(opuli) R(omani) ordinato statu Galliarum.*
269. Levick (1976), p.123.
270. Suet., *Caius* 16.1: see n.81.

## CHAPTER 6: ENFORCING PUBLIC STANDARDS

1. Suet., *Gramm.* 22.2; Dio 57.17.1.
2. Dio, 57.17.2: *καί τινος Ἀτεΐου Καπίτωνος εἰπόντος ὅτι 'εἰ καὶ μηδεὶς πρόσθεν τὸ ὄνομα τοῦτ' ἐφθέγξατο, ἀλλὰ νῦν γε πάντες διὰ σὲ ἐς τὰ ἀρχαῖα αὐτὸ καταριθμήσομεν,' Μάρκελλός τις ὑπολαβὼν ἔφη 'σύ, Καῖσαρ, ἀνθρώποις μὲν πολιτείαν Ῥωμαίων δύνασαι'.* Some translations cite the name erroneously as Marcellus: see Mallan (2020), p.225.
3. Suet., *Tib.* 71.1.
4. This may be the same story related in Suet., *Tib.* 30.1 involving a *praefectus alae*.
5. Tac., *Ann.* 2.50.
6. Dio 57.10.1.
7. Suet., *Tib.* 47.1.
8. Dio 57.10.2; Vell. Pat. 2.130.1.
9. Tac. *Ann.* 2.49. Suet., *Tib.* 50.3 relates that there was a fire at the Temple of Vesta during Tiberius' reign (date unknown, but perhaps 29 CE) during which Augusta and crowds urged the *Vigiles* to work harder to stop the fire destroying the hallowed building.
10. Six years later in 20 CE.
11. *CIL*, XI, 367: <:columna I>*[Imp(erator) Caesar D]ìvì f(ilius) Augustus pontifex maxim(us) co(n)s(ul) XIII imp(erator) XX tribunic(ia) potest(ate) XXXVII p(ater) p(atriae) [Ti(berius) Caes]ar Divi Augusti f(ilius) Dìvì Iulì n(epos) August(us) pontif(ex) maxim(us) co(n)s(ul) II II imp(erator) VIII trib(unicia) potest(ate) XXII* :columna II> *dedere*. The bridge spans 62.6 metres (205.4ft) between the abutments and the five arches span variously from 8.6 metres (28.2ft) to the widest at 10.6 metres (34.8ft). Balance (1951), n.52, remarks that the bridge was highly adorned compared to other bridges on the *Via Flaminia*.
12. Tac., *Ann.* 2.48.
13. Tac., *Ann.* 2.48.
14. Tac., *Ann.* 2.48.
15. Tac., *Ann.* 2.48: *ita prodigos et ob flagitia egentis.*
16. Tac., *Ann.* 2.51.
17. In accordance with the *Lex Papia Poppaea*.
18. Tac., *Ann.* 2.51: *laetabatur Tiberius, cum inter filios eius et leges senatus disceptaret*. For a different interpretation of Tacitus' remark, see Rogers (1943), pp.117–119.
19. Jer., *Chron.* A17; Tac., *Ann.* 2.41; Vell. Pat. 2.129.2.
20. Strabo 7.1.4: *ἐν ᾧ ἐθριαμβεύθη τῶν ἐπιφανεστάτων ἀνδρῶν σώματα καὶ γυναικῶν, Σεγιμοῦντός τε Σεγέστου υἱός, Χηρούσκων ἡγεμών, καὶ ἀδελφὴ αὐτοῦ, γυνὴ δ' Ἀρμενίου τοῦ πολεμαρχήσαντος ἐν τοῖς Χηρούσκοις ἐν τῇ πρὸς Οὐᾶρον Κουιντίλλιον παρασπονδήσει καὶ νῦν ἔτι συνέχοντος τὸν πόλεμον, ὄνομα Θουσνέλδα, καὶ υἱὸς τριετὴς Θουμέλικος: ἔτι δὲ Σεσίθακος, Σεγιμήρου υἱὸς τῶν Χηρούσκων ἡγεμόνος, καὶ γυνὴ τούτου Ῥαμίς, Οὐκρομήρου θυγάτηρ ἡγεμόνος Χάττων, καὶ Δευδόριξ, Βαιτόριγος τοῦ Μέλωνος ἀδελφοῦ υἱός, Σούγαμβρος. Σεγέστης δὲ ὁ πενθερὸς τοῦ Ἀρμενίου καὶ ἐξ ἀρχῆς διέστη πρὸς τὴν γνώμην αὐτοῦ καὶ λαβὼν καιρὸν ηὐτομόλησε καὶ τῷ θριάμβῳ παρῆν τῶν φιλτάτων, ἐν τιμῇ ἀγόμενος. ἐπόμπευσε δὲ καὶ Λίβης τῶν Χάττων ἱερεύς, καὶ ἄλλα δὲ σώματα ἐπομπεύθη ἐκ τῶν πεπορθημένων ἐθνῶν, Καούλκων Καμψανῶν Βρουκτέρων Οὐσίπων Χηρούσκων Χάττων Χαττουαρίων Λανδῶν Τουβαττίων.*
21. Tac., *Ann.* 2.42; Vell. Pat. 2.129.3.
22. Tac. *Ann.* 2.52. Tacitus is the only source for the uprising led by Tacfarinas. For a description of the region, see Strabo 17.3.4. For a discussion about the formation of Africa Proconsularis in 40–39 BCE rather than 27 BCE, see Fishwick & Shaw (1977).
23. For the causes of the revolt, see Vanacker (2015).
24. Whittaker (2009), pp.191, 198, notes that the recruitment of Musulamii into the Roman Army in the first century BCE/CE is not well understood.

25. Tac. *Ann.* 2.52; Tac., *Hist.* 8.1. Strabo 17.3.2: describes the Mauri as 'a large and prosperous Libyan tribe', *Λιβυκὸν ἔθνος μέγα καὶ εὔδαιμον.*
26. *Cf.* Vell. Pat. 2.129.4.
27. Tac., *Ann.* 2.54.
28. Tac., *Ann.* 2.42.
29. Tac., *Ann.* 2.42.
30. Dio 57.17.6.
31. Dio 57.17.7. *Cf.* Eutrop. 7.11.2; Strabo 12.1.4; Suet. *Tib.* 37.4; Tac., *Ann.* 2.42.2; Vell. Pat. 2.39.3; Vict., *Caes.* 2.3; [Vict.], *Epit.* 2.8.
32. Jer., *Chron.* A20.
33. Tac., *Ann.* 2.42.
34. Tac., *Ann.* 2.64–67.
35. Pliny, *Nat. Hist.* 19.33[110]. The story might be apocryphal.
36. Pliny, *Nat. Hist.* 2.86 (200): *maximus terrae memoria mortalium exstitit motus Tiberii Caesaris principatu.* It is sometimes called the 'AD 17 Lydia Earthquake'.
37. Tac., *Ann.* 2.47. Modern Turkey is susceptible to earthquakes: as I wrote this endnote on 6 February 2023, cities along the East Anatolian Fault (EAF) zone on the border between Turkey and Syria were struck by a 7.8-magnitude earthquake, making it the strongest since the Erzincan earthquake on the North Anatolian Fault in December 1939. It brought down 50,000 buildings, including entire city blocks, impacting an estimated 15.73 million people, killing some 50,000 in Turkey and 7,200 in Syria. Antakya (ancient Antiocheia on the Orontes) was particularly badly damaged. See P. Martin Mai, Theodoros Aspiotis, Tariq Anwar Aquib *et al*, 'The Destructive Earthquake Doublet of 6 February 2023 in South-Central Türkiye and Northwestern Syria: Initial Observations and Analyses', *The Seismic Record* 2023, 3 (2), pp.105–115.
38. Jer., *Chron.* A18; Tac., *Ann.* 2.47. For the natural disaster, see Graham (2019).
39. Strabo 12.8.18.
40. Tac., *Ann.* 2.47: *nam centies sestertium pollicitus Caesar, et quantum aerario aut fisco pendebant in quinquennium remisit.* Tiberius was not alone in singling out a city for special treatment: Strabo 12.8.18 remarks that, 'his father [Augustus] had assisted the Tralliani on the occurrence of a similar calamity, when the gymnasium and other parts of the city were destroyed'; *ἐπηνώρθωσε δ' ὁ ἡγεμὼν χρήματα ἐπιδούς, καθάπερ καὶ πρότερον ἐπὶ τῆς γενομένης συμφορᾶς Τραλλιανοῖς (ἡνίκα τὸ γυμνάσιον καὶ ἄλλα μέρη συνέπεσεν) ὁ πατὴρ αὐτοῦ καὶ τούτοις καὶ Λαοδικεῦσιν.*
41. M. Aetius: Tac., *Ann.* 2.48: *delectus est M. Ateius e praetoriis, ne consulari obtinente Asiam aemulatio inter pares et ex eo impedimentum oreretur.* Lictors: Dio, 57.17.7: *ταῖς τε ἐν τῇ Ἀσίᾳ πόλεσι ταῖς ὑπὸ τοῦ σεισμοῦ κακωθείσαις ἀνὴρ ἐστρατηγηκὼς σὺν πέντε ῥαβδούχοις προσετάχθη.*
42. Tac., *Ann.* 2.48: 'The people of Temnus, Philadelpheia, Aegae, Apollonis, the Mostenians, and Hyrcanian Macedonians, as they were called, with the towns of Hierocaesarea, Myrina, Cyme, and Tmolus'; *Temnios, Philadelphenos, Aegeatas, Apollonidenses, quique Mosteni aut Macedones Hyrcani vocantur, et Hierocaesariam, Myrinam, Cymen, Tmolum. Cf.* Orosius, *Histories Against the Pagans* 4.18; Suet., *Tib.* 48.2.
43. *RPC* I 2451: *TIBEPION CEBACTON KTICTHN.*
44. *RIC* I 48: *CIVITATIBVS ASIAE RESTITVTIS.*
45. Pliny, *Nat. Hist.* 36.67 [197] adds that 'It was a figure of Menelaüs; a circumstance which goes far towards proving that the use of this material is of more ancient date than is generally supposed, confounded as it is at the present day with glass, by reason of its resemblance', *obsianam imaginem Menelai, ex qua apparet antiquior materiae origo, nunc vitri similitudine interpolata.*
46. Tac., *Ann.* 2.1.

47. Tac., *Ann.* 2.2–3.
48. Tac., *Ann.* 2.3.
49. Tac., *Ann.* 2.4.
50. Tac., *Ann.* 2.4.
51. Tac., *Ann.* 2.68.
52. Tac., *Ann.* 2.43: *Igitur haec et de Armenia quae supra memoravi apud patres disseruit, nec posse motum Orientem nisi Germanici sapientia conponi: nam suam aetatem vergere, Drusi nondum satis adolevisse. tunc decreto patrum per missae Germanico provinciae quae mari dividuntur, maiusque imperium, quoquo adisset, quam iis qui sorte aut missu principis obtinerent.*
53. *Ex auctoritate huius ordinis ad rerum transmarinarum statum componendum* is the legal definition of Germanicus' *imperium proconsulare maius* expounded in the *Senatus Consultum de Cn. Pisone Patre* (*SCPP*), lines 30–37: see Potter (1999). On the position undertaken by Caius as *praepositus Orienti*, see Romer (1985), p.93, citing Suet., *Tib.* 12.2.
54. *Cf.* Suet., *Tib.* 25.5; Tac., *Ann.* 1.76, 1.80. Cooley (2023), pp.9–10, 168–172.
55. Drogula (2015b) makes a compelling case for Tiberius assigning Germanicus to monitor and mitigate Piso's more rash decisions in Syria.
56. Vell. Pat. 2.129.3: *Quanto cum honore Germanicum suum in transmarinas misit provincias! Cf. P.Oxy.* XXV 2435, which uses the same phrasing.
57. Rogers (1943), pp.119–121.
58. Tac., *Ann.* 3.34.13.
59. Tac., *Ann.* 2.88.
60. Tac., *Ann.* 2.62.
61. Tac., *Ann.* 2.62.
62. Tac., *Ann.* 2.63: *nam multi s nationibus clarissimum quondam regem ad se vocantibus Romanam amicitiam praetulisse.*
63. Tac., *Ann.* 2.63: *responsum a Caesare tutam ei honoratamque sedem in Italia fore, si maneret: sin rebus eius aliud conduceret, abiturum fide qua venisset. ceterum apud senatum disseruit non Philippum Atheniensibus, non Pyrrhum aut Antiochum Populo Romano perinde metuendos fuisse. extat oratio qua magnitudinem viri, violentiam subiectarum ei gentium et quam propinquns Italiae hostis, suaque in destruendo eo consilia extulit.*
64. Tac., *Ann.* 2.63.
65. Tac., *Ann.* 2.63.
66. Tac., *Ann.* 2.63 specifies that the location of the Quadi was between the rivers Marus (March or Morava) and Cusus (Waag, Gran or Gusen).
67. Tac. *Ann.* 2.88: *non fraude neque occultis, sed palam et armatum populum Romanum hostis suos ulcisci.*
68. Tac., *Ann.* 2.53: *sed fratres egregie concordes et proximorum certaminibus inconcussi.* This is in contrast to the various followers of Drusus and Germanicus in Tac., *Ann.* 2.43, who allegedly sowed division and discord. For a detailed discussion of Germanicus' voyage to the East, see Powell (2013), pp.127–152.
69. 'Decree of Assos' (*IGR* IV, 251) made on the occasion of Caius' speech.
70. Suet., *Caius* 1.2; Tac., *Ann.* 2.53.
71. Suet., *Tib.* 26.2.
72. *SIG*[3] 792.
73. Tac., *Ann.* 2.54.
74. Tac., *Ann.* 2.54.
75. For the 'Palmyra Tariff', see Butcher (2003), p.193.

76. Tac., *Ann.* 2.53; Suet., *Caius* 1.2. For Germanicus, Artabanus II of Parthia and Zenon Artaxias in Armenia, see Olbrycht (2016).
77. Tac., *Ann.* 2.64, 3.11.
78. Tac., *Ann.* 2.64. Lebek (1989b and 1991).
79. Tac., *Ann.* 2.64: *laetiore Tiberio quia pacem sapientia firmaverat quam si bellum per acies confecisset.*
80. Tac., *Ann.* 2.83; *Tabula Siarensis*, Fragment 1; Pliny, *Nat. Hist.* 5.79, spells the place name as two words, 'Epi Daphnae'. Jos., *Ant. Jud.* 14.13.1, refers to the place as Daphe by Antioch. Powell (2013), p.140, notes that his grandfather, M. Antonius, had stayed here on his way to meet Kleopatra in 42/41 BCE.
81. Tac., *Ann.* 2.87.
82. Dio 57.18.5.
83. Dio 57.18.5a; Suet., *Tib.* 36.1. For astrology in Rome, see Ripat (2011).
84. Suet., *Tib.* 36.1; Tac., *Ann.* 2.85.
85. Suet., *Tib.* 36.1.
86. The text of the edict is contained in the *Tabula Larinas*: see Lebek (1990) and Slater (1994).
87. Tac., *Ann.* 2.85: *Eodem anno gravibus senatus decretis libido feminarum coercita cautumque ne quaestum corpore faceret cui avus aut pater aut maritus eques Romanus fuisset.*
88. Tac., *Ann.* 2.86.
89. Tac., *Ann.* 2.84. Lindsay (1993) n.3 argues that Ti. Gemellus and Germanicus Gemellus were born the following year in 20 CE.
90. Tac., *Ann.* 2.84: *Quod rarum laetumque etiam modicis penatibus tanto gaudio principem adfecit ut non temperaverit quin iactaret apud patres nulli ante Romanorum eiusdem fastigii viro geminam stirpem editam.*
91. Tac., *Ann.* 2.59: *proficiscitur cognoscendae antiquitatis.*
92. A verbatim record of that speech in Greek survives on a papyrus (*P.Oxy.* XXV 2435). In the transcription, Germanicus is referred to as the *imperator*, 'commander', and Tiberius as 'my father'.
93. Age: Suet., *Caius* 1.2. Dress: Tac., *Ann.* 2.59.
94. Tac., *Ann.* 2.59: *acerrime increpuit.*
95. Tac., *Ann.* 2.59. Only the *princeps*' equestrian-grade representative (*praefectus Aegypti*) was permitted to operate in the province semi-autonomously and he needed to perform his duty of ensuring the supply of grain to feed Rome's poor without distraction.
96. Tac., *Ann.* 2.60–61, provides an account of the sights he saw on his trip along the river. For a commentary, see Powell (2013), pp.127–152, and Powell (2022b).
97. Amm. Marc. 22.14.8.
98. Tac., *Ann.* 2.43.
99. Tac., *Ann.* 2.69.
100. Tac., *Ann.* 2.55, 2.57–58. For the relationship between Tiberius, Piso and Germanicus, see Bird (1987), Shotter (1968) and Rapke (1982).
101. Tac., *Ann.* 2.57: *et erat, ut rettuli, clementior. sed amici accendendis offensionibus callidi intendere vera, adgerere falsa ipsumque et Plancinam et filios variis modis criminari.*
102. For the possible causes of Germanicus' death, see Powell (2013), pp.153–162, and Powell (2019).
103. *Ante diem VI Idus Octobres*: *Tab. Siarensis*, Frag. 2, Col. A; *Insc. Ital.* 13.2.209; Tac., *Ann.* 2.72; Suet. *Caius* 2; Dio 57.18.9.
104. Cooley (2023), p.5.
105. Tac., *Ann.* 2.82.
106. Tac., *Ann.* 2.74.

107. Tac., *Ann.* 2.82.
108. Suet., *Caius* 6.1: *Salva Roma, salva patria, salvus est Germanicus.*
109. Tac., *Ann.* 2.82.
110. Suet., *Caius* 5.1.
111. Dio 57.18.9; Tac., *Ann.* 2.74.
112. Tac., *Ann.* 2.75.
113. Tac., *Ann.* 2.69: *et reperiebantur solo ac parietibus erutae humanorum corporum reliquiae, carmina et devotiones et nomen 'Germanici' plumbeis tabulis insculptum, semusti cineres ac tabo obliti aliaque malefica quis creditur animas numinibus infernis sacrari. simul missi a Pisone incusabantur ut valetudinis adversa rimantes. Cf.* Dio 57.18.9.
114. Tac., *Ann.* 2.74: *postulantibus Vitellio ac Veranio ceterisque qui crimina et accusationem tamquam adversus receptos iam reos instruebant.*
115. Tac., *Ann.* 3.7.
116. Tac., *Ann.* 2.70.
117. Tac., *Ann.* 2.75.
118. Tac., *Ann.* 2.76–78.
119. Tac., *Ann.* 2.78: *ad Tiberium epistulis incusat Germanicum luxus et superbiae; seque pulsum, ut locus rebus novis patefieret, curam exercitus eadem fide qua tenuerit repetivisse.*
120. Tac., *Ann.* 2.80.
121. Tac., *Ann.* 2.79, 2.81.
122. Tac., *Ann.* 3.8: *Tiberius quo integrum iudicium ostentaret, exceptum comiter iuvenem sueta erga filios familiarum nobilis liberalitate auget.*
123. Tac., *Ann.* 3.8: *si vera forent quae iacerentur, praecipuum in dolore suum locum respondit: sed malle falsa et inania nec cuiquam mortem Germanici exitiosam esse.*
124. *Senatus Consultum de Honoribus Germanici Decernendis* is known today as the *Tabula Hebana* (*Tab. Heb.*) and *Tabula Siarensis* (*Tab. Siar.*), on account of the find-spots of the inscribed bronze fragments; see Lott (2012), pp.79–99, 209–37. For the full Latin text with a translation in English, see Powell (2013), Appendix, pp.220–225.
125. Tac., *Ann.* 2.83: *Cum censeretur clipeus auro et magnitudine insignis inter auctores eloquentiae, adseveravit Tiberius solitum paremque ceteris dicaturum: neque enim eloquentiam fortuna discerni et satis inlustre si veteres inter scriptores haberetur.*
126. Tac., *Ann.* 2.83.
127. Tac., *Ann.* 3.49.
128. Lott (2012), p.230, citing *Tab. Siar.* 3.9 (160–167).
129. Tac., *Ann.* 3.1.
130. Tac., *Ann.* 3.2.
131. Tac., *Ann.* 3.2.
132. Cooley (2023), p.5.
133. Tac., *Ann.* 3.3–4.
134. Tac., *Ann.* 3.2.
135. Tac., *Ann.* 2.79, 2.81.
136. Tac., *Ann.* 3.6: *utque premeret vulgi sermones, monuit edicto multos inlustrium Romanorum ob rem publicam obisse, neminem tam flagranti desiderio celebratum. idque et sibi et cunctis egregium si modus adiceretur. non enim eadem decora principibus viris et imperatori popolo quae modicis domibus aut civitatibus. convenisse recenti dolori luctum et ex maerore solacia; sed referendum iam animum ad firmitudinem, ut quondam divus Iulius amissa unica filia, ut divus Augustus ereptis nepotibus abstruserint tristitiam. nil opus vetustioribus exemplis, quotiens populus Romanus cladis exercituum, interitum ducum, funditus amissas nobilis familias constanter tulerit. principes mortalis, rem publicam aeternam esse. proin repeterent sollemnia, et quia ludorum Megalesium spectaculum suberat, etiam voluptates resumerent.* The

*Megalensia* or *Ludi Megalenses* were celebrated in Rome from 4–10 April each year in honour of the Magna Mater; they consisted of performances of scenic plays.

137. Tac., *Ann.* 3.7.138. Tac., *Ann.* 3.20, relates how Decrius dodged the incoming missiles to intercept his fleeing troops and cursed the standard-bearers who could see Roman soldiers turn their backs to a horde of undrilled men or deserters, even while taking injuries in his breast and his face – with one eye pierced – and continued to fight until he dropped dead, left abandoned by his men.
139. Tac., *Ann.* 3.21.
140. Tac., *Ann.* 3.21: *quod non eam quoque Apronius iure proconsulis tribuisset questus magis quam offensus.*
141. Tac., *Ann.* 3.21: *inritum fessumque Romanum impune ludificabatur.*
142. Tac., *Ann.* 3.22–28.
143. Tac., *Ann.* 3.28.
144. Tac., *Ann.* 3.22.
145. Tac., *Ann.* 3.23.
146. Tac., *Ann.* 3.9.
147. Tac., *Ann.* 3.10.
148. Cooley (2023), p.18.
149. Suet., *Tib.* 72.3: *Redde Germanicum!*
150. Tac., *Ann.* 3.10.
151. Tac., *Ann.* 3.11.
152. Tac., *Ann.* 3.11. Three other high-profile senators had been approached, but they declined for various reasons.
153. For the trial proceedings, see Powell (2013), pp.170–177, and Powell (2020). There are two primary sources for the trial of Piso: Tac., *Ann.* 3.10–19, and *Senatus Consultum de Cn. Pisone Patre* (*SCPP*) – an almost complete inscription in 176 lines of Latin text, which is the decree of the Senate on the case, allowing modern historians to compare Tacitus' account against the 'official record'.
154. Here Tacitus infers that Tiberius had appointed him as his legate to Syria with the consent of the Senate to help his adopted son in the East. The *SCPP* makes it plain that the appointment was Tiberius' decision alone. For a comparison of the two texts, see Mellor (2011), pp.35–41.
155. Tac., *Ann.* 3.12: *integris animis diiudicandum.*
156. Tac., *Ann.* 3.12: *sin facinus in cuiuscumque mortalium nece vindicandum detegitur, vos vero et liberos Germanici et nos parentes iustis solaciis adficite.*
157. Tac., *Ann.* 3.12: *nemo Drusi lacrimas, nemo maestitiam meam spectet, nec si qua in nos adversa finguntur.*
158. Tac., *Ann.* 3.12: *quod in curia potius quam in foro, apud senatum quam apud iudices de morte eius anquiritur.* Cases of murder with poison suspected would usually have been heard before a chief magistrate (*praetor*) presiding over crimes of poisonings (*quaestio de veneficiis*); however, Cooley (2023), p.19, notes that a case for treason would normally be held in the *quaestio maiestatis*, adjudicated by a *praetor*; from 15 CE, they were heard in the Senate.
159. Tac., *Ann.* 3.13.
160. *SCPP*, line 173.
161. The *clipeus virtutis* ('Shield of Courage') was awarded to Augustus in 27 BCE for his 'courage, clemency, justice and piety'; *virtutis clementiaeque et iustitiae et pietatis* (Aug., *Res Gest.* 34).
162. Tac., *Ann.* 3.13.

163. Tac., *Ann.* 3.13: *odio Germanici et rerum novarum studio Pisonem vulgus militum per licentiam et sociorum iniurias eo usque conrupisse ut parens legionum a deterrimis appellaretur; contra in optimum quemque, maxime in comites et amicos Germanici saevisse.*
164. Tac., *Ann.* 3.13: *postremo ipsum devotionibus et veneno peremisse; sacra hinc et immolationes nefandas ipsius atque Plancinae, peritam armis rem publicam, utque reus agi posset, acie victum.*
165. On these points, Tacitus' account aligns well with the text of the *SCPP*.
166. Tac., *Ann.* 3.14: *solum veneni crimen visus est diluisse.*
167. Tac., *Ann.* 3.14: *Senatus numquam satis credito sine fraude Germanicum interisse.*
168. Tac., *Ann.* 3.7: *Martinam subita morte Brundisii extinctam, venenumque nodo crinium eius occultatum nec ulla in corpore signa sumpti exitii reperta.*
169. Tac., *Ann.* 3.14: *Caesar ob bellum provinciae inlatum.*
170. Tac., *Ann.* 3.17: *et cum accusatores ac testes certatim perorarent respondente nullo, miseratio quam invidia augebatur.*
171. Tac., *Ann.* 3.15.
172. Tac., *Ann.* 3.16; *cf.* Suet., *Tib.* 52.3.
173. Tac., *Ann.* 3.15.
174. The *Scalae Gemoniae* was a flight of steps which went past the jail (*carcer*) in the *Forum Romanum* up to the *Arx* on the *Capitolinus* Hill. The bodies of criminals, who had been executed, were thrown down them and then left exposed at the bottom for a time. They are first mentioned in the extant documents in Tiberius' reign: see Suet., *Tib.* 53.1, 61.1, 75.1; Tac. *Ann.* 3.14, 4.4, 4.31.
175. Tac., *Ann.* 3.14; *cf.* Suet., *Caius* 2.1.
176. Tac., *Ann.* 3.15. *Cf.* Dio 57.18.9; Suet., *Tib.* 52.3.
177. Tac., *Ann.* 3.15, specifically mentions a *gladius*. It was a strange weapon to use to commit suicide; the shorter dagger (*pugio*) would have been an easier choice.
178. Tac., *Ann.* 3.16.
179. Tac., *Ann.* 3.15.
180. Tac., *Ann.* 3.17.
181. *SCPP* line 173.
182. Cooley (2023), p.18, states that *SCPP* makes no mention of Piso poisoning Germanicus.
183. Tac., *Ann.* 3.17. Cn. Piso took the *praenomen* Lucius. For the punishment as *damnatio memoriae*, see Bodel (1999) and Flower (1998) and (2006), pp.132–138, and fig.23, p.137, showing the damaged lettering of an inscription set up for Piso in the forum of Leptis Magna in 5/6 CE.
184. Tac., *Ann.* 3.18.
185. Tac., *Ann.* 3.17: *patris quippe iussa nec potuisse filium detrectare.*
186. Tac., *Ann.* 3.18: *ob externas ea victorias sacrari dictitans.*
187. Tac., *Ann.* 3.18: *domestica mala tristitia operienda.*
188. Tac., *Ann.* 3.19.
189. Tac., *Ann.* 3.19; see n.77.
190. Tac., *Ann.* 3.22.
191. Tac., *Ann.* 3.19. Vipsania was 55 or 56 years old.
192. Tac., *Ann.* 3.30. Crispus was implicated in the assassination of M. Agrippa Postumus in 14 CE; see Kehoe (1985). Volusius Saturninus was suffect consul (12 BCE), proconsul of Africa (*c.* 8–4 BCE) and *legatus Augusti propraetore* of Syria (4 BCE–5 CE), who accumulated vast wealth.
193. Tac., *Ann.* 2.88, implies a parallel with Germanicus and his relative Tiberius.

## CHAPTER 7: HOLDING A WOLF BY THE EARS

1. Tac., *Ann.* 3.31.
2. Tac., *Ann.* 3.31.
3. Suet., *Tib.* 26.2.
4. Tac., *Ann.* 3.29. The qualification for the college would usually require the candidate to first hold a quaestorship.
5. Suet., *Tib.* 54.1.
6. Tac., *Ann.* 3.29.
7. Tac., *Ann.* 3.32.
8. Tac., *Ann.* 3.33: *iudicioque patrum deligendum pro consule gnarum militiae, corpore validum et bello suffecturum.*
9. Tac., *Ann.* 3.35.
10. Vell. Pat. 2.125.5: *viro nescias utiliore in castris an meliore in toga.*
11. Tac., *Ann.* 3.38.
12. Tac., *Ann.* 3.39.
13. Drinkwater (1978), p.820.
14. Tac., *Ann.* 3.40. Drinkwater (1978), p.833, notes wide agreement among modern historians that the financial strain of Romanization on local Gallic aristocracies under Tiberius was the primary cause of discontent.
15. Tac., *Ann.* 3.41.
16. See Ch. 2, n.41.
17. Tac., *Ann.* 3.41, calls Tiberius' reaction *dubitatione*, 'doubt' or 'indecision'.
18. Tac., *Ann.* 3.42.
19. Tac., *Ann.* 3.43.
20. A similar measure was used by Shim'on Ben Kosiba in preparation for his war of 132–135/6 CE to liberate Iudaea; see Powell (2021), p.81.
21. Tac., *Ann.* 3.43.
22. Tac., *Ann.* 3.45.
23. Tac., *Ann.* 3.46.
24. Tac., *Ann.* 3.47: *Tum demum Tiberius ortum patratumque bellum senatu scripsit.* Bromwich (1993), p.186 notes that Tiberius, or veterans at *Colonia* Iulia Firma Secundanorum Arausio (Orange), may have renovated their grand triumphal arch to celebrate this victory over Sacrovir and of *Legio* II Augusta's part in supressing the rebellion since its legionary symbol – the Capricorn – appears on the arch, however he concedes that it is far from certain.
25. Tac., *Ann.* 3.47: *neque dempsit aut addidit vero, sed fide ac virtute legatos, se consiliis superfuisse. simul causas cur non ipse, non Drusus profecti ad id bellum forent, adiunxit, magnitudinem imperii extollens, neque decorum principibus, si una alterave civitas turbet omissa urbe, unde in omnia regimem. nunc quia non metu ducatur iturum ut praesentia spectaret componeretque.*
26. Dolabella appears on an inscription from Vis island (ancient *Issa*), dated 20 CE, *AE* 1964, 228; *ILJug*, 257: *Drusus Caesar, T[(iberii) Aug(usti) f(ilius), Divi] / Augusti nepos, consul de[sign(atus) II], / pontifex, augur, camp[um dedit] / Publio Dolabella leg(ato) pro[praetore].*
27. Tac., *Ann.* 3.47: *igitur secutae Caesaris litterae quibus se non tam vacuum gloria praedicabat ut post ferocissimas gentis perdomitas, tot receptos in iuventa aut spretos triumphos, iam senior peregrinationis suburbanae inane praemium peteret.*
28. Tac., *Ann.* 3.36.
29. Tac., *Ann.* 3.37.
30. Tac., *Ann.* 3.38.
31. Tac., *Ann.* 3.38.

32. The euphemism *aqua atque igni* meant denying the guilty of the essentials of life, i.e. banishment from Rome or Italy.
33. Tac., *Ann.* 3.48.
34. Consul for 12 BCE. Flor. 2.31; Strabo, 12.6.5 (shown as 'Cyrinius'); Tac., *Ann.* 2.30, 3.23, 3.48.
35. Jer., *Chron.* A21; Tac., *Ann.* 3.72. *Cf.* Dio 57.21.3; Vell. Pat. 2.130.1. Erected in 55 BCE, the Theatre of Pompeius was Rome's first permanent theatre built of stone, previous structures having been constructed of timber.
36. Dio 52.33.1, 55.24.6, 55.26.1, 55.26.4–5, 55.33.4, 58.9.3; Suet., *Div. Aug.* 25.2, 30.1; Tac., *Ann.* 13.27.1. For the *Vigiles Urbani* see Daugherty (1992).
37. Tac., *Ann.* 3.72; *cf.* Vell. Pat. 2.130.1.
38. Dio 57.20.3; Tac., *Ann.* 3.49.
39. Tac., *Ann.* 3.50.
40. Tac., *Ann.* 3.51.
41. Dio 57.20.4 states ten days. *Senatus Consulta* became operative only when deposited in the *Aerarium* at the Temple of Saturn on the *Capitolinus* Hill.
42. Tac., *Ann.* 3.58.
43. Dio 57.13.3–5 mentions that more men were wearing purple, a prescribed colour.
44. Suet., *Tib.* 46.1: *Pecuniae parcus ac tenax comites peregrinationum expeditionumque numquam salario, cibariis tantum sustentavit.*
45. Suet., *Tib.* 34.1.
46. Dio 57.13.5.
47. Tac., *Ann.* 4.7.
48. Probably the *Lex Iulia* of 22 BCE: see Dio 54.2.3–4.
49. Tac., *Ann.* 3.53–54.
50. Tac., *Ann.* 3.53–54: *Maius aliquid et excelsius a principe postulatur; et cum recte factorum sibi quisque gratiam trahant, unius invidia ab omnibus peccatur. … Patres Conscripti, curam sustinet princeps; haec omissa funditus Rem Publicam trahet.*
51. Suet., *Tib.* 34.1.
52. Tac., *Ann.* 3.56.
53. Tac., *Ann.* 3.57.
54. Tac., *Ann.* 3.59: *contra patrium morem.*
55. Jer., *Chron.* A22. Woodman (2006), p.328, sees symmetry in the way Tacitus presents the story, mirroring Tiberius' award of the power forty years before.
56. Tac., *Ann.* 3.58.
57. Tac., *Ann.* 3.59.
58. Tac., *Ann.* 3.60.
59. Tac., *Ann.* 3.61–63.
60. Tac., *Ann.* 3.63.
61. Tac., *Ann.* 3.64.
62. Tac., *Ann.* 3.66. For the law on *repetundae* see Blunt (1961).
63. Tac., *Ann.* 3.67.
64. *Cf.* Dio 57.19.2.
65. Tac., *Ann.* 3.68.
66. Tac., *Ann.* 3.69.
67. Gyarus was a bleak and uninhabited island; Cynthus is now called Cythnos, south of Keos.
68. Tac., *Ann.* 3.68, 3.70.
69. Tac., *Ann.* 3.70 states that Capito's reputation suffered greatly as a result of Tiberius' rejection, as he was seen as tarnishing his own exemplary character.

70. Tac., *Ann.* 3.71.
71. Tac., *Ann.* 3.58. Musial (2014) notes that Tiberius appeared before the Senate in a dual role; he presented the pontiffs' opinion as the *pontifex maximus*, but as the *princeps* he made a decision on its basis.
72. In 242 BCE.
73. Tac., *Ann.* 3.72. *Cf.* Vell. Pat. 2.130.1; Dio 57.21.3. Augustus had restored the theatre at great personal expense in 32 BCE.
74. Tac., *Ann.* 3.72, 4.8.
75. Dio 57.21.3.
76. Dio 57.21.6: *καὶ τὸ λοιπὸν πᾶν πόκοις τε καὶ ἱματίοις παχέσι περιλαβών, σχοίνοις τε πανταχόθεν αὐτὴν διέδησε, καὶ ἐς τὴν ἀρχαίαν ἕδραν ἀνθρώποις τε πολλοῖς καὶ μηχανήμασιν ὀνευσάμενος ἐπανήγαγε.*
77. Pliny, *Nat. Hist.* 36.66 [195]: *ne aeris, argenti, auri metallis pretia detraherentur*. He adds: 'This story, however, was, for a long time, more widely spread than well authenticated', *eaque fama crebrior diu quam certior fuit*. *Cf.* Dio 57.21.6, who takes the story at face value.
78. Tac., *Ann.* 4.23.
79. Tac., *Ann.* 3.73: *non alias magis sua populique Romani contumelia indoluisse Caesarem ferunt quam quod desertor et praedo hostium more ageret.*
80. Tac., *Ann.* 3.74.
81. See Tac., *Ann.* 1.19.
82. Presumably leading their own *centuriae* of eighty men each.
83. Vell. Pat. 2.125.5.
84. Tac., *Ann.* 3.75.
85. Tac., *Ann.* 3.76.
86. Also called the *Rostra Vetera*, 'Old Rostra' (Suet., *Div. Aug.* 100.3).
87. Suet., *Tib.* 61.1; Tac., *Ann.* 4.15.
88. Suet., *Tib.* 54.1; Tac., *Ann.* 4.4.
89. Tac., *Ann.* 4.4.
90. Tac., *Ann.* 4.4: *nam voluntarium militem deesse, ac si suppeditet, non eadem virtute ac modestia agere, quia plerumque inopes ac vagi sponte militiam sumant.*
91. Tac., *Ann.* 4.4, 4.5, which gives the earliest listing of the legions and their deployments in the extant Roman sources.
92. Pliny, *Nat. Hist.* 3.67; Suet., *Tib.* 37.1; Suet., *Nero* 48.1; Tac., *Ann.* 4.2, 4.8. *Not. Reg.* 6. Rectangular in plan, measuring a total of 440 by 380 metres (1,440ft x 1,250ft), it was surrounded by a circuit wall of brick-faced concrete, rising 4.73 metres (12.2 ft) high, where they are still preserved, with crenellations along the top and four turreted gates (Tac., *Hist.* 3.84). It was called vulgarly the *castrum praetorium* (*CIL*, XV, 7239 b, c).
93. Tac., *Ann.* 4.5.
94. Tac., *Ann.* 4.2.
95. Tac., *Ann.* 4.5. The cohorts, each of six *centuriae*, were numbered X through XII, the fourth being located at *Colonia* Munatia. For the *Cohortes Urbanae*, see Powell (2018), pp.312–313, and Ricci (2011), pp.486–487.
96. Tac., *Ann.* 4.1.
97. *Praetor*: Dio 57.19.7, *ὃ μήπω πρότερον μηδενὶ τῶν ὁμοίων οἱ ἐγεγόνει*; prior to this promotion, Seianus did not belong to the senatorial class. *Socius*: Tac., *Ann.* 4.2. *Cf.* Augustus' characterization of Tiberius as 'son, colleague in power'; *illuc cuncta vergere: filius, collega imperii* (Tac., *Ann.* 3).
98. Tac., *Ann.* 4.1: *corpus illi laborum tolerans, animus audax; sui obtegens, in alios criminator; iuxta adulatio et superbia; palam compositus pudor, intus summa apiscendi libido, eiusque causa modo largitio et luxus, saepius industria ac vigilantia, haud minus noxiae quotiens parando regno finguntur.*

99. Tac., *Ann.* 4.3. Drusus 'incessantly complained "that a stranger was invited to assist in the government while the emperor's son was alive. How near was the step of declaring the stranger a colleague?"'; *et ultor metuebatur non occultus odii set crebro querens ro incolumi filio adiutorem imperii alium vocari. et quantum superesse ut collega dicatur?* (Tac., *Ann.* 4.7).
100. Dio 57.13.2: '*ζῶντος μέν μου οὐδὲν οὔτε βίαιον οὔθ' ὑβριστικὸν πράξεις: ἂν δέ τι καὶ τολμήσῃς, οὐδὲ τελευτήσαντος.*'
101. Tac., *Ann.* 4.3.
102. For Tacitus' presentation of Livilla, see Sinclair (1990).
103. Tac., *Ann.* 4.8.
104. Tac., *Ann.* 4.3.
105. Jer., *Chron.* A23; Tac., *Ann.* 4.10. Lindsay (1993), p.85 argues the story, whether true or false, that Drusus had been poisoned by his wife could not have been in circulation before 31 CE.
106. Tac., *Ann.* 4.10–11 refutes the rumour.
107. Tac., *Ann.* 4.8.
108. Tac., *Ann.* 4.9; *CIL*, VI, 31200 (Lott (2012), pp.159–167) and *Tab. Ilicitana* (Lott (2012), pp.169–173): a silver shield (*clipeus*) bearing Drusus' image was to be carried by the *equites* in their parade on 15 July annually, and seats in theatres formerly named in honour of Germanicus would now be named after Germanicus *and* Drusus.
109. Tac., *Ann.* 4.11.
110. Sen., *Consol. Marc.* 15.3: *Ti. Caesar et quem genuerat et quem adoptauerat amisit; ipse tamen pro rostris laudauit filium stetitque in conspectu posito corpore, interiecto tantummodo uelamento quod pontificis oculos a funere arceret, et flente populo Romano non flexit uultum; experiendum se dedit Seiano ad latus stanti quam patienter posset suos perdere.*
111. Tac., *Ann.* 4.15.
112. This was a high honour: over 100 statues of famous men (*Summi Viri*) – the *Viri Illustres* and *Viri Triumphatores*, ancestors and members of Augustus' family going back to the founding ancestors, Aeneas and Romulus, down to Iulius Caesar – stood in the *Forum Augustum* (Ovid, *Fast.* 5, 12 May). Shaya. (2013).
113. Tac., *Ann.* 4.13. The relief came in the form of a three-year exemption from tribute.
114. Tac., *Ann.* 4.14.
115. Tac., *Ann.* 4.15: *magna cum adseveratione principis non se ius nisi in servitia et pecunias familiares dedisse: quod si vim praetoris usurpasset manibusque militum usus foret, spreta in eo mandata sua: audirent socios.*
116. Tac., *Ann.* 4.15.
117. Tac., *Ann.* 4.15.
118. Tac., *Ann.* 4.14: *multa ab iis in publicum seditiose, foeda per domos temptari; Oscum quondam ludicrum, levissimae apud vulgum oblectationis, eo flagitiorum et virium venisse ut auctoritate patrum coercendum sit.*
119. Tac., *Ann.* 4.17.
120. Tac., *Ann.* 4.17: *partium Agrippinae.*
121. Tac., *Ann.* 4.18.
122. Tac., *Ann.* 4.19.
123. Tac., *Ann.* 4.20.
124. Tac., *Ann.* 4.18–19.
125. See Ch. 5, n.250.
126. Tac., *Ann.* 4.21: *adiecitque in domo eius venenum esse eumque gladio accinctum introire curiam.*
127. Tac., *Ann.* 4.21.

128. Tac., *Ann.* 4.22. This may be the Servius Plautus in Jer., *Chron.* A25. For a discussion of the case, see Hicks (2013).
129. Tac., *Ann.* 4.23.
130. Vell. Pat. 2.125.5: *vir simplicitatis generosissimae.* For Dolabella's career, see *CIL*, III, 1741 = *ILS* 938. For the administration of Illyricum under Dolabella, see Kos (2022) and Kovács (2017 and 2018).
131. Tac., *Ann.* 4.23.
132. Tac., *Ann.* 4.24.
133. Tac., *Ann.* 4.25.
134. Tac., *Ann.* 4.26.
135. *Cf.* Tac., *Ann.* 3.72.
136. Tac., *Ann.* 4.26: *regemque et socium atque amicum. Cf.* the Romans' response to Maroboduus.
137. Tac., *Ann.* 4.27: *primo coetibus clandestinis apud Brundisium et circumiecta oppida, mox positis propalam libellis ad libertatem vocabat agrestia per longinquos saltus et ferocia servitia.*
138. Tac., *Ann.* 4.27: *is disposita classiariomm copia coeptantem cum maxime coniurationem disiecit.* Under Tiberius a *quaestor* was stationed in southern Italy to check the excesses of the troops of armed and mounted herdsmen (*pastores*) maintained by the great properties on their extensive ranches (*saltus*), particularly when moving flocks along the tracks (*calles*) leading from the lowland to the highland grazing-grounds. Had Lupus not acted so quickly, the consequences could have been disastrous: the last recorded slave revolt to occur in the homeland had been led by the famous gladiator Spartacus, initiating the Third Servile War (73–71 BCE).
139. Their fate is not recorded.
140. Tac., *Ann.* 4.27: *lam trepidam ob multitudinem familiarum quae gliscebat immensum, minore in dies plebe ingenua.* Urbainczyk (2008), p.23, says the 'tighter control of the imperial bureaucracy [of the principate] resulted in fewer slave revolts' since the Spartacus War.
141. See Ch. 1, n.186.
142. Suet., *Tib.* 37.1: *Stationes militum per Italiam solito frequentiores disposuit.*
143. Suet., *Tib.* 30.1.Bowersock (1999), p.136 cites Alexander Pushkin's observation of Tiberius as 'one of the greatest administrative minds of antiquity'.
144. Tac., *Ann.* 4.28.
145. Tac., *Ann.* 4.29.
146. Dio 57.24.8.
147. Dio 57.24.8: '*ἄξιός εἰμι, εἴγε καὶ Λέντουλός με μισεῖ.*'
148. The *Rupes Tarpeia* were located on the south side of the *Capitolinus* Hill.
149. Tac., *Ann.* 4.29.
150. Tac., *Ann.* 4.44.
151. Tac., *Ann.* 4.30.
152. Tac., *Ann.* 4.30: *subverterent potius iura quam custodes eorum amoverent.*
153. Dio 57.24.5.
154. Tac., *Ann.* 4.31.
155. Tac., *Ann.* 4.31.
156. Tac., *Ann.* 4.31. Firmius had ensnared M. Scribonius Libo Drusus and orchestrated his downfall through entrapment, and then produced dubious evidence.
157. Dio 57.22.5.
158. It is not clear if Saturninus actually wrote the poem he was alleged to have read. Tacitus does not mention this in his extensive litany of cases, but the stark difference with the verdict in the trial of C. Cominius, which he does report, is perplexing.
159. He did not need to; his *imperium* had been granted without term limit in 14 CE.
160. Dio 57.24.1; *cf.* celebrations held for Augustus in Dio 53.16.2–3.

161. Suet., *Tib.* 24.1.
162. Suet., *Tib.* 25.1: *lupum se auribus tenere.*
163. Suet., *Tib.* 76.1; Tac., *Ann.* 4.7. *Cf.* Suet., *Div. Aug.* 45.1, 67.1, 101.1.
164. Suet., *Tib.* 55.1.
165. Tac., *Ann.* 4.34: *Romanorum ultimum.*
166. Tac., *Ann.* 4.34.
167. Tac., *Ann.* 4.35.
168. Tac., *Ann.* 4.36.
169. These acts would be in violation of the *Leges Porciae*: see Drogula (2011b).
170. Tac., *Ann.* 4.38: *Ego me, Patres Conscripti, mortalem esse et hominum officia fungi satisque habere si locum principem impleam et vos testor et meminisse posteros volo; qui satis superque memoriae meae tribuent, ut maioribus meis dignum, rerum vestrarum providum, constantem in periculis, offensionum pro utilitate publica non pavidum credant. haec mihi in animis vestris templa, hae pulcherrimae effigies et mansurae. nam quae saxo struuntur, si iudicium posterorum in odium vertit, pro sepulchris spernuntur. proinde socios civis et deos ipsos precor, hos ut mihi ad finem usque vitae quietam et intellegentem humani divinique iuris mentem duint, illos ut, quandoque concessero, cum laude et bonis recordationibus facta atque famam nominis mei prosequantur.*
171. Tac., *Ann.* 4.39.
172. Tac., *Ann.* 4.40.
173. Tac., *Ann.* 4.41.
174. Sen., *Controv.* 7.5.12; Tac., *Ann.* 4.42.
175. *Cf.* Suet., *Tib.* 66.1.
176. Tac., *Ann.* 4.43: the *Ager Dentheliales* on the western slope of Mount Taygetos in southern Greece.
177. Tac., *Ann.* 4.43. The ruins of a Doric temple still stand just outside the city. There is some evidence that the temple was never, in fact, completed.
178. Tac., *Ann.* 4.43.
179. Tac., *Ann.* 4.45.
180. Suet., *Tib.* 59.1–2: *Asper et immitis, breviter vis omnia dicam? / Dispeream si te mater amare potest. / Non es eques, quare? non sunt tibi millia centum? / Omnia si quaras, et Rhodos exsilium est. / Aurea mutasti Saturni saecula, Caesar: / Incolumi nam te, ferrea semper erunt. / Fastidit vinum, quia jam sitit iste cruorem: / Tam bibit hunc avide, quam bibit ante merum. / Adspice felicem sibi, non tibi, Romule, Sullam: / Et Marium, si vis, adspice, sed reducem. / Nec non Antoni civilia bella moventis / Nec semel infectas adspice cada manus, / Et dic, Roma perit: regnabit sanguine multo, / Ad regnum quisquis venit ab exsilio.*
181. Suet., *Tib.* 59.2: *Oderint, dum probent.*
182. Cic., *Cat.* 14 (9 November 63 BCE): *O concidionem miseram non modo administrandae verum etiam conservandae rei publicae!*

## CHAPTER 8: RULING AS 'THE EXILE'

1. Tac., *Ann.* 4.46.
2. Tac., *Ann.* 4.47.
3. Sabinus' campaign is described in great detail in Tac., *Ann.* 4.47–51.
4. Powell (2018), pp.189–191. Tac., *Ann.* 4.47 mentions a cohort of Sugambri auxiliary infantry, presumably *Cohors* I *Sugamborum* (or *Sygambrum*) which arrived from Moesia: see Ramsay (1929), p.155.
5. Tac., *Ann.* 4.46.
6. Tac., *Ann.* 4.52.
7. Tac., *Ann.* 4.52: *non ideo laedi quia non regnaret* – a reference to Euripides' *Medea.*

8. Tac., *Ann.* 4.52.
9. Tac., *Ann.* 4.53, where Tacitus divulges his first-hand source: 'This incident, unmentioned by any historian, was discovered in the memoirs of Agrippina's daughter [Agrippina the Younger], the mother of *princeps* Nero. She passed down the story of her life and the misfortunes of her family to posterity'; *id ego, a scriptoribus annalium non traditum, repperi in commentariis Agrippinae filiae quae Neronis principis mater vitam suam et casus suorum posteris memoravit.*
10. Tac., *Ann.* 4.54.
11. On Tiberius' habit of combining 'jesting and seriousness', see Ch. 1, n.119, Appendix 1.
12. Tac., *Ann.* 4.55.
13. Hypaepa, Tralles, Laodiceia, Magnesia, Ilium, Halicarnassus, Pergamos, Ephesus, Miletus, Sardis and Smyrna.
14. Tac., *Ann.* 4.56.
15. Tac., *Ann.* 4.57: *qui crederent in senectute corporis quoque habitum pudori fuisse: quippe illi praegracilis et incurva proceritas, nudus capillo vertex, ulcerosa facies ac plerumque medicaminibus interstincta; et Rhodi secreto vitare coetus, recondere voluptates insuerat.*
16. Tac., *Ann.* 4.57: *traditur etiam matris impotentia extrusum quam dominationis sociam aspernabatur neque depellere poterat, cum dominationem ipsam donum eius accepisset.*
17. Suet., *Div. Aug.* 72.2.
18. Tac., *Ann.* 4.57.
19. Tac., *Ann.* 4.58.
20. Tac., *Ann.* 4.59. Its modern name is Sperlonga.
21. In the remains of the villa in the environs of Sperlonga, sculptures have been found and include the assault of Scylla on Odysseus' galley, the blinding of Polyphemus, the theft of the Palladium, and Odysseus lifting up the corpse of Achilles. The sculptors have been tentatively identified as Agesander, Athenedoros and Polydoros, all of Rhodes. For the purpose of the sculptures, see Stewart (1977). For a reconstruction of the sculpture groups in the cave, see Carey (2003), p.113, fig. 29.
22. Suet., *Tib.* 55.1, 61.1; Tac., *Ann.* 4.59.
23. Tac., *Ann.* 4.59.
24. Tac., *Ann.* 4.60.
25. Tac., *Ann.* 4.60.
26. Suet., *Tib.* 47.1; Tac., *Ann.* 4.62; Dio 58.1.1.
27. Tac., *Ann.* 4.62; Dio 58.1.1.
28. Tac., *Ann.* 4.62: *conferta mole, dein convulsa, dum ruit intus aut in exteriora effunditur immensamque vim mortalium, spectaculo intentos aut qui circum adstabant, praeceps trahit atque operit.*
29. Suet., *Tib.* 40.1; Tac., *Ann.* 4.62.
30. Tac., *Ann.* 4.62.
31. Suet., *Caius* 31.1: *Augusti principatum clade Variana, Tiberi ruina spectaculorum apud Fidenas memorabilem factum.*
32. Tac., *Ann.* 4.64–65.
33. Tac., *Ann.* 4.64.
34. Tac., *Ann.* 4.64; *cf.* Suet., *Tib.* 48.1, which states Tiberius himself urged the name change in recognition of his liberality.
35. Quinta may have been a granddaughter of Appius Claudius Caecus and possibly a Vestal.
36. Tac., *Ann.* 4.64: *sanctos acceptosque numinibus Claudios et augendam caerimoniam loco in quo tantum in principem honorem di ostenderint.*
37. For Pontius Pilatus, see McGing (1991) and Maier (1971).

38. Powell (2021), pp.47–50.
39. Trotter (2019).
40. The inscription, *AE* 1963 104, is now in Israel Museum, Jerusalem: 'To the Divine Augustus [this] Tiberieum … Pontius Pilatus … Prefect of Iudaea … has dedicated [this]', *[Dis Augusti]s Tiberieum [...Ponti]us Pilatus [...Praef]ectus Iuda[ea]e [...fecit d] e[dicavit].* Based on Frova (1961); Winter (1991), p.425, suggests this was erected after Seianus' fall. The date of Pilatus' appointment is confirmed in Jer., *Chron.* A26.
41. Philo, *Leg.* 299.
42. Philo, *Leg.* 301–303.
43. Philo, *Leg.* 304–305. Fuks (1982) and McGing (1991) each critique the state of scholarly debate, which variously places the event in 31, 32, 35 or even 36 CE.
44. Jos., *Bell. Iud.* 2.169–74; Jos., *Ant. Iud.* 18.55–59.
45. Jos., *Bell. Iud.* 2.175–77; Jos., *Ant. Iud.* 18.60–62. McGing (1991), p.429.
46. Matthew 26: 57–68; 27:1–2; and 27:11–26. McGing (1991), p.437. For Roman capital punishments, see Powell (2022a).
47. Tac., *Ann.* 4.66. This is not the same man who fell at Teutoburg in 9 CE, but likely a relative.
48. Jer., *Chron.* A27.
49. Suet., *Tib.* 40.1; *cf.* the *cotidiana oscula* issued forbidding kissing in Suet., *Tib.*, 34.2; Thorburn (2008), p.439; Rogers (1945).
50. Suet., *Tib.* 40; Tac., *Ann.* 4.67.
51. Tac., *Ann.* 4.67: *concursusque oppidanorum disposito milite prohiberentur, perosus tamen municipia et colonias omniaque in continenti sita.*
52. Prop., *Eleg.* 1.11, 27–30. Sen., Ep. 51.
53. Suet., *Tib.* 41.1: *Regressus in insulam*; Dio 58.1.1. Thorburn (2008), pp.438 and 444, notes Suetonius' deliberate use of *regressus* (retreat) to Capraea as distinct from *secedere* (withdrawal) to Rhodes.
54. Pliny, *Nat. Hist.* 3.12.
55. Suet., *Tib.* 40.1: *uno parvoque litore adiretur.*
56. Tac., *Ann.* 4.67: *in continenti sita Capreas se in insulam abdidit trium milium freto ab extremis Surrentini promunturii diiunctam. solitudinem eius placuisse maxime crediderim, quoniam importuosum circa mare et vix modicis navigiis pauca subsidia; neque adpulerit quisquam nisi gnaro custode. caeli temperies hieme mitis obiectu montis quo saeva ventorum arcentur; aestas in favonium obversa et aperto circum pelago peramoena; prospectabatque pulcherrimum sinum.*
57. Strabo 5.4.9: *Νεαπολῖται δὲ καὶ ταύτην κατέσχον, πολέμῳ δὲ ἀποβαλόντες τὰς Πιθηκούσσας ἀπέλαβον πάλιν, δόντος αὐτοῖς Καίσαρος τοῦ Σεβαστοῦ, τὰς δὲ Καπρέας ἴδιον ποιησαμένου κτῆμα καὶ κατοικοδομήσαντος.* The chronology of construction is not understood.
58. Tac., *Ann.* 4.67. FitzPatrick (1949), p.70, notes that not all the villas have been identified.
59. Suet., *Tib.* 65.
60. Suet., *Div. Aug.* 72.3: *qualia sunt Capreis immanium beluarum ferarumque membra praegrandia, quae dicuntur gigantum ossa, et arma heroum.* These were almost certainly fossilized bones of dinosaurs or sauropods: for a discussion of how the fossils of dinosaurs, mammoths and other extinct animals influenced some of the most spectacular creatures of classical mythology, see Mayor (2023).
61. Suet., *Tib.* 73.1.
62. Suet., *Tib.* 65.1. It is unclear if the villa was begun by Augustus and completed by Tiberius or started and finished under Tiberius, in which case he may have stayed at villas on the island while construction progressed.
63. For a full description of the site, see Krause (2003a and 2003b).

64. Houston (1985), p.180.
65. Bruce (1986), p.535.
66. Bruce (1986), p.537. Scale models and drawings show several possible reconstructions. For the most convincing recreations based on the archaeological evidence, see Jean-Claude Golvin (plate 38), Gorski (2024) and Krause (2003a and 2003b).
67. The building consumed tons of bricks and mortar, which would have been imported from the mainland. It is not clear if the exterior finish was of exposed brick and stone or faced partially or fully with plaster or marble veneer.
68. Bishop (2012), pp.27–28; Gorski (2024), pp.28–29; Houston (1985), pp.190–191; Johnson (1983), pp.132–142. The word *praetorium* derived from the title *praetor*, and originally identified his tent within an army *castrum* (encampment).
69. Houston (1985), p.180, citing Sen., *Epist.* 51.11.
70. The presence of men of the *Cohortes Praetoriae* is inferred in Suet., *Tib.* 60.1. Seianus was likely resident at Capreae from 27–28 CE (Tac., *Ann.* 4.74) and in 30 CE (Dio 58.4.9). Macro stayed in 31 CE (Dio 58.4.9) and 36 CE (Philo, *Leg.* 35–8.). Houston (1985), p.185.
71. Suet., *Tib.* 74. Bruce (1986), p.535; Krause (2003b), p.180. Postcards from 1881–1900 show its remains as Il Faro and Torre di Tiberio.
72. Houston (1985), pp.187–191.
73. Levels 6 and 7 per Gorski (2024), pp.20–23; *cf.* Krause (2003b), p.178.
74. Cic., *Fam.* 9.4 to Varro: 'If you have a garden in your library, you want for nothing', *si hortum in bibliotheca habes, deerit nihil.* Houston (1985), p.189.
75. The library would be on Level 7 per Gorski (2024), pp.22–23. Bruce (1986), p.537, notes that 'the two square rooms measure 7.8 m. long, giving each an area of 60.8 sq. m., or 121.6 sq. m. combined'. For Pappus, see Houston (1985), p.186, citing *AE* 1960.26 = *AJA* 63 (1959), 384.
76. Krause (2003b), p.179.
77. FitzPatrick (1949), p.69. Gorski (2024), fig. 15 on p.36 and fig. 16 on p.36.
78. FitzPatrick (1949), pp.68–69.
79. Gorski (2024), p.41 estimates the cisterns held c. 2,273,000 litres (*c.* 500,000 gallons). On Capri, the average amount of annual precipitation is 1,020 millimetres (40.2 inches). Rain falls heaviest in January, October, November and December – November being the wettest month with 163 millimetres (6.4 inches).
80. FitzPatrick (1949), p.68.
81. Level 2 contained the kitchen and ovens per Gorski (2024), pp.12–13; *cf.* Houston (1985), pp.180, 185. Several inscriptions dedicated to deceased *liberti* have been found on Capri, according to Kessel (1988). Gorski (2024), p.9 estimates a support staff of 140 and that the complex could accommodate a total of 150–200 people including guests.
82. Level 3 contained the bathing facilities and slaves' quarters, per Gorski (2024), pp.14–15, with additional accommodation for slaves and freedmen on Levels 4 and 5 per Gorski (2024), pp.16–19; *cf.* Krause (2003b), p.178.
83. Level 6 per Gorski (2024), pp.20–21. There was an upper and lower exedra, constructed of arches on Level 6 and of columns on Level 7 per Gorski (2924), pp.20–23; see fig. 8 on p.30, fig. 11 on p.31, fig. 12 on p.32, fig. 13 on p.33, fig. 17, fig. 18 on p.37 and fig. 20 on p.40. This architectural design feature also appears in the *praetorium* at Caesarea Maritima, the west-facing, two-storey Lower Terrace Palace built by Herod the Great in its first phase (22–15 BCE), as distinct from the Upper Palace (11/10 BCE), which was later the residence of Pontius Pilatus while he was *Praefectus Iudaeae*. The semicircular *exedra* was built on a natural promontory extending into the Mediterranean Sea, according to Gleason *et al* (2015) and Patrich (2011), pp.205–206. Similarly, there is a semicircular *exedra* at Herod's Northern Palace at Masada, per Ovadiah & Peleg (2009).

84. The site was excavated by Amedeo Maiuri in 1937.
85. It is one of the so-called *villae maritimae* or *Palazzi a Mare*: see Günther (1903), pp.133–135. In the Grotto, statues of Neptune and Tritons, cut off at the knees, were placed at water level along the walls to create the impression that they were emerging out of the sea. During a survey conducted by the environmentalist association Marevivo in 2009, divers found seven bases at a depth of 150 metres (492ft), presumably having slipped off the ledge sometime in their history. A fragment of a nondescript marble sculpture was found there at the time of writing in February 2024.
86. Remains of white and black tessellated floors remain in places. A section of mosaic made of hexagons and squares from the Villa is now displayed in the adjacent church of Santo Stefano. For a reconstruction of the decorations on the floors, walls and ceilings see Gorski (2024), fig. 19 on pp.38–39.
87. Fragments of cut marble panels, alabaster and painted plaster have been found.
88. Houston (1985), pp.182–183, 192.
89. Booms (2010), p.133.
90. Pliny, *Nat. Hist.* 19.23 [64]: *Cartilaginum generis extraque terram est cucumis, mira voluptate Tiberio principi expetitus. nullo quippe non die contigit ei, pensiles eorum hortos promoventibus in solem rotis olitoribus rursusque hibernis diebus intra specularium munimenta revocantibus.* Perhaps *Cumumis melo.* For a discussion, see Janick & Paris (2022), who note: 'The selenite [a variety of gypsum] sheets might represent the earliest greenhouse cover.'
91. FitzPatrick (1949), p.70.
92. Suet., *Tib.* 62; cf. 14.4. Tac., *Ann.* 6.20–21.
93. Tac., *Ann.* 4.58.
94. Tac., *Ann.* 4.58.
95. Suet., *Tib.* 13.1: *se deposito patrio habitu ad pallium et crepidas.* See Ch. 3, n.90.
96. Tac., *Ann.* 4.64: *feralemque annum ferebant et ominibus adversis susceptum principi consilium absentiae.*
97. Tac., *Ann.* 4.68.
98. Tac., *Ann.* 4.69.
99. Tac., *Ann.* 6.39.
100. Tac., *Ann.* 4.70.
101. Dio 58.1.3.
102. Dio 58.1.3.
103. Tac., *Ann.* 4.70.
104. Tac., *Ann.* 4.71.
105. Tac., *Ann.* 4.74.
106. Octavia was his grandmother and through her to Augustus, his great-uncle.
107. Tac., *Ann.* 4.72.
108. Tac., *Ann.* 4.73: *turmas socialis equitesque legionum.*
109. Tac., *Ann.* 4.73: *dux Romanus … multi tribunorum praefectorumque et insignes centuriones.*
110. Tac., *Ann.* 4.74: *dissimulante Tiberio damna ne cui bellum permitteret.*
111. Tac., *Ann.* 4.74.
112. Dio 58.2.7.
113. Dio 58.5.1.
114. Assuming she was born in 59 BCE; for a discussion of birth dates, see Barrett (2002), pp. 309–310.
115. Suet., *Tib.* 51.2.
116. Tac., *Ann.* 5.1. *Roman History* (Vell. Pat. 2.130.5) ends with her death; *cf.* Livy, *Peri.* 142 ends with the death and burial of her son Nero Drusus.

117. Suet., *Tib.* 51.2; Dio 58.2.1.
118. Tac., *Ann.* 5.2; Dio 58.2.1.
119. Tac., *Ann.* 5.2.
120. Tac., *Ann.* 5.2; Dio 58.2.1.
121. Dio 58.2.2.
122. Dio 58.2.3: *κἐψηφίσαντο, ὅτι τε οὐκ ὀλίγους σφῶν ἐσεσώκει, καὶ ὅτι παῖδας πολλῶν ἐτετρόφει κόρας τε πολλοῖς συνεξεδεδώκει, ἀφ᾽ οὗ γε καὶ μητέρα αὐτὴν τῆς πατρίδος τινὲς ἐπωνόμαζον.* The accolade echoed Augustus' own award of a *corona civica* for 'protecting the lives of citizens' (*ob cives servatos*).
123. Dio 58.2.6.
124. Tac., *Ann.* 5.1.
125. Tac., *Ann.* 5.1; Dio 58.2.1. For biographies of Livia, see Barrett (2002) and Kunst (2008).
126. Tac., *Ann.* 5.1: *mater impotens.*
127. Tac., *Ann.* 5.2.
128. Tac., *Ann.* 5.3.
129. Tac., *Ann.* 5.4.
130. Suet., *Tib.* 54.1.
131. Suet., *Tib.* 53.2.
132. Tac., *Ann.* 5.4.
133. Tac., *Ann.* 5.5.
134. Tac., *Ann.* 5.5 stops here. The end of Book 5 and the beginning of Book 6 are lost. The main source for events during these three years is Cassius Dio.
135. Dio 58.1.7a[8].
136. Dio 58.1.1; *cf.* Dio 58.4.1.
137. Dio 58.1.1–2; Sen., *Controv.* 2.1.36.
138. Dio 58.1.3.
139. Dio 58.1.4.
140. Dio 58.1.5.
141. Dio 58.1.7a[8].
142. Dio 58.1.6.
143. Dio 58.1.7a[8]. Either the consul of 30 CE, C. Cassius Longinus, or his brother, L. Cassius Longinus.
144. Suet., *Tib.* 54.1: *Drusum in ima parte Palatii. Cf.* Tac., *Ann.* 6.23.
145. Dio 58.4.5.
146. Dio 58.4.6.
147. Dio 58.4.6–7.
148. Dio 58.4.3: *καὶ κοινωνὸν τῶν φροντίδων ὠνόμαζε, 'Σεϊανός' τε 'ὁ ἐμός' πολλάκις ἐπαναλαμβάνων ἔλεγε, καὶ τοῦτο καὶ γράφων πρός τε τὴν βουλὴν. Cf.* Tac., *Ann.* 4.2.
149. Dio 58.4.4; *cf.* Suet., *Tib.* 65.1.
150. Dio 58.4.3.
151. Dio 58.4.4; Suet., *Tib.* 65.1.
152. Tac., *Ann.* 6.8: *tui consulatus socium.*
153. Dio 58.4.9; Suet., *Tib.* 65.1.
154. Suet., *Tib.* 26.2.
155. Dio 58.4.9–5.1.
156. Dio 58.5.3.
157. Suet., *Tib.* 26.2. On the family of Faustus Cornelius Sulla, see Syme (1986), p.267.
158. Sex. Tedius Valerius Catullus may be the Catullus mentioned in Suet., *Caius* 36.1.
159. Dio 58.4.1.
160. Jos. *Ant. Iud.* 18.6.6. Neither Tacitus, Suetonius nor Dio mention this. Antonia had a villa at Misenum: Pliny, *Nat. Hist.* 9.172[81]. For the issues with this alleged letter, see

Boddington (1963). Nicols (1975) reports that Antonia did not pass on information to Tiberius and that the story is an invention of the Claudian and Flavian decades.

161. Tac., *Ann.* 6.47; Suet., *Tib.* 65.1; Juv. 10.74ff.
162. Tac., *Ann.* 5.8.
163. Dio 58.4.2.
164. Dio 58.7.4. Caius Caligula was born on 31 August 12 CE.
165. Dio 58.7.4.
166. Suet., *Caius* 12.1.
167. Suet., *Caius* 10.1. This meant Caius Caligula did not enjoy the standard public ceremonials accorded to his brothers on their coming of age.
168. Dio 58.8.2.
169. Dio 58.8.1, 58.8.3.
170. Dio 58.8.3.
171. Dio 58.8.4. How Nero Caesar died is not explained.
172. Dio 58.9.1.
173. Dio 58.9.2; Suet., *Tib.* 65.1.
174. Dio 58.9.3.
175. Graecinius Laco was an *eques* from Verona.
176. Dio 58.9.4.
177. Dio 58.9.5.
178. Dio 58.9.6.
179. Dio 58.9.6.
180. Dio 58.10.3.
181. Dio 58.10.1.
182. Suet., *Tib.* 65.1: *senem et solum.*
183. Dio 58.10.2.
184. Dio 58.10.4.
185. Dio 58.10.5.
186. Dio 58.10.6.
187. Dio 58.10.6–7: *κἀν τούτῳ προσκαλεσαμένου αὐτὸν τοῦ Ῥηγούλου οὐχ ὑπήκουσεν, οὐχ ὅτι ὑπερεφρόνησεν 'ἤδη γὰρ ἐτεταπείνωτὸ ἀλλ' ὅτι ἀήθης τοῦ προστάττεσθαί τι ἦν. ὡς δὲ καὶ δεύτερον καὶ τρίτον γε ἐκεῖνος ἐμβοήσας οἱ καὶ τὴν χεῖρα ἅμα ἐκτείνας εἶπε 'Σεϊανέ, δεῦρο ἐλθέ,' ἐπηρώτησεν αὐτὸν αὐτὸ τοῦτο, 'ἐμὲ καλεῖς ;' ὀψὲ δ' οὖν ποτε ἀναστάντι αὐτῷ καὶ ὁ Λάκων ἐπεσελθὼν προσέστη. καὶ τέλος διαναγνωσθείσης τῆς ἐπιστολῆς πάντες ἀπὸ μιᾶς γλώσσης καὶ κατεβόων αὐτοῦ καὶ δεινὰ ἐπέλεγον.*
188. Dio 58.10.8.
189. Dio 58.11.3, 58.12.1.
190. Dio 58.11.4. Meetings of the Senate were held in the *pronaos* of the Temple of Concordia; see Rebert & Marceau (1925), pp.54–55.
191. Dio 58.11.5.
192. Dio 58.12.1. Juv., Sat. 10.61–81 describes the reaction of 'Remus' mob' (*turba Remi*) to Seianus' demise, suggesting it would have responded with as much joy and violence had the battered body been Tiberius'.
193. Dio 58.12.2.
194. Dio 58.12.4–5.
195. Dio 58.12.7.
196. Dio 58.12.8.
197. See note 170.
198. Suet., *Tib.* 65.2: *speculabundus ex altissima rupe identidem signa, quae, ne nuntii morarentur, tolli procul, ut quidque factum foret, mandaverat.* The signal would presumably be communicated from a burning pyre or lighthouse at Misenum.

199. Dio 58.13.1; Suet., *Tib.* 65.1; Tac., *Ann.* 6.23.
200. Suet., *Tib.* 61.1: *ausus est scribere Seianum se punisse, quod comperisset furere adversus liberos Germanici filii sui.*
201. Dio 58.13.2.
202. Dio 58.13.3; Suet., *Tib.* 65.1.
203. Suet., *Tib.* 65.2.
204. Tac., *Ann.* 5.11.
205. Dio 58.16.3.
206. Dio 58.14.3; Tac., *Ann.* 5.6.
207. Dio 58.14.1–2.
208. Dio 58.14.4–5, 58.16.3.
209. Dio 58.14.3.
210. Dio 58.15.1–3; Tac., *Ann.* 5.6.
211. Tac., *Ann.* 5.8.
212. Tac., *Ann.* 5.7.
213. Dio 58.16.1.
214. Tac., *Ann.* 5.8. Aelius Gallus was likely Seianus' eldest son.
215. Tac., *Ann.* 6.2.
216. Dio 58.16.1.
217. Tac., *Ann.* 5.9.
218. Dio 58.16.6.
219. Dio 58.11.6. Bellemore (1995) questions whether Seianus' wife was still Apicata; citing a misunderstanding and reconstruction of *Fasti Ostienses*, she argues that Seianus' wife by this time was actually Livilla (Livia Iulia) and that *she* was the woman commemorated on the inscription who committed suicide.
220. Dio 58.11.5; Tac., *Ann.* 4.3.
221. Tac., *Ann.* 5.9.
222. For the *Fast. Ost.* for October 31 CE recording the deaths of Seianus and his children, see Flower (2006), fig. 39, p.173.
223. Dio 58.11.6.
224. Suet., *Tib.* 62.1.
225. Dio 58.11.7.
226. Suet., *Tib.* 62.1.
227. Tac., *Ann.* 5.6, 6.2.
228. Dio 58.11.7.
229. Dio 58.11.7: *ἤδη δὲ ἤκουσα ὅτι ἐκεῖνος μὲν αὐτῆς διὰ τὴν μητέρα τὴν Ἀντωνίαν ἐφείσατο, αὐτὴ δὲ ἡ Ἀντωνία ἑκοῦσα λιμῷ τὴν θυγατέρα ἐξώλεσε.* For a discussion of Livilla and the fall of Seianus, see Flower (2006), pp.169–182.
230. Tac., *Ann.* 5.10.
231. Dio 58.25.1.
232. Tac., *Ann.* 5.10.
233. Sen., *Quaes. Nat.* 1.15.5. This episode might describe a sighting of the *Aurora Borealis* aka Northern Lights.

## CHAPTER 9: AGING DISGRACEFULLY

1. Dio 58.17.2–3. For many years, Tiberius objected to senators swearing oaths at all to support his official acts.
2. Tac., *Ann.* 6.2; Dio 58.17.4.
3. Dio 58.17.4.

4. Tac., *Ann.* 6.2: *sed quos omitti posse, quos deligi? semperne eosdem an subinde alios? et honori bus perfunctos an iuvenes, privatos an e magistratibus? quam deinde speciem fore sumentium in limine curiae gladios? neque sibi vitam tanti si armis tegenda foret.*
5. Dio 58.18.5.
6. Dio 58.18.6.
7. Dio 58.18.2.
8. Tac., *Ann.* 6.3; Dio 58.18.3. The seats were assigned to the *Ordo Equester* under the *Leges Rosciae.*
9. Tac., *Ann.* 6.3.
10. Dio 58.18.4; Tac., *Ann.* 6.3.
11. Tac., *Ann.* 6.3.
12. Tac., *Ann.* 6.4.
13. Tac., *Ann.* 6.5: '*illos quidem senatus, me autem tuebitur Tiberiolus meus.*'
14. Tac., *Ann.* 6.6: '*quid scribam vobis, patres conscripti, aut quo modo scribam aut quid omnino non scribam hoc tempore, di me deaeque peius perdant quam perire me cotidie sentio, si scio.*'
15. Tac., *Ann.* 6.5.
16. Tac., *Ann.* 6.7.
17. Tac., *Ann.* 6.7.
18. Tac., *Ann.* 6.7. For the fate of Africanus and other Gallic Iulii, see Drinkwater (1978), p.820.
19. Tac., *Ann.* 6.8.
20. Dio 58.19.3.
21. Dio 58.19.5.
22. Dio 58.19.2.
23. Dio 58.19.1–2: *ἐκείνου μὲν ὑπερφρονήσας τά τε ἄλλα πάντα διὰ φαλακρῶν ἐν τοῖς Φλωραλίοις μέχρι νυκτὸς ἐπὶ τῇ τοῦ Τιβερίου χλευασίᾳ, ὅτι τοιοῦτος ἦν, ποιήσαντος, καὶ φῶς τοῖς ἀπιοῦσιν ἐκ τοῦ θεάτρου διὰ πεντακισχιλίων παίδων ἀπεξυρημένων παρασχόντος 'τοσοῦτον γὰρ ἐδέησε δι' ὀργῆς αὐτῷ γενέσθαι ὥστ' οὐδὲ προσεποιήσατο ἀρχὴν ὅτι περὶ αὐτῶν ἠκηκόει, καίπερ Καισιανῶν ἐξ ἐκείνου πάντων τῶν φαλακρῶν ὀνομασθέντων'.* *Floralia* was a festival in honour of the goddess Flora held on 28 April each year.
24. Tac., *Ann.* 6.9.
25. Tac., *Ann.* 6.10.
26. Tac., *Ann.* 6.10.
27. Suet., *Tib.* 72.1; Tac., *Ann.* 6.1.
28. Suet., *Div. Iul.* 39.4, 44.1; Suet., *Tib.* 72.1.
29. Presumably staying at private villas, such as his resort at Spelunca.
30. Tac., *Ann.* 6.1: *saxa rursum et solitudinem maris repetiit pudore scelerum et libidinum quibus adeo indomitis exarserat ut more regio pubem ingenuam stupris pollueret.*
31. Tac., *Ann.* 6.1: *nec formam tantum et decora corpora set in his modestam pueritiam, in aliis imagines maiorum incitamen tum cupidinis habebat. tuncque primum ignota antea vocabula reperta sunt sellariorum et spintriarum ex foeditate loci ac multiplici patientia; praepositique servi qui conquirerent pertraherent, dona in promptos, minas adversum abnuentis, et si retinerent propinquus aut parens, vim raptus suaque ipsi libita velut in captos exercebant. Cf.* Dio 58.22.1 also alleges sexual relations with high-ranking members of Roman society.
32. Suet., *Tib.* 43.1–2: *Secessu vero Caprensi etiam sellaria excogitavit, sedem arcanarum libidinum, in quam undique conquisiti puellarum et exoletorum greges monstrosique concubitus repertores, quos spintrias appellabat, triplici serie conexi, in vicem incestarent coram ipso, ut aspectu deficientis libidines excitaret. Cubicula plurifariam disposita tabellis ac sigillis lascivissimarum picturarum et figurarum adornavit librisque Elephantidis instruxit, ne cui in opera edenda exemplar impe[t]ratae schemae deesset. In silvis quoque ac nemoribus*

*passim Venerios locos commentus est prostantisque per antra et cavas rupes ex utriusque sexus pube Paniscorum et Nympharum habitu, quae palam iam et vulgo nomine insulae abutentes 'Caprineum' dictitabant.* The Latin word *capra* means 'she-goat' (pl. *caprae*). *Cf.* Suet., *Vit.* 3.2.

33. Suet., *Tib.* 44.1: *Maiore adhuc ac turpiore infamia flagravit, vix ut referri audirive, nedum credi fas sit, quasi pueros primae teneritudinis, quos pisciculos vocabat, institueret, ut natanti sibi inter femina versarentur ac luderent lingua morsuque sensim adpetentes; atque etiam quasi infantes firmiores, necdum tamen lacte depulsos, inguini ceu papillae admoveret, pronior sane ad id genus libidinis et natura et aetate.* For a full discussion of Suetonius, see Wallace-Hadrill (1984), p.19: 'Suetonius is mundane … Stylistically he has no pretentions.'
34. Suet., *Tib.* 44.2: *Quare Parrasi quoque tabulam, in qua Meleagro Atalanta ore morigeratur, legatam sibi sub condicione, ut si argumento offenderetur decies pro ea sestertium acciperet, non modo praetulit, sed et in cubiculo dedicavit. Fertur etiam in sacrificando quondam captus facie ministri acerram praeferentis nequisse abstinere, quin paene vixdum re divina peracta ibidem statim seductum constupraret simulque fratrem eius tibicinem; atque utrique mox, quod mutuo flagitium exprobrarant, crura fregisse.*
35. Suet., *Tib.* 45.1: *Feminarum quoque, et quidem illustrium, capitibus quanto opere solitus sit inludere, evidentissime apparuit Malloniae cuiusdam exitu, quam perductam nec quicquam amplius pati constantissime recusantem delatoribus obiecit ac ne ream quidem interpellare desiit, 'ecquid paeniteret'; donec ea relicto iudicio domum se abripuit ferroque transegit, obscaenitate oris hirsuto atque olido seni clare exprobrata. Unde mora in Atellanico exhodio proximis ludis adsensu maximo excepta percrebruit, 'hircum vetulum capreis naturam ligurire.'* Champlin (2020) argues categorically that the story is completely fictious, 'a fabrication from first to last'; Mallan (2016) explains that the joke relates to Tiberius licking the genitals of others, in contrast to goats which lick their own (apparently), citing Aristophanes' *Plutus* 292–95.
36. Suet., *Tib.* 60.1: *In paucis diebus quam Capreas attigit piscatori, qui sibi secretum agenti grandem mullum inopinanter obtulerat, perfricari eodem pisce faciem iussit, territus quod is a tergo insulae per aspera et devia erepsisset ad se; gratulanti autem inter poenam, quod non et lucustam, quam praegrandem ceperat, obtulisset, lucusta quoque lacerari os imperavit. Militem praetorianum ob subreptum e viridiario pavonem capite puniit. In quodam itinere lectica, qua vehebatur, vepribus impedita exploratorem viae, primarum cohortium centurionem, stratum humi paene ad necem verberavit.* The phrase *primae cohortes* likely refers to the detachment of the *Cohortes Praetoriae* which was encamped on Capreae.
37. Dio 58.18.5.
38. Tac., *Ann.* 6.13.
39. Tac., *Ann.* 6.13: *quis commotus incusavit magistratus patresque quod non publica auctoritate populum coercuissent. Cf.* Suet., *Tib.* 37.2.
40. Suet., *Tib.* 8.1.
41. Tac., *Ann.* 6.13.
42. Dio 58.19.6. Hibernus is named Severus by Philo, *Flacc.* 1.
43. Perhaps a son of L. Aelius Lamia. The *praefectus urbi* had command of the *Cohortes Urbanae*.
44. Perhaps Lucius or Marcus Calpurnius Piso (Tac., *Ann.* 3.16).
45. Tac., *Ann.* 6.14.
46. Dio 58.21.1; Tac., *Ann.* 6.15.
47. Tac., *Ann.* 6.15.
48. See n.5.
49. Plut., *Moral.* On Exile 9 [602e]: *ἀλλ' ἐκείνῳ μὲν αἱ τῆς ἡγεμονίας φροντίδες ἐπιχεόμεναι καὶ προσφερόμεναι πανταχόθεν, οὐ καθαρὰν παρεῖχον οὐδ' ἀκύμονα.*

50. Butcher & Ponting (2011), pp.557–558, and fig. 1, note the coinage was essentially pure silver bullion.
51. Tac., *Ann.* 6.17.
52. Tac., *Ann.* 6.17.
53. Frank (1935), pp.337–339.
54. Frank (1935), p.340, citing Suet., *Div. Aug.* 41 and Dio 51.21.5 after the annexation of Egypt.
55. Suet., *Tib.* 46.1, 47.1; Tac., *Ann.* 6.45.
56. Frank (1935), p.340. Whether the decision was made at Tiberius' request is not clear.
57. Tac., *Ann.* 6.17: *sed creditores in solidum appellabant nec decorum appellatis minuere fidem. ita primo concursatio et preces, dein strepere praetoris tribunal, eaque quae remedio quaesita, venditio et emptio, in contrarium mutari quia faeneratores omnem pecuniam mercandis agris condiderant. copiam vendendi secuta vilitate, quanto quis obaeratior, aegrius distrahebant, multique fortunis provolvebantur; eversio rei familiaris dignitatem ac famam praeceps dabat.*
58. Declaring war on Rome, Mithridates VI of Pontus murdered so many Roman tax collectors, contractors and traders in Asia Minor and on Delos that the bonds (*nomina*) tied to their business activities there lost all of their value. The result was that asset values collapsed, and wealth vanished from Roman banks and property owners virtually overnight.
59. Dio 58.21.4.
60. Suet., *Tib.* 48.1.
61. Dio 58.21.5; Tac., *Ann.* 6.17.
62. Suet., *Tib.* 48.1: *alterum ad mitigandam temporum atrocitatem.*
63. Frank (1935), pp.337–339.
64. Dio 58.21.1. The location of the residence he used is not known. Suet., *Tib.* 72.1 mentions that he came to Rome up the *Via Appia* as far as the seventh milestone.
65. Dio 58.21.2.
66. Dio 58.21.3.
67. Tac., *Ann.* 6.18.
68. Tac., *Ann.* 6.19.1; *cf.* Dio 58.22.1–4. Sex. Marius first appears in Tac., *Ann.* 4.36 in 25 CE. For what is known of him, see Champlin (2015), who doubts the story of incest as 'unlikely in the extreme' (p.293), derived from a now lost source used by Suetonius, Tacitus and Dio who was acquainted with Tiberius and spread 'malicious fiction' about him (p.294.).
69. Tac., *Ann.* 6.19.1.
70. Dio 58.21.5.
71. Dio 58.21.6.
72. Dio 58.21.1.
73. Dio 58.23.1. This recalls the privileges granted by Augustus to Tiberius and Nero Drusus.
74. Dio 58.25.2; Suet., *Caius* 12.1.
75. Vescularius Flaccus, Iulius Marinus and L. Aelius Seianus were all now dead.
76. Tac., *Ann.* 6.20: *immanem animum subdola modestia tegens, non damnatione matris, non exitio fratrum rupta voce; qualem diem Tiberius induisset, pari habitu, haud multum distantibus verbis. unde mox scitum Passieni oratoris dictum percrebuit neque meliorem umquam servum neque deteriorem dominum fuisse. Cf.* Suet., *Caius* 10.2. Both wrote with the benefit of hindsight.
77. Suet., *Caius* 11.1.
78. Suet., *Caius* 11.1: *praedicaret exitio suo omniumque Gaium vivere et se natricem populo Romano, Phaethontem orbi terrarum educare.*

79. Dio 58.8.1.
80. Tac., *Ann.* 6.46.
81. Suet., *Div. Claud.* 30.1.
82. Suet., *Div. Claud.* 3.2: *Mater Antonia portentum eum hominis dictitabat, nec absolutum a natura, sed tantum incohatum.*
83. Suet., *Div. Claud.* 4.3.
84. Suet., *Tib.* 23.1–2; Tac., *Ann.* 6.46. Tiberius Gemellus was born on 10 October 19 CE.
85. Dio 58.23.2.
86. Dio 58.23.3: 'σύ τε τοῦτον ἀποκτενεῖς καὶ σὲ ἄλλοι', lit. 'You take this away from others as well'.
87. Sen., *Ben.* 5.25.2: '*Non memini quid fuerim*'. Seneca interprets the line to mean Tiberius desired oblivion, yet it might also suggest that Tiberius was aware of the Stoic concept of impermanence.
88. Dio 58.23.4.
89. Dio 58.23.4. *ἀναφθέγξασθαι τοῦτο δὴ τὸ ἀρχαῖον ἐμοῦ θανόντος γαῖα μιχθήτω πυρί.* The line may come from Euripdes' *Bellerophon* or *Sisyphus*.
90. Dio 58.22.4.
91. Suet., *Tib.* 54.2; Tac., *Ann.* 6.23.
92. Tac., *Ann.* 6.24.
93. Dio 58.25.4; Tac., *Ann.* 6.24.
94. Dio 58.22.4.
95. Tac., *Ann.* 6.25: *eodem die defunctam, quo biennio ante Seianus poenas luisset.*
96. Suet., *Tib.* 53.2; Tac., *Ann.* 6.25.
97. Suet., *Tib.* 53.2.
98. Suet., *Tib.* 53.2; Tac., *Ann.* 6.25: *adsimulatus est finis.*
99. Tac., *Ann.* 6.25.
100. Dio 58.22.5; Suet., *Tib.* 53.2.
101. *CIL*, VI, 886: 'Bones of Agrippina; daughter of M. Agrippa, granddaughter of *Divus* Augustus, wife of Germanicus Caesar, mother of *Princeps* C. Caesar Germanicus'; *Ossa / Agrippinae M(arci) Agrippae [f(iliae)] / divi Aug(usti) neptis uxoris / Germanici Caesaris / matris C(ai) Caesaris Aug(usti) / Germanici principis / S(enatus) p(opulus)q(ue) R(omanus) / p(opuli) R(omani) a(uctoritate).*
102. Tac., *Ann.* 6.20: '*Et tu, Galba, quandoque degustabis imperium.*' *Cf.* Dio 57.19.4 Xiph.
103. Suet., *Tib.* 61.1: *commentario, quem de uita sua summatim breuiterque composuit.* The reference to punishing Seianus means Tiberius was working on if after 31 CE.
104. Dio 58.23.6.
105. Tac., *Ann.* 6.23.
106. Dio 58.23.6.
107. Flower (2006), pp.143–148.
108. Tac., *Ann.* 6.23. Dio 58.22.5 infers she was murdered.
109. Tac., *Ann.* 6.26.
110. Tac., *Ann.* 6.27.
111. It may have been a deliberate decision by Tiberius to keep him in the city.
112. Tac., *Ann.* 6.27: *quis incusabat egregium quemque et regendis exercitibus idoneum abnuere id munus seque ea necessitudine ad preces cogi per quas consularium aliqui capessere provincias adigerentur.*
113. Tac., *Ann.* 6.27. Arruntius replaced L. Calpurnius Piso, killed by the Termestini in 25 CE: see Ch. 7, n.179. It too may have been a deliberate decision by Tiberius to keep him in the city.

114. Suet., *Tib.* 41: *Regressus in insulam rei p. quidem curam usque adeo abiecit, ut postea non decurias equitum umquam supplerit, non tribunos militum praefectosque, non provinciarum praesides ullos mutaverit, Hispaniam et Syriam per aliquot annos sine consularibus legatis habuerit, Armeniam a Parthis occupari, Moesiam a Dacis Sarmatisque, Gallias a Germanis vastari neglexerit: magno dedecore imperii nec minore discrimine.*
115. Tac., *Ann.* 6.30.
116. Tac., *Ann.* 6.29.
117. Dio 58.24.3
118. Dio 58.24.1.
119. Dio 58.24.3–4.
120. Tac., *Ann.* 6.29.
121. Dio 58.24.3–4: *'καὶ ἐγὼ οὖν Αἴαντ'.*
122. Tac., *Ann.* 6.29–30.
123. Tac., *Ann.* 6.30.
124. See Ch. 3, n.118. *Cf.* Strabo 16.1.28.
125. Dio 58.26.1; Tac., *Ann.* 6.31.
126. Dio 58.26.2; Strabo 6.4.2; Tac., *Ann.* 6.31.
127. Tac., *Ann.* 6.32.
128. Tac., *Ann.* 6.32.
129. Strabo 7.4.4.
130. Tac., *Ann.* 4.5, 6.32.
131. Tac., *Ann.* 6.33; Dio 58.26.3 states Tiberius wrote to Mithridates directing him to invade Armenia.
132. Tac., *Ann.* 6.32.
133. Tac., *Ann.* 6.34.
134. Tac., *Ann.* 6.35.
135. Tac., *Ann.* 6.36.
136. Tac., *Ann.* 6.42.
137. Tac., *Ann.* 6.37.
138. Tac., *Ann.* 6.38.
139. Tac., *Ann.* 6.38: *ipsi fluxam senio mentem et continuo abscessu velut exilium obiectando.*
140. Dio 58.25.2–3.
141. Tac., *Ann.* 6.38; *cf.* Suet., *Tib.* 28.1.
142. Tac., *Ann.* 6.39; *cf.* Suet., *Tib.* 28.1.
143. Tac., *Ann.* 6.40.
144. Suet., *Galba* 3.4. This Galba is the brother of the future emperor. *Cf.* Suet., *Tib.* 25.5.
145. Tac., *Ann.* 6.40.
146. Dio 58.22.4 (Vibullius); Tac., *Ann.* 6.40 (Vibulenus).
147. Dio 58.27.1.
148. Dio 58.27.2.
149. Tac. *Ann.* 6.4.1.
150. Tac. *Ann.* 6.41.
151. Tac. *Ann.* 6.42.
152. Tac. *Ann.* 6.43.
153. Dio 58.26.3; Tac. *Ann.* 6.43.
154. Tac. *Ann.* 6.44.
155. Dio 58.26.4.
156. Jos., *Bell. Iud.* 2.9.5[178].
157. Rogers (1943), pp.45–46, citing Rogers (1941), p.159f.

158. Jos., *Bell. Iud.* 2.9.5[178]: *καὶ δή ποτε ἑστιῶν αὐτὸν τά τε ἄλλα ποικίλως ἐφιλοφρονεῖτο καὶ τελευταῖον τὰς χεῖρας ἀνατείνας φανερῶς ηὔξατο θᾶττον αὐτὸν θεάσασθαι τῶν ὅλων δεσπότην ἀποθανόντος Τιβερίου.*
159. Jos., *Bell. Iud.* 2.9.5[178]: *τοῦτό τις τῶν οἰκετῶν αὐτοῦ διαγγέλλει τῷ Τιβερίῳ, καὶ ὃς ἀγανακτήσας εἵργνυσιν τὸν Ἀγρίππαν καὶ μετ' αἰκίας εἶχεν αὐτὸν ἐπὶ μῆνας ἓξ ἐν δεσμωτηρίῳ.*
160. Tac. *Ann.* 15.44. This is the only reference to Pilatus' sentencing in the extant non-Christian texts.
161. Euseb., *Hist. Eccl.* 2.2.3; Tac. *Ann.* 15.44.
162. Jer., *Chron.* A32.
163. Euseb., *Hist. Eccl.* 2.2.3; Jer., *Chron.* A36; Oros., *Pagan.* 7.6–7; Tert., *Apol.* 5.1.
164. Jer., *Chron.* A36; Tert., *Apol.* 5.1: *Caesar in sententia mansit, comminatus periculum accusatoribus Christianorum.*
165. Tac., *Ann.* 6.45.
166. Cn. Domitius Ahenobarbus, L. Cassius Longinus, M. Vinicius, C. Rubellius Blandus and P. Petronius.
167. Tac., *Ann.* 6.45 states that his sources did not record which of them he rejected or accepted.
168. Tac., *Ann.* 6.47.
169. Satrius Secundus had revealed Seianus' alleged plot to Tiberius: see Ch. 8, n.160.
170. Dio 58.27.2; Tac., *Ann.* 6.47.
171. Dio 58.27.4–5; Tac., *Ann.* 6.48.
172. Dio 58.27.4; Tac., *Ann.* 6.48.
173. Tac., *Ann.* 6.49.
174. Tac., *Ann.* 6.46: *non abdita ambage occidentem ab eo deseri, orientem spectari exprobravit.*
175. Suet., *Tib.* 72.1.
176. Suet., *Tib.* 72.2.
177. Suet., *Tib.* 73.1.
178. The ancient settlement of Astura on the Astura River was situated in the coastal part of the Pontine Region of Campania.
179. Presumably the soldiers were marines of the *Classis Misenensis*. There is no record of the dart striking the animal.
180. Tac., *Ann.* 6.50: Lucullus was a formidable commander and statesman connected with L. Cornelius Sulla.
181. Suet., *Tib.* 72.2.
182. Suet., *Tib.* 73.1.
183. Suet., *Tib.* 73.1.
184. Suet., *Tib.* 74.1.
185. Suet., *Tib.* 73.1.
186. Tac., *Ann.* 6.50.
187. *F. Ost.* (*EJ*, p. 43); *ILS* 164; Suet., *Tib.* 73.1. Jer., *Chron.* A37 gives no specific day or month.
188. Dio 58.28.5; Suet., *Tib.* 73.1.
189. Dio 58.28.5 erroneously states 26 March.
190. Suet., *Tib.* 73.2: *Seneca eum scribit intellecta defectione exemptum anulum quasi alicui traditurum parumper tenuisse, dein rursus aptasse digito et compressa sinistra manu iacuisse diu immobilem; subito vocatis ministris ac nemine respondente consurrexisse nec procul a lectulo deficientibus viribus concidisse.* Seneca's description begs the question – since no one came to his aid – how anyone would know precisely what he did in his last moments? Presumably if there was a witness, it was a household slave.
191. Jos., *Ant. Iud.* 18.6.8.

192. Suet., *Caius* 12.2; Suet., *Tib.* 73.2.
193. Suet., *Tib.* 74.1: *cinis e favilla et carbonibus ad calficiendum triclinium inlatis, extinctus iam et diu frigidus, exarsit repente prima vespera atque in multam noctem pertinaciter luxit.*
194. Suet., *Caius* 12.3: *gloriatum enim assidue in commemoranda sua pietate, ad ulciscendam necem matris et fratrum introisse se cum pugione cubiculum Tiberi[i] dormientis et misericordia correptum abiecto ferro recessisse; nec illum, quanquam sensisset, aut inquirere quicquam aut exsequi ausum.*
195. Tac., *Ann.* 6.50.
196. Dio 58.28.3.
197. Perhaps a black humoured reference that the body should be burned as a spectacle for the amusement of the local people for all the disruption caused by Tiberius' comings and goings, with the imposition of necessary security arrangements to ensure his privacy.
198. Suet., Tib. 75.1: '*Tiberium in Tiberim!*' – an obvious pun.
199. Dio 59.3.7.
200. Suet., *Tib.* 76.1.
201. Dio 59.1.2.
202. Dio 59.2.2: thus, a total of ~~HS~~ 300.
203. Dio 59.2.1.
204. Dio 59.2.3. Dio does not specify who 'all the others' are; he might be referring to the soldiers serving in watch towers (*turres*) or at road stations (*mansiones*) or men of the classes (naval fleets).
205. Suet., *Caius* 37.3; *cf.* Dio 59.2.6 quotes ~~HS~~ 2,300 million or, according to other sources, he used, ~~HS~~ 3,300 million.
206. Dio 59.1.2, 59.2.1.
207. Dio 58.28.5, 59.3.8; Suet., *Caius Cal.* 15.1.
208. Dio 59.3.7; Suet., *Tib.* 26 and 27; Tac., *Ann.* 2.87. Fiske (1900), pp.106, 113, notes the existence of *flamines* of a cult devoted to Tiberius in Baetica and Lusitania, and also a temple in Asia.
209. Dio 58.23.3 and 59.1.3. For Ti. Gemellus' claim to be successor and his tragic end, see Lindsay (1993).
210. Galba was emperor after Nero, reigning from 8 June 68–15 January 69 CE. He died at the age of 73.

## CHAPTER 10: REMEMBERING TIBERIUS

1. Dio 59.1.2: *καὶ οἱ ὅρκοι περὶ μὲν τῶν ὑπὸ τοῦ Τιβερίου πραχθέντων οὐκ ἐπήχθησαν, καὶ διὰ τοῦτο οὐδὲ νῦν γίγνονται ʽοὐ γὰρ ἔστιν ὅστις αὐτὸν ἐν τοῖς αὐταρχήσασιν ἐς τὴν τῆς ὁρκίας.*
2. Marsh (1931), p.222.
3. For Paterculus as a source, see Seager (1972), pp.266–269.
4. Vell. Pat. 2.101.3
5. Vell. Pat. 2.101–102.1: *haud iniucunda tot rerum, locorum, gentium, urbium recordatione perfruor.*
6. Vell. Pat., 2.104.3: *caelestissimorum eius operum per annos continuos novem praefectus aut legatus spectator, tum pro captu mediocritatis meae adiutor fui.*
7. Vell. Pat. 2.111.3: *partem exercitus ab urbe traditi ab Augusto perduxi ad filium eius.*
8. Vell. Pat. 2.104.3, 2.111.4. This biography begins with their journey to the frontier, which he recounts sentimentally in his *Roman History*.
9. Vell. Pat. 2.121.3.
10. Vell. Pat. 2.124.4: *ut neque post nos quemquam divus Augustus neque ante nos Caesar commendaret Tiberius.*
11. Vell. Pat. 1.8.1, 1.13.4.

12. Yardley & Barrett (2011). There is no evidence that he was executed in the aftermath of Seianus' fall.
13. Tiberius appears in 2.94–131. For Velleius Paterculus' literary techniques, see Starr (1980).
14. 14–29 CE, assuming work on it was completed before publication in 30 CE.
15. E.g. questions, 2.122, and exclamations, 2.129–30. Syme (1978b) denigrates Paterculus as a historian and is scathing about his selective inclusion of events, citing how he dismisses almost entirely the war against Tacfarinas in Africa. His position is contested comprehensively by Woodman (1977), arguing that Paterculus is no more panegyrical than some of the most admired products of Roman historiography such as Livy and Ammianus. Connal (2013) argues that Paterculus' *History* reveals tensions between the public attitudes of the author as a senator and as a former soldier.
16. Vell. Pat. 2.130.1–2: *Quanta suo suorumque nomine extruxit opera! Quam pia munificentia superque humanam evecta fidem templum patri molitur! Quam magnifico animi temperamento Cn. quoque Pompei munera absumpta igni restituit! Quidquid enim umquam claritudine eminuit, id veluti cognatum censet tuendum. Qua liberalitate cum alias, tum proxime incenso monte Caelio omnis ordinis hominum iacturae patrimonio succurrit suo! Quanta cum quiete hominum rem perpetui praecipuique timoris, supplementum, sine trepidatione dilectus providet!*
17. Vell. Pat. 2.124.1: *neque contra malos opus armis foret.*
18. For Velleius Paterculus' literary style, see Cowan (2009a), Ramage (1982), Starr (1980), Woodman (1975) and Yardley & Barrett (2011), pp.xxii–xxxii. A notable, but later example of the genre, is the *Panegyricus*, written for Trajan by Pliny the Younger.
19. Livy's *Ab Urbe Condita* in 142 volumes covers the years 753–9 BCE, many of which only survive as excerpts.
20. Yardley & Barrett (2011), pp.xxxi–xxxii, note Paterculus does not discuss Tiberius 'until it [*Roman History*] is around 85 per cent complete'. Christ (2001) argues that Paterculus was uniquely placed to write about Tiberius, having seen first-hand how he led men in wartime.
21. Flower (2006) makes no mention of Tiberius having been the subject of *damnatio memoriae*.
22. E.g. Strabo 7.5.3, 13.4.8. Kos (2017), pp.140, 146.
23. Strabo 6.4.2: *καὶ αὐτὴν δὲ τὴν Ἰταλίαν διαστᾶσαν πολλάκις, ἀφ' οὗ γε ὑπὸ Ῥωμαίοις ἐστί, καὶ αὐτὴν τὴν Ῥώμην ἡ τῆς πολιτείας ἀρετὴ καὶ τῶν ἡγεμόνων ἐκώλυσεν ἐπὶ πλέον προελθεῖν πλημμελείας καὶ διαφθορᾶς. χαλεπὸν δὲ ἄλλως διοικεῖν τὴν τηλικαύτην ἡγεμονίαν ἢ ἑνὶ ἐπιτρέψαντας ὡς πατρί. οὐδέποτε γοῦν εὐπορῆσαι τοσαύτης εἰρήνης καὶ ἀφθονίας ἀγαθῶν ὑπῆρξε Ῥωμαίοις καὶ τοῖς συμμάχοις αὐτῶν, ὅσην Καῖσάρ τε ὁ Σεβαστὸς παρέσχεν ἀφ' οὗ παρέλαβε τὴν ἐξουσίαν αὐτοτελῆ, καὶ νῦν ὁ διαδεξάμενος υἱὸς ἐκεῖνον παρέχει Τιβέριος, κανόνα τῆς διοικήσεως καὶ τῶν προσταγμάτων ποιούμενος ἐκεῖνον, καὶ αὐτὸν οἱ παῖδες αὐτοῦ Γερμανικός τε καὶ Δροῦσος ὑπουργοῦντες τῷ πατρί.*
24. Strabo 3.3.8: *ὅ τ' ἐκεῖνον διαδεξάμενος Τιβέριος τριῶν ταγμάτων στρατιωτικὸν ἐπιστήσας τοῖς τόποις, τὸ ἀποδειχθὲν ὑπὸ τοῦ Σεβαστοῦ Καίσαρος, οὐ μόνον εἰρηνικοὺς ἀλλὰ καὶ πολιτικοὺς ἤδη τινὰς αὐτῶν ἀπεργασάμενος τυγχάνει.*
25. Strabo 13.4.8: *ἡ δὲ τοῦ Τιβερίου πρόνοια τοῦ καθ' ἡμᾶς ἡγεμόνος καὶ ταύτην καὶ τῶν ἄλλων συχνὰς ἀνέλαβε ταῖς εὐεργεσίαις, ὅσαι περὶ τὸν αὐτὸν καιρὸν ἐκοινώνησαν τοῦ αὐτοῦ πάθους.*
26. Val. Max. 5.5.3: *princeps parensque noster*; 8.13.init: *salutaris princeps*; 1. *praef.*: *certissima salus patriae*. For Valerius Maximus on the *Domus Augusta*, Augustus and Tiberius, see Wardle (2000). For the impact of civil war on Tiberius, see Gowing (2010).
27. For the perception of Tiberius as wise, see Champlin (2008).
28. Philo, *Leg.* 142.

29. Philo, *Leg.* 33; see also 119, 159, 298. For how Philo critically engages with the idea of Roman emperorship in his descriptions of Augustus and Tiberius, see Christoforou (2021).
30. Philo, *Leg.* 142.
31. Philo, *Leg.* 167.
32. Piano (2019), p.236.
33. Sen., *Clem.* 1.1.5–6: *nemo iam divum Augustum nec Ti. Caesaris prima tempora loquitur nec*. See Malland (2020), p.12.
34. Sen., *Ben.* 5.25.2: *Tiberi Caesar inter initia dicenti cuidam: 'Meministi–' antequam plures notas familiaritatis veteris proferret: 'Non memini', inquit, 'quid fuerim'.*
35. Sen., *Ben.* 5.25.2: *Ab hoc quidni non esset repetendum beneficium? Optanda erat oblivio; aversabatur omnium amicorum et aequalium notitiam et illam solam praesentem fortunam suam adspici, illam solam cogitari ac narrari volebat. Inquisitorem habebat veterem amicum!*
36. Pliny, *Nat. Hist.* 28.6.
37. Pliny, *Nat. Hist.* 28.6: *alia nova optamus cur sternuentes salutamus quod etiam Tiberium Caesarem, tristissimum, ut constat, hominum, in vehiculo exegisse tradunt*. Vell. Pat. 2.114.3 writes that Tiberius preferred to ride on horseback.
38. Pliny, *Nat. Hist.* Preface (Apion); 7.20 (land speed record); 11.54 (night vision), also mentioned by Dio 57.2.4; and 19.23 (cucumbers).
39. Pliny, *Nat. Hist.* 15.40[135]: *Ti. principem tonante caelo coronari ea solitum ferunt contra fulminum metus*; 16.75[194]: *Tiberius item et in capillo tondendo servavit interlunia*.
40. Pliny, *Nat. Hist.* 26.6[9]: *Ti. Caesaris principatu inrepsit id malum, nec quisquam id prior imperatore ipso sensit, magna civitas ambage, cum in edicto eius excusantis valetudinem legeret nomen incognitum*. The name, symptoms and cause of the disease and the date it afflicted Tiberius are not recorded by Pliny.
41. Pliny, *Nat. Hist.* 15.16[40]: *Tiberiana appellantur quae maxime Tiberio principi placuere. colorantur magis sole grandescuntque, alioqui eadem essent quae Liceriana*.
42. Pliny, *Nat. Hist.* 10.60[121]: *Reddatur et corvis sua gratia, indignatione quoque populi Romani testata, non solum conscientia. Tiberio principe ex fetu supra Castorum aedem genito pullus in adpositam sutrinam devolavit, etiam religione commendatus officinae domino. is mature sermoni adsuefactus, omnibus matutinis evolans in rostra in forum versus, Tiberium, dein Germanicum et Drusum Caesares nominatim, mox transeuntem populum Romanum salutabat, postea ad tabernam remeans, plurium annorum adsiduo officio mirus*.
43. Bassus: Tac. *Dial.* 23; Quint., *Inst.* 10.1.103.
44. Nonianus: Tac., *Dial.* 23.2. Rufus: Tac., *Ann.* 13.20, 14.2; Plin., *Ep.* 9.19.5. Rusticus: Tac., *Ann.* 13.20.2, 15.61.
45. Jos., *Ant. Iud.* 18.2.3 (Tiberias), 18.4.6 (active engagement in Judaean affairs), 18.3.5 (banishment), 18.6.5 ('dilatory': *μαρτυρήσει δέ μου τῷ λόγῳ περὶ τῆς ἐπὶ τοιούτοις φύσεως Τιβερίου τὸ ἔργον αὐτό*), 18.6.5 (Agrippa enchained on Capreae) and 18.6.10 (Agrippa: '*τέθνηκεν ὁ λέων*'). The date of the founding of Tiberias is confirmed in Jer., *Chron.* A28. For Josephus' sources, see Goud (1996).
46. Jos., *Ant. Iud.* 18.6.10 [18.227]: *πλεῖστα γὰρ ἀνὴρ εἷς οὗτος Ῥωμαίων τοὺς εὐπατρίδας εἰργάσατο δεινὰ δυσόργητος ἐπὶ πᾶσιν ὢν καὶ ἀνήκεστος εἰς τὸ ἐργάζεσθαι καταστάς, εἰ καὶ χωρὶς λόγου τὴν αἰτίαν ἐπανέλοιτο τοῦ μισεῖν, καὶ ἐπὶ πᾶσι μὲν οἷς κρίνοιεν ἐξαγριοῦν φύσιν ἔχων, εἰς θάνατον δὲ καὶ τῶν κουφοτάτων ἀνατιθεὶς τὴν ζημίαν. ὥστε ἡδονῇ τοῦ ἐπ' αὐτῷ λόγου φέροντος τὴν ἀκρόασιν εἰς ὅσον ἐβούλοντο ἀπολαύσματι χρῆσθαι ἐπεκεκώλυντο δείμασι κακῶν, ἃ προεωρᾶτο ψευσθεῖσι τῆς ἐλπίδος.*
47. For the reliability of Josephus, see Huntsman (1996).
48. The obverses of both coins read *TI CAESAR DIVI AVG F AVGVST IMP VIII* and show a bare head of Tiberius facing left. Numismatic references: *RCV* 2591 and *RIC* II 413; Cohen 73; *BMC* (Titus) 284; Sear 2595. See Appendix 2(b).

49. The obverse reads *TI CAESAR DIVI AVG F AVGVST IMP VIII* and shows a bare head of Tiberius facing left. Numismatic reference: *RIC* II 826; *BMC* (Domitian) 509; Sear 2895. See Appendix 2(b).
50. Suet., *Dom.* 20.1: *Praeter commentarios et acta Tiberii Caesaris nihil lectitabat; epistolas orationesque et edicta alieno formabat ingenio.*
51. Marsh (1931), p.222.
52. Champlin (2008), p.418; Harrer (1920), pp.66–67.
53. Power (2014), p.205 argues that *Annales* was published, 'at least in part', by 118 CE.
54. For a forensic analysis of Tacitus' sources, see Marsh (1931), pp.233–266; *cf.* Seager (1972), pp.256–262.
55. Tac., *Ann.* 1.81: *vix quicquam firmare ausim: adeo diversa non modo apud auctores, sed in ipsius orationibus reperiuntur*; *cf.* 1.69, 2.88, 3.3, 3.16. For a discussion of Tacitus' use of written sources, see Marsh (1931), pp.233–266, who concludes that 'We should … accept his statements of fact in all cases except a few where we have strong grounds for questioning his accuracy' (p.266).
56. Tac., *Ann.* 3.16: *neque tamen occulere debui narratum ab iis qui nostram ad iuventam duraverunt.*
57. Tac., *Ann.* 13.20: *nos consensum auctorum secuturi, quae diversa prodiderint, sub nominibus ipsorum trademus*. For Tacitus' use of rumour and historiography in his account of the death of Drusus, see Feldherr (2009).
58. Harrer (1920), p.67.
59. Tac., *Ann.* 1.4: *pars multo maxima inminentis dominos variis rumoribus differebant … Tiberium Neronem maturum annis, spectatum bello, sed vetere atque insita Claudiae familiae superbia, multaque indicia saevitiae, quamquam premantur, erumpere. hunc et prima ab infantia eductum in domo regnatrice; congestos iuveni consulatus, triumphos; ne iis quidem annis, quibus Rhodi specie secessus exul egerit, aliud quam iram et simulationem et secretas lubidines meditatum.*
60. Tac., *Ann.* 6.51: *Sic Tiberius finivit octavo et septuagesimo aetatis anno. Pater ei Nero et utrimque origo gentis Claudiae, quamquam mater in Liviam et mox Iuliam familiam adoptionibus transierit. casus prima ab infantia ancipites; nam proscriptum patrem exul secutus, ubi domum Augusti privignus introiit, multis aemulis conflictatus est, dum Marcellus et Agrippa, mox Gaius Luciusque Caesares viguere; etiam frater eius Drusus prosperiore civium amore erat. sed maxime in lubrico egit accepta in matrimonium Iulia, impudicitiam uxoris tolerans aut declinans. dein Rhodo regressus vacuos principis penatis duodecim annis, mox rei Romanae arbitrium tribus ferme et viginti obtinuit. morum quoque tempora illi diversa: egregium vita famaque quoad privatus vel in imperiis sub Augusto fuit; occultum ac subdolum fingendis virtutibus donec Germanicus ac Drusus superfuere; idem inter bona malaque mixtus incolumi matre; intestabilis saevitia sed obtectis libidinibus dum Seianum dilexit timuitve: postremo in scelera simul ac dedecora prorupit postquam remoto pudore et metu suo tantum ingenio utebatur.*
61. Woodman (2006a), pp.175, 180–181, where he notes that the first half of Tiberius' principate exactly covers Books 1–3, the last half Books 4–6. *Cf.* Harrer (1920), pp.65–66, comparing Tacitus with Suetonius in dividing Tiberius' life into distinctive parts, though not in exactly the same ways.
62. For Sallust's moralistic treatment of the history of the Late Roman Republic, see Levick (1982).
63. Tac., *Ann.* 1.1: *Tiberii Gaique et Claudii ac Neronis res florentibus ipsis ob metum falsae, postquam occiderant, recentibus odiis compositae sunt. inde consilium mihi pauca de Augusto et extrema tradere, mox Tiberii principatum et cetera, sine ira et studio, quorum causas procul habeo.*

64. Harrer (1920), pp.58–59; Mellor (2011), p.41.
65. Tac. *Ann.* 3.65: *Exequi sententias haud institui nisi insignis per honestum aut notabili dedecore, quod praecipuum munus annalium reor ne virtutes sileantur utque pravis dictis factisque ex posteritate et infamia metus sit. ceterum tempora illa adeo infecta et adulatione sordida fuere ut non modo primores civitatis, quibus claritudo sua obsequiis protegenda erat, sed omnes consulares, magna pars eorum qui praetura functi multique etiam pedarii senatores certatim exsurgerent foedaque et nimia censerent. memoriae proditur Tiberium, quoties curia egrederetur, Graecis verbis in hunc modum eloqui solitum 'o homines ad servitutem paratos!' scilicet etiam illum qui libertatem publicam nollet tam proiectae servientium patientiae taedebat.*
66. Harrer (1920), p.67.
67. Strunk (2017), pp.1–6.
68. Syme (1974); Harrer (1920); Ryberg (1942).
69. Tac., *Ann.* 7.1: *At Romae ruere in servitium consules, patres, eques. quanto quis inlustrior, tanto magis falsi ac festinantes.*
70. Harrer (1920), p.67: 'Tacitus may properly be accused of failing to see, or even of not wanting to see – perhaps for the sake of the unity of his conception of Tiberius – the discrepancies between acts and the interpretations put on them, and between proper, sane interpretation and exaggeration. This is a bad fault.'
71. Mellor (2011), pp.99–100; Powell (2013), pp.214–218.
72. Tac., *Ann.* 2.5: *provinciis impositum dolo simul et casibus obiectaret.*
73. E.g. Tac., *Ann.* 2.54, 2.55, 3.19.
74. Tac., *Ann.* 1.69: *accendebat haec onerabatque Seianus, peritia morum Tiberii odia in longum iaciens.*
75. Cowan (2009b) cites Tac., *Ann.* 1.77.1–3, 2.37–38.5, 4.37–38.3, 6.3.1–3.
76. Tac., *Ann.* 6.51, 4.14: *variis dehinc et saepius inritis praetorum questibus, postremo Caesar de immodestia histrionum rettulit: multa ab iis in publicum seditiose, foeda per domos temptari; Oscum quondam ludicrum, levissimae apud vulgum oblectationis, eo flagitiorum et virium venisse ut auctoritate patrum coercendum sit. pulsi tum histriones Italia.*
77. Tac., *Ann.* 4.32: *nobis in arto et inglorius labor.*
78. Tac., *Ann.* 4.34: *Romanorum ultimum dixisset.*
79. Tac., *Ann.* 4.34: *novo ac tunc primum audito crimine.*
80. Tac., *Ann.* 4.35.
81. Tac., *Agr.* 2–3, 40–46.
82. *Cf.* Dorey (1960), Nesselhauf (1952), Fritz (1957) and Woodhead (1948).
83. For this lost work, see Georgiadou (1988) and Stadter (2014), pp.56–69.
84. In the *Lamprias Catalogue* as item no. 27, and in the *Synopsis Historion*, a concordance by the Byzantine Greek historian Georgios Kedrenos (George Cedrenus, Eleventh Century CE).
85. Tiberius also appears in the *Lives* of *Divus* Augustus, Caius, Galba and Domitian.
86. For Suetonius as a source, see Seager (1972), pp.262–264.
87. E.g. 'it is said': 62.3, 69.1; 'commonly' or 'even believed': 21.2, 52.3, 62.3; 'some think': 9.2, 10.1, 51.1, 52.3, 67.2, 73.2.
88. Suet., *Tib.* 44.1: *Maiore adhuc ac turpiore infamia flagravit, vix ut referri audirive, nedum credi fas sit.* Commenting on Suetonius' allegations about the 'Old Goat's Garden' (see Ch. 9, n.32), Brandão (2003), p.301 observes that 'Although he says it all takes place in the secrecy of the island, the biographer describes the whole scene using the perfect as if he had witnessed it, which seems suspicious.'
89. Suet., *Tib.* 21.3: *Adduci tamen nequeo quin existimem, circumspectissimum et prudentissimum principem in tanto praesertim negotio nihil temere fecisse; sed vitiis Tiberi[i] virtutibusque*

*perpensis potiores duxisse virtutes, praesertim cum et rei p. causa adoptare se eum pro contione iuraverit et epistulis aliquot ut peritissimum rei militaris utque unicum p. R. praesidium prosequatur. Ex quibus in exemplum pauca hinc inde subieci.*

90. Suet., *Tib.* 62.2: *Carnificinae eius ostenditur locus Capreis, unde damnatos post longa et exquisita tormenta praecipitari coram se in mare iubebat, excipiente classiariorum manu et contis atque remis elidente cadavera, ne cui residui spiritus quicquam inesset. Excogitaverat autem inter genera cruciatus etiam, ut larga meri potione per fallaciam oneratos, repente veretris deligatis, fidicularum simul urinaeque tormento distenderet.*
91. Suetonius includes stories of each of the Caesars' excesses. Gunderson (2014) argues that having portrayed Augustus as the flawed exemplar of imperial rule, every one of his successors are shown in turn to be lesser than him (p.131) – Tiberius, in particular, for allegedly openly indulging his vices (pp.143–44).
92. His career is recorded on *AE* 1953.73 Hippo Regius.
93. Suet., *Tib.* 21.3–6, 67.1.
94. Suet., *Tib.* 57.1, 73.2.
95. Harrer (1920), p.67.
96. Thorburn (2008), pp.436 (noting the frequency of use of the Latin word for 'return' in 4.3, 6.3, 11.1, 13.2, 14.1, 14.4, 32.2, 38.1, 39.1, 52.2, 61.5, 72.1, 72.2), 442.
97. Mitchell (2015), p.339.
98. Suet., *Tib.* 26.1: *Verum liberatus metu civilem admodum inter initia ac paulo minus quam privatum egit.*
99. E.g. Suet., *Tib.* 41–45, 57–62. *Cf.* Harrer (1920), pp.67–68.
100. For Dio as a source, see Seager (1972), pp.264–266.
101. Dio 56.45.1: *τοῦ γὰρ Τιβερίου μετ᾽ αὐτὸν οὐχ ὁμοίου πειραθέντες ἐκεῖνον ἐζήτουν.*
102. Dio, 57.1.1–6: *ταῦτα μὲν κατὰ Αὔγουστον ἐγένετο, Τιβέριος δὲ εὐπατρίδης μὲν ἦν καὶ ἐπεπαίδευτο, φύσει δὲ ἰδιωτάτῃ ἐκέχρητο. οὔτε γὰρ ὧν ἐπεθύμει προσεποιεῖτό τι, καὶ ὧν ἔλεγεν οὐδὲν ὡς εἰπεῖν ἐβούλετο, ἀλλ᾽ ἐναντιωτάτους τῇ προαιρέσει τοὺς λόγους ποιούμενος πᾶν τε ὃ ἐπόθει ἠρνεῖτο καὶ πᾶν ὃ ἐμίσει προετείνετο: ὠργίζετό τε ἐν οἷς ἥκιστα ἐθυμοῦτο, καὶ ἐπιεικὴς ἐν οἷς μάλιστα ἠγανάκτει ἐδόκει εἶναι: ἠλέει τε δῆθεν οὓς σφόδρα ἐκόλαζε, καὶ ἐχαλέπαινεν οἷς συνεγίγνωσκε: τόν τε ἔχθιστον ὡς οἰκειότατον ἔστιν ὅτε ἑώρα, καὶ τῷ φιλτάτῳ ὡς ἀλλοτριωτάτῳ προσεφέρετο. τό τε σύμπαν οὐκ ἠξίου τὸν αὐταρχοῦντα κατάδηλον ὧν φρονεῖ εἶναι: ἔκ τε γὰρ τούτου πολλὰ καὶ μεγάλα πταίεσθαι καὶ ἐκ τοῦ ἐναντίου πολλῷ πλείω καὶ μείζω κατορθοῦσθαι ἔλεγε. καὶ εἰ μὲν μόνα ταῦτ᾽ εἶχεν, εὐφύλακτος ἂν τοῖς ἐς πεῖραν αὐτοῦ ἐλθοῦσιν ἦν: πρὸς γάρ τοι τὸ ἐναντιώτατον πάντα ἂν λαμβάνοντες ἐκ τοῦ ἴσου τό τε μὴ βούλεσθαι δή τι αὐτὸν τῷ πάνυ ποθεῖν καὶ τὸ ὀρέγεσθαί τινος τῷ μὴ ἐφίεσθαι ἐνόμιζον: νῦν δὲ ὠργίζετο εἴ τις αὐτοῦ συνεὶς φανερὸς ἐγένετο, καὶ πολλοὺς οὐδὲν ἄλλο σφίσιν ἢ ὅτι συνενόησαν αὐτὸν ἐγκαλέσαι ἔχων ἀπέκτεινεν. ὥστε χαλεπὸν μὲν ἦν μηδεμίαν αὐτοῦ σύνεσιν ποιεῖσθαι ῾πολλὰ γὰρ ἅτε πρὸς τὸ λεγόμενον ἀλλὰ μὴ πρὸς τὸ βουλόμενον συναινοῦντές οἱ ἐσφάλλοντὸ, χαλεπώτερον δὲ συνιέναι: τήν τε γὰρ ἐπιτήδευσιν αὐτοῦ καταφωρᾶν κἀκ τούτου καὶ ἄχθεσθαι αὐτῇ ὑπωπτεύοντο. μόνος 1 οὖν ὡς εἰπεῖν, ὅπερ που σπανιώτατόν ἐστι, διεγένετο ὃς οὔτ᾽ ἠγνόησε τὴν φύσιν αὐτοῦ οὔτ᾽ ἤλεγξεν: οὕτω γὰρ οὔτε πιστεύσαντές οἱ ἠπατήθησαν, οὔτε ἐνδειξάμενοι νοεῖν ἃ ἔπραττεν ἐμισήθησαν. πάνυ γὰρ πολὺν ὄχλον παρεῖχεν, εἴτε τις ἐναντιοῖτο οἷς ἔλεγεν εἴτε καὶ συναίροιτο: τὸ μὲν γὰρ ἀληθῶς γενέσθαι τὸ δὲ δοκεῖν βούλεσθαι ἐθέλων, πάντως τέ τινας πρὸς ἑκάτερον ἐναντιουμένους εἶχε, καὶ διὰ τοῦτο τοὺς μὲν τῆς ἀληθείας τοὺς δὲ τῆς δοκήσεως ἕνεκα ἤχθαιρε.*
103. Dio 58.28.5: *Τιβέριος μὲν δὴ πλείστας μὲν ἀρετὰς πλείστας δὲ καὶ κακίας ἔχων, καὶ ἑκατέραις αὐταῖς ὡς καὶ μόναις κεχρημένος, οὕτω μετήλλαξε τῇ ἕκτῃ καὶ εἰκοστῇ τοῦ Μαρτίου ἡμέρᾳ.*
104. Barnes (1984), pp. 241–245; Introduction to Mallan (2020), pp.2–5, 33–34.
105. Mallan (2020), p.30.
106. Dio 1.1.2: *ἀνέγνων μὲν πάντα ὡς εἰπεῖν τὰ περὶ αὐτῶν τισι γεγραμμένα, συνέγραψα δὲ οὐ πάντα ἀλλ᾽ ὅσα ἐξέκρινα. μὴ μέντοι μηδ᾽ ὅτι κεκαλλιεπημένοις, ἐς ὅσον γε καὶ τὰ πράγματα ἐπέτρεψε, λόγοις*

*κέχρημαι, ἐς τὴν ἀλήθειαν αὐτῶν διὰ τοῦτό τις ὑποπτεύσῃ, ὅπερ ἐπ᾽ ἄλλων τινῶν συμβέβηκεν: ἐγὼ γὰρ ἀμφότερα, ὡς οἷόν τε ἦν, ὁμοίως ἀκριβῶσαι ἐσπούδασα.*

107. Bellemore (2003), p.268.
108. For Thucydides as a historian, see Banner (2021), pp.73–81, 143; for Dio, see Mallan (2020), pp.32–33.
109. Mallan (2020), p.26.
110. Dio 55.23–24.
111. *Cos.* L. Norbanus: Dio 57.18.3; Tiberius' sayings: 57.2.3, 57.2.6, 57.7.4, 57.8.2, 57.9.2, 57.10.5, 57.13.3, 57.18.2, 15.19.1, 57.19.4, 57.21.1, 57.24.8, 58.3.7, 58.23.3, 58.23.4, 58.24.4, 58.28.4.
112. Dio 2.31.1: *οὐ μέντοι καὶ ἐκφανὴς εὐθὺς ὁ θάνατος αὐτοῦ ἐγένετο: ἡ γὰρ Λιουία, φοβηθεῖσα μὴ τοῦ Τιβερίου ἐν τῇ Δελματίᾳ ἔτ᾽ ὄντος νεωτερισθῇ τι, συνέκρυψεν αὐτὸν μέχρις οὗ ἐκεῖνος ἀφίκετο. ταῦτα γὰρ οὕτω τοῖς τε πλείοσι καὶ τοῖς ἀξιοπιστοτέροις γέγραπται: εἰσὶ γάρ τινες οἳ καὶ παραγενέσθαι τὸν Τιβέριον τῇ νόσῳ αὐτοῦ καὶ ἐπισκήψεις τινὰς παρ᾽ αὐτοῦ λαβεῖν ἔφασαν.*
113. E.g. Dio 53.19.2, 57.16.2, 57.21.5, 57.23.2.
114. Townend (1961).
115. Power (2014); Mallan (2020), pp.6–9, 28.
116. For a general comparison of Tacitus, Suetonius and Dio as sources, see Marsh (1931), pp.272–283.
117. For a discussion of the events of 14 CE, see Malloch (2004); for 33 CE, see Syme (1983) and Woodman (2006a).
118. Luke 3:1.
119. See Preface, n.5.
120. Luke 3:1; Mark 15:1–15; John 19:1–22.
121. For discussions of the New Testament *Apocrypha*, see Cheek (1958) and Reed (2015).
122. The story, *Cura Sanitatis Tiberii*, is told in a supplement to the Gospel of Nicodemus in the New Testament *Apocrypha*, believed to have been composed between the fifth and seventh centuries CE.
123. For the authenticity of these two letters, see Winter (1964) and the blog of Roger Pearse (https://www.roger-pearse.com, accessed 24 March 2024), entries for 11 May 2012 and 3 October 2016.
124. Tert., *Apol.* 21.24: *Ea omnia super Christo Pilatus, et ipse iam pro sua conscientia Christianus, Caesari tunc Tiberio nuntiavit.*
125. Tert., *Apol.* 5.1: *Tiberius ergo, cuius tempore nomen Christianum in saeculum introivit, adnuntiatum sibi ex Syria Palaestina, quod illic veritatem ipsius divinitatis revelaverat, detulit ad senatum cum praerogativa suffragii sui. Senatus, quia non ipse probaverat, respuit; Caesar in sententia mansit, comminatus periculum accusatoribus Christianorum.*
126. Acts 8:4–9. Province Iudaea was renamed by Hadrian as Syria Palaestina after the Bar Kokhba War ended in 135/136 CE: Powell (2021), p.148.
127. Euseb., *Hist. Eccl.* 2.2.1: *τὰ περὶ τῆς ἐκ νεκρῶν ἀναστάσεως τοῦ σωτῆρος ἡμῶν Ἰησοῦ εἰς πάντας ἤδη καθ ὅλης Παλαιστίνης βεβοημένα Πιλᾶτος Τιβερίῳ βασιλεῖ κοινοῦται, τάς τε ἄλλας αὐτοῦ πυθόμενος τεραστίας καὶ ὡς ὅτι μετὰ θάνατον ἐκ νεκρῶν ἀναστὰς ἤδη θεὸς εἶναι παρὰ τοῖς πολλοῖς πεπίστευτο.*
128. Euseb., *Hist. Eccl.* 2.2.3: *τὸν Τιβέριον ἣν καὶ πρότερον εἶχεν γνώμην τηρήσαντα, μηδὲν ἄτοπον κατὰ τῆς τοῦ Χριστοῦ διδασκαλίας ἐπινοῆσαι.*
129. Euseb., *Hist. Eccl.* 2.2.6: *ἡ δὲ σύγκλητος, ἐπεὶ οὐκ αὐτὴ δεδοκιμάκει, ἀπώσατο: ὁ δὲ ἐν τῇ αὐτοῦ ἀποφάσει ἔμεινεν, ἀπειλήσας θάνατον τοῖς τῶν Χριστιανῶν κατηγόροις.*
130. Oros., *Pagan.* 7.6–7: *Senatus indignatione motus, cur non sibi prius secundum morem delatum esset, ut de suscipiendo cultu prius ipse decerneret, consecrationem Christi recusauit edictoque constituit, exterminandos esse urbe Christianos; praecipue cum et Seianus praefectus*

*Tiberii suscipiendae religioni obstinatissime contradiceret. Tiberius tamen edicto accusatoribus Christianorum mortem comminatus est.*

131. For a discussion of the historicity of Tertullian, see Monachino (1974), Papini (1934), pp.40ff, and Cecchelli (1956), pp.351ff. Sordi (1957, 1960 and 1965) argues strongly for the truth of Tertullian's account regarding Pilatus' report and Tiberius' proposal for deification to the Senate, and argues the negative decision of the Senate was the juridical basis of the Christians' later persecution.
132. Euseb., *Hist. Eccl.* 2.2.6.
133. Jer., *Chron.* B2, while B1 gives the year 1 BCE.
134. They include the deaths of orator Asinius Gallus and historian Livy, Germanicus' triumph, the earthquakes in Asia, the consulship of Drusus and the appointment of Pilatus.
135. The date of the crucifixion appointment is confirmed in Jer., *Chron.* A32. In B2, he writes 'and [Jesus] suffered in the 15th [year] of Tiberius', which would be 29 CE, explaining in A32 that he began teaching then for the next three years.
136. Jer., *Chron.* A36.
137. Jul., *Ad Themist.* 265c: *Θράσυλλος δὲ Τιβερίῳ πικρῷ καὶ φύσει χαλεπῷ τυράννῳ ξυγγενόμενος.*
138. Jul., *Sat.* 309c–310a: *Τρίτος ἐπεισέδραμεν αὐτοῖς Τιβέριος σεμνὸς τὰ πρόσωπα καὶ βλοσυρός, σῶφρόν τε ἅμα καὶ πολεμικὸν βλέπων. ἐπιστραφέντος δὲ πρὸς τὴν καθέδραν ὤφθησαν ὠτειλαὶ κατὰ τὸν νῶτον μυρίαι, καυτῆρές τινες καὶ ξέσματα καὶ πληγαὶ χαλεπαὶ καὶ μώλωπες ὑπό τε ἀκολασίας καὶ ὠμότητος ψῶραί τινες καὶ λειχῆνες οἷον ἐγκεκαυμέναι. εἶθ ὁ Σειληνὸς Ἀλλοῖός μοι, ξεῖνε, φάνης νέον ἢ τὸ πάροιθεν εἰπὼν ἔδοξεν αὑτοῦ φαίνεσθαι σπουδαιότερος. καὶ ὁ Διόνυσος πρὸς αὐτόν, Τί δῆτα, εἶπεν, ὦ παππίδιον σπουδάζεις; καὶ ὅς, Ἐξέπληξέ με ὁ γέρων οὑτοσί, ὁ Σάτυρος, ἔφη, καὶ πεποίηκεν ἐκλαθόμενον ἐμαυτοῦ τὰς Ὁμηρικὰς προβαλέσθαι μούσας. ἀλλά σε, εἶπεν, ἕλξει τῶν ὤτων: λέγεται γὰρ αὐτὸς καὶ γραμματιστήν τινα τοῦτο ἐργάσασθαι. οἰμώζων μὲν οὖν, εἶπεν, ἐν τῷ νησυδρίῳ: τὰς Καπρέας αἰνιττόμενος: τὸν ἄθλιον ἁλιέα ψηχέτω.*
139. Suet., *Tib.* 60.1.
140. Zos., *Hist. Nova* 1.6.2: *Τιβέριος ὁ παρὰ τούτου διαδεξάμενος τὴν ἀρχὴν εἰς ἔσχατον ὠμότητος ἐκτραπεὶς ἀφόρητός τε δόξας εἶναι τοῖς ὑπηκόοις ἀπεδιώκετο καὶ ἔν τινι νήσῳ κρυπτόμενος ἐτελεύτησεν.*
141. Tiberius II Constantinus (Ancius Thrax Flavius Constantius, 578–582 CE), Mauricius Tiberius (Maurice, 582–602 CE), Tiberius III Apsimaros (698–705 CE), Tiberius (co-ruler with Justinian II, 705–711 CE).
142. Sanford (1944), p.41.
143. Gerald, *De Principis Instructione*, c.1.17, 216–217 *De tyrannorum obitu et fine cruento*, and c.1.18, 264–309 *De principum electorum tam vita laudabili quam fine.*

## CHAPTER 11: REIMAGINING TIBERIUS

1. On the date and route by which manuscripts of Suetonius' *Caesars* entered France during the Middle Ages, see Rand (1926). Thus, the first half of the text of *The Annals* was preserved in a single manuscript at Corvey Abbey, Germany, and the second half in a single manuscript at Monte Cassino, Italy.
2. Syme (1974), p.495.
3. Greenway: Feingold (2016); Elizabeth I: Philo (2020).
4. A copy of the Prüss edition is held at Duke University Library; it incorporates pages of vellum featuring an eleventh-century manuscript of Lucan's *Pharsalia* Book 4, lines 634–59, 667–92 and 700–25.
5. The first approved English translation of the Bible known as the King James Version was commissioned in 1604 and published in 1611.
6. Macchiaveli, *Discorsi Sopra La Prima Deca De Tito Livio*, Book III, Chapter VI – *Delle Congiure* ('Of Conspiracies)'.

7. The first text was circulated from 1513 under the Latin title *De Principatibus* ('Of Principalities').
8. Beard (2020), pp.151–166: they were the usual Twelve Caesars, omitting Domitian.
9. Beard (2021), pp.151–154. The painting, inscribed 'TIBERIO•C• / •III•' (upper left), took part in the famous Art Treasures Exhibition held in Manchester, 5 May–17 October 1857. It was auctioned by Christie's on 2 December 2014 and sold to a private buyer for £3,250.
10. For the full collection, see Beard (2021), plate 5.2.
11. The painting now hangs in the Ashmolean, Oxford, England (WA1989.74).
12. Rubens' double image of a Roman imperial couple, traditionally called *Tiberius and Agrippina*, painted around 1614, and which now hangs in The National Gallery of Art in Washington (1963.8.1), is now believed to be of Germanicus and Agrippina Maior: Van Wagenberg-Ter Hoeven, (2005).
13. The painting is in the collections of Musée d'Orsay, Paris, France (MN 67). His masterpiece, *Les Exilés* won Barrisa an award at the official Salon of 1850–51.
14. The painting is in the collections of the Tretyakov Gallery, Moscow, Russian Federation.
15. The painting is in the collections of Musée Paul-Dupuy de Toulouse, France.
16. Beard (2021), p.227, argues that the figure is Macro.
17. Shakespeare's Roman plays are *The Tragedie of Julius Caesar*, first performed in 1599, and *The Tragedie of Anthonie, and Cleopatra*, staged in 1607.
18. *Sejanus His Fall*, Act 1, scene 2.
19. *Sejanus His Fall*, Act 1, scene 2; *cf.* Tac., *Ann.* 4.38.
20. *Sejanus His Fall*, Act 3, scene 1.
21. *Sejanus His Fall*, Act 3, scene 3.
22. *Sejanus His Fall*, Act 3, scene 3.
23. Gary Taylor, 'The butcher of Rome', *Guardian*, 18 July 2005.
24. Online: https://www.redbulltheater.com/sejanus (accessed 24 March 2024).
25. Anon., *The Tragedie of Claudius Tiberius Nero*, 3123–24.
26. Anon., *The Tragedie of Claudius Tiberius Nero*, 3339–40. *Cf.* Dio 58.23.4.
27. Anon., *The Tragedie of Claudius Tiberius Nero*, 3343.
28. '*Mais je ne suis pas né pour cet excès d'honneur*': *Tibère*, Act 1, Scene 4, line 239.
29. *Tibère: Tragédie avec une Analyse de Cette Piece*, par M. Népomucene Lemercier, Paris: Ponthieu (1819).
30. The five-act structure was inspired by Roman tragedy: *Acte* 1: *L'exposition* (Exposition); *Acte* 2: *Action montante* (Rising Action); *Acte* 3: *Le point culminant* (Climax); *Acte* 4: *Action en chute* (Falling Action); and *Acte* 5: *dénouement ou resolution* (Resolution). See Gustav Freytag's *Die Technik des Dramas* (1863), published in an English translation as *Technique of the Drama: An Exposition of Dramatic Composition and Art* (1894).
31. Lucien Émile Arnault, *Le Dernier Jour de Tibère*, Act 5, Scene 7: *Sous un complot perfide / Je tombe , mais je règne ; et les dieux par vos bras / Sont prêts à châtier le plus vil des ingrats.*
32. Macron: *Le monde obéira*. Cayus: *Macron sera jugé*.
33. Jules Lemaître, *Impressions de théâtre*. Huitième série *Tibère à Caprée*, 6 May 1895: '*Ce drame est amusant; il est, en quelques en droits, remarquable. … Il y a une chrétienne (déjà!): Blandine, fille de Nerva. Nerva ayant conspiré, Tibère s'empare de Blandine, et veut d'abord la déshonorer en la livrant à un esclave. Elle se tire de ce mauvais pas. Tibère, alors, la condamne aux lions, parce qu'elle a blasphémé les dieux de l'empire. Et, au quatrième acte, elle se venge du tyran en lui sauvant la vie.*'
34. Bastien (2006), p.76.
35. The drama was translated into English by the American Frank J. Morlock and published in 2010 as *Tiberius Caesar: A Play in Five Acts*.

36. Jules Lemaître, *Impressions de théâtre*. Huitième série *Tibère à Caprée*, 6 May 1895: '*un très beau drame ... Tibère ... nettement et vigoureusement dessiné ... est vivant.*'
37. Bastien (2006), pp.76–77.
38. Jules Lemaître, *Impressions de théâtre*. Huitième série *Tibère à Caprée*, 6 May 1895: '*M. Rzéwuski a fait de lui un nihiliste hypocondre qu'une hideuse expérience et le parfait mépris de l'humanité, joints au vertige de la toute-puissance, et aussi à une satiété affreuse qui n'exclut ni la peur de la mort ni la terreur de perdre ce dont il est pourtant assouvi, ont rendu en partie monstrueux.*'
39. *INTÉRIM, Revue bleue: revue politique et littéraire* no 19, 4 série – Tome 1, 12 May 1894, pp.601–602: '*Le vieillard résiste, retrouve un reste de forces, appelle, va déshériter l'assassin: mais bientôt il se ravise, car sa haine du genre humain est plus forte que le souci de sa vengeance personnelle, et il expire monstrueusement heureux de léguer aux Romains un maitre capable de leur faire regretter Tibère.*'
40. *INTÉRIM, Revue bleue: revue politique et littéraire* no 19, 4 série – Tome 1, 12 May 1894, pp.601–602: '*Ce drame plein d'obscurités, de longueurs et d'intérêt, ... honorablement joué M.M. Taillade, Tibère entaché de romantisme.*'
41. Jules Lemaître, *Impressions de théâtre*. Huitième série *Tibère à Caprée*, 6 May 1895: '*Il y a, dans ce Tibère à Caprée, un très beau drame, – mais trop de choses autour.*'
42. Jules Lemaître, *Impressions de théâtre*. Huitième série *Tibère à Caprée*, 6 May 1895: '*Quant aux rencontres de M. Rzéwuski avec Ben Johnson, Arnault, Victor Séjour, Marie-Joseph Chénier et M. Ferdinand Dugué, n'étaient-elles point inévitables? Et est-il bien utile d'en parle?*'
43. W.M. Rosetti, Introduction to Francis Adams, *Tiberius: A Drama* (1894), pp.15–16. The reference is to Adams' *Songs of the Army of the Night* (1894), a book of radical socialist ballads.
44. Francis Adams, *Tiberius: A Drama* (1894), Act 3, pp.135–136.
45. W.M. Rosetti, Introduction to Francis Adams, *Tiberius: A Drama* (1894), p.25.
46. The full text of the play with Rosetti's Introduction can be downloaded at https://archive.org/details/cu31924013205038/page/n26/mode/1up?ref=ol&_autoReadAloud=show&view=theater (accessed 24 March 2024).
47. Graves (1934), The Great Writers edition by Marshall Cavendish Ltd (1988), p.32.
48. Graves (1934), pp.32, 33.
49. Penguin Books. *I, Claudius* was first published in hardback by Arthur Baker Ltd in 1934, then by Methuen and Co. Ltd in 1939.
50. Suet., *Tib.* 61.1.
51. Retitled *Let the Emperor Speak: A Novel of Caesar Augustus* in the USA.
52. Review of *Tiberius: The Memoirs of the Emperor* in *Publisher's Weekly* (1993, https://www.publishersweekly.com/9780786700073, accessed 24 March 2024). Historian Bowersock (1999), p.134 remarks that Tiberius may have felt trapped by Roman politics and society and retired to Capreae to escape them, and seen 'in these terms ... make of Tiberius' life something more tragic than criminal.'
53. The series of novels includes Julius Caesar, Mark Antony, Augustus, Tiberius, Caligula and Nero's heirs.
54. Tom Pinch, Introduction, *Tiberius Caesar* (2023).
55. Magerstädt (2019), pp.34–36.
56. Magerstädt (2019), p.34.
57. Conrad Brunstrom, 'So, overall ... which is better – "The Caesars" (1968) or "I Claudius" (1976)?', 16 March 2019 (https://conradbrunstrom.wordpress.com/2019/03/16/so-overall-which-is-better-the-caesars-1968-or-i-claudius-1976/, accessed 24 March 2024).
58. *The Caesars*, episode 3, 'Tiberius', quoted by Magerstädt (2019), p.35.

59. Magerstädt (2019), pp.36–37.
60. Christian Niedan, *I, Claudius*, 25 August 2017: https://atlargemagazine.com/journal/i-claudius-series/.
61. Episode 2 'Family Affairs', Scene 3 'Marcus Makes a Request'. The imagined scene sees Drusus in Illyricum and Tiberius going to Germania, when the reverse was actually true.
62. Quoted from the PBS Shop (https://shop.pbs.org/XA1862.html, accessed 24 March 2024).
63. Melanie McDonagh, 'Hail the return of *I, Claudius*, the BBC's greatest-ever drama', *Evening Standard*, 7 August 2023.
64. Sarah Hemming, 'The Inn at Lydda, Sam Wanamaker Playhouse, London – review', *Financial Times*, 8 September 2016; Michael Billington, 'The Inn at Lydda review – Christ is risen for a showdown with Caesar', *Guardian*, 7 September 2016; and Peter Greystone, 'Legendary date with the Lord', *Church Times*, 9 September 2016.
65. *Barbaren*, Season 2, episode 2.
66. *Barbaren*, Season 2, episode 2.
67. Rotten Tomatoes and their Tomatometer, 'the world's most trusted recommendation resources for quality entertainment', showed that 'Reviewers' (professional film and TV critics) rated *Barbaren* more highly than the 'TV Audience' (viewers).
68. *Domina*, Series 1, episode 6: Nightshade (2021).
69. *Domina*, Series 1, episode 8: Happiness (2021).
70. The forum scenes of *Domina* were shot at Cinecittà using the set built for HBO's *Rome* (2004–2007). Ridiculously long tunics and leather armour spoil the authenticity of the production. Nevertheless, according to Rotten Tomatoes, the TV audience rated it highly, giving it about the same score as the Reviewers, rating it noticeably higher than *Barbaren*.
71. Examples: Baron Gaston de Montesquieu's *Considérations sur les causes de la grandeur des Romains et de leur décadence* (1734) devotes Chapter XIV to Tiberius, drawing heavily upon Tacitus; Carl Weichardt (1900) offers Beaux-Art-inspired reconstruction drawings of the *Villa Iovis*.
72. Mary Beard, 'Imperial Transgressions', Sather Classical Lecture for the University of California-Berkeley, 27 February 2021.
73. The adjectives 'masterly' (showing great skill or being very accomplished) and 'masterful' (powerful and the ability to control others or to perform very skilfully), in my opinion, both apply to Tiberius. The working title of this book was *Tiberius: From Masterly Commander to Masterful Caesar*.
74. This line from director John Ford's film *The Man Who Shot Liberty Valance* serves as an epigraph for the life of the legendary filmmaker.

## CHAPTER 12: ASSESSMENT

1. Text on a building inscription dated 17–37 CE from Sardis (IN63.A09); no. 414 in Petzl (2019), p.94; *cf. ILS* 113, 114, 152, 153, 155, 156, 159, 160, 164, 5818, 5829, 5829a and 6080.
2. Champlin (2008), p.418; Harrer (1920), pp.66–67.
3. The presence of sores of this kind might indicate poor blood circulation.
4. Boschung (1990) notes that art historians have seen at least three variants of hair style for Tiberius-types, depending on the parting above the forehead. Pollini (2005) identified six changes of hairstyle. For the iconography of the Julio-Claudians see Kiss (1975).
5. Brandão (2003), p.311 observes that in Suetonius' portrait, Tiberius is, from the beginning of his principate, shackled to his alleged 'cruel and cold-blooded character',

*saeua ac lenta natura* (Suet., *Tib.* 57.1). For Roman writers' understandings of character (fixed and changing), see Woodman (1989), pp.197–198.
6. Harrer (1920), p.65.
7. McCraven (2021), p.128, cites the essential capability of a leader to be resilient.
8. Hayes (1959).
9. Ripat (2011). For how Augustus used observational astronomy and astrology as political tools and emphasized his cosmically ordained destiny, see Lewis (2023).
10. Suet., *Vit.* 3.2.
11. Dio. Laert., 7.142–3. Powers (2012).
12. Balmaceda (2014).
13. Levick (1976), p.253, n.29; Noreña (2001); Pieper (2021); Westphal (2015).
14. Cowan (2016).
15. Marsh (1931), p.127.
16. Houston (1985), p.182.
17. Suet., *Tib.* 46.1.
18. Philo, *Leg.* 142.
19. Thiel (1936); Scott (1932).
20. Miller (1968), pp.12–17.
21. Marsh (1926) demonstrates how Tacitus relied on an aristocratic tradition of Rome's great families, including written sources, and eschewed gossip and rumour.
22. Dunkle (1971).
23. Edwards (2015).
24. Turner (1943) cites the example of Tiberius' retort to the jester at Augustus' funeral.
25. For *vituperatio*, see Greer (1929), Kennedy (1968), p.433, n.19, and Rebecca Mead, 'How Nasty was Nero, Really?', *The New Yorker*, 7 June 2021.
26. Cat., *Carm* 27.4: *ebrioso acino ebriosioris. Cf.* Suet., *Tib.* 59.1.
27. Hor., *Odes* 1.27.9–10 and 3.8.
28. Ruden (2000), p.166.
29. Sen., *Ep.* 83.26.
30. Sen., *Ep.* 83.21, 95.16; Pliny, *Nat. Hist.* 14.28[142].
31. Suet., *Div. Iul.* 52.3: *At ne cui dubium omnino sit et impudicitiae et adulteriorum flagrasse infamia, Curio pater quadam eum oratione omnium mulierum virum et omnium virorum mulierem appellat.*
32. Cic., *Phil.* 2.44.
33. Suet., *Div. Aug.* 68.1.
34. Suet., *Div. Aug.* 71.1: *Circa libidines haesit, postea quoque, ut ferunt, ad vitiandas virgines promptior, quae sibi undique etiam ab uxore conquirerentur.*
35. For Roman attitudes and depictions of sex, see Clarke (2003 and 2014).
36. Marañón (1956), p.211, considers the stories 'to be mere legend', whereas others, such as Mason (1960), take them as totally credible.
37. Williams (2006).
38. Suet., *Tib.* 28.
39. Tac., Ann. 3.73: *non alias magis sua populique Romani contumelia indoluisse Caesarem ferunt quam quod desertor et praedo hostium more ageret.*
40. Champlin (2011), pp.329–330.
41. Champlin (2011), p.330.
42. Rutledge (2008).
43. Carey (2002); Champlin (2013).
44. This interpretation is expounded in Champlin (2013).

45. Champlin (2011), pp.317–328, disputes the modern translations of *sellaria* and *sprintriae* arguing for 'the Brothel [place of seats]' and 'bracelet worker' respectively. At nearby Baiae on the mainland, at least one grand villa had both a theatre and an odeon constructed of stone, which can still be visited.
46. Suet., *Vit.* 3.2.
47. Decorations on the walls of Roman houses frequently depicted fantasy landscapes populated with naked figures from mythology or life: for gardens and landscapes evoked by Roman artists, see Farrar (1998) and Powers (2023).
48. Suet., *Caius.* 41.1; Tac., *Ann.* 14.15, 15.37.
49. Suet., *Tib.* 57.1.
50. Pompeius: Suet., *Tib.* 57.2. Imprisoned without trial: Jos., *Ant. Iud.* 18.6.5. Paconius: Suet., *Tib.* 61.6.
51. Plescia (2001), pp.51–52, notes that *potestas* granted the holder the right to issue edicts (*ius dicendi*) and the power to enforce them (*ius coercitionis*) through fines, confiscation of property or flogging within his purview.
52. Champlin (2008).
53. Harrer (1920), pp.62–63.
54. Weller (1958).
55. Tac., *Ann.* 6.51: *casus prima ab infantia ancipites.*
56. Powell (2018), pp.211 and 286, notes that Augustus employed investigators (*speculatores*) to seek out conspirators.
57. Tac., *Ann.* 3.53–54.
58. Tac., *Ann.* 6.6.
59. Sen., *Ben.* 5.25.2. *Cf.* Tiberius' wish in Ch. 7, n.170.
60. Pliny, *Nat. Hist.* 28.5[23].
61. Marañón (1956).
62. Romkey (2006).
63. Trentin (2011), p.201. Champlin (2008), p.420, dismisses claims of paranoia in the fisherman tale.
64. Roth (2023).
65. Suet., *Tib.* 2.4: *Praeterea notatissimum est, Claudios omnis, … optimates adsertoresque unicos dignitatis ac potentiae patriciorum semper fuisse.*
66. Barrett (2002), pp.146–147.
67. Barrett (2002), p.148.
68. Barrett (2002), p.163.
69. Freisenbruch (2010), pp.67, 73, 86.
70. Suet. *Tib.* 50.3. Barrett (2002), p.147.
71. Freisenbruch (2010), p.91.
72. *RIC* I 47; *BMC* 81–4; *BN* 63–7; Cohen 5.
73. Her consecration would have to wait until 41 CE when Claudius was *princeps.*
74. Barrett (2001).
75. Powell (2018), pp.247–250.
76. Powell (2011), pp.33–48.
77. Bannon (1997), pp.174–175; Gartrell (2021), pp.163–166.
78. Bannon (1997), pp.178–179; Gartrell (2021), pp.166–172.
79. Tac., *Ann.* 6.51.
80. Powell (2011), p.97.
81. Powell (2011), pp.114–119, 128–134.
82. Bannon (1997), p.179.
83. Freisenbruch (2010), p.56.

84. Barrett (2002), p.50; Fantham (2006), p.82.
85. Fantham (2006), p.133; Freisenbruch (2010), pp.61–62.
86. Fantham (2006), p.90.
87. Fantham (2006), pp.97–100; Powell (2018), pp.253–254, 256–257.
88. Fantham (2006), p.99.
89. Powell (2018), pp.254–255.
90. Tac., *Ann.* 2.43.7. Barrett (2002), p.90; Rogers (1943), pp.98–99.
91. Rogers (1943), p.153.
92. Rogers (1943), pp.100–101.
93. Rogers (1943), p.153.
94. Rogers (1943), pp.145, 152–153. See Ch. 8, n.218.
95. Feldherr (2009), p.175.
96. Powell (2013), p.216; Powell (2018), pp.255–256.
97. Powell (2013), pp.41–53.
98. Powell (2013), pp.71–81.
99. Powell (2013), pp.85–118.
100. Powell (2013), pp.122–127.
101. Cooley (2023), pp.116–117, citing *SCPP* lines 23–70.
102. Drogula (2015b), p.121, describes Piso as a 'prestigious-but-recalcitrant senator'. Drogula's interpretation of Germanicus being sent to watch Piso, rather than Tacitus' view of Piso watching Germanicus, is compelling. His paper was published after I had finished writing my biography of Germanicus (2013) and, thus, I could not include it.
103. Powell (2013), pp.156–162.
104. Cooley (2023), pp.72–75.
105. Powell (2013), pp.167–170.
106. Salmon (1944), p.137.
107. Fantham, E. (2006), p.121.
108. Seager (2012); Shotter (2000).
109. Fantham (2006), p.84.
110. Fantham (2006), p.122.
111. Marsh (1931), p.225.
112. Shotter (1974), pp.45–46.
113. Houston (1985), p.187.
114. Houston (1985), pp.182–187.
115. Powell (2105), pp.200–216; Powell (2018), pp.239–241.
116. Powell (2018), p.250.
117. Vervaet (2020).
118. For M. Agrippa's life and achievements, see Powell (2015).
119. For the succession, see Champlin (1989), Charlesworth (1923), Instinsky (1966), Ober (1982) and Vout (2012). Galinsky (2012), p.182, notes that for Augustus, 'power became the means to an end and not an end in itself'.
120. Vell. Pat. 2.104.1, quoting Augustus' exact words: *his ipsis Caesaris verbis*. *Cf.* Suet., *Tib.* 21.3.
121. Marsh (1931), p.218. Galinsky (2012), p.129, calls Tiberius 'Agrippa II'.
122. Aug., *Res Gest.* 34: *Post id tempus praestiti omnibus dignitate, potestatis autem nihilo amplius habui quam qui fuerunt mihi quoque in magistratu conlegae*. However, *cf.* Suet., *Div. Aug.* 28.1–2.
123. Bleicken (2015), pp.612–613; Judge (2019), p.323.
124. Suet., *Aug.* 31.5: *qui imperium p. R. ex minimo maximum reddidissent*.

125. Suet., *Aug.* 31.5: *commentum id se, ut ad illorum vitam velut ad exemplar et ipse, dum viveret, et insequentium aetatium principes exigerentur a civibus.*
126. Levick (1976), p.58.
127. Marsh (1931), pp.50, 278, asserts that Tiberius was not involved; Detweiler (1970) blames Tiberius aided by Livia. Pappano (1941) absolves Augustus of blame and implicates Tiberius. Jameson (1975) makes a case that neither Augustus nor Tiberius were responsible, but Salustius Crispinus was. Allen (1947) suggests Agrippa died a natural death.
128. Dio 57.2.1, 66.23.2; Tac., *Ann.* 1.7.
129. Marsh (1931), p.45. Wilkinson (2012), pp.14–16, observes that Tacitus and Suetonius use *Res Publica* to mean the older form of government to distinguish it from the new Principate whereas Paterculus tried to show continuity, while Dio distinguishes between the old republic and the new monarchy.
130. Vell. Pat. 2.124.1: *quae Senatus trepidatio.*
131. Vell. Pat. 2.124.2: *ut stationi paternae succederet, illius, ut potius aequalem civem quam eminentem liceret agere principem.*
132. Vell. Pat. 2.124.2: *solique huic contigit paene diutius recusare principatum, quam, ut occuparent eum, alii armis pugnaverant.*
133. Tac., *Ann.* 1.11: *plus in oratione tali dignitatis quam fidei erat.*
134. Tac. *Ann.* 1.12: *nec ideo iram eius lenivit, pridem invisus, tamquam ducta in matrimonium Vipsania M. Agrippae filia, quae quondam Tiberii uxor fuerat.*
135. Tac., *Ann.* 12.13: *fessusque clamore omnium, expostulatione singulorum flexit paulatim, non ut fateretur suscipi a se imperium, sed ut negare et rogari desineret.*
136. Suet., *Tib.* 23–24.1: *Principatum, quamvis neque occupare confestim neque agere dubitasset, et statione militum, hoc est vi et specie dominationis assumpta, diu tamen recusavit, impudentissimo mimo nunc adhortantis amicos increpans ut ignaros, quanta belua esset imperium, nunc precantem senatum et procumbentem sibi ad genua ambiguis responsis et callida cunctatione suspendens.* Syme (1974), p.486, concludes that 'what that day witnessed was not so much a debate as a ceremony'.
137. Dio 57.2.1–7: *καὶ Τιβέριος 'καὶ πῶς οἷόν τέ ἐστιν' εἶπεν 'τὸν αὐτὸν καὶ νέμειν τι καὶ αἱρεῖσθαι ;' συνεὶς οὖν ὁ Γάλλος ἐν ᾧ κακοῦ ἐγεγόνει, τῷ μὲν λόγῳ ἐθεράπευσεν αὐτόν, ὑπολαβὼν ὅτι 'οὐχ ὡς καὶ τὸ τρίτον ἕξοντός σου, ἀλλ' ὡς ἀδύνατον ὂν τὴν ἀρχὴν διαιρεθῆναι, τοῦτό σοι προέτεινα,' οὐ μέντοι καὶ τῷ ἔργῳ ἐτιθάσευσεν, ἀλλὰ πολλὰ καὶ δεινὰ προπαθὼν μετὰ ταῦτα ἐπαπεσφάγη. Καὶ γὰρ καὶ τὴν γυναῖκα αὐτοῦ τὴν προτέραν ἐγεγαμήκει, τόν τε Δροῦσον ὡς υἱὸν προσεποιεῖτο, ὅθενπερ καὶ πρότερον διὰ μίσους αὐτῷ ἦν.*
138. Tac., *Ann.* 1.3: *eadem magistratuum vocabula; iuniores post Actiacam victoriam, etiam senes plerique inter bella civium nati: quotus quisque reliquus qui rem publicam vidisset?*
139. Flower (2010) argues that the Romans created a series of republics with much more change – and much less continuity – over the 'Republican Period' than has previously been assumed.
140. Levick (1976), p.229; Wilkinson (2012), pp.17–18. For the *nobiles*, see Syme (1986), pp.32–49.
141. Judge (2019), p.324.
142. Marsh (1931), p.49, suggests 'for an indefinite period, and hence practically for life'.
143. Judge (2019), p.323.
144. Marsh (1931), p.49.
145. Scott (1932).
146. Marsh (1931), p.218.
147. Sinclair (1992), citing Tac., *Ann.* 1.73.4.

148. Tac., *Ann.* 4.37: *qui omnia facta dictaque eius vice legis observem.*
149. Levick (1967), pp.207–209.
150. Levick (1976), pp.102–103.
151. Levick (1976), pp.20–22, 27, 180.
152. *ILS* 159 (32–33 CE).
153. Vell. Pat. 2.129.2, referring to the case of Drusus Libo. Bablitz (2009).
154. 'Injuries to the Gods will be remedied by the Gods.'
155. Levick (1976), p.180.
156. Suet. *Tib.* 30: *Quin etiam speciem libertatis quandam induxit conservatis senatui ac magistratibus et maiestate pristina et potestate. Neque tam parvum quicquam neque tam magnum publici privatique negotii fuit, de quo non ad patres conscriptos referretur.*
157. Suet. *Tib.* 30: *Numquam curiam nisi solus intravit; lectica quondam intro latus aeger comites a se removit.*
158. Marsh (1931), p.106, calls it a 'blot'.
159. Flint (1912).
160. Allison & Cloud (1962).
161. Pliny, *Panegyricus* 11.
162. Flint (1912).
163. Salmon (1944), p.133; see tables listing criminal trials, defendants, prosecutors, *patroni* and witnesses in Rogers (1935), pp.206–215.
164. Tac., *Ann.* 4.20, 6.2, 6.19.
165. For elections under Tiberius, see Dettenhofer (2002), Levick (1967), p.212, Marsh (1931), pp.296–303, and Shotter (1966a).
166. Marsh pp.302–303.
167. Blunt (1961); Sutherland (1938).
168. Seager (1972), p.248, remarks that it was 'too late' since Augustus had effectively emasculated the Senate as a decision-making body.
169. For the political significance of Seianus, see Bird (1969).
170. Champlin (2010).
171. For Seianus' alleged conspiracies, see Boddington (1963) and Marsh (1931), pp.304–310.
172. Suet., *Tib.* 61.1; Shotter (1992), pp.46–47; Marsh (1931), p.309.
173. Marsh (1931), p.221, writes: 'The principate of Augustus was dead and despotism stood forth undisguised'; *cf.* Brunt (1984), p.444, who argues that since 'all real power' was in the hands of the 'First Man', the Senate now looked to him. The result was what Snyder (2017), p.18 calls 'anticipatory obedience'.
174. *Cf.* Sen., *Clem.* 1.4.3.
175. Tac., *Ann.* 4.9. Yakobson (2019) argues that restoring the *Res Publica* would require that the consuls were 'given back' (*reddenda*) their historical supreme positions in governing the Roman Commonwealth (citing Tac., *Ann.* 1.7) but, despite promises, Tiberius hesitated to yield power to them and, thus, the 'shadow of the Republic' continued through his reign.
176. Powell (2018), pp.166–169.
177. Levick (1976), p.126, notes that Tiberius served twenty-eight seasons outside Rome before 14 CE.
178. Tac. *Ann.* 2.64.2: *laetiore Tiberio quia pacem sapientia firmaverat quam si bellum per acies confecisset.*
179. Vervaet (2020).
180. Dio 56.16.3.
181. Suet., *Tib.* 32.2: *boni pastoris esse tondere pecus, non deglubere.*
182. Notably Diocletian and Constantine I.

183. Dio 53.12.2.
184. Ver., *Aen.* 279.
185. Tac., *Ann.* 1.11: *quae cuncta sua manu perscripserat Augustus addideratque consilium coercendi intra terminos imperii, incertum metu an per invidiam. Cf.* Dio 56.33.5. Ober (1982), p.312, suggests the advice to Tiberius may have been given verbally by Augustus and not in writing.
186. Tac., *Ann.* 1.9.5: *mari Oceano aut amnibus longinquis saeptum imperium – legiones, provincias, classes, cuncta inter se conexa. Cf.* Tac., *Ann.* 4.4: 'how narrow the limits of our empire', *quanto sit angustius imperitatum*. Thus, Tiberius did not invade Britain as a matter of *praeceptum* consistent with Augustus' *consilium* (Tac., *Agr.* 13.2).
187. Tac., *Ann.* 4.32: *princeps proferendi imperi incuriosus erat*. Rehman (2024), p.154 concludes: 'There was therefore an increasingly shared assumption that the Roman Empire had reached its natural perimeter, and that where those vague, porous boundaries slowly dissipated into mysterious, exotic, and primeval lands, there remained little that could – or should – be conquered. The enduring loneliness of Tiberius' genius resides, perhaps, in the fact that he uncovered the uncomfortable truth earlier than most.' For the view that Tiberius reversed Augustus' policy, see Rogers (1940).
188. Veg., *Milit.* 3 Introduction: *Qui desiderat pacem, praeparet bellum.*
189. Tac., *Ann.* 1.78.
190. Some redeployment occurred, such as *Legio* VIIII *Hispana* was moved to and from Africa Proconsularis.
191. Suet., *Tib.* 32.1.
192. Suet., *Tib.* 32.1. *Cf.* Ch. 2, n.35.
193. Dio 57.2.3.
194. Suet. *Tib.* 30: *etiam de legendo vel exauctorando milite ac legionum et auxiliorum discriptione, denique quibus imperium prorogari aut extraordinaria bella mandari.*
195. Tac., *Ann.* 6.27.
196. Suet., *Caius* 16.1. During his reign, Augustus had suspended publication of the *Acta Senatus* (Suet., *Div. Aug.* 36.1).
197. Sánchez (2014); Bloom (2019).
198. For Roman diplomacy, see Burton (2018) and Rich (2008).
199. Suet., *Tib.* 37.4: *Reges infestos suspectosque comminationibus magis et querelis quam vi repressit.*
200. Tac., *Ann.* 6.32: *consiliis et astu res externas moliri, arma procul habere*. This is still the fundament of international relations. Rehman (2024), p.127 describes Tiberius' 'Germanian policy' as 'a combination of masterly inactivity and shrewd proxy management', concluding in respect of Rome's dependence on *socii*, *clientes* and *auxilia*, notably in the East, that 'Tiberius proved singularly adept at alliance management and great power competition' (p.164).
201. Cooley (2023), p.129, citing lines 165–72.
202. Tac., *Ann.* 4.45.
203. Claudius (Britannia) and Trajan (Dacia and Arabia Petraea) were the most successful. Caligula made preparations for an invasion of Britain but aborted it, and Domitian's foray into Germania came to nothing.
204. Hadrian abandoned Trajan's conquests in Armenia, Assyria and Mesopotamia. Again seeking glory, emperors after Hadrian could not resist the temptation; among them were Septimius Severus, Caracalla and Valerian.
205. Tac., *Ann.* 1.80.1: *causae variae traduntur: alii taedio novae curae semel placita pro aeternis servavisse, quidam invidia, ne plures fruerentur; sunt qui existiment, ut callidum eius ingenium, ita anxium iudicium; neque enim eminentis virtutes sectabatur, et rursum vitia*

*oderat: ex optimis periculum sibi, a pessimis dedecus publicum metuebat. qua haesitatione postremo eo provectus est ut mandaverit quibusdam provincias, quos egredi urbe non erat passurus.* The governors detained in Rome were L. Aelius Lamia (Syria) and L. Arruntius (Hispania Tarraconensis): see Ch. 9, n.113.

206. Salmon (1942), p.131. Ios., *Ant. Iud.* 18.6.5 in which Josephus reports Tiberius telling a parable of a man with open sores who refused assistance to swat away flies.
207. Salmon (1944), p.131 and n.1.
208. Fuks (1982). Ios., *Ant. Iud.* 18.6.5 remarks that Tiberius sent just two governors to Iudaea in his entire 22-year principate.
209. Salmon (1944), p.131 and n.1.
210. *CIL*, XIII, 3026 = *ILS* 4616: *Tib(erio) Caesare / Aug(usto) Ioui Optum[o] / Maxsumo nautae Parisiaci / publice posieru / nt / Eurises / Senani U[s]eiloni.* For a discussion of the so-called *Pilier des Nautes*, see Häussler (2012), pp.156–157.
211. Suet., *Tib.* 30.1: *Neque tam parvum quicquam neque tam magnum publici privatique negotii fuit, de quo non ad patres conscriptos referretur: de vectigalibus ac monopoliis, de extruendis reficiendisve operibus.*
212. Duncan-Jones (1982), p.145.
213. Jones (2006), p.34.
214. *Cf.* Juv., *Sat.* 10.81.
215. Closs (2020), pp.74–75. After the Great Fire of Rome of 64 CE, Nero helped those impacted with food and places to stay, while after the eruption of Vesuvius in 79 CE, Titus assisted the displaced population of Campania.
216. Jones (2006), pp.204–205, citing Tac., *Ann.* 4.6.3, and p.216, citing Just., *Digest.* 41.1.26.2.
217. Powell (2024) notes Augustus left a city of brick covered with a veneer of marble.
218. Suet., *Div. Aug.* 29.4–5.
219. Bellen (1976); Thornton & Thornton (1990), pp.661–662.
220. Duncan-Jones (1990), p.62 and fig.9.
221. See Ch. 4, n.194.
222. The impressive brick and cement vaults of the *Domus Tiberiana*, which mostly date to Nero and Hadrian, reopened to visitors in late 2023.
223. Booms (2010).
224. Woodman (2006a).
225. *AE* (1979) 173: *[Ti(berio)] Caesari div[i Aug(usti) f(ilio) divi Iuli n(epoti) Augusto] / pontif(ici) max(imo) co(n)[s(uli) 3] / [L(ucius)] Mammi[us Maximus p(ecunia) s(ua)].*
226. A *denarius* of Tiberius with a hole drilled in it, so that it could be worn as an amulet or as jewellery, was found in a field in Lincolnshire, England, in 2017: it was subjected to the Treasure process under the Portable Antiquities Scheme (ref. 2017 T327). Another specimen with a hole drilled in it was found near Swindon, Wiltshire (ref. WILT-819ADE). Both pieces predate the Roman invasion of Britain in 43 CE by a decade or more. Of the 748 Iron Age and Roman coins in the Helmingham Hall Hoard (Portable Antiquities Scheme designated Treasure under the Case Numbers 2019T794 and 2020T915) found in 2019 near Stowmarket, Suffolk with coins ranging from Cunobelinus to Claudius, 83 (11 per cent) are of Tiberius (the seated Livia as *Pax* issue).
227. Gaber (2105), p.93.
228. Fishwick (1992); Taylor (1929).
229. Seager (1972), p.150, also states that *haruspices* were expelled, but Tac., *Ann.* 2.32 and Suet., *Tib.* 36 both refer to *mathematicos*, i.e. astrologers.
230. Harland (2022); Levick (1976), p.106; Smallwood (1956), pp.324–326, rejects the date of *c.* 30 CE.

231. McGing (1991), p.424.
232. Gruen (2003 and 2016); Maier (1971); Smallwood (1956), p.322.
233. Levick (1976), p.136; Smallwood (1956), p.327.
234. Fuks (1982), pp.506–507.
235. McGing (1991), p.438.
236. Kaplan (2002), pp.152–153.
237. Ver., *Ecl.* 4.5: *magnus ab integro saeclorum nascitur ordo.*
238. Tac., *Ann.* 6.46: *quippe illi non perinde curae gratia praesentium quam in posteros ambitio.*
239. Tom Holland, 'Caesars and Sopranos: The Shadow of Suetonius', *Antigone Journal*, 10 March 2021.
240. Levick (1976), p.126.
241. In a tweet posted on 24 March 2021, Tom Holland wrote: 'Tiberius was a great emperor, *princeps* by virtue of achievement as well as inheritance. Tacitus had his own reasons for giving him a bitterly unfair spin. He is effectively the tragic hero of [my book] *Dynasty*.'
242. Vell. Pat. 2.131.1: *custodite, servate, protegite hunc statum, hanc pacem, hunc principem.* Livy ended his *Ab Urbe Condita* with the death of Tiberius' brother, Nero Drusus; see Livy, *Peri.* 142.
243. Val. Max., 8.13, *Praef.*: *salutaris principis incolumitatem ad longissimos humanae condicionis terminos prorogando.*
244. Philo, *Leg.* 33, 141.
245. Tac., *Ann.* 4.32: *immota quippe aut modice lacessita pax.* For Tacitus' obituary of Tiberius, see Woodman (1989).
246. Dio 59.2.6; Suet., *Caius.* 37.3.
247. Hor., *Odes* 1.1: 'Encampments please many, and the varied / sounds of the curved trumpet, and war, / detested by mothers', *Multos castra iuvant et lituo tubae / permixtus sonitus bellaque matribus / detestata.*

# Bibliography

**Ancient Authors**

Appian, *Bellum Civile (Civil War)*

Ammianus Marcellinus, *Res Gestae a Fine Corneli Taciti (Roman History)*

Augustus, *Res Gestae (Deeds of Augustus)*

Aulus Gellius, *Noctes Atticae (Attic Nights)*

Caesar, *Commentarii de Bello Gallico (Commentaries on The Gallic War)*

Cassiodorus, *Χρονικών (Chronicles)*

Cassius Dio, *Ῥωμαϊκὴ Ιστορία (Roman History)*

Cicero, *De Oratore (On Oratory)*

Cicero, *Epistulae ad Atticum (Letters to Atticus)*

Seneca, *Consolatio ad Liviam (Condolences for Livia)*

Seneca, *Consolatio ad Marciam (Condolences for Marcia)*

Crinagoras, *Anthologia Palatina (Palatine Anthology)*

Eutropius, *Breviarium Historiae Romanae (Brief History of the Romans)*

Florus, *Epitome de T. Livio Bellorum Omnium Annorum* (*Epitome of Livy)*

Frontinus, *Strategemata* (*Stratagems*)

Horace, *Carmina (Odes)*

Horace, *Carmen Saecularum (Century Ode)*

Jerome, *Chronicon* (*Chronology*)

Josephus, *Ἰουδαϊκὴ ἀρχαιολογία (Antiquitates Iudaicae, Antiquities of the Jews)*

Josephus, *Ἱστορία Ἰουδαϊκοῦ πολέμου πρὸς Ῥωμαίους* (*Bellum Iudaicum, Jewish War)*

Josephus, *Περὶ ἀρχαιότητος Ἰουδαίων (Contra Apionem, Against Apion)*

Josephus, *Ιστορία Ἰουδαϊκοῦ Πολέμου πρός Ῥωμαίους* (*Wars of the Jews* or *The History of the Destruction of Jerusalem)*

Julian, *Saturnalia* aka *Kronia (The Caesars)*

Juvenal, *Saturae (Satires)*

Livy, *Ab Urbe Condita (History from the Foundation of Rome)*

Livy, *Periochae (Extracts)*

Macrobius, *Saturnalia (The Saturnalia)*

Manlius, *Astronomica (Astronomical Phenomena)*

Orosius, *Historiarum Adversum Paganos (History Against the Pagans)*

Ovid, *Fasti (The Book of Days)*

Ovid, *Tristia (Sorrows)*

Ovid, *Epistulae ex Ponto (Letters from Pontus)*

Philo, *In Flaccum (Against Flaccus)*

Philo, *Legatio ad Gaium (Delegation to Caius Caligula)*

Pliny the Elder, *Naturalis Historia (Natural History)*

Plutarch, *Ἀντωνίος (Life of Antonius)*

Plutarch, *Βρούτος (Life of Brutus)*

Plutarch, *Καῖσαρος (Life of Iulius Caesar)*

Plutarch, *Πομπήϊος (Life of Pompeius Magnus)*

Plutarch, *De Invidia et Odio (On Envy and Hate)*

Polybius, *Οἱ Ιστορίες (The Histories)*
Propertius, *Elegiae* (*Elegies*)
Ptolemy, *Γεωγραφικὴ Ὑφήγησις (Geographical Narrtive)*
Seneca the Younger, *Controversiae (Debates)*
Seneca the Younger, *De Beneficiis (On Benefits)*
Seneca the Younger, *De Clementia (On Clemency)*
Seneca the Younger, *Epistulae (Letters)*
Servius, *In Vergilii Carmina Commentarii (Commentaries on Vergil's Poems)*
Strabo, *Γεωγραφικά (Geography)*
Suetonius, *De Grammaticis et Rhetoribus (On Teachers of Grammar and Rhetoric)*
Suetonius, *Vita Divi Augusti (Life of the Divine Augustus)*
Suetonius, *Vita Cai (Life of Caius Caligula)*
Suetonius, *Vita Divi Claudi (Life of the Divine Claudius)*
Suetonius, *Vita Divi Iuli (Life of the Divine Iulius Caesar)*
Suetonius, *Vita Tiberi (Life of Tiberius)*
Suetonius, *Vita Neronis (Life of Nero)*
Suetonius, *Vita Vitelli (Life of Vitellius)*
Tacitus, *Ab Excessu Divi Augusti* aka *Annales (The Annals)*
Tacitus, *De Origine et Situ Germanorum (Germania)*
Tertullian, *Apologeticum (Apology)*
Vergil, *Aeneid (Aeneid)*
Ulpian, *Digesta (Digest)*
Valerius Maximus, *Factorum et Dictorum Memorabilium (Memorable Deeds and Sayings)*
Velleius Paterculus, *Historiae Romanae (Compendium of Roman History)*
Vettius Valens, *Anthologia (Anthology)*
Zonaras, *Ἐπιτομὴ Ἱστοριῶν (Extracts of History)*
Zosimos, *Ιστορία Νέα* (*New History*)

**Modern Authors**

AA.VV. (1990), *Il bimillenario di Agrippa,* Atti delle XVII Giornate Filologiche Genovesi 1989, Genoa.

Abbott, F. F. & Johnson, A. C. (1926), *Municipal Administration in the Roman Empire,* Princeton: Princeton University Press.

Adler, W. (1993), *Studien zur germansichen Bewaffnung: Waffenmitgabe und Kampfesweise im Niederelbegebiet und im Freien Germanien um Christi Geburt,* Bonn: Saarbrücker Beiträge zur Altertumskunde.

Africa, T. W. (1971), 'Urban Violence in Imperial Rome', *The Journal of Interdisciplinary History* 2.1, 3–21.

Aldrete, Gregory S. (2007), *Floods of the Tiber in Ancient Rome* (Ancient Society and History), Baltimore: Johns Hopkins University Press.

Alföldi, Andreas (1976), *Oktavians Aufstieg zur Macht,* Bonn: Habelt.

Alföldy, Géza (1974), *Noricum,* London: Routledge and Kegan Paul.

Alföldy, Géza (1996), 'Spain' in: Bowman, A. K., Champlin, E. & Lintott, A. (eds.), *The Cambridge Ancient History Volume X: The Augustan Empire, 43 B.C.–A.D. 69* (second edition), Cambridge: Cambridge University Press, 449–463.

Alföldy, Géza (2000a), 'Das neue Edikt des Augustus aus El Bierzo in Hispanien', *Zeitschrift* für *Papyrologie und Epigraphik* 131, 177–205.

Alföldy, Géza, Dobson, Brian, & Eck, Werner (2000b), *Kaiser, Heer und Gesellschaft in der Romischen Kaiserzeit,* Heidelberger Althistorische Beitrage Und Epigraphische Studien (Book 31), Stuttgart: Franz Steiner Verlag.

Allen, G. H. (1908), 'The Advancement of Officers in the Roman Army', *Supplementary Papers of the American School of Classical Studies in Rome* 2, 1–25.

Allen, S. & Reynolds, W. (2001), *Celtic Warrior, 300 BC–AD 100*, Oxford: Osprey Publishing.

Allen Jr, Walter (1941), 'The Political Atmosphere of the Reign of Tiberius', *Transactions and Proceedings of the American Philological Association* 72, 1–25.

Allen Jr, Walter (1947), 'The Death of Agrippa Postumus', *Transactions and Proceedings of the American Philological Association* 78, 131–139.

Allison, J. E. & Cloud, J. D. (1962), 'The *lex Julia Maiestatis*', *Latomus* 21.4 (October–December), 711–731.

Almagro-Gorbea, M., & Lorrio, A. J. (2004), 'War and Society in the Celtiberian World' in: Alberro, M. & Bettina Arnold, B. (eds.), *Journal of Interdisciplinary Studies* 6: The Celts in the Iberian Peninsula, 73–112.

Alonso-Núñez, J. M. (1987), 'An Augustan World History: The *Historiae Philippicae* of Pompeius Trogus', *Greece & Rome (Second Series)* 3.1 (April), 56–72.

Alston, R. (1994), 'Roman Military Pay from Caesar to Diocletian', *The Journal of Roman Studies* 84, 113–123.

Ando, C. (2000), *Imperial Ideology and Provincial Loyalty in the Roman Empire*, Berkeley: University of California Press.

Arbizu, José María (2018), *Tiberio: El republicano en el trono de los Césares*, Madrid: Editorial Letras de autor.

Ash, Rhiannon (1999), 'An Exemplary Conflict: Tacitus' Parthian Battle Narrative (*Annals* 6.34–35)', *Phoenix, 53*(1/2), 114–135.

Ashton, R. H. J. (1973), 'Some Cnossian Coins of Tiberius', *The Numismatic Chronicle (1966-)* 13, 40–43.

Atkinson, K. M. T. (1958), 'The Governors of the Province Asia in the Reign of Augustus', *Historia: Zeitschrift für Alte Geschichte* 7.3 (July), 300–330.

Austin, N. E., & Rankov, N. B. (1995), *Exploratio: Military and Political Intelligence in the Roman World from the Second Punic War to the Battle of Adrianople*, London: Routledge.

Baatz, D., & Herrmann, F.-R. (eds.) (2002), *Die Römer in Hessen*, (revised edition), Hamburg: Nikol Verlag.

Bablitz, Leanne (2009), 'Three Passages on Tiberius and the Courts', *Memoirs of the American Academy in Rome* 54, 121–133.

Babnis, Tomasz (2017), 'Augustan Poets on the Roman-Parthian Treaty of 20 BC' *Classica Cracoviensia* 20, 5–44.

Bacevic, A. J. (2005), *The New American Militarism: How Americans Are Seduced by War*, Oxford: Oxford University Press.

Badian, E. (1974), 'The Quaestorship of Tiberius Nero', *Mnemosyne* (Fourth Series) Vol. 27, Fasc. 2, 160–172.

Badian, E. (1980), 'Notes on the *Laudatio* of Agrippa', *The Classical Journal* 76.2 (December 1980-January 1981), 97–109.

Ballance, M. H. (1951), 'The Roman Bridges of the Via Flaminia', *Papers of the British School at Rome* 19, 78–117.

Baldwin, Barry (1981), 'The Authorship of the 'Aratus' Ascribed to Germanicus', *Quaderni Urbinati Di Cultura Classica* 7, Pisa: Fabrizio Serra editore, 163–172.

Baldwin Bowsky, Martha W. (2017), 'Tiberius and the Asklepieion at Lissos (Crete): Petition and Response, Image and Power', *Mediterraneo Antico* 20.1–2, 395–444.

Bálek, M., & Šedo, O. (1996), 'Das Frühkaiserzeitliche Lager bei Mušov – Zeugnis eines augusteischen Feldzugs ins Marchgebiet?', *Germania* 74, 399–414.

Ball, Joanne (2023), *Publius Quinctilius Varus: The Man Who Lost Three Roman Legions in the Teutoburg Disaster*, Barnsley: Pen & Sword Books.

Balmaceda, Catalina (2014), 'The Virtues of Tiberius in Velleius' "Histories"', *Historia: Zeitschrift für Alte Geschichte* Bd. 63, H. 3, 340–363.

Balmaceda, Catalina (2017), Virtus Romana*: Politics and Morality in the Roman Historians* (Studies in the History of Greece and Rome), Chapel Hill: The University of North Carolina Press.

Balsdon, J. P. V. D. (1933), 'The Successors of Augustus', *Greece & Rome* 2.6 (May), 161–169.

Balsdon, J. P. V. D. (1969), *Life and Leisure in Ancient Rome*, London: The Bodley Head.

Balsdon, J. P. V. D. (1979), *Romans and Aliens*, London: Duckworth.

Baker, George Philip (1929), *Tiberius Caesar, Emperor of Rome*, New York: Cooper Square Press.

Banner Jr, James M. (2021), *The Ever-Changing Past: Why All History Is Revisionist History*, New Haven: Yale University Press.

Bannon, C. J. (1997), *The Brothers of Romulus: Fraternal* Pietas *in Roman Law, Literature, and Society*, Princeton: Princeton University Press.

Barker, D. (1996), "'The Golden Age Is Proclaimed'? The *Carmen Saeculare* and the Renascence of the Golden Race', *The Classical Quarterly New Series* 46.2, 434–446.

Barnes, T. D. (1974), 'The Victories of Augustus', *The Journal of Roman Studies* 64, 21–26.

Barnes, T. D. (1984), 'The Composition of Cassius Dio's "Roman History"', *Phoenix* 38(3), 240–255.

Barnish, Jonas A. (ed.) (1965), *Ben Johnson's Sejanus: His Fall*, New Haven: Yale University Press.

Barrett, Anthony A. (1989), *Caligula: The Corruption of Power*, New Haven: Yale University Press.

Barrett, Anthony A. (2001), 'Tacitus, Livia and the Evil Stepmother', *Rheinisches Museum Für Philologie* 144(2), 171–175.

Barrett, Anthony A. (2002), *Livia: First Lady of Imperial Rome*, New Haven: Yale University Press.

Barrett, A. A. (2005), 'Aulus Caecina Severus and the Military Woman', *Historia: Zeitschrift* für Alte *Geschichte* 54.3, 301–314

Barrett, Anthony A. (2006), 'Augustus and the Governor's Wives', *Rheinisches Museum für Philologie* Vol. 149, 129–147.

Barton, C. (2007), 'The Price of Peace in Ancient Rome' in: Raaflaub, K.A. (ed.), *War and Peace in the Ancient World*, Oxford: Blackwell Publishing (2007).

Bastien, Sophie (2006), *Caligula et Camus: Interférences transhistoriques* (Faux Titre 274), Paris: Rodopi.

Bauman, R. A. (1966), 'Tiberius and Murena', *Historia: Zeitschrift Für Alte Geschichte* 15.4 420–432.

Bauman, R. A. (1994), 'Tanaquil-Livia and the Death of Augustus', *Historia: Zeitschrift für Alte Geschichte*, 2nd Qtr., Bd. 43, H. 2, 177–188.

Bay, A. (1972), 'The Letters SC on Augustan *Aes* Coinage', *The Journal of Roman Studies* 62, 111–122.

Beacham, R. C. (1999), *Spectacle Entertainments of Early Imperial Rome*, New Haven: Yale University Press.

Bean, G. E. (1979), *Aegean Turkey*, second edition, London, Ernest Benn.

Beard, Mary (2007), *The Roman Triumph,* Cambridge, Mass.: Harvard University Press.

Becker, A., & Rasbach, G. (2007) '*Städte in Germanien: Der Fundplatz Waldgirmes*' in Wiegels, R. (ed.): *Die Varusschlacht. Wendepunkt der Geschichte?* (Archäologie in Deutschland), Stuttgart: Theiss, 102–116.

Becker, Howard C. (2008), 'Alcohol Dependence, Withdrawal, and Relapse', *Alcohol Research & Health: The Journal of the National Institute on Alcohol Abuse and Alcoholism* 31.4, 348–361.

Bell, S. (2008), 'Role Models in the Roman World', in: *Memoirs of the American Academy in Rome. Supplementary Volumes* 7, Role Models in the Roman World. Identity and Assimilation, 1–39.

Bell, M. J. V. (1965), 'Tactical Reform in the Roman Republican Army', *Historia: Zeitschrift* für Alte *Geschichte* 14.4 (October), 404–422.

Bellemore, Jane (1992), 'The Dating of Seneca's *Ad Marciam De Consolatione*', *The Classical Quarterly* 42.1, 219–234.

Bellemore, Jane (1995), 'The Wife of Sejanus', *Zeitschrift für Papyrologie und Epigraphik* 109, 255–266.

Bellemore, Jane (2003), 'Cassius Dio and the Chronology of A.D. 21', *The Classical Quarterly* (New Series) 53.1 (May), 268–285.

Bellemore, Jane (2007), 'Tiberius and Rhodes', *Klio* 89.2, 417–453.

Bellemore, Jane (2012), 'The Identity of Drusus: The Making of a Princeps', in: Gibson, Alisdair (ed.), *The Julio-Claudian Succession: Reality and Perception of the 'Augustan Model'*, *Mnemosyne,* Supplements, History and Archaeology of Classical Antiquity 349 (2012), Leiden: Brill, 79–94.

Bellen, Heinz (1976), 'Die Krise der italischen Landwirtschaft unter Kaiser Tiberius (33 n. Chr.) Ursachen, Verlauf, Folgen.', *Historia: Zeitschrift Für Alte Geschichte* 25(2), 217–234.

Berke, S., Bérenger, D., & Ilisch, P., *et al* (2009), *Corpus der römischen Funde im europäischen Barbaricum, Deutschland, 7: Land Nordrhein-Westfalen, Landesteile Westfalen und Lippe*, Bonn: Habelt.

Bernegger, P. M. (1983), 'Affirmation of Herod's Death in 4 B.C.', *Journal of Theological Studies* 34, 526–531.

Berthelet, Yann, & Dalla Rosa, Alberto (2015), '*Summum Imperium Auspiciumque*: Une Lecture Critique', *Revue Historique De Droit Français Et Étranger (1922-)* 93.2, 267–284.

Besteman, J. C., Bos, J. M., Gerrets, D. A., Heidinga, H. A., & de Koning, J. (1999), *The Excavations at Wijnaldum: Reports on Frisia in Roman and Medieval Times, Volume 1*, Rotterdam: Balkema.

Bingham, S. (1997), *The Praetorian Guard in the Political and Social Life of Julio-Claudian Rome,* University of British Columbia. (Doctoral thesis, online at https://circle.ubc.ca/handle/2429/10169)

Birch, R. A. (1981), 'The Settlement of 26 June A.D. 4 and Its Aftermath', *The Classical Quarterly (New Series)* 31.2, 443–456.

Birch, R. A. (1981), 'The Correspondence of Augustus: Some Notes on Suetonius, Tiberius 21.4–7', *The Classical Quarterly* 31.1, 155–161.

Bird, H. W. (1969), 'L. Aelius Seianus and His Political Significance', *Latomus* 28.1, 61–98.

Bird, H. W. (1987), 'Tiberius, Piso, and Germanicus: Further Considerations', *Acta Classica* 30, 72–75.

Bishop, Mike C. (2002), *Lorica Segmentata Volume I: A Handbook of Articulated Roman Plate Armour*, Chirnside: The Armatura Press.

Bishop, Mike C. (2012), *Handbook to Roman Legionary Fortresses*, Barnsley: Pen & Sword Books.

Bishop, Mike C., & Coulston, J. C. N. (2006), *Roman Military Equipment from the Punic Wars to the Fall of Rome*, Oxford: Oxbow Press.

Blázquez, J. M (1992), 'The Latest Work on the Export of Baetican Olive Oil to Rome and the Army', *Greece & Rome (Second Series)* 39.2 (October), 173–188.

Bleicken, J. (2015), *Augustus: The Biography*, London: Allen Lane.

Bloom, James J. (2019), *Rome Rules the Waves. A Naval Staff Appreciation of Ancient Rome's Maritime Strategy 300 BCE–500 CE*, Barnsley: Pen & Sword Books.

Boatwright, M. T. (2000), *Hadrian and the Cities of the Roman Empire*, Princeton: Princeton University Press.

Boddington, Ann (1963), 'Whose Conspiracy?', *The American Journal of Philology* 84.1 (January), 1–16.

Bodel, John (1999), 'Punishing Piso', *The American Journal of Philology* 120(1), 43–63.

Booms, Dirk (2010), 'The *Vernae Caprenses*: Traces of Capri's Imperial History After Tiberius', *Papers of the British School at Rome* 78, 133–143.

Borzsák, S. (1969), 'Das Germanicusbild des Tacitus', *Latomus* 28, 588–600.

Boschung, Dietrich (1990), 'Prinzenporträt des Tiberius' in: Berger, E. (ed.), *Antike Kunstwerke aus der Sammlung Ludwig III. Skulpturen*, Mainz: Philipp von Zabern, 369–377.

Boschung, Dietrich (1993), *Die Bildnistypen der iulisch-claudischen Kaiserfamilie: ein kritischer Forschungsbericht*, *Journal of Roman Archaeology* 6, 39–79.

Boschung, Dietrich (2014), 'Schwert des Tiberius' in: Trier, Marcus, & Naumann-Steckner, Friederike (eds.), *14 AD: Römische Herrschaft am Rhein*, Cologne: Wienand,148–150.

Boschung, Dietrich (2015), 'Bilder des Germanicus: Die römische Staatskunst als Instrument kaiserlicher Selbstdarstellung' in: *Archäologie in Deutschland, 2015, Sonderheft: Ich Germanicus: Feldherr Priester Superstar* (2015), Darmstadt: Wissenschaftliche Buchgesellschaft, pp. 88–97.

Bosworth, B. (1999), 'Augustus, the *Res Gestae* and Hellenistic Theories of Apotheosis', *The Journal of Roman Studies* 89, 1–18.

Botsford, G. W. (1908), 'The *Lex Curiata*', *Political Science Quarterly* 23.3 (Sep.), 498–517.

Botsford, G. W. (1918), 'Roman Imperialism', *The American Historical Review* 23.4 (July), 772–778.

Boughner, Daniel C. (1960), 'Juvenal, Horace and Sejanus', *Modern Language Notes* 75.7, 545–550.

Bowersock, Glenn (1964), 'Augustus on Aegina', *Classical Quarterly* 14, 120–121.

Bowersock, Glenn (1984), 'Augustus in the East: The Problem of the Succession' in: Millar, Fergus & Segal, Erich (eds.), *Caesar Augustus: Seven Aspects*, Oxford, 169–188.

Bowersock, G. W. (1999), 'The Roman Emperor as Russian Tsar: Tacitus and Pushkin', *Proceedings of the American Philosophical Society* 143(1), 130–147.

Bowman, A. K., Champlin, E., & Linott, A. (1996) (second edition), *The Cambridge Ancient History Vol. X: The Augustan Empire, 43 BC–AD 69*, Cambridge: Cambridge University Press.

Boyce, A. A. (1942), 'The Origin of *ornamenta triumphalia*', *Classical Philology* 37.2 (April), 130–141.

Braginton, Mary V. (1944), 'Exile under the Roman Emperors', *The Classical Journal* 39(7), 391–407.

Brandão, José Luís (2023), 'Othering the Emperor in Suetonius' in: Brandão, José Luís, Teixeira Cláudia & Rodrigues, Ália (eds.), *Confronting Identities in the Roman Empire: Assumptions about the Other in Literary Evidence*, London: Bloomsbury Academic, 297–322.

Brandon, C., Hohlfelder, R. L., & Oleson, J. P. (2008), 'The Concrete Construction of the Roman Harbours of Baiae and Portus Iulius: The ROMACONS 2006 field season', *International Journal of Nautical Archaeology* 37.2 (September), 374–379.

Brännstedt Lovisa (2016), Femina princeps: *Livia's position in the Roman state*, Lund: Lund University Press.

Braund, D. C. (1984a), 'North African Rulers and the Roman Military Paradigm', *Hermes* 112.2 (Second Quarter.), 255–256.

Braund, D. C. (1984b), *Rome and the Friendly King: The Character of Client Kingship*, Beckenham: Croom Helm.

Braunert, H. (1957), 'Der römische Provinzialzensus und der Schätzungsbericht des Lukas-Evangeliums', *Historia: Zeitschrift für Alte Geschichte* 6, Stuttgart: Franz Steiner Verlag, 192–214.

Breeze, David J. (1969), 'The Organization of the Legion: The First Cohort and the *Equites Legionis*', *The Journal of Roman Studies* 59.1/2, 50–55

Breeze, David J. (1976), 'A Note on the Use of the Titles *Optio* and *Magister* below the Centurionate during the Principate', *Britannia* 7, 127–133.

Breeze, David J., Jones, Rebecca H., & Oltean, Ioana A. (2015) (eds.), *Understanding Roman Frontiers. A Celebration for Bill Hanson*, Edinburgh: John Donald.

Brent, B. D. (1990), 'Bandit Highlands and Lowland Peace: The Mountains of Isauricia-Cilicia', *Journal of the Economic and Social History of the Orient* 33.3, 237–270.

Brodersen, K. (1995), *Terra Incognita: Studien zur römischen Raumerfassung*, *Spudasmata* 59, 268–287.

Brogan, O. (1936), 'Trade between the Roman Empire and the Free Germans', *The Journal of Roman Studies* 26 Part 2, 195–222.

Bromwich, James (1993), *The Roman Remains of Southern France: A Guidebook*, London: Routledge.

Broughton, T. R. S. (1933), 'Some Notes on the War with the Homonadeis', *The American Journal of Philology* 54.2, 134–144.

Broughton, T. R. S. (1935), 'Some Non-Colonial *Coloni* of Augustus', *Transactions and Proceedings of the American Philological Association* 66, 18–24.

Bruce, Lorne (1986), Palace and Villa Libraries from Augustus to Hadrian. *The Journal of Library History (1974–1987)* 21(3), 510–552.

Brunt, P. A. (1961), 'Charges of Provincial Maladministration under the Early Principate', *Historia: Zeitschrift Für Alte Geschichte* 10(2), 189–227.

Brunt, P. A. (1962), 'The Army and the Land in the Roman Revolution', *The Journal of Roman Studies* 52 Parts 1 and 2, 69–86.

Brunt, P. A., and Moore, J. M. (1967), Res Gestae Divi Augusti: *The Achievements of the Divine Augustus*, Oxford: Oxford University Press.

Brunt, P. A. (1971), *Italian Manpower, 225 B.C.-A.D. 14*, Oxford: Oxford University Press.

Brunt, P. A. (1974), 'C. Fabricius Tuscus and an Augustan *Dilectus*', *Zeitschrift für Papyrologie und Epigraphik* 13, 161–185

Brunt, P. A. (1975), 'The Administrators of Roman Egypt', *The Journal of Roman Studies* 65, 124–147.

Brunt, P. A. (1983), '*Princeps* and *Equites*', *The Journal of Roman Studies* 73, 42–75.

Brunt, P. A. (1984), 'The Role of the Senate in the Augustan Regime', *The Classical Quarterly (New Series)* 34.2, 423–444.

Brunn, P. (1999), 'Coins and the Roman Imperial Government', in: Paul, G. M. & Ierardi, M. (eds.) *Togo Salomon Papers II*, Ann Arbor: University of Michigan Press, 19–40.

Bryce, T. (2014), *Ancient Syria: A Three Thousand Year History*, Oxford: Oxford University Press.

Buchan, J. (1937), *Augustus*, Boston: Houghton Mifflin Co.

Burgeon, Christophe (2022), *Tibère: L'empereur mal-aimé*, Paris: Ellipses.

Burmeister, Stefan & Kehne, Peter (2015), 'Germanicus: Lehrling – Feldherr – Diplomat' in: *Archäologie in Deutschland, 2015, Sonderheft: Ich Germanicus: Feldherr Priester Superstar* (2015), Darmstadt: Wissenschaftliche Buchgesellschaft pp. 60–73.

Burn, A. R. (1952), *The Government of the Roman Empire from Augustus to the Antonines*, London: Historical Association.

Burnett, Andrew (2011), 'The Augustan Revolution Seen from the Mints of the Provinces', *The Journal of Roman Studies* 101, 1–30.

Burns, Jasper (2007), *Great Women of Imperial Rome: Mothers and wives of the Caesars*, London: Routledge.

Burton, Paul. (2018), 'Roman Diplomacy' in: Martel, Gordon (ed.), *The Encyclopedia of Diplomacy*, London: John Wiley & Sons, 2–10.

Busetta, Marco (2017), *Tiberio. Il princeps inquieto*, Bologna: Area 51 Publishing.

Butcher, Kevin (2003), *Roman Syria and the Near East*, London: The British Museum Press.

Butcher, Kevin & Ponting, Matthew (2005), 'The Roman Denarius Under the Julio-Claudian Emperors: Mints, Metallurgy and Technology', *Oxford Journal of Archaeology* 24.2, 163–197.

Butcher, Kevin & Ponting, Matthew (2009), 'The Silver Coinage of Roman Syria Under the Julio-Claudian Emperors', *Levant* 41.1, 59–78.

Butcher, Kevin & Ponting, Matthew (2011), 'The denarius in the first century'. in: Holmes, N., (ed.) *Proceedings of the XIV International Numismatic Congress. Glasgow: The International Numismatic Council*, pp. 557–568.

Cairns, F. (1995), 'M. Agrippa in Horace 'Odes' 1.6', *Hermes* 123.2, 211–217.

Calomino, Dario (2015), 'Emperor or God? The Posthumous Commemoration of Augustus in Rome and the Provinces', *The Numismatic Chronicle (1966-)* 175, 57–82.

Camargo, Carlos Henrique Ferreira & Teive, Hélio Afonso Ghizoni (2018), 'Searching for neurological diseases in the Julio-Claudian dynasty of the Roman Empire', *Arquivos de Neuro-Psiquiatria* 76.1, 53–57. (Online at https://dx.doi.org/10.1590/0004-282x20170174).

Campbell, Brian (1975), 'Who Were the *Viri Militares*?', *The Journal of Roman Studies* 65, 11–31.

Campbell, Brian (1987), 'Teach Yourself How to Be a General', *The Journal of Roman Studies* 77, 13–29.

Campbell, Brian (1993), 'War and Diplomacy: Rome and Parthia, 31 BC–AD 235', in: Rich, J. & Shipley, G. (eds.), *War and Society in the Roman World*, London: Routledge, 213–240.

Campbell, Brian (1994), *The Roman Army 31 BC–AD 337: A Sourcebook*, London: Routledge.

Campbell, J. B. (1984), *The Emperor and the Roman Army 31 BC–AD 235*, Oxford: Oxford University Press.

Campbell, Duncan B. (1986), 'Auxiliary Artillery Revisited', *Bonner Jahrbücher* 186, 117–132.

Campbell, Duncan B. (2006), *Roman Legionary Fortresses 27 BC–AD 378*, Oxford: Osprey Publishing.

Campbell, Duncan B. (2009), 'Secrets from the Soil: The Archaeology of Augustus' Military bases' in: Oorthuys, Jasper (ed.), *Ancient Warfare*, Special Issue 1, 10–16.

Campbell, Duncan B. (2010), 'Women in Roman forts: residents, visitors or barred from entry?', *Ancient Warfare* 6.6, 48–53.

Carandini, Andrea (2017), *The Atlas of Ancient Rome: Biography and Portraits of the City*, (two volumes, revised edition), Princeton: Princeton University Press.

Carcopino, Jérôme (1940), *Daily Life in Ancient Rome: The People and The City at The Height of The Empire*, New Haven: Yale University Press.

Carey, Sorcha (2002), 'A Tradition of Adventures in the Imperial Grotto', *Greece & Rome* 49(1), 44–61.

Carey, Sorcha (2003), *Pliny's Catalogue of Culture: Art and Empire in the Natural History*, Oxford University Press.

Carpenter, R. (1973), *Beyond the Pillars of Hercules; The Classical World Seen Through the Eyes of its Discoveries*, London: Tandem.

Carroll. M. (2001), *Romans, Celts and Germans: The German Provinces of Rome*, Stroud: The History Press/Tempus Publishing.

Carter, J. E. (2003), *Crimean Chersonesos: City, Chora, Museum and Environs*, Institute of Classical Archaeology, Austin: University of Texas at Austin.

Carter, J. M (1970), *The Battle of Actium: The Rise and Triumph of Augustus Caesar*, New York: Weybright and Talley.

Cartledge, P. (1975), 'The second thoughts of Augustus on the *res publica* in 28/7 B.C.', *Hermathena* 119, 30–40.

Caspari, M. O. B. (1911), 'On the *Ivratio Italiae* of 32 B. C. [On the *Iuratio Italiae* of 32 B. C.]', *The Classical Quarterly* 5.4 (October), 230–235.

Casson, L. (1974), *Travel in the Ancient World*, Baltimore: The Johns Hopkins University Press.

Cecchelli, C. (1956), *Studi in onore di Aristide Calderini e Roberto Paribeni*: Vol. 1, Milan: Casa Ed. Ceschina.

Chadwick, Nora (1970), *The Celts*, London: Penguin Books.

Champlin, Edward (1989), 'The Testament of Augustus', *Rheinisches Museum für Philologie, Neue Folge* 132. Bd., H. 2, 154–165.

Champlin, Edward (2008), 'Tiberius the Wise', *Historia: Zeitschrift Für Alte Geschichte* 57.4, 408–425.

Champlin, Edward (2009), *Itinera Tiberi*, Working Papers in Classics, Princeton: Princeton/Stanford.

Champlin, Edward (2010), 'My Sejanus', *Humanities* 31.5 (September/October), 18–21, 52–53.

Champlin, Edward (2011a), 'Tiberius and the Heavenly Twins', *The Journal of Roman Studies* 101, 73–99.

Champlin, Edward (2011b), 'Sex on Capri', *Transactions of the American Philological Association (1974-)* 141.2, 315–332.

Champlin, Edward (2012), 'Seianus Augustus', *Chiron* Sonderdruck aus Band 42, 361–388.

Champlin, Edward (2013), 'The Odyssey of Tiberius Caesar', *Classica et Mediaevalia* 64, 199–246.

Champlin, Edward (2015), 'The Richest Man in Spain', *Zeitschrift Für Papyrologie Und Epigraphik* 196, 277–295.

Champlin, Edward (2020), 'Mallonia', *Histos* 9, 220–230.

Champlin, Edward (2024), *Tiberius and His Age: Myth, Sex, and Power*, Princeton: Princeton University Press.

Chandler, D. C. (1978), '*Quaestor Ostiensis*', *Historia: Zeitschrift Für Alte Geschichte* 27(2), 328–335.

Charlesworth, M. P. (1923), 'Tiberius and the Death of Augustus', *The American Journal of Philology* 44.2, 145–157.

Chase, George Davis (1897), 'The Origin of Roman *Praenomina*', *Harvard Studies in Classical Philology* 8, 103–184.

Chaumont, Marie-Louise (1992), '*Échos de la Campagne de Tibère en Arménie (20 av. J.-C.) dans une Épigramme de Krinagoras (*Anthologia Palatina, *IX, 430)*', *L'Antiquité Classique* 61, 178–191.

Cheek, John L. (1958), 'The Apocrypha in Christian Scripture', *Journal of Bible and Religion* 26.3, 207–212.

Cheesman, George Leonard (1914), *The* Auxilia *of the Roman Imperial Army*, Oxford: Oxford University Press.

Chevalier, Raymond (1976), *Roman Roads*, London: B. T. Batsford.

Chilver, G. E. F. (1949), '*Princeps* and *Frumentationes*', *The American Journal of Philology* 70.1, 7–21.

Chrisman, Timothy B. (2015), 'Jesus and Tiberius: An Examination of Source Reliability', *Eleutheria* 4:1 (Spring), 2–17

Christ, Karl (1977), 'Zur augusteichen Germanienpolitik', *Chiron*, 149–205.

Christ, Karl (2001), 'Velleius und Tiberius', *Historia: Zeitschrift Für Alte Geschichte* 50(2), 180–192.

Chrissanthos, S. G. (2001), 'Caesar and the Mutiny of 47 B.C.', *The Journal of Roman Studies* 91, Society for the Promotion of Roman Studies, 63–75.

Christopherson, A. J. (1968), 'The Provincial Assembly of the Three Gauls in the Julio-Claudian Period', *Historia: Zeitschrift* für Alte *Geschichte* 17.3, Stuttgart: Franz Steiner Verlag, 351–366.

Christoforou, Panayiotis (2021), 'An Indication of Truly Imperial Manners: The Roman emperor in Philo's *Legatio ad Gaium*', *Historia* 70.1 (March), 83–115.

Cilliers, L., and Retief, F. P. (2000), 'Poisons, Poisoning and the Drug Trade in Ancient Rome', *Akroterion* 45, 88–100.

Claridge, A. (1998), *Rome: An Oxford Archaeological Guide*, Oxford: Oxford University Press.

Clark, M. A. (1983), '*Spes* in the Early Imperial Cult: 'The Hope of Augustus'', *Numen* 30.1 (July), 80–105.

Clark, M. D. H. (2010), *Augustus. Caesar's Web – Power and Propaganda in Augustan Rome* (Bristol Phoenix Press Greece and Rome Live), Liverpool: Liverpool University Press.

Clarke, John R. (2003), *Roman Sex, 100 BC–AD 250*, New York: Harry N. Abrahms,

Clarke, John R. (2014), 'Sexuality and Visual Representation' in: Hubbard, Thomas K. (ed.), *A Companion to Greek and Roman Sexualities*, Oxford: Wiley Blackwell. 509–533.

Clausewitz, Carl von (1832), *Vom Kriege*, Berlin: Dümmlers Verlag.

Closs, Virginia M. (2020), *While Rome Burned: Fire, Leadership, and Urban Disaster in the Roman Cultural Imagination*, Ann Arbor: University of Michigan Press.

Coats, R. Morris & Pecquet, Gary M. (2013), 'The Calculus of Conquests: The Decline and Fall of the Returns to Roman Expansion', *The Independent Review* 17.4, 517–540.

Cogitore, Isabelle (2013), 'Tacite et Germanicus: Les Choix de la Mémoire', *Cahiers du Centre Gustave Glotz* 24, 157–174.

Cohen, S. T. (2008), 'Augustus, Julia and the Development of Exile *Ad Insulam*', *The Classical Quarterly*, New Series, 58.1, 206–217.

Collins-Elliott, Stephen A. (2014), ' Social Memory and Identity in the Central Appenines Under Augustus', *Historia: Zeitschrift Für Alte Geschichte* 63.2, 194–213.

Colmenero, R. (1979), *Augusto e Hispania: Conquista y organizacion del norte peninsular*, University of Deusto.

Coltman Brown, I. (1981), 'Tacitus and a Space for Freedom', *History Today* Vol. 31, issue 4.

Connal, Robert T. (2013), 'Velleius Paterculus: The Soldier and the Senator', *The Classical World* 107.1, 49–62.

Connolly, Peter (1975), *The Roman Army*, London: Macdonald.

Connolly, Peter (1978), *Hannibal and the Enemies of Rome*, London: Macdonald.

Connolly, Peter (1998), *Greece and Rome at War*, London: Macdonald.

Cooley, Alison E. (2009), Res Gestae: *Text, Translation and Commentary*, Cambridge: Cambridge University Press.

Cooley, Alison E. (2023), *The* Senatus Consultum de Cn. Pisone Patre*: Text, Translation, and Commentary*, Cambridge: Cambridge University Press.

Cooley, M. G. L. (ed.) (2013), *The Age of Augustus*, LACTOR 17, London (second edition).

Cooper, F. (1979), *Roman Realities*, Detroit: Wayne State University Press.

Corbet, J. H. (1974), 'The Succession Policy of Augustus', *Latomus* 33.1 (Janvier-Mars), 87–97.

Cordingley, R. A., and Richmond, Ian A. (1927), 'The Mausoleum of Augustus', *Papers of the British School at Rome* 10, Rome, 23–35.

Cornell, T. (1993), 'The End of Roman Imperial Expansion', in: Rich, J. & Shipley, G. (eds.), *War and Society in the Roman World*, London: Routledge.

Cowan, Eleanor (2009a), 'Tiberius and Augustus in Tiberian Sources', *Historia: Zeitschrift* für Alte *Geschichte* 58.4, 468–485.
Cowan, Eleanor (2009b), 'Tacitus, Tiberius and Augustus', *Classical Antiquity* 28.2 (October), 179–210.
Cowan, Eleanor (2016), 'Contesting *Clementia*: The Rhetoric of *Severitas* in Tiberian Rome before and after the Trial of Clutorius Priscus', *The Journal of Roman Studies* 106, 77–101.
Cowan, Ross (2007), *Roman Battle Tactics 109 BC–AD 313*, Oxford: Osprey Publishing.
Cowan, Ross (2003), *Roman Legionary 58 BC–AD 69*, Oxford: Osprey Publishing.
Cramer, Frederick H. (1945), 'Bookburning and Censorship in Ancient Rome: A Chapter from the History of Freedom of Speech', *Journal of the History of Ideas* 6.2 (Apr.), 157–196.
Cramer, Frederick H. (1954), *Astrology in Roman Law and Politics* (Memoirs of the American Philosophical Society 37), Philadelphia: The American Philosophical Society.
Crook, J. A. (1967), *Law and Life of Rome*, London: Thames and Hudson.
Crook, J. A. (1996), 'Political History, 30 B.C. to A.D. 14', in: Bowman, A. K., Champlin, E., & Lintott, A. (eds.), *The Cambridge Ancient History Volume X: The Augustan Empire, 43 B.C.–A.D. 69* (second edition), Cambridge: Cambridge University Press, 70–112.
Cuff, D. B. (2010), *The* Auxilia *in Roman Britain and the Two Germanies from Augustus to Caracalla: Family, Religion and 'Romanization'*, University of Toronto. (Doctoral thesis).
Cuff, P. J. (1964), 'Tacitus, *Annals* i. 72', *The Classical Review* 14.2 (June), 136–137.
Cunliffe, Barry W. (1975), *Rome and the Barbarians*, London: The Bodley Head.
Cunliffe, Barry W. (ed.) (1994), *Oxford Illustrated Prehistory of Europe*, Oxford: Oxford University Press.
Cunliffe, Barry W. (1997), *The Ancient Celts*, Oxford: Oxford University Press.
Cunliffe, Barry W. (1998), *Greeks, Roman and Barbarians: Spheres of Influence*, London: The Bodley Head.
Cunliffe, Barry W. (2001), *Facing the Ocean: The Atlantic and Its Peoples 8000 BC–AD 1500*, Oxford: Oxford University Press.
Cunliffe, Barry W. (2008), *Europe Between The Oceans: 9000 BC–AD 1000*, New Haven: Yale University Press.
Cüppers, H., Bernhard, H., & Boppert, W. (eds.) (1990), *Die Römer in Rheinland-Pfalz*, Stuttgart: Thomas Theiss Verlag.
Curchin, L. A. (1986), 'Marcus Agrippa's Gout', *The American Journal of Philology* 107.3 (Autumn), 406.
Curchin, L. A. (1995), *Roman Spain*, New York: Barnes and Noble Books.
Curti, Emmanuele, Dench, Emma & Patterson, John R. (1996), 'The Archaeology of Central and Southern Roman Italy: Recent Trends and Approaches', *The Journal of Roman Studies* 86, 170–89.
Dalla Rosa, Alberto (2011), 'Dominating the Auspices: Augustus, Augury and the Proconsuls', in: Richardson, James H. & Santangelo, Frederico (eds.), *Priests and State in the Roman World*, Stuttgart: Franz Steiner Verlag (2011), 241–267.
Dalla Rosa, Alberto (2015), 'P. Silius Nerva (proconsul d'Illyrie en 16 av. J.-C.) vainqueur des Trumplini, Camunni et Vennonetes sous les auspices d'Auguste', *Revue des Études Anciennes* Tome 117, n°2, 463–484.
D'Amato, Rafael, and Sumner, Graham (2009a), *Arms and Armour of the Imperial Roman Soldier: From Marius to Commodus*, Barnsley: Frontline Books.
D'Amato, Rafael, & Sumner, Graham (2009b), *Imperial Roman Naval Forces 31 BC–AD 500*, Oxford: Osprey Publishing.
Dąbrowa, Edward (2011), 'The Date of the Census of Quirinius and the Chronology of the Governors of the Province of Syria', *Zeitschrift Für Papyrologie Und Epigraphik* 178, 137–142.

Dąbrowa, Edward (2017), 'Tacitus on the Parthians', *Electrum* 24, 171–189.

Dąbrowa, Edward (2020a), 'The Roman Army in Syria under Augustus and Tiberius' in: Dąbrowa, E., *Camps, campaigns, colonies: Roman Military Presence in Anatolia, Mesopotamia, and the Near East. Selected Studies* (2020), 15–22.

Dąbrowa, Edward (2020b), '"... *ostentasse Romana arma satis* ...": The Military Factor in Roman-Parthian Relations under Augustus and Tiberius' in: Dąbrowa, E., *Camps, campaigns, colonies: Roman Military Presence in Anatolia, Mesopotamia, and the Near East. Selected Studies* (2020), 39–46.

David, J.-M. (1996), *The Roman Conquests of Italy*, Oxford: Blackwell.

Daitz, S. G. (1960), 'Tacitus' Technique of Character Portrayal', *AJP* LXXXI, 30–52.

Dalzell, A. (1956), 'Maecenas and the Poets', *Phoenix* 10.4 (Winter), 151–162.

Damon, Cynthia (1999), 'The Trial of Cn. Piso in Tacitus' *Annals* and the *Senatus Consultum de Cn. Pisone Patre*: New Light on Narrative Technique', *The American Journal of Philology* 120.1, 143–162.

Daniel, R. (1933), *M. Vipsanius Agrippa: Eine Monographie*, Breslau.

Daugherty, Gregory N. (1992). 'The *Cohortes Vigilum* and the Great Fire of 64 AD'. *The Classical Journal* 3.87 (3). 229–240.

Davies, R. (1989), *Service in the Roman Army*, Edinburgh: Edinburgh University Press.

Davis, P. J. E. (2004), *Death and the Emperor: Roman Imperial Funerary Monuments from Augustus to Marcus Aurelius*, Austin: University of Texas Press.

De Caprariis, Francesca (1993), 'Un monumento dinastico tiberiano nel Campo Marzio settentrionale', *Bullettino della Commissione Archeologica Comunale di Roma* 95.1, 93–114.

De la Bédoyère, Guy (2017), *Praetorian: The Rise and Fall of Rome's Imperial Bodyguard*, New Haven: Yale University Press.

De la Gravière, J. (1885), *La marine des Ptolémées et la marine des Romains*, Paris.

De Souza, P. (2008), '*Parta victoriis pax*: Roman emperors as peacemakers' in Souza, P. and France, J. (eds), *War and Peace in Ancient and Medieval History*, Cambridge: Cambridge University Press, 76–106.

De Souza, P. (2011), 'War, Slavery, and Empire in Roman Imperial Iconography', *Bulletin of the Institute of Classical Studies* 54(1), 31–62.

DeGrassi, A. (1947), *Consulares et Inscriptiones Italiae* XIII, *1 Triumphales*, 567–570.

De Laet, S. J. (1938), 'Hedendaagsche Stroomingen in de Studie der Geschiedene van Keizer Tiberius (1914–1937) (vervolg en slot)', *L'Antiquité Classique* 7.2, 333–42.

Delbrück, Hans (1990), *History of the Art of War: The Barbarian Invasions*, Volume 2, Lincoln: University of Nebraska Press.

Deming, D. (2010), *Science and Technology in World History, Volume 1: The Ancient World and Classical Civilization*, Jefferson: McFarland.

Demicheli, Dino (2017), 'Tiberius and His Family on the Epigraphic Monuments from Dalmatia' in: Kovács, Péter (ed.), *Tiberius in Illyricum: Contributions to the History of the Danubian Provinces under Tiberius' Reign (14–37 AD). Hungarian Polis Studies* 24, Budapest: Eötvös Loránd University, 9–39.

Desbat, A. (2005), *Lugdunum: Naissance d'une Capitale: Dossier de Presse*, Lyon-Fourvière: Rhône Le Départment.

Dettenhofer, Maria H. (2002), 'Die Wahlreform des Tiberius und ihre Auswirkungen', *Historia: Zeitschrift für Alte Geschichte* Bd. 51, H. 3 (3rd Qtr.), 349–358.

Detweiler, R. (1970), 'Historical Perspectives on the Death of Agrippa Postumus', *The Classical Journal* 65.7 (April), 289–295.

Dieckman, Hermann (1925), 'Das Fünfzehnte Jahr Des Caesar Tiberius', *Biblica* 6.1, 63–67.

Digg-Wolf, David (2009), 'Dating Kalkriese: The Numismatic Evidence' in: Lehman, Gustav Adolf & Wiegels, Rainer (eds.), *Römische Präsenz und Herrschaft im Germanien der augusteischen Zeit. Der Fundplatz von Kalriese im Kontext neuerer Forschungen und Ausgrabungsbefunde: Beiträge zu der Tagung des Fachs Alte Geschichte der Universität Osnabrück und der Kommission ‚Imperium und Barbaricum' der Göttinger Akademie der Wissenschaften in Osnabrück vom 10. bis 12. Juni 2004*, Göttingen: Vandenhoeck & Ruprecht.

Dilke, O. A. W. (1998), *Greek and Roman Maps*, Baltimore: Johns Hopkins University Press.

Dixon, K. R., and Southern, P. (1992), *The Roman Cavalry from the First to the Third Century AD*, London: B. T. Batsford.

Dobiáš, J. (1960), 'King Maroboduus as a Politician', *Klio* 38, 155–166.

Domainko, Annika (2015), 'The Conception of History in Velleius Paterculus' *Historia Romana*', *Histos* 9, 76–110.

Domergue, C. (1978), *Mines d'or romaines en Espagne*, Toulouse, 1978.

Dorey, T. A. (1960), 'Agricola and Domitian', *Greece & Rome* 7(1), 66–71.

Dörrenberg, O. (1909), *Römerspuren und Römerkriege im nordwestlichen Deutschland*, Leipzig: Kommissions-Verlag der Dieterich'schen Verlagsbuchhandlung Theodor Weicher.

Downey, G. (1983), 'Tiberiana', in Wolfgang Haase (ed.), *Aufstieg und Niedergang der römischen Welt* 2, Stuttgart: de Gruyter, 109–110.

Drinkwater, J. F. (1978), 'The Rise and Fall of the Gallic Iulii : Aspects of the Development of the Aristocracy of the Three Gauls under the Early Empire', *Latomus* 37(4), 817–850.

Drinkwater, J. F. (1983), *Roman Gaul: The Three Provinces, 58 BC–AD 260*, London: Croom Helm.

Droberjar, Eduard (2009), 'Contributions to the History and Archaeology of the Maroboduus Empire', in: Bemmann, J. & Salač, V. (eds.), *Mitteleuropa zur Zeit Marbods*. Praha – Bonn, 81–106.

Drogula, Fred K. (2007), '*Imperium*, *Potestas*, and the *Pomerium* in the Roman Republic', *Historia: Zeitschrift für Alte Geschichte* Bd. 56, H. 4

Drogula, Fred K. (2011a), 'Controlling Travel: Deportation, Islands and the Regulation of Senatorial Mobility in the Augustan Age', *The Classical Quarterly*, New Series, Vol. 61.1 (May), 230–266.

Drogula, Fred K. (2011b), 'The *Lex Porcia* and the Development of Legal Restraints on Roman Governors', *Chiron* 41, 91–124.

Drogula, Fred K. (2015a), *Commanders and Command in the Roman Republic and Early Empire* (Studies in the History of Greece and Rome), Chapel Hill: The University of North Carolina Press.

Drogula, Fred K. (2015b), 'Who Was Watching Whom?: A Reassessment of the Conflict between Germanicus and Piso', *American Journal of Philology* 136, 121–153.

Duncan-Jones, Richard (1982), *The Economy of the Roman Empire: Quantitative Studies*, Cambridge: Cambridge University Press (second edition).

Duncan-Jones, Richard (1990), *Structure and Scale in the Roman Economy*, Cambridge: Cambridge University Press.

Dunkle, J. Roger (1971), 'The Rhetorical Tyrant in Roman Historiography: Sallust, Livy and Tacitus', *The Classical World* 65(1), 12–20.

DuPont, Florence (1999), *Daily Life in Ancient Rome*, Oxford: Blackwell. (English translation)

Durry, M. (1938), *Les Cohortes Prétoriennes*, Paris: E. de Boccard.

Dušanić, S. (1994), 'Roman Mining in Illyricum: Historical Aspects', *Dall' Adriatico al Danubio: L'Illirico nell'età greca e romana. Cividale del Friuli*, 47- 70.

Dušcanić, S. (2008), 'The Valle Ponti Lead Ingots: Notes on Roman Notables, Commercial Activities in Free Illyricum at the beginning of the Principate', *Starinar* 58, 107–118.

Dusenbury, David Lloyd (2019), *The Innocence of Pontius Pilate: How the Roman Trial of Jesus Shaped History*, London: C. Hurst & Co. Publishers Ltd.

Du Toit, Lois (1980), 'The Senatorial Debate on the 17th September A.D. 14 and Drusus' Journey to Pannonia', *Acta Classica* 23, 130–133.

Džino, Danijel (2005), *Illyrian Policy of Rome in the Late Republic and Early Principate*, University of Adelaide. (Doctoral thesis). (Available online at http://hdl.handle.net/2440/37806, accessed 1 March 2024).

Džino, Danijel (2008a), 'Strabo 7, 5 and imaginary Illyricum', *Athenaeum: Studi periodici di letteratura e storie dell'Antichità* 96.1, 173–192.

Džino, Danijel (2008b), 'Deconstructing Illyrians: Zeitgeist, Changing Perceptions and the Identity of Peoples from Ancient Illyricum' in: *Croatian Studies Review*, 43–55.

Džino, Danijel (2009), 'The *Bellum Batonianum* in contemporary historiographical narratives in a search for the post-modern Bato the Daesitiate', *Arheološki radovi i rasprave* 16, 29–45.

Džino, Danijel (2010), *Illyricum in Roman Politics: 229 BC–AD 68*, Cambridge: Cambridge University Press.

Džino, Danijel (2012), '*Bellum Pannonicum*: The Roman armies and indigenous communities in southern Pannonia 16–9 BC', *Actes du Symposium international: Le livre. La Romanie. L'Europe* 3 (20–23 September 2011), 461–480. (Fourth edition).

Džino, Danijel (2016), 'Appian's Illyrike: The Final Stage of the Roman Construction of Illyricum', Istraživanja 27, 69–83.

Džino, Danijel (2017), 'The Division of Illyricum in Tiberian Era: Long Term Significance' in: Kovács, Péter (ed.), *Tiberius in Illyricum: Contributions to the History of the Danubian Provinces under Tiberius' Reign (14–37 AD). Hungarian Polis Studies* 24, Budapest: Eötvös Loránd University, 41–54.

Džino, Danijel & Kunić, Alka Domić (2018), 'A View from the Frontier Zone: Roman conquest of Illyricum' in: Bradač, Marina Milićević & Demicheli, Dino (eds.), *The Century of the Brave/ Stoljeće hrabrih*, Zagreb: FF Press, pp. 77–87

Earl, D. C. (1968), *The Age of Augustus*, London: Paul Elek Productions.

Eaton, Jonathan (2011), 'The Political Significance of the Imperial Watchword in the Early Empire', *Greece & Rome* 58(1), 48063.

Ebel-Zepauer, W. (2003), 'Die augusteischen Marschlager in Dorsten-Holsterhausen', *Germania* 81, 539–555.

Ebel-Zepauer, W. (2005), 'Römer und Germanen in Dorsten-Holsterhausen', in H.-G. Horn *et al* (eds.) *Von Anfang an. Archäologie in Nordrhein-Westfalen (Schriften zur Bodendenkmalpflege in Nordrhein-Westfalen* 8, 367–368.

Echols, E. (1958), 'The Roman City Police: Origin and Development', *The Classical Journal* 53.8 (May), 377–385.

Eck, Werner (2003), *The Age of Augustus*, Oxford: Blackwell Publishing.

Eck, Werner (2009), *Augustus und seine Zeit*, München: Verlag C. H. Beck. (Fifth edition).

Eck, Werner (2010), 'P. Quinctilius Varus, seine senatorishe Laubahn und sein Handeln in Germanien: Normalität oder aristokratishe Unfähigkeit?' in: Aßkamp, Rudolf & Esh, Tobias (eds.), *IMPERIUM – Varus und seine Zeit. Beiträge zum internationalen Kolloquium des LWL-Römermuseums am 28. und 29. April 2008 in Münster*, Münster: Aschendorff Verlag (2010), 13–28.

Eck, Werner (2014), 'Divus Augustus: Das Fortwirken seiner Politik im Imperium Romanum', in: Borster, Marietta, & Schuller, Florian (eds.), *Augustus: Herrscher an der Zeitenwende*, Regensburg: Verlag Friedrich Pustet (2014), 170–285 + 204–205.

Eck, Werner (2015), 'Tod des Germanicus: Trauerhysterie und der Prozess gegen Piso' in: *Archäologie in Deutschland, 2015, Sonderheft: Ich Germanicus: Feldherr Priester Superstar* (2015), Darmstadt: Wissenschaftliche Buchgesellschaft, 74–78.

Eck, Werner (2016), 'Das römische Heer unter Augustus' in: Negri, Giovanni & Valvo, Alfredo (eds.) *Studi su Augusto. In occasione del XX centenario della morte*, Turin: G. Giappichelli Editore (2016), 77–94.

Eck, Werner (2017), 'Das Heer als Machtfaktor im Ordnungsgefüge des augusteischen Prinzipats' in: *Augusto. La costruzione del principato (Roma, 4–5 dicembre 214. Atti dei Convegni Lincei 309),* Rome: Bardi Edizioni (2017), 239–255.

Edmondson, Jonathan (ed.) (2009), *Augustus*, Edinburgh Readings on the Ancient World, Edinburgh.

Edwards, C. (2007), *Death in Ancient Rome*, New Haven: Yale University Press.

Edwards, C. (2011), 'Tacitus, Tiberius and Capri', *Latomus* T. 70, Fasc. 4 (Décembre), 1047–1057.

Edwards, Rebecca M. (2012), 'His Father's Son and His Son's Father: Augustus and Germanicus in Tiberian Documents' in: Deroux, C. (ed.), *Studies in Latin Literature and Roman History* 16, Brussels: Editions Latomus (2012), 398–414.

Edwards, Rebecca M. (2015), 'Caesar Telling Tales: Phaedrus and Tiberius', *Rheinisches Museum für Philologie* (Neue Folge) 158. Bd., H. 2, 167–184.

Eggers, H. J. (1976), 'Zur absoluten Chronologie der Kaizerzeit im freien Germanien' in: Temporini, H. & Haase, H. (eds.) *Aufstieg und Niedergang der römischen Welt: Geschichte und Kultur Roms im Spiegel d. neueren Forschung* II.5.1, Stuttgart: de Gruyer, 3–64.

Ehrenberg, V. (1953), '*Imperium Maius* in the Roman Republic', *The American Journal of Philology* 74.2, 113–136.

Ehrenberg, V., & Jones, A. H. M. (1955), *Documents Illustrating the Reigns of Augustus and Tiberius*, Oxford: Clarendon Press. (second edition).

Eilers, C. (2004), 'The Date of Augustus' Edict on the Jews (Jos. *AJ* 16.162–165) and the Career of C. Marcius Censorinus', *Phoenix* 58.1/2 (Spring - Summer), 86–95.

Elbe, J. von (1977), *Die Römer in Deutschland: Ausgrabungen, Fundstätten, Museen*, Gütersloh: Bertelsmann.

Elder, Olivia, & Mullen, Alex (2019), 'The Language of Letters and Beyond: Greek in Suetonius' Biographies' in: *The Language of Roman Letters: Bilingual Epistolography from Cicero to Fronto* (Cambridge Classical Studies). Cambridge: Cambridge University Press, pp. 220–270.

Elsner, J. (1991), 'Cult and Sculpture: Sacrifice in the *Ara Pacis Augustae*', *The Journal of Roman Studies* 81, 50–61.

Elton, H. (1996), *Frontiers of the Roman Empire*, Bloomington: Indiana University Press.

Engel, Wilson F. (1980), 'The Iron World of *Sejanus*: History in the Crucible of Art', *Renaissance Drama* (New Series) 11, 95–114.

Engelmann, H. (2004), 'Marcus Agrippa in Patara (*SEG* 44, 1208)', *Zeitschrift für Papyrologie und Epigraphik* 146, 129.

Engels, D., (1990), *Roman Corinth: An Alternative Model for the Classical City*, Chicago: University of Chicago Press.

Erdkamp, Paul (2005), *The Grain Market in the Roman Empire: A Social, Political and Economic Study*, Cambridge: Cambridge University Press.

Erdkamp, Paul (2007) (ed.), *A Companion to the Roman Army*, Oxford: Blackwell Publishing.

Erdrich, Michael (2016), 'Maroboduus and the Consolidation of Roman Authority in the Middle Danube Region' in: Karwowski, Maciej & Ramsl, Peter C., *Boii - Taurisci. Proceedings of the International Seminar, Oberleis-Klement, June 14th-15th, 2012*, Wien: Austrian Academy of Sciences Press, 237–252.

Erdrich, Michael (2015), 'Augustan and Early Tiberian *Stationes* in Context: Fishbourne, Bentumersiel, Winsum, Devin' in: Breeze, David J., Jones, Rebecca H., & Oltean, Ioana

A. (2015) (eds.), *Understanding Roman Frontiers. A Celebration for Bill Hanson*, Edinburgh: John Donald, 3–26.

Esmonde-Cleary, S. (2007), *Rome in the Pyrenees: Lugdunum and the Convenae from the First Century B.C. to the Seventh Century A.D.*, London: Routledge.

Eubel, P. K. (1906), *Geschichte der Kölnischen Minoriten-ordensprovinz*, Köln: J. & W. Boisserée Buchhandlung.

Evans, Sir A. J. (1883), 'An Investigation of the Roman Road-Lines from Salonae to Scupi, and the Municipal Sites and Mining Centres in the Old Dalmatian and Dardanian Ranges', *Antiquarian Researches in Illyricum*, Part 3, from *The Archaeologia* 58, London: Nichols and Sons, 1–78.

Evans, R. (2011), *Roman Conquests: Asia Minor, Syria and Armenia*, Barnsley: Pen & Sword Books.

Everitt, A. (2001), *Cicero: The Life and Times of Rome's Greatest Politician*, New York: Random House.

Everitt, A. (2006), *Augustus: The Life of Rome's First Emperor*, New York: Random House.

Fagan, G. F. (2011), *The Lure of the Arena: Social Psychology, Spectatorship and the Roman Games*, Cambridge: Cambridge University Press.

Fantham, E. (2006), *Julia Augusti: The Emperor's Daughter*, London: Routledge.

Farrar, Linda (1998), *Ancient Roman Gardens*, Stroud: Sutton Publishing.

Favro, Diane (1996), *The Urban Image of Augustan Rome*, Cambridge: Cambridge University Press.

Favro, Diane (1992), '*Pater urbis*: Augustus as City Father of Rome', *Journal of the Society of Architectural Historians* 51.1 (March), 61–84.

Favro, Diane, & Johanson, Christopher (2010), 'Death in Motion: Funeral Processions in the Roman Forum', *Journal of the Society of Architectural Historians* 69, no. 1: 12–37.

Feeny, D. (2007), *Caesar's Calendar: Ancient Time and the Beginnings of History*, Berkeley: University of Califormia Press.

Feingold, Mordechai (2016), 'Scholarship and Politics: Henry Savile's Tacitus and the Essex Connection', *The Review of English Studies* 67.282, 855–874.

Feldherr, Andrew (2009), 'The Poisoned Chalice: Rumor and Historiography in Tacitus' Account of the Death of Drusus', *Materiali e Discussioni per l'analisi Dei Testi Classici* 61, 175–189.

Feldman, L. H. (1993), *Jew and Gentile in the Ancient World: Attitudes and Interactions from Alexander to Justinian*, Princeton: Princeton University Press.

Fernández-Götz, Manuel & Roymans, Nico (2024), *Archaeology of the Roman Conquest: Tracing the Legions, Reclaiming the Conquered*, Cambridge: Cambridge University Press.

Ferrari, G. B. De (1826), *A New Guide of Naples, Its Environs, Procida, Ischia and Capri: Compiled from Vasi's Guide, Several More Recent Publications, and a Personal Visit of the Compiler to the Churches, Monuments, Antiquities Etc*, Naples: Gabriel Porcelli.

Ferrary, J.-L. (2001), 'The Powers of Augustus' in: Edmondson, Jonathan (ed.), *Augustus*, Edinburgh Readings on the Ancient World, Edinburgh (2009), 90–136.

Ferrill, Arther (1971), 'Prosopography and the Last Years of Augustus', *Historia: Zeitschrift für Alte Geschichte* Bd. 20, H. 5/6 (4th Qtr.), 718–731.

Ferrill, Arther (1991), *Caligula, Emperor of Rome*, London: Thames and Hudson.

Ferris, I. M. (2000), *Enemies of Rome: Barbarians Through Roman Eyes*, Stroud: Alan Sutton Publishing/The History Press.

Fields, Nic (2009), *The Roman Army of the Principate 27 BC–AD 117*, Oxford: Osprey Publishing.

Figuera, T. J., Brennan, T. C., & Sternberg, R. H. (2001), *Wisdom of the Ancients: Leadership Lessons from Alexander the Great to Julius Caesar*, New York: Withrop.

Finley, M. I. (1985), *Ancient History: Evidence and Models*, London: Chatto & Windus.

Fischer, Moshe (2011), ‚Rome and Judaea during the First Century CE: A strange *modus vivendi*' in: Moosbauer, Günther & Wiegels, Rainer (eds.) *Römische Okkupations- und Grenzpolitik im frühen Principat Beiträge zum Kongress* ‚Fines imperii – imperium sine fine?' *in Osnabrück vom 14. bis 18. September 2009, Osnabrücker Forschungen zu Altertum und Antike-Rezeption* 14, Diepholz: Druckhaus Breyer, 143–156.

Fischer, T. (2012), *Die Armee der Caesaren*, Regensburg: F. Pustet Verlag.

Fishwick, Duncan (1987), *The Imperial Cult in the Latin West: Studies in the Ruler Cult of the Western Provinces of the Roman Empire, Volume 1, Parts 1 and 2,* Boston: Brill Academic Publishers.

Fishwick, Duncan (1988), 'Dated inscriptions and the *Feriale Duranum*', *Syria* 65 fascicule 3–4, 349–361.

Fishwick, Duncan (1999), 'Coinage and Cult: The Provincial Momuments at Lugdunum, Tarraco and Emertita' in: Paul, G. M., & Ierardi, M. (eds.), *Roman Coins and Public Life: E. Togo Salomon Papers II*, Ann Arbor: University of Michigan Press (1999), 95–121.

Fishwick, Duncan (1992), 'On the Temple of *Divus* "Augustus"', *Phoenix* 46.3 (Autumn), 232–255.

Fishwick, Duncan (2002), *The Imperial Cult in the Latin West: Studies in the Ruler Cult of the Western Roman Empire, Volume 3, Part 1*, Boston: Brill Academic Publishers.

Fishwick, Duncan (2003), *The Imperial Cult in the Latin West: Studies in the Ruler Cult of the Western Provinces of the Roman Empire, Volume 3, Part 3,* Boston: Brill Academic Publishers.

Fishwick, Duncan (2014), 'Augustus and the Cult of the Emperor', *Stvd. hist., H.a antig.* 32, 47–60.

Fishwick, Duncan & Shaw, Brent D. (1977), 'The Formation of Africa Proconsularis', *Hermes* 105(3), 369–380.

Fiske, George Converse (1900), 'Notes on the Worship of the Roman Emperors in Spain', *Harvard Studies in Classical Philology* 11, 101–139.

Fitzgibbon, J. C. (1976), '*Ergastula*', *Echos du monde classique: Classical news and views* 20.2, 55–59.

FitzPatrick, Mary C. (1949), 'Tiberius' Villa Jovis on the Isle of Capri', *The Classical Journal* 45(2), 67–70.

Flach, Dieter (1973), 'Der Regierungsanfang des Tiberius', *Historia: Zeitschrift für Alte Geschichte* Bd. 22, H. 4 (4th Qtr.), 552–569.

Flint, W. W. (1912), 'The *Delatores* in the Reign of Tiberius, as Described by Tacitus', *The Classical Journal* 8(1), 37–42.

Flower, Harriet I. (1996), *Ancestor Masks and Aristocratic Power in Roman Culture*, Oxford: Oxford University Press, 155–187.

Flower, Harriet I. (1998), 'Rethinking "*Damnatio Memoriae*": The Case of Cn. Calpurnius Piso Pater in AD 20', *Classical Antiquity* 17.2 (October), 155–187.

Flower, Harriet I. (2006), *The Art of Forgetting: Disgrace and Oblivion in Roman Political Culture*, Chapel Hill: The University of North Carolina Press.

Flower, Harriet I. (2010), *Roman Republics*, Princeton: Princeton University Press.

Flower, Harriet I. (2020), 'Augustus, Tiberius, and the End of the Roman Triumph', *Classical Antiquity* 39, 1–28.

Fontana, Benedetto (1993), 'Tacitus on Empire and Republic', *History of Political Thought* 14.1, 27–40.

Frandsen, P. S. (1835), *Über die Politik des Marcus Agrippa*, Altona.

Frank, Tenney (1921), 'The *Carmen Saeculare* of Horace', *The American Journal of Philology* 42.4, 324–329.

Frank, Tenney (1935), 'The Financial Crisis of 33 A. D.', *The American Journal of Philology* 56(4), 336–341.

Fraschetti, A. (1980), 'La mort d'Agrippa et l'autel du Belvedere: Un certain type d'hommage', *Mélanges de L'École Française de Rome* 92, 957–76.

Freisenbruch, A. (2010), *Caesar's Wives: Sex, Power and Politics in Ancient Rome*, New York: Free Press.

Frey-Kupper, S. (1991), 'Germanicus und Drusus auf einer Münze von Panormos', *Schweizer Münzblätter* 164 (1991), pp. 90–95

Frisch, P. (1980), 'Zu den Elogien des Augustusforums', *Zeitschrift für Papyrologie und Epigraphik* 39, 91–98.

Fritz, Kurt von (1957), 'Tacitus, Agricola, Domitian, and the Problem of the Principate', *Classical Philology* 52(2), 73–97.

Frothingham, A. L. (1915), 'The Roman Territorial Arch', *American Journal of Archaeology* 19.2 (April-June), 155–174.

Frova, A. (1961), 'L'iscrizione di Ponzio Pilato a Cesarea', *Rendiconti dell'Istituto Lombardo* 95, 419–34.

Fuhrmann, C. J. (2011), *Policing the Roman Empire: Soldiers, Administrators, and Public Order*, Oxford: Oxford University Press.

Fuks, Gideon (1982), 'Again on the Episode of the Gilded Roman Shields at Jerusalem', *The Harvard Theological Review* 75(4), 503–507.

Fulford, M. (1992), 'Territorial Expansion and the Roman Empire', *World Archaeology* 23.3, Archaeology of Empires (February), 294–305.

Fullerton, M. (1985), 'The *Domus Augusti* in Imperial Iconography of 13–12 B.C.', *American Journal of Archaeology* 89, 473–483.

Fumagalli, Antonio (2021), *Tiberio: Principe indesiderato, imperatore per forza*, Rome: Edizioni Efesto.

Futurell, Alison (1997), *Blood in the Arena: The Spectacle of Roman Power*, Austin: University of Texas Press.

Gabba, E. (1971), 'The Perusine War and Triumviral Italy', *Harvard Studies in Classical Philology* 75, 139–160.

Gaber, Amr (2015), 'The Enneads of the Central Halls of the Ptolemaic Period: Epigraphic and Iconographic Evidence', *Journal of Near Eastern Studies* 74(1), 91–113.

Gabriel, R. A. (2006), *Soldiers' Lives through History - The Ancient World*, Santa Barbara: Greenwood Press.

Gaillou, P., Jones, M (1991), *The Bretons*, Oxford: Blackwell.

Galinsky, Karl (1966), 'Venus in a Relief of the *Ara Pacis Augustae*', *American Journal of Archaeology* 70.3 (July), 223–243.

Galinsky, Karl (1967), 'Sol and the *Carmen Saeculare*', *Latomus* 26.3, 619–633.

Galinsky, Karl (1996), *Augustan Culture: An Interpretive Introduction*, Princeton University Press.

Galinsky, Karl (2005) (ed.), *The Cambridge Companion to the Age of Augustus*, Cambridge University Press.

Galinsky, Karl (2012), *Augustus: Introduction to the Life of an Emperor*, Cambridge University Press.

Galinsky, Karl (2015), 'Augustus' *Auctoritas* and *Res Gestae* 34.3', *Hermes* 143.2, 244–249.

Gardener, Jane F. (1988), 'Julia's Freedmen: Questions of Law and Status', *Bulletin of the Institute of Classical Studies* 35, 94–100.

Garnsey, E. R. (1924), 'The Fall of Maecenas', *The Sewanee Review* 32.2 (April), 146–161.

Garnsey, P. D. A., and Whittaker, C. R., (eds.) (1978), *Imperialism in the Ancient World*, Cambridge: Cambridge University Press.

Garnsey, P. (1988), *Famine and Food Supply in the Graeco-Roman World: Responses to Risk and Crisis*, Cambridge: Cambridge University Press.

Gartrell, Amber (2021), *The Cult of Castor and Pollux in Ancient Rome Myth, Ritual, and Society*, Cambridge: Cambridge University Press.

Gaspari, Andrej & Zidansek, Iris Bekljanov (2015), 'Augustan military graves from the area of Kongresni trg in Ljubljana' in: Istenič, Janka, Laharnar, Boštjan, & Horvat, Jana (eds.) *Evidence of the Roman Army in Slovenia*, Katalogi in monografije / Catalogi et monographiae 41, Ljubljana: Narodni muzej Slovenije, 125–169.

Gebauer, G. C., & Sommersberg, F. W. von (1717), *De M. Agrippa*, Leipzig: Zeidler.

Georgiadou, Aristoula (1988), 'The "Lives of the Caesars" and Plutarch's other "Lives"', *Illinois Classical Studies* 13(2), 349–356.

Giard, J.-B. (1967), 'Le trésor de Port-Haliguen: Contribution à l'étude du monnayage d'Auguste', *Revue Numismatique* 6.9, 121.

Gibson, Alisdair (ed.) (2012), *The Julio-Claudian Succession: Reality and Perception of the 'Augustan Model', Mnemosyne*, Supplements, History and Archaeology of Classical Antiquity 349, Leiden: Brill.

Gilliam, J. F. (1954), 'The Roman Military *Feriale*', *The Harvard Theological Review* 47.3 (July), 183–196.

Gilliver, K. (2007), 'The Augustan Reform and the Structure of the Imperial Army' in: Erdkamp, Paul (ed.), *A Companion to the Roman Army*, Oxford: Blackwell Publishing, 183–200.

Giua, M. A. (1975), 'Tiberio simulatore nella tradizione storica pretacitiana', *Athenaeum* 53, 352–363.

Giua, M. A. (1978), 'Sulla biografia suetoniana di Tiberio: Tradizione e struttura', *Athenaeum* 56, 329–345.

Gleason, K., Burrell, B., Netzer, E., Taylor, L., & Williams, J. (1998), 'The promontory palace at Caesarea Maritima: Preliminary evidence for Herod's Praetorium', *Journal of Roman Archaeology* 11, 23–52.

Goar, Robert J. (1976), 'Horace, Velleius Paterculus and Tiberius Caesar', *Latomus* T. 35, Fasc. 1 (Janvier-Mars), 43–54.

Goethert-Polaschek, Karin (1973), *Studien zur Ikonographie der Antonia Minor*, Studia archaeologica, 15, Roma: L'erma di Bretschneider.

Goldsworthy, Adrian Keith (2003), *In the Name of Rome: The Men Who Won the Roman Empire*, London: Weidenfeld and Nicholson.

Goldsworthy, Adrian Keith (2000), *Roman Warfare*, London: Cassell.

Goldsworthy, Adrian Keith (1996), *The Roman Army at War 100 BC–AD 200*, Oxford: Oxford University Press.

Goldsworthy, Adrian Keith (2010), *Antony And Cleopatra*, New Haven: Yale University Press.

Goldsworthy, Adrian Keith (2014), *Augustus: First Emperor of Rome*, Yale: Yale University Press.

Goldsworthy, Adrian Keith (2016), *Pax Romana: War, Peace and Conquest in the Roman World*, London: Weidenfeld and Nicholson.

Golz Huzar, E. (1978), *Mark Antony: A Biography*, Minneapolis: University of Minnesota Press.

Goodman, M. (1996), 'Judaea' in: Bowman, A.K., Champlin, E., & Lintott, A. (eds.), *The Cambridge Ancient History Volume X: The Augustan Empire, 43 B.C.–A.D. 69* (second edition), Cambridge: Cambridge University Press, 737–780.

Goodman, Penelope (2020), 'In omnibus regionibus? The fourteen regions and the city of Rome', in: *Papers of the British School at Rome* 88, 1–32.

Gordon, A. E. (1968), 'Notes on the *Res Gestae* of Augustus', *California Studies in Classical Antiquity* 1, 125–138.

Gordon, A. E. (1983), *Illustrated Introduction to Latin Epigraphy*, Berkeley: University of California Press.

Gordon, R., Reynolds, J., Beard, M., & Roueché, C. (1997), 'Roman Inscriptions', *Journal of Roman Studies* 87, 206–40.

Gorski, Gilbert (2023), 'Villa Jovis: Reconstructing Tiberius' Retreat on the Island of Capri', Sarver: Allegheny Valley Collaborative.

Goud, Thomas E. (1996), 'The Sources of Josephus "Antiquities" 19', *Historia: Zeitschrift Für Alte Geschichte* 45(4), 472–482.

Goudineau, C. (1996), 'Gaul' in: Bowman, A. K., Champlin, E., & Lintott, A. (eds.), *The Cambridge Ancient History Volume X: The Augustan Empire, 43 B.C.–A.D. 69*, Cambridge: Cambridge University Press, 464–502.

Goudineau, C., & Rebourg, A. (eds.) (1985), *Les villes Augustéennes de Gaule* (Actes du Coloque international d'Autun 6–8 juin 1985), Autun.

Gowing, Alain M. (2007), 'The Imperial Republic of Velleius Paterculus' in: Marincola, John (ed.), *A Companion to Greek and Roman Historiography*, London: Wiley Publishing (2007), 389–395.

Gowing, Alain M. (2010), '"Caesar grabs my pen": Writing Civil War under Tiberius' in: *Citizens of Discord: Rome and its Civil Wars*, Breed, B. W., Damon, C. & Rossi, A. (eds.), Oxford University Press (2010), 249–60.

Gowing, Alain M. (2016), 'Memory as Motive in Tacitus' in: Galinsky, Karl (ed.), *Memory in Ancient Rome and Early Christianity*, Oxford: Oxford University Press (2016), 43–64.

Grainger, John D. (2020), *The Roman Imperial Succession*, Barnsley: Pen & Sword Books.

Grant, Michael (1949), 'The Augustan 'Constitution'', *Greece & Rome* 18.54 (October), 97–112.

Grant, Michael (1950a), *Aspects of the Principate of Tiberius: Historical Comments on the Colonial Coinage Issued Outside Spain* (Numismatic Notes and Monographs), New York: American Numismatic Society. (Online at http://numismatics.org/digitallibrary/ark:/53695/nnan117329).

Grant, Michael (1950b), 'The Official Coinage of Tiberius in Galatia', *The Numismatic Chronicle and Journal of the Royal Numismatic Society* 10(37/38), 43–48.

Grant, Michael (1958), *Roman History from Coins*, Cambridge: Cambridge University Press.

Grant, Michael (1974), *The Army of the Caesars*, New York: M. Evans and Company.

Graham, Daryn (2019), 'Tacitus, Tiberius, and the CE17 Earthquake in the Roman Province of Asia', *New England Classical Journal* 46.1, 1–20.

Grapin, C. (2003), 'Tiberius Turus/Turos, un Celtibère au service de la VI[e] légion mort à Metz', *Latomus* 62.3 (July-September), 635–641.

Gray, E. W. (1970), 'The *Imperium* of M. Agrippa. A Note on P. Colon. inv. nr. 4701', *Zeitschrift für Papyrologie und Epigraphik 6*, 227–238.

Green, P. (1989), *Classical Bearings: Interpreting Ancient History and Culture*, Berkeley: University of California Press.

Geer, Russel M. (1929), 'A Lexicon of Vituperation', *The Classical Weekly* 22(26), 208–208.

Gregoratti, L. (2012), 'Between Rome and Ctesiphon: the problem of ruling Armenia' in: *Армения — Иран: Proceedings of the Conference Armenia – Iran: History. Culture. The modern perspectives of progress, June 28, 2010*, Moscow.

Gregg, W. W. (1914), *The Tragedy of Tiberius 1607*, The Malone Society Reprints, Oxford: Oxford University Press.

Grether, Gertrude (1946), 'Livia and the Roman Imperial Cult,' *The American Journal of Philology* 67(3), 222–252.

Griffin, M.T. (1985), *Nero: The End of a Dynasty*, New Haven: Yale University Press.

Griffin, M. T. (1997), 'The Senate's Story', *Journal of Roman Studies* 87, 249–253.

Grote, K. (2005), *Römerlager in Hedemünden*, Heimat- u. Geschichtsverein Sydekum.

Grote, K. (2012), *Römerlager in Hedemünden. Der augusteische Stützpunkt, seine Außenanlagen, seine Funde und Befunde*, Niedersächsisches Landesmuseum Hannover, Sandstein Verlag.

Gruen, Erich S. (1996), 'The Expansion of the Empire' in: Bowman, A. K., Champlin, E., & Lintott, A. (eds.), *The Cambridge Ancient History Volume X: The Augustan Empire, 43 B.C.-A.D. 69* (second edition), Cambridge: Cambridge University Press, 147–197.

Gruen, Erich S. (2003), 'The Emperor Tiberius and the Jews' in: Hantos, T. (ed.), *Laurea Internationalis: Festschrift für Jochen Bleicken zum 75 Geburstag*, 298–312.

Gruen, Erich S. (2005), 'Augustus and the Making of the Principate' in: Galinsky, Karl (ed.), *The Cambridge Companion to the Age of Augustus*, Cambridge: Cambridge University Press (2005).

Gruen, Erich S. (2016), 'Was There Judeophobia in Classical Antiquity?' in: *The Construct of Identity in Hellenistic Judaism: Essays on Early Jewish Literature and History*, Berlin: De Gruyter (2016), 313–332.

Grummond, N. J. de (1990), '*Pax Augusta* and the *Horae* on the *Ara Pacis Augustae*', *American Journal of Archaeology* 94.4 (October), 663–677.

Grünewald, T. (2004), *Bandits in the Roman Empire: Myth and Reality*, London: Routledge.

Gunderson, Erik (2014), 'E.g. Augustus: *exemplum* in the Augustus and Tiberius', in: Power, Tristan & Gibson, Roy K. (eds.), *Suetonius the Biographer: Studies in Roman Lives* (2014), Oxford: Oxford University Press, 130–146.

Gurval, R. A., (1995), *Actium and Augustus: The Politics and Emotions of Civil War*, Ann Arbor: The University of Michigan Press.

Günther, R. T. (1903), 'Earth Movements in the Bay of Naples', *The Geographical Journal* 22 (August), 133–135.

Günther, R. T. (1913), *Pausilypon: The Imperial Villa Near Naples*, Oxford: Oxford University Press.

Guštin, Mitja (2015), 'Roman Camps Following the Toute to Segestica and the Western Balkans' in: Istenič, Janka, Laharnar, Boštjan, & Horvat, Jana (eds.), *Evidence of the Roman Army in Slovenia*, Ljubljana: Narodni muzej Slovenije, 221–233.

Güven, S. (1998), 'Displaying the *Res Gestae* of Augustus: A Monument of Imperial Image for All', *Journal of the Society of Architectural Historians* 57.1 (March), 30–45.

Haas, R. N. (2009), *War of Necessity; War of Choice: A Memoir of Two Iraq Wars*, New York: Simon and Schuster.

Habicht, C. (1991), 'Was Augustus a Visitor at the Panathenaia?', *Classical Philology* 86, 3 (July), 226–228.

Habicht, C. (2005), 'Marcus Agrippa *Theos Soter*', *Hyperboreus* 11, 242–246.

Haight, E. H. (1922), 'Reconstruction in the Augustan Age', *The Classical Journal* 17.7 (April), 355–376.

Haley, E. W. (2003), *Baetica Felix: People and Prosperity in Southern Spain from Caesar to Septimius Severus*, Austin: University of Texas Press.

Hallett, Judith P. (1984), *Fathers and Daughters in Roman Society: Women and the Elite Family* (Princeton Legacy Library), Princeton: Princeton University Press.

Hammond, Mason (1938), 'The Tribunician Day during the Early Empire', *Memoirs of the American Academy in Rome* 15, 23–61.

Hammond, Mason (1965), 'The Sincerity of Augustus', *Harvard Studies in Classical Philology* 69, 139–162.

Hanson, A. E. (1980), 'Juliopolis, Nicopolis, and the Roman Camp', *Zeitschrift für Papyrologie und Epigraphik* 37, 249–254.

Hanson, A. E. (1982), 'Publius Ostorius Scapula: Augustan Prefect of Egypt', *Zeitschrift* für *Papyrologie und Epigraphik* 47, 243–253.

Hanson, W.S. (ed.), (2009), 'The Army and the Frontiers of Rome', *Journal of Roman Archaeology Supplementary Series* 74.

Hardy, E. G. (1887), 'The Movements of the Roman Legions from Augustus to Severus', *The English Historical Review* 2.8 (October), 625–656.

Hardy, E. G. (1889), 'Dr. Mommsen on the Recruiting System for Legionaries and Auxiliaries under the Empire in Hermes XIX', *The Classical Review* 2.3 (March), 112–114.

Hardy, E. G. (1920), 'Augustus and His Legionaries', *The Classical Quarterly* 1, 14.3/4 (July-October), 187–194.

Harland, Philip A. (2022), 'Judeans, Egyptians, and Magians: Various authors on Tiberius' actions against foreign practices 17–19 CE (first-third centuries CE)', *Ethnic Relations and Migration in the Ancient World*, https://philipharland.com/Blog/?p=9316.

Harlow, Mary, & Laurence, Ray (2017), 'Augustus *Senex*: Old Age and the Remaking of the Principate', *Greece & Rome* 64(2), 115–131.

Harley, B., & Woodward, D. (1987), *The History of Cartography: Cartography in Prehistoric, Ancient and Medieval Europe and the Mediterranean* 1, Chicago: University of Chicago Press.

Harrer, G. A. (1919), 'Rome and Her Subject Peoples', *The Classical Journal* 14.9 (June), 550–556.

Harrer, G. A. (1920), 'Tacitus and Tiberius', *The American Journal of Philology* 41.1, 57–68.

Harries, Jill (2013), 'The *Senatus Consultum Silanianum*: Court Decisions and Judicial Severity in the Early Roman Empire', in: du Plessis, Paul J. (ed.), *New Frontiers: Law and Society in the Roman World*, Edinburgh: Edinburgh University Press, pp. 51–70.

Harris, W. (1985), *War and Imperialism in Republican Rome 327–70 BC*, Oxford: Oxford University Press.

Harrison, S. J. (1989), 'Augustus, the Poets, and the *Spolia Opima*', *The Classical Quarterly (New Series)* 39.2, 408–414.

Hartley, Brian & Wacher, John (1983), *Rome and Her Northern Provinces. Papers presented to Sheppard Frere in honour of his retirement from the Chair of Archaeology of the Roman Empire, University of Oxford, 1983*, Gloucester: Alan Sutton Publishing.

Haslam, M.W. (1980), 'Augustus' Funeral Oration for Agrippa', *The Classical Journal* 75.3 (February-March), 193–199.

Haverfield, F. (1914), 'Legions and *Auxilia*', The *Classical Review* 28.7 (November), 226–227.

Häussler, Ralph (2012), '*Interpretatio indigena*. Re-inventing Local Cults in a Global World', *Mediterraneo Antico* 15(1), 143–174.

Hayes, Walter M. (1959), 'Tiberius and the Future', *The Classical Journal* 55.1 (October), 2–8.

Haynes, H. (2003), *The History of Make-Believe: Tacitus on Imperial Rome*, Berkeley: University of California Press.

Haynes, Ian P. (1993), 'The Romanisation of Religion in the '*Auxilia*' of the Roman Imperial Army from Augustus to Septimus Severus', *Britannia* 24, 141–157.

Haynes, Ian P. (2013), *Blood of the Provinces: The Roman* Auxilia *and the Making of Provincial Society from Augustus to the Severans*, Oxford: Oxford University Press.

Heinrichs, J. (1999), 'Zur Verwicklung Ubischer Gruppen in den Ambiorix-Aufstand d. J. 54 v. Chr.: Eburonische und ubische Münzen im Hortfund Fraire-2', *Zeitschrift Für Payrologie und Epigraphik*, 127, 275–293.

Henderson, M. I. (1963), 'The Establishment of the *Equester Ordo*', *The Journal of Roman Studies* 53, 1 and 2, 61–72.

Heidel, W. A. (1920), 'Why Were the Jews Banished from Italy in 19 A. D.', *The American Journal of Philology* 41.1, 38–47.

Heinrichs, Johannes (2000a), 'Überlegungen zur Versorgung augusteischer Truppen mit Münzgeld. Ein neues Modell und daraus ableitbare Indizien für einen Wandel in der Konzeption des Germanienkriegs nach Drusus' in: Mooren, L. (ed.), *Politics, Administration and Society in the Hellenistic and Roman World* (*Studia Hellenistica* 36), Leuven: Peeters Publishers (2000), 155–214.

Heinrichs, Johannes (2000b), 'Römische Perfidie unter germanischer Edelmut? Zur Umsiedlung protocugernischer Gruppen in den Raum Xanten 8 v. Chr.' in: Grünewald, T. & Schalles, H. J., (eds.) *Germania Inferior: Beiträge des deutschen-niederländischen Kolloquiums in Regionalmuseum Xanten 21.-24. September 1999*, Berlin: Walter de Gruyter, 54–92.

Heiss, A. (1870), *Description générale des monnaies antiques de l'Espagne*, Paris.

Hekster, Olivier (2008), *Rome and its Empire, AD 193–284*, Edinburgh: Edinburgh University Press.

Hekster, Olivier (2009), 'Honouring Ancestors: The Dynamic of Deification' in: Hekster, Olivier, Schmidt-Hofner, Sebstian & Witschel. Christian (eds.), *Ritual Dynamics and Religious Change in the Roman Empire: Proceedings of the Eighth Workshop of the International Network Impact of Empire* (Heidelberg, 5–7 July 2007), 95–110).

Henig, M. (1970), 'The Veneration of Heroes in the Roman Army: The Evidence of Engraved Gemstones', *Britannia* 1, 249–265.

Herm, G. (1977), *The Celts: The People Who Came Out of the Darkness*, New York: St Martin's Press.

Herz, P. (1984), 'Das Kenotaph von Limyra. Kultische und juristische Voraussetzungen', *Mitteilung des Deutschen Archäologischen Instituts* (Istanbul) 35, 178–192.

Hicks, Benjamin W. (2013), 'The Prosecution of M. Plautius Silvanus (pr. 24)', *Ancient History Bulletin* 27, 55–64.

Hickson, F.V. (1991), 'Augustus *Triumphator*: Manipulation of the Triumphal Theme in the Political Program of Augustus', *Latomus* 50.1 (January-March), 124–138.

Hill, Sir G. F, (1899), *A Handbook of Greek and Roman Coins*, London: MacMillan.

Hinge, G., and Krasilnikoff, J. A. (eds.) (2009), *Alexandria: A Cultural and Religious Melting Pot (Aarhus Studies in Mediterranean Antiquity)*, Aarhus: Aarhus University Press.

Hinz, Vinko (1993), 'Eine bekannte Tugend des Tiberius (Tab. Siar. Frg. I Z. 5)', *Zeitschrift für Papyrologie und Epigraphik* 96, 59–63.

Hoff, M. C. (1989), 'Civil Disobedience and Unrest in Augustan Athens', *Hesperia: The Journal of the American School of Classical Studies at Athens* 58.3 (July-September), 267–276.

Hoffmann, F., Minas-Nerpel, M., & Pfeiffer, S. (eds.) (2009), *Die dreisprachige Stele des C. Cornelius Gallus: Übersetzung und Kommentar*, Berlin: De Gruyter.

Hoffman, M. W. (1952), 'The college of *Quindecimviri* (*Sacris Faciundis*) in 17 B.C.', *The American Journal of Philology* 73, 289–294.

Holder, P. F. (1980), *Studies in the* Auxilia *of the Roman Army from Augustus to Trajan* (BAR international series), Oxford: Archaeopress.

Holland, Leicester B. (1946), 'The Triple Arch of Augustus', *American Journal of Archaeology* 50(1), 52–59.

Holland, Louise Adams (1947), 'Aeneas-Augustus of Prima Porta', *Transactions and Proceedings of the American Philological Association* 78, 276–284.

Holliday, P. J. (1990), 'Time, History, and Ritual on the *Ara Pacis Augustae*', *The Art Bulletin* 72.4 (December), 542–557.

Holland, Tom (2015), *Dynasty: The Rise and Fall of the House of Caesar*, London: Little, Brown.

Holland, Tom (2021), 'Caesars and Sopranos: The Shadow of Suetonius', *Antigone Journal*, 10 March (Online at https://antigonejournal.com/2021/03/10/caesars-and-sopranos/, accessed 1 March 2024).

Holmes, T. R. (1928), *The Architect of the Roman Empire*, Oxford: Clarendon Press.
Hölscher, Tonio (1985), 'Monuments of the Battle of Actium: Propaganda and Response' in: Edmondson. J. (ed.), *Augustus*, Edinburgh Readings on the Ancient World, Edinburgh (2009), 310–333.
Hölscher, Tonio (2003), 'Images of War in Greece and Rome: Between Military Practice, Public Memory, and Cultural Symbolism', *The Journal of Roman Studies* 93, 1–17.
Hölscher, Tonio (2000), 'Laokoon und das Schicksal des Tiberius', *Antike Welt* 31.3, 321–323.
Hope, V. M. (2003), 'Trophies and Tombstones: Commemorating the Roman Soldier', *World Archaeology* 35.1, *The Social Commemoration of Warfare* (June), 79–97.
Horden, P., & Purcell, N. (2000), *The Corrupting Sea: A Study of Mediterranean History*, London: Blackwell.
Horster, Mariette (2011), '*Princeps Iuventutis. Concept, realisation, representation*' in: Benoist, Stéphane, Daguet-Gagy, Anne, & Hoët-van-Couwenberghe, Christine, *Figures d'empire, fragments de mémoire. Pouvoirs et identités dans le monde romain impérial (IIe s. av. n. è - VI s. de n. è.)*, Lille: Septentrion (2011), 73–103.
Horvat, Jana (2015), 'The consolidation of Roman authority in the hinterland of the northern Adriatic' in: Marion. Yolande & Tassaux, Francis (eds.), *AdriAtlas et l'histoire de l'espace adriatique du vie s. a.C. au viiie s. p.C., Actes du colloque international de Rome (4–6 novembre 2013)* – Scripta Antiqua 79, Bordeaux: Ausonius Éditions, 273 –291.
Housman, A. E. (1913), 'Manilivs, Avgvstvs, Tiberivs, Capricornvs, and Libra [Manilius, Augustus, Tiberius, Capricornus and Libra]', *The Classical Quarterly* 7(2), 109–114.
Houston, George W. (1985). 'Tiberius on Capri', *Greece & Rome*, *32*(2), 179–196.
Houston, George W. (2008), 'Tiberius and the Libraries: Public Book Collections and Library Buildings in the Early Roman Empire', *Libraries & the Cultural Record* 43.3, 247–269.
Huntsman, Eric D. (1996), 'The Reliability of Josephus: Can He Be Trusted?', *Brigham Young University Studies* 36(3), 392–402.
Hurlet, Frédéric (1994), 'Recherches sur la durée de l' "imperium" des "co-régents" sous les principats d'Auguste et de Tibère', *Cahiers du Centre Gustave Glotz* 5, 255–289.
Hurlet, Frédéric (1997), *Les collègues du prince sous Auguste et Tibère*. (Collection de l'École française de Rome 227), Rome: École française de Rome.
Hurlet, Frédéric (2009), *Rome et l'Occident romain (IIe siècle av. J.-C. – IIe siècle ap. J.-C.). Gouverner l'Empire*, Rennes: Presses Universitaires de Rennes.
Hurlet, Frédéric (2011), 'Consulship and Consuls Under Augustus', in Beck, H., Duple, A., Jehne, M., & Polo, F. P. (eds.), *Consuls and* Res Publica*: Holding High Office in the Roman Republic*, Cambridge: Cambridge University Press: 319–335.
Hurley, Donna W. (1989), 'Gaius Caligula in the Germanicus Tradition', *American Journal of Philology* 110.2 (Summer), 316–338.
Huzar, E.G. (1995), 'Emperor Worship in Julio-Claudian Egypt', in *Aufstieg und Niedergang der römischen Welt: Geschichte und Kultur Roms im Spiegel der neuren Forschung*, Volume 1, Berlin: Walter de Gruyter, 3092–3143.
Huzar, E. G. (1978), *Mark Antony: A Biography*, Beckenham: Croom Helm.
Illarregui, E. (2005), 'Cantabrian Weapons' in: Kocsis, L. (ed.), *Journal of Roman Military Equipment 16, The Enemies of Rome: Proceedings of the 15th International Roman Military Equipment Conference*, Budapest (2005), 81–105.
Instinsky, Hans Ulrich (1966), 'Augustus und die Adoption des Tiberius', *Hermes* 94. Bd., H. 3, 324–343
Isaac, Benjamin H. (1971), 'Colonia Munatia Triumphalis and Legio Nona Triumphalis?', *Talanta* 3,11–43
Isaac, Benjamin H. (1992), *The Limits of Empire: The Roman Army in the East*, Oxford: Clarendon Press.

Isaac, Benjamin H. (2006), *The Invention of Racism in Classical Antiquity*, Princeton: Princeton University Press.

Isler, Hans Peter (1978), 'Die Residenz der römischen Kaiser auf dem Palatin: Zur Entstehung eines Bautypus', *Antike Welt* 9(2), 2–16.

Itgenshorst, T. (2004), 'Augustus und der republikanische Triumph: Triumphalfasten und *summi viri*-Galerie als Instrumente der imperialen Machtsicherung', *Hermes* 132.4, 436–458.

Jacobson, David M. (2019), 'Coins of the First Century Roman Governors of Judaea and their Motifs', *Electrum* 26, 73–96

Jahnkun, H. (1976), 'Siedlung, Wirtschaft und Gesellschaftsordnung der germanischen Stämme in der Zeit der römischen Angriffskriege', H. Temporini, W. Haase (ed.) *Aufstieg und Niedergang der römischen Welt: Geschichte und Kultur Roms im Spiegel d. neueren Forschung*, Vol. II. 5.1, Stuttgart: de Gruyer, 65–126.

James, H. (1989), *A German Identity: 1770–1990*, New York: Routledge.

Jameson, Shelagh (1968), 'Chronology of the Campaigns of Aelius Gallus and C. Petronius', *The Journal of Roman Studies* 58, Parts 1 and 2, 71–84.

Jameson, Shelagh (1975), 'Augustus and Agrippa Postumus', *Historia: Zeitschrift Für Alte Geschichte* 24(2), 287–314.

Janick, Jules, & Paris, Harry (2022), 'History of Controlled Environment Horticulture: Ancient Origins', *HortScience* 57(2), 236–238.

Johne, K.-P. (2006), *Die Römer an der Elbe: Das Stromgebiet der Elbe im geographischen Weltbild und im politischen Bewusstsein der griechisch-römischen Antike*, Berlin: Akademie Verlag.

Johnson, Anne (1983), *Roman Forts of the 1st and 2nd centuries AD in Britain and the German Provinces*, London: Adam & Charles Black.

Jomini, A. H. (1862), *The Art of War*, Westport: Greenwood Press.

Jones, A. H. M. (1950), 'The *Aerarium* and the *Fiscus*', *The Journal of Roman Studies* 40.1/2, 22–29.

Jones, A. H. M. (1951), 'The *Imperium* of Augustus', *The Journal of Roman Studies* 41, Parts 1 and 2, 112–119.

Jones, David (2006), *The Bankers of Puteoli: Finance, Trade and Industry in the Roman World*, Stroud: Tempus.

Jones, R. F. J., & Bird, D. G. (1972), 'Roman Gold-Mining in North-West Spain, II: Workings on the Rio Duerna', *The Journal of Roman Studies* 62, 59–74.

Jones, R. F. J. (1976), 'The Roman Military Occupation of North-West Spain', *The Journal of Roman Studies* 66, 45–66.

Jones, Timothy M. (2017), *A Mere Equestrian? Sejanus and the Succession to Tiberius in its Augustan Context*, Sydney: Macquarie University Department of Ancient History. (Unpublished doctoral thesis).

Jorgensen, Lars, Storgaard, Birger & Thomsen, Lone Gebauer (eds.) (2003), *The Spoils of Victory: The North in the Shadow of the Roman Empire*, Copenhagen: Nationalmuseet.

Judge, E. A, & Harrison, J. R. (eds.) (2008), *The First Christians in the Roman World: Augustan and New Testament Essays*, Tübingen: Mohr Siebeck.

Judge, E. A. (2019), *The Failure of Augustus: Essays on the Interpretation of a Paradox*, Newcastle Upon Tyne: Cambridge Scholars Publishing.

Junkelmann, Marcus (2006), Panis militaris, *Die Ernährung des römischen Soldaten oder der Grundstoff der Macht*, Mainz: Verlag Philipp von Zabern.

Junkelmann, Marcus (2014), *Die Legionen des Augustus*, München: Herbert Utz Verlag.

Kagan, K. (2006), 'Redefining Roman Grand Strategy', *The Journal of Military History* 70.2 (April), 333–362.

Kalfoglou-Kaloteraki, V. (2003), '*Μάρκῳ Ἀγρίππᾳ*', *Hellenika* 53, 299–303.

Kaplan, Robert D. (2002), *Warrior Politics: Why Leadership Demands a Pagan Ethos*, New York: Vintage Books.

Kaufman, D. B. (1932), 'Poisons and Poisoning Among the Romans', *Classical Philology* Vol. 27, no. 2, 156–167.

Kavka, Gregory S. (1983), 'Rule by Fear', *Noûs* 17(4), 601–620.

Keaveney, A. (2007), *The Army in the Roman Revolution*, Abingdon: Routledge.

Keay, S. J. (1988), *Roman Spain*, London: British Museum Publications.

Keay, S. J. (2003), 'Recent Archaeological Work in Roman Iberia (1990–2002)', *The Journal of Roman Studies* 93, 146–211.

Keegan, John (2003), *Intelligence in War: From Napoleon to Al-Qaeda*, New York: Alfred A. Knopf.

Kehoe, Dennis (1985), 'Tacitus and Sallustius Crispus', *The Classical Journal* 80(3), 247–254.

Keitel, Elizabeth (1981), 'Tacitus on the Deaths of Tiberius and Claudius', *Hermes* 109. Bd., H. 2, 206–214.

Kellum, Barbara A. (1991), 'The City Adorned: Programmatic Display at the *Aedes Concordiae Augustae*' in: Raaflaub, Kurt A. & Toher, Mark (eds.), *Between Republic and Empire: Interpretations of Augustus and His Principate*, Berkeley: University of California Press, 276–307.

Kellum, Barbara A. (1994), 'The Construction of Landscape in Augustan Rome: The Garden Room at the Villa ad Gallinas', *The Art Bulletin* 76.2 (June), 211–224.

Kelly, Gordon P. (2006), *A History of Exile in the Roman Republic*, Cambridge: Cambridge University Press.

Kennedy, D. L. (1983), 'Milliary Cohorts: The Evidence of Josephus, *BJ*, III.4.2(67) and of Epigraphy', *Zeitschrift für Papyrologie und Epigraphik* 50, 253–263.

Kennedy, D. (1996a), *The Roman Army in the East. Journal of Roman Archaeology Supplementary Series no. 18*, Ann Arbor, Michigan.

Kennedy, D. (1996b), 'Syria', in: Bowman, A. K., Champlin, E., & Lintott, A. (eds.), *The Cambridge Ancient History Volume X: The Augustan Empire, 43 B.C.–A.D. 69* (second edition), Cambridge: Cambridge University Press, 703–736.

Kennedy, George (1968), 'The Rhetoric of Advocacy in Greece and Rome', *The American Journal of Philology* 89(4), 419–436.

Kenty, Joanna (2017), 'Messalla Corvinus: Augustan Orator, Ciceronian Statesman', *Rhetorica: A Journal of the History of Rhetoric* 35(4), 445–474.

Keppie, Lawrence J. F. (1973), '*Vexilla Veteranorum*', *Papers of the British School at Rome* 41, 8–17.

Keppie, Lawrence J. F. (1984), 'Colonisation and Veteran Settlement in Italy in the First Century AD', *Papers of The British School at Rome* Vol. 52, 77–114.

Keppie, Lawrence J. F. (1984), *The Making of the Roman Army From Republic to Empire*, London: B. T. Batsford.

Keppie, Lawrence J. F. (1996), 'The Army and The Navy' in: Bowman, A. K., Champlin, E., & Lintott, A. (eds.), *The Cambridge Ancient History Volume X: The Augustan Empire, 43 B.C.–A.D. 69* (second edition), Cambridge: Cambridge University Press, 371–396.

Keppie, Lawrence J. F. (2002), 'The Origins and Early History of the Second Augustan Legion', in R. J. Brewer (ed.), *The Second Augustan Legion and the Roman Military Machine*, Cardiff: National Museum of Wales (2002).

Kessel, Humbert (1988), 'Einige Inschriften von der Insel Capri', *Zeitschrift Für Papyrologie Und Epigraphik* 71, 195–198.

Kienast, Dietmar (1966), *Untersuchungen zu den Kriegsflotten der römischen Kaiserzeit*, Bonn: Habelt.

Kienast, Dietmar (2009), *Augustus: Prinzeps und Monarch*, Darmstadt: Primus Verlag (fourth edition).

Kiessel, M., & Weidner, M. (2009), 'Defining Roman, Celtic and Germanic Ethnicity through Archaeological Monuments. Examples from Roman Provinces in North-western Europe', *GAU Journal of Social and Applied Sciences* 5, 35–51.

King, A. (1990), *Roman Gaul and Germany*, London: British Museum Publications.

Kirbihler, François (2012), 'César, Auguste et l'Asie: continuités et évolutions de deux politiques' in: Devillers, Olivier & Sion-Jenkis, Karin (eds.), *César sous Auguste*. Ausonius Scripta Antiqua 48, Bordeaux (2012), 124–144.

Kiss, Z. (1975), *L'iconographie des princes julio-claudiens au temps d'Auguste et de Tibère*, Warsaw: Travaux du Centre d'archéologie méditerranéenne de l'Académie polonaise des sciences.

Kleineburg, Andreas, Marx, Christian, Knobloch, Eberhard, & Lelgemann, Dieter (2010), *Germania und die Insel Thule: Die Entschlüsselung von Ptolemaios' "Atlas der Oikumene"*, Darmstadt: Wissenschaftliche Buchgesellschaft.

Klein, M. (2005), 'Roman Decorated Daggers and Figural Sword Fittings from Mainze-*Mogontiacum* (Germania Superior)' in Kocsis, L. (ed.), *Journal of Roman Military Equipment* 16, The Enemies of Rome: Proceedings of the 15th International Roman Military Equipment Conference, Budapest 2005, 237–248.

Kleiner, D. E. E. (1978), 'The great friezes of the *Ara Pacis Augustae*. Greek Sources, Roman Derivatives and Augustan Social Policy', *Mélanges de l'Ecole française de Rome. Antiquité* 90–2, 753–785.

Klooster, Jacqueline (2017), 'Tiberius and Hellenistic Poetry', *Aitia* [online], 7.1.

Knight, D. J. (1991), 'The Movements of the *Auxilia* from Augustus to Hadrian', *Zeitschrift* für *Papyrologie und Epigraphik* 85, 189–208.

Kober, Alice E. (1945), 'Tiberius, Master Detective', *The Classical Outlook* 22.4 (January), 37.

Koenen, L. (1970), 'Die "Laudatio funebris" des Augustus für Agrippa auf einem neuen Papyrus (P. Colon. inv. nr. 4701)', *Zeitschrift Für Papyrologie Und Epigraphik* 5, 217–283.

Koepfer, Christian (2009a), 'Arming the Warrior: Archaeological Evidence' in: Oorthuys, Jasper (ed.), *Ancient Warfare*, Special Issue 1, 48–51.

Koepfer, Christian (2009b), 'The Legionary's Equipment: Archaeological Evidence' in: Oorthuys, Jasper (ed.), *Ancient Warfare*, Special Issue 1, 37–41.

Koestermann, Erich (1955), 'Die Majestätsprozesse unter Tiberius', *Historia: Zeitschrift für Alte Geschichte* Bd. 4, H. 1, 72–106.

Koestermann, Erich (1957a), 'Die Mission des Germanicus im Orient', *Historia* 6, 331–75.

Koestermann, Erich (1957b), 'Die Feldzüge des Germanicus 14–16 n. Chr.', *Historia* 6, 429–79.

Kokkinos, Nikos (2002), *Antonia Augusta: Portrait of a Great Roman Lady*, London: Libri Publications.

Kolník, T. (1991), 'Zu ersten Römern und Germanen an der mittleren Donau im Zusammenhang mit den geplanten römischen Angriffen gegen Marbod 6 n. Chr.', in *Die römische Okkupatzion nördlich der Alpen zur Zeit des Augustus*, Münster, 71–84.

Kondoleon, C. (ed.) (2000), *Antioch: The Lost Ancient City. Exhibition Catalogue, Worcester Art Museum, October 7, 2000-February 4, 2001; The Cleveland Museum of Art, March 18-June 3, 2001; The Baltimore Museum of Art, September 16-December 30, 2001*, Princeton: Princeton University Press.

Köhne, E., & Ewigleben, E. (eds.) (2000), *Gladiators and Caesars*, Berkeley: California University Press.

Köhler, H. J., & von Schnurbein, S. (2003), 'Die Römer kommen! Die Lagerspuren auf dem Goldberg', in *Sole und Salz schreiben Geschichte. 50 Jahre Landesarchäologie. 150 Jahre Archäologische Forschung Bad Nauheim*. Mainz, 279–281.

Kösters, K. (2009), *Mythos Arminius. Die Varusschlacht und ihre Folgen*, Münster: Aschendorf Verlag.

Köstner, Elena (2020), 'Genesis and Collapse of a Network: The Rise and Fall of Lucius Aelius Seianus', *Journal of Historical Network Research* 4, 225–251.

Kornemann, E. (1930), *Doppelprinzipat und Reichsteiling im Imperium Romanum*, Teubner: Leipzig.

Kornemann, E. (1980), *Tiberius*, Frankfurt (Main): Societäts-Verlag (reprint of Stuttgart 1960 edition).

Kos, Marjeta Šašel (2010), 'Pannonia or Lower Illyricum?', *Tyche: Beiträge zur Alten Geschichte, Papyrologie und Epigraphik* 25, 123–131.

Kos, Marjeta Šašel (2011), 'The Roman Conquest of Dalmatia and Pannonia Under Augustus' in: Moosbauer, Günther & Wiegels, Rainer (eds.) *Römische Okkupations- und Grenzpolitik im frühen Principat Beiträge zum Kongress* ‚Fines imperii – imperium sine fine?' *in Osnabrück vom 14. bis 18. September 2009, Osnabrücker Forschungen zu Altertum und Antike-Rezeption* 14, Diepholz: Druckhaus Breyer, 107–117.

Kos, Marjeta Šašel (2012), 'Colonia Iulia Emona – the genesis of the Roman city', *Arheološki* vestnik 63, 79–104.

Kos, Marjeta Šašel (2014a), 'The Problem of the Border between Italy, Noricum, and Pannonia* Tafel 10–11', *Tyche: Beiträge zur Alten Geschichte, Papyrologie und Epigraphik* 29, 153–166.

Kos, Marjeta Šašel (2014b), 'What was happening in Emona in AD 14/15? An imperial inscription and the mutiny of the Pannonian legions' in: Ferle, Mojca (ed.) *EMONA: mesto v imperiju [30. maj 2014–31. maj 2015] / A City of the Empire [30 May 2014–31 May 2015]*, Ljubljana: Mestni muzej, Muzej in galerije mesta Ljubljane, 79–179.

Kos, Marjeta Šašel (2015), 'The Final Phase of the Augustan Conquest of Illyricum' in: Cuscito, Giuseppe (ed.), *Antichità Altoadriatiche* 81, Aquileia: Centro di antichità altoadriatiche, 65–87.

Kos, Marjeta Šašel (2017), 'Tiberius in Strabo's Geography: echoes of his activities in Illyricum' in: Kovács, Péter (ed.), *Tiberius in Illyricum: Contributions to the History of the Danubian Provinces under Tiberius' Reign (14–37 AD), Hungarian Polis Studies* 24, Budapest: Eötvös Loránd University, 139–155.

Kos, Marjeta Šašel (2022), 'The Creation of the Province of Dalmatia in Light of the Recent Research', *Mélanges de l'École française de Rome – Antiquité* 134–1, 61–70.

Kovács, Péter (2017), 'Velleius Paterculus on Pannonia' in: Kovács, Péter (ed.), *Tiberius in Illyricum: Contributions to the History of the Danubian Provinces under Tiberius' Reign (14–37 AD), Hungarian Polis Studies* 24, Budapest: Eötvös Loránd University, 103–119.

Kovács, Péter (2018), 'Northern Pannonia and the Roman Conquest' in: Bradač, Marina Milićević & Demicheli, Dino (eds.), *The Century of the Brave/Stoljeće hrabrih*, Zagreb: FF Press, 163–174.

Kraft, K. (1967), 'Der Sinn des Mausoleums des Augustus', *Historia: Zeitschrift für Alte Geschichte* 16.2 (April), 189–206.

Krappe, Alexander Haggerty (1927), 'Tiberius and Thrasyllus', *The American Journal of Philology* 48.4, Johns Hopkins University Press, 359–366.

Kraus, Christina Shuttleworth (2010), 'The Tiberian Hexad' in: Woodman, A.J. (ed.), *The Cambridge Companion to Tacitus*, Cambridge: Cambridge University Press (2010), 100–115.

Krause, Clemens (2003a), *Villa Jovis. Die Residenz des Tiberius auf Capri*, Mainz: Philipp von Zabern.

Krause, Clemens (2003b), 'Des Kaisers Residenz: Die Villa Jovis auf Capri', *Antike Welt* 34(2), 177–180.

Krebs, C. B. (2011), 'Tacitus: The Continuing Message', *History Today* 61.9 (online at https://www.historytoday.com/christopher-krebs/tacitus-continuing-message, accessed 1 March 2024).

Kröger, H., & Best, W. (2011), *Porta Westfalica-Barkhausen Ein Gang durch die Jahrtausende,* Förderverein Römerlager Barkhausen Porta Westfalica e.V. in Zusammenarbeit mit dem LWL – Archäologie für Westfalen.

Kruta, V. (ed.) (1999), *The Celts*, New York: Rizzoli International.

Kryśkiewicz, Hadrian (2016), 'Augustus and the 'other' *signa* — remarks on the issue of "non-Parthian" ensigns recovered in the Augustan age (*Res Gestae* 29.1)', *Mnemon: Investigations and Publications on the History of the Ancient World* 16, 173–186.

Kühlborn, J. S. (1989), 'Oberaden' in: R. Aßkamp (ed.), *2000 Jahre Römer in Westfalen*, Mainz.

Kühlborn, J. S. (ed.) (1995), *Germaniam pacavi: Germanien habe ich befriedet. Archäologische Stätten augusteischer Okkupation*, Münster.

Kühlborn, J. S. (1996), *Das römische Uferkastell Beckinghausen*, Lünen.

Kunić, Alka Dunić (2006), 'Posljednja faza osvajanja Ju'ne Panonije', *VAMZ*, 3.s., XXXIX, 59–164.

Kunić, Alka Dunić (2012), 'Literary Sources Before the Marcomannic War' in: Migotti, Branka (ed.), *The Archaeology of Roman Southern Pannonia: The state of research and selected problems in the Croatian part of the Roman province of Pannonia*, BAR International Series 2393, Oxford: Archaeo Press.

Kunst, Christiane (2008), *Livia: Macht und Intrigen am Hof des Augustus*, Stuttgart: Klett-Cotta.

Kunst, Christiane (2015), 'Patchworkfamilie und aristokratische Familienpolitik: Immer das große Ganze im Blick' in: *Archäologie in Deutschland, 2015, Sonderheft: Ich Germanicus: Feldherr - Priester - Superstar* (2015), Darmstadt: Wissenschaftliche Buchgesellschaft, pp. 79–87.

Kurkjian, V. M. (1958), *A History of Armenia*, New York: Armenian General Benevolent Union of America.

Kuttner, A. L. (1995), *Dynasty and Empire in the Age of Augustus: The Case of the Boscoreale Cups*, Berkeley: University of California Press.

Kühlborn, Johann-Sebastian (1989), 'Oberaden' in: Trier, B. (ed.) *2000 Jahre Römer in Westfalen*, Mainz: Philipp von Zabern, 44–51.

Kühlborn, Johann-Sebastian (1990), 'Die augusteischen Militärlager an der Lippe', in Horn, H.-G. (ed.) *Archäologie in Nordrhein-Westfalen. Geschichte im Herzen Europas*, Mainz: Philipp von Zabern, 169–186.

Kühlborn, Johann-Sebastian (1991), 'Die Lagerzentren der römischen Militärlager von Oberaden und Anreppen', in Aßkamp, R., Berke, S. (eds.): *Die römische Okkupation nördlich der Alpen zur Zeit des Augustus*. Münster: Aschendorff, 129–140.

Kühlborn, Johann-Sebastian (ed.) (1995), Germania pacavi*: Germanien habe ich befriedet: Archäologische Stätten augusteischer Okkupation*, Münster: Westfällisches Museum für Archäologie – Amt für Bodendenkmalpflege.

Kühlborn, Johann-Sebastian (1996), *Das römische Uferkastell Beckinghausen*, Museum der Stadt Lünen. Informationen aus dem Museum der Stadt Lünen, 1–4.

*Kühlborn,* Johann-Sebastian *(2014), 'Römer im Paderborner Land. Anreppen, das Hauptquartier des Tiberius', in Führer zur Vor- und Frühgeschichte der Hochstiftkreise Paderborn und Höxter 3 (Marsberg), 1–42.*

*Lacey, W. K. (1963), 'Nominatio and the Elections under Tiberius', Historia: Zeitschrift für Alte Geschichte (April) Bd. 12, H. 2 (April), 167–176.*

*Lange, Carsten Hjort (2009a), Res Publica Constituta: Actium, Apollo and the Accomplishment of the Triumviral Assignment, Brill: Leiden.*

Lange, *Carsten Hjort* (2009b), 'The Battle of Actium and the 'slave of passion" in Moore, J. Morris, I., & Bayliss, A. J. (eds.) *Reinventing History: The Enlightenment Origins of Ancient History*, London, Centre for Metropolitan History, 115–136.

Lange, *Carsten Hjort* (2011), 'The Battle of Actium: A Reconsideration', *Classical Quarterly* 61.2, 608–623.

Lange, *Carsten Hjort* (2015), 'Augustus' Triumphal and Triumphal-like Returns', in Ostenberg, I., Malmberg, S., & Jonas Bjørnebye, J. (eds.) *The Moving City: Processions, Passages and Promenades in Ancient Rome*, London: Bloomsbury Academic, 133–144.

Lange, Ralph (2019), *Die Macht der Gegenwart. Zur Dynamik von Präsenz und Distanz in der römischen politischen Kultur*, Universität zu Köln. (Doctoral thesis). (Online at https://kups.ub.uni-koeln.de/9416/1/Lange_Dissertation_KUPS.pdf).

Langguth, A. J. (1994), *A Noise of War; Caesar, Pompey, Octavian and the Struggle for Rome*, New York: Simon and Schuster.

Last, Hugh (1947), '*Imperivm Maivs*: A Note', *The Journal of Roman Studies* 37, Parts 1 and 2,157–164.

Le Bohec, Yann (1994), *The Imperial Roman Army*, London: B. T. Batsford.

Le Bohec, Yann (2011), 'La violence et la guerre chez les Romains au temps d'Auguste' in: Moosbauer, Günther & Wiegels, Rainer (eds.) *Römische Okkupations- und Grenzpolitik im frühen Principat Beiträge zum Kongress* 'Fines imperii – imperium sine fine?' *in Osnabrück vom 14. bis 18. September 2009, Osnabrücker Forschungen zu Altertum und Antike-Rezeption* 14, Diepholz: Druckhaus Breyer, 239–252.

Lebek, W. D. (1990), 'Standeswürde und Berufsverbot unter Tiberius: Das SC der Tabula Larinas', *Zeitschrift Für Papyrologie Und Epigraphik* 81, 37–96.

Lebek, W. D. (1986), 'Schwierige Stellen der Tabula Siarensis', *Zeitschrift für Papyrologie und Epigraphik* 66, 31–48.

Lebek, W. D. (1987), 'Die drei Ehrenbögen für Germanicus: *Tab. Siar. Frg.* I 9–34; *CIL* VI 31199a 2–17', *Zeitschrift für Papyrologie und Epigraphik* 67, 129–48.

Lebek, W. D. (1989a), 'Die Mainzer Ehrungen für Germanicus, den älteren Drusus and Domitian (*Tab. Siar. Frg.* I 26–34; Suet. *Claud.* 1, 3)', *Zeitschrift für Papyrologie und Epigraphik* 78, 45–82.

Lebek, W. D. (1989b), 'Die postumen Ehrenbögen und der Triumph des Drusus Caesar (*CIL* VI 31200 B Col. I, 1–4; Tac. Ann. 4,9,2)', *Zeitschrift für Papyrologie und Epigraphik* 78, 83–91.

Lebek, W. D. (1991), 'Ehrenbogen und Prinzentod: 9 v.Chr.–23 n. Chr.', *Zeitschrift für Papyrologie und Epigraphik* 86, 1991, 47–78.

Lehman, G. A., 1991, 'Das Ende der römischen Herrschaft *über* das "Westelbische" Germanien: Von der Varus-Katastrophe zur Abberufung des Germanicus Caesar 16/7 n. Chr.', *Zeitschrift für Papyrologie und Epigraphik* 86, 79–96.

Lendering, Jona, & Bosman, Arjen (2010), *De Rand van het Rijk: De Romeinen en de Lage Landen*, Amsterdam: uitgeverij Atheneum.

Lepper, Frank, & Frere, Sheppard (1988), *Trajan's Column*, Gloucester: Alan Sutton Publishing.

Lesquier, J. (1918), *L'Armée romaine d'Égypte d'Auguste à Dioclétien*, Cairo: L'Institut Française.

Letta, C. (1976), 'La dinastia dei Cozii e la romanizzazione delle Alpi occidentali', *Athenaeum* 54, 37–76.

Levante, Edoardo (1985), 'The Coinage of Rhosus', *The Numismatic Chronicle (1966-)* 145, 237–243.

Levick, Barbara M. (1966), 'Drusus Caesar and the Adoptions of A.D. 4.', *Latomus* 25(2), 227–244.

Levick, Barbara M. (1967), 'Imperial Control of the Elections under the Early Principate: Commendatio, Suffragatio, and "Nominatio"', *Historia: Zeitschrift Für Alte Geschichte* 16(2), 207–230.

Levick, Barbara M. (1971), 'The Beginning of Tiberius' Career', *The Classical Quarterly* 21.2 (November), 478–486.

Levick, Barbara M. (1972a), 'Tiberius' Retirement to Rhodes in 6 B.C.', *Latomus* 31 (Octobre-Décembre), 779–813.

Levick, Barbara M. (1972b), 'Abdication and Agrippa Postumus', *Historia: Zeitschrift Für Alte Geschichte* 21(4), 674–697.

Levick, Barbara (1975), 'Julians and Claudians', *Greece & Rome* 22.1, 29–38.

Levick, Barbara M. (1976a), *Tiberius the Politician*, London: Routledge.

Levick, Barbara M. (1976), 'The Fall of Julia the Younger', *Latomus* 35, 301–333.

Levick, Barbara M. (1982), 'Morals, Politics, and the Fall of the Roman Republic', *Greece & Rome* 29(1), 53–62.

Levick, Barbara M. (1985), *Government of the Roman Empire: A Source Book*, Beckenham: Croom Helm.

Levick, Barbara M. (1990), *Claudius*, London: B. T. Batsford.

Levick, Barbara M. (1999), 'Messages on Roman Coinage: Types and Inscriptions', in Paul, G.M. & Ierardi, M. (eds.), *Roman Coins and Public Life: E. Togo Salomon Papers II*, Ann Arbor: University of Michigan Press, 41–60.

Levick, Barbara M. (2010), *Augustus: Image and Substance*, Harlow: Pearson Education.

Lewis, Anne-Marie (2023), *Celestial Inclinations: A Life of Augustus*, Oxford: Oxford University Press.

Lewis, Bunnell (1907), 'Roman Antiquities at Baden (Switzerland) and Bregenz', *Archaeological Journal*, 151–167.

Lewis, M. J. T. (2001), 'Railways in the Greek and Roman World', in Guy, A., & Rees, J., (eds.) *Early Railways. A Selection of Papers from the First International Early Railways Conference*, 8–19 (10–15).

Lewis, P. R., & Jones, G. D. B. (1970), 'Roman Gold-Mining in North-West Spain', *The Journal of Roman Studies* 60 (1970), 169–185.

Lewis, R.G. (1993), 'Imperial Autobiography, Augustus to Hadrian', *Aufstieg und Niedergang der römischen Welt* 2.34.1, Berolini: De Gruyter, 629–706.

Liebenam, W. (1891), 'Bemerkungen zur Tradition über Germanicus', *Neue Jahrbücher für Philologie und Pedagogik* 143, 717–736.

Limoges, S. (2008), 'The portrayal of Germanicus in Tacitus' *Annales* and the historicity of the Germanicus-Tiberius conflict', *Hirundo* 6, 32–40.

Lindemann, K., (1967), *Der Hildesheimer Silberfund: Varus und Germanicus*, Hildesheim: Lax.

Lindenthal, J. R., & Nickel, R. (2005): 'Römische Lager Am Goldstein in Bad Nauheim', in *Hessen Archäologie 2004*. Stuttgart, 86–88.

Linderski, J. (1984), 'Rome, Aphrodisias and the *Res Gestae*: The *Genera Militiae* and the Status of Octavian', *The Journal of Roman Studies* 74, 74–80.

Linderski, J. (1988), 'Julia in Regium', *Zeitschrift Für Papyrologie Und Epigraphik* 72, 181–200.

Lindsay, Hugh (1993), 'Observations on the Career of Tiberius Gemellus' in: Lee, K., Mackie, C. & Tarrant, H. (eds.), *Multarum Artium Scientia: Festschrift for R. G. Tanner*: Prudentia Supplementary Number, Auckland: Auckland University Press, 84–88.

Lindsay, Hugh (1995), 'A Fertile Marriage: Agrippina and the Chronology of her Children by Germanicus', *Latomus* 54, 3–17.

Linsmeyer, A. (1875), *Der Triumphzug des Germanicus*, Munich.

Lintott, A. (1993), *Imperium Romanum: Politics and Administration*, London: Routledge.

Lobur, John A. (2007), '*Festinatio* (Haste), *Brevitas* (Concision), and the Generation of Imperial Ideology in Velleius Paterculus', *Transactions of the American Philological Association (1974-)*, 137.1, 211–230.

Lobur, John A. (2008), *Consensus, Concordia and the Formation of Roman Imperial Ideology*, London: Routledge

Lott, J. Bert (2012), *Death and Dynasty in Early Imperial Rome: Key Sources, with Text, Translation, and Commentary*, Cambridge: Cambridge University Press.

Lucas, H. (1904), *Zur Geschichte der Neptunsbasilica in Rom*, Berlin.

Luden, H. (1825), *Geschichte Des teutschen Volkes*, Volume 1, Gotha: Justus Perthes.

Luttwak, Edward N. (1976), *The Grand Strategy of the Roman Empire: From the First Century A.D. to the Third*, Baltimore: The Johns Hopkins University Press.

Lyasse, Emmanuel (2013), *Tibère*, Paris: Tallandier.

MacGregor, Alexander (2004), 'Which art in Heaven: the Sphere of Manilius', *Illinois Classical Studies* 29, 143–157.

MacKendrick, Paul (1971), *Roman France*, London: Bell.

MacKendrick, Paul (1970), *Romans on the Rhine: Archaeology in Germany*, New York: Funk and Wagnalls.

MacKenzie, D. C. (1983), 'Pay Differentials in the Early Empire', *The Classical World* 76.5 (May-June), 267–273.

MacMullen, R. (1984a), 'The Roman Emperors' Army Costs', *Latomus* 43.3 (July-September), 571–580.

MacMullen, R. (1984b), 'The Legion as a Society', *Historia: Zeitschrift* für Alte *Geschichte* 33.4 (Fourth Quarter), 440–456.

MacMullen, R. (2000), *Romanization in the Time of Augustus*, New Haven: Yale University Press.

Magerstädt, Sylvie (2019), *TV antiquity: Swords, sandals, blood and sand*, Manchester: Manchester University Press.

Magie, David (1920), 'Augustus' War in Spain', *Classical Philology* 15.4 (October), 323–339.

Magie, David (1908), 'The Mission of Agrippa to the Orient in 23 BC', *Classical Philology* 3.2 (April), 145–152.

Maier, Paul L. (1969), 'The Episode of the Golden Roman Shields at Jerusalem', *The Harvard Theological Review* 62(1), 109–121.

Maiuri, Amedeo (1956), *Capri: Its History and Its Monuments*, Rome: Istituto Poligrafico dello Stato.

Malissard, A. (1990), 'Germanicus, Alexandre et le début des *Annales* de Tacite. A propos de Tacite, *Annales*, 2, 73' in: Croisille, J.M. (ed.), *Neronia IV. Alejandro Magno, modelo de los emperadores romanos*, Brussels, 328–338.

Mallan, Christopher T. (2016), 'Tiberius the Goat: An Addition to Champlin's 'Mallonia', *Histos* 10, 15–16.

Mallan, Christopher T. (2021), *Cassius Dio: Roman History, Books 57–58 (The Reign of Tiberius)*, Clarendon Ancient History Series, Oxford: Oxford University Press.

Malloch, S. J. V. (2004), 'The end of the Rhine mutiny in Tacitus, Suetonius, and Dio', *The Classical Quarterly (New Series)* 54, 198–210.

Mallory, J. P. (1989), *In Search of Indo-Europeans: Language, Archaeology and Myth*, London: Thames and Hudson.

Mann, J. C. (1963), 'The Raising of New Legions during the Principate', *Hermes* 91.4, 483–489.

Manning, W. H., & Scott, I. R. (1979), 'Roman Timber Military Gateways in Britain and on the German Frontier', *Britannia* 10, 19–61.

Marañón, G. (1956), *Tiberius: The Resentful Caesar*, New York: Duell, Sloan and Pearce.
Marlowe, J. (1971), *The Golden Age of Alexandria: From its Foundation by Alexander the Great in 331 BC to its Capture by the Arabs in 642 AD*, London: Victor Gollancz.
Marsh, Frank Burr (1926), 'Roman Parties in the Reign of Tiberius', *The American Historical Review* 31.2 (Jan.), 233–250.
Marsh, Frank Burr (1928), 'Tiberius and the Development of the Early Empire', *The Classical Journal* 24.1 (Oct.), 14–27.
Marsh, Frank Burr (1931), *The Reign of Tiberius*, Oxford: Oxford University Press.
Martin-Kilcher, Stephanie (2011), ‚Römer und *gentes Alpinae* im Konflikt – archäologische und historische Zeugnissedes 1. Jahrhunderts v. Chr.' in: Moosbauer, Günther & Wiegels, Rainer (eds.) *Römische Okkupations- und Grenzpolitik im frühen Principat Beiträge zum Kongress* ‚Fines imperii – imperium sine fine?' *in Osnabrück vom 14. bis 18. September 2009, Osnabrücker Forschungen zu Altertum und Antike-Rezeption* 14, Diepholz: Druckhaus Breyer, 27–62.
Martino, E. (1982), *Roma Contra Cántabros y Astures. Nueva Lectura de las Fuentes*,Santander: Sal Terrae.
Mason, Ernst (1963), *Tiberius: The Life of Tiberius Claudius Nero, Sadist, Murderer and Tyrant*, London: Panther Books.
Matei-Popescu, Florian (2013), 'The Roman Auxiliary Units of Moesia', in: *Il Mar Nero: Annali di archeologia e storia* 8 (2010–11), 207–230.
Matijević, K. (2006), *Zur augusteischen Germanienpolitik*, Osnabrücker Online – Beiträge zu den Altertumswissenschaften.
Mattern, Susan P. (1999), *Rome and the Enemy: Imperial Strategy in the Principate*, Berkeley: The University of California Press.
Mattern, Susan P. (1999), 'Physicians and the Roman Imperial Aristocracy: The Patronage of Therapeutics', *Bulletin of the History of Medicine* 73.1 (Spring), 1–18.
Mattingly, D. J., & Hitchner, R. B. (1995), Roman Africa: An Archaeological Review', *The Journal of Roman Studies* 85, 165–213.
Mattingly, H. (1937), 'The Property Qualifications of the Roman Classes', *The Journal of Roman Studies* 27, 99–107.
Mattingly, H. (1960), *Roman Coins: From the Earliest Times to the Fall of the Western Empire*, London: Methuen (second edition).
Matyszak, Philip (2006), *The Sons of Caesar: Imperial Rome's First Dynasty*, London: Thames and Hudson.
Mayor, Adrienne (2009), *Greek Fire, Poison Arrows and Scorpion Bombs: Biological and Chemical Warfare in the Ancient World*, New York: Overlook Press.
Mayor, Adrienne (2023), *The First Fossil Hunters: Dinosaurs, Mammoths, and Myth in Greek and Roman Times*, Princeton: Princeton University Press.
Maxfield, Valerie A. (1981), *The Military Decorations of the Roman Army*, London: B. T. Batsford.
Mazzolani, Lidia Storoni (2006), *Tiberio o la spirale del potere: La Forza Irresistible Del Dispotismo*, Milan: BUR.
McAllen Green, W. (1927), 'Notes on the Augustan Deities', *The Classical Journal* 23.2 (November), 86–93.
McCall, J. B. (2002), *The Cavalry of the Roman Republic: Cavalry Combat and Elite Reputations in the Middle and Late Republic*, London: Routledge.
McCane, B. R. (2008), 'Simply Irresistible: Augustus, Herod, and the Empire', *Journal of Biblical Literature* 127.4 (Winter), 725–735.

McCracken, George (1940), 'Tiberius and the Cult of the Dioscuri at Tusculum', *The Classical Journal* 35.8 (May), 486–488.
McCraven, William H. (2021), *The Hero Code: Lessons Learned from Lives Well Lived*, New York: Hachette.
McCullough, D. W. (ed.) (1998), *Chronicles of the Barbarians; Firsthand Accounts of Pillage and Conquest, From the Ancient World to the Fall of Constantinople*, New York: History Book Club.
McDermott, W. C. (1970), '*Milites Gregarii*', *Greece & Rome* (Second Series) 17.2 (October) 184–196.
McDonnell-Staff, Paul (2009), 'The Other Invader Over the Alps: Watershed of the Second Punic War', *Ancient Warfare* 3.4 (August/September 2009), 36–41.
McGing, Brian C. (1991), 'Pontius Pilate and the Sources', *The Catholic Biblical Quarterly* 53(3), 416–438.
McHugh, John S. (2021), *Sejanus: Regent of Rome*, Barnsley: Pen & Sword Books.
McPherson, C. (2009), 'Fact and Fiction: Crassus, Augustus, and the *Spolia Opima*', *Hirundo*: McGill Journal of Classical Studies 8, 21–34.
Melchior, A. (2009), 'What Would Pompey Do? *Exempla* and Pompeian Failure in the *Bellum Africum*', *The Classical Journal* 104.3 (February-March), 241–257.
M'Elderry, R. K. (1909), 'The Legions of the Euphrates Frontier', *The Classical Quarterly* 3.1 (January), 44–53.
Meledandri, Giovanni (2022), 'The Death of Germanicus: Disease or Murder?', *Journal of Virology and Viral Diseases* 2(2) (Online, accessed 15 February 2023: https://doi.org/10.54289/JVVD2200107)
Merrill, Elmer Truesdell (1919), 'The Expulsion of Jews from Rome under Tiberius', *Classical Philology* 14.4 (October), 365–372.
Merriweather, S. (1940), 'Tacitus and the Portraits of Germanicus and Drusus', *Classical Philology* 35, 64.
Messer, William Stuart (1920), 'Mutiny in the Roman Army. The Republic', *Classical Philology* 15.2 (April), 158–175.
Metzger, E. (2004), 'Roman judges, case law, and principles of procedure', *Law and History Review* 22, 243–275.
Meyer, A. (2013), *The Creation, Composition, Service and Settlement of Roman Auxiliary Units Raised on the Iberian Peninsula* (British Archaeological Reports International Series).
Mierow, C. C. (1943), 'Germanicus Caesar Imperator', *The Classical Journal*, *39*(3), 137–155.
Mihajlović, Vladimir D. (2018), 'Imagining the Ister/Danube in Ancient Thought and Practice: River, the Scordisci, and Creation of Roman Imperialistic Space*', *Issues in Ethnography and Anthropology* 13.3, 747–780.
Milani, Luigi A. (1891), '"Nero Claudio Druso nella statua frammentaria veronese e in altri monumenti." — I rilievi dell' *Ara Pacis* Augustae', *Mittheilungen des arch. Instituts zu Rom* 6.4, 307–19.
Miles, G. B. (1990), 'Roman and Modern Imperialism: A Reassessment', *Comparative Studies in Society and History* 32.4 (October), 629–659.
Millar, Fergus (1966), 'The Emperor, the Senate and the Provinces', *The Journal of Roman Studies* 56, Parts 1 and 2, 156–166.
Millar, Fergus (1973), 'Triumvirate and Principate', *The Journal of Roman Studies* 63, 50–67.
Millar, Fergus (1982), 'Emperors, Frontiers and Foreign Relations, 31 B.C. to A.D. 378', *Britannia* 13, 1–23.
Millar, Fergus (1988), 'Government and Diplomacy in the Roman Empire during the First Three Centuries', *The International History Review* 10.3 (August), 345–377.

Millar, Fergus (1992), 'The Augustan Monarchy. Review of *Between Republic and Empire: Interpretations of Augustus and his Principate* by Kurt A. Raaflaub; Mark Toher' in: *The Classical Review (New Series)* 42.2, 378–381.
Miller, N. P. (1968), 'Tiberius Speaks: An Examination of the Utterances Ascribed to Him in the Annals of Tacitus', *The American Journal of Philology* 89.1 (January), 1–19.
Miltner, Franz (1952), 'Der Tacitusbericht Über Idistaviso', *Rheinisches Museum für Philologie* (Neue Folge) 95. Bd., 4. H., 343–356.
Mišec, Alenka (2009), 'The Augustan Conquest of Southeastern Alpine and Western Pannonian Areas: Coins and Hoards', *Arheološki vestnik* 60, 283–296.
Mitchell, S. (1976), '*Legio* VII and the Garrison of Augustan Galatia', *The Classical Quarterly (New Series)* 26.2, 298–308.
Mócsy, A. (1983), 'Civilized Pannonians' in: Hartley, Brian & Wacher, John (eds.), *Rome and Her Northern Provinces* (1983), Gloucester: Alan Sutton Publishing, 169–178.
Momigliano, A. (1942), 'The Peace of the *Ara Pacis*', *Journal of the Warburg and Courtauld Institutes* 5, 228–231.
Mommsen, T. E. (1954), 'Augustus and Britain: A Fragment from Livy?', *The American Journal of Philology* 75.2, 175–183.
Mommsen, T., & Demandt, A. (1996), *A History of Rome Under the Emperors*, London: Routledge.
Monachino, Vincenzo (1974), *Le persecuzioni e la polemica pagano-cristiana*, Rome: Edizioni P.U.G., 21–24.
Monteil, M. (2008), *La France gallo-romaine*, Paris: Editions La Découverte.
Morello, Ruth (2006), 'A Correspondence Course in Tyranny: The *Cruentae Litterae* of Tiberius', *Arethusa* (Spring) 39.2, 331–354
Morillo, Angel, & García-Marcos, V. (2002), 'Twenty Years of Roman Military Archaeology in Spain' in: Freeman, Philip, Bennett, Julian, & Fiema, Zbigniew T. (eds.), *Limes XVIIIth International Congress of Roman Frontier Studies Held in Amman, Jordan* (September 2000), Oxford, 2002, 779–789.
Morillo, Angel (2011), 'The Roman occupation of the north of *Hispania*: war, military deployment and cultural integration' in: Moosbauer, Günther & Wiegels, Rainer (eds.) *Römische Okkupations- und Grenzpolitik im frühen Principat Beiträge zum Kongress* ,Fines imperii – imperium sine fine?' *in Osnabrück vom 14. bis 18. September 2009*, *Osnabrücker Forschungen zu Altertum und Antike-Rezeption* 14, Diepholz: Druckhaus Breyer, 11–26.
Morley, Neville (2010), 'They Make a Desert and Call it Peace': The Nature of Roman Rule' in: Morely, N., *The Roman Empire: Roots of Imperialism* (2010), New York: Pluto Press, 38–69.
Mráv, Zsolt (2010), 'Graves of auxiliary soldiers and veterans in northern part of province Pannonia in the 1st Century AD' in: Sanader, M., Rendić-Miočević, A., Tončinić, D. & Radman-Livaja, I. (eds.), *Proceedings of the XVIIth Roman Military Equipment Conference (ROMEC): Weapons and Military Equipment in a Funerary Context*, Zagreb.
Mráv, Zsolt (2010–13), 'The Roman Amy along the Amber Road between Poetovio and Carnuntum in the 1st Century A.D. – Archaeological Evidence: A Preliminary Research Report', *Commucationes Archaelogicae Hungariae*, 49–100.
Mueller, H.-F. (2002), *Roman Religion in Valerius Maximus*, London: Routledge.
Müller, K. (1874), *Fragmenta Historicorum Graecorum* Vol. 3, Paris.
Musial, Danuta (2014), 'The *Princeps* as *Pontifex Maximus*. The Case of Tiberius, *Electrum* 21, 99–106.
Musilová, Margaréta (2016), 'Structural Analysis of the Celto-Roman Masonry Building on Bratisalava's Castle Hill – A Preliminary Study' in: Karwowski, M. & Ramsl, P. C. (eds.), *Boii*

– *Taurisci: Proceedings of the International Seminar, Oberleis-Klement, June 14th-15th, 2012* (1st ed.), Wien: Austrian Academy of Sciences Press, 217–236

Nagel, Barbara Natalie (2013), 'The Tyrant as Artist: Legal Fiction and Sexual Violence under Tiberius', *Law and Literature* 25.2, 286–310.

Nesselhauf, Herbert (1952), 'Tacitus und Domitian', *Hermes* 80(2), 222–245.

Newark, T., & McBride, A. (1985), *The Barbarians: Warriors and Wars of the Dark Ages*, Poole: Blandford Press.

Newark, T., & McBride, A. (1986), *Celtic Warriors 400 BC–AD 1600*, Poole: Blandford Press.

Newark, T., & McBride, A. (1998), *Celtic Warriors*, Hong Kong: The Military Book Club/ Concord Publications.

Newlands, C. E. (1995), *Playing with Time: Ovid and the* Fasti, New York: Cornell University Press.

Nicolet, C. (1984), 'Augustus, Government, and the Propertied Classes' in: Millar, Fergus and Segal, Erich (eds.), *Caesar Augustus: Seven Aspects*, Oxford, 89–128.

Nicolet, C., & Gautier Dalché, P. (1986), 'Les quatre sages de Jules César et la mesure du monde selon Julius Honorius', *Journal des Savants* (October–December), 157–218.

Nicolet, C. (1991), *Space, Geography, and Politics in the Early Roman Empire*, Ann Arbor: University of Michigan Press.

Nicholls, J. J. (1967), 'The Content of the *Lex Curiata*', *The American Journal of Philology* 88.3 (July), 257–278.

Nicols, John (1975), 'Antonia and Sejanus', *Historia: Zeitschrift Für Alte Geschichte* 24(1), 48–58.

Nigdélis, P. M. (1994), 'M. Insteius L.f. αὐτοκράτωρ et la province de Macedoine au debut du second triumvirat. À propos d'une inscription inédite d'Europos', *Bulletin de correspondance hellénique*, 118.1, 215–228.

Nippel, W. (1995), *Public Order in Ancient Rome,* Cambridge: Cambridge niversity Press.

Nock, A. D. (1952), 'The Roman Army and the Roman Religious Year', *The Harvard Theological Review* 45.4 (October), 187–252.

Nony, D. (1982), 'Sur quelques monnaies impériales romaines', *Mélanges de l'Ecole française de Rome: Antiquité* 94–2, 893–909.

Noreña, Carlos F. (2001), 'The Communication of the Emperor's Virtues', *The Journal of Roman Studies* 91, 146–168.

Norkus, J. (1963), *Die Feldzüge der Römer in Nordwestdeutschland in den Jahren 9–16 n. Chr. von einem Soldaten gesehen*, Hildesheim.

North, J. A. (1981), 'The Development of Roman Imperialism', *Journal of Roman Studies* 71, 1–9.

Nouwen, Robert (2008), 'Het Romeinse leger en het romaniseringsproces in de Lage Landen', *Kunsttijdschrift Vlaanderen* 57, 106–111.

Ober, J. (1982), 'Tiberius and the Political Testament of Augustus', *Historia: Zeitschrift* für Alte *Geschichte* 31.3 (Third Quarter), 306–328.

Oberziner, G. (1900), *Le guerre di Augusto contro i populi Alpini*, Trento: Roma E. Loescher.

Odiorne, G. S. (1961), *How Managers Make Things Happen*, Englewood Cliffs: Prentice-Hall.

Oldfather, W. A. (1916), 'The Varus Episode', *The Classical Journal* 11.4 (January), 226–236.

Oliver, J. H. (1989), *Greek Constitutions of Early Roman Emperors from Inscriptions and Papyri* no. 295, Philadelphia: American Philosophical Society.

Oliver, J. H. & Palmer, R. E. A. (1954), 'Text of the Tabula Hebana', *American Journal of Philology* 75, 225–249.

Oliver, R. P. (1951), 'The First Medicean MS of Tacitus and the Titulature of Ancient Books', *Transactions and Proceedings of the American Philological Association* 82, 232–261.

Olbrycht, Marek Jan (2016), 'Germanicus, Artabanos II of Parthia, and Zeno Artaxias in Armenia', *Klio* 98, 605–633.

Opper, Thorsten (2014), *The Meroë Head of Augustus*, London: The British Museum.

Orejas, A., & Sánchez-Palencia, F. J. (2002), 'Mines, Territorial Organization, and Social Structure in Roman Iberia: Carthago Noua and the Peninsular Northwest', *American Journal of Archaeology* 106.4 (October), 581–599.

Orlin, Eric M. (2002), 'Foreign Cults in Republican Rome: Rethinking the Pomerial Rule', *Memoirs of the American Academy in Rome* 47, 1–18.

Orlin, Eric M. (2007), 'Augustan Religion and the Reshaping of Roman Memory', *Arethusa* 40.1, 73–92.

Orlin, Eric M. (2008), 'Octavian and Egyptian Cults: Redrawing the Boundaries of Romanness', *The American Journal of Philology* 129.2, 231–253.

Orth, W. (1978), 'Zur Fabricius-Tuscus-Inschrift aus Alexandreia/Troas', *Zeitschrift für Papyrologie und Epigraphik* 28, 57–60.

Osgood, Josiah (2011), *Claudius Caesar: Image and Power in the Early Roman Empire*, Cambridge: Cambridge Unversity Press.

Osgood, Josiah (2012), 'Suetonius and the Succession to Augustus' in: Gibson, Alisdair (ed.), *The Julio-Claudian Succession: Reality and Perception of the "Augustan Model", Mnemosyne,* Supplements, History and Archaeology of Classical Antiquity 349 (2012), 19–40.

Östenberg, Ida (2009), 'From conquest to *pax romana*. The *signa recepta* and the end of the triumphal *Fasti* in 19 BC' in: Hekster, Olivier, Schmidt-Hofner, Sebastian and Witschel, Christian (eds.), *The impact of empire on the dynamics of ritual. Proceedings of the eighth workshop of the international network Impact of Empire, Heidelberg, July 5–7, 2007* (Impact of Empire 9), Leiden; Brill (2009), 53–75.

Östenberg, Ida (2014), 'War and Remembrance. Memories of defeat in Ancient Rome' in: Alroth, B., & Scheffer, C. (eds.), *Attitudes towards the past in Antiquity: Creating identities?*, Papers held at the Conference at Stockholm University 15–17 May 2009, 255–265.

Östenberg, Ida (2019), '*Damnatio Memoriae* Inscribed: The Materiality of Cultural Repression' in: Petrovic, Andrej, Petrovic, Ivana & Thomas, Edmund (eds.) *The Materiality of Text – Placement, Perception, and Presence of Inscribed Texts in Classical Antiquity*, Leiden: Brill (2019), 324–347.

Ovadiah, Aher, & Peleg, Rachel (2009), 'The "Promontory Palace" in Caesarea Maritima and the Northern Palace at Masada: Architectural Conceptions and Sources of Inspiration', *Revue Biblique (1946-)* 116(4), 598–611.

Pagán, Victoria Emma (1999), 'Beyond Teutoburg: Transgression and Transformation in Tacitus *Annales* 1.61–62', *Classical Philology* 94.3 (July), 302–320.

Pagán, Victoria Emma (ed.) (2011), *A Companion to Tacitus*, Oxford: Blackwell Publishing.

Pandey, N. B. (2014), Reading Rome from the Farther Shore: *Aeneid* 6 in the Augustan Landscape', *Vergilius* 60, 85–116.

Panter, A. (2007), 'Der Drususstein in Mainz und dessen Einordnung in die römische Grabarchitektur seiner Erbauungszeit', *Mainzer Archäologische Schriften* 6, Generaldirektion Kulturelles Erbe Rheinland-Pfalz, Direktion Landesarchäologie.

Pantle, Christian (2009), *Die Varusschlacht: Der germanische Freiheitskrieg*, Berlin: Ullstein Buchverlage.

Papini, Giovanni (1934), *II Cesare della crocifissione*, Rome: La nuova antologia.

Pappano, Albert Earl (1941), 'Agrippa Postumus,' *Classical Philology* 36(1), 30–45.

Parchami, A. (2009), *Hegemonic Peace and Empire: The* Pax Romana, Britannica and Americana, Abingdon: Routledge.

Parker, H. M. D. (1928), *The Roman Legions*, Oxford: Clarendon Press.

Patrich, Joseph (2011), *Studies in the Archaeology and History of Caesarea Maritima*. Caput Judaeae, Metropolis Palaestinae, Leiden: Brill.

Patterson, Lee E. (2015), 'Antony and Armenia', *Transactions of the American Philological Association* (*TAPA*) 145, 77–105.

Paul, G.M., & Ierardi, M., eds. (1999), *Roman Coins and Public Life Under the Empire: E. Togo Salmon Papers II*, Ann Arbor: University of Michigan Press.

Pelling, Christopher (1993), 'Tacitus and Germanicus' in: Luce, T. J., & Woodman, A. J. (eds.). *Tacitus and the Tacitean Tradition*. Princeton: Princeton University Press (1993), 59–85.

Pelling, C. B. R. (1988), *Plutarch: Life of Antony*, Cambridge University Press: Cambridge.

Pelling, C. B. R. (1996), 'The Triumviral Period', in A. K. Bowman *et al* (ed.), *CAH* $10^2$ Cambridge University Press: Cambridge, 1–69.

Perowne, Stewart (1956), *The Life and Times of Herod the Great*, London: Hodder and Stoughton Ltd.

Petrikovits, Harald von (1960), *Das römische Rheinland Archäologische Forschungen seit 1945*, *Beihefte der Bonner Jahrbücher* Band 8, Köln: Westdeutcher Verlag.

Pettegrew, D. K. (2011), 'The *Diolkos* of Corinth', *American Journal of Archaeology* 115.4, 549–574.

Pettinger, Andrew (2012), *The Republic in Danger: Drusus Libo and the Succession of Tiberius*, Oxford: Oxford University Press.

Petzl, George (2019), *Archaeological Exploration of Sardis. Monograph 14: Sardis: Greek and Latin Inscriptions, Part II: Finds from 1958 to 2017*, Cambridge, Mass.: Harvard University Press.

Phillips, Darryl (2012), 'Potestas and Auctoritas: Augustus and Elections 27–17 B.C.', *Studies in Latin Literature and Roman History* 16, 134–150.

Philo, John-Mark (2020), 'Elizabeth I's Translation of Tacitus: Lambeth Palace Library, MS 683', *The Review of English Studies* 71.298 (February), 44–73.

Piano, Valerie (2019), '*P.Hercul. 1067* Reconsidered: Latest Results and Prospective Researches', in: Nodar, Alberto, & Torallas, Tovar Sofia. (eds.), *Proceedings of the 28th Congress of Papyrology; 2016 August 1–6; Barcelona*. Barcelona: Publicacions de l'Abadia de Montserrat, Universitat Pompeu Fabra, 231–240.

Pieper, Christoph (2021), '*Tiberius aequatus Augusto*: Augustan Intertexts for Tiberius' *moderatio* in Velleius Paterculus 2.94.1 and 2.122.1', *Philologus* 165.2, 241–259.

Pietsch, M., Timpe, D., & Wamser, L. (1991), 'Das augusteische Truppenlager Marktbreit. Bisherige archäologische Befunde und historische Erwägungen', *Bericht der Römisch-Germanischen Kommission* 72, 263–324.

Pietsch, M. (1993), 'Die Zentralgebäude des augusteischen Legionslagers von Marktbreit und die *Principia* von Haltern', *Germania* 71, 355–368.

Piruli, S. (1980), 'Osservazioni sul feriale di Spello', *Tituli* 2, 47–80.

Pitassi, Michael (2011), *Roman Warships*, Woodbridge: The Boydell Press.

Pitts, L. F. (1989), 'Relations between Rome and the German 'Kings' on the Middle Danube in the First to Fourth Centuries A.D.', *The Journal of Roman Studies* 79, 45–58.

Platner, S. B. (as completed and revised by T. Ashby) (1929), *A Topographical Dictionary of Ancient Rome*, London: Oxford.

Pleket, H. W. (1958), *The Greek Inscriptions in the* Rijksmuseum van Oudheden *at Leyden*, Leiden.

Plescia, Joseph (2001), 'Judicial Accountability and Immunity in Roman Law', *The American Journal of Legal History* 45(1), 51–70.

Polak, Marinus & Kooistra, Laura I. (2013), 'A Sustainable Frontier? The Establishment of the Roman Frontier in the Rhine Delta. Part 1: From the end of the Iron Age to the death of Tiberius (*c.* 50 BC–AD 37)', *Jahrbuch des Römisch-Germanischen Zentralmuseums* 60, 355–460.

Polo, F. P. (2011), *The Consul at Rome: The Civil Functions of the Consuls in the Roman Republic*, Cambridge: Cambridge University Press.

Pollini, John (1987), *The Portraiture of Caius and Lucius Caesar*, New York: Fordham University Press.

Pollini, John (2005), 'A New Marble Portrait of Tiberius: Portrait Typology and Ideology', *Antike Kunst* 48, 57–72.

Pollini, John (2010), 'Lovemaking and Voyeurism in Roman Art and Culture: The House of the Centenary at Pompeii', *Römische Mitteilungen* 116, 289–319.

Pollini, John (2013), 'The Image of Caligula: Myth and Reality', *Digital Sculpture Project: Caligula*, Virtual World Heritage Laboratory.

Pollini, John (2017), 'The Bronze Statue of Germanicus from Ameria (Amelia)', *American Journal of Archaeology* 121.3 (July), 425–437.

Posluschny, A. (1977), 'Die hallstattzeitliche Siedlung auf dem Kapellenberg bei Marktbreit, Unterfranken', *Bayerische Vorgeschichtsblätter* 62, 29–113.

Posner, Eric A. (2020), 'The Constitution of the Roman Republic', in: Dari-Mattiacci, Giuseppe & Kehoe, Dennis P. (eds), *Roman Law and Economics: Institutions and Organizations Volume I*, Oxford: Oxford Academic.

Possanza, D. Mark (2012), 'Review: *Aratus: Phaenomena, Translated with an Introduction and Notes* by Aaron Poochigan', *Aestimatio* 9, 66–87.

Potter, D. S. (1987), 'The *Tabula Siarensis*, Tiberius, the Senate, and the Eastern Boundary of the Roman Empire', *Zeitschrift für Papyrology und* Epigraphik 69, 269–276.

Potter, D. S. (1999), 'Political Theory in the *Senatus Consultum Pisonianum*', *The American Journal of Philology* 120.1, 65–88.

Potter, D. S. & Damon, Cynthia (1999), 'The *Senatus Consultum De Cn. Pisone Patre*', *The American Journal of Philology* 120.1, 13–42.

Potter, T. W. (1987), *Roman Italy*, London: Guild Publishing/British Museum Publications.

Powell, A. (ed.) (2013), *Roman Poetry and Propaganda in the Age of Augustus* (Bristol Classical Paperbacks), London: Bloomsbury.

Powell, A., & Welch, K. (eds.) (2002), *Sextus Pompeius*, Swansea: Classical Press of Wales.

Powell, A., & Smith, C. (eds.) (2008), *The Lost Memoirs of Augustus and the Development of Roman Autobiography*, Swansea: Classical Press of Wales.

Powell, Lindsay (1988), 'The Mood of the Armies: Morale and Mutiny in the Roman Army of the First Century AD', *Exercitus* 2.4, 61–64.

Powell, Lindsay (2009), '*Bella Germaniae*: The German Wars of Drusus the Elder and Tiberius', *Ancient Warfare* Special Issue 1, 10–16.

Powell, Lindsay (2010), 'Fighting for the Gods: Historical Introduction', in J. Oorthuys (ed.), *Ancient Warfare* 4.5, 2–5.

Powell, Lindsay (2011a), *Eager for Glory: The Untold Story of Drusus the Elder*, Barnsley: Pen & Sword Books.

Powell, Lindsay (2011b), 'The Last Clash of the Cimbri and Romans: The Battle of Vercellae, 101 BC', in J. Oorthuys (ed.), *Ancient Warfare* 5.1, 27–33.

Powell, Lindsay (2013), *Germanicus: The Magnificent Life and Mysterious Death of Rome's Most Popular General*, Barnsley: Pen & Sword Books.

Powell, Lindsay (2014b), *Combat: Roman Soldier v. Germanic Warrior*, Oxford: Osprey Publishing.

Powell, Lindsay (2015), *Marcus Agrippa: Right-Hand Man of Caesar Augustus*, Barnsley: Pen & Sword Books.

Powell, Lindsay (2016), 'A Trophy Proud to Thee: Celebrating Victory the Augustan Way', *Ancient Warfare* 9.6, 16–20.

Powell, Lindsay (2018), *Augustus at War: The Struggle for the* Pax Augusta, Barnsley: Pen & Sword Books.

Powell, Lindsay (2019a), 'Follow the Roman Birds: The Battle of Idistaviso, Summer AD 16', *Ancient Warfare* 12.5 (April-May), 22–33.

Powell, Lindsay (2019b), 'Ancient Rome's 'JFK Moment': The Death of Germanicus Caesar', *Ancient History* 24 (November–December), 42–45.

Powell, Lindsay (2020), 'Avenging Germanicus: Ancient Rome's Show Trial', *Ancient History* 30 (November-December), 52–55.

Powell, Lindsay (2021), *Bar Kokhba: The Jew Who Defied Hadrian and Challenged the Might of Rome*, Barnsley: Pen & Sword Books.

Powell, Lindsay (2022a), "*Civis Romanus Sum*': Roman Citizenship and the Justice System', *Ancient History* 39, 18–21.

Powell, Lindsay (2022b), 'Germanicus in Egypt: A Roman VIP Tours Sights on the Nile', *Ancient History* 42 (January–February), 44–47.

Powell, Lindsay (2023), *Hannibal of Carthage*, London: Flame Tree Publishing.

Powell, Lindsay (2024), 'Augustus the Builder: Transforming the City of Rome', *Ancient History* 50 (July–August), 44–47.

Power, Tristan (2014), 'Suetonius' Tacitus', *Journal of Roman Studies* 104, 205–225.

Powers, Jessica (2023), *Roman Landscapes: Visions of Nature and Myth from Rome and Pompeii*, San Antonio: San Antonio Museum of Art.

Powers, Nathan (2012), 'The Stoic Argument for the Rationality of The Cosmos' in: Inwood, Brad (ed.), *Oxford Studies in Ancient Philosophy, Volume 43*, Oxford: Oxford University Press.

Pratt, K. J. (1955), 'Roman Anti-Militarism', *The Classical Journal* 51.1 (October), 21–25.

Purcell, Nicholas (1986), 'Livia and the Womanhood of Rome', *Proceedings of the Cambridge Philological Society* 32 (212), 78–105.

Questa, C. (1957), 'Il Viaggio di Germanico in Oriente e Tacito', *Maia* 9, 291–321.

Raaflaub, Kurt A. (1980), 'The political significance of Augustus' military reforms' in: Edmondson, J. (ed.), *Augustus*, Edinburgh Readings on the Ancient World, Edinburgh (2009), 203–228.

Raaflaub, Kurt A. (2007), *War and Peace in the Ancient World*, Oxford: Blackwell Publishing.

Radboud, Bernt Kerremans (2018), 'A Real Roman Defeat: Memory, Collective Trauma and the *Clades Lolliana*', *Acta Classica* 61, 69–98.

Radman-Livaja, Ivan & Vukelić, Vlatka (2018), 'The Whereabouts of Tiberius' Ditch in Siscia' in: Bradač, Marina Milićević & Demicheli, Dino (eds.), *The Century of the Brave/ Stoljeće hrabrih*, Zagreb: FF Press, 407–421.

Rageth, von Jürg & Zanier, Werner (2010), 'Crap Ses und Septimer: Archäologische Zeugnisse der römischen Alpeneroberung 16 / 15 v. Chr. aus Graubünden', *Germania* 88, 241–283.

Ramage, E. S. (1982), 'Velleius Paterculus 2.126.2–3 and the Panegyric Tradition', *Classical Antiquity* 1(2), 266–271.

Ramage, E. S. (1985), 'Augustus' Treatment of Julius Caesar', *Historia: Zeitschrift für Alte Geschichte* 34. 2 (second quarter), 223–245.

Ramsey, J. T., Licht, A. L., & Brian, G. Marsden, B. G. (ed.) (1997), *The Comet of 44 B.C. and Caesar's Funeral Games* (APA American Classical Studies, no. 39), Oxford: Oxford University Press.

Ramsey, W. M. (1916), 'Colonia Caesarea (Pisidian Antioch) in the Augustan Age', *The Journal of Roman Studies* 6, 83–134.

Ramsey, W. M. (1917), 'Studies in the Roman Province Galatia: I. The Homanadeis and the Homanadensian War', *The Journal of Roman Studies* 7, 229–283.

Ramsey, W. M. (1922), 'Studies in the Roman Province Galatia', *The Journal of Roman Studies* 12, 147–186.

Ramsey, W. M. (1924), 'Studies in the Roman Province Galatia. VI. – Some Inscriptions of Colonia Caesarea Antiochea', *The Journal of Roman Studies* 14, 172–205.

Ramsay, W. M. (1929), 'Roman Garrisons and Soldiers in Asia Minor. Part II', *The Journal of Roman Studies* 19, 155–160.

Rand, E. K. (1926), 'On the History of the *De Vita Caesarum* of Suetonius in the Early Middle Ages', *Harvard Studies in Classical Philology* 37, 1–48.

Rankov, Boris, & Hook, Richard (1994), *The Praetorian Guard*, London: Osprey Publishing.

Rapke, Terence T. (1982), 'Tiberius, Piso, and Germanicus', *Acta Classica* 25, 61–69.

Rasbach, G., & Becker, A. (2003), 'Die spätaugusteische Stadtgründung in Lahnau-Waldgirmes. Archäologische, architektonische und naturwissenschaftliche Untersuchungen', in *Germania* 81, 147–199.

Rebert, Homer F., & Marceau, Henri (1925), 'The Temple of Concord in the Roman Forum', *Memoirs of the American Academy in Rome* 5, 53–77.

Reddé, Michel (2011), ‚L'armée romaine et les peuples gaulois de César à Auguste' in: Moosbauer, Günther & Wiegels, Rainer (eds.) *Römische Okkupations- und Grenzpolitik im frühen Principat Beiträge zum Kongress,* Fines imperii – imperium sine fine?' *in Osnabrück vom 14. bis 18. September 2009, Osnabrücker Forschungen zu Altertum und Antike-Rezeption* 14, Diepholz: Druckhaus Breyer, 63–74.

Reed, Annette Yoskiko (2015), 'The Afterlives of New Testament Apocrypha', *Journal of Biblical Literature* 134(2), 401–425.

Reed, N. (1975), 'Drusus and the Classis Britannica', *Historia: Zeitschrift für Alte Geschichte* 24.2, 315–323.

Reeder, J. C. (1997), 'The Statue of Augustus from Prima Porta, the Underground Complex, and the Omen of the Gallina Alba', *The American Journal of Philology* 118.1 (Spring), 89–118.

Regev, E. (2010), 'Herod's Jewish Ideology Facing Romanization: On Intermarriage, Ritual Baths, and Speeches', *Jewish Quarterly Review* 100.2 (Spring), 197–222.

Rehak, P. (2001), 'Aeneas or Numa? Rethinking the Meaning of the *Ara Pacis Augustae*', *The Art Bulletin* 83.2 (June), 190–208.

Rehman, Iskander (2024), *Iron* Imperator*: Roman Grand Strategy Under Tiberius,* Stockholm: Bokforlaget Stolpe Ab.

Reinhold, Meyer (1933), *Marcus Agrippa: A Biography*, New York: The W. F. Humphrey Press.

Reinhold, Meyer (1972), 'Marcus Agrippa's Son-in-Law P. Quinctilius Varus', *Classical Philology* 67. 2 (April), 119–121.

Reinking, L. (1855), *Die Niederlage des Quintilius Varus und Germanicus Kriegszug Durch das Bructererland: Eine Prüfung der bisherigen Ansichten*, Warendorf: J. Schnell.

Reinmuth, O. W. (1935), *The Prefect of Egypt from Augustus to Diocletian*, Leipzig: Dieterich'schen Verlagsbuchhandlung.

Retsö, J. (2000), 'Where and What Was "Arabia Felix"?', *Proceedings of the Seminar for Arabian Studies* 30, Papers from the thirty-third meeting of the Seminar for Arabian Studies held in London, 15–17 July 1999, 189–192."

Retsö, J. (2003), 'When Did Yemen Become "Arabia Felix"?', *Proceedings of the Seminar for Arabian Studies 33*, Papers from at the thirty-sixth meeting of the Seminar for Arabian Studies held in London, 18–20 July 2002, 229–235

Rettinger, E. (ed.), (2003), *2000 Jahre Mainz: Geschichte der Stadt digital*, (CD-ROM), Institut für Geschichtliche Landeskunde an der Universität Mainz, Mainz.

Reynolds, J. (1996), 'Cyrene', in Bowman, A.K., Champlin, E., Lintott, A. (eds.), *The Cambridge Ancient History Volume X: The Augustan Empire, 43 B.C.–A.D. 69* (second edition), Cambridge: Cambridge University Press, 619–640.

Ricci, Cecilia (2011), '*In Custodiam Urbis*: Notes on the *Cohortes Urbanae* (1968–2010)'. *Historia: Zeitschrift Für Alte Geschichte* 60(4), 484–508.

Rich, J. (2008), 'Treaties, allies and the Roman conquest of Italy' in: De Souza, P. & France, J. (eds.), *War and Peace in Ancient and Medieval History*, Cambridge: Cambridge University Press, 51–75.

Rich, J. W. (1998), 'Augustus's Parthian Honours, the Temple of Mars Ultor and the Arch in the Forum Romanum', *Papers of the British School at Rome* 66, 71–128.

Rich, J. W. (1999), 'Drusus and the *Spolia Opima*', *The Classical Quarterly (New Series)* 49.2, 544–555.

Rich, J. W. (2002), 'Augustus, War and Peace' in: Edmondson, J. (ed.), *Augustus*, Edinburgh Readings on the Ancient World, Edinburgh (2009), 137–164.

Rich, John (2015), 'Consensus rituals and the origin of the principate' in: Ferrary, J.-L. & J. Scheid, J. (eds.) *Il princeps romano: autocrate o magistrato? Fattori giuridic e fattori sociali del potere imperiale da Augusto a Commodo*, Pavia: IUSS Press, 101–138.

Rich, J. W., & Shipley, G. (eds.) (1993), *War and Society in the Roman World*, London: Routledge.

Richmond, Ian A. (1933), 'Commemorative Arches and City Gates in the Augustan Age', *The Journal of Roman Studies* 23, 149–174.

Richardson, J. S. (1976), 'The Spanish Mines and the Development of Provincial Taxation in the Second Century B.C.', *The Journal of Roman Studies* 66, 139–152.

Richardson, J. S. (2012) *Augustan Rome 44 BC to AD 14: The Restoration of the Republic and the Establishment of the Empire* (The Edinburgh History of Ancient Rome), Edinburgh: Edinburgh University Press.

Richardson, P. (1996), *Herod: King of the Jews and Friend of the Romans*, University of South Carolina.

Riese, A. (1878), *Geographi latini minores collegit, recensuit, prolegomenis instruxit*, Henninger Bros, Heilbronn.

Ripat, Pauline (2011), 'Expelling Misconceptions: Astrologers at Rome', *Classical Philology* 106(2), 115–154.

Ritchie, W. F., & Ritchie, J. N. G. (1985), *Celtic Warriors*, Aylesbury: Shire Archaeology.

Robinson, H. R. (1975), *The Armour of Imperial Rome*, London: Arms and Armour Press.

Rodà de Llanza, I. (2003), in Morillo, A. & Aurrcoecha, J. (eds.), *The Roman Army in Hispania*, Leon, 53–63.

Roddaz, Jean-Michel (1984), *Marcus Agrippa*, Rome: École Française de Rome, Palais Farnèse.

Rogers, Robert Samuel (1935), *Criminal Trials and Criminal Legislation under Tiberius*, Middletown, Conn.: The American Philological Association.

Rogers, Robert Samuel (1940), 'Tiberius' Reversal of an Augustan Policy', *Transactions and Proceedings of the American Philological Association* 71, 532–536.

Rogers, Robert Samuel (1941a), 'Augustus the Man', *The Classical Journal* 36.8 (May), 449–463.

Rogers, Robert Samuel (1941b), 'The Prefects of Egypt under Tiberius', *Transactions and Proceedings of the American Philological Association* 72, 365–371.

Rogers, Robert Samuel (1943), *Studies in the Reign of Tiberius: Some Imperial Virtues of Tiberius and Drusus Julius Caesar*, Baltimore: The Johns Hopkins Press.

Rogers, Robert Samuel (1945), 'Tiberius' Travels, A.D. 26–37', *The Classical Weekly* 39.6 (November 12), 42–44.

Rogers, Robert Samuel (1959), 'The Emperor's Displeasure-*Amicitiam Renuntiare*', *Transactions and Proceedings of the American Philological Association* 90, 224–237.

Rogers, Robert Samuel (1967), 'The Deaths of Julia and Gracchus, A.D. 14.', *Transactions and Proceedings of the American Philological Society* 98, 383–390.

Roller, D. W. (1998), *The Building Program of Herod the Great*, University of California Press.

Rollo, W. (1938), 'The Franco-German Frontier', *Greece & Rome* 8.22 (October), 36–49.

Romeo, I. (1998), *Ingenuus Leo. L'immagine di Agrippa,* Rome: L'Ermadi Bretschneider.

Romer, F. E. (1978). 'A Numismatic Date for the Departure of C. Caesar?', *Transactions of the American Philological Association (1974-)* 108, 187–202.

Romer, F. E. (1985), 'A Case of Client-Kingship', *The American Journal of Philology* 106.1 (spring), 75–100.

Romkey, Stephanie (2006), 'Obsessive-Compulsive Personality Disorder and the Enigmatic Personality of Emperor Tiberius', McMaster University (unpublished PhD thesis). https://macsphere.mcmaster.ca/bitstream/11375/10319/1/fulltext.pdf

Roncaglia, Carolynn (2013), 'Client Prefects?: Rome and the Cottians in the Western Alps', *Phoenix* 67(3/4), 353–372.

Rosborough, R.R. (1920), *An epigraphic commentary on Suetonius's Life of Caius Caligula*, Philadelphia, Penn.

Rose, C. B. (1990), "Princes' and Barbarians on the *Ara Pacis*', *American Journal of Archaeology* 94.3 (July), 453–467.

Rose, C. B. (1997), *Dynastic Commemoration and Imperial Portraiture in the Julio-Claudian Period*, Cambridge University Press.

Rose, C. B. (2005), 'The Parthians in Augustan Rome', *American Journal of Archaeology* 109.1 (January), 21–75.

Ross, Anne (1970), *Everyday Life of the Pagan Celts*, London: B. T. Batsford.

Ross, D. O. (1973), 'The Tacitean Germanicus', *Yale Classical Studies* 23, 209–227.

Rossini, O. (2007), *Ara Pacis*, Rome: Mondadori Electa (collana Musei in Comune).

Rosso, E. (2000), 'Vie d'un groupe statuaire julio-claudien à Mediolanum Santonum', *Labyrinthe* 7, 103–122 (online at https://labyrinthe.revues.org/index805.html).

Rost, A. (2005), 'Conditions for the Preservation of Roman Military Equipment on Battlefields – the Example of Kalkriese' in: Kocsis, L. (ed.), *Journal of Roman Military Equipment* 16, The Enemies of Rome: Proceedings of the 15th International Roman Military Equipment Conference, Budapest 2005, 219–224.

Rost, A. (2009), 'The battle between Romans and Germans in Kalkriese: interpreting the archaeological remains from an ancient battlefield' in: Morillo, A., Hanel, N., & Martin, E. (eds.), *Limes XX, Roman Frontier Studies*. Anejo de Gladius 13, 1339–1345.

Roth, John (2023), 'Uncancelling Tiberius in History, Philosophy and Classical Tradition', Antigone Journal (online at https://antigonejournal.com/2023/02/uncancelling-tiberius/, accessed 1 March 2024).

Roth, Jonathon P. (1994), 'The Size and Organization of the Roman Imperial Legion', *Historia: Zeitschrift* für Alte *Geschichte* 43.3 (Third Quarter), 346–362.

Roth, Jonathon P. (1999), *The Logistics of the Roman Army at War (264 BC–AD 235)*, Boston: Brill Academic Publishers.

Roth, Jonathon P. (2007), 'Jews and the Roman Army: Perceptions and realities' in: de Blois, Lukas & Lo Cascio, Elio (eds.), *The Impact of the Roman Army (200 B.C.–A.D. 476): Economic, Social, Political, Religious and Cultural Aspects. Proceedings of the Sixth Workshop of the International Network Impact of Empire (Roman Empire, 200 B.C.–A.D. 476), Capri, Italy, March 29-April 2, 2005. Impact of Empire, Volume: 6*, Boston: Brill Academic Publishers (2007), 409–420.

Rothenhoffer, Peter (2020), 'Emperor Tiberius and His *praecipua legionum cura* in a New Bronze Tablet from AD 14', *Gephyra* 19 (May), 101–110.

Rowe, Gregory (2002), *Princes and Political Cultures: The New Tiberian Senatorial Decrees*, Ann Arbor: The University of Michigan Press.

Rowe, Gregory (2012), 'Reconsidering the "Auctoritas" of Augustus', *The Journal of Roman Studies* 103, 1–15.

Rowell, H. T. (1941), 'Vergil and the Forum of Augustus', *The American Journal of Philology* 62.3, 261–276.

Roxan, M. M. (1973), *The* auxilia *of the Roman Army raised in the Iberian Peninsula*, University of London. (Doctoral thesis, online at https://discovery.ucl.ac.uk/1318033/, accessed 1 March 2024)

Roymans, Nico (2000), 'The Lower Rhine *Triquetrum* Coinages and the Ethnogenesis of the Batavi', T. Grünewald, H. J., Schalles (eds.) *Germania Inferior: Beiträge des deutschen-niederländischen Kolloquiums in Regionalmuseum Xanten 21.-24. September 1999*, Berlin: Walter de Gruyter, 93–145.

Roymans, Nico (2004), *Ethnic identity and imperial power: the Batavians in the early Roman Empire*, Amsterdam: Amsterdam University Press.

Roymans, Nico, & Aarts, Joris (2009), 'Coin use in a dynamic frontier region. Late Iron Age Coinages in the Lower Rhine area', *Journal of Archaeology in the Low Countries* 1–1 (May).

Rubincam, Catherine (1992), 'The Nomenclature of Julius Caesar and the Later Augustus in the Triumviral Period', *Historia: Zeitschrift für Alte Geschichte* Bd. 41, H. 1, 88–103.

Ruden, Sarah trans. (2000), *Petronius: Satyricon*, Indianapolis: Hackett Publishing Company.

Ruffing, Kai, (ed.) & Ruttloh, Falk (2021), *Germanicus: Rom, Germanien und die Chatten (Geschichte in Wissenschaft und Forschung)*, Stuttgart: Verlag W. Kohlhammer.

Rüger, C. (1996), 'Germany' in: Bowman, A. K., Champlin, E., & Lintott, A. (eds.), *The Cambridge Ancient History Volume X: The Augustan Empire, 43 B.C.–A.D. 69* (second edition), Cambridge: Cambridge University Press, 517–534.

Rüpke, Jörg (2008), *Fasti Sacerdotum: A Prosopography of Pagan, Jewish, and Christian Religious Officials in the City of Rome, 300 BC to AD 499*, Oxford: Oxford University Press.

Rutland, L.W. (1987), 'The Tacitean Germanicus: Suggestions for a Re-evaluation', *Rheinisches Museum für Philologie* 130, 153–164.

Rutledge, Steven H. (1999), '*Delatores* and the Tradition of Violence in Roman Oratory', *The American Journal of Philology* 120.4, 555–73.

Rutledge, Steven H. (2001), *Imperial Inquisitions: Prosecutors and Informants from Tiberius to Domitian*, London: Routledge.

Rutledge, Steven H. (2008), 'Tiberius' Philhellenism', *The Classical World* 101.4 (Summer), 453–467.

Ryan, F. X. (1998), *Rank and Participation in the Republican Senate*, Franz Steiner Verlag.

Ryberg, Inez Scott (1942), 'Tacitus' Art of Innuendo', *Transactions and Proceedings of the American Philological Association*, *73*, 383–404.

Ryberg, Inez Scott (1949), 'The Procession of the *Ara Pacis*', *Memoirs of the American Academy in Rome* 19, 77–101.

Sabin, P. (2000), 'The Face of Roman War', *The Journal of Roman Studies* 90, 1–17

Saddington, D. B. (1970), 'The Roman "Auxilia" in Tacitus, Josephus and Other Early Imperial Writers', *Acta Classica* 13, 89–124.

Saddington, D. B. (1982), *The Development of the Roman Auxiliary Forces from Caesar to Vespasian (49B.C.–A.D.79)*, Harrare: University of Zimbabwe.

Saddington, D. B. (1987), 'A New Julio-Claudian Auxiliary Decurion?', *Zeitschrift für Papyrologie und Epigraphik* 68, 261–262

Saddington, D. B. (1990), 'The Origin and Nature of the German and British Fleets', *Britannia* 21, 223–232.

Saddington, D. B. (1996), 'Early Imperial *praefecti castrorum*', *Historia: Zeitschrift für Alte Geschichte* 45.2 (Second Quarter), 244–252.

Saddington, D. B. (2000), "Honouring' Tiberius on Inscriptions, and in Valerius Maximus – A Note', *Acta Classica* 43, 166–172.

Saddington, D. B. (2003), 'An Augustan Officer on the Roman Army: "Militaria" in Velleius Paterculus and Some Inscriptions', *Bulletin of the Institute of Classical Studies*. Supplement, no. 81, Documenting the Roman Army: Essays in Honour of Margaret Roxan, 19–29.

Salač, V. (2006), '2000 let od římského vojenského tažení proti Marobudovi Naše nejstarší historické výročí a metodologické problémy studia starší doby římské', *Archeologické rozhledy* 58, 462–485.

Salle, Catherine (1985), *Tibère: le Second César*, Paris: Robert Laffont.

Salmon, Edward Togo (1968), *A History of the Roman World from 30 BC to AD 138*, London: Routledge (sixth edition).

Sánchez-Ostiz Gutiérrez, A. (1999), *Tabula Siarensis*, Edición, Traducción y Comentario, Pamplona.

Sánchez, Fernando López (2014), 'Tibère à Capri et la flotte impériale de Misène' in: Devillers, Olivier (ed.), *Neronia IX*. La villégiature dans le monde romain de Tibère à Hadrien, Actes du IXe Congrès Internationnal de la SIEN (Villa Vigoni, Loveno di Menaggio, 3–6 octobre 2012), Ausonius Scripta Antiqua 62, Bordeaux (2014). 259–354.

Sanders, H. A. (1941), 'The Origin of the Third Cyrenaic Legion', *The American Journal of Philology* 62.1, 84–87.

Sandys, John Edwin & Campbell, Sidney George (1927), *An Introduction to the Study of Latin Inscriptions*, Cambridge: Cambridge University Press.

Sanford, Eva Mattews (1944), 'The Study of Ancient History in the Middle Ages', *Journal of the History of Ideas* 5(1), 21–43.

Santosuosso, A. (1997), *Soldiers, Citizens, and The Symbols of War: From Classical Greece to Republican Rome, 500–167 BC*, Boulder: Westview Press.

Šašel Kos, M. (1995), 'The 15th Legion at Emona: Some Thoughts', *Zeitschrift* für *Papyrologie und Epigraphik* 109, 227–244.

Šašel Kos, M. (2011), ‚The Roman conquest of Dalmatia and Pannonia under Augustus –some of the latest research results' in: Moosbauer, Günther & Wiegels, Rainer (eds.), *Römische Okkupations- und Grenzpolitik im frühen Principat Beiträge zum Kongress* ‚Fines imperii – imperium sine fine?' *in Osnabrück vom 14. bis 18. September 2009*, *Osnabrücker Forschungen zu Altertum und Antike-Rezeption* 14, Diepholz: Druckhaus Breyer, 107–118.

Sauer, E. (1999), 'The Augustan coins from Bourbonne-les-Bains (Haute-Marne): A mathematical approach to dating a coin assemblage', *Revue Numismatique* 6 (154), 145–182.

Savage, J. J. (1942), 'Germanicus and Aeneas again', *Classical Journal* 38, 166–167.

Savage, J. J. H. (1968), 'The *Aurea Dicta* of Augustus and the Poets', *Transactions and Proceedings of the American Philological Association* 99, 401–417.

Sayles, Wayne G. (2007) (second edition), *Ancient Coin Collecting III: The Roman World – Politics and Propaganda*, Iola: Krause Publications.

Sawiński, Paweł (2018), *The Succession of Imperial Power under the Julio-Claudian Dynasty (30 BC–AD 68)*, Berlin: Peter Lang.

Scarborough, J. (1968), 'Roman Medicine and the Legions: A Reconsideration', in *Medical History* 12.3, 254–261.

Scott, Kenneth (1932), 'Tiberius' Refusal of the Title "Augustus"', *Classical Philology* 27(1), 43–50.

Schall, Ute (2018), *Tiberius: Grausamer Kaiser – tragischer Mensch*, Hamburg: acabus Verlag.

Scheid, John (2001), 'To Honour the *Princeps* and Venerate the Gods: Public Cult, Neighbourhood Cults, and Imperial Cult in Augustan Rome' in: Edmondson, Jonathan (ed.), *Augustus*, Edinburgh Readings on the Ancient World, Edinburgh (2009), 275–309.

Scheidel, Walter (2009), 'Disease and Death in the ancient city of Rome' in: *Princeton/Stanford Working Papers in Classics* (online at https://papers.ssrn.com/sol3/papers.cfm?abstract_id=1347510, accessed 1 March 2024).

Schiller, A. A. (1978), *Roman Law: Mechanisms of Development*, Berlin: de Gruyter Mouton.

Schlüter, W. (1999), 'The Battle of the Teutoburg Forest: archaeological research at Kalkriese near Osnabrück' in: Creighton, J. D. & Wilson, R. J. A. (eds.), *Roman Germany: Studies in Culural Interaction, Journal of Roman Archaeology*, Supplementary Series 32, 125–159.

Schmitt, Hatto H. (1958), 'Der pannonische Aufstand des Jahres 14 n. Chr. und der Regierungsantritt des Tiberius', *Historia: Zeitschrift Für Alte Geschichte* 7(3), 378–383.

Schmitthenner, W. (1962), 'Augustus' spanischer Feldzug und der Kampf um den Prinzipat', *Historia: Zeitschrift* für Alte *Geschichte* 11.1 (January), 29–85.

Schmitthenner, W. (1979), 'Rome and India: Aspects of Universal History during the Principate', *The Journal of Roman Studies* 69, 90–106.

Schmitz, Michael (2019), *Roman Conquests: The Danube Frontier*, Barnsley: Pen & Sword Books.

Schneider, H. (ed.) (2006), *Feindliche Nachbarn: Rom und die Germanen*, Wien: Böhlau Verlag.

Schneider, Pierre (2015), '*Quod nunc Rubrum ad mare patescit*: the *mare Rubrum* as a frontier of the Roman Empire', *Klio* 97.1, 135–156.

Schnurbein, Siegmar von (1971), 'Ein Bleibarren der XIX. Legion aus dem Hauptlager von Haltern', in *Germania* XLIX, 132–136.

Schnurbein, Siegmar von (1974), *Die römischen Militäranlagen bei Haltern: Bericht über die Forschungen seit 1899*, Münster: Verlag Aschendorff.

Schnurbein, Siegmar von (1985), 'Die Funde von Augsburg-Oberhausen und die Besetzung des Alpenvorlandes durch die Römer' in: Bellot, J., Czysz, W., & Krahe, G. (eds.), *Forschungen zur provinzialrömschen Archäologie in Bayerisch-Schwaben*, Augusburg, 15–44.

Schnurbein, Siegmar von (2000), 'The Organization of the Fortresses in Augustan Germany' in: Brewer, R. J. (ed.), *Roman Fortresses and their Legions: Papers in Honour of George C. Boon,* London/Cardiff: Society of Antiquaries of London/National Museums and Galleries of Wales, 29–39.

Schnurbein, Siegmar von (2002), 'Neue Grabungen in Haltern, Oberaden und Anreppen' in: Freeman, P. *et al* (eds.), *Limes XVII: Proceedings of the XVIIIth International Congress of Roman Frontier Studies*, Oxford, 527–533.

Schnurbein, Siegmar von, Köhler, H.-J. (1994), 'Dorlar: Ein augusteisches Römerlager im Lahntal', in *Germania* 72, 193–703.

Schlott, Christoph & Rittershofer, Karl-Friedrich, (1999), *Zum Ende des spätlatènezeitlichen Oppidum auf dem Dünsberg (Gem. Biebertal-Fellingshausen, Kreis Giessen, Hessen)*, Montagnac: Editions Monique Mergoil.

Schön, F. (1986), *Der Beginn der römischen Herrschaft in Rätien*, Sigmaringen: Thorbecke.

Schönberger, C. (1969), 'The Roman Frontier Policy in Germany: An Archaeological Survey', *Journal of Roman Studies* 59 1/2, 144–197.

Schönberger, H., & Simon, H. G. (1976), *Römerlager Rödgen* (Limesforschungen 15), Berlin: Gebr. Mann Verlag.

Schößler, Alrun (2021), *Tiberius im taciteischen Narrativ: Gewaltarme Aushandlungen zwischen Tiberius und der senatorischen Oberschicht in den Annalen des Tacitus*, Darmstadt: wbg Academic in Wissenschaftliche Buchgesellschaft.

Schrömbges, Paul (1992), 'Zu den angeblichen Reichsteilungsplänen des Tiberius (Dio 57, 2, 4 F.)', *Rheinisches Museum Für Philologie* 135(3/4), 298–307.

Schumacher, L. (1985), 'Die imperatorischen Akklamationen der Triumvirn und die *auspicia* des Augustus', *Historia: Zeitschrift für Alte Geschichte* 34.2 (Second Quarter), 191–222.

Schußmann, M. (1993), *Die Kelten in Bayern*, Treuchtlingen-Berlin: wek-Verlag.

Scott, Kenneth (1932), 'The *Diritas* of Tiberius', *The American Journal of Philology* 53.2, 139–151.

Seager, Robin (1972), *Tiberius*, Berkeley: University of California Press.
Seager, Robin (2002), 'Tacitus *Annals* 1.7.1–5', *The Classical Quarterly* 52.2, 627–629.
Seager, Robin (2012), 'Perceptions of the *Domus Augusta*, AD 4–24' in: Gibson, Alisdair (ed.), *The Julio-Claudian Succession: Reality and Perception of the "Augustan Model"*, *Mnemosyne*, Supplements, History and Archaeology of Classical Antiquity 349 (2012), Leiden: Brill, 41–58.
Ségolène, D. (1992), *Prosopographie des chevaliers romains julio-claudiens (43 av. J.-C. - 70 ap. J.-C.)*, (Publications de l'École française de Rome, 153), Rome: École Française de Rome.
Seibert, J. (1970), 'Der Huldigungseid auf Kaiser Tiberius', *Historia: Zeitschrift für Alte Geschichte* 19.2 (April), 224–231.
Severy, B. (2000), 'Family and State in the Early Imperial Monarchy: the *Senatus Consultum de Pisone Patre*, *Tabula Siarensis*, and *Tabula Hebana*', Classical Philology 95, 318–337.
Severy, B. (2003), *Augustus and the Family at the Birth of the Roman Empire*, London: Routledge.
Shannon, K. (2011), 'Livy's Cossus and Augustus, Tacitus' Germanicus and Tiberius: a historiographical allusion', *Histos* 5, 266–282.
Shatzman, I. (1972), 'The Roman General's Authority over Booty', *Historia: Zeitschrift für Alte Geschichte* 21.2 (2nd Qtr.), 177–205.
Shaw, B. D. (1984), 'Bandits in the Roman Empire', *Past and Present* 105 (November), 3–52.
Shaw-Smith, R. (1971), 'A Letter from Augustus to Tiberius', *Greece & Rome* (Second Series) 18.2 (October), 213–214.
Shaya, J. (2013), The Public Life of Monuments: The *Summi Viri* of the Forum of Augustus', *American Journal of Archaeology* 117.1 (January), 83–110.
Sherk, R. T. (1974), 'Roman Geographical Exploration and Military Maps', *Aufstieg und Niedergang des Römisches Welt* 2.1, 534–62.
Shero, L. R. (1941), 'Augustus and His Associates', *The Classical Journal* 37.2 (November), 87–93.
Shirley, E. (2001), *Building a Roman Legionary Fortress*, Stroud: The History Press/Tempus.
Sherwin-White, A. N. (1939), '*Procurator Augusti*', *Papers of the British School at Rome*15, 11–26.
Shotter, David C. A. (1965), 'Three Problems in Tacitus' "*Annals*" I', *Mnemosyne* (Fourth Series), Vol. 18, Fasc. 4, 359–365.
Shotter, David C. A. (1966a), 'Tiberius and the Spirit of Augustus', *Greece & Rome* 13.2 (October), 207–212.
Shotter, David C. A. (1966b), 'Elections under Tiberius', *The Classical Quarterly* 16.2 (November), 321–332.
Shotter, David C. A. (1966c), 'Tiberius' Part in the Trial of Aemilia Lepida', *Historia: Zeitschrift für Alte Geschichte* Bd. 15, H. 3 (August), 312–317.
Shotter, David C. A. (1968), 'Tacitus, Tiberius and Germanicus', *Historia: Zeitschrift Für Alte Geschichte* 17(2), 194–214.
Shotter, David C. A. (1969), 'The Trial of Clutorius Priscus', *Greece & Rome* 16.1 (April), 14–18.
Shotter, David C. A. (1971), 'Julians, Claudians and the Accession of Tiberius', *Latomus* T. 30, Fasc. 4 (Octobre-Décembre), 1117–1123.
Shotter, David C. A. (1972), 'The Trial of C. Junius Silanus', *Classical Philology* 67(2), 126–131.
Shotter, David C. A. (1974), 'The Fall of Sejanus: Two Problems', *Classical Philology* 69(1), 42–46.
Shotter, David C. A. (1980), 'A Group of *Maiestas* Cases in A.D. 21', *Hermes* 108. Bd., H. 2, 230–233.
Shotter, David C. A. (1988), 'Tacitus and Tiberius', *Ancient Society* 19, 225–236.
Shotter, David C. A. (1992), *Tiberius Caesar*, London: Routledge.

Shotter, David C. A. (2000), 'Agrippina the Elder: A Woman in a Man's', World', *Historia: Zeitschrift für Alte Geschichte* Bd. 49, H. 3 (3rd Qtr.), 341–357.

Sidebotham, S. E. (1986), 'Aelius Gallus and Arabia', *Latomus* 45.3 (July–September), 590–602.

Signon, Helmut (1978), *Agrippa: Freund und Mitregent des Kaisers Augustus*, Frankfurt (Main): Societäts-Verlag.

Silvio, Panciera (1988), 'Gli «elogia» del Mausoleo di Augusto' in: *Epigrafia. Actes du colloque international d'épigraphie latine en mémoire de Attilio Degrassi pour le centenaire de sa naissance. Actes de colloque de Rome (27–28 mai 1988) Rome*: École Française de Rome (1991), 133–152.

Simeón, Maurici Pérez (2010), 'Tiberius› Solomonic Decision', *Index: Quaderni Camerti di Studi Romanistici, International Survey of Roman Law* 38, 261–279.

Simkins, M. (1984), *The Roman Army from Caesar to Trajan*, London: Osprey Publishing.

Simpson, C. J. (1977), 'The Date of Dedication of the Temple of Mars Ultor', *The Journal of Roman Studies* 67, 91–94

Simpson, C. J. (1988), 'The Change in *Praenomen* of Drusus Germanicus', *Phoenix - Journal of the Classical Association of Canada* 42.2, 173–175.

Simpson, C. J. (2005), 'Rome's 'Official Imperial Seal'? The Rings of Augustus and His First Century Successors', *Historia: Zeitschrift* für Alte *Geschichte* 54.2, 180–188.

Sinclair, Patrick (1990), 'Tacitus' Presentation of Livia Julia, Wife of Tiberius' Son Drusus', *The American Journal of Philology*, *111*(2), 238–256.

Sinclair, Patrick (1992), '*Deorum iniurias dis curae* (Tac., *Ann.* I, 73, 4)', *Latomus* 51(2), 397–403.

Singer, Mary White (1948), 'The Problem of Octavia Minor and Octavia Maior', *Transactions and Proceedings of the American Philological Association* 79, 268–274.

Sitwell, N. H. H. (1986), *Outside the Empire: The World the Romans Knew*, London: Paladin.

Slater, W. J. (1994), 'Pantomime Riots', *Classical Antiquity* 13 (1), 120–144.

Small, Michael Willoughby (2013), 'Business Practice, Ethics and the Philosophy of Morals in the Rome of Marcus Tullius Cicero', *Journal of Business Ethics 115*(2), 341–350.

Sobocinski, Melanie Grunow (2009), 'Porta Triumphalis and Fortuna Redux: Reconsidering the Evidence', *Memoirs of the American Academy in Rome* 54, 135–164.

Sommer, C. S. (2009), 'Why There? The Positioning of Forts Along the Riverine Frontiers', *Journal of Roman Archaeology* Supplement 74, 103–114.

Sonnabend, Holger (2021), *Tiberius: Kaiser ohne Volk*, Mainz: wbg Philipp von Zabern.

Smallwood, E. Mary (1956), 'Some Notes on the Jews under Tiberius', *Latomus* 15.3, 314–329.

Smith, Mark D. (2018), '*Praefectus Iudaeae*: Pontius Pilatus and His World' in: *The Final Days of Jesus: The Thrill of Defeat, The Agony of Victory: A Classical Historian Explores Jesus's Arrest, Trial, and Execution*, Cambridge: Lutterworth Press (2018), 39–79.

Smith, W. (ed.) (1867), *The Dictionary of Greek and Roman Biography and Mythology*, Boston: Little, Brown.

Snyder, Timothy (2017), *On Tyranny: Twenty Lessons from the Twentieth Century*, New York: Random House.

Sordi, Marta (1957), 'I primi rapporti fra lo Stato romano e il Christianesimo', *Rendiconti Accademia Nazionale Lincei* 12, 58–93.

Sordi, Marta (1960), 'Sui primi rapporti deli'autorita romana con il Christianesimo', *Studi Romani* 8, 393–409.

Sordi, Marta (1965), *II Christianesimo e Roma*, Bologna: Institute di Studi Romani 19, pp. 21–31.

Spaeth, B. S. (1994), 'The Goddess Ceres in the *Ara Pacis* Augustae and the Carthage Relief', *American Journal of Archaeology* 98.1 (January), 65–100.

Spaul, J. (2000), *Cohors². The Evidence for and a Short History of the Auxiliary Infantry Units of the Imperial Roman Army*, BAR International Series 841, Oxford: Oxford Archaeopress.

Speidel, Michael Alexander (1992), 'Roman Army Pay Scales', *The Journal of Roman Studies* 82, 87–106.

Speidel, Michael Alexander (2009), 'Geld und Macht. Die Neuordnung des staatlichen Finanzwesens unter Augustus' in: Speidel, M. A. (ed.) *Heer und Herrschaft im Römischen Reich der Hohen Kaiserzeit* (Mavors Roman Army Researches, Band 16), Stuttgart: Franz Steiner Verlag (2009), 53–84.

Speidel, Michael Alexander (2014), 'Actium, Allies, and the Augustan Auxilia: reconsidering the transformation of military structures and foreign relations in the reign of Augustus' in: Wolff, Catherine & Faurel, Patrice (eds.), *Les auxiliaires de l'armée romaine. Des alliés aux fédérés. Actes du sixième Congrès de Lyon (23–25 octobre 2014)*, Collection Études et Recherches sur l'Occident Romain – CEROR (2016).

Speidel, Michael P. (1976), 'Citizen Cohorts in the Roman Imperial Army. New Data on the *Cohorts Apula*, Campana, and III Campestris', *Transactions of the American Philological Association (1974–2014)* 106, 339–348.

Speidel, Michael P. (1982), 'Augustus's Deployment of the Legions in Egypt', *Chronique d'Egypte* 57.113, 120–124.

Speidel, Michael P. (1992), '*Exploratores*: Mobile Elite Units of Roman Germany', *Roman Army Studies* II, *Mavors* 8, 89–104.

Speidel, Michael P. (1981), '*Princeps* as a Title for 'ad hoc' Commanders', *Britannia* 12, 7–13

Speidel, Michael P. (1994), *Riding for Caesar: The Roman Emperor's Horseguard*, London: B. T. Batsford.

Speidel, Michael P. (2004), *Ancient Germanic Warriors: Warrior Styles from Trajan's Column to Icelandic Sagas*, Abingdon, Oxfordshire: Routledge.

Spencer, Andrew Clark (2009), 'The Value of Imperial *Virtutes* in the *Tabula Siarensis* and the *Senatus Consultum de Cn. Pisone patre*', University of North Carolina at Chapel Hill. (Doctoral thesis).

Spinosa, Antonio (1993), *Tiberio: L'imperatore che non amava Roma*, Milano: Arnoldo Mondadori Editore.

Staccioli, R. A. (1986), *Guida di Roma Antica*, Milan: RCS Rizzoli Libri.

Stadter, Philip A. (2014), *Plutarch and his Roman Reader*, Oxford: Oxford University Press.

Staley, A. (1965), 'The Landing of Agrippina at Brundisium with the Ashes of Germanicus', *Philadelphia Museum of Art Bulletin* 61 (287/288), 10–19.

Starr, Chester G. (1941), *The Roman Imperial Navy 31 BC–AD 324*, Cornell Studies in Classical Philology 26, New York: Cornell University Press.

Starr, Chester G. (1956), 'How Did Augustus Stop the Roman Revolution?', *The Classical Journal* 52.3 (December), 107–112.

Starr, Chester G. (1969), 'Review of *Untersuchungen zu den Kriegsflotten der romischen Kaiserzeit* by Dietmar Kienast', *The American Journal of Philology* 90.1 (January), 120–122.

Starr, Raymond J. (1980), 'Velleius' Literary Techniques in the Organization of His History', *Transactions of the American Philological Association (1974–)* 110, 287–301.

Steele, R. B. (1931), 'The Date of Manilius', *The American Journal of Philology* 52(2), 157–167.

Stern, Gaius (2006), *Women, Children, and Senators on the* Ara Pacis Augustae*: A Study of Augustus' Vision of a New World Order in 13 BC*, Berkeley: University of California.

Stern, Gaius (2023), 'Love and Politics 13–9 BC: The Loves of Tiberius and of Drusus and their Wives on the *Ara Pacis Augustae*', *Acta Antiqua Academiae Scientiarum Hungaricae* 61.4, 395–410.

Steuer, H. (2006), 'Warrior Bands, War Lords and the Birth of Tribes and States in the First Millenium AD in Middle Europe' in: Otto, T., Thrane, H., & Vandkilde, H. (eds.), *Warfare and Society: Archaeological and Social Anthropological Perspectives*, Aarhus: Aarhus University Press, 227–236.

Stevenson, Tom R. (2013), 'The Succession Planning of Augustus', *Antichthon* 47, 118–139.

Stewart, A. F. (1977), 'To Entertain an Emperor: Sperlonga, Laokoon, and Tiberius at the Dinner Table', *Journal of Roman Studies* 67, 76–90.

Stiles, Andrew (2018), 'Velleius Paterculus, the Adoptions of 4 CE, and the *Spes* Race' in: Kazantzidis, George & Spatharas, Dimos (eds.), *Hope in Ancient Literature, History, and Art Ancient Emotions I, Series: Trends in Classics* - Supplementary Volumes, 63 (2018), Berlin: De Gruyer, 259–274.

Stobart, J. C. (1908), 'The Senate under Avgvstvs [The Senate under Augustus]', *The Classical Quarterly* 2.4 (October), 296–303.

Stockton, David (1965), 'Primus and Murena', *Historia: Zeitschrift Für Alte Geschichte* 14.1, 18–40.

Stone, S. C. (1983), 'Sextus Pompey, Octavian and Sicily', *American Journal of Archaeology* 87, 11–22.

Stout, S. E. (1921), 'Training Soldiers for the Roman Legion', *The Classical Journal* 16.7 (April), 423–431.

Strahl, E. (2009), 'Die Dame von Bentumersiel an der Ems – Römischer Luxus für das Jenseits', *Archäologie in Niedersachsen* 12, 63–66.

Strahl, E. (2009), 'Germanische Siedler – Römische Legionäre. Die Siedlung Bentumersiel im Reiderland', *Varus-Kurier* 11, 12–15.

Strassmeir, Andreas, & Gagelman, Andreas (2009), *Das Heer des Arminius: Germanische Krieger zu Beginn des 1. nachchristlichen Jahrhunderts (Heere & Waffen)*, Berlin: Zeughaus Verlag.

Strassmeir, Andreas, & Gagelman, Andreas (2011), *Das Heer des Varus: Römische Truppen in Germanien 9 n. Chr. Teil 1: Legionen und Hilfstruppen, Bekleidung, Trachtzubehör, Schutzwaffen (Heere & Waffen)*, Berlin: Zeughaus Verlag.

Strassmeir, Andreas, & Gagelman, Andreas (2012), *Das Heer des Varus: Römische Truppen in Germanien 9 n. Chr. Teil 2: Waffen, Ausrüstung, Feldzeichen, Reiterei, Verbände und Einheiten (Heere & Waffen)*, Berlin: Zeughaus Verlag.

Strothmann, M. (2000), *Augustus – der Vater der* res publica*: zur Funktion der drei Begriffe* restitutio, saeculum, pater patriae *im augusteischen Prinzipat*, Stuttgart: Steiner.

Strauss, Barry (2012), *Masters of Command: Alexander, Hannibal, Caesar and the Genius of Leadership*, New York: Simon and Schuster.

Strauss, Barry (2019), *Ten Caesars: Roman Emperors from Augustus to Constantine*, New York: Simon & Schuster; Illustrated Edition.

Strunk, Thomas E. (2014), 'Rape and Revolution: Livia and Augustus in Tacitus' *Annales* (*)', *Latomus* 73, 126–148.

Strunk, Thomas E. (2017), *History after Liberty: Tacitus on Tyrants, Sycophants, and Republicans*, Ann Arbor: University of Michigan Press.

Stuart, M. (1940), 'Tacitus and the Portraits of Germanicus and Drusus', *Classical Philology* 35, 64–67.

Sumi, Geoffrey S. (2005), *Ceremony and Power: Performing Politics in Rome between Republic and Empire*, Ann Arbor: University of Michigan Press.

Sumi, Geoffrey S. (2009), 'Monuments and Memory: The *Aedes Castoris* in the Formation of Augustan Ideology', *The Classical Quarterly* 59(1), 167–186.

Sumi, Geoffrey (2011), Ceremony and the Emergence of Court Society in the Augustan Principate', *American Journal of Philology* 132.1 (Whole Number 525), (Spring), 81–102.

Sumner, Graham (2009), *Roman Military Dress*, Stroud: The History Press.

Sumner, G. V. (1967), 'Germanicus and Drusus', *Latomus* 26, 421–33.

Sumner, G. V. (1970a), 'The Legion and the Centuriate Organization', *The Journal of Roman Studies* 60, 67–78.
Sumner, G. V. (1970b), 'The Truth About Velleius Paterculus: Prolegomena', *Harvard Studies in Classical Philology* 74, 257–297.
Sumner, G. V. (1971), 'The *Lex Annalis* under Caesar', *Phoenix* 25.3 (Autumn), 246–271.
Suspène, Arnaud (2013), Germanicus: le Témoignages Numismatiques', *Cahiers du Centre Gustave Glotz* 24, 175–195
Sutherland, C. H. V. (1934), 'Aspects of Imperialism in Roman Spain', *The Journal of Roman Studies* 24, 31–42.
Sutherland, C. H. V. (1938), 'Two 'Virtues' of Tiberius: A Numismatic Contribution to the History of His Reign', *The Journal of Roman Studies* 28, Part 2, 129–140.
Sutherland, C. H. V. (1941a), 'C. Baebius and the Coinage of (?) Dium under Tiberius', *Journal of Roman Studies* 31(1–2), 73–81.
Sutherland, C. H. V. (1941b), '*Divus Augustus Pater*: A Study in the *Aes* Coinage of Tiberius', *The Numismatic Chronicle and Journal of the Royal Numismatic Society* 1 (3/4), 97–116.
Sutherland, C. H. V. (1942), '*Divus Augustus Pater*: Correction', *The Numismatic Chronicle and Journal of the Royal Numismatic Society* 2 (1/4), 106–106.
Sutherland, C. H. V. (1978), *Coinage in Roman Imperial Policy: 31 B.C.–A.D. 68*, New York: Numismatic Publications.
Swan, Peter Michael (1967), 'The Consular *Fasti* of 23 B.C. and the Conspiracy of Varro Murena', *Harvard Studies in Classical Philology* 71, 235–247.
Swan, Peter Michael (2004), *The Augustan Succession: An Historical Commentary on Cassius Dio's Roman History Books 55–56 (9 BC–AD 14)*, Oxford: Oxford University Press.
Swoboda, E. (1932), *Octavian and Illyricum*, Wien: Höfels.
Syme, Ronald (1933a), 'Some Notes on the Legions Under Augustus', *Journal of Roman Studies* 23, 14–33.
Syme, Ronald (1933b), 'M. Vinicius (Cos. 19 BC)', *The Classical Quarterly* 27, no. 3/4 (July-October), 142–148.
Syme, Ronald (1934a), 'The Spanish War of Augustus (26–25 B.C.)', *The American Journal of Philology* 55.4, 293–317.
Syme, Ronald (1934b), 'The Northern Frontier under Augustus', in *Cambridge Ancient History* Vol. X, Cambridge: Cambridge University Press, 358–364.
Syme, Ronald (1939a), *The Roman Revolution,* Oxford: Oxford University Press.
Syme, Ronald (1939b), 'Review of *Les Cohortes Prétoriennes* by Marcel Durry', *The Journal of Roman Studies* 29, Part 2, 242–248.
Syme, Ronald (1956), 'Seianus on the Aventine', *Hermes* 84.3, 257–266.
Syme, Ronald (1958a), *Tacitus*, Oxford: Oxford University Press.
Syme, Ronald (1958b), 'Imperator Caesar: A Study in Nomenclature' in: Edmondson, Jonathan (ed.), *Augustus*, Edinburgh Readings on the Ancient World, Edinburgh (2009), 40–59.
Syme, Ronald (1959), 'Livy and Augustus', *Harvard Studies in Classical Philology* 64, 27–87.
Syme, Ronald (1974), 'History or Biography. The Case of Tiberius Caesar', *Historia: Zeitschrift für Alte Geschichte* Bd. 23, H. 4 (4th Qtr.), 481–496.
Syme, Ronald (1978a), *History in Ovid*, Oxford: Oxford University Press.
Syme, Ronald (1978b), 'Mendacity in Velleius', *The American Journal of Philology* 99(1), 45–63.
Syme, Ronald (1979), 'Some Imperatorial Salutations', *Phoenix* 33.4 (Winter), 308–329.
Syme, Ronald (1983), 'The Year 33 in Tacitus and Dio', *Athenaeum* 61, 3–23 = *Roman Papers* 4 (Oxford, 1988), 223–244.
Syme, Ronald (1979–1991), Badian, E. & Birley, Anthony R. (eds.) *Roman Papers* Vols. I-VII, Oxford: Oxford University Press.

Syme, Ronald (1982), 'The Marriage of Rubellius Blandus', *The American Journal of Philology* 103.1, 62–85.
Syme, Ronald (1984b), 'Lurius Varus, a Stray Consular Legate', *Harvard Studies in Classical Philology* 88, 165–169.
Syme, Ronald (1986), *The Augustan Aristocracy*, Oxford: Oxford University Press.
Syme, Ronald (1988), 'Military Geography at Rome', *Classical Antiquity* 7.2 (October), 227–251.
Syme, Ronald (2016), 'M. Aemilius Lepidus (*cos.* 78 BC)', in: Santangelo, Federico (ed.), *Approaching the Roman Revolution: Papers on Republican History*, Oxford: Oxford University Press.
Syme, Ronald, & Birley, Anthony R. (eds.) (1999), *The Provincial at Rome: And Rome and the Balkans 80 BC–AD 14*, Exeter: University of Exeter Press.
Talbert, R. J. A. (1996), 'The Senate and Senatorial and Equestrian Posts', in Bowman, A. K., Champlin, E., Lintott, A. (eds.), *The Cambridge Ancient History Volume X: The Augustan Empire, 43 B.C.–A.D. 69* (second edition), Cambridge: Cambridge University Press, 324–343.
Talbert, R. J. A. (2000), *Map-by-Map Directory*, Princeton: Princeton University Press.
Talbert, R. J. A. (2001), 'Review of *Rome and the Enemy: Imperial Strategy in the Principate* by Susan P. Mattern', *The American Journal of Philology* 122.3 (Autumn), 451–454.
Tameanko, M. (1999), *Monumental Coins: Buildings and Structures on Ancient Coins*, Iola, Wis.: Krause Publications.
Tarn, W. W. (1931), 'The Battle of Actium', *The Journal of Roman Studies* 21, 173–199
Tarn, W. W. (1932), 'Antony's Legions', *The Classical Quarterly* 26.2 (April), 75–81.
Tarn, W. W. (1938), 'Actium: A Note', *The Journal of Roman Studies* 28, 165–168.
Tarver, John Charles (1902), *Tiberius the Tyrant*, London: Archibald Constable.
Taylor, Joan E. (1998), 'Pontius Pilate and the Imperial Cult in Roman Judaea', *New Testament Studies* 52.4, 555–582.
Taylor, Lily Ross (1920), 'The Worship of Augustus in Italy during His Lifetime', *Transactions and Proceedings of the American Philological Association* 51, 116–133.
Taylor, Lily Ross (1929), 'Tiberius' Refusals of Divine Honors', *Transactions and Proceedings of the American Philological Association* 60, 87–101.
Taylor, Lily Ross (1937), 'Tiberius' *Ovatio* and the *Ara Numinis Augusti*', *The American Journal of Philology* 58.2, 185–193.
Taylor, Lily Ross (1957), 'The Centuriate Assembly before and after the Reform', *The American Journal of Philology* 78.4, 337–354.
Taylor, Michael J. (2009), 'Hit and Run: The Germanic Warrior in the First Century AD' in: Oorthuys, Jasper (ed.), *Ancient Warfare*, Special Issue 1, 42–47.
Tekir, Gökhan (2020), 'Tiberius' Germania Strategy', *Journal of Universal History Studies* 3.1 (June), 85–100.
Tenney, F. (1933), 'On Augustus and the *Aerarium*', *The Journal of Roman Studies* 23, 143–148.
Thakur, Sanjaya (2014), 'Tiberius, the Varian disaster, and the dating of Tristia 2', *Materiali e discussioni per l'analisi dei testi classici* 73, 69–97.
Thiel, J. H. (1936), 'Kaiser Tiberius (Ein Beitrag zum Verständnis seiner Persönlichkeit). II. Die *Diritas* des Kaisers', *Mnemosyne* 3(3), 177–218.
Thompson, E. A. (1958), 'Early Germanic Warfare', *Past and Present* 14.1, 2–22.
Thorburn Jr, J. E. (2008), 'Suetonius' *Tiberius*: A Proxemic Approach', *Classical Philology* 103.4 (October), 435–448.
Thorley, J. (1969), 'The Development of Trade between the Roman Empire and the East under Augustus', *Greece & Rome (Second Series)* 16.2 (October), 209–223.

Thornton, M. K. (1992), 'Damage-Control in the *Aeneid*: or Rescuing the Military Reputation of Augustus', *Latomus* 51.3 (July-September), 566–570.

Thornton, M. K., & Thornton, R. L. (1990), 'The Financial Crisis of A.D. 33: A Keynesian Depression?', *The Journal of Economic History* 50(3), 655–662.

Timpe, Dieter (1998), 'Germanen, Germania, Germanische Altertumskunde', *Reallexikon der Germanischen Altertumskunde* 11. Berlin, 181–245.

Timpe, Dieter (2006), *Römisch-germanische Begegnungen in der späten Republik und frühen Kaiserzeit. Voraussetzungen - Konfrontationen - Wirkungen. Gesammelte Studien*, München/ Leipzig: Sauer.

Toher, Mark (2012), 'The *Exitus* of Augustus', *Hermes* 140. Jahrg., H. 1, 37–44.

Torelli, M. (1982), *Topology and Structure of Roman Historical Reliefs*, Ann Arbor: University of Michigan Press.

Torres-Martínez, Jesús & Fernández-Götz, Manuel (2017), 'Rome's Forgotten Battle. How Emperor Augustus Destroyed the *Oppidum* of the Cantabri at Monte Bernorio', *Current World Archaeology* 85, 24–28.

Townend, G. B. (1961), 'Traces in Dio Cassius of Cluvius, Aufidius and Pliny', *Hermes* 89(2), 227–248.

Toynbee, J. M. C. (1961). 'The *Ara Pacis Augustae*', *The Journal of Roman Studies* 51, Parts 1 and 2, 153–156.

Trillmich, Walter (1978), *Familienpropaganda der Kaiser Caligula und Claudius: Agrippina Maior und Antonia Augusta auf Münzen*, Berlin: Walter de Gruyter.

Trillmich, Walter (1990), '*Colonia Augusta Emerita*, Capital of Lusitania' in: Edmondson, Jonathan (ed.), *Augustus*, Edinburgh Readings on the Ancient World, Edinburgh (2009), 427–467.

Trotter, Michael R. (2019), 'Judea as a Roman Province' in: Blumell, Lincoln H. (ed), *New Testament History, Culture, and Society: A Background to the Texts of the New Testament*, (Religious Studies Center, Brigham Young University; Salt Lake City: Deseret Book (2019), 141–159.

Tully, G. D. (1998), 'The στρατάρχης of *Legio* VI Ferrata and the Employment of Camp Prefects as Vexillation Commanders', *Zeitschrift für Papyrologie und Epigraphik* 120, 226–232.

Turcan, Robert (2017), *Tibère*, Paris: Les Belles Lettres.

Turner, Anne (1943), 'A Vergilian Anecdote in Suetonius and Dio', *Classical Philology* 38(4), 261–261.

Turpin, W. (1994), '*Res Gestae* 34.1 and the Settlement of 27 B.C.', *The Classical Quarterly*, New Series 44.2, 427–437.

Urbainczyk, Theresa (2008), *Slave Revolts in Antiquity*, Berkeley: University of California Press.

Vanderpool, Eugene (1959), 'Athens Honors the Emperor Tiberius', *The Journal of the American School of Classical Studies at Athens* 28.1 (January- March), 86–90.

Vanvinckenroye, W. (1985), *Tongeren: Romeinse Stad*, Tielt: Uitgeverij Lannoo.

Van Dijk, Willemijn (2019), *The Successor: Tiberius and the Triumph of the Roman Empire*, Waco, Texas: Baylor University Press.

Van Nostrand, J.J. (1915), *The Reorganization of Spain by Augustus*, Berkeley: University of California Press.

Van Wagenberg-Ter Hoeven, Anke A. (2005), 'A Matter of Mistaken Identity. In Search of a New Title for Rubens's "Tiberius and Agrippina"', *Artibus Et Historiae* 26.52, 113–127.

Van der Veen, Vincent (2020), *Roman military equipment and horse gear from the Hunerberg at Nijmegen. Finds from the Augustan military base and Flavio-Trajanic castra and canabae legionis*, *Auxiliaria* 18, Nijmegen: Radboud Universiteit, Provinciaal-Romeinse Archeologie.

Vanacker, Wouter (2015), '"Adhuc Tacfarinas" Causes of the Tiberian War in North Africa (AD ca. 15–24) and the Impact of the Conflict on Roman Imperial Policy', *Historia: Zeitschrift Für Alte Geschichte* 64(3), 336–356.

Vermillion, Major John M. (1987), 'The Pillars of Generalship', *Parameters* (Summer) 2–17

Vervaet, Frederik Juliaan (2010), 'The Secret History: The Official Position of *Imperator* Caesar *Divi Filius* from 31 to 27 BCE', *Ancient Society* 40, 79–152.

Vervaet, Frederik Juliaan (2011), 'On the Order of Appearance in Imperator Caesar's Third Triumph (15 August 29 BCE)', *Latomus* 70.1, 96–102.

Vervaet, Frederik Juliaan (2014), *The High Command in the Roman Republic: The Principle of the* Summum Imperium Auspiciumque *from 509 to 19 BCE*, Stuttgart: Franz Steiner Verlag.

Vervaet, Frederik Juliaan (2020), '*Subsidia dominationi*: The Early Careers of Tiberius Claudius Nero and Nero Claudius Drusus Revisited', *Klio* 102(1), 121–201.

Viertel, A. (1901), *Tiberius und Germanicus: Eine Historische Studie*, Göttingen.

Vishnia, R. F. (2002), 'The Shadow Army: The *Lixae* and the Roman Legions', *Zeitschrift* für *Papyrologie und Epigraphik* 139, 265–272.

Vout, Caroline (2012), 'Tiberius and the Invention of Succession' in: Gibson, Alisdair (ed.), *The Julio-Claudian Succession: Reality and Perception of the "Augustan Model"*, *Mnemosyne*, Supplements, History and Archaeology of Classical Antiquity 349 (2012), Leiden: Brill, 59–78.

Vojvoda, Mirjana (2016), '*Signis Receptis* as a Reverse Motive on Roman Imperial Coins' in: Korać, Miomir (ed.), *Archaeology and Science* 11, Center for New Technology Institute of Archaeology Belgrade, 43–52.

Vulić, N. (1934), 'The Illyrian War of Octavian', *The Journal of Roman Studies* 24, 163–167.

Walker, S., & Higgs, P. (eds.) (2001), *Cleopatra of Egypt: From History to Myth*, Princeton University Press.

Wallace-Hadrill, Andrew (1981). 'The Emperor and His Virtues', *Historia: Zeitschrift Für Alte Geschichte* 30.3, 298–323.

Wallace-Hadrill, Andrew (1982), 'The Golden Age and Sin in Augustan Ideology', *Past and Present*, 95.1, 19–36.

Wallace-Hadrill, Andrew (1984), *Suetonius: The Scholar and His Caesars*, New Haven: Yale University Press.

Wallace-Hadrill, Andrew (1986), 'Image and Authority in the Coinage of Augustus', *The Journal of Roman Studies* 76, 66–87.

Wallace-Haddrill, Andrew (1993), *Augustan Rome* (Classical World Series), London: Bristol Classical Press.

Walser, G. (1994), *Studien sur Alpengeschichte in antiker Zeit*, Stuttgart: Franz Steiner Verlag.

Wamser, L., Flügel, C., & Ziegaus, B. (2004), *Die Römer zwischen Alpen und Nordmeer*, Düsseldorf: Patmos Verlag.

Ward-Perkins, J. B. (1970), 'From Republic to Empire: Reflections on the Early Provincial Architecture of the Roman West', *The Journal of Roman Studies* 60, 1–19.

Wardle, D. (2000), 'Valerius Maximus on the *Domus Augusta*, Augustus, and Tiberius', *The Classical Quarterly*, *50*(2), 479–493.

Wardle, D. (2007), 'A Perfect Send-off: Suetonius and the Dying Art of Augustus (Suetonius, Aug. 99)', *Mnemosyne* (Fourth Series) 60.3, 443–463.

Wardle, D. (2012), 'Suetonius on Augustus as God and Man', *The Classical Quarterly* (New Series) 62.1 (May), 307–326.

Wardle, D. (2014), *Suetonius: Life of Augustus*: Oxford: Oxford University Press.

Wardman, A. E. (1967), 'Description of Personal Appearance in Plutarch and Suetonius: The Use of Statues as Evidence', *The Classical Quarterly* 17(2), 414–420.

Watkins, T. H. (1983), '*Coloniae* and *Ius Italicum* in the Early Empire', *The Classical Journal* 78.4 (April-May), 319–336

Watson, G. R. (1969), *The Roman Soldier*, London: Thames and Hudson.

Watson, Richard A. (1987), 'Origins and Early Development of the Veto Power', *Presidential Studies Quarterly* 17(2), 401–412.

Weaver, P. R. C. (1965), 'Freedmen Procurators in the Imperial Administration', *Historia: Zeitschrift Für Alte Geschichte* 14(4), 460–469.

Weichardt, Carl (1900), *Das Schloß des Tiberius und andere Römerbauten auf Capri*, Leipzig: Verlag Von K. F. Koehler.

Weinrib, E. J. (1968), 'The Family Connections of M. Livius Drusus Libo' *Harvard Studies in Classical Philology* 72, 247–278.

Weinstock, S. (1957), 'The Image and the Chair of Germanicus', *Journal of Roman Studies* 47, 144–154.

Weinstock, S. (1960), '*Pax* and the "*Ara Pacis*"', *The Journal of Roman Studies* 50, Parts 1 and 2, 44–58.

Weisser, Bernhard (2015), 'Germanicus Caesar: Zur Inszenierung eines Nachkommen im Medium der Münzen zwischen 4 und 19 n. Chr.' in: 'Ich Germanicus: Feldherr, Priester, Superstar', *Archäologie in Deutschland* (Sonderheft 2015), 98–104.

Welch, Kathryn E. (1995), 'The Career of M. Aemilius Lepidus 49–44 B.C.', *Hermes* 123(4), 443–454.

Welch, Kathryn (2011), 'Velleius and Livia: Making a Portrait' in: Cowan, Eleanor (ed.), *Velleius Paterculus: Making History*, Swansea: Classical Press of Wales (2011), 309–334.

Weller, Judith Ann (1958), 'Tacitus and Tiberius' Rhodian Exile', *Phoenix* 12.1 (Spring), 31–35.

Wells, Colin M. (1971), 'The Supposed Augustan Base at Augsburg-Oberhausen: A New Look at the Evidence', *Saalburg-Jahrbuch* 27, 63–72.

Wells, Colin M. (1972), *The German Policy of Augustus: An Examination of the Archaeological Evidence*, Oxford: Oxford University Press.

Wells, Colin M. (1984), *The Roman Empire*, Cambridge: Harvard University Press.

Wells, P. S. (1999), *The Barbarians Speak: How the Conquered Peoples Shaped Roman Europe*, Princeton: Princeton University Press.

Wellesley, K. (1967), 'The *Dies Imperii* of Tiberius', *The Journal of Roman Studies* 57 1/2, 23–30.

Werner, W. (1997), 'The largest ship trackway in ancient times: the *Diolkos* of the Isthmus of Corinth, Greece, and early attempts to build a canal', *International Journal of Nautical Archaeology* Vol. 26, Issue 2 (May), 98–119.

Weski, T. (1982), *Waffe in germanischen Gräbern der älteren römischen Kaiserzeit südlich der Ostsee*, British Archaeological Reports International Series 147, Oxford.

Westphal, Heiko (2015), '*O Imperium Suum Paulatim Destruxit*: The Concept of *Moderatio* in Valerius Maximus' *Facta et Dicta Memorabilia* 4.1', *Acta Classica* 58, 191–208.

Wharton, David B. (1997), ‚Tacitus' Tiberius: The State of the Evidence for the Emperor's *Ipsissima Verba* in the *Annals*', *The American Journal of Philology* 118.1 (Spring), 119–125.

Wheeler, E. L. (1993), 'Methodological Limits and the Mirage of Roman Strategy: Part I', *The Journal of Military History* 57.1 (January), 7–41.

Wheeler, E. L. (1993), 'Methodological Limits and the Mirage of Roman Strategy: Part II', *The Journal of Military History* 57.2 (April), 215–240.

Whitby, M. (1995), 'Old Frontiers: Modern Models. Review of *Frontiers of the Roman Empire. A Social and Economic Study* by C. R. Whittaker', *The Classical Review (New Series)* 45.2, 338–339.

White, L. M. (2005), 'Epilogue as Prologue: Herod and the Jewish Experience of Augustan Rule' in: Galinsky, Karl (ed.), *The Cambridge Companion to the Age of Augustus*, Cambridge University Press (2005).

White, K. D. (1984), *Greek and Roman Technology*, Ithaca, New York: Cornell University Press.

White, P. (1988), 'Julius Caesar in Augustan Rome', *Phoenix* 42.4 (Winter), 334–356.

Whittaker, C. R. (1996a), 'Roman Africa', in Bowman, A. K., Champlin, E., & Lintott, A. (eds.), *The Cambridge Ancient History Volume X: The Augustan Empire, 43 B.C.–A.D. 69* Cambridge: Cambridge University Press, 586–618. (Second edition).

Whittaker, C. R. (1996b), *Frontiers of the Roman Empire: A Social and Economic Study*, Baltimore: The John Hopkins University.

Wigg, A. (1999), 'Neu entdeckte halternzeitliche Militärlager in Mittelhessen' in: Schlüter, W., & Wiegels, R. (eds.), *Rom, Germanien und die Ausgrabungen von Kalkriese*, Osnabrück: Rasch, 419–436.

Wightman, E. M. (1971), *Roman Trier and the Treveri*, New York: Praeger.

Wightman, E. M. (1977), 'Military Arrangements, Native Settlements and Related Developments in Early Roman Gaul', *Helinium* 17, 105–126.

Wilbers-Rost, S. (2009), 'The site of the Varus Battle at Kalkriese. Recent results from archaeological research' in: Morillo, A., Hanel, N., & Martin, E. (eds.), *Limes XX, Roman Frontier Studies*, Anejo de Gladius 13, 1347–1352.

Wilcox, P. (1982), *Rome's Enemies: Germanics and Dacians*, London: Osprey Publishing.

Wilhelm, A. B. (1826), *Die Feldzüge des Nero Claudius Drusus in nördlichen Deutschland*, Halle: Verlag von Friedrich Kuff.

Wilkes, John J. (1963), 'A Note on the Mutiny of the Pannonian Legions in A.D. 14', *The Classical Quarterly (New Series)* 13.2 (November), 268–271

Wilkes, John J. (1969), *Dalmatia: History of the Roman Provinces*, London: Routledge and Kegan Paul.

Wilkes, John J. (1972), 'Julio-Claudian Historians', *The Classical World* 65.6 (February), 177–192+197–203.

Wilkes, John J. (1992), *The Illyrians*, Oxford: Blackwell.

Wilkes, John J. (1996), 'The Danubian and Balkan Provinces' in: Bowman, A.K., Champlin, E., Lintott, A. (eds.), *The Cambridge Ancient History Volume X: The Augustan Empire, 43 B.C.–A.D. 69* (second edition), Cambridge: Cambridge University Press, 545–585.

Wilkinson, Sam (2012), *Republicanism During the Early Roman Empire*, London: Bloomsbury.

Will, W. (1983). 'Zu Velleius II.105.1', *Rheinisches Museum Für Philologie* 126(2), 189–190.

Willems, W. J. H. (1980), 'Arnhem-Meinerswijk: een Nieuw *Castellum* aan de Rijn', *Westerheem* 29, 334–348.

Willems, W. J. H. (1989), 'Early Roman Camps on the Kops Plateau at Nijmegen (NL)', in V.A. Maxfield (ed.) *et al*, *Proceedings of the XVth International Congress of Roman Frontier Studies*, University of Exeter Press, 210–214.

Willems, W. J. H. (1992), 'Roman Face Masks from the Kops Plateau, Nijmegen, The Netherlands', in *Journal of Roman Equipment Studies*, Armatura Press 3, 57–66.

Willems, W. J. H., & Enckevort, H. van (2009), 'Vlpia Noviomagus: Roman Nijmegen, The Batavian Capital at the Imperial Frontier', Supplement 73, *Journal of Roman Archaeology*, Portsmouth, Rhode Island.

Williams, D. (1998), *Romans and Barbarians*, London: Constable.

Williams, Dyfri (2006), *The Warren Cup*, London: British Museum Publications.

Williams, Guy (2014), 'Augustus and the Visionary Leadership of *Pax Romana*', *Saber and Scroll* 3.1, Article 8. (Online at http://digitalcommons.apus.edu/saberandscroll/vol3/iss1/8).

Williams, K. F. (2009), 'Tacitus' Germanicus and the Principate', *Latomus* 68(1), 117–130.

Williams, Mary Frances (1997), 'Four Mutinies: Tacitus "*Annals*" 1.16–30; 1.31–49 and Ammianus Marcellinus "Res Gestae" 20.4.9–20.5.7; 24.3.1–8, *Phoenix* 51(1), 44–74.
Winter, Paul (1964), 'A Letter from Pontius Pilate', *Novum Testamentum* 7(1), 37–43.
Winterling, Aloys (2011), *Caligula: A Biography*, Berkeley: California University Press.
Wiseman, T. P. (1970), 'The Definition of *Eques Romanus* in the Late Republic and Early Empire', *Historia: Zeitschrift* für Alte *Geschichte* 19.1 (January), 67–83.
Wiseman, T. P. (2019), *The House of Augustus: A Historical Detective Story,* Princeton: Princeton University Press.
Wolff, H. (1996), 'Raetia' in: Bowman, A. K., Champlin, E. & Lintott, A. (eds.), *The Cambridge Ancient History Volume X: The Augustan Empire, 43 B.C.–A.D. 69* (second edition), Cambridge: Cambridge University Press, 535–544.
Wolfram, H. (1997), *The Roman Empire and Its Germanic Peoples*, Berkeley: University of California Press.
Wolters, Reinhard (1990), *Römische Eroberung und Herrschaftsorganisation in Gallien und Germanien*, Bochum: Brockmeyer Verlag.
Wolters, Reinhard (2008), *Die Schlacht im Teutoburger Wald: Arminius, Varus und das römische Germanien*, München: Verlag C.H. Beck.
Woodhead, A. G. (1948), 'Tacitus and Agricola', *Phoenix* 2(2), 45–55.
Woodman, A. J. (1975), 'Questions of Date, Genre, and Style in Velleius: Some Literary Answers', *The Classical Quarterly* 25(2), 272–306.
Woodman, A. J. (1977), *Velleius Paterculus: The Tiberian Narrative (2.94–131)*, Cambridge Classical Texts and Commentaries, Series Number 19, Cambridge: Cambridge University Press.
Woodman, A. J. (1983), *Velleius Paterculus: the Caesarian and Augustan Narrative* (Cambridge Classical Texts and Commentaries), Cambridge: Cambridge University Press.
Woodman, A. J. (1989), 'Tacitus' Obituary of Tiberius', *The Classical Quarterly* 39.1, 197–205.
Woodman, A. J. (1998), *Tacitus Reviewed*, Oxford: Clarendon Press.
Woodman, A. J. (2006a), 'Tiberius and the Taste of Power: The Year 33 in Tacitus', *The Classical Quarterly* (New Series) 56.1 (May), 175–189.
Woodman, A. J. (2006b), 'Mutiny and Madness: Tacitus *Annals* 1.16–49', *Arethusa* 39, 303–329.
Woodman, A. J. (2015), 'Tacitus and Germanicus: Monuments and Models' in: Ash, Rhiannon, Mossman, Judith & Titchener, Frances B. (eds.), *Fame and Infamy: Essays on Characterization in Greek and Roman Biography and Historiography* (2015), Oxford: Oxford University Press, 255–268.
Woolf, G. (1993), 'Roman Peace' in: Rich, J. & Shipley, G. (eds.), *War and Society in the Roman World*, London: Routledge, 171–194.
Woolf, G. (1997), 'Beyond Romans and Natives', *World Archaeology* 28.3, Culture Contact and Colonialism (February), 339–350.
Woolf, G. (1998), *Becoming Roman: The Origins of Provincial Civilization in Gaul*, Cambridge: Cambridge University Press.
Woytek, Bernhard E. (2017), 'Tiberian Pseudo Medallions of the CLEMENTIAE/MODERATIONI(S) Group and the Problem of Chronology', *The Numismatic Chronicle (1966–)* 177, 83–92.
Woytek, Bernhard E. & Blet-Lemarquand, Maryse (2017), 'The C. L. CAESARES denarii *RIC* I$^2$ Augustus 208: A pseudo-Augustan unsigned restoration issue. Corpus, die study, metallurgical analyses', *Revue numismatique* 174, 183–248.
Wright, F. A. (1937), *Marcus Agrippa: Organizer of Victory*, Edinburgh: T. and A. Constable.
Wightman, E. M. (1977), 'Military Arrangements, Native Settlements and Related Developments in Early Roman Gaul', *Helinium* 17, 105–126.

Yardley, J. C. & Barrett, Anthony A. (2011), *Velleius Paterculus. The Roman History: From Romulus and the Foundation of Rome to the Reign of the Emperor Tiberius* (Hackett Classics), Indianapolis: Hackett Publishing.

Yakobson, Alexander (2019), 'Tiberius the Legacy of Augustus and the Shadow of the Republic: Accesion Debate and Beyond' in: Cecconi, G.A, Lizzi Testa, R. & Marcone, A. (eds.), *The Past as Present: Essays on Roman History in Honour of Guido Clemente*, Turnhout: Brepols Publishers, 789–808.

Yakobson, Alexander (2021). 'Augustus, the Roman Plebs and the Dictatorship: 22 BCE and Beyond' in: In Beck, H. & Vankeerberghen, G. (eds.), *Rulers and Ruled in Ancient Greece, Rome, and China*, Cambridge: Cambridge University Press, 269–299.

Yavetz, Zvi (1995), *Tiberius and Caligula: From Make-believe to Insanity*, Tel Aviv: Dvir Publishing House.

Yavetz, Zvi (1999), *Tiberius. Der traurige Kaiser. Biographie*, Munich: C.H. Beck.

Yeo, C. A. (1959), 'The Founding and Function of Roman Colonies', *The Classical World* 52.4 (January), 104–107 and 129–130.

Zanier, Werner (1994), 'Eine römische Katapultpfeilspitze der 19. Legion aus Oberammergau: Neues zum Alpenfeldzug des Drusus im Jahr 15 v. Chr.', *Germania* 72, 587–596.

Zanier, Werner (2010), 'Der römische Alpenfeldzug unter Tiberius und Drusus im Jahre 15 v. Chr. Übersicht zu den historischen und archäologischen Quellen' in: Aßkamp, Rudolf & Esh, Tobias (eds.), *IMPERIUM – Varus und seine Zeit. Beiträge zum internationalen Kolloquium des LWL-Römermuseums am 28. und 29. April 2008 in Münster*, Münster: Aschendorff Verlag (2010), 73–96.

Zanker, Paul (1990), *The Power of Images in the Age of Augustus*, Ann Arbor: University of Michigan Press.

Ziegler, Ruprecht (1998/99), 'Ergänzungen zum Münzcorpus der Stadt Anazarbos in Kilikien', *Jahrbuch Numismatik Geldgeschichte* 48/49, 101–132.

**Films, Novels, Plays and Television Series**

Adams, Francis Williams Lauderdale (1894), *Tiberius: A Drama*, London: T. Fisher Unwin.

Anon. (1607), *The Tragedie of Claudius Tiberius Nero, Rome's Greatest Tyrant* (or *The Tragicall Life and Death of Claudius Tiberius Nero*), London: Francis Burton.

Arnault, Lucien (1828), *Le Dernier Jour de Tibère: Tragédie en cinq actes et en vers*, Paris: Ladvocat; Delaunay; Ponthieu et Ce.

Bocheński, Jacek, *Tiberius Caesar* (trans. Tom Pinch) (2023), Luxembourg: Mondrala Press.

Bosławita, Bogdan (Josef-Ignacy Kraszewski) (1902), *Villa Jovis: Tibère à Caprée*, Paris: Éditions du 'Carnet'.

Burke, Simon, (2021 and 2023), *Domina*, Epix, MGM Plus and Sky Studios.

Jonson, Benjamin (Ben) (1603), *Sejanus His Fall: A Tragedie*, London: Richard Bishop (printed 1616).

Campan, Bernard (1847), *Tibère à Caprée: Tragédie en 5 actes et en verse*, Montpellier: Impr. de Boehm.

De Chénier, Marie-Joseph (1819), *Tibère: Tragédie avec une Analyse de Cette Piece, par M. Népomucene Lemercier*, Paris: Ponthieu.

Dugué, Ferdinand (1881), *Tibère: Drame en cinq actes (huit tableaux)*, Paris: Calman Lévy. (printed 1892).

Graves, Robert (1934), *I, Claudius*, London: Arthur Baker Ltd.

Panting, Jonquil (director) & Brooks, Robin (writer) (2010), *I, Claudius*, BBC Radio 4.

Bennett, Derek (director) & Mackie, Philip (writer) (1968), *The Caesars*, Granada TV.

Massie, Allan (1990), *Tiberius: The Memoirs of the Emperor*, London: Hodder and Stoughton Ltd.

Pellgrin, Abbé Simon-Joseph (1726), *Tibère: Tragédie*, Paris: Flathault (printed 1727).
Rzéwuski, Count Stanislas (1894), *Tibère à Caprée: drame en 5 actes et 7 tableaux*, Paris: Porte St-Martin.
Séjour, Victor (1849), *La chute de Séjan: Drame en cinq actes et en vers*, Paris: Michel Lévy Frères.
Wise, Herbert (director) & Pullman, Jack (writer) (1976), *I, Claudius*, BBC TV.
Wolfson, John (2016), *The Inn at Lydda: A Meeting of Caesar and Christ* (Programme), London: Shakespeare's Globe.
Young, Roger E. (director) & Lerner, Eric (writer) (2003), *Imperium: Augustus* (or *Augustus: The First Emperor*).

# Index

A Roman citizen is listed under his or her *nomen gentile*, or *cognomen* where it is not known. Gods are listed by their Latin names with the exceptions of Jove (Iovis) or Jupiter (Iupiter) and Mars (Marti). A military campaign is listed under the designation *bellum* or *clades* when there is a contemporary Roman title, or under 'battle', 'revolt' or 'siege' when there is not. A military unit is listed under its respective designation *ala*, *classis*, *cohors* or *legio*.